AGRICOLA

'Inspect the basis of the social pile:
Inquire,' said I, 'how much of mental power
And genuine virtue they possess who live
By bodily toil, labour exceeding far
Their due proportion, under all the weight
Of that injustice which upon ourselves
Ourselves entail.' Such estimate to frame
I chiefly looked (what need to look beyond?)
Among the natural abodes of men,
Fields with their rural works; recalled to mind
My earliest notices; with these compared
The observations made in later youth,
And to that day continued—For, the time
Had never been when throes of mighty Nations
And the world's tumult unto me could yield,
How far soe'er transported and possessed,
Full measure of content; but still I craved
An intermingling of distinct regards
And truths of individual sympathy
Nearer ourselves.

WORDSWORTH, *Prelude*, book XIII.

AGRICOLA

A STUDY OF AGRICULTURE AND RUSTIC LIFE IN THE GRECO-ROMAN WORLD FROM THE POINT OF VIEW OF LABOUR

BY

W E HEITLAND MA

FELLOW OF ST JOHN'S COLLEGE

GREENWOOD PRESS, PUBLISHERS
WESTPORT, CONNECTICUT

First published 1921

Reprinted by permission
of Cambridge University Press

First Greenwood Reprinting 1970

Library of Congress Catalogue Card Number 69-13929

SBN 8371-4088-9

Printed in the United States of America

PREFACE

VERY few words are needed here, for the book is meant to explain its own scope. I have only to thank those to whose kindness I am deeply indebted. Professor Buckland was so good as to help me when I was striving to utilize the evidence of the Roman jurists. Chapter XLIX in particular owes much to his genial chastisement. On chapters II and LXI Mr G G Coulton has given me most valuable criticism. Yet I thank these gentlemen with some reluctance, fearing that I may seem to connect their names with errors of my own. Mr T R Glover kindly read chapter XXIX. Professor Housman called my attention to the 'Farmer's Law,' and kindly lent me Mr Ashburner's articles, to which I have referred in Appendix B. To all these, and to the Syndics of the University Press for undertaking the publication of this unconventional work, I hereby express my sincere gratitude. My reasons for adopting the method followed in this book are given on pages 5–6 and 468.

W E HEITLAND

CAMBRIDGE
August 1920

TABLE OF CONTENTS

Table of Contents

Table of Contents

Table of Contents

INTRODUCTORY

I. EVIDENCE.

THE inquiry of which the results are set forth in these pages was undertaken in the endeavour to satisfy my own mind on a very important question in the history of the past. Circumstances have compelled me to interest myself in the civilization of the Greco-Roman world. And it has always been a painful disadvantage to students of the 'classical' systems that the available record neither provides adequate labour-statistics nor furnishes a criticism of existing labour-conditions from the point of view of the handworkers. Accustomed as we are nowadays to continual agitations for increase of wages and reduction of working hours, with centuries of strange experience in the working of Poor-laws, we are in no danger of undervaluing the importance of the wage-earner in our social fabric. We are rather in danger of forgetting other (and perhaps not less vital) considerations, under pressure of the material claims of the labourer and his hire. Power goes by votes; the handworker is now a voter; and the voice of the handworker is loud in the land. No scheme is too wild to find advocates; and those who venture to assert the right of invention organization and thrift to superior recognition as public benefits often think it necessary to adopt an apologetic tone. Now it may be that this is a passing phase, and that the so-called 'working-class'—that is, handworkers for wages—will come to see that the civilization whose comforts they enjoy, and whose discomforts they resent, does not wholly depend upon the simple repeated acts of the handworkers themselves. Perhaps there are already signs of some such reaction. But, if so, the reaction must be voluntary; for no power exists in this country to constrain the handworker to take reasonable views, in short to face facts. In these words I am not implying any denial of the reasonableness of many of his claims. To offer an opinion on questions of more or less is no business of mine.

But, when we compare modern industries in general with those of the ancient world, we find ourselves in presence of a very different situation. The largest scale of operations attainable in antiquity seems small and crude by the side of recent achievements, for instance the building of the Pyramids compared with the Panama canal. Machinery, transport, and scientific discovery in general, have made it possible to carry out colossal undertakings with comparative ease and without wholesale destruction of human life. The greatest works of the ancients are for the most part silent witnesses to the ruthless employment of forced labour, either that of captives or bought slaves or that of the impressed subjects of an autocrat. Mere brute force, applied in un-limited quantity[1] with callous indifference to the sufferings of the toilers, was the chief means at disposal: mechanical invention had got so far as to render possible some tasks that without it could not have been performed at all. It gave extended effect to the mass of forced labour, and there it stopped, for we have no reason to think that it improved the labourer's lot. The surviving evidence as to the condition[2] of slaves in mines and factories enables us to form some faint notion of the human wastage resulting from the cruel forced-labour system. We may then state the position briefly thus: to attempt great enterprises was only possible through the crude employment of labour in great masses: the supply of this labour was, or appeared to be, procurable only by com-pulsion: and compulsion was operative through the institution of slavery or the passive submission of cowed populations to the will of despots. But if slavery promoted large-scale enterprise, surely large-scale enter-prise tended to establish slavery in the form of forced labour more firmly than ever. In the modern world the necessity of employing free labour has stimulated scientific invention, in mechanical and other departments, the tendency of which is to require greater intellectual[3] development in the labourer, and in the long run to furnish him with effective means of asserting his own freedom.

Under modern conditions, the gradual displacement of small handi-craftsmen by the growth of great capitalistic combinations is going on, perhaps not always for good. The public accept this result as fate. And, if economy in production and prime-cost cheapness are the only things worth considering, it is not easy to condemn the process. But events are steadily demonstrating the fear once entertained, that handworkers in general would find their position weakened thereby, to be groundless. If the independent craftsman has lost ground, the wage-earning journeyman has gained. We need not follow out this topic in detail, but note the contrast presented by the ancient world. The 'small man' in crafts and trades was able to hold his own, for without steam-power the capitalist was not strong enough to suppress him. In a small way he was something of a capitalist himself, and commonly owned slave-apprentices. His part in ancient civilization was undoubtedly far more important than it appears in literature: for he ministered to the ordinary needs of every day, while literature, then

[1] A good specimen of such work at a late date may be found in Statius *Silvae* IV 3 on the *via Domitiana* lines 40–66.

[2] For instance Diodorus V 38 § 1, Strabo XII 3 § 40 (p 562), Apuleius *met* IX 12.

[3] Not artistic, of course.

as now and more than now, chiefly recorded the exceptional. When we turn to the wage-earner, who earns a living by hiring out his bodily powers to an employer, we are dealing with a wholly different class. These are the free men who in a slave-holding society have to compete with the slave. In the course of the present inquiry we must keep a sharp look-out for every reference or allusion to such persons in the department of agriculture, and in particular note numerous passages in which the status of labourers cannot be inferred with certainty from the language. But the importance of this special point is of course not confined to agriculture.

I have chosen to limit my inquiry to the case of agriculture for these reasons. First, because it was and is the industry on which human life, and therefore all other industries and all progress, did and do rest. Secondly, because its economic importance in the ancient world, so far from declining, manifestly increased. The problem of food-supply was always there. And it was never more pressing than in the later ages of Rome, when imperial efforts to enforce production, if successful, fed her barbarian armies, at the same time attracting the attention of barbarian invaders to lands that promised the food-crops which they themselves were too lazy to produce. Thirdly, because the importance of agriculture was and is not merely economic. Its moral value, as a nursery of steady citizens and, at need, of hardy soldiers, was and still should be recognized by thoughtful men. Therefore its conditions and its relative prosperity or decay deserve the attention of all historians of all periods. Unluckily statistical record of a scientific character is not available for the times that we call ancient, and numbers are notoriously liable to corruption in manuscripts. Therefore I have only ventured to give figures seldom and with reserve. For agriculture we have nothing on the scale of the inscriptions that record wages, for instance on public works at Athens. On the other hand we have for certain periods the evidence of specialists such as Cato Varro and Columella, to whom we owe much information as to the actual or possible conditions of rustic enterprise and labour. The relation of agriculture and agricultural labour to the state as a whole is a subject illustrated by great theorists such as Plato and Aristotle. The practical problems of landowning and farming meet us now and then in the contemporary evidence of such men as Xenophon and the younger Pliny. Even orators, though necessarily partisan witnesses, at times give valuable help: they may distort facts, but it is not their interest to lessen their own power of persuasion by asserting what is manifestly incredible. The ancient historians tell us very little, even of the past; contemporary evidence from them is especially rare. They are preoccupied with public affairs, and the conditions of rustic life and labour only concern them at moments when serious distress or disorder compels attention. Rhetoricians and poets are doubtful witnesses. Like the orators, they use their matter freely and with much colouring for their immediate purposes. But they are not, like forensic orators, in direct contact with practical emergencies. The questions arising out of Vergil's *Georgics* are problems to be discussed by themselves.

The contribution of encyclopaedic or occasional writers is in some cases of value. I will here only name the elder Pliny and Apuleius. Books of travel and geography, for instance Herodotus and Strabo, give stray details, but generally in reference to distant countries, mostly in the East and so hardly within my subject, save for purposes of comparison. There are however two topics with which I am not directly concerned, but which it is impossible wholly to ignore in speaking of ancient agriculture. First, the relation of military duty to landholding [the farmer as citizen soldier], and mercenary service [the rustic as volunteer for pay]. This has been so fully treated in modern handbooks that I need say little about it. Secondly, the various conditions of tenure of land. That rustic life and therewith rustic labour were directly and deeply affected by varieties of tenure, needs no proof. The cited opinions of Roman lawyers in the Digest are the main authority on points of this kind, and stray references elsewhere serve to illustrate them. In conclusion I have only to insist again on the fact that we have no direct witness of the labourer's, or even the working farmer's, point of view. The evidence all comes from above; and therefore generally gives us a picture of conditions as the law meant them to be and presumed them normally to be. How far the practical working corresponded to the legal position, is only to be guessed with caution from the admissions involved in the elaboration of legal remedies; and, in the case of imperial *coloni*, from the unique evidence of the notable African inscriptions.

It is I trust after the above considerations not unreasonable to devote no special chapters to certain writers whom nevertheless it is often necessary to cite in notes. Diodorus, Livy, Athenaeus, Macrobius, Gellius, Palladius, are cases of the kind. Stray references in their works are valuable, but there is nothing to require a treatment of them as several wholes. Even Livy is chiefly useful as handing down remains of past tradition : hence he (and Dionysius and Plutarch with him) have a leading place in the introductory chapter on early Rome. So too the writers of the so-called *historia Augusta* and the laws of the Theodosian and Justinian Codes find their place in the notes to certain chapters. On the other hand (to omit obvious cases) Euripides, Xenophon, the younger Seneca, Martial, the younger Pliny, Apuleius, Ammianus, Symmachus, Apollinaris Sidonius, need careful treatment with full regard to the periods and circumstances by which their evidential values are severally qualified. And in order to place each witness in his proper setting it is sometimes necessary to pause and group a number of circumstances together in a special chapter. This arises from the endeavour to preserve so far as possible the thread of continuity, which is always really there, though at times very thin, owing to the loss of many works in the course of ages. In such chapters one has to look both backward and forward, and often to digress for a moment on topics only connected indirectly with the main object.

I have tried to avoid needless repetitions, but some repetitions are unavoidable, since the same point often serves to illustrate different parts of the argument. To make a system of cross-references from chapter to chapter quite complete is hardly possible, and would add immensely to the bulk of foot-notes. It has seemed better to attempt completeness by elaboration of the Index. A few details from a period later than that with which I am concerned are given in the Appendix, as being of interest. Also the names of some books from which in a course of miscellaneous reading I have derived more or less help, particularly in noting modern survivals or analogies. For significant matter occurs in quite unexpected quarters. And the observers who record facts of rustic life and labour in Italy or France, in North or Central or South America, without attempting to manipulate them in connexion with a theory, deserve much gratitude.

It is evident that in the handling of evidence there is room for some variety of method. And it seems reasonable to hold that the choice of method should be mainly guided by two leading considerations, the nature of the evidence available and the aim of the inquiry pursued. In the present case the inquiry deals with a part, a somewhat neglected part, of Greco-Roman history: and the subject is one that can by no means be strictly confined to ascertaining the bare facts of farm life and labour. That the conditions of agriculture were not only important in connexion with food-supply, but had an extensive moral and political bearing, is surely beyond dispute. And the nature of the surviving evidence favours, or rather requires, the taking of a correspondingly wide view. Outside the circle of technical writings, the literary evidence almost always has an eye to the position of agriculture as related to the common weal; nor is this point of view ignored even by the technical writers. Therefore, in treating the subject as I have tried to treat it, it is very necessary to take each witness separately so far as possible, and not to appraise the value of his testimony without a fair consideration of his condition and environment. This necessity is peculiarly obvious in the case of the theorists, whose witness is instructive in a very high degree, but only when we bear in mind the existing state of things from observation of which their conclusions were derived. And the changes of attitude in philosophic thought are sometimes highly instructive. Take farm life and labour as it appears to Plato and Aristotle and later to Musonius: a whole volume of history, economic moral and political, lies in the interval of some 400 years. Inscriptions furnish little to the student of this subject, but that little is worth having. To conclude this paragraph, I do not apologize for putting my authorities in the witness-box and questioning them one by one. For only thus do I see a possibility of giving a true picture of the conditions with which I am concerned. It is a long method, but perhaps not uninteresting, and I see no other.

It may seem necessary to explain why I have not devoted special chapters to rustic life and labour in Oriental countries, some of which eventually became parts of the Roman empire. Such countries are for instance Egypt, Palestine and Syria. One reason is that I could do nothing more than compile conclusions of the inquirers who have lately rescued a vast mass of detail, chiefly from the Egyptian papyri. Age forbade me to undertake this task unless it seemed clear that my inquiry really depended on it. But, inasmuch as I have not been trying to produce a technical treatise upon ancient agriculture, I do not think it necessary. That there is room for such a treatise, I have no doubt: nor that its writer will need to have many years at his disposal and a good knowledge of several sciences at his back. With regard to eastern countries other than Egypt, practically the Seleucid empire, knowledge is at present very scanty, as Rostowzew has to confess. Ancient India lies quite beyond my range, as having never been a part of the Roman empire: but there is evidently much of interest to be gathered in this field. From these extensive and promising researches my limited effort is divided by a clearly marked line. I am concerned with agriculture and agricultural labour not as the occupation of passive populations merely producing so much food year by year, peoples over whom centuries might pass without ascertainable change of a moral social or political character. Such peoples, in short, as do not get beyond the conception of ruler and ruled to that of state and citizen, or at least have not yet done so. For of all conclusions to be drawn from the history of the Greco-Roman world none seems to me more certain than the fact that, while political social and moral movements affected the conditions of agriculture, agricultural changes reacted upon political social and moral conditions. Thus the general history of the peoples, comprising the rise and fall of ancient efforts towards self-government, must always be kept in view: the fluctuations of what I may call civic values, and the position of farmers as labourers or employers of labour cannot be treated in separate compartments and their reciprocal effect ignored. That in the later stages of my inquiry Oriental influences begin to dominate Roman imperial policy, is evident, and I have not left this factor out of account. But this phenomenon announces the end of the old world. The long struggle of the Empire in the East and its final overthrow by the forces of Islam, its break-up in the West and the foundation of new nation-states, are beyond my range. In the Appendix I have put some remarks on two documents of the Byzantine period, from which we get glimpses of changes that were proceeding in the eastern empire while it still held its ground and was indeed the most highly organized of existing powers. To these I have subjoined a list of some of the books I have consulted and found helpful in various degrees, particularly such as have furnished modern illustrations in the way c. analogy or survival. A few special quotations from some of these may serve to shew how very striking such illustrations can be.

II. LAND AND LABOUR.

Of the many difficult questions connected with the past history of the human race few have evoked such a difference of opinion as the practical importance of slavery. By some inquirers it has been held that the so-called 'classical' civilization of the Greco-Roman world rested upon a slavery basis, in short that slavery alone enabled that civilization to follow the lines of its actual development. In reply to this doctrine it is urged[1] that its holders have been led astray by an unhistorical method. They have been deeply impressed by the all-pervading evils of the economic and domestic slave-system during the period (say 200 BC–200 AD roughly) when it was in full extension and vigour. The prepossession thus created has led them to misinterpret the phenomena of earlier ages, and to ignore the significance of the later period of decline. Prejudiced eyes have detected slavery where it was not, and have seen in it where existent an importance greater than impartial inquiry will justify. Moreover the discussion of slavery-questions in modern times, conducted with the intemperate warmth of partisan controversy, have had an influence unfavourable to the statement of facts in their true relations, and therefore to the exercise of cool judgment. According to this view the facts of our record shew that, while slave-labour had its four centuries or so of predominance, free-labour never ceased, and on it, and not on slavery, the civilization of the 'classical' world was built up. It is argued that in primitive conditions there was little slavery, that growth of trade and exchange (and

[1] See especially Ed Meyer *Kleine Schriften* pp 80–212.

therewith of civilization) led to division of labour and the growth of larger enterprises. On this follows a time in which the employment of slave-labour becomes more and more common, and ends by being for some centuries the basis of economic and domestic life. In due course comes the period of decline, when for various reasons slaves became less numerous, and the highly-organized civilization of antiquity relapses into the primitive conditions of the early Middle Age. Slavery is not extinct, but reverts generally to various degrees of serfdom, resembling that which meets us in the early traditions of Greek slavery. Things have gone round the full circle, and the world takes a fresh start.

This version of the process is attractive. It presents to us a spectacle of cyclic movement, pleasing from its simplicity and dignity. But it seems to imply that the old civilization reached its height more or less concurrently with the growth of slavery. One is driven to ask[1] whether the concurrence was purely accidental or not. So far as concerns the manufacture of articles for export by slave-industry, it can hardly have been a mere chance: nor is it denied that in this department it was the demand created by the needs of growing civilization that called forth the supply. Luxury too is merely a name for such needs when they clearly exceed strict necessaries of life: and here too the monstrous extravagancies of domestic slavery were a characteristic feature of the civilization of the Greco-Roman world. That neither of these forms of servile employment could outlive the civilization that had produced them, is surely no wonder. The case of slavery in agriculture is less simple, and several questions may suggest themselves to anyone who considers this subject with an open mind.

Agriculture was long regarded, from a social point of view, as superior to other occupations dependent on bodily labour. This opinion dated from very early times when, as traditions agree, the land was owned by privileged nobles who as members of powerful clans formed aristocracies of a more or less military character. War was waged by men fighting hand to hand, and it was natural that hand-work of a kind likely to promote health and strength should be honoured above manual trades of a less invigorating and even sedentary character. The development of cities and urban life, which in many states led to the overthrow of the old clan aristocracies, did not make handicraftsmen the equals of agriculturists in popular esteem. Pressure to win a firm footing on the land was as marked a feature in Athenian Attica as in Roman Latium. Agriculture was a profession worthy of the free citizen, and the ownership of a plot of land stamped the citizen as a loyal and responsible member of a free and self-conscious

---

[1] To this question I return in the concluding chapter.

community. The ruin of Attic farmers in the Peloponnesian war, the disastrous changes in Italian agriculture after Rome became imperial, still left the old prepossession. The charm of country life and pursuits remained as an ineffective ideal. Greek philosophers were impressed with the virtues of farmer-folk, virtues social moral and ultimately political. From them Cicero and others learnt to praise rustic life : the Gracchi made vain efforts to revive it : the poets, led by Vergil, pictured the glories of old Italian agriculture : but the aspirations were vain. The 'classical' civilization was urban in its growth, and urban it remained. Writers on agriculture might lament that free men, capable of tilling the land, loitered idly in the city. In practice they had to take facts as they found them, and give elaborate precepts for a farm-system in which slavery was the essential factor.

It was and is possible to regard agriculture from various points of view. Three of these at least deserve a preliminary consideration. The nakedly economic view, that the production of food is necessary for any life above that of mere savages, and therefore is worthy of respect, can never have been wholly absent from men's minds in any age. It was common property, and found frequent expression. Even when various causes led to much dependence on imported corn, the sentiment still survived, and its soundness was recognized by philosophers. The military view, that the hardy peasant makes the best soldier, was generally accepted in principle, but its relation to agriculture in the strict sense of tillage was not always a direct one. The technical training of skilled combatants began early in Greece. It was not only in the Spartan or Cretan systems that such training was normal : the citizen armies of Athens consisted of men who had passed through a long course of gymnastic exercises and drill. During their training these young men can hardly have devoted much labour to the tillage of farms, even those of them who were of country birth. What percentage of them settled down in their later years to farm-life, is just what one vainly wishes to know. The helot-system supplied the tillage that fed the warrior-caste of Sparta. It would seem that the toils of hunting played a great part in producing the military fitness required of the young Spartiate. We may be pretty sure that the Thessalian cavalry—wealthy lords ruling dependent cultivators—were not tillers of the soil. Boeotia and Arcadia were both lands in which there was a large farmer class. Boeotian infantry were notable for their steadiness in the shock of battle. But they were not untrained, far from it. United action was ever difficult in Arcadia, where small cities lay scattered in the folds of mountains. Hence no Arcadian League ever played a leading part in Greece. But the rustics of these country towns and villages were man for man as good material for war-work as

Greece could produce. In the later age of professional soldering they, with the Aetolians and others in the less civilized parts, furnished numbers of recruits to the Greek mercenary armies. But the regular mercenary who had the luck to retire in comfortable circumstances, on savings of pay and loot, is portrayed to us as more inclined to luxury and wantonness in some great city than to the simple monotony of rustic life. Nor must we forget that slaves were often an important part[1] of war-booty, and that the professional warrior was used to the attendance of slaves (male and female) even on campaigns. So far the connexion of peasant and soldier does not amount to much more than the admission that the former was a type of man able to endure the hardships of a military career.

The national regular army formed by Philip son of Amyntas in Macedonia, afterwards the backbone of Alexander's mixed host, is in itself a phenomenon of great interest: for in making it Philip made a nation. That the ranks were mainly filled with country folk is certain. But, what with wastage in wars and the settlement of many old soldiers in the East, there is little evidence to shew whether any considerable number of veterans returned to Macedon and settled on the land. I believe that such cases were few. The endless wars waged by Alexander's successors with mixed and mongrel armies were hardly favourable to rustic pursuits: foundation of great new cities was the characteristic of the times. When we turn to Rome we find a very different story. Tradition represents landowners settled on the land and tilling it as the persons responsible for the defence of the state. Cincinnatus called from the plough to be dictator is the typical figure of early patriotic legend. When the Roman Plebeians dislodged the Patrician clans from their monopoly of political power, the burden of military service still rested on the *adsidui*, the men with a footing on the land. Tradition still shews us the farmer-soldier taking the risk of disaster to his homestead during his absence on campaigns. In the historical twilight of fragmentary details, coloured by later imagination, thus much is clear and credible. The connexion between land-holding and soldiering was not openly disregarded until the reforms of Marius. The age of revolution was then already begun, and one of its most striking features was the creation of a professional soldiery, a force which, as experience proved, was more easy to raise than to disband. The method of pensioning veterans by assigning to them parcels of land for settlement was in general a failure, for the men were unused to thrift and indisposed to a life of patient and uneventful labour. The problem of the Republic was inherited by the Empire, and attempts at solution were only partially successful: but the system

---

[1] A good instance is Xen *anab* IV I §§ 12–14.

of standing armies, posted on the frontiers, made the settlement of veterans in border-provinces a matter of less difficulty. From the third century AD onwards we find a new plan coming into use. Men were settled with their families on lands near the frontiers, holding them by a military tenure which imposed hereditary liability to service in the armies. Thus the difficulty was for a time met by approaching it from the other end. The superiority of the rustic recruit was as fully recognized as ever: at the end of the fourth century it was re-affirmed[1] by Vegetius.

I pass on to the third point of view, which I may perhaps call philosophic. It appears in practice as the view of the statesman, in theory as that of the speculative philosopher. Men whose life and interests are bound up with agriculture are in general a steady class, little inclined to wild agitations and rash ventures. On a farm there is always something not to be left undone without risk of loss. The operations of nature go on unceasingly, uncontrolled by man. Man must adapt himself to the conditions of soil and weather: hence he must be ever on the watch to take advantage of his opportunities, and this leaves him scant leisure for politics. We may add that the habit of conforming to nature's laws, and of profiting by not resisting what cannot be successfully resisted, is a perpetual education in patience. Working farmers as a class were not men lightly to embark in revolutionary schemes, so long as their condition was at all tolerable. It must be borne in mind that before the invention of representative systems a citizen could only vote by appearing in person at the city, where all the Assemblies were held. Assemblies might be adjourned, and two journeys, to the city and back, were not only time-wasting and tiresome, but might have to be repeated. Accordingly we hear of the encouragement of Attic farmers by Peisistratus[2] as being a policy designed to promote the stability of his government. At Rome we find reformers alarmed at the decay of the farmer-class in a great part of Italy, and straining to revive it as the sound basis of a national life, the only practical means of purifying the corrupted institutions of the state. Selfish opposition on the part of those interested in corruption was too strong for reformers, and the chance of building up a true Italian nation passed away. The working farmer had disappeared from Roman politics. The sword and the venal city mob remained, and the later literature was left to deplore the consequences.

The course of agricultural decline in Greece was different in detail from that in Italy, but its evil effects on political life were early noted, at least in Attica. The rationalist Euripides saw the danger clearly, during the Peloponnesian war; and the sympathy of the

---

[1] Veget I 3.   [2] Ἀθηναίων πολιτεία cap 16, with Sandys' notes.

conservative Aristophanes with the suffering farmers was plainly marked. The merits of the farmer-class as 'safe' citizens, the backbone of a wise and durable state-life, became almost a commonplace of Greek political theory. Plato and Aristotle might dream of ideal states, governed by skilled specialists professionally trained for their career from boyhood. In their more practical moments, turning from aspirations to facts of the world around them, they confessed the political value of the farmer-class. To Aristotle the best hope of making democracy a wholesome and tolerable form of government lay in the strengthening of this element: the best Demos is the γεωργικὸς δῆμος, and it is a pity that it so often becomes superseded by the growing population devoted to trades and commerce. I need not carry further these brief and imperfect outlines of the honourable opinion held of agriculture in the Greco-Roman world. As producing necessary food, as rearing hardy soldiers, as favouring the growth and maintenance of civic virtues, it was the subject of general praise. Some might confess that they shrank from personal labour on the land. Yet even in Caesarian Rome it is somewhat startling when Sallust[1] dismisses farming in a few words of cynical contempt.

It is clear that the respect felt for agriculture was largely due to the opinion that valuable qualities of body and mind were closely connected with its practice and strengthened thereby. So long as it was on the primitive footing, each household finding labour for its own maintenance, the separation of handwork and direction could hardly arise. This primitive state of things, assumed by theorists ancient and modern, and depicted in tradition, had ceased to be normal in the time of our earliest records. And the employment of persons, not members of the household, as hired labourers, or of bondmen only connected with the house as dependents, at once differentiated these 'hands' from the master and his family. The master could not habitually hire day-labourers or keep a slave unless he found it paid him to do so. For a man to work for his own profit or for that of another were very different things. This simple truism, however, does not end the matter from my present point of view. It is necessary to ask whether the respect felt for agriculture was so extended as to include the hired labourer and the slave as well as the working master. We shall see that it was not. The house-master, holding and cultivating a plot of land on a secure tenure, is the figure glorified in traditions and legendary scenes. The Greek term αὐτουργός, the man who does his own work, is specially applied to him as a man that works with his own hands. It crops up in literature often, from Euripides to Polybius

---

[1] *Catil* 4 § 1 *non fuit consilium...neque vero agrum colundo aut venando servilibus officiis intentum aetatem agere.*

and Dion Chrysostom; and sometimes, when the word is not used, it is represented by equivalents. But both the hired labourer and the slave were employed for the express purpose of working with their own hands. And yet, so far as agriculture is concerned, I cannot find that they were credited with αὐτουργία, the connotation[1] of which is generally favourable, seldom neutral, never (I think) unfavourable. It seems then that the figure present to the mind was one who not only worked with his own hands, but worked for his own profit—that is, on his own farm. And with this interpretation the traditions of early Rome fully agree.

To admit this does not however imply that the working house-master employed neither hired labourer nor slave. So long as he took a hand in the farm-work, he was a working cultivator for his own profit. The larger the scale of his holding, the more he would need extra labour. If prosperous, he would be able to increase his holding or supplement his farming[2] by other enterprises. More and more he would be tempted to drop handwork and devote himself to direction. If still successful, he might move on a stage further, living in the city and carrying on his farms by deputy, employing stewards, hired freemen or slaves, or freedmen, his former slaves. If he found in the city more remunerative pursuits than agriculture, he might sell his land and the live and dead stock thereon, and become simply an urban capitalist. So far as I know, this last step was very seldom taken; and I believe the restraining influence to have been the prestige attached to the ownership of land, even when civic franchises had ceased to depend on the possession of that form of property alone. If this view be correct, the fact is notable: for the system of great landed estates, managed by stewards[3] on behalf of wealthy owners who lived in the city, was the ruin of the peasant farmer class, in whose qualities statesmen and philosophers saw the guarantee for the state's lasting vigour. No longer were αὐτουργοὶ a force in politics: in military service the professional soldier, idling in the intervals of wars, superseded the rustic, levied for a campaign and looking forward to the hour of returning to his plough. It was in Italy that the consummation of this change was most marked, for Rome alone provided a centre in which the great landlord could reside and influence political action in his own interest. To Rome the wealth extorted from tributary subjects flowed in an ever-swelling stream. No small part of the spoils served to enrich the noble land-lords, directly or indirectly, and to supply them with the funds needed

[1] To this topic I return in the concluding chapter. See chapter on Aristotle.
[2] See chapter on Cato.
[3] For the existence of this system in Modern Italy see Bolton King and Okey *Italy today* pp 174-5.

for corrupting the city mob and so controlling politics. Many could afford to hold their lands even when it was doubtful whether estates managed by slaves or hirelings were in fact a remunerative investment. If we may believe Cicero, it was financial inability[1] to continue this extravagant policy that drove some men of apparent wealth to favour revolutionary schemes. The old-fashioned farmstead, the *villa*, was modernized into a luxurious country seat, in which the owner might now and then pass a brief recess, attended by his domestic slaves from Town, and perhaps ostentatiously entertaining a party of fashionable friends.

We have followed the sinister progress of what I will call the Agricultural Interest, from the 'horny-handed' peasant[2] farmer to the land-proud capitalist. No doubt the picture is a highly coloured one, but in its general outlines we are not entitled to question its truth. Exceptions there certainly were. In hilly parts of Italy a rustic population[3] of freemen survived, and it was from them that the jobbing gangs of wage-earners of whom we read were drawn. And in the great plain of the Po agricultural conditions remained far more satisfactory than in such districts as Etruria or Lucania, where great estates were common. A genuine farming population seems there to have held most of the land, and rustic slavery appeared in less revolting form. But these exceptions did not avail to stay the decline of rural Italy. True, as the supply of slave-labour gradually shrank in the empire, the working farmer reappeared on the land. But he reappeared as a tenant gradually becoming bound[4] to the soil, worried by the exactions of officials, or liable to a blood-tax in the shape of military service. He was becoming not a free citizen of a free state, but a half-free serf helplessly involved in a great mechanical system. Such a person bore little resemblance to the free farmer working with his own hands for himself on his own land, the rustic figure from whom we started. On the military side, he was, if a soldier, now soldier first and farmer afterwards: on the civic side, he was a mere subject-unit, whose virtues were of no political importance and commanded no respect. In the final stage we find the government recruiting its armies from barbarians and concerned to keep the farmer on the land. So cogent then was the necessity of insuring the supply of food for the empire and its armies.

At this point we must return to our first question, how far the agriculture of the Greco-Roman world depended on free or slave labour. It

---

[1] Cic *in Catil* II § 18. See the chapter on Cicero.
[2] Cf Valerius Maximus VII 5 § 2.
[3] For modern Italy see Appendix.
[4] Cf Caesar *B C* I 34, 56, discussed in the chapter on Varro.

is clear that, while the presence of the slave presupposes the freeman to control him, the presence of the freeman does not necessarily imply that of the slave.   Dion Chrysostom[1] was logically justified in saying that freedom comes before slavery in order of time.   And no doubt this is true so long as we only contemplate the primitive condition of households each providing for its own vital needs by the labour of its members.   But the growth of what we call civilization springs from the extension of needs beyond the limits of what is absolutely necessary for human existence.   By what steps the advantages of division of labour were actually discovered is a subject for the reconstructive theorist.   But it must have been observed at a very early stage that one man's labour might be to another man's profit.   Those who tamed and employed other animals were not likely to ignore the possibilities offered by the extension of the system to their brother men.   It would seem the most natural thing in the world.   It might be on a very small scale, and any reluctance on the bondsman's part might be lessened by the compensations of food and protection.   A powerful master might gather round him a number of such dependent beings, and he had nothing to gain by treating them cruelly.   On them he could devolve the labour of producing food, and so set free his own kinsmen to assert the power of their house.   In an age of conflict stronger units tended to absorb weaker, and the formation of larger societies would tend to create fresh needs, to encourage the division of labour, and to promote civilization by the process of exchange.   Labour under assured control was likely to prove an economic asset of increasing value.   In agriculture it would be of special importance as providing food for warriors busied with serving the community in war.

This imaginative sketch may serve to remind us that there are two questions open to discussion in relation to the subject.   First, the purely speculative one, whether the early stages of progress in civilization could have been passed without the help of slavery.   Second, the question of fact, whether they were so passed or not.   It is the latter with which I am concerned.   The defects of the evidence on which we have to form an opinion are manifest.   Much of it is not at first hand, and it will often be necessary to comment on its unsatisfactory character.   In proceeding to set it out in detail, I must again repeat that two classes of free handworkers must be clearly kept distinct—those who work for themselves, and those who work for others.   It is the latter class only that properly come into comparison with slaves.   A man habitually working for himself may of course work occasionally for others as a wage-earner.   But here, as in the case of the farmer-soldier, we have one person in two capacities.

[1] *Oratio* XV (I pp 266-7 Dind).

AUTHORITIES IN DETAIL—GREEK

III. THE HOMERIC POEMS.

The Iliad. In a great war-poem we can hardly expect to find many references to the economic labours of peace. And an army fighting far from home in a foreign land would naturally be out of touch with the rustic life of Greece. Nor was the poet concerned to offer us the details of supply-service, though he represents the commissariat as efficient. Free labour appears[1] in various forms of handicraft, and the mention of pay ($\mu\iota\sigma\theta\acute{o}\varsigma$)[2] shews wage-earning as a recognized fact. We hear of serving for hire ($\theta\eta\tau\epsilon\acute{v}\epsilon\iota\nu$)[3], and the $\emph{ἔρι}\theta οι$ or farm-labourers[4] seem to be $\theta\hat{\eta}\tau\epsilon\varsigma$ under a special name. That labour is not viewed as a great degradation may fairly be inferred from the case of Hephaestus the smith-god, from the wage-service of Poseidon and Apollo under Laomedon, and from the herdsman-service of Apollo under Admetus. Agriculture is assumed, and in the Catalogue 'works' ($\emph{ἔργα}$)[5] occurs in the sense of 'tilled lands.' But it is chiefly in similes or idyllic scenes that we get glimpses of farming[6] operations. Thus we have ploughing, reaping, binding, threshing, winnowing. Most striking of all is the passage in which the work of irrigation[7] is graphically described. There is no reason to suppose that any of the workers in these scenes are slaves: they would seem to be wage-earners. But I must admit that, if slaves were employed under the free workers, the poet would very likely not mention such a detail: that is, if slavery were a normal institution taken for granted. For the present I assume only free labour in these cases. We are made aware of a clear social difference between the rich and powerful employer and the employed labourer. The mowers are at work in the field of some rich man[8] ($\grave{a}\nu\delta\rho\grave{o}\varsigma$ $\mu\acute{a}\kappa\alpha\rho o\varsigma$ $\kappa\alpha\tau'$ $\acute{a}\rho o\nu\rho\alpha\nu$), who does not appear to lend a hand himself. Or again in the close of a ruler ($\tau\acute{\epsilon}\mu\epsilon\nu o\varsigma$ $\beta\alpha\sigma\iota\lambda\acute{\eta}\iota o\nu$)[9], with binders following them, a busy scene. The $\beta\alpha\sigma\iota\lambda\epsilon\acute{v}\varsigma$ himself stands watching them in dignified silence, staff in hand. There is nothing here to suggest that the small working farmer was a typical figure in the portraiture of rural life. Flocks and herds are of great importance, indeed the ox is a normal standard of value. But the herdsmen are mean freemen. Achilles is disgusted[10] at the prospect of being drowned by Scamander 'like a

---

[1] VI 315, XXIII 712, VII 221.   [2] XII 433–5, XXI 445, 451, X 304.
[3] XXI 444.   [4] XVIII 550.   [5] II 751.
[6] XVIII 542, 554, XI 67, XX 495–7, V 500, XIII 590.   [7] XXI 257–9.
[8] XI 68.   [9] XVIII 550–60.   [10] XXI 281–3.

young swineherd swept away by a stream in flood.' For the heroes of the poem are warrior-lords: the humble toilers of daily life are of no account beside them.

And yet the fact of slavery stands out clearly, and also its connexion with the fact of capture in war. The normal way of dealing with enemies is to slay the men and enslave the women. The wife of a great warrior has many handmaidens, captives of her lord's prowess. A slave-trade exists, and we hear of males being spared[1] and 'sold abroad': for they are sent 'to islands far away' or 'beyond the salt sea.' We do not find male slaves with the army: perhaps we may guess that they were not wanted. A single reference to δμῶες (properly slave-captives) appears in XIX 333, where Achilles, speaking of his property at home in Phthia, says κτῆσιν ἐμὴν δμῶάς τε. But we cannot be certain that these slaves are farm-hands. We can only reflect that a slave bought and paid for was not likely to be fed in idleness or put to the lightest work. In general it seems that what weighed upon the slave, male or female, was the pressure of constraint, the loss of freedom, not the fear of cruel treatment. What Hector keeps from the Trojans[2] is the 'day of constraint,' ἦμαρ ἀναγκαῖον, also expressed by δούλιον ἦμαρ. Viewed from the other side we find enslavement consisting in a taking away[3] the 'day of freedom,' ἐλεύθερον ἦμαρ. The words δούλην III 409 and ἀνδραπόδεσσι VII 475 are isolated cases of substantives in passages the genuineness of which has been questioned. On the whole it is I think not an unfair guess that, if the poet had been depicting the life of this same Greek society in their homeland, and not under conditions of present war, we should have found more references to slavery as a working institution. As it is, we get a momentary glimpse[4] of neighbour landowners, evidently on a small scale, engaged in a dispute concerning their boundaries, measuring-rod in hand; and nothing to shew whether such persons supplied the whole of their own labour in tillage or supplemented it by employing hired men or slaves.

The Odyssey is generally held to be of later date than the Iliad. A far more important distinction is that its scenes are not episodes of war. A curious difference of terms[5] is seen in the case of the word οἰκῆες, which in the Iliad seems to mean 'house-folk' including both free and slave, in the Odyssey to mean slaves only. But as to the condition of slaves there is practically no difference. A conquered foe was spared on the battlefield by grace of the conqueror, whose ownership of his slave was unlimited: and this unlimited right could be conveyed

---

[1] XXI 40-2, 78-80, 101-3, 453-4, XXII 45, XXIV 751-2.
[2] XVI 835-6, VI 463.
[3] VI 455, XVI 831, XX 193.   [4] XII 421-4.
[5] IV 245, XIV 3-4, 62-5, XVI 302-3, XVII 533. (*Iliad* V 413, VI 366.)

by sale[1] to a third party. We find Odysseus ready to consign offending slaves[2] to torture mutilation or death. In the story of his visit to Troy[3] as a spy we hear that he passed for a slave, and that part of his disguise consisted in the marks of flogging. Yet the relations of master and mistress to their slaves are most kindly in ordinary circumstances. The faithful slave is a type glorified in the Odyssey: loyalty is the first virtue of a slave, and it is disloyalty, however shewn, that justifies the master's vengeance. For they live on intimate terms[4] with their master and mistress and are trusted to a wonderful degree. In short we may say that the social atmosphere of the Odyssey is full of mild slavery, but that in the background there is always the grim possibility of atrocities committed by absolute power. And we have a trace even of secondary[5] slavery: for the swineherd, himself a slave, has an under-slave of his own, bought with his own goods from slave-dealers while his own master was abroad. Naturally enough we find slaves classed as a part of the lord's estate. Odysseus hopes[6] that before he dies he may set eyes on his property, his slaves and his lofty mansion. But another and perhaps socially more marked distinction seems implied in the suitors' question[7] about Telemachus—'who were the lads that went with him on his journey? were they young nobles of Ithaca, or his own hired men and slaves ($\theta\hat{\eta}\tau\acute{\epsilon}\varsigma$ $\tau\epsilon$ $\delta\mu\hat{\omega}\acute{\epsilon}\varsigma$ $\tau\epsilon$)?' The answer is that they were 'the pick of the community, present company excepted.' The wage-earner and the slave do not seem to be parted by any broad social line. Indeed civilization had a long road yet to travel before levelling movement among the free classes drew a vital distinction between them on the one side and slaves on the other.

Free workers of various kinds are often referred to, and we are, owing to the circumstances of the story, brought more into touch with them than in the Iliad. Handicraftsmen[8] are a part of the life of the time, and we must assume the smith the carpenter and the rest of the males to be free: female slaves skilled in working wool do not justify us in supposing that the corresponding men are slaves. Beside these are other men who practise a trade useful to the community, 'public-workers' ($\delta\eta\mu\iota\omicron\epsilon\rho\gamma\omicron\acute{\iota}$)[9], but not necessarily handworkers. Thus we find the seer, the leech, the bard, classed with the carpenter as persons whom all men would readily entertain as guests; the wandering beggar none would invite. The last is a type of 'mean freeman,' evidently common in that society. He is too much akin to the suppliant, whom religion[10]

---

[1] Selling XIV 297, XV 387, 428, 452–3, XX 382–3. Buying I 430, XIV 115, etc.

[2] XIX 488–90, XXII 173–7, 189–93, 440–5, 462–4, 465–77. (Cf XVIII 82–7.)

[3] IV 245 foll.   [4] IX 205–7, XI 430–2, XVI 14 foll, XIX 489, XXIII 227–8, etc.

[5] XIV 449–52.   [6] VII 224–5, XIX 526.   [7] IV 643–4, 652.

[8] In XIX 56–7 a $\tau\acute{\epsilon}\kappa\tau\omega\nu$, Icmalius, is even mentioned by name.

[9] XVII 382–7, XIX 134–5.   [10] XIV 56–8.

protects, to be roughly shewn the door: he is *αἰδοῖος ἀλήτης*[1], and trades on the reverence felt for one who appeals as stranger to hospitable custom. Thus he picks up a living[2] from the scraps and offals of great houses. But he is despised, and, what concerns us here, despised[3] not only for his abject poverty but for his aversion to honest work. That the poet admires industry is clear, and is curiously illustrated by his contrasted pictures of civilization and barbarism. In Phaeacia are the fenced-in gardens[4] that supply Alcinous and his people with never-failing fruits: the excellence of their naval craftsmen is expressed in the 'yarn' of ships that navigate themselves. In the land of the Cyclopes, nature provides[5] them with corn and wine, but they neither sow nor plough. They have flocks of sheep and goats. They have no ships or men to build them. They live in caves, isolated savages with no rudiments of civil life. It is not too much to say that the poet is a believer in work and a contemner of idleness: the presence of slaves does not suggest that the free man is to be lazy. Odysseus boasts of his activities (*δρηστοσύνη*)[6]. He is ready to split wood and lay a fire, to prepare and serve a meal, and in short to wait on the insolent suitors as inferiors do on nobles. Of course he is still the unknown wanderer: but the contrast[7] between him and the genuine beggar Irus is an effective piece of by-play in the poem.

Turning to agriculture, we may note that it fills no small place. Wheat and barley, pounded or ground to meal, seem to furnish the basis of civilized diet. The Cyclops[8] does not look like a 'bread-eating man,' and wine completely upsets him to his ruin. Evidently the bounty of nature has been wasted on such a savage. But the cultivation of cereal crops is rather assumed than emphasized in the pictures of Greek life. We hear of tilled lands (*ἔργα*)[9], and farm-labour (*ἔργον*)[10] is mentioned as too wearisome for a high-spirited warrior noble. The tired and hungry plowman[11] appears in a simile. But the favourite culture is that of the vine and olive and other fruits in orchards carefully fenced and tended. One of the suitors makes a jesting offer[12] to the unknown Odysseus 'Stranger, would you be willing to serve for hire (*θητευέμεν*), if I took you on, in an outlying field—you shall have a sufficient wage —gathering stuff for fences and planting tall trees? I would see that you were regularly fed clothed and shod. No, you are a ne'er-do-weel (*ἔργα κάκ' ἔμμαθες*) and will not do farm-work (*ἔργον*): you prefer to go round cringing for food to fill your insatiate belly.' This scornful proposal sets the noble's contempt for wage-earning labour in a clear light.

---

[1] XVII 578.   [2] XVII 18–9, 226–8.   [3] XVIII 403.
[4] VII 112 foll, VIII 557–63.   [5] IX 109–11, 125 foll.   [6] XV 319 foll.
[7] XVIII 1–116.   [8] IX 191.   [9] II 22, IV 318, XIV 344, XVI 139–45.
[10] XIV 222–3.   [11] XIII 31–4.   [12] XVIII 357–64.

And the shade of Achilles, repudiating[1] the suggestion that it is a great
thing to be a ruler among the dead in the ghostly world, says 'I had
rather be one bound to the soil, serving another for hire, employed by
some landless man of little property, than be king of all the dead.' He
is speaking strongly: to work for hire, a mean destiny at best, is at its
meanest when the employer is a man with no land-lot of his own
(ἄκληρος), presumably occupying on precarious tenure a bit of some
lord's estate. After such utterances we cannot wonder that as we saw
above, θῆτες and δμῶες are mentioned[2] in the same breath.

That slaves are employed on the farm is clear enough. When
Penelope sends for old Dolius[3], a *servus dotalis* of hers (to use the
Roman expression) she adds 'who is in charge of my fruit-garden.' So
too the aged Laertes, living a hard life on his farm, has a staff of slaves[4]
to do his will, and their quarters and farm duties are a marked detail
of the picture. The old man, in dirty rags like a slave, is a contrast[5]
to the garden, in which every plant and tree attests the devoted toil of
his gardeners under his own skilled direction. Odysseus, as yet un-
recognized by his father, asks him how he comes to be in such a mean
attire, though under it he has the look of a king. Then he drops this
tone and says 'but tell me, whose slave[6] are you, and who owns the
orchard you are tending?' The hero knows his father, but to preserve
for the present his own incognito he addresses him as the slave that
he appears to be. Now if garden work was done by slaves, surely the
rougher operations of corn-growing were not confined to free labour,
and slaves pass unmentioned as a matter of course. Or are we to
suppose that free labour had been found more economical in the long
run, and so was employed for the production of a staple food? I can
hardly venture to attribute so mature a view to the society of the
Odyssey. We must not forget that animal food, flesh and milk, was an
important element of diet, and that the management of flocks and herds
was therefore a great part of rustic economy. But the herdsmen in
charge are slaves, such as Eumaeus, bought in his youth by Laertes[7]
of Phoenician kidnappers. In romancing about his own past experiences Odysseus describes a raid in Egypt, and how the natives
rallied[8] and took their revenge. 'Many of our company they slew:
others they took alive into the country, to serve them in forced labour.'
As the ravaging of their 'beautiful farms' was a chief part of the raiders'
offence, the labour exacted from these captives seems most probably
agricultural.

An interesting question arises in reference to the faithful slaves,
the swineherd and the goatherd. When Odysseus promises them

[1] XI 489-91. [2] IV 644. [3] IV 735-7. [4] XXIV 208-10.
[5] XXIV 222-55. [6] XXIV 257. [7] XV 412-92. [8] XIV 271-2.

rewards in the event of his destroying the suitors with their help, does this include an offer of freedom? Have we here, as some have thought, a case of manumission—of course in primitive form, without the legal refinements of later times? The promise is made[1] so to speak in the character of a father-in-law: 'I will provide you both with wives and give you possessions and well-built houses near to me, and you shall in future be to me comrades and brothers of Telemachus.' The 'brother-hood' suggested sounds as if it must imply freedom. But does it? Eumaeus had been brought up[2] by Laertes as the playmate of his daughter Ctimene; yet he remained nevertheless a slave. Earlier in the poem Eumaeus, excusing the poor entertainment that he can offer the stranger (Odysseus), laments the absence[3] of his lord, 'who' he says 'would have shewn me hearty affection and given me possessions such as a kindly lord gives his slave ($oἰκῆϊ$), a house and a land-lot ($κλῆρον$) and a wife of recognized worth ($πολυμνήστην$), as a reward for laborious and profitable service.' Here also there is no direct reference to an expected grant of freedom: nor do I think that it is indirectly implied. It is no doubt tempting to detect in these passages the germ of the later manumission. But it is not easy to say why, in a world of little groups ruled by noble chiefs, the gift of freedom should have been a longed-for boon. However high-born the slave might have been in his native land, in Ithaca he was simply a slave. If by belonging to a lord he got material comfort and protection, what had he to gain by becoming a mere wage-earner? surely nothing. I can see no ground for believing that in the society of the 'heroic' age the bare name of freedom was greatly coveted. It was high birth that really mattered, but the effect of this would be local: nothing would make Eumaeus, though son of a king, noble in Ithaca. No doubt the slave might be at the mercy of a cruel lord. Such a slave would long for freedom, but such a lord was not likely to grant it. On the whole, it is rash to read manumission into the poet's words.

Reviewing the evidence presented by these 'Homeric' poems, it may be well to insist on the obvious truism that we are not dealing with formal treatises, charged with precise definitions and accurate statistics. The information given by the poet drops out incidentally while he is telling his tale and making his characters live. It is all the more genuine because it is not furnished in support of a particular argument: but it is at the same time all the less complete. And it is not possible to say how far this or that detail may have been coloured by imagination. Still, allowing freely for the difficulty suggested by these considerations, I think we are justified in drawing a general inference as to the position of handworkers, particularly on the land, in Greek 'heroic' society as

---

[1] XXI 213-6.   [2] XV 363-5.   [3] XIV 62-5.

conceived by the poet. If the men who practise handicrafts are freemen, and their presence welcome, this does not exalt them to anything like equality with the warrior nobles and chiefs. And in agriculture the labourer is either a slave or a wage-earner of a very dependent kind. The lord shews no inclination to set his own hand to the plough. When one of the suitors derisively invites the supposed beggar to abandon his idle vagrancy for a wage-earning 'job on the land,' the disguised Odysseus retorts[1] 'Ah, if only you and I could compete in a match as reapers hard at work fasting from dawn to dark, or at ploughing a big field with a pair of full-fed spirited oxen,—you would soon see what I could do.' He adds that, if it came to war, his prowess would soon silence the sneer at his begging for food instead of working. Now, does the hero imply that he would really be willing to reap or plough? I do not think so: what he means is that he is conscious of that reserve of bodily strength which appears later in the poem, dramatically shewn in the bending of the famous bow.

IV. HESIOD.

Hesiod, Works and Days. Whether this curious poem belongs in its present shape to the seventh century BC, or not, I need not attempt to decide. It seems certain that it is later than the great Homeric poems, but is an early work, perhaps somewhat recast and interpolated, yet in its main features representing conditions and views of a society rural, half-primitive, aristocratic. I see no reason to doubt that it may fairly be cited in evidence for my present purpose. The scene of the 'Works' is in Boeotia: the works (ἔργα) are operations of farming, and the precepts chiefly saws of rustic wisdom. Poverty[2] is the grim spectre that haunts the writer, conscious of the oppressions of the proud and the hardness of a greedy world. Debt, want, beggary, must be avoided at all costs. They can only be avoided[3] by thrift, forethought, watchfulness, promptitude that never procrastinates, and toil that never ceases. And the mere appeal to self-interest is reinforced by recognizing the stimulus of competition (ἔρις)[4] which in the form of honest rivalry is a good influence. The poet represents himself as owner of a land-lot (κλῆρος)[5], part of a larger estate, the joint patrimony of his brother Perses and himself: this estate has already been divided, but points of dispute still remain. Hesiod suggests that Perses has been wronging him with the help of bribed 'kings.' But wrong-doing is not the true road to well-being. A dinner of herbs and a clear conscience are the

[1] XVIII 366-75.   [2] 299-302, 394-5, 399-400, 403-4, 646-7.
[3] 289-90, 303-5, 308-13, 381-2, 410-3 (cf 498).   [4] 20-4.   [5] 37-41.

better way. As the proverb says 'half is more than the whole.' Perses is treated to much good advice, the gist of which is first and foremost an exhortation[1] to work (ἐργάζευ), that is, work on the land, in which is the source of honourable wealth. Personal labour is clearly meant: it is in the sweat[2] of his brow that the farmer is to thrive. Such is the ordinance of the gods. Man is meant to resemble[3] the worker bee, not the worthless drone. It is not ἔργον but idleness (ἀεργίη) that is a reproach. Get wealth[4] by working, and the idler will want to rival you: honour and glory attend on wealth. Avoid delays[5] and vain talk: the procrastinator is never sure of a living; for he is always hoping, when he should act. Whether sowing or ploughing or mowing, off with your outer[6] garment, if you mean to get your farm-duties done in due season. The farmer must rise early, and never get behindhand with his work: to be in time, and never caught napping by changes of weather, is his duty.

Here is a picture of humble and strenuous life, very different from the scenes portrayed in the 'heroic' epics. It seems to belong to a later and less warlike age. But the economic and social side of life is in many respects little changed. The free handicraftsmen seem much the same. Jealousy of rivals[7] in the same trade—potter, carpenter, beggar, or bard—is a touch that attests their freedom. The smith, the weaver, the shoemaker, and the shipwright, are mentioned[8] also. Seafaring[9] for purposes of gain illustrates what men will dare in quest of wealth. You should not cast a man's poverty[10] in his teeth: but do not fancy that men will give you[11] of their store, if you and your family fall into poverty. Clearly the beggar is not more welcome than he was in the world of the Odyssey. Suppliant and stranger are protected[12] by religion, and a man should honour his aged father, if he would see good days. A motive suggested for careful service of the gods is 'that you may buy another's estate[13] and not another buy yours'—that is, that the gods may give you increase. Just so you should keep a watch-dog, that thieves[14] may not steal your goods by night. Hesiod's farmer is to keep the social and religious rules and usages—but he is before all things a keen man of business, no Roman more so.

The labour employed by this close-fisted countryman is partly free partly slave. In a passage[15] of which the exact rendering is disputed the hired man (θῆτα) and woman (ἔριθον) are mentioned as a matter of course. For a helper (ἀνδρὶ φίλῳ)[16] his wage must be secure (ἄρκιος) as stipulated. References to slaves (δμῶες)[17] are more frequent, and

---

[1] 298–9, 397–8.　　　[2] 289–90.　　　[3] 303–5.　　　[4] 308–13.
[5] 410–3, 500–1, 554 foll, 576 foll.　　[6] 391.　　[7] 25–6.
[8] 493, 538, 544, 809.　　[9] 686.　　[10] 717–8.　　[11] 394–400.
[12] 327–34.　　[13] 341.　　[14] 605.　　[15] 602–3.
[16] 370.　　[17] 459, 469–71, 502–3, 559–60, 573, 597–8, 607–8, 765–7.

the need of constant watchfulness, to see that they are not lazy and
are properly fed housed and rested, is insisted on. The feeding of
cattle and slaves is regulated according to their requirements in different
seasons of the year: efficiency is the object, and evidently experience
is the guide. Of female slaves there is no certain[1] mention: indeed
there could be little demand for domestic attendants in the farmer's
simple home. Such work as weaving[2] is to be done by his wife. For
the farmer is to marry, though the risks[3] of that venture are not hidden
from the poet, who gives plain warnings as to the exercise of extreme
care in making a suitable choice. The operations of agriculture are
the usual ploughing sowing reaping threshing and the processes of the
vineyard and the winepress. Oxen sheep and mules form the livestock.
Corn is the staple[4] diet, with hay as fodder for beasts.

Looking on the picture as a whole, we see that the Hesiodic farmer
is to be a model of industry and thrift. Business, not sentiment, is the
note of his character. His function is to survive in his actual circumstances; that is, in a social and economic environment of normal selfishness. If his world is not a very noble one, it is at least eminently
practical. He is a true αὐτουργός, setting his own hand to the plough,
toiling for himself on his own land, with slaves and other cattle obedient
to his will. It is perhaps not too much to say that he illustrates a great
truth bearing on the labour-question,—that successful exploitation of
other men's labour is, at least in semi-primitive societies, only to be
achieved by the man who shares the labour himself. And it is to be
noted that he attests the existence of wage-earning hands as well as
slaves. I take this to mean that there were in his rustic world a number
of landless freemen compelled to make a living as mere farm labourers.
That we hear so much less of this class in later times is probably to
be accounted for by the growth of cities and the absorption of such
persons in urban occupations and trades.

V. STRAY NOTES FROM EARLY POETS.

A few fragments may be cited as of interest, bearing on our subject.
The most important are found in the remains[5] of **Solon**, illustrating the
land-question as he saw and faced it at the beginning of the sixth
century BC. The poets of the seventh and sixth centuries reflect the

---

[1] 406 is reasonably suspected.   [2] 405, 779, 800.   [3] 695–705.
[4] 32, 597, 606–7.
[5] *Solon the Athenian*, by Ivan M. Linforth of the University of California (1919) discusses
in full the conditions of Solon's time and his actual policy, with an edition of his poetic
remains.

problems of an age of unrest, among the causes of which the introduction of metallic coinage, susceptible of hoarding and unaffected by weather, played a great part. Poverty, debt and slavery of debtors, hardship, begging, the insolence and oppression of rich and greedy creditors, are common topics. The sale of free men into slavery abroad is lamented by Solon, who claims to have restored many such victims by his measures of reform. In particular, he removed encumbrances on land, thus setting free the small farmers who were in desperate plight owing to debt. The exact nature and scope of his famous reform is a matter of dispute. Whether he relieved freeholders from a burden of debt, or emancipated the clients[1] of landowning nobles from dependence closely akin to serfdom, cannot be discussed here, and does not really bear on the matter in hand. In either case the persons relieved were a class of working farmers, and the economic reform was the main thing: political reform was of value as tending to secure the economic boon. It is remarkable that Solon, enumerating a number of trades (practically the old Homeric and Hesiodic list), speaks of them merely as means of escaping the pressure of poverty, adding 'and another man[2] is yearly servant to those interested in ploughing, and furrows land planted with fruit-trees.' This man seems to be a wage-earner ($\theta\dot{\eta}s$) working for a large farmer, probably the owner of a landed estate in the rich lowland ($\pi\epsilon\delta\iota\dot{a}s$) of Attica. The small farmers were mostly confined to the rocky uplands. Evidently it is not manual labour that is the hardship, but the dependent position of the hired man working on another's land. The hard-working independent peasant, willing to till stony land for his own support, is the type that Solon encouraged and Peisistratus[3] approved.

The life of such peasant farmers was at best a hard one, and little desired by men living under easier conditions. Two fragments from Ionia express views of dwellers in that rich and genial land. **Phocylides** of Miletus in one of his wise counsels says 'if you desire wealth, devote your care to a fat farm ($\pi\acute{\iota}ovos\ \dot{a}\gamma\rhoo\hat{v}$), for the saying is that a farm is a horn of plenty.' The bitter **Hipponax** of Ephesus describes a man as having lived a gluttonous life and so eaten up his estate ($\tau\dot{o}v\ \kappa\lambda\hat{\eta}\rhoov$): the result is that he is driven to dig a rocky hillside and live on common figs and barley bread—mere slave's fodder ($\delta o\acute{\upsilon}\lambda\iota ov\ \chi\acute{o}\rho\tau ov$). Surely the 'fat farm' was not meant to be worked by the owner single-handed; and the 'slave's fodder' suggests the employment of slaves. Ionia was a home of luxury and ease.

---

[1] The view of M Clerc *Les métèques Athéniens* pp 340–5.

[2] ἄλλος γῆν τέμνων πολυδένδρεον εἰς ἐνιαυτὸν λατρεύει τοῖσιν καμπύλ' ἄροτρα μέλει. Mr Linforth takes the last four words as defining ἄλλος, the plowman. I think they refer to the employers, spoken of as a class.

[3] Aristotle 'Aθ πολ 11, 12, 16.

The oft-quoted scolion of the Cretan **Hybrias** illustrates the point of view of the warrior class in more military communities. His wealth is in sword spear and buckler. It is with these tools that he does his ploughing reaping or vintage. That is, he has command of the labour of others, and enjoys their produce. We shall speak below of the well-known lords and serfs of Crete.

VI. TRACES OF SERFDOM IN GREEK STATES.

Before passing on to the times in which the merits of a free farmer-class, from military and political points of view, became a matter of general and conscious consideration, it is desirable to refer briefly to the recorded cases of agricultural serfdom in Greek states. For the rustic serf is a type quite distinct from the free farmer, the hired labourer, or the slave; though the language of some writers is loose, and does not clearly mark the distinction. Six well-known cases present themselves, in connexion with Sparta, Crete, Argos, Thessaly, Syracuse, and Heraclea on the Pontus. Into the details of these systems it is not necessary to enter, interesting though many of them are. The important feature common to them all is the delegation of agricultural labour. A stronger or better-organized people become masters of a weaker population, conquering their country by force of arms, and sparing the conquered on certain terms. The normal effect of the compact is that the conquerors are established as a ruling warrior class, whose subsistence is provided by the labour of the subject people. These subjects remain on the land as farmers, paying a fixed quota of their produce to their masters. Some are serfs of the state, and pay their dues to the state authorities: some are serfs of individuals, and pay to their lords. In either case they are strictly attached to the land, and cannot be sold out of the country. This clearly marks off the serf from the slave held in personal bondage. In some cases certainly, probably in all, the warrior class (at least the wealthier of them) had also slaves for their own personal service. The serf-system differs from a caste-system. Both, it is true, are hereditary systems, or have a strong tendency to become so. The ruling class do not easily admit deserving subjects into their own ranks. And they take precautions to hinder the degradation of their equals into lower conditions through poverty. The warrior's land-lot ($\kappa\lambda\hat{\alpha}\rho\rho\varsigma$), the sale of which is forbidden, is a favourite institution for the purpose. That such warrior aristocracies could not be kept up in vigour for an indefinite time, was to be proved by experience. Their duration depended on external as well as internal conditions. Hostile invasion might destroy the efficiency of state regulations, however well adapted to keep the serfs under control. Sparta always feared her Helots, and it was essential to keep an enemy out of Laconia. Early in the history of Syracuse the unprivileged masses were supported by the serfs in their rising against the squatter-lords, the γαμόροι whose great estates represented the allotments of the original settlers. In Crete and Thessaly matters were complicated by lack of a central authority. There were a number of cities: subordination and cooperation were alike hard to secure, and the history of both groups is a story of jealousy, collisions, and weakness. The Thessalian Penestae often rebelled. The two classes of Cretan[1] serfs (public and private) were kept quiet partly by rigid exclusion from all training of a military kind, partly by their more favourable condition : but the insular position of Crete was perhaps a factor of equal importance. The long control of indigenous barbarian serfs by the city of Heraclea was probably the result of similar causes.

But in all these cases it is conquest that produces the relation between the tiller of the soil and his overlord. Whether the serf is regarded as a weaker Greek or as a Barbarian (non-Greek) is not at present the main question from my point of view. The notion of castes, belonging to the same society and influenced by the same racial and religious traditions, but each performing a distinct function—priestly military agricultural etc.—as in ancient India, is another thing altogether. Caste separates functions, but the division is in essence collateral. Serfdom is a delegation of functions, and is a compulsory subordination. That the Greeks of the seventh and sixth centuries BC were already becoming conscious of a vital difference between other races and themselves, is fairly certain. It was soon to express itself in the common language. Contact with Persia was soon to crystallize this feeling into a moral antipathy, a disgust and contempt that found voice in the arrogant claim that while nature's law justifies the ruling of servile Barbarians by free Greeks, a reversal of the relation is an unnatural monstrosity. Yet I cannot discover that Greeks ever gave up enslaving brother Greeks. Callicratidas in the field and Plato in his school might protest against the practice; it still remained the custom in war to sell as slaves those, Greek or Barbarian, whom the sword had spared. We shall also find cases in which the remnant of the conquered were left in their homes but reduced to the condition of cultivating serfs.

Among the little that is known of the ancient Etruscans, whose power was once widely extended in Italy, is the fact that they dwelt in cities and ruled a serf population who lived chiefly in the country. The

---

[1] See the remarks of Dareste Haussoullier and Th Reinach in the *Recueil des inscriptions juridiques Grecques* (Paris 1904) on the Gortyn Laws.

ruling race were apparently invaders not akin to any of the Italian
stocks: their subjects probably belonged to the old Ligurian race, in
early times spread over a large part of the peninsula. That the
Etruscan cities recognized a common interest, but in practice did not
support each other consistently, was the chief cause of their gradual
weakening and final fall. Noble lords with warlike traditions had little
bent for farm life or sympathy with the serfs who tilled the soil. The
two classes seem to have kept to their own[1] languages, and the
Etruscan gradually died out under the supremacy of Rome.

VII. HERODOTUS.

Herodotus, writing in the first half of the fifth century BC, partly
recording the results of his own travels, partly dependent on the work
of his predecessors, is a witness of great value. In him we find the
contrast and antipathy[2] of Greek and Barbarian an acknowledged fact,
guiding and dominating Greek sentiment. Unhappily he yields us
very little evidence bearing on the present subject. To slavery and
slave-trade he often refers without comment: these are matters of
course. The servile character of oriental peoples subject to Persia is
contemptuously described[3] through the mouth of the Greek queen of
Halicarnassus. Nor does he spare the Ionian Greeks, whose jealousies
and consequent inefficiency made them the unworthy tools of Persian
ambition; a sad contrast to those patriotic Greeks of old Hellas who,
fired by the grand example of Athens, fought for their freedom and
won it in the face of terrible odds. The disgust—a sort of physical
loathing—with which the free Greek, proud of training his body to perfection, regarded corporal mutilation as practised in the East, is illustrated by such passages[4] as that in which the Persians are astounded
at the Greek athletic competitions for a wreath of olive leaves, and that
in which he coolly tells the story of the eunuch's revenge. But all this,
interesting as giving us his point of view, does not help us in clearing
up the relations of free and slave labour. As for handicrafts, it is
enough to refer to the well-known passage[5] in which, while speaking
of Egypt, he will not decide whether the Greeks got their contempt for
manual trades from the Egyptians or not. That the Greeks, above all
the Spartans, do despise $\chi\epsilon\iota\rho\omega\nu\alpha\xi\iota\alpha\iota$, is certain; but least true of the
Corinthians.   Barbarians in general respect the warrior class among
their own folk and regard manual trades as ignoble. So the source of
Greek prejudice is doubtful. That the craftsmen are free is clear from

---

[1] See Livy X 4 § 9.

[2] See his references to the Spartan use of $\xi\epsilon\hat{\iota}\nu o\iota = \beta\acute{\alpha}\rho\beta\alpha\rho o\iota$ IX 11, 53, 55.

[3] VIII 68 γ.   [4] VIII 26, 105–6.   [5] II 164–7.

the whole context. It is remarkable that in enumerating seven classes of the Egyptian population he mentions no class[1] as devoted to the tillage of the soil, but two of herdsmen, in charge of cattle and swine. Later authorities mention[2] the γεωργοί, and connect them with the military class, rightly, it would seem: for Herodotus[3] refers to the farms granted by the kings to this class. They are farmer-soldiers. It would seem that they were free, so far as any Egyptian could be called free, and worked their land themselves. If this inference be just, we may observe that a Greek thought it a fact worth noting. Was this owing to the contrast[4] offered by systems of serfage in the Greek world?

It is curious that wage-labour is hardly ever directly mentioned. In describing[5] the origin of the Macedonian kings, who claimed descent from an Argive stock, he says that three brothers, exiles from Argos, came to Macedon. There they served the king for wages as herdsmen in charge of his horses cattle sheep and goats. The simplicity of the royal household is emphasized as illustrating the humble scale of ancient monarchies. Alarmed by a prodigy, the king calls his servants (τοὺς θῆτας) and tells them to leave his country. The sequel does not concern us here: we need only note that work for wages is referred to as a matter of course. The same relation is probably meant in the case of the Arcadian deserters[6] who came to Xerxes after Thermopylae, in need of sustenance (βίου) and wishing to get work (ἐνεργοὶ εἶναι). But the term θητεύειν is not used. And the few Athenians who stayed behind[7] in the Acropolis when Athens was evacuated, partly through sheer poverty (ὑπ' ἀσθενείης βίου), would seem to be θῆτες. It is fair to infer that hired labour is assumed as a normal fact in Greek life. For the insistence on poverty[8] as naturally endemic (σύντροφος) in Hellas, only overcome by the manly qualities (ἀρετή) developed in the conquest of hard conditions by human resourcefulness (σοφίη), shews us the background of the picture present to the writer's mind. It is his way of telling us that the question of food-supply was a serious one. Out of her own soil Hellas was only able to support a thin population. Hence Greek forces were absurdly small compared with the myriads of Persia: but the struggle for existence had strung them up to such efficiency and resolute love of freedom that they were ready to face fearful odds.

The passage occurs in the reply of Demaratus the Spartan to a question of Xerxes, and refers more particularly to Sparta. In respect

---

[1] Isocrates *Busiris* §§ 15–20 pp. 224–5 also allows for no special class of γεωργοί in Egypt.
[2] Plato *Timaeus* p 24. Diodorus I 28, 73–4 (? from Hecataeus of Abdera, latter half of 3rd cent BC).
[3] II 141, 168. See Index under *Egypt*.
[4] The passage of Isocrates just cited seems to favour this view.
[5] VIII 137.   [6] VIII 26.   [7] VIII 51.   [8] VII 102.

of courage and military efficiency the claim is appropriate: but poverty was surely characteristic of nearly all the European Hellas, and the language on that point is strictly correct, probably representing the writer's own view. It is also quite consistent with the statement[1] that in early times, before the Athenians had as yet driven all the indigenous population out of Attica, neither the Athenians nor the Greeks generally had slaves (οἰκέτας). The context seems to indicate that domestic slaves are specially meant. I do not lay much stress on this allegation, urged as it is in support of a case by one party to the dispute: but it is a genuine tradition, which appears again in the later literature. In the time of Herodotus there were plenty of domestic slaves. Accordingly he finds it worth while to mention[2] that Scythian kings are attended by persons of their own race, there being no bought servants employed.

Herodotus is a difficult witness to appraise justly, partly from the occasional uncertainty as to whether he is really pledging his own authority on a point, partly because the value of his authority varies greatly on different points. But on the whole I take his evidence to suggest that agriculture was carried on in Greece either by free labouring farmers employing hired men when needed, or by serfs. I do not see any evidence to shew that no slaves were employed. The subject of his book placed him under no necessity of mentioning them: and I can hardly believe that farm-slavery on a small scale had died out all over Greece since the days of Hesiod. Nor do I feel convinced on his authority that the poverty of Greece was, so far as mere food is concerned, as extreme as he makes Demaratus represent it. When the Spartans heard that Xerxes was offering the Athenians a separate peace, they were uneasy, and sent a counter-offer[3] on their own behalf. Not content with appealing to the Hellenic patriotism of Athens, they said 'We feel for you in your loss of two crops and the distress that will last some while yet. But you shall have all this made good. We, Spartans and confederates, will find food for your wives and your helpless families[4] so long as this war lasts.' Supposing this offer to have been actually made, and to have been capable of execution, surely it implies that there were food-stuffs to spare in the Peloponnese. It may be that I am making too much of this passage, and of the one about poverty. The dramatic touch of Herodotus is present in both, and I must leave the apparent inconsistency between them as it stands. The question of Peloponnesian agriculture will come up again in connexion with a passage of Thucydides.

---

[1] VI 137.   [2] IV 72.   [3] VIII 142.

[4] οἰκετέων here = members of the family, as often. Stein refers to VIII 4, 41, 44, 106. Compare the use of οἰκεὺς in the Iliad, and see Aesch Agam 733, Eur Suppl 870.

VIII. THE TRAGEDIANS.

The lives of **Aeschylus** (died 456 BC) **Sophocles** and **Euripides** (both died 406 BC) cover a period of stirring events in the history of Greece, particularly of Athens. **Aeschylus** had borne his part in the Persian wars: he was a fighting man when Herodotus was born, and Sophocles a boy. Euripides saw the rise of Athenian power to its greatest height, and died with Sophocles on the eve of its fall. These men had seen strange and terrible things. Hellas had only beaten off the Persian to ruin herself by her own internecine conflicts. While the hatred and contempt for 'barbarians' grew from sentiment into something very like a moral principle, Greeks butchered or enslaved brother Greeks on an unprecedented scale. Greek lands were laid waste by Greek armies: the devastation of Attica in particular had serious effects on the politics and policy of Athens. Athens at length lost her control of the Euxine corn trade and was starved out. For the moment a decision was reached: the reactionary rural powers, backed by the commercial jealousy of Corinth, had triumphed. No thoughtful man in Athens during the time when the rustic population were crowded into the city, idle and plagued with sickness, could be indifferent to the strain on democratic institutions. This spectacle suggested reflexions that permanently influenced Greek thought on political subjects. The tendency was to accept democracy in some form and degree as inevitable in most states, and to seek salvation in means of checking the foolish extravagancies of mob-rule. The best of these means was the encouragement of farmer-citizens: but the circumstances of Greek history made practical success on these lines impossible. In practice, oligarchy meant privilege, to which a scattered farming population would submit; democracy meant mob-rule sooner or later, and the dominance of urban interests. The problem which Plato and Aristotle could not solve was already present in the latter part of the Peloponnesian war. Aristophanes might ridicule Euripides, but on the country-and-town issue the two were agreed.

Aeschylus indeed furnishes very little to my purpose directly. The Greek antipathy to the Barbarian is very clearly marked; but the only points worth noting are that in the *Persae*[1] he makes Persian speakers refer to their own people as βάρβαροι, and that in a bitter passage of the *Eumenides* he expresses[2] his loathing of mutilations and tortures, referring no doubt to Persian cruelties. Agriculture can hardly be said to be mentioned at all, for the gift of weather-wisdom[3] is

---

[1] *Pers* 186–7, 255, 337, 391, 423, 434, 475, 798, 844.   [2] *Eum* 186–90.
[3] *Prom* 454–8, 708.

useful to others than the farmer, and the Scythian steppes are untilled land. A fragment, telling of a happy land[1] where all things grow in plenty unsown without ploughing or digging, reminds us of the Odyssey, minus the savages: another, referring to the advance made in domestication of beasts to relieve men of toil, make up the meagre list. All are in connexion with Prometheus. There are two interesting passages[2] in which the word γαμόρος (landholder) occurs, but merely as an expression for a man with the rights and responsibilities of a citizen. There is nothing of tillage. It was natural for the champion of the power of the Areopagus to view the citizen from the landholding side. He is a respecter of authority, but at the same time lays great stress on the duty and importance of deference to public opinion. This tone runs through the surviving plays, wherever the scene of a particular drama may be laid. Athenian conditions are always in his mind, and his final judgment appears in the *Eumenides* as an appeal to all true citizens to combine freedom with order. Ties of blood, community of religious observances, the relation between citizens and aliens, are topics on which he dwells again and again. In general it is fair to conclude that, while he cheerfully accepted the free constitution of Athens as it stood since the democratic reform of Cleisthenes, he thought that it was quite democratic enough, and regarded more recent tendencies with some alarm. Now these tendencies, in particular the reforms of Ephialtes and Pericles, were certainly in the direction of lessening the influence of the Attic farmers and increasing that of the urban citizens, who were on the spot to take advantage of them. To put it in the briefest form, Aeschylus must be reckoned an admirer of the solid and responsible citizens of the old school, men with a stake in the country.

Sophocles also supplies very little. The antipathy of Greeks to Barbarians appears in a milder form: Aeschylus was naturally more bitter, having fought against the Persian invader. The doctrine that public opinion (of citizens) ought to be respected, that obedience to constituted authorities is a duty, in short the principle that freedom should be combined with order, is set forth in various passages of dramatic debate. Yet the scenes of the plays, as those of Aeschylus, are laid in legendary ages that knew not democracy. The awful potency of ties of blood, and the relations of citizen and alien, are topics common to both. But I think it may fairly be said that political feeling is less evident in Sophocles. This is consistent with his traditional character. In their attitude towards slavery there is no striking difference: both treat it as a matter of course. But in

---

[1] Fragm 194, 198, Dind.
[2] *Suppl* 612–4, *Eum* 890–1.

Sophocles there are already signs[1] of the questioning that was soon to become outspoken, as to the justice of the relation of master and slave. Agriculture is hardly mentioned. The words γεωργός, γεωργεῖν, γεωργία, are (as in Aeschylus) not used. A reference to ploughing occurs in a famous passage[2] celebrating the resourcefulness of Man. The herdsman, usually a slave, is once[3] spoken of as perhaps a hired servant. One curious passage[4] calls for notice. In the *Trachiniae* the indifference of Heracles to his children is compared by his wife Deianira to the conduct of a farmer (γῄτης) who has got a farm at a distance (ἄρουραν ἔκτοπον) and only visits it at seed-time and harvest. The man is apparently a non-resident landowner, living presumably in the city (surely Athens is in the poet's mind) and working his farm by deputy—a steward—and only inspecting it at important seasons. Whether the labour employed is slave or free, there is nothing to shew. It is of interest to find the situation sufficiently real to be used in a simile. But I infer that the situation, like the conduct of Heracles, is regarded as exceptional.

Euripides takes us into a very different atmosphere. An age of movement was also an age of criticism and inquiry, social religious political ethical. The intellectual leaders came from various parts of the Greek world, but the intellectual centre of 'obstinate questionings' was Athens, and their poet Euripides. The use of drama, with plots drawn from ancient legend, as a vehicle for reflexions on human problems, addressed to a contemporary audience and certain to evoke assent and dissent, is the regular practice of Euripides. His plays give us a mass of information as to the questions exercising the minds of thoughtful men in a stirring period. The point of view is that of the new school, the enlightened 'thinkers' who claimed the right to challenge traditional principles, opinions, prejudices, and institutions, testing them by the canons of human reason fearlessly applied. This attitude was naturally resented by men of the old school, averse to any disturbing influence tending to undermine the traditional morality, and certain to react upon politics. Their opposition can still be traced in the comedies of Aristophanes and in various political movements during the Peloponnesian war. Among the topics to which the new school turned their attention were two of special interest to Euripides. The power of wealth was shewing itself in the growth of capitalistic enterprise, an illustration of which is seen in the case of the rich slave-owner Nicias. Poverty[5] and its

[1] *Trach* 52-3, 61-3, *O T* 763-4, Fragm 518, 677, Dind.
[2] *Antig* 338-40. The use of horses for ploughing is strange. Jebb thinks that mules are meant.
[3] *O T* 1029.   [4] *Trach* 31-3.
[5] *Electra* 37-8, 375-6, *Phoenissae* 405, fragm 143 and many more.

disadvantages, sometimes amounting to sheer degradation, was as
ever a subject of discontent: and this was closely connected with
the position of free wage-earning labour. At Athens political action
took a strong line in the direction of utilizing the wealth of the rich
in the service of the state: for the poor, its dominant tendency was
to provide opportunities of drawing state pay (μισθός), generally a
bare living wage, for the performance of various public duties. The
other topic, that of slavery, had as yet hardly reached the stage of
questioning the right or wrong of that institution as such. But the
consciousness that the slave, like his master, was a blend of human
virtues and human vices,—was a man, in short,—was evidently becoming clearer, and suggesting the conclusion that he must be judged
as a man and not as a mere chattel. Otherwise Euripides would
hardly have ventured to bring slaves on the stage[1] in so sympathetic
a spirit, or to utter numerous sayings, bearing on their merits and
failings, in a tone of broad humanity.

In such circumstances how came it that there was no sign of a
movement analogous to modern Abolitionism? If the slave was
confessedly a man, had he not the rights of a man? The answer is
plain. That a man, simply as a man, had any rights, was a doctrine
not yet formulated or clearly conceived. The antipathy[2] between
Greek and Barbarian was a practical bar to its recognition. The
Persian was not likely to moderate his treatment of Greeks in his
power from any such consideration: superior force, nothing less,
would induce him to conform to Greek notions of humanity. While
force was recognized as the sole foundation of right as against free
enemies, there could not be much serious doubt as to the right of
holding aliens in slavery. But in this questioning age another
theoretical basis of discussion had been found. Men were testing
institutions by asking in reference to each 'is it a natural[3] growth?
does it exist by nature (φύσει)? or is it a conventional status? does
it exist by law (νόμῳ)?' Here was one of the most unsettling inquiries
of the period. In reference to slavery we find two conflicting doctrines
beginning to emerge. One is[4] that all men are born free (φύσει) and
that slavery is therefore a creation of man's device (νόμῳ). The other
is that superior strength is a gift of nature, and therefore the rule of
the weaker[5] by the stronger is according to nature. The conflict
between these two views was destined to engage some of the greatest

[1] The loyalty of slaves to kind masters is referred to very often.
[2] References in Euripides are too many to cite here.
[3] Cf the oft-quoted line from Eur *Auge* ἡ φύσις ἐβούλεθ', ᾗ νόμων οὐδὲν μέλει.
[4] Cf Eur fragm 515, 828, Dind, etc.
[5] Cf Eur fragm 263, 1035, Dind, and the use of τὸ δοῦλον 'the slave-quality' in *Hecuba* 332-3, *Ion* 983, etc.

minds of Greece in later years, when the political failure of the Greek
states had diverted men's thoughts to problems concerning the individual. For the present slavery was taken for granted, but it is
evident that the seeds of future doubt had been sown. Among the
stray utterances betraying uneasiness is the oft-quoted saying[1] of the
sophist Alcidamas 'god leaves all men free : nature makes no man a
slave.' The speaker was contemporary with Euripides, whose sayings
are often in much the same tone, if less direct. A remarkable passage
is that in which he makes Heracles repudiate[2] the myths that represent slavery as existing among the gods. No god that is a real god
has any needs, and such tales are rubbish—an argument that was
destined to reappear later as bearing upon slavery among men,
particularly in connexion with the principles of the Cynic school.

I have said enough as to the point of view from which the
questioners, such as Euripides, regarded slavery. It is somewhat
surprising that the poet's references to hired labour[3] are very few,
and all of a depressing kind, treating θητεύειν as almost or quite
equivalent to δουλεύειν. The references or allusions to handicrafts
are hardly to the point: such men are doubtless conceived as θῆτες,
but they would generally direct themselves in virtue of their trade-
skill : they are not hired 'hands.' Herdsmen often appear, but
generally if not always they seem to be slaves or serfs. Nor is it
clear that the digger (σκαφεύς) is free ; he is referred to[4] as a specimen
of the meanest class of labourer. But in three of the plays there
occur passages directly descriptive of the poor working farmer, the
αὐτουργὸς of whom I have spoken above. In the *Electra*, the prologue
is put in the mouth of the poor but well-born αὐτουργὸς to whom the
crafty Aegisthus has given Electra in marriage. The scene between
husband and wife is one of peculiar delicacy and interest. The points
that concern us here are these. The princess has been united[5] to a
poor and powerless freeman. He is fully occupied[6] with the hard
labour of his farm, which he apparently cultivates single-handed. He
understands the motive of Aegisthus, and shews his respect for
Electra by refraining from conjugal rights. She in turn respects his
nobility, and shews her appreciation by cheerfully performing[7] the
humble duties of a cottar's wife. When the breadwinner (ἐργάτης)
comes home from toil, he should find all ready for his comfort. He is
shocked to see her, a lady of gentle breeding (εὖ τεθραμμένη) fetch
water from the spring and wait upon his needs. But he has to accept
the situation: the morrow's dawn[8] shall see him at his labour on the

---

[1] See Cope's note on Aristotle *rhet* 1 13 § 2.
[2] *Herc Fur* 1341–6. [3] *Alcestis* 2, 6. *Electra* 203–4. *Cyclops* 76 foll, cf 23–4.
[4] *Electra* 252. [5] *Electra* 35–9. [6] *ibid* 73–4. [7] *ibid* 75–6. [8] *ibid* 78–81.

land : it is all very well to pray for divine aid, but to get a living the
first thing needful is to work. Now here we have a picture of the
free farmer on a small scale, who lives in a hovel and depends on the
labour of his own hands. He is the ancient analogue of the French
peasant, who works harder than any slave, and whose views are apt
to be limited by the circumstances of his daily life. He has no slaves[1].
Again, the Theban herald in the *Supplices*[2], speaking of the incapacity
of a Demos for the function of government, says 'but a poor husbandman (γαπόνος ἀνὴρ πένης), even if not stupid, will be too busy to
attend to state affairs.' Here is our toiling rustic, the ideal citizen of
statesmen who desire to keep free from popular control. The same
character appears again in the *Orestes*, on the occasion of a debate in
the Argive Assembly (modelled on Athens), as defender of Orestes.
He is described[3] as 'not of graceful mien, but a manly fellow, one
who seldom visits the city and the market-place, a toiler with his
hands (αὐτουργός), of the class on whom alone the safety of the
country depends ; but intelligent and prepared to face the conflict of
debate, a guileless being of blameless life.' So vivid is this portrait,
that the sympathy of the poet with the rustic type of citizen can
hardly be ignored. Now, why did Euripides take pains to shew this
sympathy ? I take it to be a sign that he saw with regret the declining
influence of the farmer class in Attic politics.

Can we go a step further, and detect in these passages any sort of
protest against a decline in the number of small working farmers,
and a growth of exploitation-farming, carried on by stewards directing
the labour of slaves or hired hands ? In the next generation we find
this system in use, as indeed it most likely always had been to some
extent on the richer soils of lowland Attica. The concentration of
the country folk in the city during the great war would tend to promote agriculture by deputy after the return of peace. Deaths, and
the diversion of some farmers to other pursuits, were likely to leave
vacancies in the rural demes. Speculators who took advantage of
such chances to buy land would not as a rule do so with intent to
live on the land and work it themselves ; and aliens were not allowed
to hold real estate. It seems fairly certain that landlords resident in
Athens, to whom land was only one of many forms of investment,
and who either let their land to tenant-farmers or exploited its cultivation under stewards, were a class increased considerably by the
effects of the war. We shall see further reasons below for believing
this. Whether Euripides in the passages cited above is actually

---

[1] The slaves in 360 and 394 are attendants of Orestes.   [2] *Suppl* 420–2.
[3] *Orest* 918–20. Cf fragm 188 Dind where the virtue of rustic life is sketched καὶ δόξεις
φρονεῖν σκάπτων ἀρῶν γῆν ποιμνίοις ἐπιστατῶν.

warning or protesting, I do not venture to say: that he grasped the significance of a movement beginning under his very eyes, is surely a probable conjecture.

That we should hear little of the employment of slaves in the hard work of agriculture, even if the practice were common, is not to be wondered at. Assuming the existence of slavery, there was no need for any writer other than a specialist to refer to them. But we have in the *Rhesus* a passage[1] in which Hector forecasts the result of an attack on the Greeks while embarking: some of them will be slain, and the rest, captured and made fast in bonds, will be taught to cultivate (γαπονεῖν) the fields of the Phrygians. That this use of captives is nothing extraordinary appears below, when Dolon the spy is bargaining for a reward in case of success. To a suggestion that one of the Greek chiefs should be assigned to him he replies 'No, hands gently nurtured (εὖ τεθραμμέναι)[2] are unfit for farm-work (γεωργεῖν).' The notion of captive Greeks slaving on the land for Asiatic lords is a touch meant to be provocative of patriotic indignation. And the remark of Dolon would surely fall more meaningly on the ears of men acquainted with the presence of rustic slavery in their own country. To serfage we have a reference[3] in the *Heraclidae*, but the retainer (πενέστης) is under arms, 'mobilized,' not at the time working on the land. His reward, when he brings the news of victory, is to be freedom.

IX. THE 'CONSTITUTION OF ATHENS' OR 'OLD OLIGARCH.'

One of the most remarkable documents that have come down to us bearing upon Athenian politics is the 'Constitution[4] of Athens' wrongly assigned to Xenophon. It is certainly the work of an earlier writer, and the date of its composition can be fixed as between 430 and 424 BC. Thus it refers to the first years of the Peloponnesian war, during which Attica was repeatedly invaded, its rural economy upset, and the manifold consequences of overcrowding in the city of refuge were beginning to shew themselves. Not a few of the 'better classes' of Athenian citizens (οἱ βέλτιστοι) were dissatisfied with the readiness of the Demos, under the guidance of Pericles, to carry out a maritime and aggressive policy abroad at the cost of sacrificing

---

[1] *Rhesus* 74–5.   [2] *Rhesus* 176.

[3] *Heracl* 639, 788–9, 890, cf fragm 827 Dind.

[4] *Die pseudoxenophontische* Ἀθηναίων πολιτεία...*von Ernst Kalinka* (Teubner 1913). A great work.

rural interests at home. For the sacrifice fell on the landowners, more particularly on the larger owners : the compensations[1] of state-pay and chances of plunder might suffice for the peasant farmer driven into Athens. At the same time it was undeniable that the astounding energy displayed by democratic Athens had surprised the Greek world ; and the most discontented Athenian could hardly suppress an emotion of patriotic pride. The writer of the pamphlet before us—for a pamphlet it is—was under the influence of these conflicting feelings. Whether it is right to describe him as an Oligarch depends on what that term is taken to connote. That he would greatly prefer a system[2] under which the educated orderly and honest citizens should enjoy greater consideration and power, is evident : also that in his view these qualities are normal attributes of the wealthier classes. For he finds in poverty the main cause[3] of demo-cratic misdeeds. That the masses are ill-informed and lack judgment and self-control, is the result of their preoccupation with necessities of daily life. But from this conviction to aiming at a serious oli-garchic revolution is a long step. The democracy in its less aggressive form, before the recent developments owing to the presence of an idle refugee population, might conceivably have sufficed for his require-ments. He is a prejudiced contemporary witness, frank and cynical in the extreme, praising the Demos for doing the very things that he hates and despises, because those things are in the interest of the democracy such as it appears to him : they would be fools to act otherwise. For convenience sake I follow Mr Zimmern[4] in calling him the *Old Oligarch*.

His disgust at the lack of discipline in the slaves at Athens, and his ingenious explanation[5] of the causes that have led to toleration of the nuisance, are very characteristic of his whole attitude. But the slaves of whom he speaks are those labourers whom their owners allowed to work for hire in the city and Peiraeus, taking a share of their pay as rent for their services. Perhaps the state slaves are meant also. He admits that you have to put up with the airs of these fellows, who often become men of substance ($\pi\lambda o\acute{\upsilon}\sigma\iota o\iota$ $\delta o\hat{\upsilon}\lambda o\iota$) and think themselves as good as the citizens. Truth is, the master depends on the return he gets from his investment : if the rent comes in regularly, he asks no questions and the slave is given[6] a free hand. No wonder the bondman jostles his betters in the public streets, a state of things inconceivable in orderly Sparta. Now on the face of it this picture has nothing to do with the agricultural situation. But

---

[1] I § 3.   [2] I § 5 etc.   [3] This view reappears later in Isocrates.
[4] In his book *The Greek Commonwealth*.   [5] I §§ 10–12.
[6] Kalinka well points out that in I § 11 $\grave{\epsilon}\lambda\epsilon\upsilon\theta\acute{\epsilon}\rho o\upsilon\varsigma$ $\grave{\alpha}\phi\iota\acute{\epsilon}\nu\alpha\iota$ is not technical = manumit.

let us look further. The stress of the great war had increased the city population. The increased demand for imported foodstuffs and for materials of war (such as ship-timber) had undoubtedly increased the demand for dock-labourers, boatmen, porters, carters, and other 'hands.' Male citizens had enough to do in services by land and sea. From what source was the extra force of rough able-bodied labour recruited? Is it likely that a number of raw barbarian slaves were imported for the purpose? I think not; time would be needed to make them efficient, and the available shipping had already a difficult task to keep up the supply of indispensable goods. Is it not much more likely that rustic slaves, brought into Athens by their owners, were turned to account[1] in another department of labour, thus earning wages for themselves while they maintained their masters? The probability of this view will depend largely on proof that rustic slaves were employed in Attica under normal conditions at this time. We shall presently see how the evidence of Aristophanes bears on the point.

Meanwhile let us see what references to agriculture are to be found in this pamphlet. In speaking of the nautical skill[2] now a common accomplishment among Athenians, the writer remarks that the possession of estates abroad, and the duties of offices concerned with external affairs, have something to do with it. Men have to cross the water: they and their attendants ($\dot{a}\kappa\dot{o}\lambda ov\theta o\iota$) thus pick up skill by experience without intending it: for it happens time and again that both master and slave ($\kappa a\dot{\iota}$ $a\dot{v}\tau\dot{o}v$ $\kappa a\dot{\iota}$ $\tau\dot{o}v$ $o\dot{\iota}\kappa\acute{e}\tau\eta v$) have to take a turn at the oar. The estates referred to are chiefly state-lands allotted to Athenian cleruchs in confiscated districts, but also private properties. The voyages to and fro are nothing exceptional. Whether a man resided on his estate and had need to visit Athens, or whether he resided in Athens and had to visit his estate from time to time, he must go to sea. It is to be borne in mind that allottees in cleruchies often let their lands to the former owners as tenants. In another passage[3] he points out the disadvantage to Athens, as a maritime power, of not being on an island and so secure from invasion. 'As things are, those Athenians who farm land or are wealthy ($o\dot{\iota}$ $\gamma\epsilon\omega\rho\gamma o\hat{v}\nu\tau\epsilon\varsigma$ $\kappa a\dot{\iota}$ $o\dot{\iota}$ $\pi\lambda o\acute{v}\sigma\iota o\iota$) are more inclined to conciliate the enemy ($\dot{v}\pi\acute{e}\rho\chi o\nu\tau a\iota$ = cringe to), while the Demos, well aware that their own belongings are in no danger of destruction, is unconcerned and defiant.' A notable admission, confirmed by other evidence, as we shall see. It is to be observed that farmers

---

[1] In 1 § 17 it is notable that among those who gain by concentration of business at Athens is $\epsilon\dot{\iota}$ $\tau\dot{\omega}$ $\zeta\epsilon\hat{v}\gamma\acute{o}\varsigma$ $\dot{e}\sigma\tau\iota v$ $\mathring{\eta}$ $\dot{a}\nu\delta\rho\acute{a}\pi o\delta o v$ $\mu\iota\sigma\theta o\phi o\rho o\hat{v}v$. Country carts would now be plentiful in Athens.

[2] 1 § 19.   [3] 2 § 14.

and wealthy men are coupled together. The class more especially meant are probably those represented in Aristophanes by the substantial farmers of the *Peace*. But capitalists with investments in land are also included, and small-holders or tenants; these last working the land themselves, but not necessarily without employing hired or slave labour.

X. ARISTOPHANES.

Aristophanes is a witness of great importance. Of eleven surviving plays the *Acharnians* appeared in 425 BC, the *Plutus* in 388. Thus we have from this prince of wit and humour a series of comments on the social and political life of Athens and Attica from the point of view of conservative admirers of good old times. The evidence of Comedy is liable to be suspect, on the ground of a tendency to exaggerate and distort facts: but to make allowances for this tendency is not a task of extreme difficulty. Nor can it fairly be said that the political bias of the poet is such as to deprive his evidence of all authority. If he seems at times to be singularly detached from the prejudices of the war-party, dominating Athens under the democratic leaders, and able to discern and boldly to declare that the right was not solely on their own side in the war; still he was a warm patriot, devoted to the Athens whose defects he could not ignore. Among the striking events of the time nothing seems to have impressed him more forcibly than the devastation of Attica and the consequent ruin of the agricultural interest. That the cooping-up of the rural population[1] within the walls month after month was a progressive calamity, could hardly escape the notice of any one then resident. It was not merely the squalor or the appalling sickness, though these were in themselves enough to produce a terrible strain. Discontent and recklessness took hold of the masses, and other observers beside Aristophanes remarked the degeneration of the democracy. Aristophanes was an opponent of the war-policy, and strove hard to rally the farmer-folk in favour of peace. He spared no pains to discredit the noisy demagogues, accusing them of prolonging the war in order to retain or increase their own importance at the cost of the soundest element in the civic body. But, while he turned the farmers' grievances to account in political advocacy, he was no mere unscrupulous partisan. His frequent references to the homely joys of country life, sometimes in sympathetic rural vignettes, have the ring of sincerity. Like many another dweller in the unwholesome city, he sighed for the fresh air, the wholesome food, the peace and quiet of Attic farmsteads: no doubt he idealized the surroundings, though he did not depict them

---

[1] *Equites* 792-4, *Pax* 632-6, *Eccl* 243.

as scenes of spotless innocence. But the details that drop out casually are often very significant from the point of view of my inquiry, and very helpful as giving us a genuine picture of the time.

On no point is information more to be desired than the relation of agriculture to wealth. Is the typical farmer of the period a man of large estate or not? We have seen that the 'old oligarch' classed together the wealthy and the farmers as favouring a peace-policy. That such a body of opinion, large or small, existed in Athens, is also suggested by passages in Aristophanes. In the *Ecclesiazusae*, the play in which the leader of the female politicians offers to cure distress by a communistic scheme, we are told[1] that a proposal to mobilize a fleet divides the Assembly: the poor man votes for it, but the wealthy and the farmers are against it. I take it that, as in the case of the Sicilian expedition, the man who wants to get paid for service (with a chance of profit) supports the motion; those who dislike having to pay for the enterprise, or see no way of profiting by it, are in opposition. This is a phenomenon normal in politics, and does not tell us whether the 'farmers' are cultivators on a large scale or small. Later in the play we find a protest[2] against the iniquity of the present juxtaposition of wealth and destitution, the state of things in which one man farms much land while another has not enough to afford him a grave. Even a comic poet would hardly put this into the mouth of one of his characters if there were not some section of the audience to whom it might appeal. It is probable that at the time (393–2 BC) communistic suggestions were among the currents of opinion in humbled and impoverished Athens. To squeeze the rich had long been the policy of the democrats, and a jealousy of wealth in any form became endemic in the distressful city. A few years later (388 BC) the poet gave in the *Plutus* a pointed discussion[3] of economic questions, ridiculing the notion that all could be rich at the same time: for nobody would work, and so civilization would come to an end. True, the individualistic bent of the average Athenian, grasping and litigious, prevented the establishment of downright communism: but Athens was henceforth never free from the jealous and hardly patriotic demands of the clamorous poor We must remember that military service, no longer offering prospects of profit in addition to pay, was becoming unpopular; that land-allotments[4] in conquered territories had ceased; and that agriculture in a large part of Attica was toilsome and unremunerative. Poverty was widespread, and commerce declined: this implies that the supply of slaves, and the money to buy them, would be reduced. Was there then much to attract the poor man to the lonely tillage of a patch of

---

[1] *Eccl* 197–8. [2] *Eccl* 591–2. [3] *Plut* 510–626.
[4] Old Strepsiades still has his thoughts fixed on these, *Nubes* 202–3.

rocky land? The generation of small farmers before and during the great war had some outlook for themselves and their sons, serving in victorious armies or fleets, getting booty or allotments abroad. Hence they took a keen interest in politics. The fall of Athens had changed all this: the profits of empire had departed, and with them the buoyancy of an imperial pride. No wonder if there were signs of unwillingness to follow a hard rustic life. So the Informer in the *Plutus*[1], when asked 'are you a husbandman?' replies 'do you take me for a madman?' Earlier in the play[2] Chremylus, wishing to share with old cronies the profits of having captured the god of wealth, says to his slave 'invite my fellow farmers: I fancy you'll find them working themselves (αὐτοὺς) on their farms.'

I have taken this later picture first, in order to bring out more clearly the contrast presented by that given in the earlier plays. Naturally enough, many details are the same in both, but the general character of the farmers is different. The farmer class makes an important figure. They are sturdy rustics[3], old-fashioned and independent, rough in manners, fond of simple country life, and inclined (perhaps justly) to mistrust the city folk, who cheat them in business whenever they can, and take advantage of them in other ways, such as liability to military service at short notice. When driven to take refuge in Athens, their hearts are in their farms, and they have to make up their minds whether to support the war-party in hope of regaining their homes and property by force of arms, or to press for peace in order to end what is from their point of view an unnecessary war, kept going in the interest of demagogues and others who are profiting by the opportunities of offices and campaigns abroad. The issue appears in our earliest play, the *Acharnians* (425 BC). The farmers of the deme Acharnae, one of whose occupations was wood-cutting and charcoal-burning, at first come on as stubborn rustics, all for war and revenge on the enemy. But Dicaeopolis the chief character of the play, himself a farmer, and a sufferer in the same kind by the Spartan raids, succeeds in persuading[4] them that Athenian policy, provocative and grasping, is really to blame for their losses. In the end they come over to his views, and the play serves as a manifesto of the peace-party. Of course we are not to take it as history. But the conflict between the two sections of opinion is probably real enough. When Dicaeopolis describes[5] himself as 'with my eyes ever turned to my farm, a lover of peace, detesting the city and hankering after my own deme, that never yet bade me buy charcoal or rough wine or olive oil,' he is giving us a portrait of the rustic

---

[1] *Plut* 903.   [2] *Plut* 223–4.
[3] *Ach* 180, 211, *Pax* 570, 1185–6, *Eq* 316–7, *Nub* 43 foll.
[4] The gradual conversion is seen in *Ach* 557 foll, 626 foll.   [5] *Ach* 32–4.

who is resolved not to part with cash for what can be produced on the farm.

But, whatever policy may seem best adapted to achieve their purpose, the purpose itself is clearly and consistently marked. The desire of the war-time farmers is simply to return to their farms[1] and to resume the life of toil and plenty, varied by occasional festivals, that had been interrupted by the war. They long to escape from the abominations of the crowding and unhealthiness prevailing in the city. Once they get back to their old surroundings, all will be well. Time and labour will even repair the damages caused by the enemy. No misgivings suggest that a change of circumstances may be found to have robbed Attic country life of some of its charm. Nothing like the loss of the empire, the fall of Athens, and the deadly depression of economic and political life, is foreboded: they face the sequel with undisturbed faith in the stability of the existing system. Nor indeed until the Sicilian disaster (413 BC) was there much to cause uneasiness. So we find the same spirit illustrated in the *Peace* (421 BC), which may be regarded as driving home the lesson of the *Acharnians*. The agricultural interests are now represented as solidly in favour of the peace of Nicias, unsatisfactory though it soon proved to be. While other interests are slack, indifferent or even hostile, farmers are whole-hearted[2] in determination to end the war and go home. Trygaeus their leader, according to the Greek sketch of the plot an elderly rustic, describes himself[3] as a 'skilled vine-dresser, one who is no informer or fomenter of troubles (lawsuits).' Needless to say, he carries his point, and the farmers march off triumphant[4] to their farms, eager to take up the old easygoing life once more. We must not take our comic poet too literally, but we have no reason to doubt that feelings such as he depicts in this play did prevail, and perhaps widely. And, though the peace was insincere, and warfare never really ceased, the immunity of Attica from invasion for several years gave time for agriculture to revive. When Agis occupied Deceleia in the winter of 413, his marauders would find on the Attic farms all manner of improvements and new plantations to destroy. And the destruction of the fruits of a laborious revival is to be reckoned among the depressing influences that weighed upon falling and desperate Athens. It was surely at work in the year 411, when Aristophanes was preaching a policy of concord at home and sympathetic treatment of the Allies in order to save the shaken empire. In the *Lysistrata* he represents the mad war-fury of the Greek states as due to the misguided men, whom the women coerce by privation into willingness for peace. This is strung up into a passionate longing, so that neither[5] of the

---

[1] *Pax* 551-70, 1127 foll; cf fragm 100, 107, 109, 294, 387, Kock.
[2] *Pax* 509-11.   [3] *Pax* 190.   [4] *Pax* 551-70, 1318-24.   [5] *Lysistr* 1173-4.

principal parties is disposed to haggle over details. The Athenian
breaks out 'I want to strip and work my land at once.' The Spartan
rejoins 'and I want to be carting manure.' There is still no misgiving
expressed, and the poet is probably true to facts. The struggles of the
time were a fearful strain on Athenian resources, but it still seemed
possible that the empire would weather the storm.

This brief sketch leads on to the inquiry, what do we gather as to
the labour employed on the farms? We have to consider three possibilities (*a*) the farmer, including his family, (*b*) hired labourers, (*c*) slaves.
It is well to begin by remarking that frequency of reference to one of
these does not necessarily imply the same proportion in actual employment. Slavery being assumed as a fact in all departments of life (as it
is by all writers of the period), and the slave being an economic or
domestic appliance rather than a person, there was no need to call
special attention to his presence. Hence it is natural that the rustic
slave should, as such, be seldom referred to in the plays. He is in fact
mentioned several times, rather more often than the yoke of oxen. Nor
was it necessary to mention the wage-earner, the man employed for
the job under a temporary contract, and in connexion with agriculture
he hardly appears at all. But the working farmers were a class of
citizens. They had votes, and they were on political grounds a class
to whose sympathies the poet was anxious to appeal. Therefore he
had no choice but to lay stress upon their virtues and magnify their
importance. Any careful reader of Aristophanes will I think admit
that he does this consistently. In doing this with political aims he was
subject to the temptation of passing lightly over any considerations
that might, whether justly or unjustly, be turned against his case. This
may serve to explain why he refers almost solely to the small working
farmer, who himself labours on the land. We are not to infer that there
were no large estates worked by deputy, though probably there were
not many: to lay stress on the interested views of large landowners
was not likely to please the jealous Demos. Nor are we to infer that
the small farmer used no slaves: that he laboured himself is no proof,
for no man could get more out of a slave's labour than the working
owner, on whom the burden of making good his slave's neglect must
fall. I turn now to the passages from which the various details may
be gleaned.

In the *Acharnians* the working farmer Dicaeopolis is delighted at
having made a separate peace on his own account. He holds it a fine
thing[1] that he should now be able to perform religious rites and
celebrate the festival of the rustic Dionysia with his slaves. He is back
at home[2] in his own rural deme, and he calls his slave Xanthias to

---

[1] *Ach* 248–50, 259.   [2] *Ach* 266.

carry the phallus in the procession. In the *Clouds*[1] old Strepsiades says that he lives in the heart of the country, and his preference for the easy and rather squalid life on a farm is plainly expressed. And the play opens with his complaint that in war-time a man has not a free hand to punish his slaves. It is however not clear that he is supposed to be at the time living on the farm. In the *Wasps* the chorus of old dicasts are indignant[2] that their old comrade Philocleon should be dragged off by his own slaves at the order of his son. The old man himself, struggling and protesting, reminds the leading slave of the time when he caught the rogue stealing grapes (obviously in his vineyard) and thrashed him soundly. In the *Peace* a rustic scene[3] is described. The weather being unfavourable for work on the land, but excellent for the seed just sown, it is proposed to make merry indoors. Country fare is made ready, and the female slave Syra is told to call in the man slave Manes from the farm. A little below Trygaeus is mocking the workers in war-trades. To the trumpet-maker he says, fit up your trumpet differently[4] and you can turn it into a weighing-machine: 'it will then do for serving out rations of figs to your slaves on the farm.' In the *Lysistrata* the chorus, being aware that an interval of distress will follow the conclusion of peace, offers[5] to tide over the crisis by helping the fathers of large families and owners of hungry slaves by doles of food. 'Let them bring their bags and wallets for wheat: my Manes shall fill them.' After these passages the announcement of the working of the communistic scheme[6] in the *Ecclesiazusae* carries us into a very different atmosphere. 'But who is to till the soil under the new order?' asks Blepyrus. 'Our slaves,' replies Praxagora, his typical better-half. We see that this amounts to basing society on a serf-system, for the slaves will be common property like the rest. In the *Plutus* old Chremylus is a farmer, apparently a working[7] farmer, but he has a slave, indeed more than one. Age has probably led him to do most of his work by deputy. When Poverty, in the course of her economic lecture, explains to him[8] that wealth for all means slaves for none and that he will have to plough and dig for his own proper sustenance, he is indignant. The weak points of the argument do not concern us here. The solution offered in the play, the cure of the Wealth-god's blindness, enabling him to enrich only the deserving, is a mere piece of sportive nonsense, meant to amuse an audience, not to hold out a serious hope of better things.

Enough has been said to shew that the slave had a place in farm life as depicted by Aristophanes. It will be observed that in the earlier plays the references are all of a casual kind: that is to say, that slave-

---

[1] *Nub* 43 foll, 138.   [2] *Vesp* 442–52.   [3] *Pax* 1140 foll.   [4] *Pax* 1248–9.
[5] *Lys* 1203–14.   [6] *Eccl* 651.   [7] *Plut* 26–7, 253.   [8] *Plut* 517–20, 525–6.

labour calls for no particular attention or remark. The consideration
of slave-labour as such, in fact as an economic phenomenon, only
appears later. This is, I repeat, significant of the change that had come
upon Athens and Attica in consequence of exhaustion. In respect of
hired labour it is obvious that pressure of poverty, as stated[1] in the
Plutus, directly influences the supply. If the possession of a com-
petency will deter men from professional industry in trades, even more
will it deter them from the drudgery of rough labour. The hired men
($\mu\iota\sigma\theta\omega\tau\omega\ell$) were commonly employed in all departments, for instance
in the building trades, to which there is a reference[2] in the *Birds*. But
we may fairly assume that during the great war the number of such
'hands' available for civilian services was much reduced. In agriculture
there would be little or no demand for them. And any able-bodied
citizen could earn good pay from the state. Moreover rough labour
was not much to the taste of the average Athenian,—above all, digging[3].
'I cannot dig' was proverbial. On the other hand there were farm-
duties in the performance of which sufficient care and intelligence
could only be exacted through the medium of wage-paying. Such was
that of olive-pickers, to whom and their wage we have a reference[4] in the
Wasps. They are probably free persons, but it is possible that wage-
earning slaves, paying rent to their owners, might be thus employed.
That in some occupations free and slave-labour were both employed
indifferently, is certain. The carriage of burdens[5] is a case in point.
But employment in odd jobs would be far more frequent in the city,
including Peiraeus, than in country places. I do not think it rash to
conclude that hired free labourers were few on the farms of Attica in
the time of Aristophanes.

Turning to citizen agriculturists, it must be mentioned that views
differ as to the proportion of large estates held and worked by wealthy
owners in this period. Such estates would almost certainly employ
slave-labour. So far as the evidence of Aristophanes goes, I should
infer that they were few. No doubt he had reasons for not making
much of such cases; still I believe that the comfortable working farmer,
homely and independent, the poet's favourite character, was in fact the
normal type. They were not paupers,—far from it: but their capital
consisted in land, buildings, dead and live farm-stock, and the unexhausted value of previous cultivation. These items could not suddenly
be converted into money without ruinous loss: most of them could
not be carried away in the flight to Athens. Hence the dislike felt
by such men to an adventurous policy, in which their interests were

---

[1] *Plut* 510–626.   [2] *Aves* 1152.
[3] *Aves* 1431–2 (cf Vesp 959), fragm of Δαιταλεῖς 4 Dind, 221 Kock.
[4] *Vesp* 712.   [5] *Ran* 164–77.

sacrificed. The passages in which agriculture is connected[1] with large
property occur in a play produced 392 BC, at which time great changes
had happened. It is highly probable that, among these changes, much
Attic land had passed from the hands of ruined yeomen into those of
rich men possessed of ready money and able to buy in a glutted market.
In a later period we shall find γεωργεῖν used in the sense of acting the
country landowner. To illustrate the life and ways of the peasant
farmers of this period Aristophanes supplies endless references descriptive and allusive. The chief of these have been cited above. A few
more may be added here. In the *Clouds* Strepsiades, urging his son to
a rustic life, hopes to see him dressed in a leathern jerkin, like his
father before him, driving in the goats[2] from the waste (φελλέως, the
rocky hill-pasture). Here is a good instance of husbandry in the Attic
highlands, in short a case of crofters. What a refugee might hope to
save in his flight and take back to his farm on the return of peace—
it amounts to a few implements[3]—is set out in the *Peace*. Loss of oxen,
a yoke of two, driven off by Boeotian raiders, is pitifully bewailed[4] by
a farmer in the *Acharnians*. But in general the farmers of the earlier
plays are represented as tough elderly men. They are the 'elder
generation,' and the poet genuinely admires them. For the younger
generation he has a profound contempt. Evidently he thought that
the soundest breed of Athenian citizens was dying out; and I am not
sure that he was wrong.

I conclude that the evidence of Aristophanes on the whole points
to an agriculture mainly carried on by working farmers with the help
of slaves. This system was subjected to a very severe strain by the
war-conditions prevailing for many years, and I do not think that it
was possible to revive it on the same footing as before, even when
Attica was no longer exposed to frequent raids. It was not merely the
loss of fixed capital that told on the farmer class. Importation of corn
was so developed and organized to meet the necessities of the crowded
city, that it completely dominated the market, and in the production
of cereals the home agriculture could now no longer compete with
foreign harvests. There remained the culture of the olive and vine:
but it needed years to restore plantations of these and other fruit-trees,
and to wait for revival needed a capital possessed by few. The loss of
imperial revenues impoverished Athens, and the struggle with financial
difficulties runs through all her later history. It did not take the
poorer citizens long to see that how to get daily bread was the coming
problem. State-pay was no longer plentiful, and one aim of jealous
franchise-regulations was to keep down the number of claimants. Had

---

[1] *Eccl* 197–8, 591–2.   [2] *Nub* 71–2. Cf φελλέα in Isaeus VIII § 42 ₽ 73.
[3] *Pax* 552, 1318.   [4] *Ach* 1018–36.

Aristophanes any inkling of the evil days to come? At all events he was aware that poverty works in two[1] ways: if it leads one man to practise a trade for his living, it tempts another to evildoing, perhaps to crime.

XI. THUCYDIDES.

Thucydides is a writer from whom it is extremely difficult to extract any evidence on the subject of agricultural labour. The preeminent importance of the problem of food-supply in the Greece of his day may be amply illustrated from his work; but mainly in casual utterances, the full significance of which is only to be gathered by thorough examination such as has been made[2] by Dr Grundy. The economic revolution in Attica that followed the reforms of Solon, the extended culture of the vine and olive, the reduced growth of cereal crops, the development of manufactures and sea-borne trade, the growing dependence on imported corn, and the influence of these changes on the public policy of Athens, are now seen more clearly as a whole than ever before. But to the great historian these things were part of the background of his picture. They are parts of a movement taken for granted rather than understood. And the same is true of the existence and application of slave-labour. In the time of Thucydides slavery was an economic and social fact, unchallenged. It may be that it affected unfavourably the position of the free handworker in the long run, and gave opportunities to slave-owning capitalists. But this effect came about slowly, and freeman and slave could and did labour[3] side by side, for instance in the great public works promoted by Pericles. How far slave-labour was really cheaper than free is a question beyond my subject. But it is important to note the attitude of the poor citizen towards the question of what we call a living wage. Once the great outlay on public works began to fall off, and industries on a larger scale to compete with the individual craftsman, how was the poor citizen to live? Directly or indirectly, the profits of empire supplied the answer. Now it was obvious that the fewer the beneficiaries the larger would be the average dividend of each. So the policy favoured by the poorer classes was a jealous restriction of the franchise. It was not the slave as labour-competitor against whom protection was desired, but the resident freeman of doubtful origin as a potential profit-sharer.

During nearly the whole of the period covered by the history of Thucydides the public policy of Athens was controlled by urban influences. Even before the rustic citizens were cooped up in the city, it

---

[1] *Eccl* 605, *Av* 712.   [2] *Thucydides and the history of his age* chapters III–VII.
[3] See Francotte *L'industrie dans la Grèce ancienne* livre II cc 5–7.

was no doubt city residents that formed the normal majority in the Assembly, and to whom most of the paid offices and functions fell. Even allowing for the recent growth of 'seafaring rabble' in Peiraeus, these Athenians were not at all a mere necessitous mob. But it must be remembered that the commercial and industrial capitalists were interested in foreign trade. As Mr Cornford[1] points out, even metics of this class must have had considerable influence owing to wealth and connexions. Thus the urban rich as well as the urban poor were tempted to favour a policy of adventure, contrary to the wishes and interests of the Attic farmers. Now these latter were the truest representatives of the old Attic stock. Once they were crowded into the city and many of them diverted to state service, any sobering influence that they might at first exercise would become less and less marked, and they would tend to be lost in the mass. Therefore we hear only of the rustic life[2] from which they unwillingly tore themselves in 431 BC: we do not get any detailed picture of it, for the historian's attention was otherwise occupied. In the passage[3] accounting for the unpopularity of Pericles in 430 BC we read that the Demos was irritated because 'having less (than the rich) to start with, it had been deprived of that little,' while the upper class (δυνατοί) had lost their fine establishments. Here the context seems to imply that the δῆμος referred to is especially the small farmers, still dwelling on their losses and not yet otherwise employed.

One passage is so important that it must be discussed by itself. Pericles is made to encourage[4] the Athenians in resistance to the Spartan demands by pointing out the superiority of their resources compared with those of the enemy. 'The Peloponnesians' he says 'are working farmers (αὐτουργοί). They have no store of wealth (χρήματα) either private or public. Nor have they experience of protracted warfare with operations beyond the sea: for their own campaigns against each other are short, owing to poverty.' After explaining how they must be hampered by lack of means, he resumes thus 'And working farmers are more ready to do service in person than by payment. They trust that they may have the luck to survive the perils of war; but they have no assurance that their means will not be exhausted before it ends: for it may drag out to an unexpected length—and this is likely to happen.' Two questions at once suggest themselves. Is this a fair sketch of agricultural conditions in Peloponnese? Does it imply that Attic farmers were not αὐτουργοί? To take the latter first, it is held by Professor Beloch[5] that the passage characterizes the Peloponnese

---

[1] *Thucydides mythistoricus* chapter II.
[2] II 14, 16. An earlier period is referred to in I 126 §§ 7, 8. [3] II 65 § 2.
[4] I 141. [5] *Die Bevölkerung der Griechisch-Röm Welt* p 150.

as a land of free labour, in contrast with slave-holding Athens. To this
view I cannot assent. I am convinced that the Attic farmer who worked
with his own hands did often, if not always, employ slave-labour also.
He would not have a large gang of slaves, like the large-scale cultivator:
he could not afford to keep an overseer. But it might pay him to keep
one or two slaves, not more than he could oversee himself. If the contrast
be clearly limited, so as to compare the wealth of Athens, now largely industrial and commercial, with the wealth of a purely agricultural population, scattered over a wide area, and having little ready money, it is
reasonable and true. But this does not raise the question of the Attic
farmer at all. A little below[1] Pericles is made to urge that class to
submit quietly to invasion and serious loss. They are not the people
on whose resources he relies to wear out the enemy. That enemy finds
it hard to combine for common action or to raise money by war-taxes.
Athens is a compact community, able to act quickly, and has at disposal the forces and tribute of her subjects, secured by naval supremacy.
To the other question, that of Peloponnesian agriculture, I see no
simple answer. All the southern parts, the region of Spartan helotry,
can hardly be called a land of free labour in any rational sense. Nor
does it appear that Argolis, in spite of the various revolutions in local
politics, could rightly be described thus. Elis and Achaia were hardly
of sufficient importance to justify such a general description, even if it
were certain that it would apply to them locally. Arcadia, mostly
mountainous and backward, is the district to which the description
would be most applicable. But that there were slaves in Arcadia is
not only probable but attested by evidence, later in date but referring
to an established[2] state of things. At festivals, we are told, slaves and
masters shared the same table. This does not exclude rustic slaves: it
rather seems to suggest them. The working farmer entertaining his
slaves on a rural holiday is even a conventional tradition of ancient
country life. Arcadia, a land of peasant farmers, where a living had to
be won by hard work, a land whence already in the fifth century (and
still more in the fourth) came numbers of mercenary soldiers, a land
whence Sparta raised no small part of her 'Peloponnesian' armies, is
what Pericles has chiefly in mind. And that Arcadians were normally
αὐτουργοὶ did not imply that they had no slaves.

So far as Attica is concerned, Thucydides himself incidentally
attests the presence of rustic slaves. He would probably have been
surprised to hear such an obvious fact questioned. In refusing to repeal
the 'Megarian decree' the Athenians charged[3] the Megarians with
various offences, one of which was the reception of their runaway slaves.
In the winter 415–4 BC Alcibiades, urging the Spartans to occupy

---

[1] I 143.   [2] Theopompus in Athenaeus 149 d.   [3] I 139 § 2.

Deceleia, is made to state[1] the advantages of that move thus 'For of all the farm-stock in the country the bulk will at once come into your possession, some by capture, and the rest of its own accord ($a\dot{v}\tau\acute{o}\mu a\tau a$).' I take the last words to refer especially to slaves,—rustic slaves. In recording the success of the plan, the historian tells[2] us that more than 20000 slaves, a large part of whom were artisans ($\chi\epsilon\iota\rho o\tau\acute{\epsilon}\chi\nu a\iota$), deserted to the enemy. We may guess that many or most of the artisan slaves had escaped from Athens. Their loss would be felt in the reduction of manufacturing output, so far as such enterprise was still possible at the time, and perhaps in the dockyards. But the rest would be rustic slaves, many of them (to judge by the map) from a district[3] in which there were probably many small farms. On the other hand, the slaves welcomed by the Megarians were probably from larger estates in the Thriasian plain. Turning from Attica, we find references to rustic slaves[4] in Corcyra (427 BC) and Chios (412 BC), where they were numerous and important in their effect on operations. And in other passages where the slaves belonging to the people of this or that place are mentioned we are not to assume that only urban slaves are meant. For to live in a town, and go out for the day's work on the land, was and is a common usage in Mediterranean countries. An extreme case[5] is where people live on an island and cross water to cultivate farms elsewhere. It is perhaps hardly necessary to remark that rich slave-owners, who could afford overseers, did not need to reside permanently on their estates. Such a man might have more than one farm, and in more than one district, not necessarily in Attica at all, as Thucydides himself exploited a mining concession in Thrace. In any case a well-equipped 'country place' was a luxury, and is characterized as such[6] in words put into the mouth of Pericles, who as the democratic statesman was concerned to stifle discontent by insinuating that it was a mere expression of the selfishness of the rich.

The settlement of Athenians in colonies ($\dot{a}\pi o\iota\kappa\acute{\iota}a\iota$) or on allotments of conquered land ($\kappa\lambda\eta\rho o\nu\chi\acute{\iota}a\iota$), in the islands or on the seaboard has been fully treated[7] by Dr Grundy. He shews that this movement had two aims, the occupation of strategic points as an imperial measure of security, and the provision of land-lots for poorer citizens as a measure of economic relief. The latter purpose is part of a general plan for reducing the financial liabilities of the state with respect to its citizen population, the necessity for which Dr Grundy explains. By these settlements abroad some surplus population was removed and provided with means of livelihood. If the assumption of a surplus citizen

---

[1] VI 91 § 7.   [2] VII 27 § 5.
[3] Trygaeus in Aristoph *Pax* is a farmer from this district.
[4] III 73, VIII 40 § 2.   [5] III 88 § 3.   [6] II 62 § 3.
[7] *opus cit* chapters IV, VII.

population be sound (and I am not in a position to challenge it), we must also assume a certain degree of genuine land-hunger, at least more than the Attic territory could satisfy. If there was such land-hunger, it is perhaps not unreasonable to connect it with the survival of old Attic traditions of country life. And it would seem that the settlers, cleruchs or colonists, did as a rule[1] stay and live in their settlements. They would probably work their lands on much the same general plan as their brethren in Attica, and their labour-arrangements would be much the same. But in 427 BC, when Pericles was dead and there was surely no surplus population, at least of able-bodied men, owing to the war, we find a curious record. Reconquered Lesbos[2] had to be dealt with. It was not subjected to an assessed tribute ($\phi\acute{o}\rho o\varsigma$), but parcelled into 3000 allotments, 2700 of which were reserved for 2700 Athenian citizens, those who drew the lucky lots ($\tau o\grave{v}\varsigma \lambda a\chi\acute{o}\nu\tau a\varsigma$), and these 2700 were sent out. But they did not stay[3] there. They let their shares to the old inhabitants as cultivating tenants, at a rent of two minae per share per annum, and evidently returned to Athens. By this arrangement a sum of about £21000 a year would come in to the shareholders in Athens, who would have a personal interest in seeing that it was punctually paid. Whether these non-resident landlords were chosen by lot from all citizens, rich or poor, is not stated. We know that in some cases[4] at least the choice of settlers was confined to members of the two lowest property-classes; and it may well be that on this occasion the opportunity[5] was taken to compensate to some extent members of rural families, who had suffered loss from the invasions of Attica, but did not wish to go abroad. In any case their tenants would farm as they had done before, employing or not employing slave labour according to their means and the circumstances of the several farms. So too in cases of lands let on lease, and in the confiscations and re-distributions of lands, proposed or carried out, it was simply their own profit and comfort that attracted the lessees or beneficiaries. We are entitled to assume that if it paid to employ slaves, and slaves were to be had, then slaves were employed. In short, the scraps of evidence furnished by Thucydides leave us pretty much where we were.

[1] For instance, in Euboea and Aegina.
[2] III 50. Herodes, whose murder was later the occasion of a speech of Antiphon, is thought to have been one of the cleruchs.
[3] Arnold's note explains the situation well, and Beloch p 83 agrees.
[4] See the inscription relative to Brea, G F Hill *Sources* III 317.
[5] See the hint in the speech of Pericles I 143 § 4.

XII. XENOPHON.

Xenophon, who lived somewhere between 440 and 350 BC, introduces us to a great change in the conditions of the Greek world. The uneasiness and sufferings of the Greek states from the fall of Athens in 404 to the time of exhaustion resulting from the battle of Mantinea in 362 do not concern us here. Of such matters we hear much, but very little directly of the economic changes that were undoubtedly going on. Poverty was as before a standing trouble in Greece. In the more backward parts[1] able-bodied men left their homes to serve as hired soldiers. The age of professional mercenaries was in full swing. Arcadians Achaeans Aetolians Acarnanians Thessalians and other seekers after fortune became more and more the staple material of armies. Athens could no longer support imperial ambitions on imperial tributes, and had to depend on the sale of her products to procure her supplies of food. These products were chiefly oil and wine and urban manufactures, and there is reason to think that in general the most economical method of production was by slave labour under close and skilful superintendence. Slaves were supplied by kidnappers from the Euxine and elsewhere, but prisoners captured by armies were another source of supply. This living loot was one of the perquisites that made military life attractive, and the captives found their way to such markets as the industrial centres of Athens and Corinth. What happened in the rural districts of Attica, how far there was a revival of the small farmer class, is a point on which we are very much in the dark. The indirect evidence of Xenophon is interesting but not wholly conclusive.

It is perhaps important to consider what significance should be attached to the mention of agricultural work done by men of military forces on land or sea. In 406 BC we hear of hardships[2] endured by the force under the Spartan Eteonicus who were cut off in Chios after the defeat of Arginusae. During the summer months they 'supported themselves on the fruits of the season and by working for hire in the country.' This is meant to shew that they were in sad straits, as the sequel clearly proves. Again, in 372 BC Iphicrates was with a force in Corcyra, and naval operations were for the time over. So he 'managed[3] to provide for his oarsmen (ναύτας) chiefly by employing them in farm-work for the Corcyraeans,' while he undertook an expedition on the mainland with his soldiers. In both these cases want

---

[1] That there was normally much insecurity in rustic life in some parts of Greece, may be inferred from the dance-scene of the farmer and the robber, acted by men from north central Greece in *Anabasis* VI 1 §§ 7, 8. Daubeny's Lectures pp 17, 18.

[2] *Hellenica* II 1 § 1.   [3] *Hellenica* VI 2 § 37.

of pay was no doubt one reason for emergency-labour. In the earlier
case the destitution of the men led them to look for any paid work:
in the second the general had to do his best in spite of irregular and
insufficient supplies from home.   In both cases it is the exceptional
nature of the arrangement that makes it worth mentioning.   It can
hardly be viewed as having any economic significance.   But it is of
some interest in connexion with a passage of Aristotle[1] that will require notice below.

In the *Anabasis* Xenophon reports his own arguments, urging the
Greek army to fight their way out of the Persian empire. He feared
that, now Cyrus was dead, and they were cut off far from home in an
enemy's country, they might in despair surrender to the King and
take service under him. At best this meant giving up Greece and
settling in Persia on the King's terms. This he begged them not to
do: that they could under Greek discipline cut their way out was
evident from the independence of many peoples of Asia Minor, who
lived and raided as they chose in defiance of the Persian power. He
added 'Therefore I hold[2] that our right and proper course is first to
make a push to reach Hellas and our own kinsmen, and to demonstrate
to the Greeks that their poverty is their own fault: for, if they would
only convey to these parts those of their citizens who are now living
in want at home, they could see them in plenty (πλουσίους).' But he
reminds them that the good things of Asia are only to be had as the
reward of victory.   For my present purpose the one important point
is that a mixed host of Greek mercenaries are said to have been
appealed to by a reference to the fact of poverty and land-hunger
among their folks at home, and that this reference is said to have been
made by an Athenian. Writing this in later life, Xenophon would
hardly have set down such an argument had it not then, as on the
occasion recorded, had considerable force. In another passage[3] he
gives an interesting account of the motives that had induced most of
the men to join the expedition. He is explaining why they were irritated at a rumour that they were to be pressed to settle down at a
spot on the Euxine coast. 'It was not lack of subsistence that had led
most of the soldiers to go abroad on this paid service: they had been
told of the generosity of Cyrus. Some had other men following them,
some had even spent money for the cause: others had run away
from their parents, or left children behind, meaning to win money
and return to them, on the faith of the reported prosperity of those
already in the service of Cyrus. Such was the character of the men,
and they were longing to get safe home to Greece.' In short, full-
blooded men were not content to drag on poor ill-found stagnant lives

[1] Ar *Pol* VII 6 § 8.   [2] *Anab* III 2 § 26.   [3] *Anab* VI 4 § 8.

in corners of Greece. And we may add that nothing stimulated the enterprises of Greek adventurers in the East, and led up to the conquests of Alexander, more effectually than the experiences of the Ten Thousand.

Among these experiences was of course the capture of booty, more particularly[1] in the form of marketable prisoners. So many of these were sometimes in hand that they were a drag on the march: in a moment of peril[2] they had to be abandoned. Even so, a considerable sum had been raised by sales[3] and was shared out at Cerasus. The Greek cities on the Pontic seaboard would all no doubt be resorts of slave-dealers. One of the Ten Thousand himself, formerly a slave[4] at Athens, recognized as kinsmen by their speech the people of a mountain tribe in Armenia. In Thrace too we hear of the chieftain Seuthes, when short of cash, offering[5] to make a payment partly in slaves. Nor was selling into slavery a fate reserved for barbarians alone. Greeks[6] had been treated thus in the great war lately ended; and now the Spartan harmost, anxious to clear the remainder of the Ten Thousand[7] out of Byzantium safely, made them an offer of facilities for a raid in Thrace: any that stayed behind in the town were to be sold as slaves. And more than 400 were accordingly sold. It seems reasonable to infer that at this time the slave-markets were as busy as ever, perhaps more so than had been the case during the great war. It may be going too far to say that in some parts of Greece people were now trying to restore a broken prosperity by industrial exploitation of slave-labour, while from other parts soldiers of fortune and kidnappers went forth to enlarge the supply of slaves. But that there is some truth in such a statement I do not doubt. It was evidently no easy matter for persons of small means to live in any sort of comfort at Athens. We hear of Socrates[8] discussing with a friend the embarrassments of a genteel household. The late civil disorders have driven a number of this man's sisters cousins and aunts to take refuge in his house. In the present state of things neither land nor house property are bringing in anything, and nobody will lend. How is he to maintain a party of 14 free persons in all? Socrates points to the case of a neighbour who provides for a still larger household without difficulty. Questions elicit the fact that this household consists of slave-artisans trained to useful trades. The distressed party have been brought up as ladies, to do nothing. Socrates suggests that they had better work for bread than starve.

[1] *Anab* I 2 § 27, V 6 § 13, VII 3 § 48, 8 §§ 12–19.   [2] *Anab* IV I §§ 12, 13.
[3] *Anab* V 3 § 4.
[4] *Anab* IV 8 § 4. It does not appear that the man rejoined his native tribe.
[5] *Anab* VII 7 § 53.
[6] See the protest of Callicratidas, *Hellen* I 6 § 14, with Breitenbach's note.
[7] *Anab* VII 1 § 36, 2 § 6, 3 § 3.   [8] *Memorab* II 7.

The adoption of this suggestion produced the happiest results in every way. Such was the way in which Socrates led his friend. He drew from him the assertion that free people are superior to slaves, and so brought him round to the conviction that superiority could not be shewn by mere incapacity for work.

In this conversation of Socrates may be detected the germ of a complete revolution in thought on labour-subjects. It avoids the topic of common humanity. That the slave is a man and brother, only the victim of misfortune, had been hinted by Euripides and was to become a theme of comic poets. But Socrates lets this point alone, and argues from natural economic necessity. Elsewhere he denounces[1] idleness and proclaims that useful labour is good for the labourer, taking a moral point of view. Again, he suggests[2] that the shortcomings of slaves are largely due to their masters' slackness or mismanagement. But he accepts slavery as a social and economic fact. All the same he makes play at times with the notion of moral worthlessness, which many people regarded as characteristic of slaves in general. It is the knowledge of the true qualities[3] of conduct, in short of the moral and political virtues, that makes men honourable gentlemen (καλοὺς κἀγαθούς), and the lack of this knowledge that makes them slavish (ἀνδραποδώδεις). But, if the difference between a liberal and an illiberal training, expressed in resulting habits of mind, is thus great, the slavish must surely include many of those legally free. Hence he even goes so far as to say 'Therefore we ought to spare no exertions to escape being slaves (ἀνδράποδα).' And he lays stress on the need of moral qualities[4] in slaves as well as freemen: we should never be willing to entrust our cattle or our store-houses or the direction of our works to a slave devoid of self-control. His position suggests two things: first, that the importance of the slave in the economic and social system was a striking fact now recognized: second, that the unavoidable moral degradation generally assumed to accompany the condition of slavery was either wrongfully assumed or largely due to the shortcomings of masters. The conception of the slave as a mere chattel, injury to which is simply a damage to its owner, was proving defective in practice, and the philosopher was inclined to doubt its soundness in principle. Xenophon had been brought into touch with such questionings by his intercourse with Socrates. It remains to see how far he shews traces of their influence when he comes to treat labour-problems in connexion with agriculture.

References to agriculture[5] are few and unimportant in the *Memora-*

---

[1] *Memor* I 2 § 57, II 7 §§ 4–11, 8.   [2] *Memor* III 13 § 4.
[3] *Memor* I 1 § 16, IV 2 §§ 22–31.   [4] *Memor* I 5 § 2.
[5] *Memor* III 7 § 6, 9 §§ 11, 15.

bilia. The *Economicus* deals directly with the subject. A significant passage throws light on the condition of rural Attica at the end of the fifth century BC. The speaker Ischomachus tells[1] how his father made money by judicious enterprise. He bought up farms that were let down or derelict, got them into good order, and sold them at a profit when improved. Clearly he was a citizen, able to deal in real estate, and a capitalist. There can hardly be a doubt that he operated by the use of slave-labour on a considerable scale. All through the *Economicus* slavery is presupposed, but the attitude of Xenophon is characteristically genial and humane. The existence of a slave-market[2], where you may buy likely men, even skilled craftsmen, is assumed. But the most notable feature of the book is the seriousness with which the responsibility of the master[3] is asserted. There is no querulous evasion of the issue by laying the blame of failure on the incorrigible vices of slaves. Prosperity will depend on securing good service: good service cannot be secured by any amount of chains and punishments, if the master be slack and fitful: both in the house and on the farm, good sympathetic discipline, fairly and steadily enforced, is the secret of success. Carelessness malingering and desertion must be prevented or checked. And to achieve this is the function of the economic art, operating through the influence of hope rather than fear. The training of slaves[4] is a matter needing infinite pains on the part of the master and mistress. She must train her housekeeper (ταμία) as he trains his steward (ἐπίτροπος), and both are to act in a humane and kindly spirit. Yet the strictly animal view of slaves[5] appears clearly in a passage where the training of slaves is compared with that of horses or performing dogs. 'But it is possible to make men more obedient by mere instruction (καὶ λόγῳ), pointing out that it is to their interest to obey: in dealing with slaves the system which is thought suitable for training beasts has much to recommend it as a way of teaching obedience. For by meeting their appetites with special indulgence to their bellies you may contrive to get much out of them.' We gather that the better and more refined type of Athenian gentleman with a landed estate, while averse to inhumanity, and aware that slaves were human, still regarded his slaves as mere chattels. His humanity is prompted mainly by self-interest. As for rights, they have none.

The system of rewards and punishments on the estate of course rests wholly on the master's will. The whole success of the working depends on the efficiency of the steward or stewards. Accordingly the passage in which Ischomachus explains how he deals with these trusted slaves is of particular interest. Having carefully trained a man, he

---

[1] *Econ* 20 §§ 22 foll.   [2] *Econ* 12 § 3.   [3] *Econ* 3 §§ 1–5, 5 §§ 15, 16, 12 § 19.
[4] *Econ* 7–9, 12–14, 21.   [5] *Econ* 13 § 9, cf 9 § 5.

must judge him[1] according to a definite standard—does he or does he not honestly and zealously discharge his trust? 'When I find that in spite of good treatment they still try to cheat me, I conclude that their greediness is past curing, and degrade them[2] from their charge.' This seems to mean that they are reduced to the position of the ordinary hands. 'But when I observe any induced to be honest[3] not merely because honesty pays best, but because they want to get a word of praise from me, these I treat as no longer slaves (ὥσπερ ἐλευθέροις ἤδη). I not only enrich them, but shew them respect as men of honour.' One is tempted to interpret these last words as implying that actual manu-mission takes place, the services of the men being retained as freedmen. But the words do not say so plainly, and it is safer to read into them no technical sense. That the men are trusted and allowed to earn for themselves, is enough. The agriculture depicted in the *Economicus* is that of a landowner with plenty of capital, not that of the peasant farmer. The note of it is superintendence[4] (ἐπιμέλεια), not bodily labour (αὐτουργία). In one place αὐτουργία is mentioned, when agri-culture is praised, one of its merits being the bodily strength that those gain who work with their own hands. It is as well to repeat here that the fact of a farmer labouring himself does not prove that he employs no other labour. On the other hand there is good reason to infer that the other class, those who 'do their farming by superintendence,' are not manual labourers at all. The benefit to them is that agriculture 'makes them early risers and smart in their movements.' The master keeps a horse, and is thus enabled to ride out[5] early to the farm and stay there till late.

It is remarkable that in this book we hear nothing of hired labourers. There are two references[6] to the earning of pay, neither of them in connexion with agricultural labour. Yet the existence of a class of poor people who have to earn their daily bread[7] is not ignored. Socrates admires the economic skill[8] of Ischomachus. It has enabled him to be of service to his friends and to the state. This is a fine thing, and shews the man of substance. In contrast, 'there are numbers of men who cannot live without depending on others: numbers too who are content if they can procure themselves the necessaries of life.' The solid and strong men are those who contrive to make a surplus and use it as benefactors. I read this passage as indirect evidence of the depression of small-scale free industry and the increase of slave-owning capitalism in the Athens of Xenophon's time. And I find another in-dication[9] of this in connexion with agriculture. In the course of the

---

[1] *Econ* 12–15.
[2] *Econ* 14 § 8.
[3] *Econ* 14 § 9.
[4] *Econ* 5 § 4, 14 § 2, 20 *passim*.
[5] *Econ* 5 § 6.
[6] *Econ* 1 § 4, 4 § 6.
[7] cf *Memor* II 7 §§ 7–10.
[8] *Econ* 11 §§ 9, 10.
[9] *Econ* 20 *passim*.

dialogue it appears that the chief points of agricultural knowledge are simple enough: Socrates knew them all along. Why then do some farmers succeed and others fail? The truth of the matter is, replies Ischomachus, that the cause of failure is not want of knowledge but want of careful superintendence. This criticism is in general terms, but it is surely inapplicable to the case of the working peasant farmer: he who puts his own labour into the land will not overlook the short-comings of a hired man or a slave. In the agriculture of which this book treats it is the practical and intelligent self-interest of the master that rules everything. His appearance on the field[1] should cause all the slaves to brighten up and work with a will: but rather to win his favour than to escape his wrath. For in agriculture, as in other pursuits, the ultimate secret of success[2] is a divine gift, the power of inspiring a willing obedience.

I have kept back one passage which needs to be considered with reference to the steward[3]. Can we safely assume that an ἐπίτροπος was always, or at least normally, a slave? Of those who direct the labourers, the real treasure is the man who gets zealous and steady work out of the hands, whether he be steward or director (ἐπίτροπος or ἐπιστάτης). What difference is connoted by these terms? In the *Memorabilia*[4] Socrates meets an old friend who is impoverished by the results of the great war, and driven to earn his living by bodily labour. Socrates points out to him that this resource will fail with advancing age: he had better find some employment less dependent on bodily vigour. 'Why not look out for some wealthy man who needs an assistant in superintendence of his property? Such a man would find it worth his while to employ you as director (or foreman, ἔργων ἐπιστατοῦντα), to help in getting in his crops and looking after his estate.' He answers 'it would gall me to put up with a servile position (δουλείαν).' Clearly the position of ἐπιστάτης appears to him a meaner occupation than free wage-earning by manual labour. In another place[5] we hear of an ἐπιστάτης for a mine-gang being bought for a talent (£235). That superintendents, whatever their title, were at least normally slaves, seems certain. As to the difference between 'steward' and 'director' I can only guess that the former might be a slave promoted from the ranks, but might also be what the 'director' always was, a new importation. It seems a fair assumption that, as a free superintendent must have been a new importation, a specially bought slave 'director' would rank somewhat higher than an ordinary 'steward,' whose title

---

[1] *Econ* 21 § 10.   [2] *Econ* 21 § 12.   [3] *Econ* 21 § 9.

[4] *Memor* II 8 especially § 3. For this suggestion that a free man should be steward of a rich man's estate I can find no parallel. See the chapters on the Roman agricultural writers. The case of the shepherd in Juvenal I 107–8 is not parallel.

[5] *Memor* II 5 § 2. See *Vect* 4 § 22 for suggested employment of free citizens or aliens.

ἐπίτροπος at once marked him as a slave. In relation to the general employment of slave-labour there is practically no difference: both are slave-driving 'overseers.' As the pamphlet on the Revenues has been thought by some critics not to be the work of Xenophon, I pass it by, only noting that it surely belongs to the same generation. It fully attests the tendency to rely[1] on slave-labour, but it is not concerned with agriculture.

The romance known as *Cyropaedia* wanders far from fact. Its purpose is to expound or suggest Xenophon's own views on the government of men: accordingly opportunities for drawing a moral are sought at the expense of historical truth. But from my present point of view the chief point to note is that it does not touch the labour-question with which we are concerned. True, we hear[2] of αὐτουργοί, and of the hardship and poverty of such cultivators, gaining a painful livelihood from an unkind soil. That the value of a territory depends on the presence of a population[3] able and willing to develop its resources, is fully insisted on by Cyrus. But this is in connexion with conquest. The inhabitants of a conquered district remain as tributary cultivators, merely changing their rulers. That the labour of the conquered is to provide the sustenance of the conquering race, is accepted as a fundamental principle. It is simply the right of the stronger: if he leaves anything to his subject, that is a voluntary act of grace. The reason why we hear little of slavery is that all are virtually slaves save the one autocrat. The fabric of Xenophon's model government is a very simple one: first, an oriental Great King, possessed of all the virtues: second, a class of warrior nobles, specially trained and dependent on the King's favour: third, a numerous subject population, whose labour supports the whole, and who are practically serfs. A cynical passage[4] describes the policy of Cyrus, meant to perpetuate the difference of the classes. After detailing minutely the liberal training enjoined on those whom he intended to employ in governing (οὓς...ἄρχειν ᾤετο χρῆναι), Xenophon proceeds to those whom he intended to qualify for servitude (οὓς...κατεσκεύαζεν εἰς τὸ δουλεύειν). These it was his practice not to urge to any of the liberal exercises, nor to allow them to possess arms. He took great care to spare them any privations: for instance at a hunt: the hunters had to take their chance of hunger and thirst, being freemen, but the beaters had ample supplies and halted for meals. They were delighted with this consideration, the design of which was to prevent their ever ceasing to be slaves (ἀνδράποδα). The whole scheme is frankly imperial. All initiative and power rests with the autocrat, and all depends on his virtues. That a

---

[1] *Vectigalia* ch 4 *passim*.
[2] *Cyrop* VII 5 § 67, VIII 3 §§ 36–41.
[3] *Cyrop* IV 4 §§ 5–12, VII 5 §§ 36, 73.
[4] *Cyrop* VIII 1 §§ 43–4.

succession of such faultless despots could not be ensured, and that the scheme was consequently utopian, did not trouble the simple Xenophon. Like many other thoughtful men of the time, he was impressed by the apparent efficiency of the rigid Spartan system, and distrusted the individual liberty enjoyed in democratic states, above all in Athens. In Persia, though he thought the Persians were no longer what Cyrus the Great had made them, he had seen how great was still the power arising from the control of all resources by a single will. These two impressions combined seem to account for the tone of the *Cyropaedia*, and the servile position of the cultivators explains why it has so very little bearing on the labour-question in agriculture.

XIII. THE COMIC FRAGMENTS.

In pursuing our subject from period to period, and keeping so far as possible to chronological order, it may seem inconsistent to take this collection[1] of scraps as a group. For Attic Comedy covers nearly two centuries, from the age of Cratinus to the age of Menander. Many changes happened in this time, and the evidence of the fragments must not be cited as though it were that of a single witness. But the relevant passages are few; for the writers, such as Athenaeus and Stobaeus, in whose works most of the extracts are preserved, seldom had their attention fixed on agriculture. The longer fragments[2] of Menander recently discovered are somewhat more helpful. The adaptations of Plautus and Terence must be dealt with separately.

That country life and pursuits had their share of notice on the comic stage is indicated by the fact that Aristophanes produced a play[3] named Γεωργοί, and Menander a Γεωργός. That the slave-market was active is attested by references in all periods. So too is wage-earning labour of various kinds: but some of these passages certainly refer to wage-earning by slaves paying a rent (ἀποφορά) to their owners. Also the problems arising out of the relation between master and slave, with recognition of the necessity of wise management. The difference between the man who does know how to control slaves[4] and the man who does not (εὔδουλος and κακόδουλος) was early expressed, and indirectly alluded to throughout. The good and bad side of slaves, loyalty treachery honesty cheating etc, is a topic constantly handled. But these passages nearly always have in view the close relation of domestic slavery. I think we are justified in inferring that the general tone steadily becomes more humane.

[1] Cited from Kock's edition 1880–8.   [2] *Menandrea*, ed Körte 1910, Teubner.
[3] Fragments 100–24. From other plays, 294, 387.
[4] Cratinus 81, Pherecrates 212.

Common humanity gains recognition as a guide of conduct. Many of the fragments have been handed down as being neatly put moral sentences, and of these not a few[1] recognize the debt that a slave owes to a good master. These are utterances of slaves, for the slave as a character became more and more a regular figure of comedy, as comedy became more and more a drama of private life. Side by side with this tone is the frank recognition of the part played by chance[2] in the destinies of master and slave; a very natural reflexion in a state of things under which you had but to be captured and sold out of your own country, out of the protection of your own laws, to pass from the former condition to the latter. A few references to manumission also occur, and the Roman adaptations suggest that in the later Comedy they were frequent. On the other hand several fragments seem to imply that circumstances were working unfavourably to the individual free craftsmen, at least in some trades. The wisdom of learning a craft (τέχνη), as a resource[3] that cannot be lost like external possessions, is insisted on. But in other passages a more despairing view[4] appears; death is better than the painful struggle for life. No doubt different characters were made to speak from different points of view.

It is to be noted that two fragments of the earlier Comedy refer to the old tradition[5] of a golden age long past, in which there were no slaves (see under Herodotus), and in which the bounty of nature[6] provided an ample supply of food and all good things (see the passages cited from the *Odyssey*). Athenaeus, who has preserved[7] these extracts, remarks that the old poets were seeking by their descriptions to accustom mankind to do their own work with their own hands (αὐτουργοὺς εἶναι). But it is evident that the subject was treated in the broadest comic spirit, as his numerous quotations shew. When in the restoration of good old times the articles of food are to cook and serve themselves and ask to be eaten, we must not take the picture very seriously. These passages do however suggest that there was a food-question at the time when they were written, of sufficient importance to give point to them : possibly also a labour-question. Now Crates and Pherecrates flourished before the Peloponnesian war and during its earlier years, Nicophon was a late contemporary of Aristophanes. The evidence is too slight to justify a far-reaching conclusion, but it is consistent with the general inferences drawn from other authorities. In the fragments of the later Comedy we begin to find passages bearing on agriculture,

---

[1] e.g. Antiphanes 265, Philemon 227, Menander 581, etc.
[2] Philemon 95.
[3] Philemon 213, Menander 68, 716, Hipparchus 2.
[4] Menander 14, Posidippus 23 with Kock's note.
[5] Pherecrates 10, Crates 14.   [6] Nicophon 13, 14.
[7] Athenaeus VI pp 263, 267 e–270 a.

and it is surely a mere accident that we do not have them in those of the earlier.

The contrast between life in town and life in the country is forcibly brought out[1] by Menander. The poor man has no chance in town, where he is despised and wronged: in the country he is spared the galling presence of witnesses, and can bear his ill fortune on a lonely farm. The farm then is represented as a sort of refuge from unsatisfactory surroundings in the city. When we remember that in Menander's time Athens was a dependency of one or other of Alexander's Successors, a community of servile rich and mean poor, fawning on its patrons and enjoying no real freedom of state-action, we need not wonder at the poet's putting such a view into the mouths of some of his characters. The remains of the play Γεωργός are of particular interest. The old master is a tough obstinate old fellow, who persists in working[2] on the land himself, and even wounds himself by clumsy use of his mattock. But he has a staff of slaves, barbarians, on whom he is dependent. These paid no attention to the old man in his misfortune; a touch from which we may infer that the relations between master and slaves were not sympathetic. But a young free labourer in his employ comes to the rescue, nurses him, and sets him on his legs again. While laid up, the old man learns by inquiry that this youth is his own son, the fruit of a former amour, whom his mother has reared in struggling poverty. Enough of the play remains to shew that the trials of the free poor were placed in a strong light, and that, as pointed out above, the struggle for existence in the city was felt to be especially severe. In this case whether the old man is rich or not does not appear: at all events he has enough property to make amends for his youthful indiscretions by relieving the necessities of those who have a claim on him. He is probably the character in whose mouth[3] were put the words ‘ I am a rustic (ἄγροικος); that I don't deny; and not fully expert in affairs of city life (lawsuits etc?): but I was not born yesterday.’

The functions of the rustic slaves may give us some notion of the kind of farms that Menander had in mind. In the Γεωργός, the slave Davus, coming in from his day's labour, grumbles[4] at the land on which he has to work: shrubs and flowers of use only for festival decorations grow there as vigorous weeds, but when you sow seed you get back what you sowed with no increase. This savours of the disappointing tillage of an upland farm. In the Ἐπιτρέποντες[5], Davus is a shepherd,

---

[1] Menandrea pp 159–61 (fragments of Γεωργός).
[2] Menandrea pp 157, 159.
[3] opus cit and Menander 97 Kock. For ἄγροικος connoting simplicity cf 794 ἄγροικος εἶναι προσποιεῖ πονηρὸς ὤν.
[4] Menandrea p 155, 96 Kock.   [5] Menandrea p 15 (lines 26, 40).

Syriscus a charcoal-burner, occupations also proper to the hill districts.
We must not venture to infer that Attic agriculture was mainly of this
type in the poet's day. The favourite motive of plots in the later
Comedy, the exposure of infants in remote spots, their rescue by casual
herdsmen or other slaves, and their eventual identification as the very
person wanted in each case to make all end happily, would of itself
suggest that lonely hill-farms, rather than big estates in the fat lowland,
should be the scene. From my point of view the fact of chief interest is
that slave-labour appears as normal in such an establishment. Rustic
clothing[1] and food served out in rations[2] are minor details of the
picture, and the arrangement by which a slave can work as wage-
earner[3] for another employer, paying over a share to his own master
(the ἀποφορά), surely indicates that there was nothing exceptional
about it. There are one or two other fragments directly bearing on
agricultural labour. One of uncertain age[4] speaks of a tiresome hand
who annoys his employer by chattering about some public news from
the city, when he should be digging. I doubt whether a slave is meant:
at least he is surely a hired one, but why not a poor freeman, reduced
to wage-earning? Such is the position of Timon[5] in Lucian—μισθοῦ
γεωργεῖ—a passage in which adaptations from Comedy are reasonably
suspected. That rustic labour has a better side to it, that 'the bitter of
agriculture has a touch of sweet in it,' is admitted[6] by one of Menander's
characters, but the passage which seems the most genuine expression
of the prevalent opinion[7] is that in which we read that a man's true
part is to excel in war, 'for agriculture is a bondman's task' (τὸ γὰρ
γεωργεῖν ἔργον ἐστὶν οἰκέτου).

The nature and condition of the evidence must be my excuse for
the unsatisfactory appearance of this section. The number of passages
bearing on slavery in general, and the social and moral questions connected therewith, is large and remote from my subject. They are of
great interest as illustrating the movement of thought on these matters,
but their bearing on agricultural labour is very slight. To the virtues
of agriculture as a pursuit tending to promote a sound and manly
character Menander[8] bears witness. 'A farm is for all men a trainer in
virtue and a freeman's life.' Many a town-bred man has thought and
said the same, but praise is not always followed by imitation. Even
more striking is another[9] remark, 'farms that yield but a poor living
make brave men.' For it was the hard-living rustics from the back-
country parts of Greece that succeeded as soldiers of fortune, the famous

---

[1] Menandrea p 13 (line 12, cf 111).   [2] Menandrea p 5.
[3] Menandrea p 25.   [4] Kock III p 473 (adespota 347).
[5] Lucian, Timon 7, 8. Kock adesp 1434, note.
[6] Menander 795.   [7] Menander 642.   [8] Menander 408.
[9] Menander 63, τὰ κακῶς τρέφοντα χωρὶ' ἀνδρείους ποιεῖ.

Greek mercenaries whose services all contemporary kings were eager to secure. In short, to the onlooker it seemed a fine thing to be bred a healthy rustic, but the rustic himself was apt to prefer a less monotonous and more remunerative career.

XIV. EARLY LAWGIVERS AND THEORISTS.

The treatises of the two great philosophers on the state (and therefore on the position of agriculture in the state) did not spring suddenly out of nothing; nor was it solely the questionings of Socrates[1] that turned the attention of Plato and Aristotle to the subject. Various lawgivers had shewn in their systems a consciousness of its importance, and speculative thinkers outside[2] the ranks of practical statesmen had designed model constitutions in which a reformed land-system played a necessary part. It is to Aristotle, the great collector of experience, that we owe nearly all our information of these attempts. It is convenient to speak of them briefly together. All recognize much the same difficulties, and there is a striking similarity in the means by which they propose to overcome them. The lawgivers[3] referred to are **Pheidon** of Corinth and **Philolaus**, also a Corinthian though his laws were drafted for Thebes, and thirdly[4] **Solon**. The dates of the first two are uncertain, but they belong to early times. The two constitution-framers[5] are **Hippodamus** of Miletus, whose birth is placed about 475 BC, and **Phaleas** of Chalcedon, probably somewhat later. Both witnessed the growth of imperial Athens, and Phaleas at least is thought to have been an elder contemporary of Plato. Very little is known about them. If we say that the attempt to design ideal state systems shews that they were not satisfied with those existing, and that the failure of past legislation may have encouraged them to theorize, we have said about all that we are entitled to infer.

On one point there was general agreement among Greek states: all desired to be 'free' or independent of external control. For some special purpose one people might for a time be recognized as the Leaders (ἡγεμόνες) of a majority of states, or more permanently as Representatives or Patrons (προστάται). But these unofficial titles only stood for a position acquiesced in under pressure of necessity. Each community wanted to live its own life in its own way, and the extreme jealousy of interference remained. Side by side with this was an

---

[1] Stobaeus *flor* LVI 16 preserves an utterance of Socrates on labour, especially agricultural labour, as the basis of wellbeing, in which he remarks that ἐν τῇ γεωργίᾳ πάντα ἔνεστιν ὧν χρείαν ἔχομεν.

[2] ἰδιωτῶν Aristotle *Pol* II 7 § 1.   [3] Arist *Pol* II 6 § 13, 12 § 10.

[4] Arist *Pol* II 7 § 6 and Newman's note.   [5] Arist *Pol* II 7, 8.

internal jealousy causing serious friction in most of the several states, at first between nobles and commons, later between rich and poor. The seditions (στάσεις) arising therefrom were causes, not only of inner weakness and other evils, but in particular of intervention from without. Therefore it was often the policy of the victors in party strife to expel or exterminate their opponents, in order to secure to themselves undisputed control of their own state. This tendency operated to perpetuate the smallness of scale in Greek states, already favoured by the physical features of the land. That the Greeks with all their cleverness never invented what we call Representative Government is no wonder. Men's views in general were directed to the independence of their own state under control of their own partisans. The smaller the state, the easier it was to organize the control: independence could only be maintained by military efficiency, and unanimous loyalty was something to set off against smallness of numbers. Moreover the Greek mind had an artistic bent, and the sense of proportion was more easily and visibly gratified on a smaller scale. The bulk of Persia did not appear favourable to human freedom and dignity as understood in Hellas. In the Persian empire there was nothing that a Greek would recognize as citizenship. The citizen of a Greek state expected to have some voice in his own government: the gulf between citizen and non-citizen was the line of division, but even in Sparta the full citizens were equals in legal status among themselves. We may fairly say that the principle of equality (τὸ ἴσον) was at the root of Greek notions of citizenship. Privilege did not become less odious as it ceased to rest on ancestral nobility and became more obviously an advantage claimed by wealth.

Since the light thrown on the subject[1] by Dr Grundy, no one will dispute the importance of economic considerations in Greek policy, and in particular of the ever-pressing question of the food-supply. The security of the land and crops was to most states a vital need, and necessitated constant readiness to maintain it in arms. Closely connected therewith was the question of distribution. Real property was not only the oldest and most permanent investment. Long before Aristotle[2] declared that 'the country is a public thing' (κοινόν), that is an interest of the community, that opinion was commonly held, whether formulated or instinctive. The position of the landless man was traditionally a dubious one. The general rule was that only a citizen could own land in the territory of the state. From this it was no great step to argue that every citizen ought to own a plot of land within the borders. This was doubtless not always possible. In such a state as Corinth or Megara or Miletus commercial growth in a narrow territory

---

[1] In *Thucydides and the history of his age* chapters III–VII.
[2] *Politics* III 13 § 2.

had led to extensive colonization from those centres. And the normal procedure in the foundation of Greek colonies was to divide the occupied territory into lots (κλῆροι) and assign them severally to settlers. In course of time the discontents generated by land-monopolizing in old Hellas were liable to reappear beyond the seas, particularly in colonial states of rapid growth: a notorious instance is found in the troubles arising at Syracuse out of the squatter-sovranty created by the original colonists. We meet with plans for confiscation and redistribution of land as a common phenomenon of Greek revolutions. The mischievous moral effects of so unsettling a process on political wellbeing did not escape the notice of thoughtful observers. But on one important point we have practically no evidence. Did the new allottees wish to be, and in fact normally become, working farmers (αὐτουργοί)? Or did they aim at providing for themselves an easy life, supported by the labour of slaves? I wish I could surely and rightly decide between these alternatives. As it is, I can only say that I believe the second to be nearer the truth.

Under such conditions Greek lawgivers and theorists alike seem to have looked to much the same measures for remedying evils that they could not ignore. The citizen as landholder is the human figure with which they are all concerned. To prevent destitution arising from the loss[1] of his land-lot is a prime object. Some therefore would forbid the sale of the lot. To keep land in the same hands it was necessary to regulate numbers of citizen households, and this was attempted[2] in the laws of Pheidon. Families may die out, so rules to provide for perpetuity by adoptions[3] were devised by Philolaus. Again, there is the question of the size of the lots, and this raises the further question of a limit to acquisition. Such a limitation is attributed[4] to certain early lawgivers not named, and with them apparently to Solon. Phaleas would insist on equality of landed estate[5] among his citizens: a proposal which Aristotle treats as unpractical, referring to only one form of wealth, and leaving out of account slaves, tame animals, coin, and the dead-stock tools etc. His exclusive attention to internal civic wellbeing is also blamed, for it is absurd to disregard the relations of a state to other states: there must be a foreign policy, therefore you must provide[6] military force. The fanciful scheme of Hippodamus, a strange doctrinaire genius, seems to have been in many points inconsistent from want of attention to practical detail. From Aristotle's account he appears not to have troubled himself with the question of equal land-lots, but his fixing the number[7] of citizens (10,000) is evidence that his

[1] See Newman on Ar *Pol* II 7 § 7.   [2] Ar *Pol* II 6 § 13.
[3] Ar *Pol* II 12 § 10.   [4] Ar *Pol* II 7 §§ 3–7.   [5] *Pol* II 7 *passim*.
[6] *Pol* II 7 §§ 14, 15.   [7] μυρίανδρον *Pol* II 8 §§ 2, 3, with notes in Newman.

point of view necessitated a limit. He proceeds on a system of triads.
The citizens are grouped in three classes, artisans (τεχνῖται), husbandmen (γεωργοί), and the military, possessors of arms. The land is either
sacred (for service of religion, ἱερά), public (δημοσία or κοινή) or the
property of the husbandmen (ἰδία). The three classes of land and
citizens are to be assumed equal. The military are to be supported by
the produce of the public land. But who cultivates it? Aristotle shews
that the scheme is not fully thought out. If the soldiers, then the distinction, obviously intended, between soldier and farmer, is lost. If the
farmers, then the distinction between the public and private land is
meaningless. If neither, a fourth class, not allowed for in the plan, will
be required. This last is probably what Hippodamus meant: but to
particularize the employment of slaves may have appeared superfluous.
Into the purely constitutional details I need not enter, but one criticism
is so frankly expressive of Greek ideas that it can hardly be omitted.
What, says Aristotle, is the use of political rights to the artisans and
husbandmen? they are unarmed, and therefore will practically be slaves
of the military class. This was the truth in Greek politics generally,
and is one of the most significant facts to be borne in mind when
considering the political failure of the Greeks.

A curious difference of economic view is shewn in the position
assigned to the artisan[1] or craftsman element by Hippodamus and
Phaleas respectively. Phaleas would have them state-slaves (δημόσιοι),
Hippodamus makes them citizens, though unarmed. On the former
plan the state would no doubt feed them and use their produce, as we
do with machinery. Of the latter plan Aristotle remarks that τεχνῖται
are indispensable: all states need them, and they can live of the earnings of their crafts, but the γεωργοί as a distinct class are superfluous.
We may reply that, if the craftsmen live of their earnings and stick to
their several crafts, they will need to buy food, and the farmers are
surely there to supply it. The reply is so obvious that one feels as if
Aristotle's meaning had been obscured through some mishap to the
text. For the present purpose it suffices that the professional craftsmen
in these two Utopias are to be either actual slaves or citizens *de iure*
who are *de facto* as helpless as slaves. In the scheme of Hippodamus
the farmer-class also are virtually the slaves of the military. Another
notable point, apparently neglected by Hippodamus, is the trust reposed
in education[2] or training by both Phaleas and his critic. How to implant in your citizens the qualities needed for making your institutions
work well in practice, is the problem. Phaleas would give all the same

[1] 'Artisan' is not quite = τεχνίτης. All professional work is included.
[2] *Pol* II 7 §§ 8, 9. The probable influence of Spartan precedents is pointed out in Mr Newman's note.

training, on the same principle as he gives equal land-lots. To Aristotle this seems crude nonsense: the problem to him is the discovery of the appropriate training, whether the same for all or not. This insistence on training as the main thing in citizen-making is, as we shall see, a common feature of Greek political speculation. But in the artistic desire to produce the 'complete citizen,' and thereby make possible a model state, the specializing mania outruns the humbler considerations of everyday human society, and agriculture, for all its confessed importance, is apt to be treated with something very like contempt. The tendency to regard farmer and warrior as distinct classes is unmistakeable. The peasant-soldier of Roman tradition is not an ordinary Greek figure. How far the small scale of Greek states may have favoured this differentiation is very hard to say. But Greek admiration for the athlete type had probably something to do with the growth of military professionalism.

The recognition of a land-question and attempts to find a solution were probably stimulated by observation of contemporary phenomena, especially in the two leading states of the fifth century. Sparta had long held the first place, and even the rise of Athens had not utterly destroyed her ancient prestige. That her military system was effective, seemed proved by the inviolability of Laconian territory and the successes of her armies in external wars. That it was supported by the labour of a Greek population reduced to serfdom, was perhaps a weak point in her institutions; but that Greek opinion was seriously shocked by the fact can hardly be maintained. It was now and then convenient to use it as a passing reproach, but even Athens did not refuse to aid in putting down Helot rebellions. And this weak point was set off by a strong one. Whatever the reasons[1] for her policy, she interfered very little in the internal affairs of her allies and did not tax them. To be content with the leadership of confederates, and not to convert it into an empire of subjects, assured to her a certain amount of respectful sympathy in the jealous Greek world. Thus she afforded an object-lesson in the advantages of rigid specialization. She provided her own food in time of peace, and took her opponents' food in time of war. The disadvantages of her system were yet to appear. Athens on the other hand was becoming more and more dependent on imported food. She was the leader of the maritime states and islands: she had become their imperial mistress. However easy her yoke might be in practice, it left no room for independent action on the part of her subject allies: what had been contributions from members of a league had become virtually imperial taxation, and to Greek prejudices such taxation appeared tyranny. Nor was this prejudice allowed to die out. The

[1] See the valuable discussion in Grundy *op cit* chapter VIII.

rival interests of commercial Corinth saw to it that the enslavement, not of Greeks but of Greek states, should be continually borne in mind. The contrast between the two leading powers was striking. But, if many Greek states feared in Athens a menace to their several independence, on the other hand they shrank from copying the rigid discipline of Sparta. No wonder that some of the more imaginative minds had dreams of a system more congenial to Greek aspirations. But the land-question was a stumbling-block. That a citizen should take an active personal share in politics was assumed, and that he should do this tended to make him depute non-political duties to others. Thus the notion that all citizens should be equal in the eye of the law and share in government—democracy in short—was not favourable to personal labour on the land. No distribution of land-lots could convert the city politician into a real working farmer. Therefore either there must be a decline in agriculture or an increase of slave-labour, or both. From these alternatives there was no escape: but ingenious schemers long strove to find a way. And from those days to these no one has succeeded in constructing a sound and lasting civilization on a basis of slavery.

XV. PLATO.

An Athenian who died in 347 BC at the age of 80 or 82 years had witnessed extraordinary changes in the Hellenic world, more particularly in the position of Athens. With the political changes we are not here directly concerned. But they were closely connected with economic changes, both as cause and as effect. The loss of empire[1] entailed loss of revenue. The amounts available as state-pay being reduced, the poorer citizens lost a steady source of income: that their imperial pride had departed did not tend to make them less sensitive to the pinch of poverty. Athens, thrown back upon her own limited resources, had to produce what she could in order to buy what she needed, and capital, employing slave-labour, found its opportunity. In this atmosphere discontent and jealousy grew fast: conflicting interests of rich and poor were at the back of all the disputes of political life. Athens it is true avoided the crude revolutionary methods adopted in some less civilized states. The Demos did not massacre or banish the wealthy Few, and share out their lands and other properties among the poor Many. But they consistently regarded the estates of the rich as the source from which the public outlay should as far as possible be drawn. They left the capitalist free to make money in his own way, and squeezed him when he had made it. Whether he were citizen or

---

[1] Cf Isocr *de pace* § 69 p 173, §§ 129–131 p 185.

metic[1] mattered not from the economic point of view. Capitalistic industry was really slave-industry. The 'small man' had the choice of either competing, perhaps vainly, with the 'big man' on the land or in the workshop, or of giving up the struggle and using his political power to make the 'big man' disgorge some of his profits. Moreover military life no longer offered the prospects of conquest and gain that had made it attractive. The tendency was to treat the citizen army as a defensive force, and to employ professional mercenaries (of whom there was now[2] no lack) on foreign service. To a thoughtful observer these phenomena suggested uneasy reflexions. Demos in Assembly was a dispiriting spectacle. Selfish[3] and shortsighted, he cared more for his own belly and his amusements than for permanent interests of state. Perhaps this was no new story. But times had changed, and the wealthy imperial Athens, able to support the burden of her own defects, had passed away. Bad government in reduced circumstances might well be productive of fatal results.

It was not Athens alone that had failed. Fifteen years before Plato's death the failure of both Sparta and Thebes had left Hellas exhausted[4] and without a leading state to give some sort of unity to Greek policy. There was still a common Hellenic feeling, but it was weak compared with separatist jealousy. Antipathy to the Barbarian remained: but the Persian power had been called in by Greeks to aid them against other Greeks, and this was a serious danger to the Greek world. Things were even worse in the West. How anarchic democracy had paved the way for military tyranny at Syracuse, how the tyranny had lowered the standard of Greek civilization in Sicily and Italy, and had been the ruin of Greek cities, no man of that age knew better than Plato. Plato was not singular in his distrust of democracy: that attitude was common enough. Among the companions of Socrates I need only refer to Xenophon and Critias. Socrates had insisted that government is a difficult art, for success in which a thorough training is required. Now, whatever might be the case in respect of tyrannies or oligarchies, democracy was manifestly an assertion of the principle that all citizens were alike qualified for a share in the work of government. Yet no craftsman would dream of submitting the work of his own trade to the direction of amateurs. Why then should the amateur element, led by amateurs, dominate in the sphere of politics? It was easy to find

---

[1] Plato was evidently uneasy at the growing influence of metics, to judge from the jealous rule of *Laws* p 850. This is in striking contrast with the view of Xenophon.

[2] *Laws* 630 *b*, cf 697 *e*.

[3] See *Republic* 565 *a* on the indifference of the handworking δῆμος. Cf Isocr *de pace* § 52 p 170.

[4] Cf Xenophon *hell* VII 5 § 27 on the ἀκρισία καὶ ταραχὴ intensified after Mantinea, 362 BC.

instances of the evil effects of amateurism in public affairs. It is true that this line of argument contained a fallacy, as arguments from analogy very often do. But it had a profound influence on Plato, and it underlay all his political speculations. It was reinforced by an influence that affected many of his contemporaries, admiration of Sparta on the score of the permanence[1] of her system of government. That this admiration was misguided, and the permanence more apparent than real, matters not: to a Greek thinker it was necessarily attractive, seeking for some possibly permanent principle of government, and disgusted with the everlasting flux of Hellenic politics. Nor was there anything strange in imagining an ideal state in which sound principles might be carried into effect. The foundation of colonies, in which the settlers made a fresh start as new communities, was traditionally a Greek custom. Such was the foundation, logical and apparently consistent with experience, on which Plato designed to build an Utopia. Avoiding the unscientific *laisser-faire* of democratic politics, functions were to be divided on a rational system, and government placed in the hands of trained specialists.

It is well to note some of the defects of Greek civilization as Plato saw it, particularly in Athens. The confusion and weakness of democratic government, largely the fruit of ignorance haste and prejudice, has been referred to above. In most states the free citizen population were born and bred at the will of their fathers under no scientific state-regulation, not sifted out in youth by scientific selection, and only trained up to the average standard locally approved. Something better was needed, if more was to be got out of human capacity. But it seems certain that Plato found the chief and most deep-seated source of social and political evils in the economic situation. The unequal distribution of wealth and the ceaseless struggle between rich and poor lay at the root of that lack of harmonious unity in which he saw the cause of the weakness and unhappiness of states. To get rid of the plutocrat and the beggar[2] was a prime object. Confiscation and redistribution[3] offered no lasting remedy, so long as men remained what they were. A complete moral change was necessary, and this could only be effected by an education that should train all citizens cheerfully and automatically to bear their several parts in promoting the happiness of all. There must be no more party-strivings after the advantage of this or that section: the guiding principle must be diversity of individual functions combined with unity of aim. An ideal state must be the Happy Land

---

[1] Even Isocrates, who hated Sparta, says of it τὴν μάλιστα τὰ παλαιὰ διασώζουσαν, *Helen* § 63 p 218, and attributes the merits of the Spartan government to imitation of Egypt, *Busiris* § 17 p 225. He notes the moral change in Sparta, *de pace* §§ 95 foll pp 178-180.

[2] *Republic* p 421 e, *Laws* 936 c, 744 e.　　　　[3] *Laws* 736 c, cf *Rep* 565 a, b.

of the Expert, and each specialist must mind his own business. Thus each will enjoy his own proper happiness: friction competition and jealousy will pass away. There will be no more hindrance to the efficiency of craftsmen: we shall not see one tempted by wealth[1] to neglect his trade, while another is too poor to buy the appliances needed for turning out good work. The expert governors or Guardians must be supplied with all necessaries[2] by the classes engaged in the various forms of production. Thus only can they be removed from the corruptions that now pervert politicians. To them at least all private property must be denied. And, in order that they may be as expert in their own function of government as other craftsmen are in their several trades, they must be bred selected and educated on a strictly scientific system the very opposite of the haphazard methods now in vogue.

This brief sketch of the critical and constructive scope of the *Republic* must suffice for my purpose. Plato laid his finger on grave defects, but his remedies seem fantastic in the light of our longer and more varied experience. Any reform of society had to be carried out by human agency, and for the difficulty of adapting this no adequate allowance is made. He recognizes the difficulty of starting an ideal community on his model. Old prejudices will be hard to overcome. So he suggests[3] that it will be necessary for the philosophical rulers to clear the ground by sending all the adult inhabitants out into the country, keeping in the city only the children of ten years and under: these they will train up on their system. He implies that with the younger generation growing up under properly regulated conditions the problems of establishment will solve themselves by the effect of time. This grotesque proposal may indicate that Plato did not mean his constructive design to be taken very seriously. But a more notable weakness appears in the narrowness of outlook. It was natural that a Greek should think and write as a Greek for Greeks, and seek lessons in Greek experience. But the blight of disunion and failure was already on the little Greek states; and their experience, not likely to recur, has in fact never really recurred. Hence the practical value of Plato's stimulating criticism and construction is small. In the labour-question we find no advance. Slavery is assumed as usual, but against the enslavement of Greeks, of which recent warfare supplied many examples, he makes a vigorous protest. Euripides had gone further than this, and questionings of slavery had not been lacking. Another very Greek limitation of view comes out in the contempt[5] for βαναυσία, the assumed

---

[1] *Republic* 421 d.   [2] *Republ* 416 d, e, 417, 464 c, 543 b.
[3] *Republ* 540 e–541 a.   [4] *Republ* 469–471.
[5] *Republ* 495 d, 590 c, 522 b. *Laws* 741.

physical and moral inferiority of persons occupied in sedentary trades.
That such men were unfitted for the rough work of war, and therefore
unfitted to take part in ruling an independent Greek state, was an
opinion not peculiar to Plato. But this objection could not well be
raised against the working farmer. Why then does Plato exclude the
farmer-class from a share in the government of his ideal state? I think
we may detect three reasons. First, the husbandman, though necessary
to the state's existence, has not the special training required for government, nor the leisure to acquire it. Second, it is his intense occupation
that alone secures to the ruling class the leisure needful for their responsible duties. Third, the belief[1] that a man cannot be at the same
time a good husbandman and a good soldier. These three may be
regarded as one: the philosopher would get rid of haphazard amateurism
by making the expert specialist dominant in all departments of civil
and military life. The influence of the Spartan system (much idealized),
and the growth of professional soldiering, on his theories is too obvious
to need further comment.

Reading the *Republic* from the labour-question point of view, one
is struck by the lack of detail as to the condition of the classes whose
labour feeds and clothes the whole community. We must remember
that the dialogue starts with an attempt to define Justice, in the course
of which a wider field of inquiry is opened up by assuming an analogy[2]
between the individual and the state. As the dominance of his nobler
element over his baser elements is the one sure means of ensuring the
individual's lasting happiness, so the dominance of the nobler element
in the state alone offers a like guarantee. On these lines the argument
proceeds, using an arbitrary psychology, and a fanciful political criticism
to correspond. The construction of a model state is rather incidental
than essential to the discussion. No wonder that, while we have much
detail as to the bodily and mental equipment of the 'Guardians' (both
the governing elders and the warrior youths) we get no information as
to the training of husbandmen and craftsmen. Like slaves, they are
assumed to exist: how they become and remain what they are assumed
to be, we are not told. We are driven to guess that at this stage of
his speculations Plato was content to take over these classes just as
he found them in the civilization of his day. But he can hardly have
imagined that they would acquiesce in any system by which they would
be excluded from all political power. The hopeless inferiority of the
husbandman is most clearly marked when contrasted with the young
warriors of the 'Guardian' class. Duties are so highly specialized that
men are differentiated for life. The γεωργὸς cannot be a good soldier.
But if a soldier shews cowardice he is to be punished[3] by being made

---

[1] *Republ* 374 c, d.   [2] *Republ* 433-4.   [3] *Republ* 468 a.

a γεωργὸς or δημιουργός—a degradation in itself, and accompanied by
no suggestion of a special training being required to fit him for his
new function.   It is unnecessary to enlarge on such points: constructors
of Utopias cannot avoid some inconsistencies and omissions.   The
simple fact is that the arrangements for differentiation of classes in the
model state are not fully worked out in detail.

Plato's Guardians are to have no private property; for it is private
property[1] that seems to him the cause of sectional and personal interests which divide and weaken the state and lead to unhappiness.
But the other classes are not so restricted.   They can own land and
houses etc; on exactly what tenure, is less clear.   Meanwhile, what is
it that the Guardians have in common?   It is the sustenance (τροφὴ)
provided as pay (μισθὸς) for their services by the mass of workers
over whom they rule.   It is expressly stated[2] that in the model state
the Demos will call the Rulers their Preservers and Protectors, and
the Rulers call the Demos their Paymasters and Sustainers.   In existing states other than democracies their mutual relation is too often
expressed as that of Masters and Slaves.   I cannot refrain from noting
that, if the pay of the Guardians consists in their sustenance, this is
so far exactly the case of slaves.   That power and honour should be
reserved for men maintained thus, without private emoluments, is remarkable.   The Spartiates, however much an idealizing of their system
may have suggested the arrangement, were maintained by the sulky
labour of Helot serfs.   Are the husbandmen in Plato's scheme really
any better than Helots?   In describing the origin of states in general,
Plato finds the cause[3] of that development in the insufficiency of individuals to meet their own needs.   But in tracing the process of the
division of labour, and increasing complexity of civilization, he ignores
slavery, though slavery is often referred to in various parts of the book.
Now, if the husbandman has under him no slaves, and is charged with
the food-supply of his rulers, he comes very near to the economic
status of a serf.   He works with his own hands, but not entirely at
his own will or for his own profit.   And in one respect he would, to
Greek critics, seem inferior to a Spartan[4] Helot: he is, by the extreme
specializing system, denied all share in military service, and so can
hardly be reckoned a citizen at all.   How came Plato to imagine for a
single moment that a free Greek would acquiesce in such a position?
I can only guess that the present position of working farmers and
craftsmen in trades seemed to him an intolerable one.   If, as I believe

---

[1] That the speculations of Greek political writers were influenced by the traditions of a
primitive communism is the view of Emil de Laveleye *Primitive property* ch 10.

[2] *Republ* 463 *b*.   [3] *Republ* 369 *b*—373 *c*.

[4] Cf Isocrates *Panath* § 180 p 271.

from the indications in Xenophon and other authorities, agriculture and the various industries of Attica were now steadily passing into the hands of slave-owning capitalists, and small men going to the wall, there would be much to set a philosopher thinking and seeking some way of establishing a wholesomer state of things. On this supposition speculations, however fantastic and incapable of realization in fact, might call attention to practical evils and at least prepare men's minds for practical remedies. In admitting the difficulty of making a fresh start, and the certainty that even his model state would in time lose its purity[1] and pass through successive phases of decay, Plato surely warns us not to take his constructive scheme seriously. But whether he really believed that free handworkers could (save in an oligarchy, which[2] he detests,) be induced to submit to a ruling class, and be themselves excluded on principle from political interests of any kind, is more than I can divine.

That the scheme outlined in the *Republic* was not a practical one was confessed by Plato in his old age by producing the *Laws*, a work in which the actual circumstances of Greek life were not so completely disregarded. The main points that concern us are these. Government is to be vested in a detailed code of laws, administered by magistrates elected by the citizens. There is a Council and an Assembly. Pressure is put upon voters, especially[3] on the wealthier voters, to make them vote. The influence of the Solonian model is obvious. Provision is made[4] for getting over the difficulties of the first start, while the people are still under old traditions which the new educational system will in due course supersede. But, so far from depending on perfect Guardians with absolute power, and treating law as a general pattern[5] modifiable in application by the Guardians at their discretion, we have law supreme and Guardians dependent on the people's will. It is a kind of democracy, but Demos is to be carefully trained, and protected from his own vagaries by minute regulations. The number of citizens[6] is by law fixed at 5040. Each one has an allotment of land, a sacred κλῆρος that cannot be sold. This passes by inheritance from father to son as an undivided whole. Extinction of a family may be prevented by adoptions under strict rules. Excess of citizen population may be relieved by colonies. Poverty is excluded[7] by the minimum guaranteed in the inalienable land-lot, excessive wealth by laws fixing a maximum. It is evident that in this detailed scheme of the *Laws* agriculture must have its position more clearly defined than in the *Republic*.

---

[1] *Republ* 547 *b* foll.

[2] *Republ* 550–2.

[3] *Laws* 756　See *Rep* 565 *a* with Adam's note.

[4] *Laws* 754.

[5] See *Politicus* 293–7, Grote's *Plato* III pp 309–10.

[6] *Laws* 737 foll, 922 *a*—924 *a*, called γεωμόροι 919 *d*.

[7] *Laws* 744 *d*, *e*.

So indeed it has. In order that all may have a fair share, each citizen's land-lot[1] is in two parts, one near the city, the other near the frontier. Thus we see that all citizens will be interested in cultivating the land. We see also that this will be absolutely necessary: for it is intended[2] that the model state shall not be dependent on imported food (like Athens), but produce its own supply. Indeed commerce is to be severely restricted. What the country cannot produce must if necessary be bought, and for this purpose only[3] will a recognized Greek currency be employed: internal transactions will be conducted with a local coinage. The evil effects[4] seen to result from excessive commercial dealings will thus be avoided. When we turn to the agricultural labour-question, we find that wholesale employment of slaves[5] or serfs is the foundation of the system. For Plato, holding fast to the principle of specialization, holds also that leisure[6] is necessary for the citizens if they are to bear their part in politics with intelligent judgment. As, in this second-best Utopia, the citizens are the landowners, and cannot divest themselves of their civic responsibilities, they must do their cultivating by deputy. And this practically amounts to building the fabric of civilization on a basis of slavery—nothing less. In the matter of agriculture, the industry on which this self-sufficing community really rests, this dependence on slave-labour is most striking. It even includes a system[7] of serf-tenants (probably for the borderland farms) who are to be left to cultivate the land, paying a rent or quota of produce (ἀπαρχή) to the owners. The importance of not having too large a proportion[8] of the slaves in a gang drawn from any one race is insisted on as a means of preventing combinations and risings. At the same time careful management is enjoined, sympathetic[9] but firm: a master should be kind, but never forget that he is a master: no slave must be allowed to take liberties. To implant a sound tradition of morality is recognized as a means of promoting good order in the community, and this influence should be brought to bear[10] on slaves as well as on freemen. Yet the intrinsic chattelhood of the slave appears clearly in many ways; for instance, the damage to a slave is made good by compensating[11] his owner. The carelessness of ill-qualified practitioners[12] who treat slaves, contrasted with the zeal of competent doctors in treating freemen, is another significant touch.

It seems then that Plato, the more he adapts his speculations to the facts of existing civilization, the more positively he accepts slave-

---

[1] *Laws* 745 *c–e*.   [2] *Laws* 842 *c–e*.   [3] *Laws* 742.
[4] *Laws* 705.   [5] Rustic slaves, *Laws* 760 *e*, 763 *a*.
[6] *Laws* 832 *d*. The artisans are not citizens, 846 *d–847 b*.
[7] *Laws* 806 *d*.   [8] *Laws* 777 *c*.   [9] *Laws* 777 *d–778 a*, cf 793 *e*.
[10] *Laws* 838 *d*.   [11] *Laws* 865 *c, d*, cf 936 *c–e*.
[12] *Laws* 720. See *Rep* 406 on medical treatment of δημιουργοί.

labour as a necessary basis. The conception of government as an art is surely the chief cause of this attitude. The extreme specialization of the *Republic* is moderated in the *Laws*, but there is not much less demand for leisure, if the civic artists are to be unhampered in the practice of their art. Of the dangers[1] of servile labour on a large scale he was well aware, and he had evidently studied with attention[2] the awkward features of serfdom, not only in the old Hellas, but in the Greek colonial states of the East and West. Nevertheless he would found his economy on the forced labour of human chattels. A system that had grown up in the course of events, extending or contracting according to changes of economic circumstance, was thus presented as the deliberate result of independent thought. But the only theory at the back of traditional slavery was the law[3] of superior force—originally the conqueror's will. Plato was therefore driven to accept this law as a principle of human society. To accept it was to bring his speculations more into touch with Greek notions; for no people have surpassed the Greeks in readiness to devolve upon others the necessary but monotonous drudgery of life. This attitude of his involves the conclusion that the Barbarian is to serve the Greek, a position hardly consistent with his earlier[4] doctrine, that no true line could be drawn distinguishing Greek and Barbarian. Such a flux of speculative opinion surely weakens our respect for Plato's judgment in these matters. We can hardly say that he offers any effective solution of the great state-problems of his age. But that these problems were serious and disquieting his repeated efforts bear witness. And one of the most serious was certainly that of placing the agricultural interest on a sound footing. Its importance he saw : but neither of his schemes, neither passive free farmers nor slave-holding landlords, was likely to produce the desired result. To say this is not to blame a great man's failure. Centuries have passed, and experience has been gained, without a complete solution being reached : the end is not yet.

A few details remain to be touched on separately. The employment of hired labourers is referred to as normal[5] in the *Politicus Republic* and *Laws*. They are regarded simply as so much physical strength at disposal. They are free, and so able to transfer their labour from job to job according to demand. Intellectually and politically they do not count. But the μισθωτὸς is neither a chattel like the slave, nor bound to the soil like the serf. I have found no suggestion of the employment of this class in agriculture ; and, as I have said above, I believe that they were in fact almost confined to the towns, especially

---

[1] Case of domestics, *Republ* 578–9.
[2] *Laws* 776–7.
[3] *Laws* 690 *b*.
[4] *Politicus* 262 *d*.
[5] *Politicus* 289–90, *Republ* 371, *Laws* 742 *a*.

such as the Peiraeus. It is also worth noticing that we find favourable
mention of apprenticeship[1] as a method of learning a trade. But this
principle also seems not applied to agriculture. Again, we are told[2] in
the *Laws* that one who has never served (δουλεύσας) will never turn
out a creditable master (δεσπότης). From the context this would seem
to refer only to the wardens of the country (ἀγρονόμοι), who must be
kept under strict discipline in order to perform very responsible duties.
It does not apply to farmers. Another curious rule[3] is that kidnapping
of men is not to be allowed. Yet there are bought slaves, and therefore a market. That the dealer in human flesh should be despised[4] by
his customers is a feeling probably older than Plato, and it lasted down
to the days of *Uncle Tom's Cabin*. In view of Plato's acceptance of the
sharp line drawn between Greek and Barbarian (and this does touch
rustic slavery) it is interesting to note that he observed[5] with care the
different characters of alien peoples. He also refers[6] to them without
contempt in various contexts side by side with Greeks, and cites[7] their
common belief as a proof of the existence of the gods.

If I may venture to make a general comment on Plato's position
in relation to the labour-question, I would remark that he is already in
the same difficulty which proved embarrassing to Aristotle, and which
has always beset those who seek to find a theoretical justification for
slavery. True, he is less definite and positive than Aristotle: but the
attempt to regard a human being as both a man and a chattel is a
failure. This point need not be further pressed here. But it is well to
observe that agriculture is the department in which the absurdity most
strikingly appears. Heavy farm-labour without prospect of personal
advantage was recognized as a function that no man would willingly
perform. Hence to be sent to labour on a farm was one of the punishments that awaited the offending domestic slave. Hence overseers
were employed to exact from rustic slaves their daily task under the
menace of severe and often cruel punishments. Hence the humaner
masters (as Xenophon shews us) tried to secure more cheerful and
effective service by a system of little rewards for good work. In short
there was in practical life a miserable attempt to treat the slave both
as a brute beast and as a moral being capable of weighing consequences
and acting accordingly. One form of reward, manumission, was
apparently not at this time common[8] in Greece: and it was one not

[1] *Republ* 467 a, *Laws* 720 a, b.   [2] *Laws* 762 e.
[3] *Laws* 823.   [4] *Republ* 344 b.
[5] *Republ* 435 e–436 a, *Laws* 747 c.   [6] *Rep* 423 b, 452 c, 544 d, *Laws* 840 e.
[7] *Laws* 886 a, 887 e.
[8] It is not easy to reach a firm opinion on this matter. The inscribed records are nearly
all of a much later age. But even a more informal method of manumission would surely, if
common, have left more clearly marked traces in literature. See Index, *Manumission*.

easy to apply in agriculture. It was not easy to know what to do with
a worn-out farm-hand, unless he was transferred to lighter duties on
the farm ; for he would be useless elsewhere. Sooner or later a time
would come when he could no longer do anything of any value. What
then? Was he charitably fed by the master[1] whom he had served, or
was he cast adrift in nominal freedom? From the fragments of Comedy
one may perhaps guess that the humaner practice generally prevailed.
But the silence of Plato seems to suggest that to him, and indeed to
Greeks generally, the point was not an important one. Even for a
citizen, if destitute in old age, the state-relief was very small. We must
therefore not wonder at the silence generally maintained as to the
treatment of the worn-out rustic slave. Slave artisans, and those whose
services were let out to other employers with reservation of a rent to
their own masters, could scrape together the means of sustenance in
their old age. It is possible that manumission of rustic slaves may
have occasionally taken place, and that they too may have scraped together some small savings: but I can find no ground for thinking that
such cases were normal or even frequent. In the *Laws* Plato allows
for the presence of freedmen[2], and frames regulations for their control,
probably suggested by experience of the Attic laws and their defects.
Manumission by the state[3] as reward of slave-informers is also mentioned. But there is nothing in these passages to weaken the natural
inference that town slaves, and chiefly domestics, are the class to
whom in practice such rules would apply. In short, we must not look
to a philosopher reared in a civilization under which manual labour
tended to become the burden of the unfree and the destitute, and to
be despised as mean and unworthy of the free citizen, for a wholesome
solution of the problem of farm-labour.

XVI. THE EARLIER ATTIC ORATORS.

It is convenient to take the speeches and pamphlets of the masters
of Attic oratory in two sections, though there can be no exact chronological division between the two. The political background is different
in the two cases. To **Isocrates** the urgent problem is how to compose
Greek jealousies by uniting in an attack on the common enemy,
Persia: to **Demosthenes** it is how to save the separate independence
of the weary Greek states from the control of the encroaching king of
Macedon. True, the disunion of Greece was not to be ended by either

---

[1] The problem of the worn-out plantation slave was much discussed in the United States
in slavery days. An interesting account of the difficulties arising from emancipation in
British Guiana is given in J Rodway's *Guiana* (1912) pp 114 foll.

[2] *Laws* 914–5, and an allusion in *Republ* 495 e.   [3] *Laws* 914 a, 932 d.

effort. But the difficulties of Isocrates lay largely outside Athens: the
states did not want to have a leader; Philip, to whom he turned in his
old age, was no more welcome to them than the rest of his proposed
leaders. Demosthenes had to face the fact of a Macedonian party in
Athens itself, as well as to overcome the apathy and inertia which had
been growing continually since the fall of the Athenian empire. His
opponents were not all mere corrupt partisans of the Macedonian king.
Athens was now no longer a great power, and they knew it: Demosthenes is forgiven by historians for his splendid defiance of facts.
Naturally enough, in the conflicts of political opinion from the time of
the revolution of the Four Hundred to the death of Demosthenes
(411–322 BC) we have few references to agriculture. Yet we know that
the question of food-supply was still a pressing one for many Greek
states, above all for Athens. Some of the references have a value as
being contemporary. But a large part of these are references to litigation, and deal not with conditions of cultivation but with claims to
property. Among the most significant facts are the importance attached
to the control of the Hellespontine trade-route and the careful regulations affecting the import and distribution[1] of corn.

The period on which we get some little light from passages in the
earlier orators is roughly about 410–350 BC. It includes the general
abandonment of agricultural enterprises abroad, owing to the loss of
empire and therewith of cleruchic properties. By this shrinkage the
relative importance of home agriculture must surely have been increased.
Yet I cannot find a single direct statement or reference to this effect.
It seems reasonable to suppose that it was not necessary to assert
what was only too obvious. Corn had to be imported, and imported
it was from various[2] sources of supply. To guard against failure of
this supply was a chief preoccupation of the Athenian government.
But that some corn was still grown in Attica is clear. **Isocrates** says[3]
that one act of hostility to the Thirty was the destruction of corn in
the country by the democrats. And in another place[4] he lays stress
upon the mythical legend of the earliest introduction of corn-growing,
the civilizing gift of Demeter to her favoured Attica. Yet there are
signs that the culture of the olive and vine was more and more dis-
placing cereal crops: the fig tree, often a sacred thing, was, and had
long been, a regular feature of the country-side. Live stock, goats sheep
and cattle, were probably abundant, though there was seldom need
for an orator to mention them. If we judge by the remaining references,

---

[1] See Lysias XXII, speech against the corn-dealers.
[2] See for instance Andocides *de reditu* §§ 20–1 p 22 (Cyprus), Isocrates *Trapeziticus* § 57
p 370 (Bosporus).
[3] Isocr *de bigis* § 13 p 349.
[4] Isocr *Panegyricus* § 28 p 46, cf Plato *Menex* 237 e.

it would seem that land was not generally cultivated by its owners. Letting to tenant farmers[1] was the plan adopted by the state in dealing with public lands, and the collection of the rents was farmed out in its turn to capitalist speculators by public auction. We have several specimens[2] of mixed estates, described by an orator in connexion with some litigation. From these we may fairly infer that the policy of not putting all their eggs into one basket found favour with Athenian capitalists.   Landed estate is in such cases but one item, side by side with house-property, mortgages and money at interest on other securities, slaves and other stock employed or leased to employers, stock in hand, specie and other valuables, mentioned in more or less detail.   Consistently with this picture of landlord and tenant is the statement[3] that formerly, in the good old times before Athens entered upon her ill-starred career of imperialism, the country houses and establishments of citizens were superior to those within the city walls; so much so, that even the attraction of festivals could not draw them to town from their comfortable country-seats. Evidently a great change had come over rural Attica, if the writer is to be trusted.   We are not to suppose that personal direction of a farm by the owner of the land was altogether a thing of the past.   Suburban farms at least were, as we learn from Xenophon, sometimes managed by men living in the city and riding out to superintend operations and give orders.   The injured husband[4] defended by **Lysias** may even have gone to and fro on foot.   He does not seem to have been a wealthy man, and he may have been a αὐτουργός, taking part in the labours of his farm: that he earned his night's rest and slept sound seems suggested by the context of his curious story.

That there was no lack of interest in the prospects of agriculture generally may be inferred from various references to the different qualities of soils not only in Attica but in other parts of Greece and abroad.   The smallness of the cultivable area in rocky Samothrace[5] was noted by **Antiphon**. **Isocrates** remarked[6] that in Laconia the Dorian conquerors appropriated not only the greater part of the land but the most fertile.   The results of their greed and oppression had not been wholly satisfactory in the long run: adversity carried with it the peril[7] of Helot risings.   No fertility of soil can compensate for the ill effects of bad policy and lack of moderation: the independence and well-being of cramped rocky Megara, contrasted[8] with the embarrassments of wide

---

[1] Andoc *de myster* §§ 92–3 p 12, Böckh-Fränkel *Staatsh* I 372–7.   For private letting of farm-lands see Lysias VII § 4–10 pp 108–9 (one tenant was a freedman), Isaeus XI § 42.

[2] Isaeus VI §§ 19–22, VIII § 35, XI §§ 41–4.   [3] Isocr *Areopagiticus* § 52 p 150.

[4] Lysias I §§ 11, 13, p 92.   [5] Antiphon fragm 50 Blass.

[6] Isocr *Panath* § 179 p 270.   [7] Isocr *Philippus* §§ 48–9 pp 91–2.

[8] Isocr *de pace* §§ 117–8 p 183.

fruitful Thessaly, is an object-lesson. The Greek race needs to expand[1], as it did of old, when Athens led the colonization of the Asiatic seaboard. It is monstrous to try and wring contributions from ($\delta\alpha\sigma\mu o$-$\lambda o\gamma\epsilon\hat{\iota}\nu$)[2] the islanders, who have to till mountain sides for lack of room. It is in Asia that the new Greece must find relief, at the expense of Persia, whose subjects let vast areas lie idle, while the parts that they do cultivate keep them in great plenty; so fertile is the land. Attica itself was once a prosperous farming country. In the good old days, before the unhappy dissension between selfish rich and grudging poor, agriculture was one of the chief means[3] used to avert poverty and distress. Farms let at fair rents kept the people profitably employed, and so out of mischief. Men could and did[4] live well in the country: they were not jostling each other in the city to earn a bare subsistence by pitiful state-fees—beggars all—as they are doing now. The great pamphleteer may be overdrawing his picture, but that it contains much truth is certain, and it seems pretty clear that he saw no prospect of a local revival. Athens had run her course of ambitious imperialism, and the old country life, developed in long security, could not be restored. Any man who felt inclined to live a farmer's life would, if I read the situation aright, prefer some cheap and profitable venture abroad to the heavy and unremunerative struggles of a crofter in upland Attica. Small farms in the rich lowland were I take it very seldom to be had. And, if he had the capital to work a large farm, he was under strong temptation to employ his capital in urban industries, state-contracts, loans at interest, etc, and so to distribute his risks while increasing his returns. For his main object was to make money, not to provide himself and his family with a healthy and comfortable home. The land-question in Attica is illustrated by a passage of **Isaeus** in which he refers to the fraud of a guardian. The scoundrel, he says, has robbed his nephew of the estate: he is sticking to the farm ($\tau\grave{o}\nu$ $\dot{\alpha}\gamma\rho\acute{o}\nu$) and has given him a hill pasture[5] ($\phi\epsilon\lambda\lambda\acute{e}\alpha$).

Farming enterprise abroad had been a product of the Athenian empire with its cleruchies and colonies, and probably private ventures of individuals, unofficial but practically resting on imperial protection. The collapse of this system would ruin some settlers and speculators, and impoverish more. Even those who returned to Athens still possessed of considerable capital would not in all cases take to Attic farming, even supposing that they were willing to face its risks and that suitable farms were available. It was to Athens a most important

---

[1] Isocr *Paneg* §§ 34-7 pp 47–8, *de pace* § 24 p 164, *Panathen* §§ 13, 14, p 235, §§ 43–4 p 241, etc.

[2] Isocr *Paneg* § 132 pp 67–8. [3] Isocr *Areopag* § 44 p 148.

[4] Isocr *de pace* § 90 p 177, *Areopag* §§ 54–5 pp 150–1, § 83 p 156.

[5] Isaeus VIII § 42 p 73, cf Aristophanes *Nub* 71–2.

object to retain or recover all she could of her island territories, partly
no doubt in order to control the cultivable lands in them. In the peace-
negotiations of 390 BC the extreme opposition party at Athens were
not content[1] with the proposals by which she was to recover the islands
of Lemnos Imbros and Scyros: they demanded also the restitution of
the Thracian Chersonese and estates and debts elsewhere. So strong
was the feeling of dependence on these investments abroad. And
Isocrates, in depicting the evil results of imperial ambition, recalls[2] to
the citizens that, instead of farming the lands of others, the Peloponnesian war had for years prevented them from setting eyes upon their
own.

Thus far I have said nothing of the labour-question. Orators and
pamphleteers were not likely to concern themselves much with this
topic, for there was nothing in the nature of an Abolitionist controversy
to bring them into discussion of the subject. Slavery is in this department of Greek literature more a fundamental assumption than ever.
The frequent arguments on the torture of slave witnesses and the moral
value of evidence so extracted are plain proof of this. But what about
agricultural labour? In the case of the sacred olive-stump we hear from
Lysias[3] that the farm in question several times changed hands by sale.
Some of the purchasers let it to tenants. The words used of the persons
who actually farmed it from time to time are the usual ones, $\dot{\epsilon}\gamma\epsilon\dot{\omega}\rho\gamma\epsilon\iota$
$\epsilon\dot{\iota}\rho\gamma\acute{a}\sigma a\tau o$ etc. That these tenants were not merely $a\dot{\upsilon}\tau o\upsilon\rho\gamma o\acute{\iota}$, but
employers of labour, may fairly be guessed from the case of the
present tenant, accused of sacrilege. He at least is an owner of
slaves, and argues[4] that he could never have been so mad as to put
himself at their mercy. They would have witnessed his sacrilege,
and could have won their freedom by informing against their master.
Isocrates[5] draws no real distinction between serfs and slaves in the
case of Sparta. Here too the slave was dangerous, though in a
different way: but he was on the land. A fragment of **Isaeus**[6]
runs 'he left on the farm old men and cripples.' The context is
lost, but the persons referred to must surely be slaves: no one would
employ wage-labour of this quality. In another place he casually mentions[7] the sale of a flock of goats with the goatherd. These little scraps
of evidence all serve to strengthen the impression, derived from other
sources, of slave-labour as the backbone of Attic agriculture in this
period. To free labour there are very few references, and none of these
seem to have any connexion with agriculture. This does not prove

[1] Andocides *de pace* § 15 p 25, § 36 p 28.   [2] Isocr *de pace* § 92 p 177.
[3] Lysias VII especially §§ 4–11 pp 108–9.   [4] Lysias VII § 16 p 109.
[5] See especially the *Archidamus* §§ 8, 28, 87, 88, 96, 97.
[6] Isaeus fragm 3 Scheibe.   [7] Isaeus VI § 33 $\sigma\dot{\upsilon}\nu$ $\tau\hat{\omega}$ $a\dot{\iota}\pi\acute{o}\lambda\omega$.

that no hired freemen were employed on farms. For special jobs, as we shall see later, they were called in: but this was only temporary employment. The μισθωτοὶ or θῆτες were a despised[1] class: some of them were freedmen. The competition with slave-labour doubtless had something to do with this, and to be driven by necessity to such labour was galling to a citizen, as we have already learnt from Xenophon.

XVII. ARISTOTLE.

The great founder of the philosophy of experience is a witness[2] of exceptional value. He collected and recorded the facts and traditions of the past, judging them from the point of view of his own day. Stimulated by the theories of his master Plato, he also strove, by sketching the fabric of a model state, to indicate the lines on which Greek political development might be conducted with advantage. Inasmuch as ideal circumstances were rather to be desired than expected, he did not restrict his interest in the future to the mere designing of an ideal: taking states as he found them, conditioned by their situation and past history, he sought for the causes of their growth and decay, and aimed at discovering cures for their various maladies. But throughout, whether looking to the past or the future, he was guided by a characteristic moral purpose. For him 'good living' (τὸ εὖ ζῆν) is the aim and object of political institutions. It is in the state that man finds the possibility of reaching his full development: for he is by nature a 'political animal.' That is, he cannot live alone. Each step in association (household, village,) brings him nearer to that final union of the city. In this he attains the highest degree of manhood of which he (as Man, differentiated from other animals by reason and speech,) is capable. This completion of his potentialities is the proof of his true nature ; that he realizes his best self in the πόλις shews that he is a πολιτικὸν ζῷον. The animal needs met in the more primitive associations are of course met in the city also. But there is something more, and this something more is a moral element, from which is derived the possibility of 'good living,' as contrasted with existence of a more predominantly animal character. Therefore, though in point of time the man comes before the state, in logical order the state comes first: for the man can only exist in the fulness of his nature when he is a citizen. He is by the law of his nature part of a state, potentially: as such a part he is to be

---

[1] See Isocrates *Plataicus* § 48 p 306 (of Plataeans), and Isaeus v § 39 with Wyse's note.

[2] I should mention that for simplicity sake I refer to the *Politics* by the books in the old order. Also that I do not raise the question of the authorship of the first book of the so-called *Economics*, as the point does not affect the argument. In common with all students of the *Politics* I am greatly indebted to the edition of Mr W L Newman.

regarded. As states vary, so do the several types of citizens. In the best state the qualities of good man and good citizen are identical and complete.

The aim of political science (πολιτική) is to frame and employ the machinery of states so as to promote the perfection of human excellence (ἀρετή), and to train the citizens on such principles as will insure the effective working and permanence of their institutions. We may call it Aristotle's response to the Greek yearning after a stability which was in practice never attained. To design a model state was one way of approaching the problem. But Aristotle was surely not the man to believe that such an ideal could be practically realised. To make the best of existing systems was a more promising enterprise. Now in either procedure it was evident that material equipment[1] could not be left out of account. Without food clothing and shelter men cannot live at all, and therefore cannot live well. Experience also shewed that the means of defence against enemies could not safely be neglected. It is under the head of equipment (χορηγία) that we get the philosopher's view of the proper position of agriculture in the life of a state. We must bear in mind the general Greek conception of citizenship common to states- men and theorists, present to Plato and Aristotle no less than to Cleisthenes or Pericles. Residence gave no claim to it. Either it was hereditary, passing from father to son on proof of citizen descent and certain religious qualifications; or it was deliberately conferred on a person or persons as a privilege. That beside the citizens there should be resident within the state[2] a number of persons, not citizens or likely to become citizens, was a necessity generally admitted. They might be free aliens, more or less legally connected with the state, or slaves public or private. These alien persons were very numerous in some states, such as Athens or Corinth. Subject or serf populations of Greek origin, as in Laconia or Thessaly, are not to be distinguished from them for the present purpose. One common mark of citizenship was the right of owning land within the territory of the state. We know that the Attic landowner must be an Athenian citizen, and such was the general rule. Who did the actual work of cultivation, or tended the flocks and herds, is another question. We have seen reason for believing that personal labour[3] of the owner on his farm had at one time been usual, and that the practice still in the fourth century BC prevailed in those parts of Greece where there had been little develop- ment of urban life. And that slave-labour was employed by farmers

---

[1] This χορηγία includes a population limited in number and of appropriate qualities. *Politics* VII 4, and 8 §§ 7–9.

[2] *Pol* VII 4 § 6.

[3] See the story of Peisistratus and the peasant in Ἀθην πολ c 16.

on a greater or less scale, according to the size of their estates, seems
as certain as certain can be. In Attica the slave overseer, entrusted
with the direction of a gang of slave labourers, had become[1] a well-
recognized figure, and farming by deputy, as well as labouring by
deputy, was an ordinary thing. Citizens resided in the city more than
ever. Rich men visited their country estates to keep an eye on their
overseers, or paid the penalty of their neglect. Poor citizens, resident
and able to attend meetings of the Assembly, had to be kept quiet by
systematic provision of fees for performance of civic functions. It may
be too strong to say that squeezing the wealthy was the leading fact
of politics: but there was too much of that sort of thing, and the
scramble for state pay was demoralizing. Immediate personal interest
tended to deaden patriotism in a state that within human memory had,
whatever its faults, been the most public-spirited community among
the leading states of Greece.

In treating of politics, and therewith in assigning a position to
agriculture, Aristotle was affected by three main influences. First,
the historical; the experience of Greek states, and more particularly
of Athens. Secondly, the theoretical; the various attempts of earlier
philosophers, particularly of Plato, to find a solution of political problems
on speculative lines. Thirdly, his own firm conviction that the lasting
success of state life depended on devotion to a moral end. It will be
the simplest and best plan to consider his utterances on agriculture
from these three points of view.

The supply of food being the first of necessities, and being in fact
(as we have seen) an ever-pressing problem in Greece, it is no wonder
that land-hunger, leading to wars for territory, and land-grabbing, a
fertile cause of internal dissension and seditions in states, were normal
phenomena of Greek history. And what happened in old Hellas was
reproduced abroad, as the Greek colonists overflowed into lands beyond
the seas. Once the possession of territory was secured by war, and
the means of its defence organized, two problems soon presented themselves for solution. It was at once necessary to decide by what labour
the land was to be cultivated. Greek colonists, desirous no doubt of
an easier life than they had led in the old country, generally contrived
to devolve this labour upon others at a very early stage of their
establishment. Either they reduced natives to the condition of serfs,
or they employed slaves, whom the profits of growing trade and commerce enabled them to procure in larger and larger numbers. Meanwhile in the mother country various systems went on side by side.
There were large districts of agricultural serfage, in which a race of
conquerors were supported by the labour of the conquered. In other

---

[1] *Economics* 1 5 § 1, 6 § 5, *Pol* 1 7 § 5, and see the chapter on Xenophon.

parts independent peoples, backward in civilization, lived a free rustic life of a largely pastoral character.   Others again devoted themselves more to the tillage of the soil, with or without the help of slaves.   It was known that in earlier times a population of this kind in Attica had long existed, and that after the unification of Attica and the reforms of Solon it had for a time been the backbone of the Athenian state.   But in fertile lowland districts there was a not unnatural tendency towards larger estates, worked by hireling or slave-labour.   It seems fairly certain that in Attica before the time of Aristotle the supply of free wage-earners for farm-work was failing: the development of the city and the Peiraeus, and the growing number of those in receipt of civil and military pay, had drawn the poor citizen away from rustic labour.   Nor is there reason to think that after the loss of empire there was any marked movement back to the land on the part of free labourers or even small farmers.   It would rather seem that Attic land was passing into fewer hands, and that the employment of stewards or overseers, free or slave, was one of the features of a change by which the farming of land was becoming a symptom of considerable wealth.

But beside the decision as to labour there was the question as to a means of checking land-monopoly.   Such monopoly, resulting in the formation of a discontented urban mob, was a serious menace to the stability of a constitution.   For all poor citizens to get a living by handicrafts was perhaps hardly possible; nor would the life of an artisan suit the tastes and wishes of all.   Nature does (or seems to do) more for the farmer on his holding than for the artisan in his workshop, and the claim to a share of the land within the boundaries of their states had led to seditions and revolutions, ruinous and bloody, followed by ill feeling, and ever liable to recur.   Colonial states, in which the first settlers usually allotted the land (or most of it) among themselves and handed down their allotments to their children, were particularly exposed to troubles of this kind.   The various fortunes of families, and the coming of new settlers, early raised the land-question there in an acute form, as notoriously at Syracuse.   No wonder that practical and theoretical statesmen tried to find remedies for a manifest political evil.   Stability was only to be assured by internal peace.   To this end two main lines of policy[1] found favour.   Security of tenure was promoted by forbidding the sale of land-lots or making it difficult to encumber them by mortgages: while the prohibition of excessive acquisition[2] was a means of checking land-grabbers and interesting a larger number of citizens in the maintenance of the land-system.   But

---

[1] *Pol* VI 4 §§ 8–10.

[2] We have a modern analogue in the recent legislative measures in New Zealand and Australia, not to speak of movements nearer home.

there is no reason to think that measures of this kind had much success. Nor were vague traditions[1] of the equality of original land-lots in some Greek states of any great importance. Some theoretical reformers might aim at such an arrangement, but it was a vain aspiration. Indeed, regarded from the food-producing point of view, nothing like a true equality was possible in practice. Confiscation and redistribution were only to be effected at the cost of civil war, and the revered wisdom of Solon[2] had rejected such a proceeding. Communistic schemes had little attraction for the average Greek, so far as his own labour or interests might be involved: even the dream of Plato was far from a thoroughgoing communism.

Of the farmer in his character of citizen[3] Aristotle had a favourable impression formed from the experience of the past. The restless activity of Assemblies frequently meeting, and with fees for attendance, was both a cause and an effect of the degeneration of democracies in his day. It meant that political issues were now at the mercy of the ignorant and fickle city-dwellers, a rabble swayed by the flattery of self-seeking demagogues. Athens was the notable instance. Yet tradition alleged (and it can hardly be doubted) that in earlier times, when a larger part of the civic body lived and worked in the country, a soberer and steadier policy[4] prevailed. The farmers, never free from responsibilities and cares, were opposed to frequent Assemblies, to attend which involved no small sacrifice of valuable time. For this sacrifice a small fee would have been no adequate compensation, and in fact they had none at all. Naturally enough Aristotle, admitting[5] that in the states of his day democratic governments were mostly inevitable, insists on the merits of the farmer-democracies of the good old times, and would welcome their revival. But the day for this was gone by, never to return. Another important point arises in connexion with the capacity of the state for war, a point seldom overlooked in Greek political speculation. In discussing the several classes out of which the state is made up, Aristotle observes[6] that individuals may and will unite in their own persons the qualifications of more than one class. So the same individuals may perform various functions: but this does not affect his argument, for the same persons may be, and often are, both hoplites and cultivators, who yet are functionally distinct parts of the state. Just below, speaking of the necessity of 'virtue' ($\dot{a}\rho\epsilon\tau\dot{\eta}$) for the discharge of certain public duties (deliberative and judicial), he

---

[1] See note on Plato, p 75.   [2] 'Αθην πολ cc 11, 12.

[3] A most interesting treatment of this topic is to be found in Bryce's *South America* (1912) pp 330–1, 533, where we get it from the modern point of view, under representative systems.

[4] See the general remarks *Pol* IV 6 § 2, VI 4 §§ 1, 2, 13, 14. For historical points 'Αθην πολ cc 16, 24.

[5] *Pol* III 15 § 13.   [6] *Pol* IV 4 §§ 15, 18, cf VII 9.

adds 'The other faculties may exist combined in many separate individuals; for instance, the same man may be a soldier a cultivator and a craftsman, or even a counsellor of state or a judge; but all men claim to possess virtue, and think they are qualified to hold most offices. But the same men cannot be at once rich and poor. The common view therefore is that Rich and Poor are the true *parts* of a state.' That is to say, practical analysis can go no further. In another passage[1], discussing the formation of the best kind of democracy, he says 'for the best Demos is that of farmers (ὁ γεωργικός): so it is possible to form (a corresponding?) democracy where the mass of the citizens gets its living from tillage or pasturage (ἀπὸ γεωργίας ἢ νομῆς).' After considering the political merits of the cultivators, busy and moderate men, he goes[2] on 'And after the Demos of cultivators the next best is that where the citizens are graziers (νομεῖς) and get their living from flocks and herds (βοσκημάτων): for the life in many respects resembles that of the tillers of the soil, and for the purposes of military campaigning these men are peculiarly hardened[3] by training, fit for active service, and able to rough it in the open.' The adaptability of the rustic worker is further admitted[4] in a remark let fall in a part of his treatise where he is engaged in designing a model state. It is to the effect that, so long as the state has a plentiful supply of farm-labourers, it must also have plenty of seamen (ναυτῶν). Having just admitted that a certain amount of maritime commerce will be necessary, and also a certain naval power, he is touching on the manning of the fleet. The marine soldiers will be freemen, but the seamen (oarsmen) can be taken from unfree classes working on the land. Their social status does not at this stage concern us: that such labourers could readily be made into effective oarsmen is an admission to be noted. To the philosopher himself it is a comfort to believe that he has found out a way of doing without the turbulent 'seafaring rabble' (ναυτικὸς ὄχλος) that usually throngs seaport towns and embarrasses orderly governments. In other words, it is a relief to find that in a model state touching the sea it will not be necessary to reproduce the Peiraeus.

In considering the proposals of earlier theorists for the remedy of political defects it is hardly possible and nowise needful to exhaust all the indications of dissatisfaction with existing systems. Of Euripides and Socrates, the two great questioners, enough has been said above. The reactionary Isocrates was for many years a contemporary of Aristotle. What we can no longer reproduce is the talk of active-minded

[1] *Pol* VI 4 §§ 1, 2, 13. [2] *Pol* VI 4 § 11.
[3] Whether the πεπονημένη ἕξις (favourable to eugenic paternity) of *Pol* VII 16 §§ 12, 13, may include this class, is not clear. In Roman opinion it certainly would.
[4] *Pol* VII 6 § 8. Xenophon (see p 53) records cases of seamen ashore and in straits working for hire on farms.

critics in the social circles of Athens. It happens that Xenophon has left us a sketch of the ordinary conversations of Socrates. No doubt these were the most important examples of their kind, and his method a powerful, if sometimes irritating, stimulus to thought. But we are not to assume a lack of other questioners, acute and even sincere, more especially among men of oligarchic leanings. That Aristotle came into touch with such persons is probable from his connexion with Plato. Certain passages in the *Constitution of Athens*, in which he is reasonably suspected[1] of giving a partisan view of historical events, point to the same conclusion. We shall never know all the criticisms and suggestions of others that this watchful collector heard and noted. But it is both possible and desirable to recall those to which his own record proves him to have paid attention.

Both Hippodamus and Plato based their schemes on a class-system, in which the farmer-class form a distinct body: but the former made them citizens with voting rights. Being unarmed, and so at the mercy of the military class, Aristotle held that their political rights were nugatory. In the *Republic*, Plato gave them no voice in state-affairs, but in the *Laws* he admitted them to the franchise. While these two reformers made provision for a military force, Phaleas, ignoring relations with other states, made none. To Phaleas, equality in landed estate seemed the best means of promoting harmony and wellbeing in the community; and he would effect this equality by legal restrictions. This proposition Aristotle rejected as neither adequate nor suited to its purpose. Moral[2] influences, hard work, discretion, even intellectual activity, can alone produce the temper of moderation that promotes concord and happiness. In short, if you are to effect any real improvement, you must start from the doctrine of the Mean[3] and not trust to material equalizing. The several tenure of land-lots was generally recognized, with variations in detail; Plato in the *Laws* abandoned the impracticable land-system of the *Republic*, and not only assigned a κλῆρος to each citizen household, but arranged it in two[4] sections, for reasons given above. The attempt to ensure the permanence of the number of land-lots and households by strict legal regulation, as some legislators had tried to do, is also a general feature of these speculations. Plato in the *Laws* even went further, and would place rigid restrictions on acquisition of property of all kinds. All agree in the usual Greek contempt for those engaged in manual or sedentary trades. Such 'mechanical' (βάναυσοι) workers were held to be debased in both body and mind below the standard of 'virtue' required of the good soldier or citizen. Phaleas made these 'artisans' public slaves *de iure*:

---

[1] See Sandys on ʼΑθην πολ c 4.   [2] *Pol* II 7 § 12.   [3] *Pol* II 7 § 7.
[4] Severely criticized in *Pol* II 6 § 15, though adopted by himself. See below.

Hippodamus placed them, with the farmers, in nominal citizenship but *de facto* bondage. Plato tolerates them because he cannot do without them. In the matter of hard bodily labour, free or slave, the position of Plato is clear. He would devolve it upon slaves; in agriculture, with a coexisting alternative system of serf-tenants. But both classes are to be Barbarians. It seems that Hippodamus meant the public, if not the private, land of his model state to be worked by slaves. Most striking is the fact that Plato in his later years combined the aim of self-sufficiency with dependence on servile labour. Commerce is, for the moral health of the state, to be strictly limited. The supply of necessary food-stuffs is to be a domestic industry, carried on by alien serfs or slaves for the most part. Such communism as exists among the Guardians in the *Republic* is a communism of consumers who take no part in material production: and it is abandoned in the *Laws*.

The above outlines must suffice as a sketch of the situation both in practice and in theory when Aristotle took the matter in hand. The working defects of Greek constitutions were obvious to many, and the incapacity of the ignorant masses in democracies was especially evident to thoughtful but irresponsible critics. Yet the selfishness of the rich in oligarchies was not ignored, and the instability of governments supported by only a minority of the citizens was an indisputable fact. The mass of citizens (that is, full members of the state according to the qualification-rules in force) had to come in somewhere, to give numerical strength to a government. How was governing capacity to be placed in power under such conditions? Experience suggested that things had been better for Athens when a larger part of her citizens lived on the land. Use could no doubt be made of this experience in case an opening for increasing the number of peasant farmers[1] should occur. But it was precisely in states where such a policy was most needed that an opening was least likely to occur. It would seem then that the only chance of improving government lay in persuading the average citizen to entrust wider powers to a specially selected body of competent men, in short to carry into politics the specializing principle[2] already developed by the advance of civilization in other departments. Now the average citizen was certain to test the plans of reformers by considering how their operation would affect cases like his own. It was therefore necessary to offer him a reassuring picture of projects of this kind, if they were to receive any hearing at all. To own a plot of land, inalienable and hereditary, was a security against indigence. To have the labour of cultivating it performed as a matter of course by others was a welcome corollary. To be relieved of mechanical drudgery

---

[1] See *Pol* VI 5 §§ 8–10, on the measures that may be taken to secure lasting εὐπορία.
[2] Cf IV 15 § 6, etc.

by aliens and slaves was a proposal sure to conciliate Greek pride. And the resulting leisure for the enlightened discharge of the peculiarly civic functions of war and government was an appeal to self-esteem and ambition. But that the creation of a ruling class of Guardians with absolute power, such as those of Plato's *Republic*, would commend itself to democratic Greeks, was more than any practical man could believe. Nor would the communism of those Guardians appear attractive to the favourers of oligarchy. Therefore Plato himself had to recast his scheme, and try to bring it out of dreamland by concessions to facts of Greek life. Not much was gained thereby, and the great difficulty, how to make a start, still remained. That much could be done by direct legislative action was a tradition in Greek thought fostered by tales of the achievements of early lawgivers. But to remodel the whole fabric of a state so thoroughly that an entire change should be effected in the political atmosphere in which the citizens must live and act, while the citizens themselves would be the same persons, reared in old conditions and ideas, was a project far beyond the scope of ordinary legislation. To Aristotle it seemed that the problem must be approached differently.

This is not the place to discuss the two distinct lines taken by him; first, that the character of the state depends on that of its members, and secondly, that the individual only finds his true self as member of a state. The subject has been fully[1] treated, better than I could treat it; and in constructing a model there remains the inevitable difficulty, where to begin. The highest development of the individual is only attainable under the training provided by the model state, and this state is only possible as an association of model citizens. If we may conjecture Aristotle's answer from a rule[2] laid down in the *Ethics*, he would say 'first learn by doing, and then you can do what you have learnt to do.' That is, effort (at first imperfect) will improve faculty, and by creating habit will develope full capacity. But even so it would remain uncertain whether the individual, starting on a career of self-improvement, is to work up to the making of a model state, or the imperfect state to start training its present citizens to perfection. The practical difficulty is there still. Nor is it removed by putting the first beginnings of training so early[3] that they even precede the infant citizen's birth, in the form of rules for eugenic breeding. Aristotle's procedure is to postulate favourable equipment, geographical and climatic, a population of high qualities (that is, Greek,) and then to consider how he would organize the state and train its members—if the postulated conditions were realized and he had a free hand. In

---

[1] E Barker *The political thought of Plato and Aristotle.*
[2] *Ethics* II 1 § 4.
[3] *Pol* VII 16.

this new Utopia it is most significant to observe what he adopts from
historical experience and the proposals of earlier theorists, and in what
respects he departs from them. It is in particular his attitude towards
ownership and tillage of land, and labour in general, that is our present
concern.

As it follows from his doctrine of the Mean that the virtue of the
state and its several members must be based on the avoidance of extremes, so it follows[1] from the moral aim of the state that its component
elements are not all 'parts' of the state in the same strict sense.
Economically, those who provide food clothing etc are parts, necessary
to the existence of the community. Politically (for politics have a
moral end) they are below the standard of excellence required for a
share in the government of a perfect state. They cannot have the
leisure or the training to fit them for so responsible a charge. Therefore they cannot be citizens. To maintain secure independence and
internal order the citizens, and the citizens only, must bear arms. And,
since the land must belong to the possessors of arms, none but citizens
can own land. This does not imply communism. There will have to
be public[2] land, from the produce of which provision will be made for
the service of religion and for the common tables at which citizens will
mess. To maintain these last by individual contributions would be
burdensome to the poor and tend to exclude them. For rich and poor
there will be. But the evil of extreme poverty will be avoided. There
will be private land, out of which each citizen (that is evidently each
citizen-household) will have an allotment of land. This κλῆρος will be
in two[3] parcels, one near the city and the other near the state-frontier,
so that issues of peace and war may not be affected by the bias of
local interests. The cultivation of these allotments will be the work
of subjects, either inhabitants of the district (περίοικοι) or slaves; in
any case aliens, not Greeks; and in the case of slaves care must be
taken not to employ too many of the same race together or such as
are high-spirited. He is concerned to secure the greatest efficiency
and to leave the least possible facilities for rebellion. The labourers
will belong to the state or to individual citizens according to the proprietorship of the land on which they are severally employed. By these
arrangements he has provided for the sustenance of those who in the
true political sense are 'parts' of the state (πόλις), and for their enjoyment of sufficient leisure[4] to enable them to conduct its government
in the paths of virtue and promote the good life (τὸ εὖ ζῆν) which is
the final cause of state existence.

[1] *Pol* VII 8, 9, etc.   [2] *Pol* VII 10.
[3] This adoption of the split land-lots (see above p 91) is perhaps explained by the fact that
the landowners are not αὐτουργοί, so the difficulty of dual residence does not arise.
[4] *Pol* IV 8 § 5, 9 § 4, etc.

The citizens then have the arms and the land and all political power. Among themselves they are on an equal footing, only divided functionally according to age: deliberative and judicial duties belonging to the elder men, military activities to the younger. It is impossible to overlook the influence of the Spartan system on the speculations of Aristotle as well as those of Plato. The equality of Spartan citizens was regarded as evidence[1] of a democratic element in their constitution, and we find this same theoretical equality among the full citizens at any given moment in the developing constitution of Rome. It is significant that Aristotle felt the necessity of such an equality. He remarks[2] that the permanence of a constitution depends on the will of the possessors of arms. We may observe that he seldom refers to the mercenaries so commonly employed in his day, save as his bodyguard of usurping tyrants. But in one passage[3] he speaks of oligarchies being driven to employ them at a pinch for their own security against the Demos, and of their own overthrow in consequence. Therefore he did not ignore the risk run by relying on hirelings: naturally he would prefer to keep the military service of his model state in the hands of his model citizens. But he had no belief[4] in the blind devotion of Sparta to mere preparation for warfare. Peace is the end of war, not war of peace. If you do not learn to make a proper use of peace, in the long run you will fail in war also: hence the attainment of empire was the ruin of Sparta: she had not developed the moral qualities needed for ruling in time of peace. But in his model state he seems not to make adequate provision for the numbers required in war. His agricultural labourers are not to be employed in warfare, as the Laconian Helots regularly were. He only admits them to the service of the oar, controlled by the presence of marine soldiers, who are free citizens like the poorer class of Athenians who generally served in that capacity. The servile character of rustic labour on his plan is thus reasserted, and with it the superior standing of land forces as compared with maritime. The days were past when Athenians readily served at the oar in their own triremes, cruising among the subject states and certain of an obsequious reception in every port. Hired rowers had always been employed to some extent, even by Athens: in this later period the motive power of war-gallies of naval states was more and more obtained from slaves. There was an economic analogy between farm-labour and oar-labour. The slave was forced to toil for practically no more[5]

[1] *Pol* II 6 § 17, 9 §§ 21-2, IV 9 §§ 7-9. The same view is found in Isocrates.
[2] *Pol* VII 9 § 5.   [3] *Pol* V 6 §§ 12, 13.
[4] *Pol* VII 14, 15, VIII 4, cf II 9 § 34.
[5] *Economics* I 5 § 3 δούλῳ δὲ μισθὸς τροφή. Cf the saying about the ass, *Ethics* X 5 § 8.

than his food : the profits of the farm and the profits of war-booty
fell to be shared in either case by few.

Aristotle, who was well aware of the merits of the working farmer,
the peasant citizen, and recognized that such men had been a sound
and stable element in the Athens of former days, would surely not
have treated agriculture as a work reserved for servile hands, had he
not been convinced that the old rural economy was gone and could
never be revived.   For, if suggestions from Sparta influenced him
when designing Utopian institutions, it is no less clear that the
Utopian setting—territory, city, port-town,—are merely modifications
of Attica, Athens, Peiraeus.   In Greece there was no state so favoured
geographically, so well equipped by nature for independence prosperity and power.   If a Greek community was ever to realize an
artistic ideal, and live in peaceful and secure moderation a model
life of dignity and virtue, it could hardly have a better chance of
success than in some such advantageous position as that enjoyed by
Athens.   Her defects lay in her institutions, such as he viewed them
at their present stage of development.   These could not be approved
as they stood : they needed both political and economic reform.   Into
the former we need not enter here : the later democracy could not
but disgust one who judged merit from the standpoint of his doctrine
of the Mean.   Economically, we may infer from his own model project
that two great changes would be required.   Citizens must all have an
interest in the land, though farmed by slave labour.   The port-town
must no longer be a centre of promiscuous commerce, thronged with
a cosmopolitan population of merchants seamen dock-labourers etc
and the various purveyors who catered for their various appetites.   In
truth the Peiraeus was a stumbling-block to him as to Plato, and
probably to most men[1] who did not themselves draw income from its
trade or its iniquities, or who did not derive political power from the
support of its democratic citizens.   To have a state 'self-sufficing' so
far as to get its necessary food from its own territory, and to limit
commerce to a moderate traffic sufficient to procure by exchange such
things as the citizens wanted but could not produce (for instance[2]
timber), was a philosopher's aspiration.

While proposing to restrict commercial activity as being injurious
in its effect, when carried to excess, on the higher life of the state,
Aristotle like Plato admits[3] that not only slaves but free aliens, permanently or temporarily resident, must form a good part of the

---

[1] Deinarchus refers (in Dem § 69 p 99) to Demosthenes' ownership of a house in Peiraeus,
and goes on to denounce him as heaping up money and not holding real property, thus
escaping taxation.   Yet the laws enjoin that a man who is a political leader ought γῆν ἐντὸς
ορων κεκτῆσθαι.   This wild abuse at least is a sign of existent feelings.

[2] We may at least add slaves.   [3] *Pol* VII 4 § 6.

population. He does not even[1] like Plato propose to fix a limit to
the permissible term of metic residence. Apparently he would let
the resident alien make his fortune in Utopia and go on living there
as a non-citizen of means. But he would not allow him to hold real
property within the state, as Xenophon or some other[2] writer had
suggested. That the services of aliens other than slaves were required
for the wellbeing of the state, is an important admission. For it
surely implies that there were departments of trade and industry in
which slave-labour alone was felt to be untrustworthy, while the model
citizens of a model state could not properly be so employed. The
power of personal interest[3] in promoting efficiency and avoiding waste
is an elementary fact not forgotten by Aristotle. Now the slave,
having no personal interest involved beyond escaping punishment, is
apt to be a shirker and a waster. The science of the master ($\delta\epsilon\sigma\pi o\tau\iota\kappa\acute{\eta}$)[4],
we are told, is the science of using slaves ; that is, of getting out of
them what can be got. It is a science of no great scope or dignity.
Hence busy masters employ overseers. He suggests that some
stimulus to exertion may be found in the prospect of manumission[5]
for good service. This occurs again in the *Economics,* but the question
of what is to become of the worn-out rustic slave is not answered by
him[6] any more than it is by Plato. My belief is that, so far as farm
staffs are concerned, he has chiefly if not wholly in view cases[7] of stewards
overseers etc. These would be in positions of some trust, perhaps
occasionally filled by freemen, and to create in them some feeling of
personal interest would be well worth the master's while. Domestic
slavery was on a very different footing, but it too was often a worry[8]
to masters. Here manumission played an obvious and important
part, and perhaps still more in the clerical staffs of establishments
for banking and other businesses. These phenomena of Athenian
life were interesting and suggestive. Yet Aristotle is even more
reticent[9] than Plato (and with less reason) on the subject of manumission : which is matter for regret.

The model state then will contain plenty of free aliens, serving
the state with their talents and labour, an urban non-landholding
element. They set the model citizens free for the duties of politics
and war. Whether they will be bound to service in the army or the

---

[1] Aristotle, like most of the philosophers at Athens, was a metic. See Bernays' *Phokion*
note 8, in which the notable passage *Pol* VII 2 §§ 3–7 is discussed.
[2] The author of *Revenues* ($\pi\acute{o}\rho o\iota$).   [3] *Pol* II 3 § 4, 5 § 8.   [4] *Pol* I 7.
[5] *Pol* VII 10 § 14, *Econ* I 5 § 5.
[6] But perhaps to some extent by the author of *Econ* I 6 § 9.
[7] See *Econ* I 5 §§ 1, 2, 6 § 5.   [8] *Pol* II 3 § 4, 5 § 4.
[9] He only once (III 5 § 2) in the *Politics* mentions ἀπελεύθεροι, and once in the *Rhetoric*
(III 8 § 1).

fleet, like the Athenian metics, we are not told. Nor is it easy to guess how Aristotle would have answered the question. Their main function is to carry on the various meaner or 'mechanical' trades and occupations, no doubt employing or not employing the help of slaves according to circumstances. All such trades were held to have a degrading effect[1] on both body and mind, disabling those practising them from attaining the highest excellence, that is the standard of model citizens in war and peace. Aristotle finds the essence of this taint in transgression of the doctrine of the Mean. Specialization carried to extremes produces professionalism which, for the sake of perfecting technical skill, sacrifices the adaptability, the bodily suppleness and strength and the mental all-round alertness and serene balance,—qualities which every intelligent Greek admired, and which Aristotle postulated in the citizens of his model community. So strong is his feeling on the point that it comes[2] out in connexion with music. The young citizens are most certainly to have musical training, but they are not to become professional performers; for this sort of technical excellence is nothing but a form of βαναυσία.

If neither the farmer nor the artisan are to be citizens, and the disqualification of the latter rests on his narrow professionalism, we are tempted to inquire whether the claim of the farmer may not also have been regarded as tainted by the same disability. That agriculture afforded scope for a high degree of technical skill is a fact not missed by Aristotle. He is at pains to point out[3] that this most fundamental of industries is a source of profit if scientifically pursued, as well as a means of bare subsistence. For the exchange[4] of products (such as corn and wine) by barter soon arises, and offers great opportunities, which are only increased to an injurious extent by the invention of a metallic currency. Now the founder of the Peripatetic school was not the man to ignore the principles of scientific farming, and the labour of collecting details had for him no terrors. Accordingly he refers to the knowledge[5] required in several departments of pastoral and agricultural life. He sketches briefly the development of the industry, from the mere gathering of nature's bounty, through the stage of nomad pasturage, to settled occupation and the raising of food-crops by tillage of the soil. But in the *Politics* he does not follow out this topic. His preoccupation is the development of man in political life: so he dismisses further detail with the remark[6] (referring to the natural branch of χρηματιστική, the art of profit-

---

[1] Too often asserted to need references. But *Pol* III 5 §§ 4–6 is notable as pointing out that τεχνῖται were generally well-to-do, but θῆτες poor.

[2] *Pol* VIII 6 §§ 3–8.   [3] *Pol* I 8 §§ 3 foll.   [4] *Pol* I 9.

[5] *Pol* I 10, 11.   [6] *Pol* I 11 § 1, and Mr Newman's note.

making, which operates with crops and beasts) that in matters of this kind speculation is liberal (= worthy of a free man) but practice is not. This seems to imply that to be engrossed in the detailed study of various soils or breeds of beasts, with a view to their appropriate and profitable management, is an illiberal and cramping pursuit. He does not apply to it the term βαναυσία, and the reason probably is that the bodily defects of the sedentary artisan are not found in the working farmer. But the concentration upon mean details of no moral or political significance is common to both. That all unskilled[1] wage-earners fall under the same ban is a matter of course, hardly worth mentioning. In short, all those who depend on the custom of others for a living are subject to a sort of slavery in a greater or less degree, and unfit to be citizens.

The value attached to 'self-sufficiency' as evidence of freedom and of not living 'in relation to another' (that is, in dependence[2] on another,) is in striking contrast to views that have enjoyed a great vogue in modern economic theory. Neither the man nor the state can be completely[3] self-sufficing: that Aristotle, and Plato before him, saw. Man, feeling his way upward through the household to the state, needs help. He first finds[4] a helper (I am omitting the sex-union) in the ox, the forerunner of the slave, and still in primitive rustic life the helper of the poor. Growing needs bring division of labour and exchange by barter, and so on. As a political animal he can never be quite independent as an individual, but it is the law of his being that the expanding needs which draw him into association with his fellows result in making him more of a man. Here lies a pitfall. If through progress in civilization his daily life becomes so entangled with those of other men that his freedom of action is hampered thereby, surely he has lost something. His progress has not been clear gain, and the balance may not be easy to strike. It is therefore a problem, how to find a position in which man may profit by the advantages of civilization without risking the loss of more than he has gained. Aristotle does not state it in terms so brutally frank. But the problem is there, and he does in effect attempt a solution. The presence in sufficient numbers of slaves legally unfree, and workers legally free but virtually under a defined or special kind[5] of servitude (ἀφωρισμένην τινὰ δουλείαν), is the only means by which a privileged class can get all the good that is to be got out of human progress. His model citizens are an aristocracy of merited privilege, so trained to virtue that to be governed by them will doubtless

---

[1] *Pol* I 11 §§ 3–5.   [2] *Rhetoric* I 9 § 27 πρὸς ἄλλον ζῆν, and Cope's note.
[3] *Pol* VI 8 § 3, VII 6 §§ 1–5.   [4] *Pol* I 2 § 5, 5 §§ 8, 9, cf *Ethics* VIII 11 § 6.
[5] *Pol* I 13 § 13, cf II 5 § 28.

enable their subjects to enjoy as much happiness as their inferior natures can receive. This solution necessitates the maintenance of slavery[1] as existing by nature, and the adoption of economic views that have been rightly called reactionary. The student of human nature and experience unwisely departed from the safer ground of his own principles and offered a solution that was no solution at all.

As the individual man cannot live in complete isolation, supplying his own needs and having no relations with other men,—for his manhood would thus remain potential and never become actual—so it will be with the state also. It must not merely allow aliens to reside in it and serve its purposes internally : it will have to stand in some sort of relations to other states. This is sufficiently asserted by the provision made for the contingency of war. But in considering how far a naval force would be required[2] in his model state he remarks ' The scale of this force must be determined by the part (τὸν βίον) played by our state : if it is to lead a life of leadership and have dealings with other states (ἡγεμονικὸν καὶ πολιτικὸν βίον), it will need to have at hand this force also on a scale proportioned to its activities.' Then, jealous ever of the Mean, he goes on to deny the necessity of a great 'nautical rabble,' in fact the nuisance of the Peiraeus referred to above. On the protection of such maritime commerce as he would admit he does not directly insist ; but, knowing Athens so well, no doubt he had it in mind. Another illustration of the virtuous Mean may be found in the rules of education. The relations of the quarrelsome Greek states had been too often hostile. The Spartan training had been too much admired. But it was too one-sided, too much a glorification of brute force, and its inadequacy had been exposed since Leuctra. Its success had been due to the fact that no other state had specialized in preparation for war as Sparta had done. Once others took up this war-policy in earnest, Sparta's vantage was gone. This vantage was her all. Beaten in war, she had no reserve of nonmilitary qualities to assuage defeat and aid a revival. The citizens of Utopia must not be thus brutalized. Theirs must be the true man's courage (ἀνδρία)[3], as far removed from the reckless ferocity of the robber or the savage as from cowardice. It is surely not too much to infer[4] that military citizens of this character were meant to pursue a public policy neither abject nor aggressive.

It is in connexion with bodily training that we come upon views that throw much light on the position of agricultural labour. There is, he remarks, a general agreement[5] that gymnastic exercises do promote

[1] *Pol* I 5, 6.   [2] *Pol* VII 6 §§ 7, 8.
[3] *Pol* VII 15 §§ 1–6, VIII 4 §§ 1–5, and a number of passages in the *Ethics*.
[4] Indeed in *Pol* VII 15 §§ 2–3 he practically says so.   [5] *Pol* VIII 3 § 7.

manly courage, or as he puts it below 'health and prowess.' But at the present time there is, in states where the training of the young is made a special object, a tendency[1] to overdo it: they bring up the boys as regular athletes, producing a habit of body that hinders the shapely development and growth of the frame. The Thebans in particular are thought to be meant. His own system does not thus run to excess. Gentle exercises gradually extended will develop fine bodies to match fine souls. Now his labouring classes receive no bodily training of the kind. The frame of the artisan is left to become cramped and warped by the monotonous movements of his trade. So too the farm-labourer is left to become hard and stiff-jointed. Neither will have the supple agility needed for fighting as an art. We have seen that this line had already been taken by Plato in the *Republic*; indeed it was one that a Greek could hardly avoid. Yet the shock-tactics of heavy columns were already revolutionizing Greek warfare as much as the light troops organized by Iphicrates. Were Aristotle's military principles not quite up to date? Philip made the Macedonian rustic into a first-rate soldier. But the northern tribesman was a free man. The rustic of the model state was to be a slave or serf: therefore he could not be a soldier. To keep him in due subjection he must not be allowed to have arms or trained to use them skilfully. This policy is nothing more or less than the precautionary device[2] resorted to in Crete; the device that he twits Plato with omitting in the *Republic*, though without it his Guardians would not be able to control the landholding Husbandmen. And yet the weakness of the Cretan system is duly noted[3] in its place. The truth is, Aristotle was no more exempt from the worship of certain ill-defined political terms than were men of far less intellectual power. The democrat worshipped 'freedom' in the sense[4] of 'do as you please,' the mark of a freeborn citizen. The philosopher would not accept so crude a doctrine, but he is none the less determined to mark off the 'free' from the unfree, socially as well as politically. Adapting an institution known in Thessalian[5] cities, he would have two open 'places' (ἀγοραί) in his model state; one for marketing and ordinary daily business, the other reserved for the free citizens. Into the latter no tradesman (βάναυσον) or husbandman (γεωργόν), or other person of like status (τοιοῦτον), is to intrude—unless the magistrates summon him to attend.

It is a pity that Aristotle has left us no estimate of the relative numerical strength of the various classes of population in Utopia. He neglects this important detail more completely even than Plato. Yet I fancy that an attempt to frame such an estimate would very soon

---

[1] *Pol* VIII 4.   [2] *Pol* II 5 § 19.   [3] *Pol* II 10 § 16.
[4] *Pol* VI 2 § 3, cf 4 § 20, and *Ethics* X 10 § 13.   [5] *Pol* VII 12 §§ 3-6.

have exposed the visionary and unpractical nature of the whole fabric
constructed on his lines. It would, I believe, have been ultimately
wrecked on the doctrine of the Mean. Restriction of commerce had
to be reconciled with financial strength, for he saw that wealth was
needed[1] for both peace and war. This εὐπορία could only arise from
savings, the accumulated surplus of industry. The labouring classes
would therefore have to provide not only their own sustenance etc and
that of their rulers, but a considerable surplus as well. This would
probably necessitate so numerous a labouring population that the
citizens would have enough to do in controlling them and keeping
them to their work. To increase the number of citizens would add to
the unproductive[2] mouths, and so on. Foreign war would throw everything out of gear, and no hiring of mercenaries is suggested. It is the
carrying to excess of the principle of specialization that demands excess
of 'leisure,' nothing less than the exemption of all citizens (all persons
that count, in short,) from manual toil. Yet it was one who well knew
the political merits of peasant farmers that was the author of this extravagant scheme for basing upon a servile agriculture the entertainment
of a hothouse virtue.

The general effect produced by reviewing the evidence of Aristotle
on agriculture and the labour-question is that he was a witness of the
decay of the working-farmer class, and either could not or would not
propose any plan for reviving it. The rarity of the words αὐτουργὸς
and cognates is not to be wondered at in his works. They do not occur
in the *Politics*. The *Rhetoric* furnishes two[3] passages. One refers to
the kinds of men especially liable to unfair treatment (ἀδικία) because
it is not worth their while to waste time on legal proceedings, citing as
instances aliens and αὐτουργοί. Rustics may be included, but are not
expressly mentioned. The other[4] refers to qualities that men generally
like and respect, as justice. 'Popular opinion finds this character in
those who do not make their living out of others; that is, who live of
their own labour, for instance those who live by farming (ἀπὸ γεωργίας),
and, in other pursuits, those most of all who work with their own hands.'
Here we have the working farmer expressly cited as a type worthy of
respect. But to single him out thus certainly does not suggest that the
type was a common one. The great Aristotelian index of Bonitz
supplies three[5] more passages, all from the little treatise *de mundo*.
They occur in a special context. God, as the cause that holds together
the universe, is not to be conceived as a power enduring the toil of a

---

[1] *Pol* VII 8 § 7.   [2] II 6 § 6 ἀργοί (in his criticism of Plato's *Laws*).
[3] *Rhet* I 12 § 25, cf Plato *Rep* 565 a αὐτουργοί τε καὶ ἀπράγμονες.
[4] *Rhet* II 4 § 9, cf Euripides *Orestes* 918–20.
[5] *de mundo* 6 §§ 4, 7, 13.

self-working laborious animal (αὐτουργοῦ καὶ ἐπιπόνου ζῴου). Nor must we suppose that God, seated aloft in heaven and influencing all things more or less directly in proportion as they are near or far, pervades and flits through the universe regardless of his dignity and propriety to carry on the things of earth with his own hands (αὐτουργεῖ τὰ ἐπὶ γῆς). The third passage is in a comparison, illustrating the divine power by the Persian system, in which the Great King sitting on his throne pervades and directs his vast empire through his ministering agents. Such *a fortiori* is the government of God.

XVIII. THE LATER ATTIC ORATORS.

It has already been remarked that no clear chronological line can be drawn to divide this famous group into two sections, but that there is nevertheless a real distinction between the period of hostility to Persia and that in which fear of Macedon was the dominant theme. The jealousies and disunion of the Greek states are the background of both. Isocrates[1] had appealed in vain for Greek union as a means of realizing Greek ambitions and satisfying Greek needs. Demosthenes, so far as he did succeed in combining Greek forces to resist the encroachments of Philip, succeeded too late. In the fifth century BC we see the Greek states grouped under two great leading powers. The conflict of these powers leaves one of them the unquestioned head of the Greek world. The next half century witnessed the fall of Sparta, earned by gross misgovernment, and the rise and relapse of Thebes. In the same period Athens made another bid for maritime empire, but this second Alliance had failed. Isolation of Greek states was now the rule, and the hopelessness of any common policy consummated the weakness of exhaustion. At Athens the old fervent patriotism was cooling down, as we learn from the growing reluctance to make sacrifices in the country's cause. Demos was no longer imperial, and he was evidently adapting himself to a humbler role. His political leaders had to secure his food-supply and provide for his festivals, and this out of a sadly shrunken income. To provide efficient fighting forces on land and sea was only possible by appropriating the Festival fund (θεωρικόν), and the mob of Athens was unwilling either to fight in person or to surrender its amusements in order to hire mercenaries. Too often the result was that mercenaries, hired but not paid, were left to pillage friend and foe alike for their own support. The truth is,

[1] Even after the ruin of Phocis and the peace of 346 BC the old man wrote in the same strain. But it was to Philip, in whom he recognised the real master of Greece, that he now appealed.

individualism was superseding old-fashioned patriotism. The old simple views of life and duty had been weakened by the questionings of many thinkers, and no new moral footing had yet been found to compete with immediate personal interest. Athens was the chief centre of this decline, for the intellectual and moral influences promoting it were strongest there: but it was surely not confined to Athens. The failure of Thebes after the death of Epaminondas was one of many symptoms of decay. She had overthrown Sparta, but she could not herself lead Greece: her utmost achievement was a fatal equilibrium of weak states, of which the Macedonian was soon to take full advantage. And everywhere, particularly in rural districts, the flower of the male population was being drained away, enlisting in mercenary armies, lured by the hope of gain and willing to escape the prospect of hard and dreary lives at home. In short, each was for his own hand.

Such an age was not one to encourage the peaceful and patient toil of agriculture. The great cities, above all Athens, needed cheap corn. Their own farmers could not supply this, and so importation[1] was by law favoured, and as far as possible inforced. Thus times of actual dearth seldom occurred, and home-grown corn was seldom a paying crop. Thrown back all the more on cultivation of the olive and vine the products of which were available for export, the farmer needed time for the development of his planted ($\pi\epsilon\phi\upsilon\tau\epsilon\upsilon\mu\acute{\epsilon}\nu\eta$) land, and the waiting for returns necessitated a larger capital. He was then exposed to risk of greater damage in time of war. For his capital was irretrievably sunk in his vineyard or oliveyard, and its destruction would take years to repair—that is, more waiting and more capital. This was no novel situation. But its effect in reducing the number of small peasant farmers was probably now greater than ever. Not only were mercenary armies relentless destroyers and robbers (having no fear of reprisals and no conventional scruples to restrain them), but their example corrupted the practice of citizen forces. Even if no fighting took place in this or that neighbourhood, the local farmers[2] must expect to be ruined by the mere presence of their own defenders. When we bear in mind the risks of drought in some parts or floods in others, the occasional losses of live stock, and other ordinary misfortunes, it is fair to imagine that the farmer of land needed to be a man of substance, not liable to be ruined by a single blow. And the sidelights thrown on the subject by the indirect references in the orators are quite consistent with this view.

The loss of the Thracian Chersonese in the disasters of 405 BC had

---

[1] References are too numerous to be given here. A *locus classicus* is Dem *Lept* §§ 30-3 pp 466-7, on the case of Leucon the ruler of Bosporus. We hear also of corn imported from Sicily and Egypt, and even (Lycurg § 26 p 151) from Epirus to Corinth.

[2] Demosthenes *Olynth* 1 § 27 p 17.

not only dispossessed the Athenian settlers there, but made that region a source of continual anxiety to Athens. She was no longer in secure control of the strait through which the corn-ships passed from the Pontus. A considerable revival of her naval power enabled her in 365 to occupy the island of Samos and to regain a footing in the Chersonese. To both of these cleruchs were sent. But the tenure of the Chersonese was disputed by Thracian princes, and it was necessary to send frequent expeditions thither. The success or failure of these enterprises is recorded in histories of Greece. The importance of the position justified great efforts to retain it. Greek cities on the Propontis and Bosporus, not Thracian chiefs only, gave trouble. If short of supplies, as in 362, they were tempted to lay hands[1] on the corn-ships, and consume what was meant for Athens. But the result of much confused warfare was that in 358 the Chersonese became once more a part of the Athenian empire. Even after the dissolution of that empire in the war with the Allies 358–6, part of the peninsula still remained Athenian. But it was now exposed to the menace of the growing power of Macedon under Philip. To induce the Demos, who needed the corn, to provide prompt and adequate protection for the gate of Pontic trade, was one of the many difficult tasks of Demosthenes.

Demosthenes is by far the most important witness to the circumstances of his age; though much allowance must be made for bias and partisan necessities, this does not greatly affect references to agricultural matters. Unfortunately his supreme reputation caused the works of other authors to be attributed to him in later times. Thus the total number of speeches passing under his name is a good deal larger than that of the undoubtedly genuine ones. But, if we set aside a few mere forgeries of later rhetoricians, the speeches composed by contemporary authors are no less authorities for stray details of rural life than those of Demosthenes himself. It is therefore not necessary to discuss questions of authorship, on which even the ablest specialists are often not agreed. But it is of interest to bear in mind that we are gleaning little items, from a strictly Athenian point of view, bearing on the condition of the same Athens and Attica as came under the cool observation of the outsider Aristotle. The lives of Aristotle and Demosthenes, from 384–3 to 322 BC, are exactly contemporary. And, as in matters of politics the speeches of the orators often illustrate the philosopher's criticisms of democracy, so it is probable that the matters of food-supply and rural economy, referred to by speakers for purposes of the moment, were among the particulars noted by Aristotle when forming his conclusions on those subjects.

The right of owning real estate in Attica being reserved for

[1] (Dem) *c Polycl* §§ 5, 6 pp 1207–8.

Athenian citizens, aliens were debarred from what was sometimes a
convenient form[1] of investment. If the possible return on capital so
placed was lower than in more speculative ventures, the risk of total
loss was certainly much less, of partial loss comparatively small.
Moreover it gave the owner a certain importance[2] as a citizen of known
substance. It enabled a rich man to vary[3] his investments, as references
to mixed estates shew. And he had a choice of policies in dealing
with it: he could reside on his own property and superintend the
management himself, or entrust the charge to a steward, or let it to a
tenant. And, if at any time he wanted ready money for some purpose,
he could raise it by a mortgage on favourable terms. If the land lay
in a pleasant spot not too far from the city, he was tempted to make
himself a 'place in the country' for his own occasional retirement and
the entertainment of friends. That landowning presented itself to
Athenians of the Demosthenic period in the aspects just sketched is
manifest from the speeches belonging to the years from 369 to 322 BC.
Of the small working farmer there is very little trace. But that some
demand for farms existed seems indicated by the cleruchs sent to the
Chersonese and Samos. No doubt these were meant to serve as resident
garrisons at important points, and it is not to be supposed that they
were dependent solely on their own labour for tillage of their lots.
Another kind of land-hunger speaks for itself. The wars and wastings
of this period placed large areas of land at the disposal of conquerors.
Olynthian, Phocian, Boeotian territory was at one time or another
confiscated and granted out as reward for this or that service. No
reproaches of Demosthenes are more bitter than the references to these
cruel and cynical measures of Philip's corrupting policy. Individuals
shared[4] these and other spoils: the estates of Aeschines and Philocrates
in Phocis, and later of Aeschines in Boeotia, are held up as the shame-
ful wages of treachery. These estates can only have been worked by
slave-labour under stewards, for politicians in Athens could not reside
abroad. They are specimens of the large-scale agriculture to which the
circumstances of the age were favourable.

A dispute arising out of a case of challenge to exchange properties[5]
(ἀντίδοσις), in order to decide which party was liable for performance
of burdensome state-services, gives us a glimpse of a large holding in
Attica. It belongs to 330 BC or later. The farm is an ἐσχατιά, that is

---

[1] A good case of such investment by guardians is Dem *Nausim* § 7 p 986.

[2] Dem *F Leg* § 314 p 442, εἶτα γεωργεῖς ἐκ τούτων καὶ σεμνὸς γέγονας.

[3] See cases in Aeschines *Timarch* § 97 p 13, Dem *pro Phorm* §§ 4, 5 p 945. The
inheritance of Demosthenes himself included no landed property, *c Aphob* 1 §§ 9–11
p 816.

[4] Dem *F Leg* § 146 p 386, cf § 114 p 376, § 265 p 426, *de cor* § 41 p 239.

[5] [Dem] *c Phaenipp* §§ 5–7 pp 1040–1.

a holding near[1] the frontier. It is stated to have been more than 40
stadia (about 5 miles) in circuit. The farmstead included granaries
(οἰκήματα) for storing the barley and wheat which were evidently the
chief crops on this particular farm. It included also a considerable
vineyard producing a good quantity of wine. Among the by-products
was brushwood (ὕλη, not timber ξύλα)[2]. The faggots were carried to
market (Athens, I presume) on the backs of asses. The ass-drivers are
specially mentioned. The returns from the faggot-wood are stated at
over 12 drachms a day. The challenging speaker declares that this
estate was wholly unencumbered: not a mortgage-post (ὅρος) was to
be seen. He contrasts his own position, a man who has lost most of
his property in a mining venture, though he has even toiled with his
own[3] hands, with that of the landlord (I presume not an αὐτουργός)
enriched by the late rise of the prices of corn and wine. He may be
grossly exaggerating the profits of this border-farm: his opponent
would probably be able to cite very different facts from years when
the yield had been poor or prices low. Still, to impress an Athenian
jury, the picture drawn in this speech must at least have seemed a
possible one. The labour on the farm would be mainly that of slaves:
but to this I shall return below. In another speech[4] we hear of a farmer
in the far north, on the SE Crimean coast. The sea-carriage of 80 jars
of sour wine is accounted for by his wanting it for his farm-hands
(ἐργάται). Slaves are probably meant, but we cannot be sure of it in
that slave-exporting part of the world. At any rate he was clearly
farming on a large scale. If he was, as I suppose, a Greek settler, the
case is an interesting one. For it would seem to confirm the view of
Isocrates, that Greek expansion was a feasible solution of a felt need,
provided suitable territory for the purpose could be acquired; and that
of Xenophon, when he proposed to plant necessitous Greeks in Asiatic
lands taken from Persia.

The type of farmer known to us from Aristophanes, who works a
holding of moderate size, a man not wealthy but comfortable, a well-
to-do peasant proprietor who lives among the slaves whose labour he
directs, is hardly referred to directly in the speeches of this period.
Demosthenes[5] in 355 BC makes the general remark 'You cannot deny
that farmers who live thrifty lives, and by reason of rearing children
and domestic expenses and other public services have fallen into arrear

[1] Aeschines mentions two ἐσχατιαί in the estate of Timarchus.
[2] The lack of ξύλα in Attica made timber, like wheat, a leading article of commerce, and
dealing in it was a sign of a wealthy capitalist. Cf Dem *F Leg* § 114 p 376, *Mid* § 167
p 568.
[3] I suspect this is an exaggeration.
[4] [Dem] *Lacrit* §§ 31-3 P 933.
[5] Dem *Androt* § 65 p 613, repeated in *Timocr* § 172 P 753.

with their property-tax, do the state less wrong than the rogues who embezzle public funds.' But he does not say that there were many such worthy citizen-farmers, nor does he (I think) imply it. In a similar passage[1] three years later he classes them with merchants, mining speculators, and other men in businesses, as better citizens than the corrupt politicians. Such references are far too indefinite, and too dependent on the rhetorical needs of the moment, to tell us much. In one of the earlier private speeches[2] Demosthenes deals with a dispute of a kind probably common. It is a neighbours' quarrel over a wall, a watercourse, and right of way. To all appearance the farms interested in the rights and wrongs were not large holdings. They were evidently in a hilly district. The one to protect which from floods the offending wall had been built had at one time belonged to a 'town-bred[3] man' who disliked the place, neglected it, and sold it to the father of Demosthenes' client. There is nothing to shew that this farm was the whole of the present owner's estate: so that it is hardly possible to classify him economically with any exactitude. We do by chance learn that he had a staff of slaves, and that vines and fig-trees grew on the land.

The author of one of the earlier speeches[4] (between 368 and 365 BC) furnishes much more detail in connexion with estates of what was apparently a more ordinary type. Neighbours are quarrelling as usual, and we have of course only *ex parte* statements. The farms, worked by slave-labour, produce vines and olives and probably some corn also. The enclosure and tending of valuable plants is represented as kept up to a high standard. Incidentally we learn that the staff used to contract[5] for the gathering of fruit (ὀπώραν) or the reaping and carrying of other crops (θέρος ἐκθερίσαι), clearly on other estates. The contract was always made by a person named, who is thereby proved to have been the real owner of these slaves,—a point in the case. According to his own account, the speaker had for some time been settled (κατῴκουν) on the estate. That is, he had a house there and would sometimes be in residence. The amenities of the place are indicated by the mention of his young rose-garden, which was ravaged by trespassers, as were his olives and vines. The house from which they carried off 'all the furniture, worth more than 20 minas,' seems to have been in Athens, and the mention of the lodging-house (συνοικία) that he mortgaged for 16 minas shews that his estate was a mixed one. Country houses were no exceptional thing. A mining speculator speaks of an opponent[6] as coming to his house in the country and intruding

---

[1] Dem *Aristocr* § 146 p 668.
[2] Dem *c Callicl passim*.
[3] ἀστικοῦ, Dem *Callicl* § 11 p 1274.
[4] [Dem] *Nicostr passim*.
[5] [Dem] *Nicostr* § 21 p 1253.
[6] Dem *Pantaen* § 45 p 979.

into the apartments of his wife and daughters. A party protesting against being struck off the deme-register says[1] that his enemies made a raid on his cottage in the country (οἰκίδιον ἐν ἀγρῷ). He is probably depreciating the house, in order not to have the dangerous appearance of a rich man.

We hear also of farms near Athens, the suburban position of which no doubt enhanced their value. In the large mixed estate inherited and wasted by Timarchus, Aeschines[2] mentions (344 BC) a farm only about a mile and a half from the city wall. The spendthrift's mother entreated him to keep this property at least: her wish was to be buried there. But even this he sold, for 2000 drachms (less than £80). In the speech against Euergus and Mnesibulus the plaintiff tells[3] how his opponents raided his farm and carried off 50 soft-wooled sheep at graze, and with them the shepherd and all the belongings of the flock, also a domestic slave, etc. This was not enough: they pushed on into the farm and tried to capture the slaves, who fled and escaped. Then they turned to the house, broke down the door that leads to the garden (κῆπον), burst in upon his wife and children, and went off with all the furniture that remained in the house. The speaker particularly points out[4] that he had lived on the place from childhood, and that it was near the race-course (πρὸς τῷ ἱπποδρόμῳ). It must then have been near Athens. The details given suggest that it was a fancy-farm, devoted to the production of stock valued for high quality and so commanding high prices. The garden seems to be a feature of an establishment more elegant than that of a mere peasant farmer. It corresponds to the rose-bed in a case referred to above: Hyperides[5] too mentions a man who had a κῆπος near the Academy, doubtless a pleasant spot. The farm in the plain (ὁ ἐν πεδίῳ ἀγρός)[6] belonging to Timotheus, and mortgaged by him to meet his debts, is only mentioned in passing (362 BC) with no details: we can only suppose it to have been an average holding in the rich lowland.

A few passages require separate consideration in connexion with the labour-question. In the speech on the Crown (330 BC) Demosthenes quotes[7] Aeschines as protesting against being reproached with the friendship (ξενίαν) of Alexander. He retorts 'I am not so crazy as to call you Philip's ξένος or Alexander's φίλος, unless one is to speak of reapers or other wage-earners as the friends of those who hire them ...but on a former occasion I called you the hireling (μισθωτὸν) of Philip, and I now call you the hireling of Alexander.' Here the reaper

---

[1] Dem *Eubulid* § 65 p 1319.   [2] Aeschin *Timarch* § 99 p 14.
[3] [Dem] *Euerg Mnes* §§ 52–3 p 1155.   [4] Twice, §§ 53, 76.
[5] Hyperid *in Demosth* fragm col 26.   [6] [Dem] *c Timoth* § 11 p 1187.
[7] Dem *de Cor* §§ 51–2 p 242.

($\theta\epsilon\rho\iota\sigma\tau\dot{\eta}s$) is contemptuously referred to as a mere hireling. Such was the common attitude towards poor freemen who lived by wage-earning labour,—$\theta\hat{\eta}\tau\epsilon s$ in short. But is it clear that the $\mu\iota\sigma\theta\omega\tau\dot{o}s$ is necessarily a freeman? The passage cited above from an earlier speech makes it doubtful. If a gang of slaves could contract to cut and carry a crop ($\theta\acute{\epsilon}\rho os\ \mu\iota\sigma\theta o\hat{\iota}\nu\tau o\ \grave{\epsilon}\kappa\theta\epsilon\rho\acute{\iota}\sigma a\iota$), their owner acting for them, surely they were strictly $\mu\iota\sigma\theta\omega\tau o\grave{\iota}$ from the point of view of the farmer who hired them. They were $\grave{a}\nu\delta\rho\acute{a}\pi o\delta a\ \mu\iota\sigma\theta o\phi o\rho o\hat{\upsilon}\nu\tau a$, to use the exact Greek phrase. In the speech against Timotheus an even more notable passage[1] (362 BC) occurs. Speaking of some copper said to have been taken in pledge for a debt, the speaker asks 'Who were the persons that brought the copper to my father's house? Were they hired men ($\mu\iota\sigma\theta\omega\tau o\acute{\iota}$), or slaves ($o\grave{\iota}\kappa\acute{\epsilon}\tau a\iota$)?' Here, at first sight, we seem to have the hireling clearly marked off as free. For the argument[2] proceeds 'or which of my slave-household ($\tau\hat{\omega}\nu\ o\grave{\iota}\kappa\epsilon\tau\hat{\omega}\nu\ \tau\hat{\omega}\nu\ \grave{\epsilon}\mu\hat{\omega}\nu$) took delivery of the copper? If slaves brought it, then the defendant ought to have handed them over (for torture): if hired men, he should have demanded our slave who received and weighed it.' Strictly speaking, slaves, in status $\delta o\hat{\upsilon}\lambda o\iota$, are $o\grave{\iota}\kappa\acute{\epsilon}\tau a\iota$[3] in relation to their owner, of whose $o\grave{\iota}\kappa\acute{\iota}a$ they form a part. But if A in a transaction with B employed some slaves whom he hired for the purpose from C (C being in no way personally involved in the case), would not these[4] be $\mu\iota\sigma\theta\omega\tau o\acute{\iota}$, in the sense that they were not his own $o\grave{\iota}\kappa\acute{\epsilon}\tau a\iota$, but procured by $\mu\iota\sigma\theta\grave{o}s$ for the job? It is perhaps safer to assume that in the case before us the hirelings meant by the speaker are freemen, but I do not think it can be considered certain. Does not their exemption from liability to torture prove it? I think not, unless we are to assume that the slaves hired from a third person, not a party in the case, could be legally put to question. That this was so, I can find no evidence, nor is it probable. The regular practice was this: either a party offered his slaves for examination under torture, or he did not. If he did not, a challenge ($\pi\rho\acute{o}\kappa\lambda\eta\sigma\iota s$) was addressed to him by his opponent, demanding their surrender for the purpose. But to demand the slaves of any owner, not a party in the case, was a very different thing, and I cannot discover the existence of any such right. I am not speaking of state trials, in which the claims of the public safety might override private

[1] [Dem] c Timoth § 51 p 1199.   [2] Ibid § 52.
[3] Of course $o\grave{\iota}\kappa\acute{\epsilon}\tau\eta s$ is often loosely used as merely 'slave.' But here the antithesis seems to gain point from strict use.
[4] I have not found this question distinctly stated anywhere. Beauchet Droit privé IV 222 treats the $\mu\iota\sigma\theta\omega\tau o\acute{\iota}$ of this passage as freemen. But in II 443 he says that slaves hired from their owners were generally designated $\mu\iota\sigma\theta\omega\tau o\acute{\iota}$. Nor do I find the point touched in Meier-Schömann-Lipsius (edition 1883-7, pp 889 foll), or any evidence that the $\pi\rho\acute{o}\kappa\lambda\eta\sigma\iota s$ could be addressed to others than parties in a case. Wallon I 322 foll also gives no help.

interests, but of private cases, in which the issue lay between clearly defined adversaries. In default of direct and unquestionable authority, I cannot suppose that an Athenian slaveowner could be called upon to surrender his property (even with compensation for any damage thereto) for the purposes of a case in which he was not directly concerned.

Stray references to matters of land-tenure, such as the letting of sacred lands[1] (τεμένη) belonging to a deme, are too little connected with our subject to need further mention here. And a curious story[2] of some hill-lands (ὄρη) in the district of Oropus, divided by lot among the ten Tribes, apparently as tribal property, is very obscure. Such allotments would probably be let to tenants. What is more interesting in connexion with agriculture is the references to farming as a means of getting a livelihood, few and slight though they are. Demosthenes[3] in 349 BC tells the Assembly that their right policy is to attack Philip on his own ground, not to mobilize and then await him in Attica: such mobilization would be ruinous to 'those of you who are engaged in farming.' The speech against Phaenippus[4] shews us an establishment producing corn and wine and firewood and alleged to be doing very well owing to the prices then ruling in the market. We have also indications of the presence of dealers who bought up crops, no doubt to resell at a profit. From the expressions[5] ὀπώραν πρίασθαι and ὀπωρώνης it might seem that fruit-crops in particular were disposed of in this way. Naturally a crop of this sort had to be gathered quickly, and a field gang would be employed—slaves or freemen, according to circumstances. For that in these days poverty was driving many a free citizen[6] to mean and servile occupations for a livelihood, is not only a matter of certain inference but directly affirmed by Demosthenes in 345 BC. Aeschines[7] in 344 also denies that the practice of any trade to earn a bare living was any political disqualification to a humble citizen of good repute. From such poor freemen were no doubt drawn casual hands at critical moments of farm life, analogues of the British hop-pickers[8]. But, with every allowance for possible occasions of employing free labour, particularly in special processes where servile apathy was plainly injurious, the farm-picture in general as depicted in these speeches is one of slave-

---

[1] Dem *Eubulid* § 63 p 1318.
[2] Hyperides *pro Euxen*, fragm §§ 16, 17, col 12, 13.
[3] Dem *Olynth* I § 27 p 17.
[4] [Dem] *c Phaenipp* §§ 5–7 pp 1040–1, §§ 19–21 pp 1044–5.
[5] ὀπωρώνης, Dem *de Cor* § 262 p 314.
[6] Dem *Eubulid* § 45 p 1313, speaking of an old woman.
[7] Aeschin *Timarch* § 27 p 4.
[8] We have already seen the case of olive-pickers in Aristoph *Vesp* 712.

labour. And this suggests to me a question in reference to the disposal of Greek slaves. For the vast majority of slaves[1] in Greece, whether urban or rustic, were certainly Barbarians of several types for several purposes. The sale of the people of captured cities had become quite an ordinary thing. Sparta had sinned thus in her day of power, and the example was followed from time to time by others. The cases of Olynthus in 348 BC and Thebes in 335 fall in the present period. Aeschines mentions[2] some captives working chained in Philip's vineyard; but these can only have been few. The mass were sold, and a large sum of money realized thereby. At Thebes the captives sold are said to have numbered 30,000. What markets absorbed these unhappy victims? I can only guess that many found their way to Carthage and Etruria.

XIX. THE MACEDONIAN PERIOD 322–146 BC.

The deficiency of contemporary evidence illustrating the agricultural conditions of this troubled age in the Greek world makes it necessary to combine the various scraps of information in a general sketch. Hellas had now seen its best days. The break-up of the great empire of Alexander did not restore to the little Greek states the freedom of action which had been their pride and which had been a main influence in keeping up their vitality. The outward and visible sign of their failure was the impossibility of an independent foreign policy. The kingdoms of Alexander's Successors might rise and fall, but Greek states could do little to affect the results. A new world was opened to Greek enterprise in the East, and Greek mercenaries and Greek secretaries traders and officials were carrying the Greek language and civilization into wide lands ruled by Macedonian kings. But these were individuals, attracted by the prospect of a gainful military or civil career. Either they settled abroad, and drained Greece of some of her ablest sons; or they returned home enriched, and formed an element of the population contrasting painfully with those who had stayed behind. In either case it seems certain that the movement tended to lower the standard of efficiency and patriotism in their native states. Citizen armies became more and more difficult to maintain. The influx of money no longer locked up in Oriental treasuries only served to accentuate the old social distinction[3] of Rich and Poor. Men who came back with fortunes meant to enjoy themselves, and they

---

[1] See Dem *Mid* § 48 p 530, etc.

[2] Aeschin *F Leg* § 156 p 59. The passage of Dem *F L* to which he refers is not in our text, for §§ 194–5 pp 401–2 is different.

[3] See Plut *Aratus* 14, 25, 27, 36, 39, 40, *Philopoemen* 7, 15.

did : the doings of the returned soldier of fortune were proverbial, and
a fruitful theme for comic poets. But the spectacle of wanton luxury
was more likely to lure enterprising individuals into ventures abroad
than to encourage patient industry at home. And there is little doubt
that such was the general result. The less vigorous of the poor citizens
remained, a servile mob, ever ready by grovelling compliments to earn
the bounties of kings.

Political decay and changes of social circumstance were accompanied by new movements in the sphere of thought. It is generally
observed that in this period philosophy more and more appeals to the
individual man, regardless of whether he be a citizen or not. How far
this movement arose out of changed conditions may be open to
difference of opinion: but, as usual in human affairs, what began as an
effect continued to operate as a cause. The rapid spread of the Greek
tongue and Greek civilization eastwards, known as Hellenizing, was
a powerful influence promoting cosmopolitan views. Alien blood could
no longer form an unsurmountable barrier: the Barbarian who spoke
Greek and followed Greek ways had won a claim to recognition, as had
already been foreseen by the mild sincerity[1] of Isocrates. But these
half-Greeks, some of them even of mixed blood, were now very
numerous. They competed with genuine Hellenes at a time when the
pride of the genuine Hellene was ebbing: even in intellectual pursuits,
in which the Hellene still claimed preeminence, they were serious and
eventually successful rivals. It is no wonder that earlier questionings
took new life, and that consciousness of common humanity tended to
modify old-established sentiment, even on such subjects as the relation
of master and slave. It was not merely that the philosophic schools
from different points of view, Cynic Cyrenaic Stoic Epicurean, persistently regarded man as a mental and moral unit, whatever his
political or social condition might be. The fragments and echoes of
the later Comedy suffice to shew how frankly the slave could be presented on the public stage as the equal, or more than equal, of his master.

The foundation of new cities by the Successor-kings was another
influence acting in the same direction. These were either royal capitals
or commercial centres, or both, like Alexandria. Others were important from their situation as strategic posts, such as Lysimacheia by
the Hellespont or Demetrias commanding the Pagasaean gulf. Competing powers could not afford to wait for gradual growth; so great
efforts were made to provide populations for the new cities without
delay. Sometimes multitudes were transplanted wholesale from older
communities. In any case no strict inquiry into the past condition of
transplanted persons can have taken place. In Sicily we know that

[1] Isocr *paneg* § 50 p 50.

Syracuse had become the one great centre of what remained of Greek power in that island. But, what with incorporation of foreign mercenaries and enfranchisement of slaves, what with massacres of Greek citizens, the population of Syracuse was a mongrel mob. Such, if in a less degree, were the populations of the new cities of the kings. There was nothing national about them. In some, for instance Alexandria, a rabble wavering between apathy and ferocity was a subject of concern to the government. Others were more noted as centres of industry: such were some of those in Asia Minor. But common to them all was the condition, a momentous change from a Greek point of view, of dependence. They were not states, with a policy of their own, but parts of this or that kingdom. However little their overlord might interfere with their internal affairs, still it was he, not they, that stood in relation to the world outside. They were not independent: but as a rule they were prosperous. In the new world of great state-units they filled a necessary place, and beside them the remaining state-cities of the older Greek world were for the most part decaying. These for their own protection had to conform their policy to that of some greater power. Patriotism had little material in which to find expression: apathy and cosmopolitan sentiment were the inevitable result. Such was in particular the case at Athens, which remained eminent as a centre of philosophic speculation, attracting inquirers and students from all parts. But the 'fierce democracy' of her imperial days was a thing of the past, and she lived upon her former glories and present subservience.

If academic distinction and cosmopolitanism went easily together, commercial activity was hardly likely to foster jealous state-patriotism of the old sort. The leading centre of commerce in the eastern Mediterranean was Rhodes. The island city was still a state. Its convenient position as a port of call on the main trade routes gave it wealth. Its usefulness to merchants from all parts enabled it to play off the kings against one another, and to enjoy thereby much freedom of action. Its steady conservative government and its efficient navy made it a welcome check on piracy in time of peace, and a valued ally in war. It was also a considerable intellectual centre. No power was so closely in touch with international questions generally, or so often employed as umpire in disputes. Till an unfortunate blunder at the time of the war with Perseus (168 BC) put an end to their old friendship with Rome, and led to their humiliation, the wise policy of the Rhodians preserved their independence and earned them general goodwill. But it was surely not in a state thriving on trade and traffic that the old narrow Greek patriotism could find a refuge. It is not necessary to refer to more cases in particular. The main point of interest is that in this age of cities and extensive maritime intercourse urban life was generally developing and rural life shrinking. Now it had been, and still was, the case that mixture of population normally took place in active cities, especially in seaport towns. It was in quiet country towns and hamlets that native purity of blood was most easily preserved.

If the general outline of circumstances has been fairly sketched in the above paragraphs, we should expect to find that agriculture on a small scale was not prospering in this period. Unhappily there is hardly any direct evidence on the point. Even indirect evidence is meagre and sometimes far from clear. One notable symptom of the age is seen in the rise of bucolic poetry. This is not a rustic growth, the rude utterance of unlettered herdsmen, but an artificial product of town-dwelling poets, who idealize the open-air life to amuse town-bred readers somewhat weary of the everlasting streets. In the endeavour to lend an air of reality to scenes of rural life, it was convenient to credit the rustics (shepherds goatherds etc) with a grossness of amorosity that may perhaps be exaggerated to suit the taste of urban readers. Of this tendency the idylls of **Theocritus** furnish many instances. We need not accept them as accurate pictures of the life of herds and hinds in Sicily or elsewhere, but they give us some notion of the ideas of rural life entertained by literary men of the Alexandrian school. Beside the guardians of flocks and herds with their faithful dogs, their flutes and pan-pipes, idling in the pleasant shade and relieving the tiresome hours with musical competition, we have the hinds ploughing mowing or busy with vintage and winepress. Some are evidently freemen, others are slaves; and we hear of overseers. There is milking and making of cheese, and woodmen[1] are not forgotten. The bloom of flowers, the murmur of streams, the song of birds, the whisper of the refreshing breeze, form the setting of these rural scenes, and might almost persuade us that we are privileged spectators of a genuine golden age. But the sayings and doings of the rustics undeceive us. And the artificiality of this poetry is further betrayed by that of the panegyric and pseudo-epic poems of the same author. His admiration of Hiero[2] of Syracuse may be mainly sincere, but his praises of Ptolemy[3] Philadelphus are the utterances of a courtier. His excursions into the region of mythology are brief, for the reading public of his day could not stand long epics on the adventures[4] of Heracles or the Dioscuri. And the literary apparatus is antiquarian, a more or less direct imitation of the old Homeric diction, but unable to reproduce the varied cadences. It is generally remarked that the genius of Theocritus finds its happiest and liveliest expression in the fifteenth idyll, which depicts urban scenes. In this respect that idyll may be compared with the mimes of

---

[1] v 64–5, cf XVII 9, 10.   [2] XVI.   [3] XVII.   [4] XXII, XXV.

Herodas, which illustrate, probably with truth, the shadier sides of urban life in cities of the period, which Theocritus ignores.

It is in a miniature epic[1] of mythological setting that we find the most direct references to tillage of the soil combined with the keeping of live stock—general agriculture, in short. We read of the plowman[2] in charge of the crops, of the hard-working diggers[3] (φυτοσκάφοι οἱ πολυεργοί), of the herdsmen[4], of an overseer[5] or steward (αἰσυμνήτης). The staff seems to consist entirely of slaves. But it is not easy to say how far the picture is meant as a reproduction of the primitive labour-conditions of the traditional Heroic age, how far the details may be coloured by the conditions of Theocritus' own day. In the Idylls we find a shepherd, free presumably, in charge of a flock the property[6] of his father. On the other hand ἐριθακὶς in one passage[7] seems not to be a wage-earner, but a black slave. The ἐργάτης of the tenth idyll[8] is probably a free man, but he is enamoured of a slave girl. No conclusion can be drawn from a reference[9] to coarse but filling food meant for labourers. Roughness and a certain squalor are conventional rustic attributes: a town-bred girl repulses the advances of a herdsman[10] with the remark ' I'm not used to kiss rustics, but to press town-bred lips,' and adds further detail. Nor is the mention of Thessalian[11] serfs (πενέσται) in the panegyric of Hiero anything more than a part of the poet's apparatus. And the reference[12] to the visit of Augeas to his estate, followed by a comment on the value of the master's personal attention to his own interests, is a touch of truism common to all peoples in every age. To Theocritus, the one poet of learned Alexandria who had high poetic genius, the life and labour of farmers was evidently a matter of little or no concern. He could hardly idealize the Egyptian fellah. And the one passage[13] in which he directly illustrates the position of the Greek contemporary farmer is significant. Discontented owing to a disappointment in love, the man is encouraged by his friend to enter the service of the generous Ptolemy as a mercenary soldier.

One or two small references may be gleaned from the *Characters* of Aristotle's successor **Theophrastus.** That the bulk of these typical portraits are drawn from town-folk is only to be expected, but this point is not to be pressed overmuch, for philosophers did not frequent country districts. The general references to treatment of slaves, the slave-market, and so forth, are merely interesting as illustrative of the general prevalence of slavery, chiefly of course in Athens. But we do

[1] xxv.   [2] xxv 1, 51.   [3] xxv 27, cf xxiv 137.
[4] xxv 86–152.   [5] xxv 47–8.   [6] vii 15–6.
[7] iii 35, cf xv 80.   [8] x 9, cf i, xxi 3.   [9] xxiv 136–7.
[10] xx 3, 4.   [11] xvi 34–5.   [12] xxv 56–9.
[13] xiv 58–9, cf 13, 56, where στρατιώτας is a professional soldier.

get to the farm in the case[1] of the rustic boor (ἄγροικος). His lack of dignity and proper reserve is shewn in talking to his slaves on matters of importance: he makes confidants of them, and so far forgets himself as to lend a hand in grinding the corn. It has been remarked that Greek manners allowed a certain familiarity[2] in the relations of master and slave. But this person overdoes it: in Peripatetic language, he transgresses the doctrine of the Mean. He employs also hired men (μισθωτοί), and to them he recounts all the political gossip (τὰ ἀπὸ τῆς ἐκκλησίας), evidently a sign of his awkwardness and inability to hold his tongue. I take these wage-earners to be poor freemen. They might be slaves hired from another owner: this practice appears else-where in connexion with town slaves. But the general impoverishment of the old Greece, save in a few districts, is beyond doubt: and the demand for slaves in new cities would raise the price of slaves and tend to drive the free poor to manual labour.

The exact dates of the birth and death of **Polybius** are uncertain, but as an observer of events his range extended from about 190 or 189 to 122 or 121 BC. Though his references to agriculture are few and separately of small importance, they have a cumulative value on certain points. He wrote as historian of the fortunes of the civilized world of his day, treated as a whole, in which a series of interconnected struggles led up to the supremacy of Rome. His Greece is the Greece of the Leagues. No leading state of the old models had been able to unite the old Hellas effectively under its headship, but the Macedonian conquest had plainly proved that in isolation[3] the little separate states had no future open to them but slavery. The doings of Alexander's Successors further inforced the lesson. It was clear that the only hope of freedom lay in union so far as possible, for thus only could Greek powers be created able to act with any sort of independence and self-respect in their relations with the new great powers outside. Accordingly there took place a revival of old local unions in districts where a community of interest between tribes or cities had in some form or other long been recognized. Such were the tribal League of Aetolia and the city League of Achaia. But these two were but notable instances of a federative movement much wider. The attempt to unite the scattered towns of Arcadia, with a federal centre at Megalopolis, seems to have been less successful. But the general aim of the movement towards federalism in Greece is clear. That it did not in the end save Greek freedom was due to two defects: it was too partial and too late. For no general union was achieved. Greek jealousy remained, and Leagues fought with Leagues in internal strife: then they were

[1] *Char* IV (XIV Jebb).   [2] See Plutarch *de garrulitate* 18.
[3] Plut *Aratus* 24, *Philopoemen* 8.

drawn into quarrels not their own, as allies of great foreign powers. It was no longer possible to remain neutral with safety. No League was strong enough to face the risk of compromising itself with a victorious great power. Achaean statesmen did their best, but they too could not save their country from ruin, once the League became entangled in the diplomacy of Rome. Nor was it the old Hellas alone that thus drifted to its doom. Between Rome and Carthage the western Greeks lost whatever power and freedom their own disunion and quarrels had left them. The Rhodian republic and its maritime League of islanders had to become the subject allies of Rome.

One point stands out clearly enough. In the Greece of the third century BC the question of food-supply was as pressing as it had ever been in the past. The operations of King Philip were often conditioned by the ease or difficulty of getting supplies[1] of corn for his troops: that is, he had to work on an insufficient margin of such resources. In 219, after driving the Dardani out of Macedonia, he had to dismiss his men[2] that they might get in their harvest. In 218, the success of his Peloponnesian campaign was largely dependent[3] on the supplies and booty captured in Elis, in Cephallenia, in Laconia; and on the subsidies of corn and money voted by his Achaean allies. The destruction of crops[4] was as of old a principal means of warfare. And when he had to meet the Roman invasion in 197, the race to secure what corn[5] was to be had was again a leading feature of the war. It is true that the feeding of armies was a difficulty elsewhere[6], as in Asia, and in all ages and countries: also that difficulties of transport were a considerable part of it. But the war-indemnities[7] fixed by treaties, including great quantities of corn, shew the extreme importance attached to this item. And the gifts of corn[8] to the Rhodian republic after the great earthquake (about 225 BC), and the leave granted them[9] in 169 by the Roman Senate to import a large quantity from Sicily, tell the same story. Another article in great demand, only to be got wholesale from certain countries, such as Macedonia, was timber. It was wanted for domestic purposes and for construction of military engines, which were greatly developed in the wars of the Successors; but above all for shipbuilding, commercial and naval. Rhodes in particular[10] needed a great supply; and the gifts of her friends in 224 BC were largely in the form of timber. There was no doubt a great demand for it at Alexandria, Syracuse, Corinth, and generally in seaport towns. It is evident that in strictly Greek lands the wood grown was chiefly of small size, suitable for fuel. There is

---

[1] Polyb IV 63.   [2] IV 66.   [3] IV 75, V I, 3, 19.   [4] X 42, etc.
[5] XVIII 20.   [6] XVI 24, XXI 6, etc.   [7] XXI 34, 36, 43, 45.
[8] V 89.   [9] XXVIII 2.   [10] V 89, cf XXV 4, XXI 6.

no sign of an advance on the conditions of an earlier time in the way of afforestation: nor indeed was such a policy likely.

But food had to be found somehow. Agriculture therefore had to go on. Outside the commercial centres, where food-stuffs could be imported by sea, there was no alternative: the population had to depend on the products of local tillage and pasturage. A few cities celebrated as art-centres might contrive to live by the sale of their works, but this hardly affects the general situation. We should there-fore very much like to know how things stood on the land. Was the tendency towards large landed estates, or was the small-farm system reviving? Was farm-labour chiefly that of freemen, or that of slaves? If of freemen, was it chiefly that of small owners, or that of wage-earners? In default of any authoritative statement, we have to draw what inferences we can from slight casual indications. That the career of Alexander was directly and indirectly the cause of great disturbances in Greek life, is certain. Of the ways in which it operated, two are of special importance. The compulsory restoration of exiles[1] whose properties had been confiscated led to claims for restitution; and in the matter of real estate the particular land in question was easily identified and made the subject of a bitter contest. Now un-certainty of tenure is notoriously a check on improvement, and the effect of the restorations was to make tenures uncertain. At the same time the prospects of professional soldiering in the East were a strong temptation to able-bodied husbandmen who were not very prosperous. From the rural parts of Greece a swarm of mercenaries went forth to join the host of Alexander, and the movement continued long. In the stead of one Alexander, there arose the rival Successor-kings, who competed in the military market for the intelligent Greeks. It was worth their while, and they paid well for a good article. So all through the third century there was a draining away of some of the best blood of Greece. Some of these men had no doubt parted with farms before setting out on the great venture. Of those who survived the wars, some settled down abroad as favoured citizens in some of the new cities founded by the kings. The few who returned to Greece with money saved did not come home to labour on a small farm: they settled in some city where they could see life and enjoy the ministrations of male and female slaves. Now it is not likely that all lands disposed of by these men were taken up by husbandmen exposed to the same temptations. Probably the greater part were bought up by the wealthier residents at home, and so went to increase large hold-ings.

How far do stray notices bear out this conclusion? At Athens in

---

[1] This topic is well treated by Mahaffy *Greek Life and Thought* chapter I.

322 BC a constitution was imposed by Antipater, deliberately framed
for the purpose of placing power in the hands of the richer classes.
He left 9000 citizens in possession of the full franchise, excluding
12000 poor. For the latter he offered to provide allotments of land in
Thrace. Accounts[1] vary, but it seems that some accepted the offer
and emigrated. It was not a compulsory deportation, but it was exile.
Economically it may have been a relief to Athens by reducing the
number of citizens who shared civic perquisites. But it had no tendency to bring more citizens back on to Attic land: such a move
would have implied displacement of present landholders, whom it was
Antipater's policy to conciliate. In the course of the third century
we get a glimpse of the agrarian situation at Sparta. It is clear that
the movement, already noted by Aristotle, towards land-monopoly[2]
in the hands of a few rich, had been steadily going on. It ended by
provoking a communistic reaction under the reforming kings Agis IV
and Cleomenes III. Blood was shed, and Sparta became a disorderly
state, the cause of many troubles in Greece down to the time of the
Roman conquest. The growing Achaean League, in the side of which
revolutionary Sparta was a thorn, was essentially a conservative
federation. However democratic its individual members might be,
the constitution of the League worked[3] very effectively in the interest
of the rich. On the occasion of the capture of Megalopolis by Cleomenes Polybius is at pains to warn his readers[4] against believing
stories of the immense booty taken there. Though the Peloponnese
had enjoyed a period of prosperity, still these stories are gross ex-
aggerations. Megalopolis, an important member of the League, had
been from the first laid out on too ambitious[5] a scale. That the 'Great
City' was a great desert, had found proverbial expression in a verse.
A little later, when Philip was campaigning in Peloponnesus, we hear
of the great prosperity[6] of Elis, especially in agriculture. The Eleans
had enjoyed a great advantage in the protection afforded them by
religion as guardians of Olympia. We may add that they were allied
with the Aetolian League, whose hostility other Greek states were
not forward to provoke. A class of wealthy resident landlords existed
in Elis, and much of the country was good farming land under tillage.

---

[1] The best treatment of this matter known to me is in Bernays' *Phokion* pp 78–85. See
Diodorus XVIII 18, Plutarch *Phoc* 28.

[2] According to Plut *Cleomenes* 18, Sparta was very helpless before that king's reforms.
The Aetolians in a raid carried off 50000 slaves, and an old Spartan declared that this was a
relief.

[3] Freeman's *Federal Government* chapter v.   [4] II 62.

[5] See Strabo VIII 8 § 1 p 388, and cf Plut *Philopoemen* 13.

[6] Polyb IV 73. Theocritus had spoken of ἱππήλατος Ἇλις (XXII 156). Keeping horses
was a mark of wealth.

But in most of the Achaean and Arcadian[1] districts pastoral industry, and therefore sparse population, was the rule, owing to the mountainous nature of those parts. In central Greece we need only refer to the restored Thebes, centre once more of a Boeotian confederacy. The fertile lowland of Boeotia supplied plenty of victual; and among Greek delicacies the eels of the lake Copais were famous. Boeotians were known as a well-nourished folk. In the fragments of the comic poet Eubulus[2] (assigned to the fourth century BC) we have them depicted as gluttonous, with some grossness of detail. Such being their tradition, I can see nothing strange in the picture[3] given of the Boeotians in his own day by **Polybius**. The ceaseless guzzling, the idleness and political corruption of the people, may be overdrawn. I admit that such qualities were not favourable to lasting prosperity; but their prosperity was not lasting. In the view of Polybius the subjection of Greece by the Romans was rather an effect than a cause of Greek degeneracy, and I dare not contradict him. Moreover a piece of confirmatory evidence relative to the third century BC occurs in a fragment of **Heraclides Ponticus**. In a traveller's description[4] of Greece Boeotia is thus referred to. Round Tanagra the land is not very rich in corn-crops, but stands at the head of Boeotian wine-production. The people are well-to-do, but live simply: they are all farmers ($\gamma\epsilon\omega\rho\gamma\omicron\acute{\iota}$), not labourers ($\grave{\epsilon}\rho\gamma\acute{a}\tau\alpha\iota$). At Anthedon on the coast the people are all fishermen ferrymen etc: they do not cultivate the land, indeed they have none. Of Thebes he remarks that the territory is good for horse-breeding, a green well-watered rolling country, with more gardens than any other Greek city owns. But, he adds, the people are violent undisciplined and quarrelsome. I think we may see here an earlier stage in the degeneracy that disgusted Polybius.

In all this there is nothing to suggest that small farming was common and prosperous during the Macedonian period in Greece. The natural inference is rather that agriculture in certain favoured districts was carried on by a limited number of large landowners on a large scale, pastoral industry varying locally according to circumstances. The development of urban life and luxury, and the agrarian troubles in the Peloponnese, are both characteristic phenomena of the age. In town and country alike the vital fact of civilization was the conflict of interests between rich and poor. Macedonia presents a contrast.

---

[1] Theocritus XXII 157 Ἀρκαδία τ' εὔμαλος Ἀχαιῶν τε πτολίεθρα. Polyb IX 17, and IV 3 (Messenia).

[2] Eubulus fragm 12, 34, 39, 53, 66, Kock. Also other references in Athenaeus X pp 417 foll.

[3] Polyb xx 6. Otherwise Mahaffy in *Gk Life and Thought* chapter XIII.

[4] *FHG* II pp 254–64, formerly attributed to Dicaearchus. Cited by E Meyer *Kleine Schriften* p 137.

There no great cities drew the people away from the country. A hardy and numerous population supplied the material for national armies whenever needed, and loyalty to the reigning king gave unity to national action. Hence the long domination of Macedon in Greece; the only serious opposition being that of the Aetolian League. Of all the Successor-kingdoms, Macedon alone was able to make any stand against the advance of Rome.

It remains to consider the few indications—I can hardly call them references—from which we can get a little light on the labour-question. The passages cited from Theophrastus and Theocritus point to the prevalence of slave-labour. And the same may be said of **Polybius**. In speaking[1] of the blunder in exaggerating the value of the booty taken at Megalopolis, he says 'Why, even in these more peaceful and prosperous days you could not raise so great a sum of money in all the Peloponnese out of the mere movables (ἐπίπλων) unless you took slaves into account (χωρὶς σωμάτων).' His word for live-stock not human is θρέμματα. Evidently to him slave-property is a large item in the value of estates. Again, speaking of the importance of Byzantium[2] on the Pontic trade-route, he insists on the plentiful and useful supply of bestial and human stock to Greece by this traffic. The high farming of rural Elis[3] is shewn in its being full of σώματα and farm-stock (κατασκευῆς). Hence these 'bodies' formed a considerable part of the booty taken there by Philip. And in the claims[4] made at Rome in 183 BC against Philip a part related to slave-property. References to the sale of prisoners of war, to piracy and kidnapping, are frequent: but they only concern us as indicating time-honoured means of supplying the slave-market. As for rowing ships, so for heavy farm-work, able-bodied men were wanted. At a pinch such slaves could be, and were, employed in war[5], with grant or promise of manumission: but this was a step only taken in the last resort. A curious remark[6] of **Polybius** when speaking of Arcadia must not be overlooked. In 220 BC an Aetolian force invaded Achaia and penetrated into northern Arcadia, where they took the border town of Cynaetha, and after wholesale massacre and pillage burnt it on their retreat. The city had for years suffered terribly from internal strife, in which the doings of restored exiles had played a great part. Polybius says that the Cynaethans were thought to have deserved the disaster that had now fallen upon them. Why? Because of their savagery (ἀγριότητος). They were Arcadians. The Arcadians as a race-unit (ἔθνος) enjoy a

---

[1] II 62.　　　　[2] IV 38.　　　　[3] IV 73, 75.　　　　[4] XXIII I § 11.

[5] In the famous case of the siege of Rhodes in 305-4 BC (Diodorus XX 84, 100) freedom seems to have been a *reward*, as has been pointed out by A Croiset.

[6] IV 20, 21. Compare Vergil *Buc* X 32-3 *soli cantare periti Arcades*, VII 4-5.

reputation for virtue throughout Greece, as a kindly hospitable and religious folk. But the Cynaethans outdid all Greeks in cruelty and lawlessness. This is to be traced to their neglect of the time-honoured Arcadian tradition, the general practice of vocal and instrumental music. This practice was deliberately adopted as a refining agency, to relieve and temper the roughness and harshness incidental to men living toilsome lives in an inclement climate. Such was the design of the old Arcadians, on consideration of the circumstances, one point in which was that their people generally worked in person (τὴν ἑκάστων αὐτουργίαν). On this I need only remark that he is referring to the past, but may or may not include the Arcadians of his own day: and repeat what I have said before, that to be αὐτουργὸς does not exclude employment of slaves as well. That there was still more personal labour in rural Arcadia than in many other parts of Greece, is probable. But that is all.

That the slavery-question was a matter of some interest in Greece may be inferred from the pains taken by **Polybius**[1] to refute an assertion of **Timaeus**, that to acquire slaves was not a Greek custom. The context is lost, and we cannot tell whether it was a general assertion or not. If general, it was no doubt nonsense. A more effective piece of evidence is the report[2] of **Megasthenes**, who visited India early in the third century. He told his Greek readers that in India slavery was unknown. The contrast to Greece was of course the interesting point. It is also affirmed[3] that in this period manumissions became more common, as a result of the economic decline of Greece combined with the moral evolution to be traced in the philosophic schools. Calderini, from whom I take this, is the leading authority on Greek manumission. And, so far as the records are concerned, the number of inscribed 'acts' recovered from the important centre of Delphi[4] confirms the assertion. From 201 to 140 BC these documents are exceptionally numerous. But the not unfrequent stipulation found in them, that the freed man or woman shall remain in attendance[5] on his or her late owner for the owner's life or for some fixed period, or shall continue to practise a trade (or even learn a trade) on the profits of which the late owner or his heirs shall have a claim, suggest strongly that these manumissions were the rewards of domestic service or technical skill. I do not believe that they have any connexion with rustic[6] slavery.

---

[1] In a fragment cited by Athenaeus p 272 *a*, cf 264 *c*. In Hultsch's text Polyb XII 6.

[2] Cited by Diodorus II 39, and by Arrian *Indica* 10 §§ 8, 9.

[3] Calderini *la manomissione* etc chapter V.

[4] See table in Collitz *Dialectinschriften* II pp 635–42.

[5] παραμονά, παραμένειν.

[6] In 432 acts of manumission given in Wescher and Foucart *Inscriptions de Delphes* 1863, I could not find one case of a rustic slave.

Calderini also holds that as Greek industries and commerce declined
free labour competed more and more with slave-labour. So far as
urban trades are concerned, this is probably true : and likewise a certain decline in domestic slavery due to the straitened circumstances
of families and experience of the waste and nuisance of large slave-
households. This last point, already noticed[1] e.g. by Aristotle, is to be
found expressed in utterances of the comic poets. Rustic slavery
appears in the fragments of Menander's Γεωργός, but the old farmer's
slaves are Barbarians, who will do nothing to help him when acci-
dentally hurt, and who are hardly likely to receive favours. The
ordinary view of agriculture in Menander's time seems most truly expressed in his saying[2] that it is a slave's business.

Mention of the comic poets may remind us that most of the surviving matter of the later Comedy has reached us in the Latin versions
and adaptations of **Plautus** and **Terence**. It is necessary to speak of
their evidence separately, in particular where slavery is in question,
for the relative passages are liable to be touched with Roman colouring.
In the case of manumission this is especially clear, but to pursue the
topic in detail is beyond my present purpose. The passages of **Plautus**
bearing on rustic life are not many, but the picture so far as it goes is
clear and consistent. In general the master is represented as a man of
means with a house in town and a country estate outside. The latter
is worked by slaves under a slave-bailiff or steward (*vilicus*). The
town-house is staffed by slaves, but the headman is less absolute than
the steward on the farm : departmental chiefs, such as the cook, are
important parts of the household. This is natural enough, for the
master generally resides there himself, and only pays occasional[3] visits
to the farm. The two sets of slaves are kept apart. If the steward[4] or
some other trusted farm-slave has to come to town, he is practically a
stranger, and a quarrel is apt to arise with leading domestics : for his
rustic appearance and manners are despised by the pampered menials.
But he is aware that his turn may come: some day the master in
wrath may consign the offending town-slave to farm-labour, and
then—. Apart from slavery, rustic life is regarded[5] as favourable to
good morals : honest labour, frugal habits, freedom from urban temptations, commend it to fathers who desire to preserve their sons from
corrupting debauchery. In short, the urban moralist idealizes the farm.
Whether he would by choice reside there, is quite another thing. Clearly
the average young citizen would not. That the farm is occasionally used[6]

---

[1] Ar *Pol* II 3 § 4, cf saying of Diogenes in Stob *flor* LXII 47. Menander fragm 760 K
εἶς ἐστι δοῦλος οἰκίας ὁ δεσπότης.

[2] See above, chapter XIII p 64.   [3] So Jove *Poenulus* 944-5.

[4] *Casina* 97 foll, *Poenulus* 170-1, *Mostellaria* 1-83.

[5] *Mercator* 65 foll.   [6] *Mercator passim.*

as a retreat, is no more than a point of dramatic convenience. In one passage[1] we have a picture of a small farm, with slave-labour employed on it. Freemen as agricultural labourers hardly appear at all. But a significant dialogue[2] between an old freeman and a young one runs thus: 'Country life is a life of toil.' 'Aye, but city indigence is far more so.' The youth, who has offered to do farm-work, is representative of that class of urban poor, whose lot was doubtless a very miserable one. Very seldom do we hear anything of them, for our records in general only take account of the master and the slave. In the play just referred to[3] there occur certain terms more or less technical. The neutral *operarius* seems equivalent to ἐργάτης, and *mercennarius* to μισθωτός, distinct from[4] *servus*. But these terms are not specially connected with agriculture.

The references in **Terence** give us the same picture. An old man of 60 or more is blamed[5] by a friend. 'You have a first-rate farm and a number of slaves: why will you persist in working yourself to make up for their laziness? Your labour would be better spent in keeping them to their tasks.' The old man explains[6] that he is punishing himself for his treatment of his only son. In order to detach the youth from an undesirable amour, he had used the stock reproaches of fathers to erring sons. He had said 'At your time of life I wasn't hanging about a mistress: I went soldiering in Asia for a living, and there I won both money and glory.' At length the young man could stand it no longer: he went off to Asia and entered the service of one of the kings. The old man cannot forgive himself, and is now busy tormenting himself for his conduct. He has sold off[7] all his slaves, male or female, save those whose labour on the farm pays for its cost, and is wearing himself out as a mere farm hand. Another[8] old farmer, a man of small means who makes his living by farming, is evidently not the owner but a tenant. Another[9] has gone to reside on his farm, to make it pay; otherwise the expenses at home cannot be met. In general country life is held up as a model[10] of frugality and industry. In one passage[11] we hear of a hired wage-earner employed on a farm (*a villa mercennarium*) whom I take to be a free man, probably employed for some special service. Such are the gleanings to be got from these Roman echoes of the later Attic comedy. I see no reason to believe that they are modified by intrusion of details drawn from Italy. The period in which Plautus and Terence wrote (about 230–160 BC)

[1] *Trinummus* 508–61.
[2] *Vidularia* 31–2.
[3] *Vidularia* 21–55, text is fragmentary.
[4] But not excluding it, since slaves were hired.
[5] *Hautontimorumenos* 62–74.
[6] *Hautont* 93–117.
[7] *Hautont* 142–4.
[8] *Phormio* 362–5, cf *Adelphoe* 949.
[9] *Hecyra* 224–6.
[10] *Adelphoe* 45–6, cf 95, 401, 517–20, 845–9.
[11] *Adelphoe* 541–2.

included many changes in Roman life, particularly in agriculture. In large parts of Italy the peasant farmers were being superseded by great landlords whose estates were worked by slave-labour, and the conditions of farm life as shewn by the Attic playwrights were not so strange to a Roman audience as to need recasting. And we can only remark that the evidence drawn from the passages above referred to is in full agreement with that taken from other sources.

A very interesting sidelight on conditions in Greece, agriculture included, towards the end of the third century BC, is thrown by the correspondence[1] of **Philip V of Macedon** with the authorities of Larisa. An inscription found at Larisa preserves this important record. Two points must first be noted, to give the historical setting of the whole affair. Thessaly was under Macedonian overlordship, and its economic and military strength a matter of concern to Philip, who had succeeded to the throne of Macedon in 220 BC. Moreover, the defeat of Carthage in the first Punic war (264–41), the Roman occupation of the greater part of Sicily and Sardinia, the Gallic wars and extension of Roman dominion in Italy, the Illyrian war (230–29) and intervention of Rome beyond the Adriatic, had attracted the attention of all the Greek powers. The western Republic had for some years been carefully watched, and the admission of Corcyra Epidamnus and Apollonia to the Roman alliance was especially disquieting to the Macedonian king. So in 219 BC, just before the second Punic war, Philip sent a **letter to Larisa**, pointing out that the number of their citizens had been reduced by losses in recent wars and urging them to include in their franchise the Thessalians and other Greeks resident in the city. Among other advantages, the country[2] would be more fully cultivated. The Larisaeans obeyed his injunctions. In 217 the war in Greece was ended by his concluding peace with the Aetolians, his chief antagonists. Hannibal was now in Italy, and the victory of Cannae in 216 raised hopes in Philip of using the disasters of the Romans to drive them out of Illyria. In 215 he concluded an alliance with Hannibal. The Romans replied by naval activity in the Adriatic and later by stirring up Greek powers, above all the Aetolians, to renew the war against him. Meanwhile things had not gone on quietly at Larisa. The old Thessalian noble families had given way to the king's pressure unwillingly for the moment, but internal troubles soon broke out. The nobles regained control and annulled the recent concessions. Philip therefore addressed to them a **second letter** in 214, censuring their conduct, and calling upon them to give effect to the enfranchisement-policy previously agreed to. Thus they would not only conform to his

---

[1] Collitz I No. 345, Dittenberger 238–9. Mommsen's notes in Hermes XVII.
[2] καὶ τὴν χώραν μᾶλλον ἐξεργασθήσεσθαι.

decision as their overlord, but would best serve their own interests. Their city would gain strength by increasing the number of citizens, and they would not have their territory disgracefully[1] lying waste (καὶ τὴν χώραν μὴ ὥσπερ νῦν αἰσχρῶς χερσεύεσθαι). He went on to refer to the advantageous results of such incorporations elsewhere: citing in particular the experience of Rome, whose growth and colonial expansion were the fruits of a franchise-policy so generous as to grant citizenship even to manumitted slaves. He called upon the Larisaeans to face the question without aristocratic prejudice (ἀφιλοτίμως). And the Larisaeans again complied.

Now here we have a glimpse of agricultural decline in one of the most fertile parts of Greece. The stress laid upon it by Philip shews that to him it seemed a very serious matter. He saw trouble coming, and wished to keep his dependent allies strong. That his difficulty lay in controlling the aristocratic families, who still retained much of their former power, is clear. After his defeat in 197 the Romans restored[2] the aristocratic governments in Thessalian cities; indeed all through the wars of this period in Greece the popular parties inclined to Macedon, while the propertied classes favoured Rome. In Thessaly the private estates of the nobles were cultivated by serfs. How would an incorporation of more citizens tend to promote a fuller cultivation of the land? I think we may take it for granted that the new citizens were not expected to till the soil in person. That they were to have unemployed serfs assigned to them, and so to enter the ranks of cultivating landlords, is a bold assumption: for we do not know that there were any unemployed serfs or that any distribution of land was contemplated. I can only suggest that the effect of receiving citizenship would be to acquire the right of holding real estate. Then, if we suppose that there were at the time landed estates left vacant by the war-casualties to which the king refers, and that each of these carried with it a right to a certain supply of serf labour, we do get some sort of answer to the question. But so far as I know this is nothing but guesswork. More owners interested in the profits of farming would tend, if labour were available, to employ more labour on the farms. In short, we have evidence of the decay of agriculture in a particular district and period, but as to the exact causes of this decay, and the exact nature of the means proposed for checking it, we are sadly in the dark.

The garden or orchard had always been a favourite institution in

---

[1] That this neglect was not a new thing seems shewn by the saying of Alexander that the Thessalians deserved no consideration, ὅτι τὴν ἀρίστην κεκτημένοι οὐ γεωργοῦσι. Plut apophth Alex 22.

[2] Livy XXXIV 51 §§ 4–6.

Greek life, and the growth of cities did not make it less popular. The land immediately beyond the city walls was often laid out in this manner. When Aratus in 251 BC took Sicyon and attached it to the Achaean League, the surprise was effected by way of a suburban[1] garden. And we have no reason to suppose that holdings near a city lacked cultivators. Even in the horrible period of confusion and bloodshed at Syracuse, from the death of Dionysius the elder to the victory of Timoleon, we hear[2] of Syracusans living in the country, and of the usual clamour for redistribution of lands. In the endeavour to repopulate the city an invitation to settlers was issued, with offer[3] of land-allotments, and apparently the promise was kept. These notices suggest that there was a demand for surburban holdings, but tell us nothing as to the state of things in the districts further afield, or as to the class of labour employed on the land. In any case Syracuse was a sea-port, and accustomed to get a good part of its supplies by sea. Very different was the situation in Peloponnesus, where the up-country towns had to depend chiefly on the produce of their own territories. There land-hunger was ever present. The estates of men driven out in civil broils were seized by the victorious party, and restoration of exiles at once led to a fresh conflict over claims to restitution of estates. One of the most difficult problems[4] with which Aratus had to deal at Sicyon was this ; and in the end he only solved it by the use of a large sum of money, the gift of Ptolemy Philadelphus. The restored exiles on this occasion are said to have been not less than 580 in all. They had been expelled by tyrants who had in recent years ruled the city, and whose policy it had evidently been to drive out the men of property— sworn foes of tyrants—and to reward their own adherents out of confiscated lands. To reverse this policy was the lifelong aim of Aratus. In the generation following, the life of his successor Philopoemen gives us a little light on agriculture from another point of view, that of the soldier. He was resolved to make the army of the Achaean League an efficient force. As a young man he concluded[5] that the Greek athletic training was not consistent with military life, in which the endurance of hardship and ability to subsist on any diet were primary necessities. Therefore he devoted his spare time to agriculture, working[6] in person on his farm, about 2½ miles from Megalopolis, sharing the labour and habits of the labourers (ἐργατῶν). The use of the neutral word leaves a doubt as to whether freemen or slaves are meant: taken in connexion with the passages cited from Polybius, it is perhaps more likely that the reference is to slaves. But the chief interest of the story as pre-

---

[1] Plutarch *Aratus* 5–8.   [2] Plut *Dion* 27, 37, 48.
[3] Plut *Timoleon* 23, 36.   [4] Plut *Aratus* 9, 12, 14.
[5] Plut *Philopoemen* 3, 4.   [6] In fact became an αὐτουργός.

served by **Plutarch** lies in the discovery that, compared with athletes, husbandmen are better military material.

The conclusions of Beloch[1] as to the population of Peloponnesus in this period call for serious consideration. His opinion is that the number capable of bearing arms declined somewhat since the middle of the fourth century, though the wholesale emancipation of Spartan Helots must be reckoned as an addition. But on the whole the free population was at the beginning of the second century about equal to the joint total of free and Helot population at the end of the fifth century. On the other hand, the slave population had in the interval greatly increased. He points to the importance of a slave corps[2] in the defence of Megalopolis when besieged in 318 BC: to the Roman and Italian[3] slaves (prisoners sold by Hannibal) in Achaean territory, found and released in 194 BC, some 1200 in number: and to the levy[4] of manumitted home-born slaves in the last struggle of the League against Rome. I must say that this evidence, taken by itself, hardly seems enough to sustain the great historian's broad conclusion. But many of the passages cited in preceding sections lend it support, and I am therefore not disposed to challenge its general probability. It may be added that increase in the number of slaves suggests an increase of large holdings cultivated by slave labour; and that the breeding of home-born (οἰκογενεῖς) slaves could be more easily practised by owners of a large staff than on a small scale. Moreover the loss of slaves levied for war purposes would fall chiefly on their wealthy owners. The men of property were rightly or wrongly suspected of leaning to Rome, and were not likely to be spared by the demagogues who presided over the last frantic efforts of 'freedom' in Greece. The truth seems to be that circumstances were more and more unfavourable to the existence of free husbandmen on small farms, the very class of whose solid merits statesmen and philosophers had shewn warm appreciation. The division between the Rich, who wanted to keep what they had and get more, and the Poor, who wanted to take the property of the Rich, was the one ever-significant fact. And the establishment of Roman supremacy settled the question for centuries to come. Roman capitalism, hastening to exploit the world for its own ends, had no mercy for the small independent worker in any department of life. In Greece under the sway of Rome there is no doubt that free population declined, and the state of agriculture went from bad to worse.

At this point, when the Greek world passes under the sway of Rome, it is necessary to pause and turn back to consider the fragmentary

[1] *Bevölkerung der Griechisch-Römischen Welt* pp 156–8.
[2] Diodorus XVIII 70 § 1.   [3] Livy XXXIV 50, Plut *Flamininus* 13.
[4] Polyb XXXIX 8 §§ 1–5.

record of early Italian agriculture. This one great staple industry is represented as the economic foundation of Roman political and military greatness. No small part of the surviving Latin literature glorifies the soundness of the Roman farmer-folk and the exploits of farmer-heroes in the good old days, and laments the rottenness that attended their decay. How far this tradition is to be accepted as it stands, or what reservations on its acceptance should be made, and in particular the introduction or extension of slave-labour, are the questions with which it will be our main business to deal.

ROME—EARLY PERIOD

XX. THE TRADITIONS COMBINED AND DISCUSSED.

When we turn to Roman agriculture, and agricultural labour in particular, we have to deal with evidence very different in character from that presented by the Greek world. This will be most clearly seen if we accept the very reasonable division of periods made by Wallon in his *History of Slavery*—the first down to 201 BC, the end of the second Punic war, the second to the age of the Antonine emperors, 200 BC to the death of Marcus Aurelius in 180 AD, and the third that of the later Empire. For of the first we have no contemporary or nearly contemporary pictures surviving. Traditions preserved by later writers, notes of antiquaries on words and customs long obscured by time and change, are the staple material at hand. Even with the help of a few survivals in law, inference from such material is unavoidably timid and incomplete. In collecting what the later Romans believed of their past we get vivid impressions of the opinions and prejudices that went to form the Roman spirit. But it does not follow that we can rely on these opinions as solid evidence of facts. An instance may be found in the assertion[1] that a clause requiring the employment of a certain proportion of free labourers to slaves was included in the Licinian laws of 367 BC. This used to be taken as a fact, and inferences were drawn from it, but it is now with reason regarded as an 'anticipation,' transferring the fact of a later attempt of the kind to an age in which the slave-gangs were not as yet an evident economic and social danger. In the second period, that of Roman greatness, we have not only contemporary witness for much of the time in the form of references and allusions in literature, but the works of the great writers on agriculture, Cato Varro and Columella, not to mention the great compiler Pliny, fall within it, and give us on the whole a picture exceptionally complete. We know more of the farm-management and labour-conditions in this period than we do of most matters of antiquity. The last period sees the development of a change the germs of which are no doubt to be detected in the preceding one. The great strain on the Empire, owing to the internal decay and the growing pressure of financial necessities, made the change inevitable ; economic freedom and proprietary slavery died down, and we have before us the transition to predial serfdom, the system of the unfree tenant bound to the soil. The record of this change is chiefly preserved in the later Roman Law.

[1] Only in Appian *civ* I 8 § 2. The provision is ascribed by Suet *Jul* 42 to Julius Caesar. The two writers were contemporary. Whence did Appian get his story?

My first business is therefore to inquire what the tradition of early times amounts to, and how far it may reasonably be taken as evidence of fact. And it must be borne in mind that my subject is not the technical details of agriculture in general, but the nature of the labour employed in agriculture. In ages when voluntary peace between empires and peoples on *bona fide* equal terms was never a realized fact, and as yet hardly a dream, the stability of a state depended on the strength of its military forces,—their number, efficiency, and means of renewal. Mere numbers[1] were tried and failed. The hire of professional soldiers of fortune[2] might furnish technical skill, but it was politically dangerous. Their leaders had no personal sentiment in favour of the state employing them, and their interest or ambition disposed them rather to support a tyrant, or to become tyrants themselves, than to act as loyal defenders of the freedom of the state. Mercenaries[3] hired in the mass, barbarians, were less skilled but not less dangerous. That a well-trained army of citizens was the most trustworthy organ of state-protection, was not disputed: the combination of loyalty with skill made it a most efficient weapon. The ratio of citizen enthusiasm to the confidence created by exact discipline varied greatly in the Greek republics of the fifth century BC. But these two elements were normally present, though in various proportions. The common defect, most serious in those states that played an active part, was the smallness of scale that made it difficult to keep up the strength of citizen armies exposed to the wastage of war. A single great disaster might and did turn a struggle for empire into a desperate fight for existence. The constrained transition to employment of mercenary troops as the principal armed force of states was both a symptom and a further cause of decay in the Greek republics. For the sturdy soldiers of fortune were generally drawn from the rustic population of districts in which agriculture filled a more important place than political life. There is little doubt that a decline of food-production in Greece was the result: and scarcity of food had long been a persistent difficulty underlying and explaining most of the doings of the Greeks. The rise of Macedon and the conquests of Alexander proved the military value of a national army of trained rustics, and reasserted the superiority of such troops to the armed multitudes of the East. But Alexander's career did not leave the world at peace. His empire broke up in a period of dynastic wars; for to supply an imperial army strong enough to support a single control and guarantee internal peace was beyond the resources of Macedonia.

If an army of considerable strength, easily maintained and recruited, loyal, the servant of the state and not its master, was necessary for

---

[1] Case of Persia.　　　[2] Cases of Messana, Syracuse, etc.　　　[3] Case of Carthage.

defence and as an instrument of foreign politics, there was room for a
better solution of the problem than had been found in Greece or the
East. It was found in Italy on the following lines. An increase of
scale could only be attained by growth. Growth, to be effective, must
not consist in mere conquest: it must be true expansion, in other words
it must imply permanent occupation. And permanent occupation
implied settlement of the conquering people on the conquered lands.
A growing population of rustic citizens, self-supporting, bound by ties
of sentiment and interest to the state of which they were citizens, conscious of a duty to uphold the state to which they owed their homesteads
and their security, supplied automatically in response to growing needs
the growing raw material of power. Nor was Roman expansion confined
to the assignation of land-allotments to individuals (*viritim*). Old
towns were remodelled, and new ones founded, under various conditions
as settlements (*coloniae*). Each settler in one of these towns received
an allotment of land in the territory of the township, and was officially
speaking a tiller of the soil (*colonus*). The effect of these Colonies was
twofold. Their territories added to the sum of land in occupation of
Romans or Roman Allies: so far the gain was chiefly material. But
they were all bound to Rome and subjected to Roman influences. In
their turn they influenced the conquered peoples among whom they
were planted, and promoted slowly and steadily the Romanizing of
Italy. Being fortified, they had a military value from the first, as
commanding roads and as bases of campaigns. But their moral effect
in accustoming Italians to regard Rome as the controlling centre of
Italy was perhaps of even greater importance.

We must not ignore or underrate the advantages of Rome's position
from a commercial point of view. Little though we hear of this in
tradition, it can hardly be doubted that it gave Rome a marked superiority in resources to her less happily situated neighbours, and enabled
her to take the first great step forward by becoming dominant in central
Italy. But the consolidation and completion of her conquest of the
peninsula was carried out by means of an extended Roman agriculture.
It was this that gave to Roman expansion the solid character that
distinguished republican Rome from other conquering powers. What
she took, that she could keep. When the traditional story of early
Rome depicts the Roman commons as hungry for land, and annexation
of territory as the normal result of conquest, it is undoubtedly worthy
of belief. When it shews us the devastation of their enemies' lands as
a chief part—sometimes the whole—of the work of a campaign, it is in
full agreement with the traditions of all ancient warfare. When we
read[1] that the ruin of farms by raids of the enemy brought suffering

---

[1] Livy II 23 etc.

farmers into debt, and that the cruel operation of debt-laws led to serious internal troubles in the Roman state, the story is credible enough. , The superior organization of Rome enabled her to overcome these troubles, not only by compromises and concessions at home, but still more by establishing her poorer citizens on farms at the cost of her neighbours. As the area under her control was extended, the military force automatically grew, and she surpassed her rivals in the cohesion and vitality of her power. At need, her armies rose from the soil. So did those of other Italian peoples. But in dealing with them she enjoyed the advantage of unity as compared with the far less effective cooperation of Samnite cantons or Etruscan cities. Even the capture of Rome by the Gauls could not destroy her system, and she was able to strengthen her moral position by proving herself the one competent defender of Italy against invasion from the North. When the time came for the struggle with Carthage, she had to face a different test. But no blundering on the part of her generals, no strategy of Hannibal, could avail to nullify the solid superiority of her military strength. And this strength was in the last resort derived from the numbers and loyalty of the farm-population: it was in fact the product of the plough rather than the sword.

The agricultural conditions of early Rome[1] are a subject, and have been the subject, of special treatises. Only a few points can be noticed here. That a communal system of some kind once existed, whether in the form of the associations known to inquirers as Village Communities or on a gentile basis as Clan-estates, is a probable hypothesis. But the evidence for it is slight, and, however just the general inferences may be, they can hardly be said to help us much in considering the labour-question. It may well be true that lands[2] were held by clans, that they were cultivated in common, that the produce was divided among the households, that parcels of the land were granted to the dependants (*clientes*) of the clan as tenants at will (*precario*) on condition of paying a share of their crops. Or it may be that the normal unit was a village in which the members were several freeholders of small plots, with common rights over the undivided common-land, the waste left free for grazing and miscellaneous uses. And it is possible that at some stage or other of social development both these systems may have existed side by side. In later times we find Rome the mistress of a vast territory in Italy, a large part of which was reserved as state-domain (*ager publicus populi Romani*), the mismanagement of which was a source of

---

[1] Referred to in Iwan Müller's *Handbuch* IV ii 2, ed 3 pp 533 foll, article by H Blümner.

[2] That the household as a vigorous unit outlived the *gens* is I think clear. I guess that this was because production for the supply of life-needs was more closely correlated with the former. Labour was more easily divorced from the clan-system than property was.

grave evils. But in Rome's early days there cannot have been any great amount of such domain-land. That there was land-hunger, a demand for several allotments in full ownership, on which a family might live, is not to be doubted. And the formation of communities, each with its village centre and its common pasture, was a very natural means to promote mutual help and protection. That men so situated worked with their own hands, and that the labour was mainly (and often wholly) that of the father and his family, is as nearly certain as such a proposition can be. But this does not imply or suggest that no slave-labour was employed on the farms. It merely means that farms were not worked on a system in which all manual labour was performed by slaves. We have to inquire what is the traditional picture of agricultural conditions in the early days of Rome, and how far that picture is worthy of our belief.

Now it so happens that three striking figures stand out in the traditional picture of the Roman farmer-soldiers of the early Republic. Others fill in certain details, but the names of Lucius Quinctius Cincinnatus, Manius Curius Dentatus, and Gaius Fabricius Luscinus, were especially notable in Roman legend as representing the strenuous patriotic and frugal lives of the heroes of old. The story of Cincinnatus[1] is told by Cicero Livy Dionysius and Pliny the elder, and often referred to by other writers. The hero is a Patrician of the old simple frugal patriotic masterful type, the admiration and imitation of which these edifying legends seek to encourage. He had owned seven *iugera* of land, but had been driven to pledge or sell three of these[2] in order to provide bail for his son, who had been brought to trial for disturbance of the public peace and had sought safety in flight. The forfeit imposed on the father left him with only four *iugera*. This little farm, on the further side of the Tiber, he was cultivating, when deputies from the Senate came to announce that he had been named Dictator to deal with a great emergency. They found him digging or ploughing, covered with dust and sweat: and he would not receive them till he had washed and gowned himself. Then he heard their message, took up the duties of the supreme office, and of course saved the state. It is to be noted that he chose as his Master of the Horse (the Dictator's understudy) a man of the same[3] sort, Patrician by birth, poor, but a stout warrior. We may fairly suspect that a definite moral purpose has been at work, modelling and colouring this pretty story. In a later age, when the power of moneyed interests was overriding the prestige of Patrician blood, the reaction of an 'old-Roman' party was long a vigorous force

---

[1] Cic *Cato mai* § 56, Liv III 26, Dionys x 8, 17, Plin *NH* XVIII 20, Valer Max IV 7. The discrepancies in the versions do not concern us here.

[2] Liv III 13 §§ 8–10, Dionys x 8.   [3] Liv III 27 § 1.

in Roman life, as we see from the career of the elder Cato. Cato was a Plebeian, but any Plebeian who admired the simple ways of early Rome was bound to recognize that Patricians were the nobility of the olden time.

Now the fact of Cincinnatus working with his own hands is the one material point in the story. We need not doubt that there were many such men, and that a name (perhaps correct) was necessary in order to keep the story current and to impress later generations with the virtues of their ancestors. But, if the man had under him a slave or slaves, the fact would be quite unimportant for the purpose of the legend. Therefore it is no wonder that the versions of the story in general say nothing of slaves. It is more remarkable that in the version of Dionysius we read that Cincinnatus, after selling off most of his property to meet the liabilities incurred through his son, 'kept for himself one small farm beyond the Tiber, on which there was a mean cabin: there he was living a life of toil and hardship, tilling the soil with a few slaves.' That Dionysius was a rhetorician with an eye for picturesque detail, and liable to overdraw a picture, is certain: but it is not evident how the mention of the slaves is to be accounted for by this tendency. The impression of the hero's poverty and personal labour is rather weakened by mention of slaves. The writer derived his story from Roman sources. Now, did the original version include the slaves or not? Did Livy and the rest leave them out, or did Dionysius put them in? Were they omitted as useless or embarrassing for the uses of edifying, or were they casually inserted owing to the prepossessions of a Greek familiar only with a developed slave-system, to whom 'with a few slaves' would fitly connote poverty? To answer these questions with confidence is perhaps unwise. But to me it seems far more likely that Roman writers left the detail out than that a Greek student put it in.

If the tradition of the early wars is of any value at all, it may give a general support to this opinion through the frequent references to the existence of rustic slavery. The devastation of an enemy's country is the normal occupation of hostile armies. The capture of slaves[1], as of flocks and herds and beasts of burden, is a common item in the tale of booty from the farms. That writers of a later age may have exaggerated the slave-element in the farm-labour of early times is highly probable. The picturesque was an object, and it was natural to attempt it with the use of touches suggested by daily circumstances of the world in which they were living. But that they so completely misrepresented the conditions of a past age as to foist into the picture so important a figure as the slave, without authority or probability, is hardly to be believed, unless there is good reason for thinking that

[1] Liv x 36 § 17, Dionys VI 3, etc.

slavery was unknown in the age and country of which they speak. And the contrary is the case. The dawn of Roman history shews us a people already advanced in civilization to the stage of family and clan organization, and the tradition allows for the presence of the slave in the *familia* from the first. True, he does not appear as the despised human chattel of later times, but as a man whom misfortune has placed in bondage. His master is aware that fortune may turn, and that his bondman is quite capable of resuming his former position if restored in freedom to his native home. The slave seems to be normally an Italian[1], a captive in some war; he may have passed by sale from one owner to another. But he is not a mere foreign animal, good bad or indifferent, a doubtful purchase from a roguish dealer. He bears a name[2] that connects him with his master, *Publipor Lucipor Marcipor Olipor* and so on, formed by adding the suffix *por* to the forename of Publius Lucius Marcus or Aulus. But, granting that all households might include a slave or two, and that many so did, also that agriculture was a common and honourable pursuit,—is it likely that a farming owner would himself plough or dig and leave his slave[3] to look on? I conclude therefore that the age was one in which agriculture prevailed and that the ordinary farmer worked himself and employed slave-labour side by side with his own so far as his means allowed. All was on a small scale. Passages of Livy or Dionysius that imply the presence of great slave-gangs, and desertions on a large scale in time of war are falsely coloured by 'anticipation' of phenomena well known from the experience of more recent times. But, on however small a scale, slavery was there. Until there came an impulse of an 'industrial' kind, prompting men to engage in wholesale production for a large market, the slave remained essentially a domestic, bearing a considerable share of the family labours, whatever the nature of those labours might be.

As there is no difficulty in believing that Cincinnatus and others of his type in the fifth century BC worked with slaves beside them, so it is evident that Curius and Fabricius in the first half of the third century are meant to illustrate the same frugal life and solid patriotism. In both cases the story lays particular stress on the hero's incorruptibility and cheerful endurance of poverty. A well-known scene[4] represents Curius at his rustic villa eating a dinner of herbs and refusing a gift of gold from Samnite ambassadors. He is an honest farmer-citizen of the good old sort. Fabricius is another, famed especially for his calm

---

[1] Liv II 22 §§ 5–7.

[2] Varro *sat Men* fr 59 and title of his satire *Marcipor*. Quintilian I 4 § 26, Festus p 306 L = 257 M *Marcipor Oppii* in title of Plaut *Stichus*. Sallust *hist* fr III 99 Maurenbrecher. Inscriptions CIL I 1076, 1034, 1386, Dessau 7822–3. For Pliny see below.

[3] Argument as in Luke's gospel 17 §§ 7–9.

[4] Cic *Cato mai* §§ 55–6, etc.

defiance of the threats and cajolery of Pyrrhus, and impervious to bribes. Both these traditions received much legendary colouring in course of time. The passage bearing most directly on my present inquiry is a fragment[1] of Dionysius, in which Fabricius is spurning the offers of king Pyrrhus, who is very anxious to secure the good man's services as his chief minister on liberal terms. He says 'nor need I tell you of my poverty, that I have but a very small plot of land with a mean cottage, and that I get my living neither from money at interest (ἀπὸ δανεισμάτων) nor from slaves (ἀπ' ἀνδραπόδων).' Below he declares that living under Roman conditions he holds himself a happy man, 'for with industry and thrift I find my poor little farm sufficient to provide me with necessaries.' And his constitution (φύσις) does not constrain him to hanker after unnecessary things. Here we have a good specimen of the moral stories with which the later rhetoricians edified their readers. But what does 'from slaves' mean? Is Fabricius denying that he employs slave-labour on his farm? If so, I confess that I do not believe the denial as being his own genuine utterance. I take it to be put into his mouth by Dionysius, writing under the influence of the agricultural conditions of a much later time, when great slave-owners drew large incomes from the exploitation of slave-labour on great estates. But I am not sure that Dionysius means him to be saying more than 'I am not a big capitalist farming on a large scale by slave-gangs.' How far this writer really understood the state of things in the third century BC, is hard to say. In any case he is repeating what he has picked up from earlier writers and not letting it suffer in the repetition. Taken by himself, he is no more a sufficient witness to the practice of Fabricius than to that of Cincinnatus. That there was slavery is certain: that Fabricius had scruples against employing slaves is hardly credible.

In the ages during which Rome gradually won her way to the headship of Italy the Roman citizen was normally both farmer and soldier: the soldier generally a man called up from his farm for a campaign, the farmer of military age always potentially a soldier. This state of things was evidently not peculiar to Rome. What makes it striking in the case of Rome is the well-considered system by which the military machine was kept in working order. The development of fortress colonies and extension of roads gave to Roman farmers in the border-lands more security than any neighbouring power could give to its own citizens on its own side of the border. Mobilization was more prompt and effective on the Roman side under a central control: the fortresses served as a hindrance to hostile invaders, as refuges to the rustics at need, and as bases for Roman armies. It is no great stretch

[1] Dionys XIX 15.

of imagination to see in this organization a reason for the prosperity of Roman agriculture. Farms were no doubt laid waste on both sides of the border, but the balance of the account was in the long run favourable to Rome. Among the numerous legends that gathered round the name of king Pyrrhus is a story[1] that in reply to some discontent on the part of his Italian allies, to whom his strategy seemed over-cautious, he said 'the mere look of the country shews me the great difference between you and the Romans. In the parts subject to them are all manner of fruit-trees and vineyards: the land is cultivated and the farm-establishments are costly: but the estates of my friends are so laid waste that all signs of human occupation have disappeared.' The saying may be not authentic or merely overdrawn in rhetorical transmission. But it probably contains the outlines of a true picture of the facts. It was the power of giving to her farmer-settlers a more effective protection than her rivals could give to their own farmers that enabled Rome to advance steadily and continuously. The organization was simple enough: the sword was ready to guard the plough, and the plough to occupy and hold the conquests of the sword.

From the time of the first Punic war we have a remarkable story relating to M Atilius Regulus, the man around whose name so much patriotic legend gathered. He appears as one of the good old farmer-heroes. His farm[2] of seven *iugera* lay in an unhealthy part of the country, and the soil was poor. His advice to agriculturists, not to buy good land in an unhealthy district nor bad land in a healthy one, was handed down as the opinion of a qualified judge. We are told[3] that after his victory in Africa he desired to be relieved and return home; but the Senate did not send out another commander, and so he had to stay on. He wrote and complained of his detention. Among other reasons he urged in particular his domestic anxiety. In the epitome of Livy XVIII this appears as 'that his little farm had been abandoned by the hired men.' In Valerius Maximus[4] we find a fuller account, thus 'that the steward in charge of his little farm (seven *iugera* in the *Pupinia*) had died, and the hired man (*mercennarium*) had taken the opportunity to decamp, taking with him the farm-stock: therefore he asked them to relieve him of his command, for he feared his wife and children would have nothing to live on now the farm was abandoned.' On hearing this, the Senate ordered that provision should at once be

---

[1] Preserved in a fragment of Dion Cassius, fr 40 § 27.
[2] Columella I 4 § 2, Pliny *NH* XVIII §§ 27–8, cf Valer Max IV 4 § 4.
[3] Livy *epit* XVIII.
[4] Valer Max IV 4 § 6. The version given in Seneca *ad Helv* 12 § 5 is much the same, but ends characteristically *fuitne tanti servum non habere, ut colonus eius populus Romanus esset?* Here *colonus* = tenant farmer.

made at the cost of the state (*a*) for cultivation of his farm[1] by contract (*b*) for maintenance of his wife and children (*c*) for making good the losses he had suffered. The reference of Pliny[2] rather confirms the details of Valerius, who by himself is not a very satisfactory witness. Livy is probably the source of all these versions. They are part of the Roman tradition of the first Punic war. Polybius, whose narrative is from another line of tradition, says not a word of this story. Indeed, he declares[3] that Regulus, so far from wishing to be relieved, wanted to stay on, fearing that he might hand over the credit of a final victory to a successor. The two traditions cannot be reconciled as they stand. Probably neither is complete. If we suppose the account of Polybius to be true, it does not follow as a matter of course that the other story is a baseless fiction. In any case, the relation of Regulus to the agriculture of his day, as represented by the story, seemed credible to Romans of a later age, and deserves serious consideration.

We are told that in the middle of the third century BC a man of such position and recognized merit that he was specially chosen to fill the place of a deceased consul in the course of a great war was a farmer on an estate of seven *iugera*, from which he was supporting his wife and family. In his absence on public duty he had left the farm in charge of a *vilicus*. The only reference to the labour employed there speaks of hired men (wage-earners, *mercennarii*). It does not say that there were no slaves. But the natural inference is that the *vilicus* had the control of a staff consisting wholly or largely of free labourers. Now that a slave *vilicus* might in the ordinary run of business be left in control of labourers, slave or free, seems clear from directions given by Cato[4] in the next century. The *vilicus* in this story was therefore probably a slave, as they were generally if not always. His death left the hired men uncontrolled, and they took the opportunity of robbing their employer. Roused by the absent consul's complaints (whether accompanied by a request for relief or not), the Senate took up the matter and arranged to secure him against loss. We do not hear of the punishment of the dishonest hirelings, or even of a search for them. This may be merely an omitted detail: at any rate they had probably left the neighbourhood. The curious thing is that we hear nothing of the wife of Regulus: that a Roman matron submitted tamely to such treatment is hard to believe. Was it she who made the complaints and set the Senate in motion? The general outcome of the story is a conclusion that hired labour was freely employed in this age, not to exclusion of slave labour, but combined with it: that is, that the wage-

---

[1] *colendum locari.*   [2] Plin *NH* XVIII § 39.   [3] Polyb I 31 § 4.
[4] Cato 5 § 4 (of duties of *vilicus*) *operarium mercennarium politorem diutius eundem ne habeat die.*

earning work of landless men, such as appears in the earlier traditions, still went on. It was not yet overlaid by the plantation-system, and degraded by the associations of the slave-gang and the *ergastulum*.

When we pass on to the second Punic war, of which we have a fuller and less legendary record, we find the circumstances somewhat changed, but the importance of the Roman farmer's grip of the land is recognized as clearly as before. It is not unlikely that since the time of the Pyrrhic war the practise of large-scale farming with slave-labour had begun to appear[1] in Italy, but it can hardly as yet have been widespread. Large or small, the farms in a large part of the country had suffered from the ravages of Hannibal, and it would be the land of Romans and their faithful allies that suffered most. Many rustics had to seek shelter in walled towns, above all in Rome, and their presence was no doubt in many ways embarrassing. Naturally, as the failure of Hannibal became manifest, the Roman Senate was desirous of restoring these refugees to the land and relieving the pressure on the city. Livy, drawing no doubt from an earlier annalist, tells us[2] that in 206 BC the Senate instructed the consuls, before they left for the seat of war, to undertake the bringing back of the common folk (*plebis*) on to the land. They pointed out that this was desirable, and possible under the better conditions now prevailing. 'But it was for the people (*populo*) not at all an easy matter; for the free farmers (*cultoribus*) had perished in the war, there was a shortage of slaves (*inopia servitiorum*), the live stock had been carried off, and the farmsteads (*villis*) wrecked or burnt. Yet under pressure from the consuls a good many did go back to the land.' He adds that what had raised the question at this particular juncture was the appeal of a deputation from Placentia and Cremona. These two Latin colonies, founded twelve years before as fortresses to hold the region of the Po, had suffered from Gaulish raids and had no longer a sufficient population, many settlers having gone off elsewhere. The Roman commander in the district was charged to provide for their protection, and the truant colonists ordered to return to their posts. It was evidently thought that with full numbers and military support there would be an end to the derelict condition of their territories, and that the two colonies would soon revive.

This attempt to reestablish the rustic population lays stress upon the general identity of farmer and soldier and the disturbance of agriculture by the ravages of war. But most notable is the mention of the shortage of slave-labour as a hindrance to resumption of work

[1] How far we can infer this from references to slaves such as Livy XXIII 32 § 15 (215 BC), XXV 1 § 4 (213 BC), XXVI 35 § 5 (210 BC), is not quite certain. The Licinian law to check the grabbing of state domain land certainly does not prove it, for that land was probably for the most part pasture.

[2] Liv XXVIII 11 § 9.

on derelict farms. It has been held[1] that this clause refers only to large estates worked by slave-gangs, while the free farmers stand for the men on small holdings, who presumably employed no slaves. Now it is quite conceivable that this contrast may have been in Livy's mind as he wrote in the days of Augustus. That it was the meaning of the older author from whom he took the facts is not an equally probable inference. No doubt lack of slaves would hinder or prevent the renewal of tillage on a big estate. But what of a small farm whose owner had fallen in the war? The absence of the father in the army would be a most serious blow to the efficient working of the farm. If the raids of the enemy drove his family to take refuge in Rome, and the farm was let down to weeds, more labour than ever would be needed to renew cultivation. When there was no longer any hope of his return, the supply of sufficient labour was the only chance of re- viving the farm. Surely there must have been many cases in which the help of one or two slaves was the obvious means of supplying it. Therefore, if we recognize that slave-labour had long been a common institution in Roman households, we shall not venture to assert that only large estates are referred to. That such estates, worked by slave- gangs, were numerous in 206 BC, is not likely: that small farmers often (not always) eked out their own labour with the help of a slave, is far more so. The actual shortage of slaves[2] had been partly brought about by the employment of many in military service. Some had no doubt simply run away. And the period of great foreign conquests and a full slave-market had yet to come.

I do not venture to dispute that the accumulation of capital in the form of ready money available for speculation in state leases, farming of revenues, and other contracts, had already begun at Rome in the age of the great Punic wars. In the second war, contracts for the supply of necessaries to the armed forces played a considerable part, and we hear of contractors[3] who practised shameless frauds on the state. Greed was a plant that throve in the soil of Roman life: the scandals of the later Republic were merely the sinister developments of an old tendency favoured by opportunities. Land-grabbing in par- ticular was, if consistent tradition may be believed, from early times a passion of Roman nobles: and the effect of a law[4] forbidding them to become ship-owners and engage in commerce was to concentrate their enterprise on the acquisition of great landed estates. Another notable fact is the large voluntary loans[5] which the government was

---

[1] Weissenborn's note on the passage.
[2] Liv XXII 57 § 11, and index to Livy under *volones*.
[3] Liv XXIII 49 §§ 1–4, XXIV 18 § 11, XXV 1 § 4, 3 § 8—4 § 11.
[4] Liv XXI 63 §§ 3, 4, Cic II *in Verr* V § 45.   [5] Liv XXVI 36.

able to raise in the critical period of the great war. In the year 210, when the financial strain was extreme, a very large contribution of the kind took place. In 204 the Senate arranged a scheme[1] for repayment in three instalments. In 200 the lenders, apparently alarmed by the delay in paying the second instalment, became clamorous. The Punic war was at an end, and war with Philip of Macedon just declared: they wanted to get their money back. We are told[2] that the state was not able to find the cash, and that the cry of many creditors was 'there are plenty of farms for sale, and we want to buy.' The Senate devised a middle way of satisfying them. They were to be offered the chance of acquiring the state domain-land within fifty miles of Rome at a valuation fixed by the consuls. This seems to mean, up to the amount of the instalment then in question. But they were not thereby to receive the land in full private[3] property. A quit-rent of one *as* was to be set on each *iugerum*, in evidence that the property still belonged to the state. Thus, when the state finances should admit, they might get back their ready money if they preferred it and give back the land to the state. The offer was gladly accepted, and the land taken over on these terms was called 'third-part land' (*trientabulum*) as representing ⅓ of the money lent. The final instalment appears to have been paid in cash[4] in the year 196.

That these patriotic creditors were men with a keen eye for a bargain, and that they made a good one in the above arrangement, is pretty clear. This is the only occasion on which we hear of the *trientabula* plan of settling a money claim by what was in effect a perpetual lease at a nominal rent terminable by reconversion into a money claim at the pleasure of the lessee. No doubt the valuation was so made as to give the creditor a good margin of security over and above the sum secured. There was therefore no temptation to call for the cash and surrender the land. From the reference[5] to *trientabula* in the agrarian law of 111 BC it would seem that some at least of these beneficial tenancies were still in existence after the lapse of nearly 90 years. They would pass by inheritance or sale as the ordinary *possessiones* of state domains did, and eventually become merged in the private properties that were the final result of the land-legislation of the revolutionary age. For the capitalists, already powerful in 200 BC, became more and more powerful as time went on. And this use of public land to discharge public debts was undoubtedly a step tending to promote the formation of the great estates (*latifundia*) which were the ruin of

---

[1] Liv XXIX 16 §§ 1–3.   [2] Liv XXXI 13.
[3] See Rudorff *gromatische Institutionen* pp 287–8.
[4] Liv XXXIII 42 § 3.
[5] *lex agraria*, line 31, in Bruns' *fontes* or Wordsworth's *Specimens*.

the wholesome old land-system in a great part of Italy. With this
tendency the wholesale employment of slave-labour went hand in hand.

But we must not forget that the creditors in 200 BC are made to
press for their money on the ground that they wanted to invest it in
land, of which there was plenty then in the market. This may be a
detail added by Livy himself: but surely it is more likely that he is
repeating what he found in his authorities. In any case the land referred to can hardly be other than the derelict farms belonging to those
who had suffered by the war. In earlier times we have traditions of
men losing their lands through inability to pay the debts for which
they stood pledged. In a somewhat later time we hear[1] of small
farmers being bought out cheaply by neighbouring big landlords, and
bullied if they made difficulty about leaving their farms. The present
case is different, arising directly out of the war. The father of a family
might be dead, or disinclined to go back to monotonous toil after the
excitements of military life, or unable to find the extra labour for
reclaiming a wasted and weed-grown farm, or means of restocking it.
He or his heir would probably not have capital to tide him over the
interval before the farm was again fully productive: his immediate
need was probably ready money. No wonder that farms were in the
market, and at prices that made a land-grabber's mouth water. The
great war certainly marked a stage in the decay of the small-farm
agriculture, the healthy condition of which had hitherto been the
soundest element of Roman strength.

Before we leave the traditions of the early period it is necessary
to refer to the question of free wage-earning labour. Have we any
reason to think that under the conditions of early Rome there was
any considerable class of rustic[2] wage-earners? Nearly all the passages
that suggest an affirmative answer are found in the work of Dionysius,
who repeatedly uses[3] the Greek word θητεύειν of this class of labour.
It is represented as being practically servile, for it meant working with
slaves or at least doing the work which according to the writer[4] was
(even in the regal period) done by slaves. The poor Plebeians appear
as loathing such service: their desire is for plots of land on which each
man can work freely for himself. This desire their protectors, kings
or tribunes, endeavour to gratify by allotments as occasion serves.

---

[1] Appian *civ* I 7 § 5. But the account given in this passage of the spread of *latifundia*
and slave-gangs is too loose to be of much value. In particular, the assertion that slave-
breeding was already common and lucrative is not to be believed. Appian was misled by
the experience of his own day. See Sallust *Iug* 41 § 8 *interea parentes aut parvi liberi
militum, uti quisque potentiori confinis erat, seaibus pellebantur.*

[2] The urban artisans engaged in the sedentary trades do not concern us here. See
Weissenborn on Liv VIII 20 § 4 *opificum vulgus et sellularii.*

[3] Dionys III 31, IV 9, 13, etc.

[4] Dionys VI 79, a passage much coloured by later notions.

Now that there was land-hunger from the earliest times, and that agriculture was in itself an honourable trade, we have no good reason for doubting. But that the dislike of wage-earning labour as such was the main motive of land-hunger is a more doubtful proposition. It may be true, but it sounds very like an explanation supplied by a learned but rhetorical historian. We know that Dionysius regarded Rome as a city of Greek origin. The legends of early Attica were doubtless familiar to him. We may grant that there was probably some likeness between the labour-conditions of early Rome and early Athens. But historians are ever tempted to detect analogies in haste and remodel tradition at leisure. I suspect that the two features of the same picture, the prevalence of rustic slavery and also of rustic wage-earning, are taken from different lines of tradition, and both overdrawn.

In connexion with this question it is necessary to turn back to a remarkable passage[1] of Livy referring to the year 362 BC. The famous L Manlius the martinet (*imperiosus*) was threatened with a public prosecution by a tribune for misuse of his powers as dictator in the year just past. To create prejudice against the accused, the prosecutor further alleged that he had treated his son Titus with cruel severity. The young man was slow of wit and speech, but no wrongdoing had been brought home to him. Yet his father had turned him out of his city home, had cut him off from public life and the company of other youths, and put him to servile work, shutting him up in what was almost a slaves' prison (*ergastulum*). The daily affliction of such a life was calculated to teach the dictator's son that he had indeed a martinet for his father. To keep his son among the flocks in the rustic condition and habit of a country boor was to intensify any natural defects of his own offspring, conduct too heartless for even the brute beasts. But the young Manlius upset all calculations. On hearing what was in contemplation he started for Rome with a knife, made his way into the tribune's presence in the morning and made him solemnly swear to drop the prosecution by a threat of killing him then and there if he did not take the oath. The tribune swore, and the trial fell through. The Roman commons were vexed to lose the chance of using their votes to punish the father for his arbitrary and unfeeling conduct, but they approved the dutiful act of the son, and took the first opportunity of electing him a military officer. This young man was afterwards the renowned T Manlius Torquatus, who followed his father's example of severity by putting to death his own son for a breach of military discipline.

The story is a fine specimen of the edifying legends kept in circu-

---

[1] Liv VII 4, 5. A slightly different and shorter version in Cic *de off* III § 112.

lation by the Romans of later days. That the greatness of Rome was
above all things due to their grim old fathers who endured hardness
and sacrificed all tender affections to public duty, was the general moral
of these popular tales. Exaggeration grew with repetition, and details
became less and less authentic. In particular the circumstances of their
own time were foisted in by narrators whose imagination did not suffice
to grasp the difference of conditions in the past. In the above story
we have a reference to *ergastula*, the barracoons in which the slave-
gangs on great estates were confined when not actually at work. Now
the system of which these private prisons were a marked feature certainly belongs to a later period, when agriculture on a large scale was
widely practised, not to make a living for a man and his family, but to
make a great income for a single individual by the labour of many.
Here then we have a detail clearly not authentic, which throws doubt
on the whole setting of the story. Again, we have agricultural labour
put before us as degrading (*opus servile*). It is a punishment, banishing
a young Roman from his proper surrounding in the life of Rome, and
dooming him to grow up a mere clodhopper. There may have been
some points in the original story of which this is an exaggerated version:
for it is evident that from quite early days of the Republic men of the
ruling class found it necessary to spend much time in or quite close to
the city. But the representation of agriculture as a servile occupation
is grossly inconsistent with the other legends glorifying the farmer-
heroes of yore. It is of course quite impossible to prove that no isolated
cases of a young Roman's banishment to farm life ever occurred. But
that such a proceeding was so far ordinary as fairly to be reckoned
typical, is in the highest degree improbable. That later writers should
invent or accept such colouring for their picture, is no wonder. In the
Attic New Comedy, with which Roman society was familiarized[1] in the
second century BC, this situation was found. The later conditions of
Roman life, in city and country, tended to make the view of agriculture
as a servile trade, capable of being rendered penal, more and more intelligible to Romans. Accordingly we find this view cynically accepted[2]
by Sallust, and warmly protested against[3] by Cicero. In order to
weaken the case of his client Sextus Roscius, it was urged that the
young man's father distrusted him and sent him to live the life of a
boor on his farm in Umbria. Cicero, evidently anxious as to the possible
effect of this construction of facts on the coming verdict, was at great
pains to counter it by maintaining that the father's decision was in truth
a compliment: in looking for an honest and capable manager of his
rustic estate he had found the right man in this son. The orator surely

[1] Cic *pro Sex Roscio* § 46 recognizes this familiarity.
[2] Sallust *Catil* 4 § 1.   [3] Cic *pro Sex Roscio* §§ 39–51.

did not enlarge on this point for nothing. And it is to be noted that in insisting on the respectability of a farmer's life he sees fit to refer to the farmer-consuls of the olden time. He feels, no doubt, that un-supported assertions[1] as to the employment of sons in agriculture by his contemporaries were not likely to carry much weight with the jury.

After the above considerations I come to the conclusion that Livy's representation of agriculture as a servile occupation in the case of Manlius is a coloured utterance of no historical value. A minute con-sistency is not to be looked for in the writings of an author to whom picturesqueness of detail appeals differently at different moments. For Livy was in truth deeply conscious of the sad changes in Italian country life brought about by the transition to large-scale agriculture. Under the year 385 he is driven to moralize[2] on the constant renewal of Volscian and Aequian wars. How ever did these two small peoples find armies for the long-continued struggle? He suggests possible answers to the question, the most significant of which is that in those days there was a dense free population in those districts,—districts which in his own time, he says, would be deserted but for the presence of Roman slaves. To describe vividly the decay of free population, he adds that only a poor little nursery of soldiers is left (*vix seminario exiguo militum relicto*) in those parts. The momentous results of the change of system are not more clearly grasped by Lucan or Pliny himself. Livy then is not to be cited as a witness to the existence of great numbers of rustic slaves in Italy before the second Punic war, nor even then for the highly-organized gang-system by which an in-dustrial character was given to agriculture.

One more story, and a strange one, needs to be considered, for it bears directly on the labour-question. The time in which it is placed is the latter part of the period of the Roman conquest of Italy. In a fragment[3] of one of his later books Dionysius tells us of the arbitrary doings of a consul Postumius, a Patrician of high rank who had already been twice consul. After much bullying he made his colleague, a Plebeian of recent nobility, resign to him the command in the Samnite war. This was an unpopular act, but he went on to worse. From his army he drafted some 2000 men on to his own estate, and set them to cut away brushwood without providing cutting tools (ἄνευ σιδήρου). And he kept them there a long time doing the work of wage-earners or slaves (θητῶν ἔργα καὶ θεραπόντων ὑπηρετοῦντας). Into the tale of his further acts of arbitrary insolence we need not enter here, nor into

---

[1] Cic *pro Sex Roscio* §§ 50–1. [2] Livy VI 12 § 5, cf VII 25 § 8.

[3] Dionys XVII [XVIII] 4. L Postumius Megellus was consul 305, 294, 291 BC. The story relates to his third consulship. His earlier career may be followed in Liv IX 44, X 26 § 15, 32 § 1, 37, 46 § 16.

the public prosecution and condemnation to a heavy fine that awaited him at the end of his term of office. Suffice it that the story is in general confirmed[1] by Livy, and that the hero of it seems to have been remembered in Roman tradition as a classic instance of self-willed audacity and disregard of the conventions that were the soul of Roman public life. So far as the labour is concerned, it seems to me that what was objected to in the consul's conduct was the use of his military supreme power (*imperium*) for his own private profit. He treated a fatigue-party as a farm labour-gang. Freemen might work on their own land side by side with their slaves: they might work for wages on another man's land side by side with his slaves. Any objection they might feel would be due to the unwelcome pressure of economic necessity. But to be called out for military service (and in most cases from their own farms), and then set to farm-labour on another man's land under military discipline, was too much. We must bear in mind that a Roman army of the early Republic was not composed of pauper adventurers who preferred a life of danger with hopes of loot and licence to hard monotonous toil. The very poor were not called out, and the ranks were filled with citizens who had at least some property to lose. Therefore it might easily happen that a soldier set to rough manual labour by Postumius had to do for him the service that was being done at home for himself by a wage-earner or a slave. He was a soldier because he was a free citizen; he was being employed in place of a slave because he was a soldier under martial law. In no free republic could such a wrong be tolerated. The words of the epitome of Livy state the case with sufficient precision. *L Postumius consularis, quoniam cum exercitui praeesset opera militum in agro suo usus erat, damnatus est.* It is remarkable that, among the other epitomators and collectors of anecdotes who drew from the store of Livy, not one, not even Valerius Maximus, records this story. To Livy it must have seemed important, or he would not have laid enough stress on it to attract the attention of the writer of the epitome. So too the detailed version of Dionysius, probably drawn from the same authority as that of Livy, struck the fancy of a maker of extracts and caused his text to be preserved to us. It surely descends, like many other of the old stories, in a line of Plebeian tradition, and is recorded as an illustration of the survival of Patrician insolence in a headstrong consul after the two Orders had been politically equalized by the Licinian laws.

Beside these fragments of evidence there are in the later Roman literature many passages in which writers directly assert that their forefathers lived a life of simple frugality and worked with their own hands on their own little farms. But as evidence the value of such

---

[1] Liv *epit* XI.

passages is not very great. They testify to a tradition: but in most cases the tradition is being used for the purposes of moralizing rhetoric. Now the glorification of 'good old times' has in all ages tempted authors to aim rather at striking contrast between past and present than at verification of their pictures of the past. To impute this defect to satirists is a mere commonplace. But those who are not professed satirists are often exposed to the same influence in a less degree. The most striking phenomenon in this kind is the chorus of poets in the Augustan age. The Emperor, aware that the character of Reformer is never a very popular one, preferred to pose as Restorer. The hint was given, and the literary world acted on it. Henceforth the praises of the noble and efficient simplicity of the ancients formed a staple material of Roman literature.

XXI. ABSTRACT OF CONCLUSIONS.

In reference to the early period down to 201 BC I think we are justified in coming to the following conclusions.

1. The evidence, consisting of fragmentary tradition somewhat distorted and in some points exaggerated by the influence of moral purpose on later writers, is on the whole consistent and credible.

2. From it we get a picture of agriculture as an honourable trade, the chief occupation of free citizens, who are in general accustomed to work with their own hands.

3. The Roman citizen as a rule has an allotment of land as his own, and an early classification of citizens (the 'Servian Constitution') was originally based on landholding, carrying with it the obligation to military service.

4. The Roman family had a place for the slave, and the slave, a domestic helper, normally an Italian, was not as yet the despised alien chattel of whom we read in a later age.

5. As a domestic he bore a part in all the labours of the family, and therefore as a matter of course in the commonest of all, agriculture.

6. In this there was nothing degrading. Suggestions to that effect are the echoes of later conditions.

7. Under such relations of master and slave it was quite natural that manumission should (as it did) operate to make the slave not only free but a citizen. That this rule led to very troublesome results in a later period was owing to change of circumstances.

8. Slavery then was, from the earliest times of which we have any tradition, an integral part of the social and economic system, as much in Italy as in Greece. It was there, and only needed the stimulus

of prospective economic gain for capitalists to organize it on a crudely industrial basis, without regard to considerations of humanity or the general wellbeing of the state.

9. Of wage-earning labour on the part of freemen we have little trace in tradition. The reported complaints of day-labour performed for Patrician nobles in early times are probably not unconnected with the institution of clientship, and in any case highly coloured by rhetoric.

ROME—MIDDLE PERIOD

XXII. INTRODUCTORY GENERAL VIEW.

The overthrow of Carthage put an end to a period of terrible anxiety to the Roman government, and the first feeling was naturally one of relief. But the sufferings of the war-weary masses had produced an intense longing for peace and rest. It might be true that a Macedonian war was necessary in the interest of the state: but it was only with great difficulty that the Senate overcame opposition to a forward policy. For the sufferings of the people, more particularly the farmers, were not at an end. The war indemnities from Carthage might refill the empty treasury, and enable the state to discharge its public obligations to contractors and other creditors. So far well: but receipts of this kind did little or nothing towards meeting the one vital need, the reestablishment of displaced peasants on the land. The most accessible districts, generally the best suited for tillage, had no doubt suffered most in the disturbances of war; and the future destinies of Rome and Italy were depending on the form that revival of agriculture would take. The race of small farmers had been hitherto the backbone of Roman power. But the wars of the last two generations had brought Rome into contact with an agricultural system of a very different character. Punic agriculture[1] was industrial: that is, conducted for profit on a large scale and directed by purely economic considerations. Cheap production was the first thing. As the modern large farmer relies on machinery, so his ancient predecessor relied on domesticated animals; chiefly on the animal with hands, the human slave.

It is to be borne in mind that during the second Punic war the Roman practice of employing contractors for all manner of state services (*publica*) had been greatly developed. Companies of *publicani* had played an active part and had thriven on their enterprises. These companies were probably already, as they certainly were in later times, great employers of slaves. In any case they represented a purely industrial and commercial view of life, the 'economic' as opposed to the 'national' set of principles. Their numbers were beyond all doubt greater than they had ever been before. With such men the future interests of the state would easily be obscured by immediate private interests, selfish appetite being whetted by the

[1] See the precept of Mago cited by Pliny *NH* XVIII § 35.

recent taste of profits. If a large section of the farmer class seemed in danger of extinction through the absorption of their farms in great estates, legislation to prevent it was not likely to have the warm support of these capitalists. That financial interests were immensely powerful in the later Roman Republic is universally admitted, but I do not think sufficient allowance is made for their influence in the time of exhaustion at the very beginning of the second century BC. The story of the *trientabula*, discussed above, is alone enough to shew how this influence was at work ; and it was surely no isolated phenomenon. We have therefore reason to believe that many of the farmers dispossessed by the war never returned to their former homes, and we naturally ask what became of them. Some no doubt were unsettled and unfitted for the monotonous toil of rustic life by the habits contracted in campaigning. Such men would find urban idleness, or further military service with loot in prospect, more to their taste : some of these would try both experiences in turn. We trace their presence in the growth of a city mob, and in the enlistment of veterans to give tone and steadiness to somewhat lukewarm armies in new wars. But it is not to be assumed that this element constituted the whole, or even the greater part, of those who did not go back to their old farms. The years 200–180 saw the foundation of 19 new *coloniae*, and it is reasonable to suppose that the *coloni* included a number of the men unsettled by the great war. The group founded in 194–2 were designed to secure the coast of southern Italy against attack by an Eastern power controlling large fleets. Those of 189–1 were in the North, the main object being to strengthen the Roman grip of Cisalpine Gaul. But already in 198–5 it had been found necessary to support the colonies on the Po (Placentia and Cremona) against attacks of the Gauls, and in 190 they were reinforced with contingents of fresh colonists. For the firm occupation of northern Italy was a policy steadily kept in view, and only interrupted for a time by the strain of Eastern wars.

In trying to form a notion of the condition of agriculture in the second century BC, and particularly of the labour question, we must never lose sight of the fact that military service was still obligatory[1] on the Roman citizen, and that this was a period of many wars. The farmer-soldier, liable to be called up at any time until his forty-sixth year, might have to break off important work which could not without risk of loss be left in other hands. At the worst, a sudden call might

---

[1] That is, on those possessed of a certain minimum of property, which was lowered in course of time. Originally reckoned on land only, thus reckoning only those settled on farms (*adsidui*). See Mommsen *Staatsrecht* index. The rise in the census numbers between 131 and 125 BC is explained by Greenidge *History* p 150 as due to the increase of *adsidui* through effect of Gracchan legislation.

mean ruin. Pauper wage-earners, landless men, were not reached by the military levy in the ordinary way. How soon they began to be enrolled as volunteers, and to what extent, is uncertain. But conscription of qualified citizens remained the staple method of filling the legions[1] until the famous levy held by Marius in 107. Conscription had for a long time been becoming more and more unpopular and difficult to enforce, save in cases where easy victory and abundant booty were looked for. The Roman government fell into the habit of employing chiefly the contingents of the Italian Allies in hard and unremunerative campaigns. This unfair treatment, and other wrongs to match, led to the great rebellion of 90 BC. But the grant of the Roman franchise to the Italians, extorted by force of arms, though it made more Roman citizens, could not make more Roman farmers. The truth is, a specializing process was going on. The soldier was becoming more and more a professional: farming was becoming more and more the organized exploitation of labour. Long and distant wars unfitted the discharged soldiers for the monotonous round of rustic life: while they kept the slave-market well supplied with captives, thus making it easy for capitalists to take advantage of great areas of land cheaply acquired from time to time. Moreover, the advance of Roman dominion had another effect beside the mere supply of labouring hands. It made Rome the centre of the Mediterranean world, the place where all important issues were decided, and where it was necessary to reside. The wealthy landowner was practically compelled to spend most of his time in the ruling city, in close touch with public affairs. Now this compelled him to manage his estates by stewards, keeping an eye on them so far as his engagements in Rome left him free to do so. And this situation created a demand for highly-qualified stewards. The supply of these had to come mainly from the eastern countries of old civilization. But if technical skill could thus be procured (and it was very necessary for the variety of crops that were taking the place of corn), it was generally accompanied by an oriental subtlety the devices of which were not easy to penetrate. From the warnings of the agricultural writers, as to the need of keeping a strict watch on a *vilicus*, we may fairly infer that these favoured slaves were given to robbing their masters. The master, even if he had the knowledge requisite for practical control, seldom had the leisure for frequent visits to his estate. What he wanted was a regular income to spend: and the astute steward who was always ready with the expected cash on the appointed day had little fear of reprimand or punishment. His own interest was that his own master should expect as little as possible,

[1] See Greenidge *History* pp 60-1, 424-5.

and it is obvious that this would not encourage a sincere effort to get the most out of the estate in a favourable year. His master's expectations would then rise, and the disappointment of poor returns in a bad year might have serious consequences for himself.

These considerations may help us to understand why the history of the later Roman Republic gives so gloomy a picture of agriculture. We find the small farmer, citizen and soldier too, dying out as a class in a great part of Italy. We find the land passing into the hands of a few large owners whose personal importance was vastly increased thereby. Whether bought cheap on a glutted market or ' possessed ' in a sort of copyhold tenancy from the state, whether arable or pasture, it is at all events clear that the bulk of these *latifundia* (if not the whole) had been got on very easy terms. The new holders were not hampered by lack of capital or labour, as may often have been the case with the old peasantry. Slave-labour was generally cheap, at times very cheap. Knowledge and skill could be bought, as well as bone and muscle. Like the ox and the ass, the slave was only fed and clothed and housed sufficiently to keep him fit for work: his upkeep while at work was not the canker eating up profits. With the influx of wealth, the spoils of conquest, the tribute of subject provinces, the profits of blackmail and usury, prices of almost everything were rising in the second century BC. Corn, imported and sold cheap to the Roman poor, was an exception: but the Italian landlords were ceasing to grow corn, save for local consumption. Some authorities, if not all, thought[1] that grazing paid better than tillage: and it was notorious that pasturage was increasing and cultivation declining. The slave-herdsmen, hardy and armed against wolves and brigands, were a formidable class. When combined with mutinous gladiators they were, as Spartacus shewed in 73–1 BC, wellnigh irresistible save by regular armies in formal campaigns. The owner of a vast estate, controlling huge numbers of able-bodied ruffians who had nothing to lose themselves and no inducement to spare others, was in fact a public danger if driven to desperation. He could mobilize an army of robbers and cutthroats at a few days notice, live on the country, and draw recruits from all the slave-gangs near. It was not want of power that crippled the representatives of large-scale agriculture.

And yet in the last days of the Republic, when the fabric of the state was cracking under repeated strains, we are told that, among the various types of men led by financial embarrassments to favour revolutionary schemes, one well-marked group consisted of great

---

[1] See Cato's opinion cited by Cic *de off* II § 89, Columella VI *praef* §§ 3–5, Plin *NH* XVIII §§ 29, 30.

landlords. These men, says[1] Cicero, though deep in debt, could quite well pay what they owe by selling their lands. But they will not do this : they are 'land-proud.' The income from their estates will not cover the interest on their debts, but they go on foolishly trying to make it do so. In this struggle they are bound to be beaten. In other words, the return on their landed estates is not enough to support a life of extravagance in Rome. So they borrow, at high interest. The creditors of course take good security, with a margin for risks. So, in order to keep the social status of a great landlord, the borrower takes a loan of less than the capital value of his land, while he has to pay for the accommodation more than the income from the land. Ruin is the certain end of such finance, and it is only in a revolution that there is any hope of 'something turning up' in favour of the debtor. We must not suppose that all or most of the great landlords of the day had reached the stage of embarrassment described by Cicero. That there were some in that plight, is not to be doubted, even when we have allowed freely for an orator's overstatements. But it is hardly rash to suppose that there were some landlords who were not in debt, at least to a serious extent, either through good returns from their lands or from other investments, or even from living thriftily. What seems quite clear is that large-scale farming of land was by no means so remunerative financially as other forms of invest-ment ; and that though, as pointed out above, it was carried on with not a few points in its favour.

In the same descriptive passage[2] the orator refers to another class of landowners ripe for revolution. These were the veterans of Sulla, settled by him as *coloni* on lands of farmers dispossessed on pretext of complicity with his Marian opponents. Their estates were no doubt on a smaller scale than those of the class just spoken of above. But they were evidently comfortable allotments. The discharged soldiers made bad farmers. They meant to enjoy the wealth suddenly bestowed, and they had no notion of economy. Their extravagance, one form of which was the keeping of a number[3] of slaves, soon landed them hopelessly in debt. So they also saw their only chance of recovery in a renewal of civil war and fresh confiscations. It was said that a number of necessitous rustics (probably some of the very men ejected from the farms) were ready to join them in a campaign of plunder. Here we have a special picture of the military colonist, one of the most sinister figures in the last age of the Republic. It is

---

[1] Cic *in Catil* II § 18.

[2] Cic *in Catil* II § 20, cf *de lege agr* II § 78 *fundos quorum subsidio familiarum magnitu-dines sustentare possint.*

[3] *familiis magnis.*

no doubt highly coloured, but the group settled in Etruria were probably some of the worst specimens. In such hands agriculture could not flourish, and the true interests of Rome could hardly have suffered a more deadly blow than the transfer of Italian lands from those who could farm them to those who could not. It was not merely that lands were 'let down.' Italy was made less able to maintain a native population, fitted and willing to serve the state in peace and war. The effects of this diminution of the free rustic population were most seriously felt under the Empire. Writers of the Augustan age deplore[1] the disappearance of the old races in a large part of Italy, displaced by alien slaves; and their cry is repeated by later generations. The imperial country that had conquered the Mediterranean world became dependent on subjects and foreigners for her own defence.

The evil plight of agriculture in Cicero's day was merely a continuation and development of the process observable in the second century. Experience had probably moderated some of the crude and blundering methods of the landgrabbers whose doings provoked the agrarian movement of the Gracchi. But in essence the system was the same. And it was a failure, a confessed evil. Why? It is easy to reply that slave-labour is wasteful; and this is I believe an economic truism. But it is well to look a little further. Let me begin by quoting from an excellent book[2] written at a time when this subject was one of immediate practical interest. 'The profitableness which has been attributed to slavery is profitableness estimated exclusively from the point of view of the proprietor of slaves....The profits of capitalists may be increased by the same process by which the gross revenue of a country is diminished, and therefore the community as a whole may be impoverished through the very same means by which a portion of its number is enriched. The economic success of slavery therefore is perfectly consistent with the supposition that it is prejudicial to the material well-being of the country where it is established.' These propositions I do not dispute: I had come to the same conclusion long before I read this passage. I further admit that in the case of Rome and Italy the community as a whole was impoverished by the slave-system: it was the constant influx of tributes from the provinces that kept up the appearance of wealth at the centre of empire. But whether, in the case of agriculture, the capitalist landlords were really enriched by the profits of plantation slavery, is surely a question open to doubt.

Those of them whose capital sunk in great estates and gangs of

[1] Livy VI 12 § 5, cf VII 25 § 8.
[2] Cairnes *The Slave Power* ch III. [1862, second edn. 1863.]

slaves brought in only a moderate return, while they were borrowing at a higher rate of interest, were certainly not the richer for their landed investments. To keep up a fictitious show of solid wealth for the moment, they were marching to ruin. But the man who made his income from landed estates suffice for his needs,—can we say that he was enriched thereby? Hardly, if he was missing the chance of more remunerative investments by having his money locked up in land. He made a sacrifice, in order to gratify a social pride which had in Roman public life a certain political value. Under the Republic, this political value might be realized in the form of provincial or military appointments, profitable through various species of blackmail. But the connexion of such profits with ownership of great plantations is too remote to concern us here. A smart country-place, where influential friends could be luxuriously entertained, was politically more to the point. Now if, as seems certain, the great plantations were not always (perhaps very seldom were) a strictly economic success, though protected against Transalpine competition[1] in wine and oil, can we discern any defects in the system steadily operating to produce failure?

When we admit that slave-labour is wasteful, we mean that its output as compared with that of free labour is not proportionate to the time spent. Having no hope of bettering his condition, the slave does only just enough to escape punishment; having no interest in the profits of the work, he does it carelessly. If, as we know, the free worker paid by time needs constant watching to keep him up to the mark, much more is this true of the slave. Hence a system of piece-work is disliked by the free man and hardly applicable in practice to the case of the slave. But we are not to forget that the slave, having been bought and paid for, draws no money wage. The interest on his prime cost is on the average probably much less than a free man's wage; but the master cannot pay him off and be rid of him when the job is done. The owned labourer is on his owner's hands so long as that owner owns him. Against this we must set the very low standard of feeding clothing housing etc allowed in the case of the slave. Nor must we ignore the economic advantage of slavery as ensuring a permanent supply of labour: for the free labourer was (and is) not always to be had when wanted. These were pretty certainly the considerations that underlay the organization described by the Roman writers on *res rustica*; a regular staff of slaves for everyday work, supplemented by hired labour at times of pressure or for special jobs. And the growing difficulty of getting hired help probably furnished the motive for developing the system of *coloni*. By letting parcels of an estate to small tenants a landlord could secure the presence of resident freemen in his neigh-

[1] Cic *de republ* III § 16.

bourhood. These in their spare time could be employed as labourers. At how early a date stipulation for labour in part payment of their rents placed such tenants on a 'soccage' footing is not certain. It has, rightly or not, been detected in Columella. At all events it contained the germ of predial serfdom.

Now, so long as slave-labour was the permanent and vital element in agriculture, success or failure depended entirely on the efficiency of direction and control. Accordingly the regular organization of a great estate was a complete hierarchy. At the head was the *vilicus*, having under him foremen skilled in special branches of farm work and head-shepherds and the like. Even among the rank and file of the slaves many had special duties occupying all or part of their time, for it was an object to fix responsibility. But it is clear that the efficiency of the whole organization depended on that of the *vilicus*. And he was a slave, the chattel of a master who could inflict on him any punishment he chose. The temptation to rob his master[1] for his own profit was probably not nearly so strong as we might on first thoughts suppose. If he had contrived to hoard the fruits of his pilferings in portable cash, what was he to do with it? He was not free to abscond with it. He would be well known in the neighbourhood: if any slave could escape detection as a runaway, it would not be he. And detection meant the loss of all his privileges as steward, with severe punishment to boot. His obvious policy was to cling to his stewardship, to induce his master to let him keep a few beasts of his own (as *peculium*)[2] on some corner of the estate, and to wait on events. It might be that he looked forward to manumission after long service. But I cannot find any authority for such a supposition, or any concrete instance of a manumitted *vilicus*. This inclines me to believe that in practice to such a man manumission was no boon. He was in most cases a native of some distant country, where he had long been forgotten. The farm of his lord was the nearest thing he had to a home. I am driven to suppose that as a rule he kept his post as long as he could discharge its duties, and then sank into the position of a quasi-pensioned retainer who could pay for his keep by watching his successor. Ordinary slaves when worn out may have been put to light duties about the farm, care of poultry etc, and he might direct them, so far as the new steward allowed. I am guessing thus only in reference to average cases. The brutal simplicity of selling off worn-out slaves for what they would fetch was apparently not unknown, and is approved[3] by Cato.

---

[1] But see the oratorical picture of the bad steward, Cic II *in Verrem* III § 119. That remarkable passage still leaves my questions unanswered, for the comparison with Verres is superficial and only serves a temporary purpose.

[2] Varro I 2 § 17, 17 §§ 5, 7.   [3] Cato 2 § 7, cf Martial XI 70.

It has been briefly hinted above that the steward's obvious interest lay in preventing his master from expecting too much in the way of returns from the estate. The demand for net income, that is to say the treatment of agriculture as an investment yielding a steady return year in and year out, was economically unsound. A landlord in public life wanted a safe income; interest on good debentures, as we should say. But to guarantee this some capitalist was needed to take the risks of business, of course with the prospect of gaining in good years more than he lost in bad ones. Now the Roman landlord had no such protection. In a business subject to unavoidable fluctuations he was not only entitled to the profits but liable to the losses. Imagine him just arrived from Rome, pledged already to some considerable outlay on shows or simple bribery, and looking for a cash balance larger than that shewn at the last audit. Let the steward meet him with a tale of disaster, and conceive his fury. Situations of this kind must surely have occurred, perhaps not very seldom: and one of the two men was in the absolute power of the other. We need not imagine the immediate[1] sequel. Stewards on estates for miles round would be reminded of their own risks of disgrace and punishment, and would look to their own security. I suggest that the habitual practice of these trusted men was to keep the produce of an estate down to a level at which it could easily be maintained; and, if possible, to represent it as being even less than it really was. Thus they removed a danger from themselves. This policy implied an easy-going management of the staff, but the staff were not likely to resent or betray it. A master like Cato was perhaps not to be taken in by a device of the kind: but Catos were rare, and the old man's advice to look sharply after your *vilicus* sounds as if he believed many masters to be habitually fooled by their plausible stewards. If such was indeed the case, here we have at once a manifest cause of the decline of agriculture. The restriction of production would become year by year easier to arrange and conceal, harder and harder to detect. The employment of freemen[2] as stewards seems not to have been tried as a remedy; partly perhaps because they would have insisted on good salaries, partly because they were free to go,—and, if rogues[3], not empty-handed.

The cause to which I have pointed is one that could continue operating from generation to generation, and was likely so to continue until such time as the free farmer should once more occupy the land. The loving care that agriculture needs could only return with him. It was not lack of technical knowledge that did the mischief; Varro's treatise is enough to prove that. It was the lack of personal devotion

[1] As Cato 5 § 2 says, *dominus inpune ne Sinat esse.*
[2] Foreshadowed in Xenophon *memor* II 8.
[3] Compare the case of the *mercennarius* and Regulus referred to above.

in the landlords and motive in the stewards. Principles without practice
failed, as they have failed and will fail. Nor must we lay much stress
on the disturbances of the revolutionary period. Had these, damaging
though they were, been the effective cause of decline, surely the long
peace under the early Empire would have led to a solid revival. But,
though a court poet might sing of revival to please his master, more
serious witnesses tell a different tale. In the middle of the first century
AD we have Lucan Columella and the elder Pliny. If Lucan's pictures
of the countryside peopled with slave-gangs, and of the decay of free
population, are suspected as rhetorically overdrawn, at least they agree
with the evidence of Livy in the time of Augustus, so far as the parts
near Rome are concerned. Columella[1] gravely deplores the neglect of
agriculture, in particular the delegation of management to slaves. The
landlord and his lady have long abdicated their interest in what was
once a noble pursuit: it is now a degrading one, and their places are
taken by the *vilicus* and *vilica*. Yet all he can suggest is a more perfect
organization of the slave-staff, and the letting of outlying farms to
tenants. Pliny tells the same woeful story. And while he vents his
righteous indignation on the *latifundia* that have ruined Italy, he also
mentions instances of great profits[2] made by cultivators of vines and
olives on estates of quite moderate size. But these successful men were
not of the social aristocracy: they were freedmen or other humble folks
who themselves looked sharply after their own business.

Therefore, when we are told[3], and rightly, that with establishment
of the Empire the political attraction of Rome was lessened, and that
the interest of wealthy landlords became more strictly economic in
character, we must not be in haste to identify this change with a return
of genuine prosperity. That a sort of labour-crisis followed the restoration of peace is reasonably inferred from the fact that the kidnapping[4] of freemen, and their incorporation in the slave-gangs of great
estates, was one of the abominations with which the early Principate
had to deal. In a more peaceful world the supply of new slaves fell off,
and the price doubtless rose. It would seem that at the same time free
wage-earners were scarce, as was to be expected after the civil wars.
So the highwayman, probably often a discharged soldier, laid hands
on the unprotected wayfarer. After taking his purse, he made a profit
of his victim's person by selling him as a slave to some landowner
in need of labourers, who asked no questions. Once in the *ergastulum* the man had small chance of regaining his freedom unless and

[1] Columella I *praef* §§ 3, 12, 13, 20, XII *praef* §§ 8–10.
[2] Pliny *NH* XVIII §§ 41–3 (of earlier times), XIV §§ 48–50 (speculations), XVIII §§ 273–4.
[3] M Weber *Römische Agrargeschichte* pp 242 foll.
[4] Sueton *Aug* 32, *Tib* 8, cf Seneca the elder *contr* X 4 § 18. Later, Spart *Hadr* 18. In
law, Digest XXXIX 4 § 12[2].

until an inspection of these private prisons was undertaken by the government. Such phenomena are not likely to be the inventions of sensational writers; for the government, heavily weighted with other responsibilities, was driven to intervene and put down the scandal. But to do this was not to supply the necessary labour. That problem remained, and in the attempt to solve it an important development in the organization of large estates seems to have taken place. While the regular labour was as before furnished by the slave-staff, and greater care taken[1] to avoid losses by sickness, and while even the breeding of slaves under certain restrictions was found worthy of attention, the need of extra hands at certain seasons was met by an arrangement for retaining potential free labourers within easy reach. This was an extension of the system of tenant *coloni*. Parcels of the estate were let to small farmers, whose residence was thereby assured. Columella[2] advises a landlord in dealing with his tenants to be more precise in exacting from them work (*opus*) than rent (*pensiones*), and Weber[3] takes *opus* to mean not merely the proper cultivation of their several plots but a stipulated amount of labour on the lord's farm. The practice of exacting labour from debtors[4] in discharge of their debt was not a new one, and this arrangement seems to be the same in a more systematic form. By taking care to keep the little farm sufficiently small, and fixing the rent sufficiently high, the tenant was pretty certain to be often behind with his rent. In such conditions, even if the tenant did not encumber himself by further borrowing, it is clear that he was very liable to sink into a 'soccage' tenant, bound to render regular services without wage. Nominally free, he was practically tied to the soil; while the landlord, nominally but the owner of the soil, gradually acquired what was of more value than a money rent,—the ownership of his tenant's services. In the growing scarcity of slave labour the lord had a strong motive for insisting on his rights, and so the free worker travelled down the road to serfdom.

In reviewing the history of rustic slavery, and its bearing on the labour-question, from the end of the second Punic war to the time of Marcus Aurelius, it is not necessary to refer to every indication of the discontents that were normal in the miserable slave-gangs. A few actual outbreaks of which we have definite records will serve to illustrate the sort of sleeping volcano, ever liable to explode, on which thousands of Italian landlords were sitting. The writers on agriculture were fully conscious of the peril, and among various precepts designed

[1] Even a *valetudinarium* is provided. See Columella XI 1 § 18, XII 1 § 6, 3 §§ 7, 8.
[2] Columella I 7.
[3] Weber *op cit* pp 244–5. See the chapter on Columella for this interpretation. It can hardly be considered certain, but it is not vital to the argument.
[4] Varro I 17 § 2, cf Colum I 3 § 12.

to promote order (and, so far as posible, contentment) none is more significant than the advice[1] not to have too many slaves of the same race. Dictated by the desire to make rebellious combinations difficult, this advice is at least as old as Plato[2] and Aristotle.

So early as 196 BC we hear[3] of a slave-rising in Etruria, put down with great severity by a military force. In 185 there was a great rising[4] of slave-herdsmen (*pastores*) in Apulia, put down by the officer then commanding the SE district. In about another half-century we begin the series of slave-wars which troubled the Roman world for some 60 or 70 years and caused a vast destruction of lives and property. It was the growth of the plantation system under a weak and distracted government that made such horrors possible. In 139 we hear of a rising in Sicily, where the plantation system was in full swing. From 135 there was fierce war[5] in the island, not put down till 131 after fearful bloodshed. The war of Aristonicus[6] in the new province of Asia, from 132 to 130, seems to have been essentially a slave-war. In Sicily the old story[7] was repeated 103–99 with the same phenomena and results. And in the last age of the Republic, 73 to 71 BC, Italy was devastated by the bands of Spartacus, a joint force of gladiators[8] and rustic slaves. For many months the country was at their mercy, and their final destruction was brought about more by their own disunion than by the sword of Roman legions. It is recorded[9] to the credit of Catiline that he refused to enlist rustic slaves in the armed force with which he fought and fell at Pistoria, resisting the less scrupulous advice of his confederates in Rome. During the upheaval of the great civil wars the slaves enjoyed unusual license. Many took arms: probably many others escaped from bondage. But the establishment of the Empire, though the supply of slave labour was not equal to the demand, did not put an end to slave-risings. For instance, in 24 AD a former soldier of the Imperial Guard planned an insurrection[10] in the neighbourhood of Brundisium. By promising freedom to the bold slave-herdsmen scattered about the Apennine forests he got together what was evidently a force of considerable strength. The lucky arrival of a squadron of patrol vessels enabled the local quaestor to break up the conspiracy before it could make head. But Tiberius did not dally with so serious a matter: a detachment of troops carried off the ringleader

---

[1] Varro I 17 §§ 3–6.

[2] Plato *Laws* 777 *d*, Arist *Pol* VII 10 § 13, [Ar] *Oec* I 5 § 6.

[3] Livy XXXIII 36 § 1.   [4] Livy XXXIX 29 §§ 8, 9, cf 41 § 6.

[5] Diodorus book XXXIV, and other authorities enumerated in my *Roman Republic* § 683.

[6] Strabo XIV 1 § 38 [p 646], Diodorus XXXIV 2 § 26.

[7] Diodorus XXXVI.

[8] According to Appian *civ* 1 116 § 2 he was at first joined by some free rustics. The same seems to have been the case in Sicily and Asia.

[9] Sallust *Catil* 44 §§ 5, 6, 56 § 5.   [10] Tacitus *ann* IV 27.

and his chief accomplices to Rome. Tacitus remarks that there was in the city a widespread uneasiness, owing to the enormous growth of slave-gangs while the freeborn population was declining.

These specimens are enough to illustrate a public danger obvious *a priori* and hardly needing illustration. The letter of Tiberius[1] to the Senate in 22 AD shews how he had brooded over the social and economic condition of Italy. He saw clearly that the appearance of prosperity in a country where parks and mansions multiplied, and where tillage was still giving way to pasturage, was unsound. He knew no doubt that these signs pointed to the decline of the free rural population as still in progress. As an experienced general he could hardly ignore the value of such a free population for recruiting armies to serve the state, or regard its decline with indifference. He refers to the burden of imperial responsibilities. Now the system inherited from Augustus set Italy in a privileged position as the imperial land. Surely Tiberius cannot have overlooked the corresponding liability of Italy to take a full share in the defence of the empire. Yet in present circumstances her supply of vigorous manhood was visibly failing. If the present tendencies continued to act, the present system would inevitably break down. But, however much Tiberius was inclined to do justice to the Provinces, he could not escape his first duty to Italy without a complete change of system : and for this he was not prepared. Such misgivings of course could not be expressed in a letter to the Senate; but that an Emperor, temperamentally prone to worry, did not foresee the coming debility and degradation of Italy, and fret over the prospect, is to me quite incredible.

The movement for checking luxury, which drew this letter from Tiberius, resulted according to Tacitus in a temporary reduction of extravagance in entertainments. The influence of senators brought in from country towns or the Provinces helped in promoting a simpler life. It was example, not legislation, that effected whatever improvement was made. It was the example of Vespasian that did most to reform domestic economy. But the historian was well aware that reforms depending on the lead of individuals are transient. We have no reason to believe that any lasting improvement of agriculture was produced by these fitful efforts. From stray references in Tacitus, from the letters of the younger Pliny, from notices in Juvenal and Martial, it is evident that in the great plain of the Cisalpine and in the Italian hill country farming of one kind or another went on and prospered. In such districts a real country life might be found. But this was no new development: it had never ceased. Two conditions were necessary, remoteness from Rome and difficulty of access, which

---

[1] Tacitus *ann* III 53–5.

often coincided. Estates near the city (*suburbana*) were mostly, if not in all cases, held as resorts for rest or pleasure. If a steward could grow a fair supply of farm-produce, so much the better: but the duty of having all ready for visits of the master and his friends was the first charge on his time and attention. Even at some considerable distance from the city the same condition prevailed, if an estate lay near a main road and thus could be reached without inconvenient exertion.

XXIII. CATO.

The book *de agri cultura*[1] of **M Porcius Cato** (234–149 BC) is a remarkable work by a remarkable man. It is generally agreed that it represents his views, though the form in which it has come down to us has led to differences of opinion as to the degree in which the language has been modified in transmission. We need only consider some of the contemporary facts and movements with which Cato was brought into contact and which affected his mental attitude as a public man. He took part in the second Punic war, and died just as the third war was beginning: thus he missed seeing the destruction of the great city which it had in his later years been his passion to destroy. The success of the highly organized Punic agriculture is said[2] to have been one of the circumstances that alarmed his keen jealousy: but we can hardly doubt that he like others got many a hint from the rustic system of Carthage. Another of his antagonisms was a stubborn opposition to Greek influences. In the first half of the second century BC, the time of his chief activities, these influences were penetrating Roman society more and more deeply as Roman supremacy spread further and further to the East. We need not dwell on his denunciations of Greek corruption in general and warnings against the menace to Roman thrift and simplicity. A good instance may be found in the injunction[3] to his son, to have nothing whatever to do with Greek doctors, a pack of rascals who mean to poison all 'barbarians,' who charge fees to enhance the value of their services, and have the impudence to apply the term 'barbarians' to us. The leader of the good-old-Roman party was at least thorough in his hates. And his antipathies were not confined to foreigners and foreign ways, but found ample scope at home in opposition to the newer school of politicians, whose views were less narrow and hearty than his own.

In Cato's time the formation of great landed estates, made easy by the ruin of many peasant farmers in the second Punic war, was in

[1] Text edited by Keil 1895.   [2] Plutarch *Cato maior* 27.
[3] Jordan's edition of his remains, p 77, Plut *Cat mai* 23.

full swing. The effective government of Rome was passing more and more into the hands of the Senate, and the leading nobles did not neglect their opportunities of adding to their own wealth and power. Sharing the military appointments, they enriched themselves with booty and blackmail abroad, particularly in the eastern wars : and, being by law excluded from open participation in commerce, they invested a good part of their gains in Italian land. From what we learn as to the state of Italy during the last century of the Republic, it seems certain that this land-grabbing process took place chiefly if not wholly in the more accessible parts of the country, so far as arable lands were concerned. Etruria and the districts of central Italy near Rome were especially affected, and also Lucania. Apulia soon became noted for its flocks and herds, which grazed there in winter and were driven in the summer months to the mountain pastures of Samnium. The pasturage of great private 'runs' (*saltus*) was thus supplemented by the use of wastes that were still state-property, and the tendency to monopolize these latter on favourable terms was no doubt still growing. With the troubles that arose later out of this system of *possessiones* we are not here concerned. But the increase of grazing as compared with tillage is an important point ; for that it was the most paying sort of farming was one of the facts expressly recognised[1] by Cato. The working of estates on a large scale was promoted by the plentiful supply of slaves in this period. On arable lands they were now employed in large gangs, sometimes working in chains, under slave overseers whose own privileges depended on their getting the utmost labour out of the common hands. In pastoral districts they enjoyed much greater freedom. The time was to come when these *pastores*, hardy ruffians, often armed against wild beasts, would be a public danger. But for the present it is probable that one of their chief recommendations was that they cost next to nothing for their keep.

No man knew better than Cato that it was not on such a land-system as this that Rome had thriven in the past and risen to her present greatness. He was proud[2] of having worked hard with his own hands in youth, and he kept up the practice of simple living on his own estate, sitting down to meals with the slaves[3] whom he ruled with the strictness of a practical farmer. Around him was going on the extension of great ill-managed properties owned by men whom political business and intrigues kept nearly all the year in Rome, and who gave little personal attention to the farming of their estates. When the landlord rebuilt his *villa*, and used his new country mansion mainly for entertaining friends, the real charge of the farm more and more

---

[1] Pliny *NH* XVIII §§ 29, 30, and Cicero *de off* II § 89, Columella VI *praef* §§ 3–5.
[2] Jordan *op cit* p 43. Plutarch *Cat mai* 4.   [3] Plut *Cat mai* 3–5, 20–1.

passed to the plausible slave who was always on the spot as steward. Cato knew very well that these *vilici* did not as a rule do the best for their lords. They had no real interest in getting the most out of the land. The owner, who wanted ready money for his ambitions and pleasures, was hardly the man to spend it on material improvements in hope of an eventual increase of income: thus a steward could easily find excuses for a low standard of production really due to his own slackness. All this demoralizing letting-down of agriculture was anathema to the champion of old-Roman ideas and traditions. It was a grave factor in the luxury and effeminacy that to his alarm were undermining the solid virtues of the Roman people. Above all things, it had what to his intensely Roman nature was the most fatal of defects—it did not pay. Roman nobles were in fact making their chief profits out of plundering abroad, and ceasing to exercise old-fashioned economy at home. With the former evil Cato waged open war as statesman and orator. How he dealt with the latter as a writer on agriculture I proceed to inquire.

We may classify the several points of view from which agriculture could be regarded under a few heads, and see what position in relation to each of these was taken up by Cato. First, as to the scale of farming operations. He does not denounce great estates. He insists on the maintenance of a due proportion[1] between the house and the land. Neither is to be too big for the other. A decent dwelling[2] will induce the landlord to visit his estate more often; a fine mansion will be costly and tempt him to extravagance. Secondly, it is on this frequent personal attention that successful management depends. For your steward needs the presence of the master's eye to keep him to his duty. Thirdly, he accepts the position that the regular staff of labourers are to be slaves, and some at least of these[3] are in chains (*compediti*). For special work, in time of harvest etc, extra labour is to be hired, and of this some is free labour, perhaps not all. For contractors employing gangs of labourers play a considerable part. Their remuneration may be in cash, or they may receive a share[4] of the produce (*partiario*). Some of their labourers are certainly free: if they do not pay the wages regularly, the *dominus* is to pay them and recover from the contractor. But it is not clear that contractors employed freemen exclusively, and there is some indication[5] of the contrary. Fourthly, there is no suggestion of a return to quite small peasant holdings, though he opens the treatise with an edifying passage[6] on the social political and military virtues of farmers, and cites the

---

[1] Cato *agr* 3 § 1, Pliny *NH* XVIII § 32.   [2] Cato *agr* 4.

[3] Cato *agr* 56–7.   [4] Cato *agr* 16, 136–7, 146.

[5] In 147 the *emptor* of a season's lambs seems to be bound to provide a *pastor*, who is held as a pledge to secure the final settlement.   [6] Cato *agr praef.*

traditional description of *virum bonum* as being *bonum agricolam bonumque colonum.* For his own scheme is not one for enabling a poor man to win a living for himself and family out of a little patch of ground. It is farming for profit; and, though not designed for a big *latifundium,* it is on a considerable scale. He contemplates[1] an oliveyard of 240 *iugera* and a vineyard of 100 *iugera,* not to mention all the other departments, and the rigid precepts for preventing waste and getting the most out of everything are the most striking feature of his book. The first business[2] of an owner, he says, is not to buy but to sell. Fifthly, it is important to notice that he does not suggest letting all or part of the estate to tenants. He starts by giving good advice as to the pains and caution[3] needed in buying a landed property But, once bought, he assumes that the buyer will keep it in hand and farm it for his own account. It has been said on high authority[4] that the plan of letting farms to tenant *coloni* was 'as old as Italy.' I do not venture to deny this. But my inquiry leads me to the conviction that in early times such an arrangement was extremely rare: the granting of a plot of land during pleasure (*precario*) by a patron to a client was a very different thing. Cato only uses the word[5] *colonus* in the general sense of *cultivator,* and so far as he is concerned we should never guess that free tenant farmers were known in Italy. Sixthly, whereas in Varro and Columella we find the influence of later Greek thought shewn in a desire to treat even rustic slaves as human and to appeal to the lure of reward rather than the fear of punishment, to Cato the human chattel seems on the level of the ox. When past work, both ox and slave are to be sold[6] for what they will fetch. This he himself says, and his doctrine was duly recorded by Plutarch as a mark of his hard character. It is therefore not surprising that he makes no reference to slaves having any quasi-property (*peculium*) of their own, though the custom of allowing this privilege was surely well known to him, and was probably very ancient. If the final fate of the slave was to be sold as rubbish in order to save his keep, there was not much point in letting him keep a few fowls or

---

[1] Cato *agr* 10 § 1, 11 § 1.

[2] 2 § 7 *patrem familias vendacem non emacem esse oportet.*

[3] Cato *agr* 1. [4] Mommsen in *Hermes* XV p 408.

[5] *praef* § 2, 1 § 4. According to a speaker in Seneca *controv* VII 6 § 17 Cato's later wife was *coloni sui filiam...ingenuam.* Plut *Cat mai* 24 makes her πελάτιν, that is daughter of a client. There seems to be no real contradiction. The *cliens* might be his patron's tenant.

[6] 2 § 7 *boves vetulos...servum senem, servum morbosum...vendat.* Cf Plut *Cat mai* 5, Martial XI 70, Juvenal X 268-70. In Terence *Hautont* 142-4 the Old Man, on taking to farming, sells off all his household slaves save such as are able to pay for their keep *opere rustico faciundo.* His motive for giving up domestic comfort and taking to hard manual labour on the land is to punish himself. So *ibid* 65-74 he appears as neglecting to keep his farm-hands at work.

grow a few vegetables in some waste corner of the farm. But another characteristic story raises some doubt in this matter. We are told that, having remarked that sexual passion was generally the cause of slaves getting into mischief, he allowed them[1] to have intercourse with the female slaves at a fixed tariff. Now, to afford himself this indulgence, a slave must have had a *peculium*. But Cato did not think it worth mentioning,—unless of course we assume that a reference has dropped out of the text. Nor does he refer to manumission: but we hear of his having a freedman—probably not a farm-slave at all.

Cato's position, taken as a whole, shews no sign of a reactionary aim, no uncompromising desire of reversion to a vanished past. Nor does he fall in with the latest fashion, and treat the huge *latifundium* as the last word in landowning. His precepts have in view a fairly large estate, and perhaps we may infer that he thought this about as much as a noble landlord, with other calls upon his energies, could farm through a steward without losing effective control. He does not, like the Carthaginian Mago, insist on the landlord residing[2] permanently on the estate. In truth he writes as an opportunist. For this man, who won his fame as the severest critic of his own times, knew very well that contemporary Romans of good station and property would never consent to abdicate their part in public life and settle down to merely rustic interests. Nor indeed would such retirement have been consistent with Roman traditions. But conditions had greatly changed since the days of the farmer-nobles who could easily attend the Senate or Assembly at short notice. The far greater extent of territory over which modern estates were spread made it impossible to assume that they all lay near the city. And yet the attraction of Rome was greater than ever. It was the centre and head of a dominion already great, and in Cato's day ever growing. The great critic might declaim against the methods and effects of this or that particular conquest and denounce the iniquities of Roman officials: but he himself bore no light hand in advancing the power of Rome, and thereby in making Rome the focus of the intrigues and ambitions of the Mediterranean world. So he accepted the land-system of the new age, and with it the great extension of slave-labour and slave-management, and tried to shew by what devotion and under what conditions it could be made to pay. It must be borne in mind that slave-labour on the land was no new thing. It was there from time immemorial, ready for organization on a large scale; and it was this extension of an existing institution that was new. Agriculture had once been to the ordinary Roman citizen the means of livelihood. It was now, in great part of the most strictly

[1] Plut *Cat mai* 21.   [2] Pliny *NH* XVIII § 35.

Roman districts of Italy, becoming industrialized as a field for investment of capital by the senatorial class, who practically controlled the
government and were debarred from openly engaging in commerce.
The exploitation of rustic properties as income-producing securities
was merely a new phase of the grasping hard-fisted greed characteristic
of the average Roman. Polybius, observing Roman life in this very
age with Greek eyes, was deeply impressed[1] by this almost universal
quality. And Cato himself was a Roman of Romans. Plutarch[2] has
preserved for us the tradition of his economic career. As a young
man of small means he led the hard life of a farmer, as he was not
shy of boasting[3] in later years, and was a strict master of slaves. But
he did not find farming sufficiently remunerative, so he embarked on
other enterprises. Farming remained rather as a pastime than a
source of income : but he took to safe and steady investments, such
as rights over lakes, hot springs, fullers' premises, and land that could
be turned to profit[4] through the presence of natural pasture and woodland. From these properties he drew large returns not dependent on the
weather. By employing a freedman as his agent, he lent money on
bottomry, eluding the legal restriction on senators ; and by combining
with partners in the transaction he distributed and so minimized the
risks of a most profitable business. And all through life he dealt in
slaves[5], buying them young, training them, and selling at an enhanced
price any that he did not want himself. He bred some on his estate,
probably not many. It is said that, in addition to her own children,
his wife would suckle[6] slave-babies, as a means of promoting good
feeling in the household towards her son.

In these details, of the general truth of which there is no reasonable doubt, we have a picture of a man of astounding versatility and
force : for of his political and military activities I have said nothing.
But as a writer on agriculture how are we to regard him ? Surely not
as a thoroughgoing reformer. His experience had taught him that,
if you must have a good income (a point on which he and his contemporaries were agreed), you had better not look to get it from
farming. But if for land-pride or other reasons you must needs farm,
Cato is ready to give you the best practical advice. That many (if indeed
any) men of property would take the infinite trouble and pains that
his system requires from a landlord, he was probably too wise to
believe. But that was their business. He spoke[7] as an oracle ; as in
public life 'take it or leave it' was the spirit of his utterances. The
evidence of his life and of his book, taken together, is more clear as

---

[1] Polyb XXXII 13 §§ 10, 11.
[3] Jordan *op cit* p 43.
[5] Plut *Cat mai* 21, 4.
[7] Pliny even refers to his precepts as *oracula*.

[2] Plut *Cat mai* 21, 25, 4.
[4] Cf Plin *epist* III 19 § 5.
[6] Plut *Cat mai* 20.

shewing the unsatisfactory position of rustic enterprise than from any
other point of view.

A few details relative to the staff employed on the estate are
worthy of a brief notice. Cato is keenly alive to the importance of
the labour-question. In choosing an estate you must ascertain that
there is a sufficient local supply[1] of labour. On the face of it this
seems to mean free wage-earning labour, though the word *operarius*
is neutral. But in a notable passage, in which he sets forth the advantage of being on friendly terms with neighbours (neighbouring landlords), he says 'Don't let your household (*familiam*) do damage: if
you are in favour with the neighbourhood, you will find it easier to
sell your stock, easier[2] to get employment for your own staff at a
wage, easier to hire hands: and if you are engaged in building they
(the *vicini*) will give you help in the way of human and animal
labour and timber.' Here we seem to come upon the hiring, not of
free labourers, but of a neighbour's slave hands on payment of a rent
to their owner. The case would arise only when some special rough
job called for a temporary supply of more labour. It would be the
landlord's interest to keep his neighbours inclined to oblige him.
Thus by mutual accommodation in times of pressure it was possible
to do with a less total of slaves than if each farm had had to be provided with enough labour for emergencies. We may also remark
that it made the slave-owner less dependent on free wage-earners, who
would probably have raised their demands when they saw the landlord at their mercy. It must always be borne in mind that Cato is
writing solely from the landlord's point of view.

The leading fact relative to the staff is that the steward or head
man (*vilicus*) under whom the various workers, slave or free, are
employed is himself a slave. So too the *vilica*, usually his consort.
Their position is made quite clear by liability to punishment and by
their disqualification[3] from performance of all save the most ordinary
and trivial religious ceremonies. Their duties are defined by jealous
regulations. But in order to keep the steward up to the mark the
master must often visit the estate. It is significant that he is advised
on arrival to make a round of the place[4] without delay, and not to
question his steward until he has thus formed his own impressions
independently. Then he can audit accounts, check stores, listen to
excuses, give orders, and reprimand failure or neglect. That the
master needed to be a man of knowledge and energy in order to
make his estate a source of profit when in charge of a steward, is

---

[1] Cato *agr* 1 § 3 *operariorum copia siet.*
[2] Cato *agr* 4 *operas facilius locabis, operarios facilius conduces.*
[3] Cato *agr* 5, 83, 143.   [4] Cato *agr* 2 § 1.

evident. It may well be that Cato insists so strongly on the need of
these qualities because they were becoming rare among the nobles of
his day. But, though he knew that the efficiency of a slave steward
could only be maintained by constant and expert watching, he never
suggests the employment of a free man in that capacity. The truth
seems to be that the ' Manager,' a man paid by salary or percentage
and kept up to the mark by fear of 'losing his place,' is a comparatively modern figure. In antiquity the employment of Freedmen in
positions of trust was a move in that direction, though patrons kept a
considerable hold, beyond the purely economic one, on their freedmen. But for charge of a farm Cato does not suggest employment of
a freedman.

The blending of free and slave labour might well have been
brought out more clearly than it is : but to the author writing for his
own contemporaries it would seem needless to enlarge upon a condition which everyone took for granted. Yet there are passages
where it is indicated plainly enough. Thus in the olive-press room
a bed is provided[1] for two free *custodes* (apparently foremen) out of
three : the third, a slave, is put to sleep with the *factores*, who seem
to be the hands employed[2] to work the press, probably slaves, whose
labour is merely bodily exertion. The *leguli* who gather up the olives
are probably free, for they are interested[3] in making the amount so
gathered as large as possible. Strippers, *strictores*, who pluck the
olives from the tree, are also mentioned[4] in the chapter dealing with
the harvesting of a hanging crop by a contractor. As the need of care
to avoid damaging the trees is insisted on, and all the workers are
to take a solemn oath[5] that they have stolen none of the crop, we
may fairly infer that they are freemen. When the process of manufacture is let to a contractor, his *factores* are to take a similar oath,
and are probably free. So too when a crop is sold hanging : if the
buyer neglects to pay[6] his *leguli* and *factores* (which would cause
delay) the landlord may pay them himself and recover the amount
from the buyer. On the other hand in the grazing department the
underlings are slaves. In case of the sale of winter grazing, provision
is made[7] for an arbitration for settlement of damages done by the
emptor aut pastores aut pecus emptoris to the *dominus*, or by the *dominus aut familia aut pecus* to the *emptor*. And, until the compensation
awarded is paid, the *pecus aut familia* on the ground is to be held in
pledge by the party to whom compensation is due. This would
generally be the landlord, and the *familia* of the *emptor* would be his

[1] Cato *agr* 13 § 1 *duo custodes liberi...tertius servus...*etc.
[2] Ibid 66 *ubi factores vectibus prement.*   [3] Ibid 64 § 1.   [4] Ibid 144.
[5] Ibid 144-5.   [6] Ibid 146.   [7] Ibid 149 § 2.

pastores. Even so, when a speculator buys the season's lambs, he provides a *pastor* for two months, and the man is held in pledge[1] by the landlord until the account is finally settled.

There are casual references to other persons employed on the estate whose condition has to be inferred from various indications with more or less certainty. Thus the *capulator,* who draws off the oil from the press into vessels, is connected with the *custos*[2] and is not clearly distinct from him. He may be a slave, but the call for strict cleanliness and care at this stage of the operations rather suggests the free wage-earner. An *epistates* is mentioned[3] in a chapter on food-rations (*familiae cibaria*), and grouped with the *vilicus* and *vilica* and the *opilio.* They receive less food than the common hands engaged in rough manual labour. They are probably all slaves, the *epistates* being a foreman of some sort, and the *opilio* the head shepherd, the *magister pecoris* of whom we often hear later. In the estimates[4] of the equipment required for a farm with oliveyard or vineyard the human staff is included with the other live and dead stock. The *operarii* mentioned in this connexion are evidently slave hands, and the *bubulcus*[5] *subulcus asinarius opilio* and *salictarius* are the same, only specialized in function. For an oliveyard of 240 *iugera* the human staff is put at 13 (*summa homines xiii*), for a vineyard of 100 *iugera* it is 16, and the *operarii* in particular are 10 as against 5. The greater amount of digging[6] needed on a farm chiefly devoted to vines is the reason of the difference. These estimates are for the permanent staff, the *familia,* owned by the landlords in the same way as the oxen asses mules sheep goats or pigs. So far as common daily labour is concerned, this staff should make the farm self-sufficing.

But there were many operations, connected with the life of the farm, for performing which it was either not desirable or not possible to rely on the regular staff. It would never have paid to maintain men skilled in the work of special trades only needed on rare occasions. Thus for erecting buildings the *faber*[7] is called in: the landlord finds materials, the builder uses them and is paid for his work. Lime is needed for various purposes, and it may be worth while[8] to have a kiln on the estate and do the burning there. But even so it is well to employ a regular limeburner (*calcarius*) for the job. The landlord finds limestone and fuel, and a way of payment is to work on shares (*partiario*) each party taking his share of the lime. The same share-system (according to Keil's text) is proposed for the operation known as *politio,* which

---

[1] Ibid 150.   [2] Ibid 66–7.   [3] Ibid 56.   [4] Ibid 10 § 1, 11 § 1.

[5] It is to be noted that *bubulci* are to be indulgently treated, in order to encourage them to tend the valued oxen with care. 5 § 6.

[6] Ibid 56 *compeditis...ubi vineam fodere coeperint.* Cf Columella 1 9 § 4.

[7] Ibid 14.   [8] Ibid 16, 38.

seems to include[1] weeding and 'cleaning' of the land, at least for cereal crops, and also is prescribed for the skilled tending of a vineyard. For such works as these it is fairly certain that the persons employed were assumed to be living in the neighbourhood. In the case of the blacksmith[2] (*faber ferrarius*) there can be no doubt, for his forge is spoken of as a fit place for drying grapes, hung presumably in the smoke of his wood fire. Now all these skilled men are evidently free, and work on agreed terms. Some of them are certainly not singlehanded, but whether their underlings are freemen or slaves or both we are left to guess. In all cases their work is such as calls not only for skill and industry but also for good faith, which cannot be expected from slaves. It is in short contract-work, whether the bargain be made in a formal agreement or not.

The employment of contractors, each with his own staff, at times of pressure such as the getting in and disposal of crops, has been referred to above, and it has been remarked that some at least of this emergency-labour was performed by freemen. We must therefore conclude that in Cato's time there was a considerable supply of casual labourers in country districts, on whose services landlords could rely. The contractor would seem to have been either a 'ganger' who bargained for terms with the landlord on behalf of his work-party, or a capitalist owning a gang of slaves. What made the difference would be the nature of the job in hand, according as skill or mere brute strength was chiefly required. But that slave labour was the essential factor, on which Catonian agriculture normally depended, is beyond all doubt. The slave steward is not only responsible[3] for the control of the slave staff (*familia*) and their wellbeing and profitable employment. He is authorized to employ other labour, even free labour, at need; only he must not keep such persons hanging about the place. He is to pay them off and discharge them without delay, no doubt in order to prevent them from unsettling the slaves by their presence. And slaves must never be idle. When a master calls his steward to account for insufficient results on the farm, the latter is expected to plead in excuse not only the weather but shortage of hands; slaves have been sick or have run away; or they have been employed[4] on state-work (*opus publicum effecisse*),—probably in mending the roads, for this is recognized below.

---

[1] Ibid 136. In 5 § 4 the *politor* appears as a hired wage-earner, apparently paid by the job. In Varro III 2 § 5 we find *fundo...polito cultura*. See Nonius p 66 M for *politiones = agrorum cultus diligentes*. Greenidge *hist* p 79 regards the *politores* as métayer tenants, why, I do not know.   [2] Ibid 7 § 2, 21 § 5.

[3] Ibid 5, especially § 4 *operarium, mercennarium, politorem diutius eundem ne habeat die.* This is taken by Wallon II pp 100, 345, to mean that these hired men are to be paid off at the end of their stipulated term. Keil thinks they are to be dischargeable at a day's notice. *eundem* seems to imply that it was convenient to change your hired men often.

[4] Ibid 2 § 2, and § 4 *viam publicam muniri.*

XXIV. AGRICULTURE IN THE REVOLUTIONARY PERIOD.

From the death of Cato in 149 BC to the date of Varro's book *de re rustica* (about 37 BC) is a space of more than a century. The one great fact of this momentous period in relation to agriculture is the public recognition of the decay of the small farmers over a large part of Italy, and the vain attempt to revive a class well known to have been the backbone of Roman strength. But the absorption of small holdings in large estates had already gone so far in the affected districts that there was practically only one direction in which land-reformers could move. To confiscate private property was forbidden by Roman respect for legal rights: it appears in Roman history only after the failure of the Gracchan movement, and as a phenomenon of civil war. There were however great areas of land of which the state was still in law proprietor, held by individuals (often in very large blocks) under a system of recognized occupation known as *possessio*. Tradition alleged that in Rome's early days this *ager publicus* had been a cause of quarrels between the needy Commons who hungered for land and the rich nobles who strove to monopolize the land annexed by war and now state-property. It was known that one of the effects produced by the political equalization of the Orders in the fourth century BC had been legislation to restrain land-monopoly. But the Licinian laws of 367 BC had not made an end of the evil. Soon evaded, they had become in course of time wholly inoperative. The new Patricio-Plebeian nobility quieted the claims of the poor by colonial foundations and allotments of land in newly-conquered districts, while they continued to enrich themselves by 'possession' of the public land. Undisturbed possession gradually obscured the distinction between such holdings and the estates held in full ownership as *ager privatus*. Boundaries were confused: mixed estates changed hands by inheritance or sale without recognition of a legal difference in the tenure of different portions: where improvements had been carried out, they applied indistinguishably to lands owned or possessed. The greater part of these *possessiones* was probably not arable but pasture, grazed by numerous flocks and herds in charge of slave herdsmen. Now in Cato's time the imports of foreign corn were already rendering the growth of cereal crops for the market an unremunerative enterprise in the most accessible parts of Italy. Grazing paid better. It required fewer hands, but considerable capital and wide areas of pasturage. It could be combined with the culture of the vine and olive; for the live-stock, brought down to the farmstead in the winter months, supplied plentiful manure. Moreover, the wholesale employment of slaves enabled a landlord to rely on a regular supply of labour. The slave was not liable to military service: so the master was not liable to have his staff called up at short notice. In short, economic influences, aided by selfish or corrupt administration of the laws under the rule of the nobility, gave every advantage to the rich landlords. No wonder that patriotic reformers viewed the prospect with alarm, and sought some way of promoting a revival of the peasant farmers.

The story of the Gracchan movement and the causes of its failure are set forth from various points of view in histories[1] of Rome and special monographs. What concerns us here is to remark that its remedial legislation dealt solely with land belonging to the state and occupied by individuals. Power was taken to ascertain its boundaries, to resume possession on behalf of the state, and to parcel it out in allotments among needy citizens. How far success in the aim of restoring a free citizen population in the denuded districts was ever possible, we cannot tell. But we know that it did not in fact succeed. By 111 BC whatever had been achieved[2] was finally annulled. The bulk of the *ager publicus* had disappeared. The sale of land-allotments, at first forbidden, had been permitted, and the process of buying out the newly created peasantry went on freely. But large estates formed under the new conditions were subject to no defect of title. They were strictly private property, though the term *possessiones* still remained in use. Slave-labour on such estates was normal as before. Indeed rustic slavery was now at its height. This short period of attempted land-reform comes between the two great Sicilian slave-wars (135–2 and 103–99 BC), in the events of which the horrors of contemporary agriculture were most vividly expressed. It was also a time of great wars abroad, in Gaul, in Africa, and against the barbarian invaders from the North. Roman armies suffered many defeats, and the prestige of Roman power was only restored by the military remodelling under Marius. When Marius finally threw over the principle that military service was a duty required of propertied citizens, and raised legions from the poorest classes, volunteering with an eye to profit, he in effect founded the Empire. We can hardly help asking[3] from what quarters he was able to draw these recruits. Some no doubt were idlers already living in

---

[1] The account given in Greenidge's *History of Rome* deserves special reference here. On pp 266–7 he well points out that it was not the Gracchan aim to revive the free labourer but the peasant proprietor.

[2] This is known from the *lex agraria* of which a large part is preserved. See text in Bruns' *Fontes* or Wordsworth's *Specimens*. Translated and explained in Dr E G Hardy's *Six Roman Laws*.

[3] Perhaps some inference may be drawn from Sallust *Iug* 73 § 6 *plebes sic accensa uti opifices agrestesque omnes, quorum res fidesque in manibus sitae erant, relictis operibus frequentarent Marium*...etc, though this refers directly to political support, not to the recruiting of troops.

Rome attracted by the distributions of cheap corn provided by the Government in order to keep quiet the city mob. But these can hardly have been a majority of the recruits of this class. Probably a number came in from rural districts, hearing that Marius was calling for volunteers and prepared to disregard altogether the obsolete rules which had on occasion been evaded by others before him. It is perhaps not too bold a conjecture to suggest that the casual wage-earners, the *mercennarii* referred to by Cato, were an important element in the New Model army of Marius. This landless class, living from hand to mouth, may have been declining in numbers, but they were by no means extinct. We meet them later in Varro and elsewhere. And no man knew better than Marius the military value of men hardened by field-labour, particularly when led to volunteer by hopes of earning a higher reward in a career of more perils and less monotony.

It can hardly be supposed that agriculture throve under the conditions prevailing in these troubled years. The tendency must have been to reduce the number of free rustic wage-earners, while each war would bring captives to the slave-market. We can only guess at these economic effects. The following period of civil wars, from the Italian rising in 90 BC to the death of Sulla in 78, led to a further and more serious disturbance of the land-system. The dictator had to reward his soldiery, and that promptly. The debt was discharged by grants of land, private land, the owners of which were either ejected for the purpose or had been put to death. Of the results of this wholesale confiscation and allotment we have abundant evidence, chiefly from Cicero. Making full allowance for exaggeration and partisan feeling, it remains sufficient to shew that Sulla's military colonists were economically a disastrous failure, while both they and the men dispossessed to make room for them soon became a grave political danger. The discharged soldiers desired an easy life as proprietors, and the excitements of warfare had unfitted them for the patient economy of farming. They bought slaves; but slaves cost money, and the profitable direction of slave-labour was an art calling for a degree of watchfulness and skill that few landlords of any class were willing or able to exert. So this substitution of new landowners for old was an unmixed evil: the new men failed as farmers, and we hardly need to be told that the feeling of insecurity produced by the confiscations was a check on agricultural improvements for the time. Those of the 'Sullan men' who sold their allotments (evading the law) would certainly not get a good price, and the money would soon melt away.

It will be seen that the old Roman system, under which the ordinary citizen was a peasant farmer who served the state as a soldier when needed, was practically at an end. Compulsory levies were on certain occasions resorted to, for no abolition of the old liability to service had taken place: but voluntary enlistment of young men, and their conversion into professional soldiers by technical training, was henceforth the normal method of forming Roman armies. Armies were kept on foot for long campaigns, and the problem of their peaceful disbandment was one of the most serious difficulties of the revolutionary age. The treasury had no large income to spend on money-pensions, so the demand for allotments of land became a regular accompaniment of demobilization. Meanwhile the desperate condition of landlords in important districts, and the danger from the slave-gangs, were forcibly illustrated in the rising under Spartacus (73–1 BC) and the Catilinarian conspiracy. It is unfortunate that the scope of the land-bill of Rullus[1] in 63, defeated by Cicero, is uncertain, and the effect of Caesar's land-law of 59 hardly less so. But one thing seems clear. In default of sufficient lands suitable for allotment, legislators were driven to propose the resumption of the rich Campanian domain. This public estate had long been let to tenants, real farmers, in small holdings; and the rents therefrom were one of the safest sources of public income. To disturb good tenants, and give the best land in Italy to untried men as owners, was surely a bad business. It shews to what straits rulers were driven to find land for distribution. To enter into the details of the various land-allotments between the abortive proposal of Rullus and the final settlement of Octavian would be out of place here. But it is well to note that the plan of purchasing private land for pension-allotments, proposed in the bill of Rullus, was actually carried out by the new Emperor and proudly recorded[2] by him in his famous record of the achievements of his life. The violent transfer of landed properties from present holders to discharged soldiers of the triumviral armies had evidently been both an economic failure and a political evil. To pay for estates taken for purpose of distribution was a notable step towards restoration of legality and public confidence. Whether it immediately brought about a revival of agriculture on a sound footing is a question on which opinions may justifiably differ. Much will depend on the view taken by this or that inquirer of the evidence of Varro and the Augustan poets Horace and Vergil.

NOTE—In Prendergast's *Cromwellian Settlement of Ireland* (ed 2, 1870), chapter IV a, much interesting matter may be found. Cruel expulsions, corrupt influences, and the sale of their lots by soldiers to officers, their frequent failure as cultivators, etc, stand out clearly. The analogy to the Roman cases must of course not be too closely pressed, as the conditions were not identical.

[1] See the important paper by Dr E G Hardy *Journ Phil* 1913.
[2] *Monum Ancyr* III 22 [cap XVI].

XXV. VARRO.

M Terentius Varro wrote his treatise *de re rustica* in 37–6 BC at the age of 80. The subject was only one of an immense number to which he devoted his talents and wide learning when not actively engaged in public duties. The last republican rally under Brutus and Cassius had failed at Philippi in 42, and the Roman world was shared out between the Triumvirs. In 36 the suppression of Lepidus declared what was already obvious, that Antony and Octavian were the real holders of power and probable rivals. Proscriptions, confiscations, land-allotments to soldiers, the wars with Antony's brother Lucius and the great Pompey's son Sextus, had added to the unsettlement and exhaustion of Italy. If it appeared to Varro that a treatise on farming would be opportune (and we may fairly conjecture that it did), there was surely much to justify his opinion in the distressful state of many parts of the country. But at this point we are met by a passage[1] in the work itself which seems to prove that he took a very different view of present agricultural conditions in Italy. Some of the speakers (the book is in form a dialogue) declare that no country is better cultivated than Italy, that no other country is so fully cultivated all through (*tota*), that Italian crops are in general the best of their several kinds, and in particular that Italy is one great orchard. Instances in point are given. That Varro, like Cicero, took great care[2] to avoid anachronisms and improbabilities, that his characters are real persons, and that he tries hard to fit the several topics to the several characters, is not to be denied. But it is perhaps too much to assume that such general remarks as those just cited are meant to represent the known personal opinions of the speakers. If we could be sure of the date at which the dialogue is supposed to be held, we might have a more satisfactory standard for estimating the significance and historical value of these utterances. Unluckily we have no convincing evidence as to the intended date. The scene of the second book can be laid in 67 BC with reasonable certainty, and that of the third in 54 BC. But no passage occurs in the first book sufficient to furnish material for a like inference. When Stolo refers[3] to Varro's presence with the fleet and army at Corcyra, some have thought that he has in mind the time of the civil war in 49 BC. It is much more likely that the reference is to Varro's service[4]

---

[1] Varro *RR* I 2 §§ 3, 6. I find since writing this that Heisterbergk *Entstehung des Colonats* p 57 treats this utterance, rightly, as rhetorical.

[2] See Mr Storr-Best's translation, Introduction pp xxvii–xxx.

[3] *RR* I 4 § 5. Surely in 49 Varro was in Spain.

[4] As in *RR* II *praef* § 6.

as one of Pompey's lieutenants in the pirate war of 67 BC. The dialogue of Book I would then be placed after the summer of that year, probably not much later. The boast of the speakers as to the splendid cultivation of Italy in general would refer to the time when the disturbance caused by the confiscations and assignations of Sulla was dying down and the rising of Spartacus had lately been suppressed. It would be placed before the later disturbances caused by measures designed to satisfy the claims of Pompeian Caesarian and Triumviral armies. Vergil had not yet been driven from his Cisalpine farm.

Whether by placing Book I in this interval, and by supposing that the circumstances of that time would fit the utterances of Varro's characters, I am exceeding the limits of sober guesswork, I cannot judge. But I am convinced that in any case upland pastures and forest-lands[1] accounted for a very large part of the surface of Italy then, as they do still. Indeed Varro recognizes this in his references to the migration of flocks and herds according to the seasons, and particularly when he notes not only the great stretches of rough land to be traversed but also the need of active and sturdy *pastores* able to beat off the assaults of wild beasts and robbers. Surely the complete cultivation of Italy, compared as it is with that of other countries, is a description not to be taken literally, but as a natural exaggeration in the mouth of a self-complacent Roman agriculturist. Be this as it may, the treatise marks a great advance on that of Cato in some respects. Many details are common to both writers, in particular the repeated insistence on the main principle that whatever the farmer does must be made to pay. Profit, not sentiment or fancy, was their common and truly Roman aim. But in the century or more that had elapsed since Cato wrote other authors (such as Saserna) had treated of farming, and much had been learnt from Greek and Punic authorities. Knowledge of the products and practices of foreign lands had greatly increased, and Varro, who had himself added to this store, made free use of the wider range of facts now at the service of inquirers. And the enlarged outlook called for a systematic method. Accordingly Varro's work is clearly divided into three discussions, of tillage (Book I), grazing and stock-breeding (II), and keeping fancy animals (III) chiefly to supply the market for table-luxuries. And he goes into detail in a spirit different from that of Cato. Cato jerked out dogmatic precepts when he thought fit, for instance his wonderful list of farm-requisites. Varro is more concerned with the principles, the reasons for preferring this or that method, derived from the

---

[1] The wild hill-pastures are referred to by Varro *RR* II I § 16 as still leased to *publicani* to whom the *scriptura* or registration fees had to be paid. I have given further references in my *Roman Republic* § 1351. See M Weber *Römische Agrargeschichte* pp 135 foll.

theories and experience of the past. For instance, in estimating the staff required, he insists[1] on its being proportioned to the scale of the work to be done : as the average day's work (*opera*) varies in efficiency according to the soil, it is not possible to assign a definite number of hands to a farm of definite area. Nor is he content simply to take slave-labour, supplemented by hired free labour and contract-work, for granted. In a short but important passage he discusses the labour-question, with reasons for the preference of this or that class of labour for this or that purpose, of course preferring whichever is likely to give the maximum of profit with the minimum of loss.

It is this passage[2] that is chiefly of interest from my present point of view, and I will therefore translate it in full.

'So much for the four conditions[3] of the farm that are connected with the soil, and the second four external to the farm but bearing on its cultivation. Now for the appliances used in tillage. Some classify these under two heads (*a*) men (*b*) the implements necessary for their work. Others under three[4] heads (*a*) the possessed of true speech (*b*) the possessed of inarticulate speech (*c*) the speechless. In these classes respectively are included[5] (*a*) slaves (*b*) oxen (*c*) waggons, and such are the three kinds of equipment. The men employed in all tillage are either slaves or freemen or both. Free labour is seen in the case of those who till their[6] land themselves, as poor peasants[7] with the help of their families mostly do : or in that of wage-earners[8], as when a farmer hires free hands to carry out the more important operations on his farm, vintage or hay-harvest and the like : such also are those who were called "tied men"[9] in Italy, a class still numerous in Asia Egypt and Illyricum. Speaking of these[10] as a class, I maintain that in the tillage of malarious land[11] it pays better to employ free wage-earners than slaves ; even in a healthy spot the more important operations, such as getting in vintage or harvest, are best so managed. As to their qualities, Cassius writes thus : in buying[12] labourers you are to choose men fit for heavy work, not less than 22 years of age and ready to learn farm-duties. This you can infer from giving them other tasks and seeing how they perform them, or by

---

[1] *RR* I 18.   [2] *RR* I 17.   [3] *RR* I 6–16.
[4] [*genus*] *vocale, semivocale, mutum.*
[5] These are specimens only. Others would be hired freemen, asses, and (near a river) barges.
[6] *ipsi* suggests peasant owners.   [7] *pauperculi cum sua progenie.*
[8] *mercennariis...conducticiis liberorum operis.*
[9] *obaerarios* or *obaeratos*, who work off a debt by labour for a creditor.
[10] *de quibus universis.* This seems to refer to all human workers.
[11] *gravia loca.* Cf I 12 § 2.
[12] *operarios parandos esse*, not *conducendos*, for these are clearly slaves. Cf I 16 § 4.

questioning[1] new slaves as to the work they used to do under their former owner. Slaves should be neither timid nor high-spirited. Their overseers[2] should be men able to read and write, in fact with a touch of education, honest fellows, somewhat older than the mere labourers just mentioned. For these are more willing to obey their elders. Above all things the one indispensable quality in overseers is practical knowledge of farming. For the overseer is not only to give orders, but to take part in carrying them out; so that the slave may do as he sees the overseer do, and note the reasonableness of his own subordination to one his superior in knowledge. On the other hand the overseer should not be allowed to enforce obedience by the lash rather than by reprimand,—of course supposing that the same effect[3] is produced. Again, you should not buy too many slaves of the same race, for nothing breeds trouble in the household[4] more than this. For the overseers there should be rewards to make them keen in their work: care should be taken to allow them a private store[5] and slave concubines to bear them children, a tie which steadies them and binds them more closely to the estate. It is these family ties that distinguish the slave-gangs from Epirus and give them a high market-value. You should grant favours to overseers to gain their goodwill, and also to the most efficient of the common hands; with these it is also well to talk over the work that is to be undertaken, for it makes them think that their owner takes some account of them and does not utterly despise them. They can be given more interest in their work by more generous treatment in the way of food or clothing, or by a holiday or by leave to keep a beast or so of their own at grass on the estate, or other privileges: thus any who have been overtasked or punished may find some comfort[6] and recover their ready goodwill towards their owner.'

This passage well illustrates the advance in scientific treatment of the subject since the time of Cato. The analysis and classification may not be very profound, but it tends to orderly method, not to oracles. The influence of Greek writings is to be traced, for instance in the rules for the choice and treatment of slaves. The writings of Aristotle and his school had been studied in Rome since the great collection had been brought by Sulla from the East. How far Varro actually borrows from Aristotle or Plato or Xenophon is not always easy to say. The advice to avoid getting too many slaves of one race

---

[1] The text here is damaged. I give the apparent meaning.

[2] *qui praesint*, a very general expression.

[3] That is, obedience.

[4] *offensiones domesticas*. Varro may have in mind the Syrians in the Sicilian slave-wars and the Thracians and Gauls under Spartacus.

[5] *peculium*.   [6] Here also the text is doubtful.

or too spirited, and to use sexual relations as a restraining tie, were by this time common-places of slave-management, and appear under Cato in somewhat cruder practical forms. But Varro is involved in the difficulties that have ever beset those who try to work on double principles, to treat the slave as at once the chattel of an owner and a partner in common humanity. So he tells his reader 'manage your slaves as men, if you can get them to obey you on those terms; if not,—well, you must make them obey—flog them.' Humanitarian principles have not gone far in the system of Varro, who looks solely from the master's point of view. The master gets rather more out of his slaves when they work to gain privileges than when they work merely to escape immediate punishment. So he is willing to offer privileges, and the prospect of promotion to the higher ranks of the staff. Overseers and the best of the common hands may form a little quasi-property of their own by the master's leave. But these *peculia* do not seem to be a step on the road to manumission, of which we hear nothing in this treatise. We are left to infer that rustic slaves on estates generally remained there when past active work, tolerated hangers-on, living on what they could pick up, and that to have acquired some *peculium* was a comfortable resource in old age. In short, the hopes of the worn-out rustic bondman were limited indeed.

When we note Varro's attitude towards free labour we cannot wonder that humanitarianism is not conspicuous in his treatment of slavery. Hired men are more to be trusted than slaves, so you will employ them, as Cato advised, for jobs that need care and honesty and that cannot wait. But he adds a sinister hint as to employing them on work dangerous to health. Your own slaves for whom you have paid good money are too valuable to be exposed to such risks. The great merit of the *mercennarius* is that, when the job is done and his wage paid, you have done with him and have no further responsibility. This brutally industrial view is closely connected with the legal atmosphere of Roman civilization, in which Varro lived and moved. The debtor discharging his debt by serving his creditor as a farm-hand, once an ordinary figure in Italy, was now only found abroad: Varro mentions this unhappy class, for he is not thinking of Italy alone. It is interesting to hear from him that peasant-farmers were not extinct in Italy. But we are not told whether they were still numerous or whether they were mostly to be found in certain districts, as from other authorities we are tempted to infer. Nor do we learn whether men with small farms of their own often went out as wage-earners; nor again whether landless *mercennarii* were in his time a numerous class. These omissions make it very difficult for us to form any clear and trustworthy picture of rural conditions as they presented themselves to Varro. It would seem that they were in general much the same as in Cato's time, but that Varro is more inclined to discuss openly some details that Cato took for granted. So in his turn Varro takes some things for granted, passing lightly over details that we cannot but wish to know.

There is however one important matter, ignored by Cato (at least in his text as we have it), to which reference is found in Varro. It is the presence of the free tenant farmer (*colonus*) in the agricultural system of Italy. He tells us that the formal lease[1] of a farm usually contained a clause by which the *colonus* was forbidden to graze a she-goat's offspring on the farm. In another passage[2] the same prohibition is mentioned, but with this limitation, that it applies only to land planted with immature saplings. So poisonous were the teeth of nibbling goats thought to be. The restriction imposed on the tenant suggests that the landlord was bargaining at an advantage ; the lessor could dictate his terms to the lessee. That the tenant farmers of this period were at least in some cases humble dependants of their landlords is clearly shewn by a passage[3] of Caesar. In order to hold Massalia for Pompey in 49 BC, Domitius raised a squadron of seven ships, the crews for which he made up from his own[4] slaves freedmen and tenants. Soon after he refers to this force[5] as the tenants and herdsmen brought by Domitius. These herdsmen are no doubt some of the slaves before mentioned. It is evident that the free retainers called tenants are not conceived as having much choice in the matter when their noble lord called them out for service. Probably their effective freedom consisted in the right to own property (if they could get it), to make wills, to rear children of their own, and other like privileges. But their landlord would have so great a hold[6] on them that, though in theory freemen, they were in practice compelled to do his bidding. In later times we shall find the tenant farmer a common figure in rural life, but very dependent on his landlord ; and it is by no means clear that his position had ever been a strong and independent one. Of Varro all we can say is that he does refer to farm-tenancy as a business-relation, and infer from his words that in that relation the landowner had the upper hand.

Beside what we may call the legal sense of 'tenant,' Varro also uses *colonus* in its older sense of 'cultivator.' In discussing the convenience of being able to supply farm needs, and dispose of farm surplus, in the neighbourhood, he points out that the presence or absence of this

---

[1] *RR* II 3 § 7 *in lege locationis fundi excipi solet ne colonus capra natum in fundo pascat.*
[2] *RR* I 2 § 17 *leges colonicas...etc.*
[3] Caesar *BC* I 34, 56.
[4] *servis libertis colonis suis.*
[5] *colonis pastoribusque.*
[6] As a creditor on a debtor.

advantage may make all the difference whether a farm can be made to pay or not. For instance, it is seldom worth while to keep skilled craftsmen[1] of your own: the death of one such specialist sweeps away the (year's) profit of the farm. Only rich landowners can provide for such services in their regular staff. So the usual practice of *coloni* is to rely on local men for such services, paying a yearly fee and having a right to their attendance at call. The *coloni* here are simply 'farmers,' and there is nothing to shew that they do not own their farms. The connexion with the verb *colere* appears even more strongly where *pastor* is contrasted[2] with *colonus*, grazier with tiller: and in that passage the *colonus* is apparently identical with the *dominus fundi* just below. The *coloni* of these passages can hardly be mere tenants, but on the other hand they are certainly not great landowners. They seem to be men farming their own land, but in a small way[3] of business. Whether there were many such people in Varro's Italy, he does not tell us. Nor do we find any indication to shew whether they would normally take part in farm work with their own hands. When he deplores[4] the modern tendency to crowd into the city, where men use their hands for applauding shows, having abandoned the sickle and the plough, he is merely repeating the common lament of reformers. There is no sign of any hope of serious reaction against this tendency: the importation and cheap distribution of foreign corn is a degenerate and ruinous policy, but there it is. Varro admired the small holdings and peasant farmers of yore, but no man knew better that independent rustic citizens of that type had passed away from the chief arable districts of Italy never to return.

That small undertakings were still carried on in the neighbourhood of Rome and other urban centres, is evident from the market-gardens of the Imperial age. A notable case[5] is that of the bee-farm of a single *iugerum* worked at a good profit by two brothers about 30 miles north of Rome. Varro expressly notes that they were able to bide their time so as not to sell on a bad market. He had first-hand knowledge of these men, who had served under him in Spain. Clearly they were citizens. They can hardly have kept slaves. It seems to have been a very exceptional case, and to be cited as such: it is very different from that of the peasant farmer of early Rome, concerned first of all to grow food for himself and his family. Agriculture as treated by Varro is based on slave labour, and no small part of his work deals with the

[1] *RR* I 16 § 4 *itaque in hoc genus coloni potius anniversarios habent vicinos, quibus imperent, medicos fullones fabros, quam in villa suos habeant.*

[2] *RR* II *praef* § 5, cf I 2 § 13 foll, and Columella VI *praef* §§ 1, 2.

[3] They evidently own slaves, though not special craftsmen, and are distinct from the *pauperculi* of I 17 § 2.

[4] *RR* II *praef* §§ 3, 4.
     [5] *RR* III 16 §§ 10, 11.

quarters, feeding, clothing, discipline, sanitation, and mating, of the slave staff. True to his legal bent, he is careful to safeguard the rights of the slaveowner by explaining[1] the formal details necessary to effect a valid purchase, with guarantee of bodily soundness, freedom from vice, and flawless title. Again, to keep slaves profitably it was urgently necessary to keep them constantly employed, so that the capital sunk in them should not lie idle and the hands lose the habit of industry. Therefore, while relying on local craftsmen for special skilled services occasionally needed, he insists that a number of rustic articles should be manufactured on the farm. 'One ought not to buy anything that can be produced on the estate[2] and made up by the staff (*domesticis = familia*), such as wicker work and things made of rough wood.' Moreover, the organization of the staff in departments is an elaborate slave-hierarchy. Under the general direction of the *vilicus*, each separate function of tillage or grazing or keeping and fattening fancy-stock has its proper foreman. Such posts carried little privileges, and were of course tenable during good behaviour. Some foremen would have several common hands under them: none would wish to be degraded back to the ranks. It seems that some wealthy men kept[3] birdcatchers huntsmen or fishermen of their own, but Varro, writing for the average landlord, seems to regard these as being properly free professionals. As for the common hands, the 'labourers' (*operarii*), on whose bone and sinew the whole economic structure rested, their condition was much the same as in Cato's time, but apparently somewhat less wretched. Varro does not propose to sell off worn-out slaves; this let us credit to humaner feelings. He shews a marked regard for the health and comfort of slaves; this may be partly humanity, but that it is also due to an enlightened perception of the owner's interest is certain. He does not provide for an *ergastulum*, though those horrible prisons were well known in his day. Why is this? Perhaps partly because slave-labour was no longer normally employed on estates in the extremely crude and brutal fashion that was customary in the second century BC. And partly perhaps owing to the great disturbances of land-tenure since the measures of the Gracchi and the confiscations of Sulla. The earlier *latifundia* had been in their glory when the wealthy nobles sat securely in power, and this security was for the present at an end. But, if the slave *operarii* were somewhat better treated, their actual field labour was probably no less hard. Many pieces of land could not be worked with the clumsy and superficial plough then in use. Either the slope of the ground forbade it, or a deeper turning of the soil was needed,

---

[1] *RR* II 10 §§ 4, 5.

[2] *RR* I 22 § 1. Basket work is often referred to in scenes of country life. Cf Verg *buc* II 71-2, *georg* I 266.

[3] *RR* III 3 § 4, 17 § 6.

as for growing[1] vines. This meant wholesale digging, and the slave
was in effect a navvy without pay or respite. No wonder that *fossor*
became a proverbial term for mere animal strength and dull unadapta-
bility. An interesting estimate of the capability of an average digger
is quoted[2] from Saserna. One man can dig over 8 *iugera* in 45 days.
But 4 day's work is enough for one *iugerum* (about ⅝ of an acre). The
13 spare days allowed are set to the account[3] of sickness, bad weather,
awkwardness, and slackness. Truly a liberal margin to allow for waste.
It cannot have been easy to farm at a profit with slave-labour on
such terms; for the slave's necessary upkeep was, however meagre, a
continual charge.

And yet we do not find Varro suggesting that free wage-earning
labour might in the long run prove more economical than slave-labour
even for rough work. Nay more, he does not refer to the employment
of contractors with their several gangs, each interested in getting his
particular job done quickly and the price paid. He only refers to
mercennarii in general terms, as we saw above. Nor does he speak[4] of
politio as a special process, as Cato does. It may be that he did not
think it worth while to enter into these topics. But it is more probable
that the results of agrarian legislation and civil warfare in the revolutionary period had affected the problems of rustic labour. The attempt
to revive by law the class of small cultivating owners had been a failure.
Military service as a career had competed with rustic wage-earning.
Men waiting to be hired as farm hands were probably scarce. Otherwise,
how can we account for the great armies raised in those days? To refer
once more to a point mentioned above, Varro does not suggest that
the charge of an estate might with advantage be entrusted to a freeman
as *vilicus*. That we can discover all the reasons for the preference of
slaves as stewards is too much to hope for. That it seemed to be a
guarantee of honesty and devotion to duty, the manager being wholly
in his master's power, is a fairly certain guess. And yet Varro like
others saw the advisability of employing free labour for occasional
work of importance. Perhaps the permanent nature of a steward's
responsibilities had something to do with the preference. It may well
have been difficult to keep a hold on a free manager. In management
of a slave staff no small tact and intelligence were needed as well as a
thorough knowledge of farming. General experience needed to be
supplemented by an intimate knowledge[5] of the conditions of the neighbourhood and the capacities of the particular estate. And a free citizen,

---

[1] Cf Cato 56, Columella I 9 § 4.   [2] *RR* I 18 §§ 2, 6.

[3] *valetudini tempestati inertiae indiligentiae.*

[4] In *RR* III 2 § 5 *cum villa non sit sine fundo magno et eo polito cultura* the reference is
quite general.

[5] This is well illustrated by the words of Cicero *de republ* v § 5.

whose abilities and energy might qualify him for management of a big
landed estate, had endless opportunities of turning his qualities to his
own profit elsewhere. Whether as individuals or in companies, enterprising Romans found lucrative openings in the farming of revenues, in
state-contracts, in commerce, or in money-lending, both in Italy and
in the Provinces. Such employments, compared with a possible estate-
stewardship, would offer greater personal independence and a prospect
of larger gains. And freemen of a baser and less effective type would
have been worse than useless: certainly far inferior to well-chosen
slaves.

XXVI. CICERO.

It is hardly possible to avoid devoting a special section to the evidence of **Cicero**, though it must consist mainly of noting a number of
isolated references to particular points. With all his many country-
houses, his interest in agriculture was slight. But his active part in public
life of all kinds makes him a necessary witness in any inquiry into the
facts and feelings of his time; though there are few witnesses whose
evidence needs to be received with more caution, particularly in matters
that offer opportunity for partisanship. For our present purpose this
defect does not matter very much. It is chiefly as confirming the statements of others that his utterances will be cited.

When we reflect that Cicero was himself a man of generous instincts,
and that he was well read in the later Greek philosophies, we are tempted
to expect from him a cosmopolitan attitude on all questions affecting
individuals. He might well look at human rights from the point of
view of common humanity, differentiated solely by personal virtues
and vices and unaffected by the accident of freedom or servitude. But
we do not find him doing this. He might, and did, feel attracted by
the lofty nobility of the Stoic system; but he could not become a Stoic.
No doubt that system could be more or less adapted to the conditions
of Roman life: it was not necessary to make the Stoic principles ridiculous by carrying[1] priggishness to the verge of caricature. But the
notion that no fundamental difference existed between races and classes,
that for instance the Wise Man, human nature's masterpiece, might be
found among slaves, was more than Cicero or indeed any level-headed
Roman could digest. The imperial pride of a great people, conscious
of present predominance through past merit, could not sincerely accept
such views. To a Roman the corollary of accepting them would be the
endeavour (more or less successful) to act upon them. This he had no
intention of doing, and a mere theoretical assent[2] to them as philo-

---

[1] As in his opinion the younger Cato did.
[2] See *pro Murena* § 62, where *disputandi causa* is opposed to *ita vivendi*.

sophical speculations was a detail of no serious importance. Taking this as a rough sketch of the position occupied by Romans of social and political standing, we must add to it something more to cover the case of Cicero. He was a 'new man.' He was not a great soldier. He was not a revolutionary demagogue. He was ambitious. In order to rise and take his place among the Roman nobles he had to fall in with the sentiments prevailing among them: the newly-risen man could not afford to leave the smallest doubt as to his devotion to the privileges of his race and class. Thus, if there was a man in Rome peculiarly tied to principles of human inequality, it was Cicero.

Therefore we need not be surprised to find that this quick-witted and warm-hearted man looked upon those engaged in handwork with a genial contempt[1] sometimes touched with pity. To him, as to the society in which he moved, bodily labour seemed to deaden interest[2] in higher things, in fact to produce a moral and mental degradation. In the case of slaves, whose compulsory toil secured to their owners the wealth and leisure needed (and by some employed) for politics or self-cultivation, the sacrifice of one human being for the benefit of another was an appliance of civilization accepted and approved from time immemorial. But the position of the freeman working for wages, particularly of the man who lived by letting out his bodily strength[3] to an employer for money, was hardly less degrading in the eyes of Roman society, and therefore in those of Cicero. We have no description of the Roman mob by one of themselves. That the rough element[4] was considerable, and ready to bear a hand in political disorder, is certain. But they were what circumstances had made them, and it is probable that the riotous party gangs of Cicero's time were not usually recruited among the best of the wage-earners. It is clear that many slaves took part in riots, and no doubt a number of freedmen also. In many rural districts disputes between neighbours easily developed into acts of force and the slaves of rival claimants did battle for their several owners. Moreover, slaves might belong, not to an individual, but to a company[5] exploiting some state concession of mineral or other rights. In such cases 'regrettable incidents' were always possible. And the wild herdsmen (*pastores*) roaming armed in the lonely hill-country were a ready-made soldiery ever inclined to brigandage or servile

---

[1] See *Brutus* § 257, *de orat* I §§ 83, 263, II § 40, *de finibus* V § 52, *Tusc disp* I § 34, III § 77, V § 104. The *messores* whose rustic brogue is referred to in *de orat* III § 46 surely are free Italians.

[2] From lack of the *ingenuae artes* and *liberales doctrinae* etc.

[3] *de offic* I § 150 *inliberales autem et sordidi quaestus mercennariorum omnium quorum operae non quorum artes emuntur: est enim in illis ipsa merces auctoramentum servitutis.*

[4] The *operae* often referred to.

[5] The *familiae publicanorum*. The *publicani* complained loudly when their slave-staff was in danger from the violence of others. Cf *de imperio Pompei* § 16.

rebellions, a notorious danger. It was an age of violence in city and country. Rich politicians at last took to keeping private bands[1] of swordsmen (*gladiatores*). And it is to be borne in mind that, while a citizen might be unwilling to risk the life of a costly[2] slave, his own property, a slave would feel no economic restraint to deter him from killing his master's citizen enemy.

The employment of slaves in the affrays that took place in country districts over questions of disputed right is fully illustrated in the speeches[3] delivered in cases of private law. The fact was openly recognized in the legal remedies provided, for instance in the various *interdicta* framed to facilitate the trial and settlement of disputes as to *possessio*. The forms contemplated the probability of slaves being engaged in assailing or defending possession on behalf of their masters, and the wording even varied according as the force in question had been used by men armed or unarmed. Counsel of course made much or little of the happenings in each case according to the interest of their clients. But that bloodshed occurred at times in these fights is certain. And there was no regular police force to keep order in remote corners of the land. When slaves were once armed and set to fight, they would soon get out of hand, and a slaveowner might easily lose valuable men. Nay more, an epidemic of local brigandage might result, particularly in a time of civil war and general unrest, and none could tell where the mischief would end. We can only form some slight notion of the effect of such conditions as these on the prospects of peaceful agriculture. The speech *pro Quinctio* belongs to 81 BC, the *pro Tullio* to 71, the *pro Caecina* to 69. When we reflect that the slave rising under Spartacus lasted from 73 to 71, and swept over a large part of Italy, we may fairly conclude that this period was a bad one for farming.

The most striking picture of the violence sometimes used in the disputes of rustic life meets us in the mutilated speech *pro Tullio*, of which enough remains to make clear all that concerns us. First, the form of action employed in the case was one of recent[4] origin, devised to check the outrages committed by bands of armed slaves, which had increased since the disturbances of the first civil war. The need for such a legal remedy must have been peculiarly obvious at the time of the trial, for the rising of Spartacus had only just been suppressed. Cicero refers to the notorious scandal of murders committed by these

---

[1] Cf the famous case of Clodius and Milo.
[2] Cf *pro Rosc com* §§ 32, 49, 54, *pro Tullio* § 21.
[3] For a discussion of these see Greenidge in the Appendix to *The legal procedure of Cicero's time*.
[4] *pro Tullio* §§ 7-12.

armed bands, a danger to individuals and even to the state, that had
led to the creation of the new form of action at law. In stating the
facts of the case, of course from his client's point of view, he gives us
details[1] which, true or not, were at least such as would not seem incredible to a Roman court. Tullius owned an estate in southern Italy.
That his title to it was good is taken for granted. But in it was reckoned
a certain parcel of land which had been in undisputed possession of
his father. This strip, which was so situated as to form a convenient
adjunct to a neighbouring estate, was the cause of trouble. The neighbouring estate had been bought by two partners, who had paid a fancy
price for it. The bargain was a bad one, for the land proved to be
derelict and the farmsteads all burnt down. One of the partners induced
the other to buy him out. In stating the area of the property he included
the border strip of land claimed by Tullius as his own. In the process of
settlement of boundaries for the transfer to the new sole owner he would
have included the disputed ground, but Tullius instructed[2] his attorney
and his steward to prevent this: they evidently did so, and thus the ownership of the border strip was left to be determined by process of law.
The sequel was characteristic of the times. The thwarted claimant
armed a band of slaves and took possession[3] of the land by force, killing
the slaves who were in occupation on behalf of Tullius, and committing
other murders and acts of brigandage by the way. We need not follow
the case into the law-court. What concerns us is the evidence of unfortunate land speculation, of land-grabbing, of boundary-disputes, and
of the prompt use of violence to supersede or hamper the legal determination of rights. The colouring and exaggeration of counsel is to be
allowed for; but we can hardly reject the main outlines of the picture
of armed slave-bands and bloodshed as a rural phenomenon of the
sorely tried South of Italy.

The speech *pro Caecina* shews us the same state of things existing
in Etruria. The armed violence alleged in this case is milder in form:
at least the one party fled, and nobody was killed. Proceedings were
taken under a possessory interdict issued by a praetor, and Cicero's
artful pleading is largely occupied with discussion of the bearing and
effect of the particular formula employed. Several interesting transactions[4] are referred to. A man invests his wife's dowry in a farm, land
being cheap, owing to bad times, probably the result of the Sullan civil
war. Some time after, he bought some adjoining land for himself.
After his death and that of his direct heir, the estate had to be liquidated

---

[1] *pro Tullio* §§ 14–22.

[2] § 17 *mittit ad procuratorem litteras et ad vilicum.*

[3] To conduct of this kind Cicero makes a general reference in *Paradoxa* VI § 46 *expul-
siones vicinorum...latrocinia in agris.*

[4] *pro Caecina* §§ 10–19.

for purpose of division among legatees. His widow, advised to buy in
the parcel of land adjoining her own farm, employed as agent a man
who had ingratiated himself with her. Under this commission the land
was bought. Cicero declares that it was bought for the widow, who
paid the price, took possession, let it to a tenant, and held it till her
death. She left her second husband Caecina heir to nearly all her
property, and it was between him and the agent Aebutius that troubles
now arose. For Aebutius declared that the land had been bought by
him for himself, and that the lady had only enjoyed the profits of it
for life in usufruct under her first husband's will. This was legally
quite possible. At the same time he suggested that Caecina had lost
the legal capacity of taking the succession at all. For Sulla had
degraded the citizens belonging to Volaterrae, of whom Caecina was
one. Cicero is more successful in dealing with this side-issue than in
establishing his client's claim to the land. The dispute arising out of
that claim, the armed violence used by Aebutius to defeat Caecina's
attempt to assert possession, and the interdict granted to Caecina, were
the stages by which the case came into court. Its merits are not certain.
But the greedy characters on both sides, the trickery employed by one
side or other (perhaps both), and the artful handling of the depositions
of witnesses, may incline the reader to believe that the great orator had
but a poor case. At all events farming in Etruria appears as bound up
with slave labour and as liable to be disturbed by the violence of slaves
in arms.

In the above cases it suited Cicero's purpose to lay stress on the
perils that beset defenceless persons who were interested in farms in
out-of-the-way[1] places. Yet the use of armed force was probably most
habitual on the waste uplands, and his references to the lawless doings
of the brigand slave-bands fully confirm the warnings of Varro. His
tone varies according to the requirements of his client's case, but he has
to admit[2] that wayfarers were murdered and bloody affrays between
rival bands ever liable to occur. He can on occasion[3] boldly charge a
political opponent with deliberate reliance on such forces for revolutionary ends. Thus of C Antonius he asserts 'he has sold all his live
stock and as good as parted with his open pastures, but he is keeping
his herdsmen; and he boasts that he can mobilize these and start a
slave-rebellion whenever he chooses.' There was no point in saying

[1] *pro Caecina* § 1 *in agro locisque desertis.*
[2] *pro Vareno* fragm 5, *pro Cluentio* § 161, cf *pro Tullio* § 8.
[3] *in toga candida* fragm 11 *alter pecore omni vendito et saltibus prope addictis pastores
retinet, ex quibus ait se cum velit subito fugitivorum bellum excitaturum.* For the *fugitivi* in
Sicily cf II *in Verrem* II § 27, III § 66, IV § 112, V *passim*, and the famous inscription of
Popilius, Wilmanns 797 and Wordsworth *specimens* pp 221, 475, CIL I 551, referring to
first Sicilian slave-war.

this if it had been absurdly incredible. Another glimpse of the utter lawlessness prevalent in the wilds appears in the story[1] of murders committed in Bruttium. Suspicion rested on the slaves employed by the company who were exploiting the pitch-works in the great forest of Sila under lease from the state. Even some of the free agents of the company were suspected. The case, which was dealt with by a special criminal tribunal, belongs to the year 138 BC, and attests the long standing of such disorders. And it is suggestive of guilty complicity on the part of the lessees that, though they eventually secured an acquittal, it was only after extraordinary exertions on the part of their counsel.

Indeed these great gangs of slaves in the service of *publicani* were in many parts of Italy and the Provinces a serious nuisance. Wherever the exploitation of state properties or the collection of dues was farmed out to contractors, a number of underlings would be needed. The lower grades were slaves: a few rose to higher posts as freedmen of the various companies. Now some of the enterprises, such as mines quarries woodlands and the collection of grazing dues on the public pastures, were generally in direct contact with rural life, and employed large staffs of slaves. The managers of a company were concerned to produce a high dividend for their shareholders: so long as this resulted from the labours of their men, it was a matter of indifference to them whether neighbouring farmers were robbed or otherwise annoyed. That we hear little or nothing of such annoyances is probably owing to the practice of locking up slave-labourers at night in an *ergastulum*, for fear of their running away, not to keep them from doing damage. Runaways do not appear singly as a rustic pest. But in bands there was no limit to the harm that *fugitivi* might do; witness the horrors of the slave-wars. In short, wherever slaves were employed in large numbers, the possibility of violence was never remote. Their masters had always at hand a force of men, selected for bodily strength and hardened by labour, men with nothing but hopeless lives to lose, and nothing loth to exchange dreary toil for the dangers of a fight in which something to their advantage might turn up. No doubt the instances of slaves called to arms in rustic disputes were far more numerous than those referred to by Cicero: he only speaks of those with which he was at the moment concerned.

Is it then true that in the revolutionary period farming depended on slave-labour while its security was ever menaced by dangers that arose directly out of the slave-system? I fear it is true, absurd though the situation may seem to us. Between the great crises of disturbance were spells of comparative quiet, in which men could and did farm

[1] *Brutus* § 85.

profitably in the chief agricultural districts of Italy. But it must be remembered that many an estate changed hands in consequence of civil war, and that many new landlords profited economically by appropriating the capital sunk in farms by their predecessors. The case of Sextus Roscius of Ameria gives us some light on this point. The picture drawn[1] by Cicero of the large landed estate of the elder Roscius, of his wealth and interest in agriculture, of his jealous and malignant relatives, of the reasons why he kept his son Sextus tied to a rustic life, is undoubtedly full of colouring and subtle perversions of fact. Let it go for what it may be worth. The accused was acquitted of the crime laid to his charge (parricide), but there is no sign that he was ever able to recover the estate and the home from which his persecutors had driven him. They had shared the plunder with Chrysogonus the favoured freedman of Sulla, who himself bought the bulk of the property at a mere fraction of its market value, and it is practically certain that the rogues kept what they got. It was easy to make agriculture pay on such terms. But what of the former owners of such properties, on whose ruin the new men's prosperity was built? Can we believe that genuine agricultural enterprise was encouraged by a state of things in which the fruits of long patience and skill were liable to sudden confiscation?

In Cicero, as in other writers, we find evidence of a wage-earning class living by bodily labour alongside of the slave-population. But in passages where he speaks[2] of *mercennarii* it is often uncertain whether freemen serving for hire, or slaves hired from another owner, are meant. In his language the associations[3] of the word are mean. It is true that you may buy for money not only the day's-work (*operae*) of unskilled labourers but the skill (*artes*) of craftsmen. In the latter case even Roman self-complacency will admit a certain dignity; for men of a certain social status[4] such professions are all very well. But the mere 'hand' is the normal instance; and for the time of his employment he is not easily distinguished from a slave. Therefore Cicero approves[5] a Stoic precept, that justice bids you to treat slaves as you would hirelings—don't stint their allowances (food etc), but get your day's-work out of them. In passages[6] where the word *mercennarius* is not used, but implied, there is the same tone of contempt, and it is not always clear whether the workers are free or slaves. In short the word is not as neutral as *operarius*, which connotes mere manual labour, whether the labourer be free or not, and is figuratively used[7] to connote

---

[1] *pro Roscio Amer* §§ 39–51.   [2] *pro Caecina* §§ 58, 63.
[3] Thus in *pro Cluentio* § 163 a disreputable tool is *mercennarius Oppianici.*
[4] *de officiis* I § 151 *quorum ordini conveniunt.*   [5] *de officiis* I § 41.
[6] II *in Verrem* I § 147, IV § 77.
[7] Thus of orators, *Brutus* § 297, *de orat* I §§ 83, 263, cf II § 40. Also *opifex* in *Tusc disp* v § 34.

a merely mechanical proficiency in any art. Our 'journeyman' is
sometimes similarly used.

There are other terms in connexion with land-management the use
of which by Cicero is worth noting. Thus a landlord may have some
order to give in reference to the cultivation of a farm. If he gives it
to his *procurator*[1], it is as an instruction, a commission authorizing him
to act ; if to his *vilicus*, it is simply a command. For the former is a
free attorney, able at need to represent his principal even in a court of
law : the latter is a slave steward, the property of his master. The *procurator* is hardly a 'manager' : he seldom occurs in connexion with
agriculture, and seems then to be only required when the principal is
a very 'big man,' owning land on a large scale, and probably in scattered blocks. In such cases it would be convenient for (say) a senator
to give a sort of 'power of attorney' to an agent and let him supervise
the direction of a number of farms, each managed by a steward. I take
this policy to be just that against which the writers on agriculture
warn their readers. It sins against the golden rule, that nothing is a
substitute for the Master's eye. Whether the agent referred to in the
speech *pro Tullio*, who as well as the steward received[2] written instructions from Tullius, was guilty of any neglect or blunder, we cannot
tell. That any act done to a *procurator* or by him was legally equivalent
to the same done to or by his principal, is a point pressed in the *pro
Caecina*, no doubt because it was safe ground and an excuse for not
dwelling on weak points in a doubtful case.

The *colonus* as a tenant[3] farmer, whom we find mentioned in Varro
but not in Cato, appears in Cicero. In the *pro Caecina* we read[4] that
the widow lady took possession of the farm and let it (*locavit*) ; also
that the tenant was after her death still occupying the farm, and that
a visit of Caecina, in which he audited the accounts of the tenant, is a
proof that Caecina himself was now in possession. That is, by asserting
control of the sitting tenant Caecina made the man his agent so far as
to retain possession through the presence of his representative. If the
facts were as Cicero states them, the contention would be legally sound.
For, as he points out in another passage, any representative[5] will serve
for these purposes of keeping or losing possession. If the interdict-
formula only says 'attorney' (*procurator*), this does not mean that only

---

[1] *de orat* 1 § 249 *si mandandum aliquid procuratori de agri cultura aut imperandum vilico
est.*

[2] *pro Tullio* § 17 *mittit ad procuratorem litteras et ad vilicum.*

[3] Cicero's own estate at Arpinum seems to have been let in *praediola* to tenants. See *ad
Att* XIII 9 § 2.

[4] *pro Caecina* §§ 17, 57, 94.

[5] *pro Caecina* § 57, cf 63. So in § 58 the word *familia* is shewn not to be limited to
slaves personally owned by the litigant referred to.

an attorney in the technical sense, a plenipotentiary agent appointed
by an absentee principal with full legal formalities, is contemplated.
No, the brief formula covers agency of any kind : it will apply to your
tenant your neighbour your client or your freedman, in short to any
person acting on your behalf. In the great indictment of Verres[1] we
find a good instance of tenancy in Sicily, where it seems to have been
customary for large blocks of land to be held on lease from the state
by tenants-in-chief (*aratores*) who sometimes sublet parcels to *coloni*.
In this case the trouble arose out of the tithe to which the land was
liable. Verres, in order to squeeze an iniquitous amount out of a
certain farm, appointed a corrupt court charged to inquire whether the
(arable) acreage had been correctly returned by the *colonus*. Of course
they were instructed to find that the area had been fraudulently under-
stated. But the person against whom judgment was to be given was
not the *colonus*, but Xeno, who was not the owner of the farm. He
pleaded that it belonged to his wife, who managed her own affairs ;
also that he had not been responsible for the cultivation (*non arasse*).
Nevertheless he was not only compelled to pay a large sum of money
to meet the unfair damages exacted, but subjected to further extortion under threat of corporal punishment. The returns on which
the tithes were assessed would seem to have been required from the
actual cultivators, and the lessees of the year's tithe to have had a
right of action against the owners or chief-tenants of the land, if the
tenant farmer defaulted in any particular. So far we are able to
gather that tenant farmers were no exception at this time, though
perhaps not a numerous class ; and that they were not persons of
much social importance. That they were to a considerable extent
dependent on their landlords is probable, though not actually attested
by Cicero, for we have seen evidence of it in a passage of Caesar.
Cicero's reference[2] to the case of a lady who committed adultery with
a *colonus* is couched in such terms as to imply the man's social inferiority.
In another passage[3] we hear of a man in the Order of *equites equo
publico* being disgraced by a censor taking away his state-horse, and
of his friends crying out in protest that he was *optimus colonus*, thrifty
and unassuming. Here we have a person of higher social quality, no
doubt : but I conceive *colonus* to be used in the original sense of
'cultivator.' To say 'he is a good farmer' does not imply that he is a
mere tenant, any more than it does in the notable passage of Cato.

The *vilicus* generally appears in Cicero as the slave steward familiar
to us from other writers. In one place[4] he is contrasted with the

[1] II *in Verrem* III §§ 53–5, and *passim*. These *arationes* paid *decumae*.
[2] *pro Cluentio* §§ 175, 182.   [3] *de orat* II § 287.
[4] *de republ* v § 5, where the perfect ruler is a sort of blend of *dispensator* and *vilicus*.

dispensator, who seems to be a sort of slave clerk charged with registering stores and serving out rations clothing etc. As this functionary seldom meets us in the rustic system of the period, we may perhaps infer that only large estates, where the *vilicus* had no time to spare from purely agricultural duties, required such extra service. In saying that he can read and write (*litteras scit*) Cicero may seem to imply that this is not to be expected from the *vilicus* : but the inference is not certain, for the agricultural writers require stewards to read at least. In another passage[1] we read that in choosing a slave for the post of steward the one thing to be kept in view is not technical skill but the moral qualities, honesty industry alertness. Here it is plain that the orator is warping the truth in order to suit his argument : Varro would never have disregarded technical skill. For Cicero's point is that what the state needs most in its 'stewards' (that is, magistrates) is good moral qualities. On the same lines he had some 16 years before compared[2] Verres to a bad steward, who has ruined his master's farm by dishonest and wasteful management, and is in a fair way to be severely punished for his offence. The tone of this passage is exactly that of old Cato, put in the rhetorical manner of an advocate.

A few words must be said on the subject of manumission. In his defence of Rabirius, accused of high treason, Cicero launches[3] out into a burst of indignation at the attempted revival of an obsolete barbarous procedure designed for his client's destruction. The cruel method of execution to which it points, long disused, is repugnant to Roman sentiment, utterly inconsistent with the rights of free humanity. Such a prospect[4] would be quite unendurable even to slaves, unless they had before them the hope of freedom. For, as he adds below, when we manumit a slave, he is at once freed thereby from fear of any such penalties as these. Taken by itself, this passage is better evidence of the liability of slaves to cruel punishment than of the frequent use of manumission. But we know from Cicero's letters and from other sources that freedmen were numerous. And from a sentence[5] in one of the *Philippics* we may gather that it was not unusual for masters to grant freedom to slaves after six years of honest and painstaking service. I suspect that this utterance, in the context in which it occurs, should not be taken too literally. That Romans of wealth and position liked to surround themselves with retainers, humble and loyal, bound to their patron by ties of gratitude and interest, is certain : and early manumissions were naturally promoted by this motive. But the most pleasing instances

---

[1] *pro Plancio* § 62.   [2] II *in Verrem* III § 119.   [3] *pro Rabirio* §§ 10–17.

[4] *hanc condicionem...quam servi, si libertatis spem propositam non haberent, ferre nullo modo possent.*

[5] *Philippic* VIII § 32.

were of course those in which a community of pursuits developed a
real sympathy, even affection between owner and owned, as in the
case of Tiro, on whose manumission[1] Quintus Cicero wrote to congratulate his brother. In all these passages, however, there is one
thing to be noted. They do not look to the conditions of rustic life;
and, so far as the evidence of Cicero goes, they do not shake my conviction that manumission was a very rare event on country estates.

A topic of special interest is the evidence of the existence of farmers
who, whether employing slaves or not, worked on the land in person.
What does Cicero say as to αὐτουργία in his time? It has been pointed
out above that, when it suits his present purpose, he not only enlarges
on the homely virtues of country folk but refers to the old Roman
tradition of farmer-citizens called from the plough to guide and save
the state in hours of danger. He made full use of this topic in his
defence of Sextus Roscius, and represented his client as a simple rustic,
reeking of the farmyard,—how far truly, is doubtful. But he does not
go so far as to depict him ploughing or digging or carting manure. It
is reasonable to suppose that the slaves to whom he refers[2] did the
rough farm-work under his orders. When he can make capital out of
the wrongs of the humble labouring farmer, the orator does not shrink
from doing so. One of the iniquities laid to the charge[3] of Verres is
that he shifted the burden of taking legal proceedings from the lessees
of the Sicilian tithes (*decumani*) to the tithe-liable lessees of the land
(the *aratores*). Instead of the tithe-farmer having to prove that his
demand was just, the land-farmer had to prove that it was unjust.
Now this was too much even for those farming on a large scale: it
meant in practice that they had to leave their farms and go off to make
their appeals at Syracuse. But the hardship was far greater in the case
of small farmers (probably sub-tenants), of whom he speaks thus:
'And what of those whose means of tillage[4] consist of one yoke of
oxen, who labour on their farms with their own hands—in the days
before your governorship such men were a very numerous class in
Sicily—when they have satisfied the demands of Apronius, what are
they to do next? Are they to leave their tillages, leave their house
and home, and come to Syracuse, in the hope of reasserting their rights
at law against an Apronius[5] under the impartial government of a
Verres?' No doubt the most is made of these poor men and their
wrongs. But we need not doubt that there were still some small

[1] Cic *ad fam* XVI 16 § 1 *eum indignum illa fortuna nobis amicum quam servum esse
maluisti.*
[2] *pro Roscio Amer* § 120 *homines paene operarios.*
[3] II *in Verrem* III § 27.
[4] *quid, qui singulis iugis arant, qui ab opere ipsi non recedunt...etc.*
[5] The infamous henchman of Verres.

working farmers in Sicily. In the half-century or so before the time
of Verres we hear[1] of free Sicilians who were sorely disturbed by the
great servile rebellions and even driven to make common cause with
the insurgent slaves. Some such 'small men' were evidently still to
be found wedged in among the big plantations.

Another important passage occurs in the artful speech against the
agrarian bill of Rullus. It refers to the *ager Campanus*, on the value
of which as a public asset[2] Cicero insists. This exceptionally fertile
district was, and had long been, let by the state to cultivating tenants,
whose regularly-paid rents were one of the safest items in the Roman
budget. These farms were no *latifundia*, but apparently of moderate
size, such that thrifty farmers could make a good living in this favoured
land. With the various political[3] changes, carrying with them disturbances of occupancy, caused by wars in the past, we are not here
concerned. Cicero declares that one aim of the bill was the assignation
of this district to new freeholders, which meant that the state treasury
would lose a sure source of revenue. This, in the interest of the aristocratic party, he was opposing, and undoubtedly misrepresented facts
whenever it suited his purpose. In matters of this kind, he says, the
cry is often raised[4] that it is not right for lands to lie depopulated
with no freemen left to till them. This no doubt refers to the Gracchan
programme for revival of the peasant farmers. Cicero declares that
such a cry is irrelevant to the present issue, for the effect of the bill
will be to turn out the excellent sitting tenants[5] only to make room
for new men, the dependants and tools of a political clique. The reason
why, after the fall of Capua in the second Punic war, that city was
deprived of all corporate existence, and yet the houses were left standing, was this: the menace of a disloyal Capua had to be removed, but
a town-centre of some sort could not be dispensed with. For marketing, for storage[6] of produce, the farmers must have some place of
common resort: and when weary with working on their farms they
would find the town homesteads a welcome accommodation. Allowing
for rhetorical colouring in the interests of his case, perhaps we may
take it from Cicero that a fair number of practical working farmers

---

[1] Diodorus fragm XXXIV 2 § 48, XXXVI 5 § 6.

[2] *de lege agr* II §§ 80–3.

[3] See Beloch *Campanien* pp 304–6.

[4] *de lege agr* II § 84 *agros desertos a plebe atque a cultura hominum liberorum esse non oportere.*

[5] *genus...optimorum et aratorum et militum...illi miseri, nati in illis agris et educati, glaebis subigendis exercitati...*etc.

[6] *de lege agr* II §§ 88–9 *locus comportandis condendisque fructibus, ut aratores cultu agrorum defessi urbis domiciliis uterentur...receptaculum aratorum, nundinas rusticorum, cellam atque horreum Campani agri...*etc.

were settled on the Campanian plain. His prediction[1] that, if this
district were to be distributed in freehold allotments, it would presently
pass into the hands of a few wealthy proprietors (as the Sullan allotments had been doing) suggests a certain degree of sincerity. But
taken as a whole the utterances of Cicero are too general, and too
obviously meant to serve a temporary purpose, to furnish trustworthy
data for estimating the numerical strength and importance of the
working farmers in the Italy of his day.

XXVII. SALLUST AND OTHERS.

In the writings of Cicero's contemporaries other than Varro there
is very little to be found bearing upon rustic life and labour as it went
on in their time. Literature was occupied with other themes appropriate
to the political conflicts or social scandals or philosophic questionings
that chiefly interested various individuals and the circles in which they
moved. The origins of civilization formed a fascinating problem for
some, for instance the Epicurean **Lucretius**: but his theory of the
development of agriculture deals with matters outside of our subject.
The one helpful passage of **Caesar**[2] has been noticed already. So too
has the contemptuous reference[3] of **Sallust** to agriculture as slaves'
work. This writer in a few places touches on points of interest. For
instance, in speaking[4] of the various classes of men who were ripe for
revolution, he says 'moreover there were the able-bodied men who
had been used to earn a hard living as hired labourers on farms; the
attraction of private and public bounties had drawn them into Rome,
where they found idle leisure preferable to thankless toil.' Such statements, unsupported by statistics, must be received with caution, but
this assertion is so far backed up by what we learn from other sources,
that we can accept it as evidence. How many such rustic immigrants
of this class there were at any given moment, is what we want to
know, and do not. Again, in a passage[5] describing the popularity of
Marius in 108 BC, he says 'in short, the commons were fired with such
enthusiasm that the handworkers and the rustics of all sorts, men
whose means and credit consisted in the labour of their hands, struck
work and attended Marius in crowds, putting his election before their

---

[1] *de lege agr* II § 82 *deinde ad paucos opibus et copiis adfluentis totum agrum Campanum perferri videbitis.*
[2] See above, chap XXV p 183.   [3] Sallust *Cat* 4 § 1.
[4] Sallust *Cat* 37 § 7 *iuventus, quae in agris manuum mercede inopiam toleraverat*...etc.
[5] Sallust *Iug* 73 § 6 *opifices agrestesque omnes, quorum res fidesque in manibus sitae erant* ...etc.

own daily needs.' In this there is perhaps some exaggeration, but the picture is probably true in the main. The *agrestes* may include both small farmers and labourers. But they can hardly have come from great distances, and so were probably not very numerous. The description is as loose as passages of the kind were in ancient writers, and are still. The references to rustic slave-gangs, and Catiline's refusal to arm them in support of his rising, have been cited above.

We now pass into the period in which the last acts of the Roman Republican drama were played and the great senatorial aristocrats, in whose hands was a great share of the best lands in Italy, lost the power to exploit the subject world. Not only by official extortion in provincial governorships, but by money-lending at usurious interest[1] to client princes or provincial cities, these greedy nobles amassed great sums of money, some of which was employed in political corruption to secure control of government at home. Civil wars and proscriptions now thinned their ranks, and confiscations threw many estates into the market. The fall of Antony in 31 BC left Octavian master of the whole empire of Rome, an emperor ruling under republican disguises. Now it was naturally and properly his aim to neutralize the effects of past disorders and remove their causes. He looked back to the traditions of Roman growth and glory, and hoped by using the lessons thus learnt to revive Roman prosperity and find a sound basis for imperial strength. He worked on many lines : that which concerns us here is his policy towards rustic life and agriculture. As he persuaded and pressed the rich to be less selfish[2] and more public-spirited, to spend less on ostentation and the adornment of their mansions and parks, and to contribute liberally to works of public magnificence or utility, a duty now long neglected ; even so he strove to rebuild Italian farming, to make it what it had been of yore, the seed-bed of simple civic and military virtues. But ancient civilization, in the course of its development in the Roman empire, had now gone too far for any ruler, however well-meaning and powerful, to turn the tide. Socially it was too concentrated and urban, economically too individualistic and too dependent on the manipulation of masses of capital. In many directions the policy of the judicious emperor was marvellously successful: but he did not succeed in reviving agriculture on the old traditional footing as a nursery of peasant farmers. He sought to bring back a traditional golden age, and court-poets were willing to assert[3] that the golden age had indeed returned. This was not true. The ever-repeated praises of country life are unreal. Even when sincere, they are the voice of town-bred men, weary of the fuss and follies of urban life, to which

---

[1] Two notorious instances are Pompey and M Brutus.
[2] Horace *Odes* II 15, III 6, etc.   [3] Horace *Odes* IV 5, 15, etc.

nevertheless they would presently come back refreshed but bored[1]
with their rural holiday. That the science and art of agriculture were
being improved, is true ; hence the treatise of Varro, written in his old
age. But technical improvements could not set the small farmers as a
class on their legs again. The small man's vantage lay (and still lies)
in minute care and labour freely bestowed, without stopping to inquire
whether the percentage of profit is or is not an adequate return for his
toil. Moreover, technical improvements often require the command
of considerable capital. The big man can sink capital and await a
return on the investment : but this return must be at a minimum rate
or he will feel that it does not 'pay.' For in his calculations he cannot
help comparing the returns[2] on different kinds of investments.

Under such conditions it is no wonder that we find *latifundia* still
existing under the early Empire in districts suited for the plantation
system. No doubt much of the large landholding was the outcome of
social ambitions. Men who had taken advantage of civil war and its
sequels to sink money in land took their profit either in a good percentage on plantations, or in the enhanced importance gained by
owning fine country places, or in both ways. A new class was coming
to the front under the imperial regime and among them were wealthy
freedmen. These had not yet reached the predominant influence and
colossal wealth that marked their successors of the next generation.
But they had begun to appear[3] in the last age of the Republic, and
were now a force by no means to be ignored. Such landowners were
not likely to favour the revival of peasant farmers, unless the presence
of the latter could be utilized in the interest of the big estates. There
were two ways in which this result could be attained. A small free-
holder might, from the small size of his farm, have some spare time,
and be willing to turn it to account by working elsewhere for wages.
Such a man would be a labourer of the very best kind, but he could
not be relied upon to be disengaged at a particular moment ; for, if
not busy just then on his own farm, some other employer might have
secured his services. A small tenant farmer, to whom part of a great
estate was let, would be governed by any conditions agreed upon between him and his landlord. That these conditions might include a
liability to a certain amount of actual service at certain seasons on his
landlord's estate, is obvious. That the *coloni* of later times were normally in this position, is well known. That this system, under which
a tenant retaining personal freedom was practically (and at length
legally) bound to the soil, suddenly arose and became effective, is most

---

[1] A picture forestalled by Lucretius III 1053–75.
[2] Already illustrated in the case of Cato noted above.
[3] See Cic *de legibus* III § 30. Cf Horace *epodes* IV.

improbable. Whether we can detect any signs of its gradual introduction will appear as our inquiry proceeds. We have already noted the few references to tenant *coloni* under the Republic. It is enough to remark here that, whatever degree of improvement in agriculture may have taken place owing to the reestablishment of peace and order, it could hardly have been brought about without employing the best labour to be had. If therefore we find reason to believe that the supply of skilled free labour for special agricultural work was gradually found by giving a new turn to the tenancy-system, we may hazard a guess that the first tentative steps in this direction belong to the quiet developments of the Augustan peace.

ROME—THE EMPIRE

XXVIII. AGRICULTURE AND AGRICULTURAL LABOUR UNDER THE ROMAN EMPIRE. GENERAL INTRODUCTION.

That the position of the working farmer in the fourth and fifth centuries AD was very different from what it had been in the early days of the Roman Republic, is hardly open to question. That in the last two centuries of the Republic his position had been gravely altered for the worse in a large (and that in general the best) part of Italy, is not less certain. This period, from 241 to 31 BC, had seen the subjection to Rome of the Mediterranean countries, and the Italian peninsula was an imperial land. It was inevitable that from a dominion so vast and various there should be some sort of reaction on its mistress, and reaction there had been, mostly for evil, on the victorious Roman state. The political social and moral effects of this reaction do not concern us here save only in so far as the economic situation was affected thereby. For instance, the plunder of the Provinces by bad governors and the extortions practised by subordinate officials, the greed of financiers and their agents, were the chief sources of the immense sums of money that poured into Italy. The corruption promoted by all this ill-gotten wealth expressed itself in many forms; but in no way was it more effective than in degradation of agriculture. It was not merely that it forwarded the movement towards great aggregations of *latifundia*. It supplied the means of controlling politics by bribery and violence and rendering nugatory all endeavours to reform the land-system and give legislative remedies a fair trial. The events of the revolutionary period left nearly all the land of Italy in private ownership, most of it in the hands of large owners. The Sullan and Triumviral confiscations and assignations were social calamities and economic failures. Of their paralysing effect on agriculture we can only form a general notion, but it is clear that no revival of a free farming peasantry took place.

Changes there had been in agriculture, due to influences from abroad. Farming on a large scale and organization of slave labour had given it an industrial turn. The crude and brutal form in which this at first appeared had probably been somewhat modified by experience. The great plantations clumsily adapted from Punic models were not easily made to pay. More variety in crops became the fashion, and the specializing of labour more necessary. In this we may surely trace

Greek and Greco-oriental influences, and the advance in this respect is reflected in the more scientific precepts of Varro as compared with those of Cato. But, so long as the industrial aim, the raising of large crops for the urban market, prevailed, this change could not tend to revive the farming peasantry, whose aim was primarily an independent subsistence, and who lacked the capital needed for agricultural enterprise on industrial lines. Meanwhile there was the large-scale slavery system firmly established, and nothing less than shrinkage of the supply of slaves was likely to shake it.

But the course of Roman conquest and formation of Provinces had brought Italy into contact with countries in which agriculture and its relation to governments stood on a very different footing from that traditional in Roman Italy. The independent peasant farmer living by his own labour on his own land, a double character of citizen and soldier, untroubled by official interference, was a type not present to the eyes of Romans as they looked abroad. Tribal ownership, still common in the West, had been outgrown in Italy. The Carthaginian system, from which much had been learnt, was an exploitation-system, as industrial as a government of merchant princes could make it. In Sicily it met a Hellenistic system set up by the rulers of Syracuse, and the two seem to have blended or at least to have had common characteristics. The normal feature was the payment of a tithe of produce ($\delta\epsilon\kappa\acute{a}\tau\eta$) to the State. For the State claimed the property of the land, and reserved to itself a regular 10°/₀ in acknowledgement thereof. This royal title had passed to Rome, and Rome accordingly levied her normal *decumae*, exemption from which was a special favour granted to a few communities. Now the principle that the ultimate ownership of land is vested in the King[1] was well known in the East, and is to be traced in several of the monarchies founded by the Successors of Alexander. In the Seleucid and Attalid kingdoms there have been found indications of it, though the privileges of cities and temples checked its general application. But in Egypt it existed in full vigour, and had done so from time immemorial. It was in fact the most essential expression of oriental ideas of sovranty. Combined with it was the reservation of certain areas as peculiarly 'royal lands' the cultivators of which were 'royal farmers,' $\beta\alpha\sigma\iota\lambda\iota\kappa o\grave{\iota}\ \gamma\epsilon\omega\rho\gamma o\acute{\iota}$, standing in a direct relation to the King and controlled by his administrative officials. The interest of the sovran was to extract a regular revenue from the crown-lands: hence it was the aim of government to secure the residence of its

---

[1] See Rostowzew, *Röm Colonat*, for detailed inquiry into Eastern phenomena, Egyptian in particular. For the case of China see reference to Macgowan [Appendix D 6]. A very interesting account of the system in Hindustan in the 17th century, with criticism of its grave abuses, may be found in the *Travels in the Mogul empire* by François Bernier, ed 2 by V A Smith, Oxford 1914, pages 226-38. I believe the legal phrase is 'Eminent Domain.'

farmers and the continuous cultivation of the soil. The object was attained by minute regulations applied to a submissive people of small needs.

It is evident that agriculture under conditions such as these was based on ideas fundamentally different from those prevalent in Italy. There private ownership was the rule, and by the end of the Republic it was so more than ever. The *latifundia* had grown by transfers of property[1] in land, whether the holdings so absorbed were original small freeholds or allotments of state land granted under agrarian laws. Present estates, whether large or small, were normally held under a full proprietary title; and the large ones at least were valued as an asset of social and political importance rather than as a source of economic profit. The owner could do what he would with his own, and in Italy[2] there was no tax-burden on his land. We may ask how it came about that the Italian and Provincial systems stood thus side by side, neither assimilating the other. The answer is that the contrast suited the interests of the moneyed classes who controlled the government of Rome. To exploit the regal conditions taken over by the Republic abroad was for them a direct road to riches, and the gratification of their ambitions was achieved by the free employment of their riches at home. The common herd of poor citizens, pauperized in Rome or scattered in country towns and hamlets, had no effective means of influencing policy, even if they understood what was going on and had (which they had not) an alternative policy of their own. So the Empire took over from the Republic a system existing for the benefit of hostile aristocrats and capitalists, with whom it was not practicable to dispense and whom it was not easy to control.

We cannot suppose that the classes concerned with agriculture had any suspicion how far-reaching were the changes destined to come about under the new government. They could not look centuries ahead. For the present, the ruler spared no pains to dissemble his autocratic power and pose as a preserver and restorer of the Past. Caution and a judicious patronage inspired literature to praise the government and to observe a discreet silence on unwelcome topics. The attitude of Augustus towards agriculture will be discussed below. Here it is only necessary to remark that the first aim of his policy in this as in other departments was to set the machine working with the least possible appearance of change. As the republican magistracies were left standing, and gradually failed through the incompetence of senatorial guidance, so no crude agrarian schemes were allowed to upset existing conditions,

---

[1] In Greenidge, *History* pp 292–3, there are some good remarks on the process.

[2] Frontinus grom I p 35, Columella III 3 § 11, and Heisterbergk's remarks cited below. See Index, *Italian land and taxation*.

and development was left to follow the lines of changing economic and
political needs. It is well to take a few important matters and see very
briefly how imperial policy set going tendencies that were in course of
time to affect profoundly the position of agriculture.

In the first place it was clear that no stable reconstruction was
possible without a large and steady income. To this end a great reform
of the old methods of revenue-collection was necessary. The wasteful
system of tax-farmers practically unchecked in their exactions was
exchanged for collection by officials of the state or of municipalities.
In the case of land-revenue this change was especially momentous,
for in no department had the abuses and extortions of *publicani* been
more oppressive. And it was in the Emperor's Provinces that this
reform was first achieved. Agriculture was by far the most widespread
occupation of the subject peoples; and the true imperial interest was,
not to squeeze the most possible out of them at a given moment, but
to promote their continuous well-being as producers of a moderate but
sure revenue. That this wise policy was deliberately followed is indicated by the separate[1] treatment of Egypt. Augustus did not present
his new acquisition to the Roman state. He stepped into the position
of the late Ptolemies, and was king there without the name. As he
found the cash of Ptolemaic treasure a means of paying off debts and
avoiding initial bankruptcy, so by keeping up the existing financial
system he enjoyed year by year a large income entirely at his own
disposal, and avoided the risk of disturbing institutions to which the
native farmers had been used from time immemorial. The possession
of this vast private revenue undoubtedly had much to do with the successful career of Augustus in establishing the empire.

So long as the empire was secure from invasion, and the collection
of taxes on a fair and economical plan afforded sufficient and regular
returns, general prosperity prevailed over a larger area than ever before.
The boon of peace was to the subject peoples a compensation for the
loss of an independence the advantages of which were uncertain and
in most cases probably forgotten. If the benumbing of national feelings
was in itself not a good thing, the central government was able to pay
its way, and emperors could at need appear as a sort of benign provi-
dence, by grants of money or temporary remissions of taxation in relief
of extraordinary calamities. And yet, as we can now see in retrospect,
the establishment of the new monarchy had set in motion tendencies
that were destined to upset the social and economic structure and
eventually to give it a more Oriental character. Italy long remained a

---

[1] Tacitus *ann* II 59 *seposuit Aegyptum hist* I 11 *domi retinere*. This need not be taken
to mean that he treated it strictly as part of his private estate, as Mommsen thought. See on
the controversy a note of E Meyer *Kl Schr* p 479.

favoured metropolitan land. But the great landowning nobles no longer ruled it and the Provinces also. No dissembling could conceal the truth that their political importance was gone. It may be[1] that some of the great landlords gave more attention to their estates as economic units. It is much more certain that large-scale landholding abroad[2] was more attractive than that in Italy. It was not a new thing, and under the republican government great provincial Roman landlords had enjoyed a sort of local autocratic position, assured by their influence in Rome. But an emperor's point of view was very different from that of the old republican Senate. He could not allow the formation of local princi- palities in the form of great estates under no effective control. These landlords had been bitter opponents of Julius Caesar: Augustus had been driven to make away with some of them: the uneasiness of his successors at length found full vent in the action of Nero, who put to death six great landlords in Africa, and confiscated their estates. Half Africa, the Province specially affected, thus passed into the category of Imperial Domains, under the control of a departmental bureau, and later times added more and more to these *praedia Caesaris* in many parts of the empire.

The convenient simplicity of having great areas of productive land administered by imperial agents more or less controlled by the officials of a central department, into which the yearly dues were regularly paid, cannot have escaped the notice of emperors. But the advantages of such a system had been a part of their actual experience[3] from the first in the case of Egypt. Egypt too was the special home of finance based on a system of regulated agriculture and hereditary continuity of occu- pation. In particular, the interest of the government in the maintenance and extension of cultivation was expressed in minute rules for land- tenure and dues payable, and the care taken to keep the class of 'royal farmers' in a prosperous condition. Thus there was recognized a sort of community of interest between peasant and king. That middlemen should not oppress the former or defraud the latter was a common concern of both. Now in the Roman empire we note the growth of a system resembling this in its chief features. We find the tillage of imperial domains[4] carried on by small farmers holding parcels of land,

[1] See M Weber *Agrargeschichte* pp 243 foll.
[2] The estates of Atticus in Epirus are a leading case of this. Horace *epist* I 12 refers to those of Agrippa in Sicily. Such cases have nothing to do with emigration of working farmers, in which I do not believe. Surely Greenidge *History* p 270 is right in saying that the Gracchan scheme of colonization was commercial rather than agricultural. Also the municipalities, beside their estates in Italy, held lands in the Provinces. See Tyrrell and Purser on Cic *ad fam* XIII 7 and 11. In general, Seneca *epist* 87 § 7, 89 § 20, Florus II 7 § 3.
[3] We may perhaps carry this back into the time of the Republic. See the references to the royal domains of Macedon, Livy XLV 18 § 3, and with others Cic *de lege agr* II § 50.
[4] See the chapter on the African inscriptions.

generally as subtenants of tenants-in-chief holding direct from the emperor. These small farmers were evidently workers, whether they to some extent used slave-labour or not. Imperial policy favoured these men as steady producers turning the land to good account, and thus adding to the resources of the empire without being (like great landlords) a possible source of danger. Hence great care was taken to protect the *coloni Caesaris* from oppression by middlemen: and, so long as head-tenants and official agents did not corruptly combine to wrong the farmers, the protection seems to have been effective. Moreover, the advantage of retaining the same tenants on the land whose conditions they understood by experience, and of inducing them to reclaim and improve further portions of the waste, was kept clearly in view. A policy of official encouragement in these directions was in full swing in the second century AD and may perhaps have been initiated by Vespasian.

It is not necessary to assume that these arrangements were directly copied from Oriental, particularly Egyptian, conditions. The convenience of permanent tenants and the ever-pressing need of food-supply are enough to account for the general aim, and experience of the East would naturally help to mature the policy. The establishment of the Empire made it possible. But we must plainly note the significance of new ideas in respect of residence and cultivation. In the Roman land-system of Italy private ownership was the rule, and the general assumption that the owner cultivated on his own account: stewards and slave-gangs were common but not essential phenomena. It is true that the practice of letting farms to cultivating tenants existed, and that in the first two centuries of the Empire it was on the increase, probably promoted by the comparative scarcity of slaves in times of peace. But tenancy was a contract-relation, and the law, while protecting the tenant, gave to the landlord ample means of enforcing regular and thorough cultivation. And this automatically ensured the tenant's residence in any conditions short of final despair. We shall see that as agriculture declined in Italy it became more and more difficult to find and keep satisfactory tenants: but the tenant was in the last resort free to go, and the man who had to be compelled to cultivate properly was just the man on whom the use of legal remedies was least likely to produce the desired practical effect. Now on the imperial domains abroad we find a growing tendency to insist on residence, as a rule imposed from above. The emperor could not leave his *coloni* simply at the mercy of his head-tenants. He was very ready to protect them, but to have them flitting at will was another matter. And this tendency surely points to Egyptian analogies; naturally too, as the Empire was becoming more definitely a Monarchy.

Tenants becoming dependent 209

We shall also find reason to think that both in Italy and in the Provinces there was a tendency to reduce farm-tenants to a considerable degree of *de facto* dependence by manipulation of economic relations. A landlord could let a farm on terms apparently favourable but so arranged that it was easy for the tenant to fall into arrears and become his debtor. The exploitation of debtors' necessities[1] was a practice traditionally Roman from very early times. True, it was seldom politic to sell up a defaulting tenant in the declining state of Italian agriculture. But the gradual acceptance of a liability to small burdens in lieu of cash payment might rob him of his effective independence before he was well aware of the change in his position. On a great provincial domain, the emperor being far away, a head-tenant could deal with the sub-tenants on much the same lines. A trifling requirement, just exceeding what was actually due, would be submitted to as not worth the trouble and risk of setting the appeal-machinery in motion. Further encroachments, infinitesimal but cumulative, might reduce the *colonus* to a semi-servile condition: and, the poorer he became, the less his prospect of protection from the emperor's local agents, too often men of itching palms. Still the *coloni* were freemen, and we have evidence that they sometimes appealed to their imperial lord, and with success. It seems that in some respects *coloni Caesaris* were at an advantage as compared with *coloni* of private landlords, at least in the means of protection. Roman law was very chary of interference with matters of private contract, and the principles guiding the courts were well known. An astute landlord could see to it that his encroachments on a tenant's freedom did not entitle the man to a legal remedy. But the imperial domains abroad were often, if not always, governed by administrative procedure under the emperor's own agents; and these gentry could quickly be brought to order, and compelled to redress grievances, by a single word from headquarters. That the word was forthcoming on occasion is not wonderful. The policy of an emperor was to cherish and encourage the patient farmers whose economic value was a sound imperial asset, while the head-tenant was only a convenient middleman. But the private landowner had no imperial interest to guide him, and looked only to his own immediate profit.

In tracing the influences that changed the condition of the working farmer we must not forget the establishment of a new military system. The standing army created by Augustus was an absolute necessity for imperial defence. At the same time it was a recognition of the fact that the old system of temporary levies, long proved inadequate, must henceforth be abandoned. Frontier armies could not be formed by

---

[1] For the cases of India and China see references to Sir A Fraser and Macgowan [Appendix D 6].

H. A. 14

simply mobilizing free peasants for a campaign. The strength of the armies lay in military skill, not in numbers. Long service and special training made them uniformly professional, and provision was duly made for regular conditions of retirement. The Italian peasant-farmers, much fewer than of yore, and no longer all potential soldiers, were left to become simply professional farmers. That agriculture nevertheless did not really prosper was due to causes beyond their control; but that they, both tenant *coloni* and any remaining small owners, should tend to become a purely peasant class was inevitable. Augustus may have wished to rebuild Italian agriculture on a sound foundation of the peasant-elements, but circumstances were too contrary for the successful prosecution of any such design. Meanwhile the marked differentiation[1] of soldier and farmer, and the settlement of veterans on allotments of land, mainly in frontier Provinces, was proceeding. Analogies from the East, particularly from Egypt, where such arrangements[2] were traditional, can hardly have been ignored. In ancient Egypt the division of military and farming classes had been so marked as to present the appearance of a caste-system. But this was not peculiar to Egypt. It was in full vigour in ancient India, where it impressed[3] Greek observers, to whom the general absence of slaves, there as in Egypt, seemed one of its notable phenomena.

I do not venture to suggest that Roman emperors set themselves deliberately to substitute a fixed attachment of working farmers to the soil for a failing system of rustic slave-labour. But it is not likely that, as labour-problems from time to time arose, the well-known Oriental solutions were without some influence on their policy. We must not forget that Greek thinkers had long ago approved the plan of strict differentiation of functions in ideal states, and that such notions, popularized in Latin, were common property in educated circles. Tradition[4] even pointed to the existence of some such differentiation in primitive Rome. Therefore, when we find under the later Empire a rigid system of castes and gilds, and the *coloni* attached to the soil with stern penalties to hinder movement, we must not view the situation with modern eyes. The restraint, that to us seems a cruel numbing of forces vital to human progress, would come as no great shock to the world of

---

[1] Tacitus *ann* XIV 27 records the failure of Nero's colonization of veterans singly in Italy, who mostly returned to the scenes of their service. He strangely regrets the abandonment of the old plan of settling them in whole legions. It is to be remembered that in the later Empire the army was more and more recruited from the barbarians.

[2] The γῆ κληρουχική, assigned in κλῆροι to soldiers.

[3] See Herodotus II 165–7, cf 141, Strabo XV 1 § 40 (p 704), § 34 (p 701), § 54 (p 710), cf Diodorus II 40–1, Arrian *Indica* 10 §§ 8, 9. The references to slave-traffic in the *Periplus maris Erythraei* do not really imply existence of a slave-system in India. See Rapson *Ancient India* p 97. Much of interest in Sir J D Rees, *The real India*, on the Land-system etc. In *The early history of India* by V A Smith the existence of slavery in India is maintained.   [4] See Dionysius II 28, cf 8, 9.

the fourth century, long prepared for the step by experience not encountered by theory. To us it is a painful revolution that, instead of the land belonging to the cultivator, the cultivator had become an appendage of the land. But it was the outcome of a long process: as for progress in any good sense, it had ceased. Government had become a series of vain expedients to arrest decay. And the rule of fixed *origo*, a man's officially fixed domicile, was nothing more than the doctrine of the ἰδία long prevalent in the East.

The true significance of the change binding the tiller to the soil he tilled is to be found in the fact that it was a desperate effort to solve a labour-question. To secure a sufficient supply of food had been a cause of anxiety to the imperial government from the first. The encouragement of increased production had become an important part of imperial policy in the second century. It looked to the small working farmers as the chief producing agency, men who provided all or most of the labour on their farms, and in at least some cases a certain amount of task-work[1] on the larger farms of the head-tenants. But in the wars and utter confusion of the third century the strain on the system was too great. The peaceful and prosperous parts of the empire suffered from increased demands on their resources to make good the deficiencies of the Provinces troubled with invasions or rebellions. And there can be no doubt that the working of governmental departments was interrupted and impeded by the general disorder. In such times as those of Gallienus and the so-called Thirty Tyrants the protection of the small farmers by intervention of the central authority must have been pitifully ineffective. Naturally enough, we do not get direct record of this failure, but the change of conditions that followed on the restoration of order by Diocletian shews what had been happening. The increase of taxation, rendered necessary by the costly machinery of the new government, led to increased pressure on the farmers, and evasions had to be checked by increased restraints. In a few years the facts were recognized and stereotyped by the law of Constantine, and the *coloni* were henceforth bound down to the soil by an act of state. Another notable change[2] was introduced by requiring payment of dues to be made in kind. The motive of this was to provide a certain means of supporting the armies and the elaborate civil service; for the currency, miserably debased in the course of the third century, was a quite unsuitable medium for the purpose. That Diocletian, in these institutions of a new model, was not consciously applying oriental usage to the empire generally, is hardly credible. It only remained to reduce Italy

---

[1] The *operae* referred to in the African inscriptions.

[2] It is possible to see a beginning of this system in the tenancy-on-shares (the *colonia partiaria*) which we find not only in Italy but in Africa as a recognized plan.

to the common level by subjecting Italian land to taxation. This he did, and the new Oriental Monarchy was complete.

That a labour-question underlay the policy of attaching the *coloni* to the land, is to be gathered from the following considerations. The development of the plan of promoting small tenancies, particularly on the imperial domains, was undoubtedly calculated to take the place of large-scale cultivation by slave labour. It was a move in the direction of more intensive tillage, and economically sound. So long as a firm hand was kept on large head-tenants and imperial officials, the plan seems to have been on the whole a success. But all depended on the protection of the small working farmers, and of course on the moderation of government demands. The disorders of the third century tended to paralyse the protection while they increased demands. Therefore the head-tenants, aided by the slackness or collusion of officials, gained a predominant power, which imperial policy had been concerned to prevent. By the time of Diocletian their position was far stronger than it had been under Hadrian. To restore the former relations by governmental action would be certainly difficult, perhaps impossible. As middlemen, through whose agency the collection of dues in non-municipal areas could be effected, they were useful. It was a saving of trouble to deal with a comparatively small number of persons, and those men of substance. The remodelling of the disordered Empire was no doubt a complicated and laborious business, and anything that promised to save trouble would be welcomed. So the government accepted[1] the changed position as accomplished fact, and left the *coloni*, its former clients, to the mercies of the men of capital. But the big men, controlling ever more lands, whether as possessors or as imperial head-tenants or as 'patrons' of helpless villagers, could not meet their obligations to the government without having the disposal of a sufficient and regular supply of labour. And to the authorities of the later Empire, deeply committed to a rigid system of castes and gilds, no way of meeting the difficulty seemed open but to extend the system of fixity to the class of toilers on the land. The motive was a financial one, naturally. Non-industrial, and so unable to pay for imports by export of its own manufactures, the civilization of the empire was financially based upon agriculture. Looking back on the past, we can see that the deadening of hope and enterprise in the farming population was a ruinous thing. But the empire drifted into it as the result of circumstances and influences long operative and eventually irresistible. To displace the free peasant by the slave, then the slave by the small tenant, only to end by converting the small tenant into a serf, was a part of the Roman fate.

[1] This is the view of Rostowzew *Röm Colonat* p 397.

ROME—AUGUSTUS TO NERO

XXIX. HORACE AND VERGIL.

For literary evidence bearing on agriculture in the time of Augustus we naturally look to Vergil and Horace. Now these two witnesses, taken separately and construed literally, might convey very different, even inconsistent, impressions of farm life and labour in the world around them. And Vergil is the central figure of Roman literature, the poet who absorbed the products of the past and dominated those of many generations to come. His quality as a witness to the present is what concerns us here. I have tried to discuss this problem thoroughly and fairly in a special section. In order to do this, it has been necessary to deal *pari passu* with most of the evidence of Horace, the rest of which can be treated first by itself.

Horace, the freedman's son, himself an illustration of the way in which the ranks of Roman citizenship were being recruited from foreign sources, yields to none in his admiration of the rustic Romans of old[1] and the manly virtues of the genuine stock. In the dialogue between himself and his slave Davus the latter is made to twit him with his praises of the simple life and manners of the commons of yore, though he would never be content to live as they did. A palpable hit, as Horace knew: but he did not change his tone. With due respect he speaks of the farmers of olden time, men of sturdy mould and few wants. It was as poor men on small hereditary farms[2] that M' Curius and Camillus grew to be champions of Rome. In those far-off days the citizen might have little of his own, but the public treasury[3] was full; a sharp contrast to present selfishness and greedy land-grabbing. Those old farmer folk put their own hand to the work. Their sons were brought up to a daily round of heavy tasks, and the mother of such families[4] was a strict ruler and an active housewife. For the scale of all their operations was small, and personal labour their chief means of attaining limited ends. They are not represented as using slave labour, nor is the omission strange. For the military needs of the great world-empire were never far from the minds of the Augustan writers, conscious as they were of their master's anxieties on this score. Now the typical peasant of old time was farmer and soldier too, and it is of the *rusticorum mascula militum proles* that Horace is thinking.

---

[1] Hor *Sat* II 7 23, *Epist* II 1 139-40. [2] Hor *Odes* I 12.
[3] *Odes* II 15, 18, *Sat* II 6 6-15. [4] *Odes* III 6.

There was no need to refer to farm-slaves even in the case of Regulus[1], whom tradition evidently assumed to have been a slaveowner. But, when he refers to circumstances of his own day, the slave meets us everywhere; not only in urban life and the domestic circle, but on the farm and in the contractor's[2] labour-gang. We then hear of great estates, of great blocks of land mostly forest (*saltus*)[3] bought up by the rich, of the sumptuous *villae* of the new style, all implying masses of slave labour: also of the great estates outside[4] Italy, from which speculators were already drawing incomes.

Side by side with these scenes of aggressive opulence, we find occasional mention of a poorer class, farming small holdings, who are sometimes represented[5] as cultivators of land inherited from their fore-fathers. How far we are to take these references literally, that is as evidence that such persons were ordinary figures in the rustic life of Italy, may be doubted. The poet in need of material for contrasts, which are inevitably part of his stock-in-trade, has little in common with the statistician or even the stolid reporter. Nor can we be sure that the man who 'works his paternal farm with oxen of his own' or 'delights to cleave his ancestral fields with the mattock,' are workers doing the bodily labour in person. Even Horace, inclined though he is to realism, cannot be trusted so far: such words[6] as *arat* and *aedificat* for instance do not necessarily mean that the man guides the plough or is his own mason or carpenter. When he speaks of 'all that the tireless Apulian[7] ploughs'—that is, the harvests he raises by ploughing—he does not seem to have in mind the small farmer. For the context clearly suggests corn raised on a large scale. And yet else-where[8] he gives us a picture of an Apulian peasant whose hard toil is cheered and eased by the work and attentions of his sunburnt wife, a little ideal scene of rural bliss. Apulia is a large district, and not uniform[9] in character, so we need not assume that either of these passages misrepresents fact. And there is a noticeable difference be-tween the style of the Satires and Epistles on the one hand and that of the Odes on the other. In vocabulary, as in metre and rhythm, the former enjoy an easy license denied to the severer lyric poems on which he stakes his strictly poetic reputation. In the Odes[10] for instance

---

[1] *Odes* III 5. See above pp 139–40.　　[2] *Odes* III 1 *redemptor cum famulis.*
[3] *Odes* II 3, *Epist* II 2 177–8.　　[4] *Odes* I 1, II 16, III 16.
[5] *Odes* I 1 *patrios...agros*, *Epode* II 3 *paterna rura bobus exercet suis.*
[6] *Epode* IV 13 *arat Falerni mille fundi iugera*, etc.
[7] *Odes* III 16 *quicquid arat impiger Apulus.*　　　[8] *Epode* II 39 foll.
[9] A fact recognized by Horace himself in lines 14–16 of *Odes* III 4, and *Sat* I 5 lines 77 foll.
[10] *Odes* I 35 *pauper...ruris colonus*, II 14 *inopes coloni. Sat* II 2 115, where the fact of expulsion in favour of a military pensioner is judiciously ignored. See below.

colonus bears the old general sense 'tiller of the soil': in the Satires we find it in the legal sense of 'tenant-farmer' as opposed to 'owner,' *dominus*. He refers in both groups of poems to the military colonists[1] pensioned by Augustus with grants of land. In neither place is the word *coloni* used; this is natural enough. We need only note the care with which the court-poet refers to the matter. His master doubtless had many an anxious hour over that settlement: the poet refers to the granting of lands, and does not touch on the disturbance caused thereby. Nor is Horace peculiar in this respect. The caution that marks the utterances of all the Augustan writers is very apt to mislead us when we try to form a notion of the actual situation. The general truth seems to be that the beginning of the Empire was a time of unrest tempered by exhaustion, and that things only calmed down gradually as the sufferers of the elder generation died out. Wealth was now the one aim of most ambitions, and the race to escape poverty was extreme. The merchant[2] in Horace is a typical figure. For a while he may have had enough of seafaring perils and turn with joy to the rural quiet of his country town: but to vegetate on narrow means is more than he can stand, and he is off to the seas again. He is contrasted with the farmer content to till his ancestral fields, whom no prospect of gain would tempt to face the dangers of the deep: and he is I believe a much more average representative of the age than the acquiescent farmer.

One passage in the works of Horace calls for special discussion by itself, for the value of its evidence depends on the interpretation accepted, and opinions have differed. In the fourteenth epistle of the first book the poet expresses his preference for country life in the form of an address to the steward of his Sabine estate, beginning with these lines

> *Vilice silvarum et mihi me reddentis agelli,*
> *quem tu fastidis habitatum quinque focis et*
> *quinque bonos solitum Variam dimittere patres,*

thus rendered by Howes

> Dear Bailiff of the woody wild domain
> Whose peace restores me to myself again,—
> (A sprightlier scene, it seems, thy taste requires,
> To Varia though it send five sturdy sires
> The lords of five good households)—

and the question at once arises, what sort of persons are meant by these 'five good fathers.' In agreement with the excellent note of

---

[1] These *coloni* of course owned their farms; that is, were *domini*. *Odes* III 4 lines 37-8, *Sat* II 6 55-6.

[2] *Odes* I 1 *mercator...indocilis pauperiem pati*, cf III 2.

Wilkins I hold that they are free heads of households, and that they are persons existing in the then present time, not imagined figures of a former age. It seems also clear that they were living on the modest estate (*agellus*) of Horace. If so, then they can hardly be other than tenants of farms included therein. Therefore it has naturally been inferred that the estate consisted of a *villa* with a home-farm managed by a steward controlling the staff of eight slaves of whom we hear elsewhere: and that the outlying portions were let to free farmers[1] on terms of money rent or shares of produce. Horace would thus be the landlord of five *coloni*, and his relations with them would normally be kept up through the agency of the resident slave-steward of the home-farm. All this agrees perfectly with other evidence as to the customary arrangements followed on rural estates ; and I accept it as a valuable illustration of a system not new but tending to become more and more prevalent as time went on. But it is well to note that the case is one from a hill district, and that we must not from it draw any inference as to how things were moving on the great lowland estates, the chief latifundial farm-areas of Italy.

The *patres* referred to are virtually *patres familias*[2], free responsible persons, probably Roman citizens, but tenants, not land-owning yeomen of the ancient type. Whether their visits to Varia (Vicovaro) were to bear their part in the local affairs of their market-town, or to buy and sell, or for both purposes, is not quite clear; nor does it here concern us. But we should much like to know whether these five farmers, or some of them, employed[3] any slaves. I do not see how this curiosity is to be gratified. Perhaps we may argue that their assumed liberty to come and go points to the employment of some labour other than their own: but would this labour be slave or free? If we assume (as I think we fairly may) that the labour needed would be mainly regular routine-work and not occasional help, this points rather to slave-labour. Nor is there any general reason for distrusting that conclusion ; only it would probably mean slave-labour on a small scale. There is more-over no reason to think that free wage-labourers for regular routine work were plentiful in the Sabine hills. And these small farmers were not likely to be creditors, served by debtors (*obaerati*) working off arrears of debt, a class of labour which according to Varro seems to have been no longer available in Italy. There I must leave this question, for I can add no more.

[1] So Cicero's estate at Arpinum is spoken of as *ad Att* XIII 9 § 2 as *praediola* and was per-haps let in the same way.

[2] Cf Seneca *epist* 47 § 14, 86 § 14.

[3] The ownership of the slaves is another matter, for in letting farms the *dominus* often supplied the slaves. See Index, *instrumentum*.

It remains to ask whether the identification of *patres* with *patres familias* exhausts the full meaning of the word. In the *Aeneid* (XII 520) a combatant slain is described as by craft a poor fisherman of Lerna, no dependant of the wealthy, and then follow the words *conductaque pater tellure serebat*. Now most commentators and translators seem determined to find in this a reference to the man's father, which is surely flat and superfluous. The stress is not on *pater* but on *conducta*. Is not *pater* an honourable quality-term, referring to the man[1] himself? He would not be always fishing in the lake. He had a dwelling of some sort, most probably a patch of land, to grow his vegetables. The point is that even this was not his own, but hired from some landowner. I would render 'and the land where the honest man used to grow a crop from seed was rented from another.' That *pater* (Aeneas etc) is often used as a complimentary prefix, is well known, and I think it delicately expresses the poet's kindly appreciation of the poor but honest and independent rustic. In the passage of Horace I am inclined to detect something of the same flavour. Some have supposed that the five 'fathers' were decurions of the local township of Varia, who went thither to meetings of the local senate. I shrink from reading this into the words of Horace, all the more as Nissen[2] has shewn good reason for doubting whether Varia was anything more than a subordinate hamlet (*vicus*) of Tibur.

The general effect of the words, taken in context with the rest of the epistle, is this: the *vilicus*, once a common slave-labourer (*mediastinus*) in Rome, hankers after town life, finding his rustic stewardship dull on a small estate such as that of Horace. To Horace the place is a charming retreat from the follies and worries of Rome. To him the estate with its quiet homestead and the five tenants of the outlying farms is an ideal property: he wants[3] a retreat, not urban excitements. To the steward it seems that there is 'nothing doing,' while the grandeur of a great estate is lacking. So the master is contented, while the slave is discontented, with this five-farm property looked at from their different points of view.

But the most serious problem that meets us in endeavouring to appraise the evidence of the Augustan literature is connected with the *Georgics* of Vergil. Passages from Horace will be helpful in this inquiry, in the course of which the remarkable difference between these two witnesses will appear. The stray references in other writers of the

[1] I find that Mr Warde Fowler, *The death of Turnus* p 105, also takes this view. But he understands *pater* to imply that the man brought up a family, which I do not. I agree that it gives the idea of headship of a household.

[2] *Italische Landeskunde* II p 615.

[3] The description of such an *agellus* in Plin *epist* I 24 illustrates the wants of a literary landowner excellently.

period are for the most part not worth citing. **Tibullus** speaks of the farmer[1] who has had his fill of steady ploughing, but this is in an ideal picture of the origins of agriculture. His rural scenes are not of much significance. In one place, speaking of hope[2] that sustains a man in uncertainties, for instance a farmer, he adds 'Hope it is too that comforts one bound with a strong chain: the iron clanks on his legs, yet he sings as he works.' A rustic slave, no doubt. But that his hope is hope of manumission is by no means clear: it may be hope of escape, and the words are indefinite, perhaps left so purposely. That **Ovid**[3] refers to the farmer statesmen and heroes of yore, who put their hands to the plough, is merely an illustration of the retrospective idealism of the Augustan age. Like Livy and the rest, he was conscious of the decay of Roman vitality, and amid the glories and dissipations of Rome recognized the vigour and simplicity of good old times. For him, and for **Manilius**, speculation[4] as to the origins of civilization, imaginings of a primitive communism, had attraction, as it had for Lucretius and Vergil. It was part of the common stock: and in connexion with the development of building it forms a topic of some interest[5] in the *architectura* of **Vitruvius**.

Vergil. All readers of Vergil's *Georgics* are struck by the poet's persistent glorification of labour and his insistence on the necessity and profit of personal action on the farmer's part. Yet on one very important point there is singular obscurity. Is slave-labour meant to be a part of his *res rustica*, or not? When he bids the farmer do this or that, is he bidding him to do it with his own hands, or merely to see to the doing of it, or sometimes the one and sometimes the other? So far as I know, no sufficient attention[6] has been given to the curious, and surely deliberate, avoidance of direct reference to slavery in this poem. To this subject I propose to return after considering the references in his pastoral and epic poetry. For in the artificial world of piping shepherds and in the surroundings of heroic legend the mention of slaves and slavery is under no restraint. This I hope to make clear; and, in relation to the contrast presented by the *Georgics*, to emphasize, if not satisfactorily to explain, one of the subtle reticencies of Vergil.

The *Bucolics* place us in an unreal atmosphere. The scenic setting is a blend of Theocritean Sicily and the poet's own lowlands of the Cisalpine. The characters and status of the rustics are confused in a remarkable degree. Thus in the first eclogue Tityrus appears as a slave

---

[1] Tibullus II 1 51 *agricola adsiduo...satiatus aratro.*
[2] Tibullus II 6 25-6.　　　　[3] Ovid *fasti* I 207, III 779-82, IV 693-4.
[4] Ovid *metam* I 135-6, Manilius I 73-4.　　[5] Vitruvius II 1.
[6] I cannot accept Prof. Richmond's view (Inaugural lecture 1919 p 25) of the *Georgics* as 'concerned with every side of husbandry.'

who has bought his freedom late in life (lines 27–9), having neglected to amass a *peculium* in earlier years (31–2). It was only by a visit to Rome, and the favour of Octavian, that he gained relief. But this relief appears, not as manumission, but as the restoration of a land-owner dispossessed by a military colonist. The inconsistency cannot be removed by treating the first version as symbolic or allegorical. It is there, and the poet seems to have felt no sufficient inducement to remove it. Corydon in the second eclogue has a *dominus*, and is there-fore *servus* (2). Yet he boasts of his large property in flocks, which are presumably his *peculium* (19–22). His dwelling is a lowly cot in the rough grubby surroundings of the countryside (28–9). He is *pastor* (1), but there are evidently *aratores* on the estate (66). He is warned that, if it comes to buying favours with gifts, he cannot compete with his master Iollas (57). Had he not better do some basket-work and forget his passion (71–3)?

In the third eclogue the status of Damoetas is far from clear. He appears as *alienus custos* of a flock, the love-rival of the owner (*ipse*), whom he is robbing, profiting by the latter's preoccupation with his amour (1–6). He is in short head-shepherd (101 *pecoris magistro*), and Tityrus (96) seems to be his underling. Menalcas in staking the cups explains that he dare not risk any of the flock under his charge, which belongs to his father and is jealously counted (32–43). He is owner's son, with no opportunities of fraud; probably free, for we can hardly assume that the flock is a slave's *peculium*. But whether Damoetas is (*a*) a free hireling or (*b*) a slave hired from another owner or (*c*) a slave of the flock-owner, is not to be inferred with confidence from so indis-tinct a picture. In the ninth eclogue we are again[1] brought across the rude military colonist (4) of the first eclogue. Moeris, who seems to be the steward of Menalcas, speaks of *nostri* (*agelli*, 2) and *nostra* (*carmina*, 12). Menalcas is *ipse* (16), and supposed to represent Vergil. I incline to believe that Moeris is a slave *vilicus*, but cannot feel sure. So also in the tenth, we hear of *opilio* and *subulci* (19), of *custos gregis* and *vinitor* (36). These would in the Italy of Vergil's time be normally slaves. But it is not the question of their status that is uppermost in the poet's mind. They appear in the picture merely as figures suggesting the rustic environment on which he loves to dwell. As for the fourth eclogue, it is only necessary to remark that, however interpreted, it points to the return (6) of a blissful age, and accordingly assumes the former existence of good old times.

It has been justly noted that the merry singing and easy life of the swains in the *Bucolics* are incongruous with the notorious condition of

---

[1] Whether Vergil suffered two expulsions, and what is the chronological order of eclogues I and IX, are questions that do not affect my inquiry.

the rustic slaves of Italy. No doubt the contrast is painful. But we must not presume to impute to the great and generous poet a light-headed and callous indifference to the miseries daily inflicted by capitalist exploiters of labour on their human chattels. We must not forget that in hill districts, where large-scale farming did not pay, rural life was still going on in old-fashioned grooves. Nor must we forget that in his native Cisalpine slavery was probably of a mild character. Some hundred years later we hear[1] that chained gangs of slave-labourers were not employed there: and the great armies recruited there in Caesar's time do not suggest that the free population had dwindled there as in Etruria or Lucania. The song-loving shepherds are an importation from the Sicily of Theocritus, an extinct past, an artificial world kept alive in literature by the genius of its singer. In the hands of his great imitator the rustic figures become even more unreal. Hence the extreme difficulty of extracting any sure evidence on the status of these charac-ters, or signs of the poet's own sentiments, from the language of the *Bucolics*.

In the *Aeneid* we have the legends of ancient Italy and the origin of Rome subjected to epic treatment. The drift of the poem is condi-tioned by modern influence, the desire of Augustus to gain support for the new Empire by fostering every germ of a national sentiment. The tale of Troy has to be exploited for the purpose, and with the tale of Troy comes the necessity of reproducing so far as possible the atmo-sphere of the 'heroic' age. There is therefore hardly any reference to the matters with which I am now concerned. When the poet speaks[2] of the peoples of ancient Italy it is in terms of general praise. Their warlike vigour and hardihood, the active life of hunters and farmers, can be admired without informing the reader whether they employed slave-labour or not. And in the rare references[3] to slavery in his own day Vergil has in mind the relation of master and slave simply, without any regard to agriculture. But in depicting the society of the 'heroic' times, in which the adventures of Aeneas are laid, a substratum of slavery was indispensable. It was therefore drawn from the Greek epic, where it lay ready to hand. Yet the references to slaves are less numerous than we might have expected. We find them employed in table-service (I 701-6), or as personal attendants (II 580, 712, IV 391, V 263, IX 329, XI 34). We hear of a woman skilled in handicrafts (V 284) given as a prize, and Camilla is dedicated as a *famula* of Diana (XI 558). These are not very significant references. But that slavery is assumed as an important element in the social scheme may be in-ferred from the references to captives in war (II 786, III 323, IX 272-3). They are liable to be offered up as *inferiae* to the dead (XI 81-2),

---

[1] Pliny *epist* III 19 § 7.   [2] *Aen* VII 641-817, IX 603-13.   [3] e.g. *Aen* VI 613.

and the victor takes the females as concubines at will (III 323–9, IX 546). A discarded concubine is handed over to a slave-consort (III 329), and the infant children of a *serva* form part of a common unit with their dam (V 285).

Two passages are worth notice from an economic point of view. In VIII 408–12, in a simile, we have the picture of a poor hard-working housewife who rises very early to set her *famulae* to work on their allotted tasks of wool, to 'keep the little home together.' One can hardly say that no such scene was possible in real life under the conditions of Vergil's time, though we may fairly doubt the reality of a picture in which grim poverty and the desire to bring up a family of young children are combined with the ownership and employment of a staff of domestic slaves. For we find the not owning a single slave[1] used as the most characteristic sign of poverty. And I shrink from describing the situation industrially as the sweating of slave-labour to maintain respectability. I do not think any such notion was in the poet's mind. That the simile is suggested by Greek models is pointed out by Conington, and to regard it as a borrowed ornament is probably the safest conclusion in general. It is however to be noted that the *famulae* are not borrowed, but an addition of Vergil's own. The other passage, XII 517–20, relates the death in battle of an Arcadian, who in his home was a fisherman, of humble station. The last point is brought out in the words[2] *conductaque pater tellure serebat*. This seems to mean that he was a small tenant farmer, a *colonus* of the non-owning class. Such a man might or might not have a slave or two. But, even were there any indication (which there is not) to favour either alternative, the man's home is in Arcadia, though the picture may be coloured by the poet's familiarity with Italian details. Take it all in all, we are perhaps justified in saying that in the *Aeneid* the realities of slavery and of humble labour generally are very lightly touched. Is this wholly due to the assumed proprieties of the heroic epic, dealing with characters above the ordinary freeman in station or natural qualities? Or may we surmise that to Vergil, with his intense human sympathies, the topic was in itself also distasteful, only to be referred to when it was hardly possible to avoid it?

If little, in fact almost nothing, can be gleaned bearing on the subject of labour from the *Bucolics* and *Aeneid*, we might hope to find plenty of information in the didactic poem specially addressed to farmers. In the opening of the *Georgics* (I 41) Vergil plainly says that he feels sorry for the rustic folk, who know not the path to success in their vocation: he appeals to the gods interested in agriculture, and above all to Augustus, to look kindly on his bold endeavour to set farmers in

---

[1] Ellis on Catullus XXIII 1.   [2] See page 217.

the right way. When he comes to speak of the peace and plenty, the security and joys, of country life, he grows enthusiastic (II 458–74). But among the advantages he does not omit to reckon the freedom from the extravagance and garish display of city life, the freedom to drowse under trees, the enjoyment of rural sights and sounds, in short the freedom to take your ease with no lack of elbow-room (*latis otia fundis*). This hardly portrays the life of the working farmer, to whom throughout the poem he is ever preaching the gospel of toil and watchfulness. True, he adds 'there you find forest-lands (*saltus*) with coverts for wild beasts, and a population inured to toil and used to scanty diet,' among whom yet linger survivals of the piety and righteousness of old. It is fair to ask, who are these and what place do they fill in the poet's picture? Surely they are not the men who have fled from the vain follies of the city: for they are genuine rustics. Surely not gang-slaves, driven out to labour in the fields and back again to be fed and locked up, like oxen or asses. To the urban slave transference to such a life was a dreaded punishment. Are they free small-scale farmers? No doubt there were still many of that class remaining in the upland parts of Italy. But were they men of leisure, able to take their ease at will on broad estates? I cannot think of them in such a character, unless I assume them to own farms of comfortable size (of course not *latifundia*) and to employ some labour of slaves or hirelings. And there is nothing in the context to justify such an assumption. Lastly, are they poor peasants, holding small plots of land and eking out a meagre subsistence by occasional wage-earning labour? Such persons seem to have existed, at least in certain parts of the country: but we know that some at least of this labour hired for the job was performed[1] by bands of non-resident labourers roaming in search of such employment. No, peasants of the 'crofter' type do not fit in with this picture of a rural life passed in plenty and peaceful ease. I am therefore driven to conclude that the poet was merely idealizing country life in general terms without troubling himself to exercise a rigid consistency in the combination of details. He has had many followers among poets and painters, naturally: but the claim of the *Georgics* to rank as a didactic treatise is exceptionally strong, owing to the citations of Columella and Pliny. If then the poem seems in any respect to pass lightly over questions of importance in the consideration of farming conditions, we are tempted rather to seek for a motive than to impute neglect.

But before proceeding further it is well to inquire in what sense the *Georgics* can be called didactic. What is the essential teaching of the poem, and to whom is that teaching addressed? In outward form it professes to instruct the bewildered farmers, suffering at the time

[1] Sueton *Vespas* 1.

from effects of the recent civil wars as well as from economic difficulties
of old standing; and to convey sound precepts for the conduct of
agriculture in its various branches. But there is little doubt that the
precepts are all or most of them taken directly from earlier[1] writers,
Roman or Greek; and we may reasonably suppose that most of them
(and those the most practical ones) were well known to the very classes
most concerned in their application. It is absurd to suppose that
agricultural tradition had utterly died out. The real difficulty was to
put it in practice. Now, what class of farmers were to be benefited by
the new poem? Was the peasant of the uplands, soaked in hereditary
experience, to learn his business over again with the help of the poet-
laureate's fascinating verse? Surely he spoke a rustic[2] Latin, and
sometimes hardly that. Was it likely that he would gradually absorb
the doctrines of the Vergilian compendium, offered in the most refined
language and metre of literary Rome? It is surely inconceivable. Nor
can we assume that any remaining intensive farmers of the Campanian
plain were in much need of practical instruction: what was needed
there was a respite from the unsettling disturbances of the revolutionary
period. To suggest that a part of the poet's design was to supply
much-needed teaching to the new *coloni* from the disbanded armies,
would be grotesque in any case, and above all in that of Vergil. If
we are to find a class of men to whom the finished literary art of the
Georgics would appeal, and who might profit by the doctrines so
attractively conveyed, we must seek them in social strata[3] possessed
of education enough to appreciate the poem and sympathize with its
general tone. Now all or most of such persons would be well-to-do
people, owners of property, often of landed property: people of more
or less leisure: in short, the cultured class, whose centre was Rome.
These people would view with favour any proposal for the benefit of
Italian agriculture. Many landowners at the time had got large estates
cheaply in the time of troubles, and to them anything likely to improve
the value of their lands, and to draw a curtain of returning prosperity
over a questionable past, would doubtless be welcome. They would
applaud the subtle grace with which the poet glorified the duty and

[1] Keightley includes Mago, whether rightly or not I am not sure. Conington's Introduction treats this matter fully.

[2] The futility of addressing rustic readers in polished literary language (*diserte*) is commented on by Palladius [4th cent AD] in his opening sentences. He has been thought to
have in view Columella, who by the by is Vergil's great admirer. I cannot accept the views
of Daubeny in his *Lectures* pp 3–5. It is possible that the use of fire in improving land
may be a bit of Vergil's own advice, but I doubt it. See Daubeny pp 91–4, *georg* 1 84 foll.

[3] E Meyer *Kl Schr* p 488 describing the hopeless task of Augustus in attempting the
moral and physical regeneration of Italy makes the general remark 'Nur an die höheren
Stände, nur an die Elite, konnte Augustus sich wenden.' This is a true picture of the situation as a whole. To have to begin building at the top was fatal.

profit of personal labour. But that they meant to work with their own hands I cannot believe. In the true spirit of their age, they would as a matter of course take the profit, and delegate the duty to others.

Two alternatives[1] presented themselves to a landowner. He might let his estate whole or in parcels to a tenant or tenants. Or he might work it for his own account, either under his own resident direction, or through the agency of a steward. All the evidence bearing on the revolutionary period tends to shew that the resident landlord of a considerable estate, farming his own land, was a very rare type indeed. It was found most convenient as a general rule to let an out-of-the-way farm to a cultivating tenant at a money rent or on a sharing system. A more accessible one was generally put under a steward and so kept in hand by the owner. The dwelling-house was in such cases improved so as to be a fit residence for the proprietor on his occasional visits. Growing luxury often carried this change to an extreme, and made the *villa* a 'place in the country,' a scene of intermittent extravagance, not of steady income-producing thrift. True, it seems that the crude and wasteful system of the earlier *latifundia* had been a good deal modified by the end of the Republic. A wealthy man preferred to own several estates of moderate size situated near main routes of traffic. But this plan required more stewards. And the steward (*vilicus*), himself a slave, was the head of a slave-staff proportioned to the size of the farm. Now the public effectually reached by the *Georgics* may be supposed to have included the landowners of education and leisure, whether they let their land to tenants or kept it in hand. I cannot believe that the *coloni* farming hired land[2] came under the poet's influence. In other words, the *Georgics*, in so far as the poem made its way beyond purely literary circles, appealed chiefly if not wholly to a class dependent on slave-labour in every department of their lives.

Maecenas, to whom the poem is in form addressed, had put pressure on Vergil to write it. At the back of Maecenas was the new Emperor, anxious to enlist all the talents in the service of the new dispensation. The revival of rural Italy was one of the praiseworthy projects of the Emperor and his confidential minister. It was indeed on every ground manifestly desirable. But was it possible now to turn Romans of property into working farmers? Would the man-about-Rome leave urban pleasures for the plough-tail? Not he! Nor are we to assume that Augustus was fool enough to expect it. Then what

---

[1] Most clearly stated in Columella I 7.

[2] For *coloni* of Cicero's time see II *in Verr* III § 55, *pro Caecina* § 94, *pro Cluent* §§ 175, 182. The references in Horace are given below. That letting to tenants was practised about 100 BC or earlier, appears certain from the reference to Saserna's opinion on this policy in Columella I 7 § 4.

about Maecenas? His enjoyment of luxurious ease[1] was a byword: that he retained his native commonsense under such conditions is one of his chief titles to fame. No one can have expected him to wield the spade and mattock or spread manure. The poet writing with such a man for patron and prompter was not likely to find his precepts enjoining personal labour taken too seriously. His readers were living in a social and moral atmosphere in which to do anything involving labour meant ordering a slave to do it. That the Emperor wished to see more people interested in the revival of Italian agriculture was well understood. But this interest could be shown by investing capital in Italian land; and this is what many undoubtedly did. Recent proscriptions and confiscations had thrown numbers of estates on the market. It was possible to get a good bargain and at the same time win the favour of the new ruler by a well-timed proof of confidence in the stability of the new government. Now it is to say the least remarkable that Dion Cassius, doubtless following earlier authorities, puts into the mouth of Maecenas some suggestions[2] on this very subject. After advising the Emperor to raise a standing army by enlisting the able-bodied unemployed men in Italy, and pointing out that with the security thus gained, and the provision of a harmless career for the sturdy wastrels who were at present a cause of disorders, agriculture and commerce would revive, he proceeds as follows. For these measures money will be needed, as it would under any government: therefore the necessity of some exactions must be faced. 'The very first thing[3] then for you to do is to have a sale of the confiscated properties, of which there are many owing to the wars, reserving only a few that are specially useful or indispensable for your purposes: and then to employ all the money so raised by lending it out at moderate interest. If you do this, the land will be under cultivation ($\dot{\epsilon}\nu\epsilon\rho\gamma\delta\varsigma$), being placed in the hands of owners who themselves work ($\delta\epsilon\sigma\pi\delta\tau\alpha\iota\varsigma$ $a\dot{v}\tau o\nu\rho\gamma o\hat{\iota}\varsigma$ $\delta o\theta\epsilon\hat{\iota}\sigma a$): they will become more prosperous, having the disposal of capital: and the treasury will have a sufficient and perpetual income.' He then urges the necessity of preparing a complete budget estimate of regular receipts from the above and other sources, and of the prospective regular charges both military and civil, with allowance for unforeseen contingencies. 'And your next step should be to provide for any deficit by imposing a tax on all properties whatsoever that bring a profit ($\dot{\epsilon}\pi\iota\kappa\alpha\rho\pi\dot{\iota}a\nu$ $\tau\iota\nu\dot{a}$) to the owner, and by a system of tributary dues in all our subject provinces.'

---

[1] Velleius II 88, and many passages in Seneca and other authors.

[2] Dion Cass LII 27–8.

[3] Compare Suet *Aug* 41 for the Emperor's actual policy. It seems that the influx of specie captured at Alexandria sent the rate of interest down and the price of land up.

That this long oration attributed by Dion to Maecenas is in great part made up from details of the policy actually followed by the Emperor, is I believe generally admitted. But I am not aware that the universal income-tax suggested was imposed. The policy of encouraging agriculture certainly formed part of the imperial scheme, and the function of the *Georgics* was to bring the power of literature to bear in support of the movement. The poet could hardly help referring in some way to the crying need of a great agricultural revival. He did it with consummate skill. He did not begin by enlarging on the calamities of the recent past, and then proceed to offer his remedies. Such a method would at once have aroused suspicion and ill-feeling. No, he waited till he was able to glide easily into a noble passage in which he speaks of the civil wars as a sort of doom sanctioned by the heavenly powers. No party could take offence at this way of putting it. Then he cries aloud to the Roman gods, not to prevent the man of the hour (*hunc iuvenem*) from coming to the relief of a ruined generation. The needs of the moment are such that we cannot do without him. The world is full of wickedness and wars : 'the plough is not respected as it should be ; the tillers of the soil have been drafted away, and the land is gone to weeds ; the crooked sickles are being forged into straight swords.' The passage comes at the end of the first book, following a series of precepts delivered coolly and calmly as though in a social atmosphere of perfect peace. The tone in which the words recall the reader to present realities, and subtly hint at the obvious duty of supporting the one possible restorer of Roman greatness, is an unsurpassed feat of literary art. It is followed up at the end of the second book in another famous passage, in which he preaches with equal delicacy the doctrine that agricultural revival is the one sure road not only to personal happiness but to the true greatness of the Roman people.

That this revival was bound up with the return to a system of farming on a smaller scale, implying more direct personal attention on the landlord's part, is obvious. But the poet goes further. His model farmer is to be convinced of the necessity and benefit of personal labour, and so to put his own hand to the plough. The glorification of unyielding toil[1] as the true secret of success was (and is) a congenial topic to preachers of the gospel of 'back to the land.' It may well be that the thoughtful Vergil had misgivings as to the fruitfulness of his doctrine. A cynical critic might hint that it was easy enough for one man to urge others to work. But a man like Maecenas would smile at such remarks. To set other people to do what he would never dream of doing himself was to him the most natural thing in the world.

---

[1] This is admirably dealt with in Sellar's *Virgil*, and need not be reproduced here.

So the pressure of the patron on the poet continued, and the *Georgics* were born.

Let me now turn to certain passages of the poem in which farm-labour is directly referred to, and see how far the status of the labourers can be judged from the expressions used and the context. And first of *aratores*. In I 494 and II 513 the *agricola* is a plowman ; free, for all that appears to the contrary. In II 207, where he appears as clearing off wood[1] and ploughing up the land, the *arator* is called *iratus* : this can hardly apply to an indifferent slave. The *arator* of I 261, represented as turning the leisure enforced by bad weather to useful indoor work, odd jobs in iron and wood work etc, may be one of a slave-staff whom his master will not have idle. Or he may be the farmer himself. The scene implies the presence of a staff of some kind, driven indoors by the rain. And that the poet is not thinking of a solitary peasant is further indicated by mention of sheep-washing, certainly not a 'one-man-job,' in line 272. Why Conington (after Heyne) takes *agitator aselli* in 273 to be 'the peasant who happens to drive the ass to market,' and not an *asinarius* doing his regular duty, I cannot say. On III 402, a very similar passage, he takes the *pastor* to be probably the farm-slave, not the owner, adding 'though it is not always easy to see for what class of men Virgil is writing.' A remark which shews that my present inquiry is not uncalled for. To return, there is nothing to shew whether the ass-driver is a freeman or a slave. Nor is the status of *messores*[2] clear. In I 316–7 the farmer brings the mower on to the yellow fields ; that is, he orders his hands to put in the sickle. What is their relation to him we do not hear. So too in II 410 *postremus metito* is a precept addressed to the farmer as farmer, not as potential labourer. On the other hand the *messores* in the second and third eclogues seem to be slaves, for there is reference to *domini* in both poems.

The *fossor* is in literature the personification of mere heavy manual labour. In default of evidence to the contrary, we must suppose him to be normally[3] a slave. Thus the *fossor* of Horace *odes* III 18 is probably one of the *famuli operum soluti* of the preceding ode. But the brawny digger of *Georgics* II 264, who aids nature's work by stirring and loosening the caked earth, is left on a neutral footing. Nothing is said. The reader must judge whether this silence is the result of pure inadvertency. That *pastores* very often means slave-herdsmen, is well

---

[1] Mr T R Glover, *Virgil* p 14, reminds us that the poet's father is said to have done some business in timber at one time.

[2] When Cicero *de orat* III § 46 credits *messores* with a rustic brogue he can hardly be thinking of foreign slaves.

[3] As in Lucan VII 402 *vincto fossore*.

known. But Vergil seems to attribute to them a more real and intelligent interest in the welfare of their charge than it is reasonable to expect from rustic slaves. The *pastores* of IV 278, who gather the medicinal herb used in the treatment of bees, may be slaves: if so, they are not mere thoughtless animals. And the scene is in the Cisalpine, where we have noted that slavery was probably of a mild type. In III 420 the *pastor* is called upon to protect his beasts from snakes. But we know[1] that it was a part of slave-herdsmen's duty to fight beasts of prey, and that they were commonly armed for that purpose. In III 455 we find him shrinking from a little act of veterinary surgery, which the context suggests he ought to perform. But we know that the *magister pecoris* on a farm was instructed[2] in simple veterinary practice, and it is hardly likely that other slaves, specially put in charge of beasts, had no instructions. The *pastores* (if more than one, the chief,) appear as *pecorum magistri* (II 529, III 445, cf *Buc* III 101), a regular name for shepherds: they are not the same as the *magistri* of III 549, who are veterinary specialists disguised under mythical names. In II 529–31 we have a holiday scene, in which the farmer (*ipse*) treats the *pecoris magistri* to a match of wrestling and throwing the javelin. If slaves are meant, then Vergil is surely carrying back rustic slavery to early days as part and parcel of the 'good old times' to which he points in the following lines *hanc olim veteres vitam coluere Sabini* etc. The *ipse* will then be a genial farmer of the old school, whose slaves are very different from the degraded and sullen chattels of more recent years. But in this as in other cases the poet gives us no clear sign.

A passage[3] in which the reticence of which I am speaking has a peculiar effect occurs in the description of the grievous murrain that visited northern Italy some time before. One of a pair of oxen falls dead while drawing the plough. The *tristis arator*[4] unyokes the other, sorrow-stricken at the death of its fellow; he leaves the plough where it stopped, and goes his way. Then follows a piece of highly-wrought pathos[5] describing the dejection and collapse of the surviving ox. 'What now avail him his toil or his services, his past work in turning up the heavy land with the ploughshare?' And the hardness of the poor beast's lot is emphasized by the reflexion that disease in cattle is not induced by gluttony and wine-bibbing, as it often is in the case of mankind, nor by the worries (*cura*) that rob men of refreshing

[1] Varro *RR* II 10.

[2] See Varro *RR* II 2 § 20, 5 § 18, 7 § 16, even for treatment of *homines* 10 § 10. Written books of prescriptions were provided.

[3] *Georg* III 515–30.

[4] *tristis* suggests the owner. A slave was not likely to care.

[5] In Sellar's *Virgil* chapter VI § 5 there is an excellent treatment of this episode, with a discussion of V's relation to Lucretius and a most apposite quotation from G Sand.

sleep. This much-admired passage may remind us of the high value set upon the ox in ancient Italy, traditionally amounting to a kind of sanctity; for it is said[1] that to kill an ox was as great a crime as to kill a man. We may wonder too what the luxurious but responsible Maecenas thought of the lines contrasting the simple diet and untroubled life of the ox with the excesses and anxieties of man. But, if civilization owed much to the labours of the ox, and if gratitude was due to man's patient helper, what about the human slave? Is it not a remarkable thing that the *Georgics* contain not a word of appreciative reference to the myriads of toiling bondsmen whose sweat and sufferings had been exploited by Roman landlords for at least 150 years? Can this silence on the part of a poet who credits an ox with human affection be regarded as a merely accidental omission?

Of poets in general it may I think be truly said that the relation between the singer and his vocabulary varies greatly in various cases. Personal judgments are very fallible: but to me, the more I read Vergil, the more I see in him an extreme case of the poet ever nervously on his guard[2] against expressing or suggesting any meaning or shade of meaning beyond that which at a given moment he wishes to convey. This is no original discovery. But in reaching it independently I have become further convinced that the limitations of his vocabulary are evidence of nice and deliberate selection. The number of well-established Latin words, adaptable to verse and to the expression of ideas certain to occur, that are used by other poets of note but not by him, is considerable. I have a long list: here I will mention only one, the adjective *vagus*. The word may have carried to him associations below the pure dignity of his finished style. Yet Horace used it freely in the *Odes*, and Horace was surely no hasty hack careless of propriety, and no mean judge of what was proper. Now, when I turn to the *Georgics*, Vergil's most finished work, I am struck by the absence of certain words the presence of which would seem natural, or even to be expected, in any work professedly treating of agriculture in Roman Italy. Thus *servus* does not occur at all, *serva* in the *Aeneid* only, and *servitium* in the strict sense only *Buc* I 40 and *Aen* III 327. In *Georg* III 167–8 *ubi libera colla servitio adsuerint* he is speaking of the breaking-in of young oxen[3] in figurative language. So too *dominus* and *domina* occur in the *Bucolics* and *Aeneid* but not in the *Georgics*. The case of *opera* and the plural *operae* may seem to be on a somewhat different footing in so far as the special sense of *opera* = 'the average

---

[1] Varro II 5 § 4, Columella VI *praef* § 7, Plin *NH* VIII § 180.

[2] The *molle atque facetum* attributed to V by Horace is I think rightly explained by Quintilian VI 3 § 20, and amounts to easy and fastidious taste, of course the result of careful revision, his practice of which is attested in the Suetonian biography.

[3] So Tibullus II 1 41–2.

day's work[1] of a labourer' would perhaps have too technical and prosaic a flavour. In the single instance (*Aen* VII 331–2), where it occurs in the familiar phrase *da operam*, it is coupled with *laborem*, which rather suggests a certain timidity in the use of a colloquial expression. The plural, frequent in the writers on agriculture, he does not use at all, whether because he avoids the statistical estimates in which it most naturally comes, or from sheer fastidiousness due to the disreputable associations of *operae* in political slang. Perhaps neither of these reasons is quite enough to account for the absence of the word from the *Georgics*. That *famulus* and *famula* occur in the *Aeneid* only is not surprising, for they represent the δμῶες and δμωαί of Greek heroic poetry. But *famula* appears in the *Moretum*, of which I will speak below.

That Vergil is all the while pointing the way to a system of small farms and working farmers, though some topics (for instance stock-keeping) seem to touch on a larger scale of business, may be gathered from his references to *coloni*. The word is in general used merely as the substantive corresponding to *colere*, and its place is often taken by *agricola* (I 300, II 459) or *rusticus* (II 406) or other substitutes. In II 433 *homines* means much the same as the *agrestis* of I 41, only that the former need stimulus and the latter guidance. The typical picture of the *colonus* comes in I 291–302, where the small farmer and his industrious wife are seen taking some relaxation in the winter season, but never idle. It is surely a somewhat idealized picture. The parallel in Horace (*epode* II) is more matter-of-fact, and clearly includes slaves, an element ignored by Vergil. The *colonus* is not a mere tenant farmer, but a yeoman tilling his own land, like the *veteres coloni* of the ninth eclogue, a freeman, and we may add liable to military service, like those in I 507 whose conscription left the farms derelict. A curious and evidently exceptional case is that of the *Corycius senex* (IV 125–46), said to be one of Pompey's pirate colonists. The man is a squatter on a patch of unoccupied land, which he has cultivated as a garden, raising by unwearied industry quite wonderful crops of vegetables fruit and flowers, and remarkably successful[2] as a bee-keeper. Perhaps this transplanted Oriental had no slave, at least when he started gardening. But I note that his croft was more than a *iugerum* (*pauca relicti iugera ruris*) at the time when Vergil saw it, and I imagine the process of reclaiming the waste to have been gradual. When this small holding was complete and in full bearing, would the work of one elderly man suffice to carry it on? I wonder. But we get no hint of a slave or a hireling, or even of a wife. All I can venture to say is that this story is meant to be significant of the moral and material wellbeing of the

---

[1] Cf Cic *de off* I §§ 41, 150, passages in which the growth of the technical sense is seen.

[2] See the interesting story of the bee-farm in Varro *RR* III 16 §§ 10, 11.

small cultivator. It is curious that just above (118, cf 147–8) the poet is at pains to excuse his omission to discuss in detail the proper management of *horti*, on the pretext of want of space. For he was no mean antiquary, and Pliny tells[1] us that in the Twelve Tables *hortus* was used of what was afterwards called *villa*, a country farm, while *heredium* stood for a garden; and adds that in old time *per se hortus ager pauperis erat.* But *hortus* is to Vergil strictly a garden, and the old Corycian is cited expressly as a gardener: his land, we are told, was not suited for growing corn or vines.

The mention of gardening invites me to say a few words on the short descriptive idyll *Moretum* which has been regarded as a youthful composition of Vergil (perhaps from a Greek original) with more justice than some other pieces attributed to him. I see no strong objection to admitting it as Vergilian, but it is of course crude and far removed from the manner and finish of the mature *Georgics*. The peasant Simylus, *exigui cultor rusticus agri*, is a poor small farmer whose thrift and industry enable him to make a living 'in a humble and pottering way,' as Gilbert puts it. His holding is partly ordinary arable land, but includes a *hortus* as well. In the latter he skilfully grows a variety of vegetables, for which he finds a regular market in the city. Poor though he is, and accustomed to wait on himself, apparently unmarried, he yet owns a slave (*famulam*, 93) and she is a negro, fully described (31–5), woolly hair, thick lips, dark skin, spindle shanks, paddle feet, etc. She probably would do the house-work, but the preparation of food is a duty in which her master also bears a part. We hear of no male slave, and the ploughing of fields and digging the garden are apparently done by himself singlehanded. The yoke of oxen are mentioned in the last lines. The picture is such as may have been true of some humble homesteads in Italy, but the tradition of a Greek original, and the names Simylus and Scybale, must leave us in some doubt as to whether the scene be really Italian. The position is in fact much the same as it is in regard to the *Bucolics*.

Whatever may be the correct view as to the authorship and bearing of the *Moretum*, there are I think certain conclusions to be drawn from an examination of the *Georgics*, which it is time to summarize. First, the tendency of the poem is to advocate a system of smaller holdings and more intensive cultivation than had for a long period been customary in a large part of Italy. This reform is rather suggested by implication than directly urged, though one precept, said to be borrowed[2] from old Cato, recommends it in plain words. For the glorification of labour in general is all the while pointing in this direction. Secondly, the policy

---

[1] Pliny *NH* XIX §§ 50–1.

[2] II 412–3 *laudato ingentia rura, exiguum colito.* Not found in surviving text of Cato.

of the new Emperor, who posed as Restorer and Preserver rather than Reformer, finds a sympathetic or obedient expression in this tendency. For it is delicately conveyed that the reform of an evil agricultural present virtually consists in the return to the ways of a better past. And the poet, acting as poet simply, throws on this better past the halo of a golden age still more remote. The virtues of the Sabines of old[1] are an example of the happiness and honour attainable by a rustic folk. But to Vergil, steeped in ancient legend, the historic worthies of a former age are not the beginning of things. They come 'trailing clouds of glory' from the mythical origin[2] of mankind, from a world of primeval abundance and brotherly communism, a world which he like Lucretius pauses to portray. Thirdly, the reaction of Augustus against the bold cosmopolitanism of Julius Caesar has I think left a mark on the *Georgics* in the fact that the poem is, as Sellar says, so thoroughly representative of Italy. Roman Italy was not yet ready to become merely a part of an imperial estate. If people were to acquiesce in a monarchy, it had to be disguised, and one important disguise was the make-believe that the Roman people were lords of the world. A very harmless method of ministering to Roman self-complacency was excessive praise of Italy, its soil, its climate, its natural features, its various products, its races of men and their works, and all the historic associations of the victorious past. It is a notable fact that this panegyric[3] breaks out in the utterances of four very dissimilar works that still survive: for beside the *Georgics* I must place[4] the so-called *Roman Antiquities* of Dionysius, the *Geography* of Strabo, and the *de re rustica* of Varro. These four are practically contemporaries. It seems to me hardly credible that there was not some common influence operative at the time and encouraging utterances of this tone.

The actual success or failure of the attempt to revive Roman agriculture on a better footing is not only a question of fact in itself historically important: its determination will throw light on the circumstances in which Vergil wrote, and perhaps help somewhat in suggesting reasons for his avoidance of certain topics. If we are to believe Horace[5], the agricultural policy of Augustus was a grand success: security, prosperity, virtue, good order, had become normal: fertility had returned to the countryside. I had better say at once that I put little faith in these utterances of a court poet. Far more significant is the statement, preserved by Suetonius[6], of the evils dealt

---

[1] II 532.   [2] I 125–8, II 336–42.   [3] II 136–76.

[4] Dionys *Hal* I 36–7, Strabo VI 4 § I, p 286, Varro *RR* I 2 §§ I–7.

[5] Horace *Odes* IV 5, 15, published about 14 BC. So Martial V 4 declares that Domitian has made Rome *pudica*.

[6] Sueton *Aug* 32 (cf *Tib* 8), and the elder Seneca *contr* X 4 § 18. Even in the second

with by Augustus in country districts. Parties of armed bandits infested the country. Travellers, slaves and freemen alike, were kidnapped and *ergastulis possessorum supprimebantur.* He checked the
brigandage by armed police posted at suitable spots, and *ergastula
recognovit.* But it is not said that he did away with them: he cleared
out of them the persons illegally held in bondage (*suppressi*). Not
only is rustic slavery in full swing in the treatise of Varro: some 80
years later the *ergastulum* is adopted as a matter of course by Columella, and appears as a canker of agriculture in the complaints of
Pliny. The neglect of rustic industry is lamented by all three writers,
and to the testimony of such witnesses it is quite needless to add
quotations from writers of merely literary merit. There is no serious
doubt that the reconstruction of agriculture on the basis of small
farms tilled by working farmers was at best successful in a very
moderate degree; and this for many a long year. Organized slave-
labour remained the staple appliance of tillage until the growing
scarcity of slaves and the financial policy of the later Empire brought
about the momentous change by which the free farmer gradually became the predial serf.

   Another point to be noted in the *Georgics* is the absence of any
reference to *coloni* as tenants under a landlord. Yet we know that this
relation existed in Cicero's time, and tenant farmers appear in Varro[1]
and Columella[2]. Vergil, but for a stray reference in the *Aeneid*, might
seem never to have heard of the existence of such people. It is easy
to say that the difference between an owner and a tenant is a difference in law, and unsuited for discussion in a poem. But it also
involves economic problems. The landlord wants a good return on his
capital, the tenant wants to make a good living, and the conditions of
tenancy vary greatly in various cases. The younger Pliny[3] had to deal
with awkward questions between him and his tenants, and there is no
reason to suppose that his case was exceptional. Surely the subject
was one of immediate interest to an agricultural reformer, quite as
interesting as a number of the details set forth here and there in the
Georgics; that is, assuming that the author meant his farmer to be
economically prosperous as well as to set a good example. It may be
argued that the operations enjoined on the farmer would greatly im-

---

century AD, Spart *Hadr* 18 § 9 *ergastula servorum et liberorum tulit.* Perhaps the *ergastula*
in Columella I 3 § 12 refer to the same practice.
   [1] H Blümner in Müller's *Handbuch* IV 2 2 p 543 says that Varro does not refer to the
Kolonat als Pacht. But that sense seems clearly implied in I 2 § 17, II 3 § 4 *in lege locationis
fundi.* In I 16 § 4 it surely includes tenants, even if the application is more general. In II
praef § 5 *colonus* is simply = *arator*, opposed to *pastor.*
   [2] Columella I 7.
   [3] Pliny *epist* III 19, IX 37.

prove the farm and enhance the value of the land, and that no man in his senses would do this unless the land were his own: there was therefore no need to discuss tenancy, ownership being manifestly implied. The argument is fair, so far as it goes. But it does not justify complete silence on what was probably at the moment a question of no small importance in the eyes of landowners.

Some passages of Horace may serve to shew that circumstances might have justified or even invited some reference to this topic. In the seventh *epistle* of the first book he tells the story of how Philippus played a rather scurvy trick on a freedman in a small way of business as an auctioneer. As a social superior, his patronage turned the poor man's head. Taking him for an outing to his own Sabine country place, he infected him with desire of a rustic life. He amused himself by persuading him to buy a small farm, offering him about £60 as a gift and a loan of as much more. The conversion of a regular town-bred man into a thoroughgoing farmer was of course a pitiful failure. Devotion and industry availed him nothing. The losses and disappointments incidental to farming were too much for him. He seems to have had no slave: he probably had not sufficient capital. He ended by piteously entreating his patron to put him back into his own trade. The story is placed about two generations before Horace wrote. But it would be pointless if it were out of date in its setting, which it surely is not; it might have happened to a contemporary, nay to Horace himself. It is addressed to his own patron Maecenas, the generous donor of his own Sabine estate. Here we have a clear intimation that to buy a little plot and try to get a living out of it by your own labour was an enterprise in which success was no easy matter. In the second *satire* of the second book we have the case of Ofellus, one of the yeomen of the old school. He had been a working farmer on his own land, but in the times of trouble his farm had been confiscated and made over to a discharged soldier. But this veteran wisely left him in occupation as cultivator on terms. Whether he became a sort of farm-bailiff, working for the new owner's account at a fixed salary, or whether he became a tenant, farming on his own account and paying a rent, has been doubted. I am strongly of the second opinion. For it was certainly to the owner's interest that the land should be well-farmed, and that his own income (the endowment of his later years) should be well-secured by giving the farmer every motive for industry. These considerations do not suit well with the former alternative, which also makes *colonus* hardly distinguishable from *vilicus*. Again, the *colonus* is on the farm[1] *cum pecore et gnatis.*

[1] This reminds us of Varro's words, speaking (1 17 § 2) of free workers ...*cum ipsi colunt, ut plerique pauperculi cum sua progenie.*

The *pecus*, like the children, is surely the farmer's own, and it is much more likely that the live-stock should belong to a rent-paying tenant than to a salaried bailiff. Moreover, there is no mention of slaves. The man works the farm with the help of his family. Is it likely that he would turn them into a household of serfs? Therefore I render line 115 *fortem mercede colonum* 'a sturdy tenant-farmer sitting at a rent'; that is, on a holding that as owner he formerly occupied rent-free. He can make the farm pay even now: as for the mere fact of ground-landlordship, that is an idle boast, and in any case limited by the span of human life. I claim that these two passages are enough to prove the point for which I am contending; namely, that questions of the tenure under which agriculture could best be carried on were matters of some interest and importance about the time when Vergil was writing the *Georgics*.

But the help of Horace is by no means exhausted. He refers to a story of a wage-earning labourer (*mercennarius*) who had the luck to turn up a buried treasure, a find which enabled him to buy the very farm on which he was employed, and work it as his own. There is no point in this 'yarn' unless it was a well-known tale, part of the current stock of the day. The famous *satire* in which it occurs (11 6) seems to be almost exactly contemporary with the appearance of the *Georgics*. In it the restful charm of country life is heartily preferred to the worries and boredom of Rome. His Sabine estate, with its garden, its unfailing spring of water, and a strip of woodland, is of no great size, but it is enough: he is no greedy land-grabber. When in Rome he longs for it. There he can take his ease among spoilt young slaves, born[1] on the place, keeping a sort of Liberty Hall for his friends. The talk at table is not *de villis domibusve alienis* but of a more rational and improving kind: envy of other men's wealth is talked out with an apposite fable. Here we have mention of wage-earning, land-purchase, and slaves. And the poet's estate is evidently in the first place a residence, not a farm worked on strict economic lines. That the number of slave hands (*operae*) employed there on the Home Farm[2] was eight, we learn from another *satire* (11 7 118). To the smart country seats, which advertise the solid wealth of rich capitalists, he refers in express terms in *epistles* 1 15 45-6, and by many less particular references. The land-grabbers are often mentioned, and the forest-lands (*saltus*) used for grazing, in which much money was invested by men 'land-proud,' as a sign of their importance. In short, the picture of rural Italy given by Horace reveals to us a state of things wholly unfavourable to the reception of the message of the *Georgics*. When he speaks of *pauper ruris colonus* or of *inopes coloni* he is surely not betraying envy of these

---

[1] Cf Tibullus 11 1 23 *turbaque vernarum saturi bona signa coloni.*   [2] See above, p 216.

toilers' lot. Far from it. When enjoying a change in his country place, he may occasionally divert himself with a short spell[1] of field-work, at which his neighbours grin. On the other hand the spectacle of a disreputable freedman, enriched by speculations in time of public calamity, and enabled through ill-gotten wealth to become a great landlord, is the cause of wrathful indignation (*epode* IV). And these and other candid utterances come from one whose father was a freedman in a country town, farming in quite a small way, to whose care and self-denial the son owed the education that equipped him for rising in the world. Horace indeed is one of the best of witnesses on these points.

There are points on which Vergil and Horace are agreed, though generally with a certain difference of attitude. Thus, both prefer the country to the town, but Horace frankly because he enjoys it and likes a rest: he does not idealize country life as such, still less agricultural labour. Both disapprove *latifundia*, but Horace on simple common-sense grounds, not as a reformer. Both praise good old times, but Horace without the faintest suggestion of possible revival of them, or anything like them. Both refer to the beginnings of civilization, but Vergil looks back to a golden age of primitive communism, when *in medium quaerebant* and so forth; a state of things ended by Jove's ordinance that man should raise himself by toil. Horace, less convinced of the superiority of the past, depicts[2] the noble savage as having to fight for every thing, even acorns; and traces steps, leading eventually to law and order, by which he became less savage and more noble. Horace is nearer to Lucretius here than Vergil is. Neither could ignore the disturbing effect of the disbanding of armies and ejectment of farmers to make way for the settlement of rude soldiers on the land. But to Horace, personally unconcerned, a cool view was more possible. So, while hinting at public uneasiness[3] as to the detailed intentions of the new ruler in this matter, he is able to look at the policy in general merely as the restoration of weary veterans to a life of peace and the relief of their chief's anxieties. Vergil, himself a sufferer, had his little fling in the *Bucolics*, and was silent[4] in the *Georgics*. Again, Vergil shuns the function of war as a means of supplying the slave-market. He knows it well enough, and as a feature of the 'heroic' ages the fate of the captive appears in the *Aeneid*. Horace makes no scruple[5] of stating the time-honoured principle that a captive is to the conqueror a valuable asset: there is a market for him as a serviceable drudge,

---

[1] Hor *epist* I 14 39, cf II 2 184–6.
[2] Hor *Sat* I 3 99 foll, where *animalia* seems to mean little more than *homines*.
[3] Hor *Sat* II 6 55–6, *Odes* III 4 37–40.
[4] The one reference to the assignations [*G* II 198] only speaks of the misfortune of Mantua, not of his own.
[5] Hor *Epist* I 16 69–72.

and not to spare his life is sheer waste. That there may be sarcasm underlying the passage does not impair its candour. And it distinctly includes rustic slavery in the words *sine pascat durus aretque*. Lastly, while both poets praise the restfulness of the countryside with equal sincerity, it is Horace who recognizes[1] that the working farmer himself, after his long labours at the plough, looks forward to retirement and ease when he has saved enough to live on. His is a real rustic, Vergil's an ideal.

It will be admitted that all writers are, as sources of evidence, at their best when they feel free to say or to leave unsaid this or that according to their own judgment. If there is in the background some other person whom it is necessary to please, it is very hard to divine the reason of an author's frankness, and still more of his reticence. For instance, the omission of a topic naturally connected with a subject need not imply that a patron forbade its introduction. I cannot believe that such a man as Maecenas[2] banned the free mention of slavery in the *Georgics*. But, if a whole subject is proposed for treatment under conditions of a well-understood tendency, the writer is not unlikely to discover that artistic loyalty to that tendency will operate to render the introduction of this or that particular topic a matter of extreme difficulty. If the task of Vergil was to recommend a return to a more wholesome system of agriculture, reference to the labour-question or to land-tenure bristled with difficulties. My belief is that the poet shirked these topics, relevant though they surely were, because he did not see how to treat them without provoking controversy or ill-feeling; a result which Maecenas and the Emperor were undoubtedly anxious to avoid. It was simpler and safer not to refer to these things. True, the omission was a restraint on full-blooded realism. An indistinct picture was produced, and modern critics have some reason to complain of the difficulty of understanding many places of the *Georgics*.

Whether chronological considerations may throw any light on the influences to which this indistinctness is due, and, if so, what is their exact significance, are very difficult questions, to which I cannot offer a definite answer. The completion of the *Georgics* is placed in the year 30 BC, after seven years more or less spent on composition and revision. Now it was in that year that the new ruler, supreme since the overthrow of Antony, organized the great disbandment of armies of which he speaks in the famous inscription[3] recording the events of

[1] Hor *Sat* I 1 28, 32.
[2] For the story of the φιάλη (freedman's offering) sent yearly by Maecenas to Augustus as a recognition of his restoration of Roman freedom, see Gardthausen *Augustus* VII 7 and notes.
[3] *Monum Ancyr* ed Mommsen, I 16–9, III 22–8.

his career. He tells us that he rewarded all the discharged men, either with assignations of land or with sums of money in lieu thereof. The lands were bought by him (not confiscated) and the money-payments also were at his cost (*a me dedi*). Below he refers to the matter again, and adds that to pay for lands taken and assigned to soldiers was a thing no one had ever done before. That he paid in all cases, and paid the full market value, he does not expressly say ; Mommsen shews cause for doubting it. The only remark I have to make is that in the years between Philippi and Aetium there was plenty of fighting and negotiations. Maecenas was for most of the time in a position of great trust, and pretty certainly in touch with all that went on. The fact that a wholesale discharge of soldiers was surely coming, and that the future of agriculture in Italy was doubtful, was perhaps not likely to escape the forecast of so far-sighted a man. Is it just possible that Vergil may have had a hint from him, to stick to generalities and avoid controversial topics? We are credibly in-formed[1] that Maecenas was well rewarded by his master for his valuable services, and it has been pointed out[2] that his position of authority offered many opportunities of profitable transactions on his own account. There is even an express tradition that he was concerned in the liquidation of one estate. In short, he was one of the land-speculators of the time. To such a man it would seem not untimely to praise the virtues of the rustic Romans of old and to recommend their revival in the coming age ; but to call attention to the uncertainties of the present, involving many awkward problems, would seem imprudent. In sug-gesting, doubtfully, that a patron's restraining hand may have had something to do with the poet's reticence, I may be exaggerating the pressure exercised by the one on the other. But that Maecenas interested himself in the slowly-growing poem is hardly to be doubted. Early in each of the four books he is addressed by name. His *haud mollia iussa* (III 41) may imply nothing more than the general difficulty of Vergil's task : but may it not faintly indicate just the least little restive-ness under a guidance that could not be refused openly?

To reject the suggestion of actual interference on Maecenas' part is not to say that the *Georgics* exhibits no deference to his wishes. That many a veiled hint could be given by a patron in conversation is obvious. That Maecenas would be a master of that judicious art, is probable from what we know of his character and career. But, while it is plain that questions of land-tenure would from his point of view be better ignored, how would his likes and dislikes affect the mention

---

[1] Tacitus *ann* XIV 53.

[2] Gardthausen *Augustus* VII 7, pp 768–9. He quotes Schol ad Juvenal v 3 (Maecenas) *ad quem sectio bonorum Favoni pertinuerat.*

of slavery and the labour-question? Here I must refer to the three
great writers on agriculture. Cato, about 150 years earlier, and Columella, about 80 years later, both contemplate the actual buying of
land, and insist on the care necessary in selection. The contemporary
Varro seems certainly to assume purchase. All three deal with slave-
labour, Cato like a hard-fisted *dominus* of an old-Roman generation
just become consciously imperial and bent on gain, Columella as a
skilful organizer of the only regular supply of labour practically available: Varro, who makes more allowance[1] for free labour beside that
of slaves, reserves the free man for important jobs, where he may be
trusted to use his wits, or for unhealthy work, in which to risk slaves
is to risk your own property. All the ordinary work in his system is
done by slaves. The contemporary Livy[2] tells us that in his time large
districts near Rome had scarce any free inhabitants left. The elder
Pliny, reckoning up the advantages of Italy for the practice of agriculture, includes[3] among them the supply of *servitia*, though no man knew
better than he what fatal results had issued from the plantation-system.
It is to be borne in mind that this evidence relates to the plains and
the lower slopes of hills, that is to the main agricultural districts. It
is to these parts that Gardthausen[4] rightly confines his remarks on the
desolation of Italy, which began before the civil wars and was accelerated
by them. Other labour was scarce, and gangs of slaves, generally
chained, were almost the only practicable means of tillage for profit.
Speaking broadly, I think the truth of this picture is not to be denied.
If then the word had gone forth that a return to smaller-scale farming
was to be advocated as a cure for present evils, it was hardly possible
to touch on slavery without some unfavourable reference to the plantation-system. Now surely it is most unlikely that Maecenas, a cool
observer and a thorough child of the age, sincerely believed in the
possibility of setting back the clock. The economic problem could
not be solved so simply, by creating a wave of 'back-to-the-land'
enthusiasm. I suggest that he saw no good to be got by openly
endeavouring to recreate the race of small working farmers by artificial
means. Would it be wise to renew an attempt in which the Gracchi
had failed? Now to Vergil, who had passed his youth in a district of
more humane agriculture, the mere praise of farming, with its rich
compensations for never-ending toil and care, would be a congenial
theme. The outcome of their combination was that a topic not easily
idealized in treatment was omitted. The realistic value of the picture
was impaired to the relief of both poet and patron. But what the poem
gained as a beautiful aspiration it lost as a practical authority.

[1] Varro *RR* I 17, a notable chapter.   [2] Livy VI 12, VII 25.
[3] Plin *NH* XXXVII §§ 201–3.   [4] *Augustus* VI 3, p 547.

Can we suppose that Vergil did not know how important a place in contemporary agriculture was filled by slave-labour? I think not: surely it is inconceivable. What meets us at every turn in other writers cannot have been unknown to him. Macrobius[1] has preserved for us a curious record belonging to 43 BC, when the great confiscations and assignations of land were being carried out in the Cisalpine by order of the Triumvirs. Money and arms, needed for the coming campaign of Philippi, were being requisitioned at the same time. The men of property threatened by these exactions hid themselves. Their slaves were offered rewards and freedom if they would betray their masters' hiding-places, but not one of them yielded to the temptation. The commander who made the offer was Pollio. No doubt domestics are chiefly meant, but there were rustic slaves, and we have reason to think that they were humanely treated in those parts. Dion Cassius[2] tells us that in 41 BC Octavian, under great pressure from the clamorous armies, saw nothing to be done but to take all Italian lands from present owners and hand them over to the soldiers μετά τε τῆς δουλείας καὶ μετὰ τῆς ἄλλης κατασκευῆς. Circumstances necessitated compromise, which does not concern us here. But it is well to remember that it was just the best land that the soldiers wanted, and with it slaves and other farm-stock. For it was a pension after service, not a hard life of bodily drudgery, that was in view. The plan of letting the former owner stay on as a tenant has been referred to above.

I hold then that Vergil's silence on the topics to which I have called attention, however congenial it may have been to him, was intentional: and that the poem, published in honorem Maecenatis[3], was limited as to its practical outlook with the approval, if not at the suggestion, of the patron. It is essentially a literary work. In it Vergil's power of gathering materials from all quarters and fusing them into a whole of his own creation is exemplified to a wonderful degree. His own deep love of the country, with its homely sights and sounds, phenomena of a Nature whose laws he felt unable to explore, helped him to execute the task of recommending a social and economic reform through the medium of poetry. By ignoring topics deemed unsuitable, he left his sympathies and enthusiasm free course, and without sympathies and enthusiasm the Georgics would not have been immortal. Even when digressing from agriculture, as in his opening address to the Emperor, there is more sincerity than we are at first disposed to grant. He had not been a Republican, like Horace, and probably had been from the first attached to the cause of the Caesars.

---

[1] Macrob Sat I 11 § 22.   [2] Dion Cass XLVIII 6 § 3.
[3] The words of Donatus (after Suetonius) in his life of Vergil. Reifferscheid's Suetonius P 59.

I can discover no ground for thinking[1] that Vergil was ever himself a farmer. That Pliny and Columella cite him as an authority is in my opinion due to the predominance of his works in the literary world. As writers of prose dealing with facts often of an uninspiring kind, it would seem to raise the artistic tone of heavy paragraphs if the first name in Latin literature could be introduced with an apposite quotation in agreement with their own context. Vergil-worship began early and lasted long; and indeed his admirers in the present day are sometimes so absorbed in finding[2] more and more in what he said that they do not trouble themselves to ask whether there may not be some significance[3] in his silences. Rightly or wrongly, I am persuaded that this question ought at least to be asked in connexion with the *Georgics*. I have reserved till the last a passage[4] of Seneca, in which he challenges the authority of Vergil in some points connected with trees, speaking of him as *Vergilius noster, qui non quid verissime sed quid decentissime diceretur aspexit, nec agricolas docere voluit sed legentes delectare.* Now Seneca was devoted to the works of Vergil, and is constantly quoting them. He has no prejudice against the poet. The view of the *Georgics* set forth in these words implies no literary dispraise, but a refusal to let poetic excellence give currency to technical errors. Seneca is often tiresome, but in this matter his criticism is in my opinion sound. In the matter of labour my contention is not that the poet has inadvertently erred, but that he has for some reason deliberately dissembled.

XXX. THE ELDER SENECA AND OTHERS.

The comparatively silent interval, between the Augustan circle and the new group of writers under Claudius and Nero, furnishes little of importance. The one writer who stands out as giving us a few scraps of evidence is the **elder Seneca**, the earliest of the natives of Spain who made their mark in Latin literature. But the character of his work, which consists of examples of the treatment of problem-cases in the schools of rhetoric, makes him a very peculiar witness. When he tells us how this or that pleader of note made some point neatly, the words have their appropriate place in the texture of a particular argument. Often they contain a fallacious suggestion or a misstatement useful for the purpose of *ex parte* advocacy, but having as statements no authority

---

[1] Keightley (1846) says the same.

[2] With much respect and regret, I cannot accept the views of Prof Conway in his inaugural lecture of 1903.

[3] The absence of reference to Cicero has of course been noted. But this was general in the Augustan age.

[4] Seneca *epist* 86 § 15.

whatever. Still there are a few references of significance and value. Thus, when the poor man's son refuses the rich man's offer to adopt him, and his own father approves the proposal, one rhetorician made the young man[1] say 'Great troops of slaves whom their lord does not know by sight, and the farm-prisons echoing to the sound of the lash, have no charm for me: my love for my father is an unbought love.' Again, a poor man, whose property has been outrageously damaged by a rich neighbour, protests[2] against the whims of modern luxury. 'Country districts' he says 'that once were the plough-lands of whole communities are now each worked by a single slave-gang, and the sway of stewards is wider than the realms of kings.' Now, we cannot cite the old rhetorician as an authority on agriculture directly: but he gives us proof positive that references to estates worked by gangs[3] of slaves, and the *ergastula* in which the poor wretches were shut up after the hours of labour, would not in his time sound strange to Roman audiences. Another passage[4] touches on a very typical lecture-room theme, an unnatural son. A father is banished for unintentional homicide. The law forbids the sheltering and feeding of an exile. But the father contrives to return and haunt an estate adjoining the main property, now controlled by his son. The son hears of these visits, flogs the *vilicus* for connivance, and compels him to exclude the old man. The piece is one of which only a brief abstract remains, but there is enough to shew that, while the gist of it was a casuistic discussion of a moral problem, it assumes as a matter of course the liability of a trusted slave to the lash. The faithful and kindly slave is contrasted with the unnatural son. There are in these curious collections other utterances indicative of the spread of humanitarian notions. Thus in the piece first cited[5] above, the poor man's son in refusing the rich man's offer of adoption, as a situation to which he could never accommodate himself, is made to add 'If you were selling a favourite slave, you would inquire whether the buyer was a cruel man.' Such ideas come from the later Greek philosophies, chiefly Stoic, the system on which Seneca brought up his more famous son. In one place[6] we find an echo of an earlier Greek sentiment, when a rhetorician propounds the doctrine that Fortune only, not Nature, distinguishes freemen from slaves.

Indeed it is evident, from the many passages that touch on slavery and expose some of its worst horrors, that the subject was at this time beginning to attract more general attention than heretofore. And the

---

[1] Seneca *controversiae* II 1 § 26.   [2] Seneca *excerpt contr* V 5
[3] Compare the reference to unruly *servorum agmina* in Calabria, Tac *ann* XII 65, in the time of Claudius.
[4] Seneca *excerpt contr* VI 2.   [5] Seneca *contr* II 1 § 5.
[6] Seneca *contr* VII 6 § 18.

relations of patron and freedman, also discussed in these artificial school-debates, are a further illustration of this tendency. Milder and more humane principles were germinating, though as yet they had not found expression in law. In arguing on a peculiarly revolting case (the deliberate mutilation of child-beggars) a speaker incidentally refers[1] to wealthy landowners recruiting their slave-gangs by seizing freemen. The hearers are supposed to receive this reference to kidnapping as no exceptional thing extravagantly suggested. We have seen that both Augustus and Tiberius had to intervene to put down this *suppressio*. One little note of interest deserves passing mention. In a discussion on unequal marriages the question is raised whether even the very highest desert on a slave's part could justify a father in taking him as a son-in-law. A speaker cites the case[2] of Old Cato, who married the daughter of his own *colonus*. Here we clearly have the tenant farmer in the second century BC. In Plutarch the man appears as a client. Neither writer makes him a freedman in so many words. But it is probably the underlying fact. That the daughter was *ingenua* does not rule out this supposition.

Velleius and **Valerius Maximus** also belong to the reign of Tiberius. The former in what remains of his history supplies nothing to my purpose. Valerius made a collection of anecdotes from Roman and foreign histories illustrating various virtues and vices, classifying the examples of good and bad action under heads. They are 'lifted' from the works of earlier writers: many are taken from Livy, already used as a classic quarry. The book is pervaded by tiresome moralizing, and points of interest are few. There is the story of the farm[3] of Regulus, of the patriotic refusal[4] of M' Curius to take more than the normal seven *iugera* of land as a reward from the state, of the horny-handed rustic voter[5] being asked whether he walked on his hands; also reference to the simple habits of the famous Catos, and a passing remark that the men of old had few slaves. Those of the above passages that are of any value at all have been noticed in earlier sections. The freedman **Phaedrus** gives us next to nothing in his fables, unless we care to note the items[6] of a farm-property, *agellos pecora villam operarios boves iumenta et instrumentum rusticum*, and a fable specially illustrating the fact that a master's eye sees what escapes the notice of the slave-staff, even of the *vilicus*.

---

1 Seneca *contr* X 4 § 18 *solitudines suas isti beati ingenuorum ergastulis excolunt.* See above p 233 and below on Columella p 263.

2 Seneca *contr* VII 6 § 17, cf Plut *Cat mai* 24.

3 Val Max IV 4 § 6.   4 Val Max IV 3 § 5, cf 4 § 7, 8 § 1.   5 Val Max VII 5 § 2.

6 Phaedr IV 5, II 8.

XXXI. SENECA THE YOUNGER.

The chief literary figure of the reigns of Claudius and Nero was **L Annaeus Seneca**, a son of the rhetorician above referred to, and like his father born in Spain. His life extended from 4 BC to 65 AD. For the purpose of the present inquiry his surviving works are mainly of interest as giving us in unmistakeable tones the point of view from which a man of Stoic principles regarded slavery as a social institution. The society of imperial Rome, in which he spent most of his life, was politically dead. To meddle with public affairs was dangerous. Even a senator needed to walk warily, for activity was liable to be misinterpreted by the Emperor and by his powerful freedmen[1], who were in effect Imperial Ministers. To keep on good terms with these departmental magnates, who had sprung from the slave-market to be courted as the virtual rulers of freeborn Roman citizens, was necessary for all men of note. Under such conditions it is not wonderful that the wealthy were tempted to assert themselves in ostentatious luxury and dissipation: for a life of careless debauchery was on the face of it hardly compatible with treasonable conspiracy. The immense slave-households of Rome were a part and an expression of this extravagance; and the fashion of these domestic armies was perhaps at its height in this period. Now, nothing kept the richer Romans in subjection more efficiently than this habit of living constantly exposed to the eyes and ears of their menials. Cruel laws might protect the master from assassination by presuming[2] the guilt of all slaves who might have prevented it. They could not protect him from the danger of criminal charges, such as treason[3], supported by servile evidence: indeed the slave was a potential informer, and a hated master was at the mercy of his slaves. Under some Emperors this possibility was a grim reality, and no higher or more heartfelt praise could be bestowed[4] on an Emperor than that he refused to allow masters to be done to death by the tongue of their slaves.

Meanwhile the slave was still legally[5] his (or her) master's chattel, and cases of revolting cruelty[6] and other abominations occurred from time to time. Yet more humane and sympathetic views were already affecting public sentiment, chiefly owing to the spread of Stoic doctrines among the cultivated classes. Of these doctrines as adapted to Roman

---

[1] Such as Polybius the influential freedman of Claudius, to whom Seneca addressed a *consolatio*.

[2] *Epist* 77 § 7 is a notable passage.   [3] Cf *de benef* III 26.

[4] As by the younger Pliny *paneg* 42 on Trajan.

[5] *de benef* V 18 § 2, 19 § 1, VII 4 § 4.   [6] *de clement* I 18, *nat quaest* I 16 § 1.

minds Seneca was the leading preacher. Thus he cites the definition of 'slave' as 'wage-earner for life,' propounded[1] by Chrysippus: he insists on the human quality common to slave and free alike: he re-asserts the equality of human rights, only upset by Fortune, who has made one man master of another: he sees that the vices of slaves are very often simply the result of the misgovernment of their owners: he reckons them as humble members[2] of the family circle, perhaps even the former playmates of boyhood: he recommends a kindly considera-tion for a slave's feelings, and admits[3] that some sensitive natures would prefer a flogging to a box on the ear or a harsh and contemptuous scolding. We need not follow up his doctrines in more detail. The general tone is evident and significant enough. But it is the relations of the domestic circle that he has primarily in view. His references to agriculture and rustic labour are few, as we might expect from the cir-cumstances of his life. But we are in a better position to judge their value having considered his attitude towards slavery in general. It should be noted, as a specimen of his tendency to Romanize Greek doctrine, that he lays great stress on the more wholesome relations[4] of master and slave in the good old times of early Rome,—here too without special reference to the rustic households of the rude forefathers round which tradition centred.

Judged by a modern standard, a defect in Stoic principles was the philosophic aloofness from the common interests and occupations of ordinary workaday life. To the Wise Man all things save Virtue are more or less indifferent, and in the practice of professions and trades there is little or no direct connexion with Virtue. Contempt for manual labour, normal in the ancient world and indeed in all slave-owning societies, took a loftier position under the influence of Stoicism. Hence that system, in spite of its harsh and tiresome features, appealed to many of the better Romans of the upper class, seeming as it did to justify their habitual disdain. Seneca's attitude towards handicrafts is much the same as Cicero's, only with a touch of Stoic priggishness added. Wisdom, he says[5], is not a mere handworker (*opifex*) turning out appliances for necessary uses. Her function is more important: her craft is the art of living, and over other arts she is supreme. The quality of an artist's action[6] depends on his motive: the sculptor may make a statue for money or to win fame or as a pious offering. Arts, as Posi-donius[7] said, range from the 'liberal' ones to the 'common and mean' ones practised by handworkers: the latter have no pretence of moral

---

[1] *de benef* III 22 § 1, cf Athenaeus 276 b.   [2] *de benef* V 19 § 9, *epist* 12 § 3.
[3] *de constant* (ad Serenum) 5 § 1.   [4] *epist* 47 § 14.
[5] *epist* 90 § 27, *artificem vides vitae* etc.   [6] *epist* 65 § 6.
[7] *epist* 88 § 21. The contrast of *liberalis* and *sordidus* often occurs.

dignity. Indeed many of these trades are quite unnecessary, the outcome of modern[1] extravagance. We could do without them, and be all the better for it: man's real needs are small. But to work for a living is not in itself a degradation: did not the Stoic master Cleanthes draw water[2] for hire? In short, the Wise Man may be a king or a slave, millionaire or pauper. The externals cannot change his true quality, though they may be a help or a hindrance in his growth to perfect wisdom.

In his references to agriculture and country matters it is to be remarked that Seneca confirms the impression derived from other sources, that the letting of land to tenant farmers was on the increase. Discoursing on the greedy luxury of the rich, their monstrous kitchens and cellars, and the toiling of many to gratify the desires of one, he continues 'Look at all the places where the earth is being tilled, and at all the thousands[3] of farmers (*colonorum*) ploughing and digging; is this, think you, to be reckoned one man's belly, for whose service crops are being raised in Sicily and in Africa too?' The *coloni* here mentioned may be merely 'cultivators' in a general sense. But I think they are more probably tenants of holdings on great estates. In speaking of his arrival at his Alban villa, and finding nothing ready for a meal, he philosophically refuses to let so small an inconvenience make him angry with his cook and his baker. 'My baker[4] has got no bread; but the steward has some, and so have the porter and the farmer.' A coarse sort of bread, no doubt, but you have only got to wait, and you will enjoy it when you are really hungry. Here we seem to have an instance of what was now probably an ordinary arrangement: the *villa*, homestead with some land round it, kept as a country 'box' for the master by his steward, who would see to the garden and other appurtenances, while the rest of the land is let to a humble tenant farmer. In another passage we have an interesting glimpse of a tenant's legal position[5] as against his landlord. 'If a landlord tramples down growing crops or cuts down plantations, he cannot keep his tenant, though the lease may be still in being: this is not because he has recovered what was due to him as lessor, but because he has made it impossible for him to recover it. Even so it often happens that a creditor is cast in damages to his debtor, when he has on other grounds taken from him more than the amount of the debt claimed.' I gather from this passage

[1] *epist* 90 § 15. [2] *epist* 44 § 3 *aquam traxit et rigando horto locavit manus.*
[3] *epist* 114 § 26 *quot millia colonorum arent fodiant...*etc.
[4] *epist* 123 § 2 *non habet panem meus pistor: sed habet vilicus, sed habet atriensis, sed habet colonus. atriensis* = head of domestics, porter or butler.
[5] *de benef* VI 4 § 4 *colonum suum non tenet, quamvis tabellis manentibus, qui segetem eius proculcavit, qui succidit arbusta, non quia recepit quod pepigerat sed quia ne reciperet effecit. ic debitori suo creditor saepe damnatur, ubi plus ex alia causa abstulit quam ex crediti petit.*

that damage done by the lessor to the lessee's interest in the farm deprived him of right of action against the lessee, in case he wanted to enforce some claim (for rent or for some special service) under the terms of the existing contract[1] of lease. If this inference be just, the evidence is important. For the *colonus* is conceived as a humble person, whose interest a brutal inconsiderate landlord would be not unlikely to disregard, and to whom a resort to litigation would seem a course to be if possible avoided.

To this question of the rights of landlord and tenant Seneca returns later, when engaged in reconciling the Stoic thesis that 'all things belong to the Wise Man' with the facts of actual life. The Wise Man is in the position of a King to whom belongs the general right of sovranty (*imperium*) while his subjects have the particular right of ownership (*dominium*). Illustrating the point he proceeds[2] thus. 'Say I have hired a house from you. Of its contents some belong to you and some to me. The thing (*res*) is your property, but the right of user (*usus*) of your property is mine. Just so you must not meddle with crops, though grown on your own estate, if your tenant forbids it; and in a season of dearness or dearth you will be like the man in Vergil wistfully gazing at another's plenteous store, though the land where it grew, the yard where it is stacked, and the granary it is meant to fill, are all your own property. Nor, when I have hired a lodging, have you a right to enter it, owner though you be: when a slave of yours is hired for service by me, you have no right to withdraw him: and, if I hire a trap from you and give you a lift, it will be a good turn on my part, though the conveyance belongs to you.' I have quoted this at some length, in order to make the farm-tenant's position quite clear. His rights are presumed to be easily ascertainable, and his assertion of them will be protected by the law. His contract, whether a formal lease or not, is also presumed to guarantee him complete control of the subject for the agreed term. Whether encroachments by landlords and legal proceedings for redress by tenants were common events in rural Italy, Seneca need not and does not say. I suspect that personal interest on both sides was in practice a more effective restraint than appeals to law.

There are other references to agricultural conditions, which though of less importance are interesting as confirming other evidence as to the *latifundia* of this period. A good specimen is found in his denunciation of human greed as the cause of poverty, by bringing to an end

[1] The *pactum* implied in *pepigerat*.
[2] *de benef* VII 5 §§ 2, 3, *conduxi domum a te ; in hac aliquid tuum est, aliquid meum; res tua est, usus rei tuae meus est. itaque nec fructus tanges colono tuo prohibente, quamvis in tua possessione nascantur...nec conductum meum, quamquam sis dominus, intrabis, nec servum tuum, mercennarium meum, abduces...etc.* See the chapter on the Jurists of the Digest.

the happy age of primitive communism, when all shared the ownership of all. Cramped and unsatisfied, this *avaritia* can never find the
way back to the old state of plenty and happiness. 'Hence, though
she now endeavour to make good[1] what she has wasted; though she
add field to field by buying out her neighbours or wrongfully ejecting
them; though she expand her country estates on the scale of provinces, and enjoy the sense of landlordism in the power of touring
mile after mile without leaving her own domains; still no enlargement
of bounds will bring us back to the point from whence we started.'
Again, in protesting against the luxurious ostentation of travellers and
others, he shews that they are really in debt. 'So-and-so is, you fancy,
a rich man...because he has arable estates[2] in all provinces of the
empire...because his holding of land near Rome is on a scale one
would grudge him even in the wilds of Apulia.' Such a man is in debt
to Fortune. In these as in other passages the preacher illustrates his
sermon by references calculated to bring home his points. Naturally
he selects for the purpose matters familiar to his audience; and it is
this alone that make the passages worth quoting. The same may be
said of his sympathetic reference[3] to the hard lot of a slave transferred
from the easy duties of urban service to the severe toil of farm labour.
In general it may be remarked that the evidence of Seneca and other
literary men of this period is to be taken in connexion with the treatise of Columella, who is the contemporary specialist on agriculture.
The prevalence of slave labour and the growth of the tenant-farmer
class are attested by both lines of evidence.

XXXII. LUCAN, PETRONIUS, AND OTHERS.

Lucan, Seneca's nephew, has a few interesting references in his
poem on the great civil war. Thus, in the eloquent passage[4] lamenting
the decay of Roman vital strength, a long process to be disastrously
completed in the great Pharsalian battle, he dwells on the shrinkage
of free Roman population in Italy. The towns and the countryside
alike are empty, houses deserted, and it is by the labour of chained[5]
slaves that Italian crops are raised. Elsewhere[6] he looks further back,

---

[1] *epist* 90 § 39 *licet itaque nunc conetur reparare quod perdidit, licet agros agris adiciat vicinum vel pretio pellens vel iniuria, licet in provinciarum spatium rura dilatet et possessionem vocet per sua longam peregrinationem*...etc. For *iniuria* cf Columella I 3 §§ 6, 7. The violent expulsion of poor farmers by the rich is an old topic. Cf Sallust *Iug* 41 § 8, Appian *civ* I 7 § 5 and see index.

[2] *epist* 87 § 7 *quia in omnibus provinciis arat...quia tantum suburbani agri possidet quantum invidiose in desertis Apuliae possideret.*

[3] *de ira* III 29 § 1.

[4] Lucan VII 387–439.

[5] *vincto fossore coluntur Hesperiae vegetes.*

[6] I 1 158–82.

and traces this decay to the effect of luxury and corruption caused by the influx of vast wealth, the spoils of Roman conquests. Among the symptoms of disease he notes the *latifundia*, which it was now becoming the fashion to denounce, the land-grabbing passion that prompted men to monopolize great tracts of land and incorporate in huge estates, worked by cultivators unknown[1] to them, farms that once had been ploughed and hoed by the rustic heroes of old. But all such utterances are merely a part of a declaimer's stock-in-trade. We may fairly guess that they are echoes of talk heard in the literary circle of his uncle Seneca. That they are nevertheless consistent with the land-system of this period, is to be gathered from other sources, such as Petronius and Columella. It remains to note that the word *colonus* is used by Lucan in the senses of 'cultivator' and 'farmer,' rather suggesting ownership, and of 'military colonist,' clearly implying it. That of 'tenant' does not occur: there was no need for it in the poem. Again, he has *servire servilis* and *servitium*, but *servus* occurs only in a suspected[2] line, and as an adjective. His regular word for 'slave' is *famulus*.

The bucolic poems of this period are too manifestly artificial to serve as evidence of value. For instance, when **Calpurnius** declares[3] that in this blessed age of peace and prosperity the *fossor* is not afraid to profit by the treasure he may chance to dig up, we cannot infer that a free digger is meant, though it is hardly likely that a slave would be suffered to keep treasure-trove.

Petronius, in the curious mixed prose-verse satire of which part has come down to us, naturally says very little bearing directly on agriculture. But in depicting the vulgar freedman-millionaire Trimalchio he refers pointedly to the vast landed estates belonging to this typical figure of the period. He owns estates 'far as the kites[4] can fly.' This impression is confirmed in detail by a report delivered by the agent for his properties. It is a statement[5] of the occurrences in a domain of almost imperial proportions during a single day. So many children, male and female, were born: so many thousand bushels of wheat were stocked in the granary: so many hundred oxen broken in: a slave was crucified for disloyalty to his lord: so many million sesterces were paid in to the chest, no opening for investment presenting itself. On one park-estate (*hortis*) there was a great fire, which began in the steward's house. Trimalchio cannot recall the purchase of this estate, which on inquiry

---

[1] *longa sub ignotis extendere rura colonis.* Cf Seneca *de vita beata* 17 § 2 *cur trans mare possides? cur plura quam nosti?* and Petron 37.

[2] VI 152 *o famuli turpes, servum pecus.*   [3] Calpurn *ecl* IV 118.

[4] Petron § 37 *fundos habet qua milvi volant.* A proverbial phrase, cf Persius IV 26 *dives arat...quantum non milvus oberret,* Juvenal IX 55.

[5] Petron § 53.

turns out to be a recent acquisition not yet on the books. Then comes the reading of notices issued by officials[1] of the manors, of wills[2] made by rangers, of the names of his stewards; of a freedwoman's divorce, the banishment of an *atriensis*, the committal of a cashier for trial, and the proceedings in court in an action between some chamberlains. Of course all this is not to be taken seriously, but we can form some notion of the state of things that the satirist has in mind. Too gross an exaggeration would have defeated his purpose. The book is full of passages bearing on the history of slavery, but it is domestic slavery, and that often of the most degrading character.

XXXIII. COLUMELLA.

The great interest taken in agriculture after the establishment of the Roman peace by Augustus is shewn by the continued appearance of works on the subject. The treatise of **Celsus**, who wrote in the time of Tiberius, was part of a great encyclopaedic work. It was probably one of the most important books of its kind: but it is lost, and we only know it as cited by other writers, such as Columella and the elder Pliny. It is from the treatise of **Columella**, composed probably under Nero, that we get most of our information as to Roman husbandry (*rusticatio*, as he often calls it) in the period of the earlier Empire. The writer was a native of Spain, deeply interested, like other Spanish Romans, in the past present and future of Italy. It is evident that in comparing the present with the past he could not avoid turning an uneasy eye to the future. Like others, he could see that agriculture, once the core of Roman strength, the nurse of a vigorous free population, was in a bad way. It was still the case that the choicest farm-lands of Italy were largely occupied by mansions and parks, the property of non-resident owners who seldom visited their estates, and hardly ever qualified themselves to superintend their management in-telligently. The general result was hideous waste. In modern language, those who had command of capital took no pains to employ it in business-like farming: while the remaining free rustics lacked capital. Agriculture was likely to go from bad to worse under such conditions. The Empire would thus be weakened at its centre, and to a loyal Pro-vincial, whose native land was part of a subject world grouped round that centre, the prospect might well seem bewildering. Columella was from the first interested in agriculture, on which his uncle[3] at Gades

---

[1] *edicta aedilium.*

[2] *saltuariorum testamenta.* They were evidently slaves and could only make wills by leave of their owner. See Dig XXXIII 7 § 12[4].

[3] Many times referred to in the book.

(Cadiz) was a recognized authority, and his treatise *de re rustica* is his contribution to the service of Rome.

The serious consequences of the decay of practical farming, and the disappearance of the small landowners tilling their own land, had long been recognized by thoughtful men. But the settlement of discharged soldiers on allotted holdings had not repopulated the countryside with free farmers. The old lamentations continued, but no means was found for solving the problem how to recreate a patient and prosperous yeoman class, firmly planted on the soil. Technical knowledge had gone on accumulating to some extent, though the authorities on agriculture, Greek Carthaginian or Roman, appealed to by Columella are mainly the same as those cited by Varro some eighty years before. The difficulty at both epochs was not the absence of knowledge but the neglect of its practical application. Columella, like his forerunners, insists on the folly[1] of buying more land than you can profitably manage. But it seems that the average wealthy landowner could not resist the temptation to round off[2] a growing estate by buying up more land when a favourable opportunity occurred. It is even hinted that ill-treatment[3] of a neighbour, to quicken the process by driving him to give up his land, was not obsolete. Moreover, great estates often consisted of separate holdings in different parts of the country. For owners of vast, and sometimes[4] scattered, estates to keep effective control over them was an occupation calling for qualities never too common, technical skill and indefatigable industry. The former could, if combined with perfect honesty, be found in an ideal deputy; but the deputy, to be under complete control, must be a slave: and, the more skilled the slave, the better able he was to conceal dishonesty. Therefore, the more knowledge and watchful attentiveness was needed in the master. Now it is just this genuine and painstaking interest in the management of their estates that Columella finds lacking in Roman landlords. They will not live[5] in the country, where they are quickly bored and miss the excitements of the city, and My Lady detests country life even more than My Lord. But they will not even take the trouble to procure good[6] Stewards, let alone watching them so as to keep them industrious and honest. Thus the management of estates has generally passed from masters to *vilici*, and the domestic part of the duties even more completely from house-mistresses to *vilicae*. As to the disastrous effect of the change upon rustic economy, the writer entertains no doubt. But the evil was no new phenomenon. It

[1] I 3 §§ 8–13.

[2] Cf Plin *epist* III 19 § 2 *pulchritudo iungendi*, and Mayor's note. Petron § 77.

[3] I 3 §§ 6, 7, where he even refers to a very disobliging neighbour of his own estate.

[4] I 1 § 20 *longinqua ne dicam transmarina rura*...etc.

[5] I *praef* §§ 13–15, XII *praef* §§ 8–10.   [6] I *praef* § 12.

may well be that it was now more widespread than in Varro's time; but in both writers we may perhaps suspect some degree of overstatement, to which reformers are apt to resort in depicting the abuses they are wishing to reform. I do not allow much for this consideration, for the picture, confirmed by general literary evidence, is in the main unquestionably true.

So much for the case of estates administered by slave stewards for the account of their masters. But this was not the only way of dealing with landed properties. We have already noted the system of letting farms to cultivating tenants, and commented on the fewness of the references to it in literature. This plan may have been very ancient in origin, but it was probably an exceptional arrangement even in the time of Cicero. The very slight notice of it by Varro indicates that it was not normal, indeed not even common. In Columella we find a remarkable change. In setting out the main principles[1] of estate management, and insisting on the prime importance of the owner's attention (*cura domini*), he adds that this is necessary above all things in relation to the persons concerned (*in hominibus*). Now the *homines* are *coloni* or *servi*, and are unchained or chained. After this division and subdivision he goes on to discuss briefly but thoroughly the proper relations between landlord and tenant-farmer, the care needed in the selection of satisfactory tenants, and the considerations that must guide a landlord in deciding whether to let a piece of land to a tenant or to farm it for his own account. He advises him to be obliging and easy in his dealings with tenants, and more insistent in requiring their work or service (*opus*)[2] than their rent (*pensiones*): this plan is less irritating, and after all it pays better in the long run. For, barring risks of storms or brigands, good farming nearly always leaves a profit, so that the tenant has not the face to claim[3] a reduction of rent. A landlord should not be a stickler for trifles or mean in the matter of little perquisites, such as cutting firewood, worrying his tenant unprofitably. But, while waiving the full rigour of the law, he should not omit to claim his dues in order to keep alive his rights: wholesale remission is a mistake. It was well said by a great landowner that the greatest blessing for an estate is when the tenants are natives[4] of the place, a sort of hereditary occupiers, attached to it by the associations of their childhood's home. Columella agrees that frequent changes of tenant

---

[1] I 7 *passim*.

[2] If we are to hold that *opus* here refers only to work on the particular farm hired by the tenant, I presume it includes improvements, as in Digest XIX 2 § 24³.

[3] *remissionem petere non audet.*

[4] *felicissimum fundum esse qui colonos indigenas haberet et tamquam in paterna possessione natos iam inde a cunabulis longa familiaritate retineret.*

are a bad business. But there is a worse; namely the town-bred[1] tenant, who prefers farming with a slave staff to turning farmer himself. It was a saying of Saserna, that out of a fellow of this sort you generally get not your rent but a lawsuit. His advice then was, take pains to get country-bred farmers[2] and keep them in permanent tenancy: that is, when you are not free to farm your own land, or when it does not suit your interest to farm it with a slave staff. This last condition, says Columella, only refers to the case of lands derelict[3] through malaria or barren soil.

There are however farms on which it is the landlord's own interest to place tenants rather than work them by slaves for his own account. Such are distant holdings, too out-of-the-way for the proprietor to visit them easily. Slaves out of reach of constant inspection will play havoc with any farm, particularly one on which corn is grown. They let out the oxen for hire, neglect the proper feeding of live stock, shirk the thorough turning of the earth, and in sowing tending harvesting and threshing the crop they waste and cheat you to any extent. No wonder the farm gets a bad name thanks to your steward and staff. If you do not see your way to attend in person to an estate of this kind, you had better let it to a tenant. From these remarks it seems clear that the writer looks upon letting land to tenant farmers as no more than an unwelcome alternative, to be adopted only in the case of farms bad in quality or out of easy reach. Indeed he says frankly that, given fair average conditions, the owner can always get better returns by managing a farm himself than by letting it to a tenant: he may even do better by leaving the charge to a steward, unless of course that steward happens to be an utterly careless or thievish fellow. Taking this in connexion with his remarks about stewards elsewhere, the net result seems to be that a landlord must choose in any given case what he judges to be the less of two evils.

A few points here call for special consideration. In speaking of the work or service (*opus*) that a landlord may require of a tenant, as distinct from rent, what does Columella precisely mean? It has been held[4] that he refers to the landlord's right of insisting that his land shall be well farmed. This presumably implies a clause in the lease under which such a right could be enforced. But there are difficulties. In the case of a distant farm, let to a tenant because it has 'to do without the presence[5] of the landlord,' the right would surely be

[1] *urbanum colonum, qui per familiam mavult agrum quam per se colere.*
[2] *rusticos et eosdem adsiduos colonos.*
[3] *in his regionibus quae gravitate caeli solique sterilitate vastantur.* Cf I 5 § 5, *gravibus*, and Varro I 17 § 2.
[4] By H. Blümner in Müller's *Handbuch.* So also Gummerus in *Klio* 1906 pp 85-6.
[5] *domini praesentia cariturum.*

inoperative in practice. In the case of a neighbouring farm, why has the landlord not kept it in hand, putting in a steward to manage it? This interpretation leaves us with no clear picture of a practical arrangement. But this objection is perhaps not fatal. The right to enforce proper cultivation is plainly guaranteed to landlords in Roman Law, as the jurists constantly assert in discussing tenancies. And *opus* is a term employed[1] by them in this connexion. It is therefore the safer course to take it here in this sense, and to allow for a certain want of clearness in Columella's phrase. At the same time it is tempting to accept another[2] view, namely this, that the writer has in mind service rendered in the form of a stipulated amount of auxiliary labour on the landlord's 'Home Farm' at certain seasons. That a *corvée* arrangement of this kind existed as a matter of course on some estates, we have direct evidence[3] in the second century, evidence that suggests an earlier origin for the custom. True, it implies that landlords were in practice able to impose the burden of such task-work on their free tenants, in short that they had the upper hand in the bargain between the parties. But this is not surprising: for we read[4] of a great landlord calling up his *coloni* to serve on his private fleet in the great civil war, a hundred years before Columella. Still, it is perhaps rash to see in this passage a direct reference to the custom of making the supply of auxiliary labour at certain seasons a part of tenant's obligations. Granting this, it is nevertheless reasonable to believe that the first beginnings of the custom may belong to a date at least as early as the treatise of Columella. For it is quite incredible that such a practice should spring up and become prevalent suddenly. It has all the marks of gradual growth.

Another point of interest is the criticism of the town-bred *colonus*. He prefers to work the farm with a slave staff, rather than undertake the job himself. I gather from this that he is a man with capital, also that he means to get a good return on his capital. He fears to make a loss on a rustic venture, being well aware of his own inexperience. So he will put in a steward with a staff of slaves. The position of the steward will in such a case be peculiarly strong. If he is slack and thievish and lets down the farm, he can stave off his master's anger by finding fault with the soil or buildings, and involve the tenant and landlord in a quarrel over the rent. To devise pretexts would be easy for a rogue, and a quarrel might end in a lawsuit. That Saserna, writing

[1] Dig xxxiii 7 § 25¹, xix 2 § 24, § 25³.
[2] M Weber *Rom Agrargeschichte* p 244. Of course *opus* is a general term, not technical as *operae* (=labour units) often is. See Vinogradoff *Growth of the Manor* note 94 on p 110. From Horace epist I 1 21 *opus debentibus* I can get no help.
[3] See below, in the chapter on the African inscriptions.   [4] Caesar *civ* I 34, 56.

probably about 100 BC, laid his finger on this possible source of trouble, is significant. It is evidence that there were tenant-farmers in his time, and bad ones among them : but not that they were then numerous, or that their general character was such as to make landlords let their estates in preference to managing them through their own stewards for their own account. And this agrees with Columella's own opinion some 150 years later. If you are to let farms to tenants, local men who are familiar with local conditions are to be preferred, but he gives no hint that such tenants could readily be found. His words seem rather to imply that they were rare.

One point is hardly open to misunderstanding. In Columella's system the typical tenant-farmer, the *colonus* to be desired by a wise landlord, is a humble person, to whom small perquisites are things of some importance. He is not a restless or ambitious being, ever on the watch for a chance of putting his landlord in the wrong or a pretext for going to law. Such as we see him in the references of Seneca, and later in those of the younger Pliny and Martial, such he appears in Columella. For the landlord it is an important object to keep him— when he has got him—and to have his son ready as successor in the tenancy. From other sources we know[1] that the value of long undisturbed tenancies are generally recognized. But we have little or nothing to shew whether the tenant-farmers of this age usually worked with their own hands or not. That they employed slave labour is not only *a priori* probable, but practically certain. We have evidence that at a somewhat later date it was customary[2] for the landlord to provide land farmstead (*villa*) and equipment (*instrumentum*), and we know that under this last head slaves could be and were concluded. It is evident that the arrangement belongs to the decisive development of the tenancy system as a regular alternative to that of farming by a steward for landlord's own account. The desirable country-bred tenant would not be a man[3] of substantial capital, and things had to be made easy for him. It is not clear that a tenant bringing his own staff of slaves would have been welcomed as lessee: from the instance of the town-bred *colonus* just referred to it seems likely that he would not.

While Columella prescribes letting to tenants as the best way of solving the difficulties in dealing with outlying farms, he does not say that this plan should not be adopted in the case of farms near the main estate or 'Home Farm.' I think this silence is intentional. It is hard

---

[1] Wallon, *Esclavage* II 99, 100, refers to the long leasing of municipal estates, held in virtual perpetuity so long as the rent was paid. He cites Gaius III 145. So too estates of temples, and later of the *fiscus*.

[2] Wallon II 120, cf Digest XXXIII 7 § 19, an opinion of Paulus. It seems to be a sort of *métayer* system. See index.

[3] But such as the *imbecilli cultores* of Plin *epist* III 19 § 6.

to believe that there were no instances of landlords either wholly non-resident or who so seldom visited their estates that they could not possibly keep an eye on the doings of stewards. In such cases there would be strong inducement to adopt the plan by which they could simply draw rents and have no stewards to look after. That stewards needed to be carefully watched was as clear to Columella as to Cato or Varro. True, letting to tenants was a policy liable to bring troubles of its own. We shall see in the case of the younger Pliny what they were and how he met them. Meanwhile he may serve as an example of the system. It is also plain that a large continuous property could be divided[1] into smaller parcels for convenience of letting to tenants. Whether the later plan of keeping a considerable Home Farm in hand under a steward, and letting off the outer parcels of the same estate to tenants, was in vogue already and contemplated by Columella, is not easy to say. In connexion with this question it is to be noted that he hardly refers at all to free hired labour[2] as generally available. The migratory gangs of wage-earners, still known to Varro, do not appear, nor do the itinerant *medici*. When he speaks of hiring hands at any price, or of times when labour is cheap, he may mean hiring somebody's slaves, and probably does. Slave labour is undoubtedly the basis of his farm-system, and its elaborate organization fills an important part of his book. Yet two marked consequences of the Roman Peace had to be taken into account. Fewer wars meant fewer slaves in the market, and a rise of prices: peace and law in Italy meant that big landowners could add field to field more securely than ever, while great numbers of citizens were settling in the Provinces, taking advantage of better openings[3] there. To keep some free labour within call as an occasional resource was an undeniable convenience for a large owner with a farm in hand. Small tenants[4] under obligation to render stipulated service at certain seasons would obviously supply the labour needed. And, if we picture to ourselves a Home Farm round the lord's mansion, worked by steward and slave staff, with outlying 'soccage' tenants on holdings near, we are already in presence of a rudimentary Manor. As time went by, and the system got into regular working order, the landlord had an opportunity of strengthening his hold on the tenants. By not pressing them too severely for arrears of rent, and occasionally granting abatements, he could gradually increase their services. What he thus

---

[1] See case referred to by Paulus in Digest XXXI § 86[1].

[2] I *praef* § 12 *ex mercennariis aliquem*. In II 2 § 12 *operarum vilitas*, and IV 6 § 3 *operarum paenuria*, III 21 § 10 *plures operas quantocumque pretio conducere*, the hands hired may be slaves.

[3] Of course not necessarily agricultural, in fact generally not. See my article in *Journal of Roman Studies* 1918, and Index under *Emigration*.

[4] Very different from the small farmers of old time, who were owners.

saved on his own labour-bill might well be more than a set-off against the loss of money-rents. More and more the tenants would become dependent on him. Nominally free, they were becoming tied to the soil on onerous terms, and the foundation was laid of the later relation of Lord and Serf.

Such I conceive to be the rustic situation the beginnings of which are probably to be placed as early as Columella's time, though we do not find him referring to it. He says nothing of another point, which was of importance[1] later, namely the admission of slaves or freedmen as tenants of farms. It has all the appearance of a subsequent step, taken when the convenience of services rendered by resident tenants had been demonstrated by experience. It is no great stretch of imagination to suggest that, as the supply of slaves fell off, it was the policy of owners to turn their slave-property to the best possible account. When a steward or a gang-foreman was no longer in his prime, able (as Columella enjoins) to turn to and shew the common hands how work should be done, how could he best be utilized? A simple plan was to put him on a small farm with a few slave labourers. This would secure the presence of a tenant whose dependence was certain from the first, while a younger man could be promoted to the arduous duties of the big Home Farm. Be this as it may, it is certain that problems arising from shortage of slaves were presenting themselves in the middle of the first century AD. For slave-breeding, casual in Cato's day and incidentally mentioned by Varro, is openly recognized by Columella, who allows for a larger female element in his farm staff and provides rewards for their realized fertility.

If the system of farm-tenancies was already becoming a part of land-management so important as the above remarks may seem to imply, why does the management of a landed estate for landlord's account under a steward occupy almost the whole of Columella's long treatise? I think there are several reasons. First, it is management of tillage-crops and gardens and live stock with which he is chiefly concerned, not tenures and labour-questions: and technical skill in agriculture is of interest to all connected with it, though the book is primarily addressed to landlords. Secondly, the desirable tenant was (and is) a man not much in need of being taught his business: as for an undesirable one, the sooner he is got rid of the better. Thirdly, the plan of steward-management was still the normal one: the only pity was that the indolence of owners led to appointment of bad stewards and left them too much power. Only sound knowledge can enable landlords to choose good stewards and check bad management. Seeing agriculture in a bad way, Columella writes to supply this knowledge,

---

[1] See for instance Digest XXXIII 7 § 18[4], and § 20[1], opinions of Scaevola.

as Cato Varro and others had done before him. Accordingly he begins
with the general organization of the normal large estate, and first discusses the choice and duties of the *vilicus*, on whose character and
competence everything depends. To this subject he returns in a later
part of the treatise, and the two passages[1] enforce the same doctrine
with very slight variations in detail.

The steward[2] must not be a fancy-slave, a domestic from the master's
town house, but a well-tried hardy rustic, or at the very least one used
to hard labour. He must not be too old, or he may break down under
the strain; nor too young, or the elder slaves will not respect him. He
must be a skilled farmer (this is most important)[3], or at least thoroughly
painstaking, so as to pick up the business quickly: for the functions of
teaching and giving orders cannot be separated. He need not be able
to read and write, if his memory be very retentive. It is a remark of
Celsus, that a steward of this sort brings his master cash more often
than a book: for he cannot make up false accounts himself, and fears
to trust an accomplice. But, good bad or indifferent, a steward must
have a female partner[4] allotted him, to be a restraining influence on him
and in some respects a help. Being[5] his master's agent, he must be
enjoined not to live on terms of intimacy with any of the staff, and still
less with any outsider. Yet he may now and then invite a deserving
worker to his table on a feast-day. He must not do sacrifice[6] without
orders, or meddle with divination. He must attend markets only on
strict business, and not gad about, unless it be to pick up wrinkles[7] for
the farm, and then only if the place visited be close at hand. He must
not allow new pathways to be made on the farm, or admit as guests any
but his master's intimate friends. He must be instructed to attend
carefully[8] to the stock of implements and tools, keeping everything in
duplicate and in good repair, so that there need be no borrowing from
neighbours: for the waste of working time thus caused is a more serious
item than the cost of such articles. He is to see to the clothing[9] of the
staff (*familiam*) in practical garments that will stand wet and cold:
this done, some work in the open is possible in almost any weather. He
should be not only an expert in farm labour, but a man of the

---

[1] I 8 and XI I.   [2] I 8 §§ 1–3, XI I §§ 3, 4, 7.

[3] I 8 §§ 3, 4, where he says that a man who learns how to do things *ab subiecto* is not
fitted *opus exigere*. XI I §§ 9–13 is not inconsistent with this, but lays more stress on the
necessity of training the *vilicus*.

[4] I 8 § 5 *contubernalis mulier*. She is to be *vilica*, cf XII I §§ 1, 2. Apuleius *met* VIII 22.

[5] *eidemque actori* = him in his capacity of *actor*. Cf XI I §§ 13, 19. See Index, *actor*.

[6] I 8 §§ 6, 7, XI I §§ 22–3.

[7] *nisi ut addiscat aliquam culturam*. He is in a sense *colonus*, and hence his sphere of
duty is called *colonia* in XI I § 23. In I 4 §§ 4, 5 the value of experiments is recognized.

[8] I 8 § 8, XI I §§ 20–1.   [9] I 8 § 9, XI I § 21.

highest mental and moral character[1] compatible with a slave-tempera-
ment. For his rule should be sympathetic but firm: he should not be
too hard[2] upon the worse hands, while he encourages the better ones,
but aim at being feared for his strictness rather than loathed for harshness. The way to achieve this is to watch and prevent, not to overlook
and then punish. Even the most inveterate rogues are most effectively
controlled by insisting on performance[3] of their tasks, ensuring them
their due rights, and by the steward being always on the spot. Under
these conditions the various foremen[4] will take pains to carry out their
several duties, while the common hands, tired out, will be more inclined
to go to sleep than to get into mischief. Some good old usages tending
to promote content and good feeling are unhappily gone beyond recall,
for instance[5] the rule that a steward must not employ a fellow-slave's
services on any business save that of his master. But he must not suffer
them to stray off the estate unless he sends them on errands; and this
only if absolutely necessary. He must not do any trading[6] on his own
account, or employ his master's cash in purchase of beasts etc. For
this distracts a steward's attention, and prevents the correct balancing
of his accounts at the audit, when he can only produce goods instead
of money. In general, the first[7] requisite is that he should be free from
conceit and eager to learn. For in farming mistakes can never be
redeemed: time lost is never regained: each thing must be done right,
once for all.

The above is almost a verbal rendering of Columella's words. At
this point we may fairly pause to ask whether he seriously thought that
an ordinary landlord had much chance of securing such a paragon of
virtue as this pattern steward. That all these high bodily mental and
moral qualities combined in one individual could be bought in one lot
at an auction[8] must surely have been a chance so rare as to be hardly
worth considering as a means of agricultural development. I take it
that the importance of extreme care in selecting the right man, and in
keeping him to his duties, is insisted on as a protest against the culpable
carelessness of contemporary landlords, of which he has spoken severely
above. If, as I believe, in the great majority of cases a new steward
required much instruction as to the details of his duties and as to the
spirit in which he was both to rule the farm-staff and to serve his master,

---

[1] I 8 § 10 *animi, quantum servile patitur ingenium, virtutibus instructus.*

[2] I 8 § 10, XI I § 25.

[3] I 8 § 11 *operis exactio, ut iusta reddantur, ut vilicus semper se repraesentet,* XI I
§§ 25-6.

[4] *magistri singulorum officiorum,* XI I § 27.   [5] I 8 § 12, XI I § 23.

[6] I 8 § 13, XI I § 24.   [7] I 8 §§ 13-4, XI I §§ 27-30.

[8] In XI I §§ 4 foll this notion is, with citation of Xenophon, repudiated, and the need of
training a steward emphasized.

surely the part to be played by the master himself[1] was of fundamental importance: indeed little less so than in the scheme of old Cato. To Columella I am convinced that his recommendations stood for an ideal seldom, if ever, likely to be realized. To say this is not to blame the good man, but rather to hint that his precepts in general must not be taken as evidence of a state of things then normally to be found existing on farms. To express aspirations confesses the shortcomings of achievement.

To return to our author's precepts. He goes on to tell us of his own way of treating[2] his farm-hands, remarking that he has not regretted his kindness. He talks to a rustic slave (provided he is a decent worker) more often, and more as man to man (*familiarius*) than he does to a town slave. It relieves the round of their toil. He even exchanges pleasantries with them. He discusses new work-projects with the skilled hands and so tests their abilities: this flatters them, and they are more ready to work on a job on which they have been consulted. There are other points of management on which all prudent masters are agreed, for instance the inspection[3] of the slaves in the lock-up. This is to ascertain whether they are carefully chained, and the chamber thoroughly secured, and whether the steward has chained or released any of them without his master's knowledge. For he must not be permitted to release the chained on his own responsibility. The *paterfamilias* should be all the more particular in his inquiries as to slaves of this class, to see that they are dealt with fairly in matters of clothing and rations, inasmuch as they are under the control[4] of several superiors, stewards foremen and warders. This position exposes them to unfair treatment, and they are apt to be more dangerous through resenting harshness and stinginess. So a careful master should question them as to whether they are getting[5] their due allowance. He should taste their food and examine their clothes etc. He should hear and redress grievances, punish the mutinous, and reward the deserving. Columella then relates[6] his own policy in dealing with female slaves. When one of them had reared three or more children she was rewarded: for 3 she was granted a holiday, for 4 she was manumitted. This is only fair, and it is a substantial increment[7] to your property. In general, a landlord is enjoined to observe religious duties, and to inspect the whole estate immediately

---

[1] In XI 1 § 4 he cites a saying of Cato, *male agitur cum domino quem vilicus docet.*

[2] 1 8 § 15.

[3] 1 8 § 16 *ut ergastuli mancipia recognoscant*...etc. In XI 1 § 22 this appears as part of the steward's daily duty.

[4] 1 8 §§ 17–8 *quanto et pluribus subiecti, ut vilicis ut operum magistris ut ergastulariis, magis obnoxii perpetiendis iniuriis, et rursus saevitia atque avaritia laesi magis timendi sunt.*

[5] *an ex sua constitutione iusta percipiant. sua* = the scale allowed by himself as *dominus.*

[6] 1 8 § 19.   [7] *multum confert augendo patrimonio.*

on his arrival from Town, checking all items carefully. This done
regularly year after year, he will enjoy order and obedience on his estate in his old age.

Next comes a general statement of the proper classification of the
slave staff according to varieties[1] of function. For departmental foremen you should choose steady honest fellows, watchfulness and skill
being needed rather than brute strength. The hind or plowman must
be a big man with a big voice, that the oxen may obey him. And the
taller he is the better will he throw his weight on the plough-tail. The
mere unskilled labourer[2] only needs to be fit for continuous hard work.
For instance, in a vineyard you want a thickset type of labourer to
stand the digging etc, and if they are rogues it does not matter much,
as they work in a gang under an overseer (*monitore*[3]). By the by, a
scamp is generally more quick-witted than the average, and vineyard
work calls for intelligence: this is why chained hands[4] are commonly
employed there. Of course, he adds, an honest man is more efficient
than a rogue, other things being equal: don't charge me with a preference for criminals. Another piece of advice is to avoid[5] mixing up the
various tasks performed by the staff on the plan of making every
labourer do every kind of work. It does not pay in farming. Either
what is every one's business is felt to be nobody's duty in particular;
or the effort of the individual is credited to the whole of the gang. This
sets him shirking, and yet you cannot single out the offender; and
this sort of thing is constantly happening. Therefore keep plowmen
vineyard-hands and unskilled labourers apart. Then he passes to
numerical[6] divisions. Squads (*classes*) should be of not more than ten
men each, *decuriae* as the old name was, that the overseer may keep
his eye on all. By spreading such squads over different parts of a large
farm it is possible to compare results, to detect laziness, and to escape
the irritating unfairness of punishing the wrong men.

The general impression left on a reader's mind by Columella's
principles of slave-management is one of strict control tempered by
judicious humanity. It pays not to be harsh and cruel. Whether we
can fairly credit him with disinterested sympathy on grounds of a
common human nature, such as Seneca was preaching, seems to me
very doubtful. That he regarded the slave as a sort of domesticated
animal, cannot so far as I know be gathered from direct statements,
but may be inferred by just implication from his use of the same language in speaking of slaves and other live stock. Thus we find[7] the

[1] 1 9 §§ 1–6. Cf XI 1 §§ 8, 9.   [2] *mediastinus.*   [3] Cf Dig XXXIII 7 § 8 pr.
[4] *vineta plurimum per alligatos excoluntur.*
[5] *ne confundantur opera familiae, sic ut omnes omnia exequantur.*   [6] 1 9 §§ 7, 8.
[7] VI 2 § 15 *pecoris operarii* (the very word also used =labourer), 3 § 3 *iumentis iusta operum reddentibus.*

'labouring herd,' and 'draught-cattle when they are putting in a good spell of work.' So too the steward is to drive home his slave-gang at dusk 'after the fashion[1] of a first-rate herdsman,' and on arrival first of all to attend to their needs 'like a careful shepherd.' The motive of this care is to keep the staff in good working order. Both steward and stewardess are required to pay great attention to the health of the staff. Not only are there prescriptions given for treatment of ailments and injuries, but the slave really stale from overwork is to have a rest; of course malingering must be checked. For the sick there is a special[2] sick-room, always kept clean and aired, and the general sanitation of the farmstead is strictly enforced. This too is dictated by enlightened self-interest, a part of the general rule[3] that upkeep is as important as acquisition. The position of the female staff of the farm has also a bearing on this subject. They do not appear to be numerous, though perhaps proportionally more so than in the scheme of Varro. The *vilica* has a number of maids under her for doing the various house-work[4] and spinning and weaving. We have already noted the rewards of fertility on their part. For the production of home-bred slaves (*vernae*), always a thing welcomed by proprietors, is most formally recognized by Columella. Why it needed encouragement may perhaps receive some illustration from remarks upon the behaviour of certain birds in the matter of breeding. Thus peafowl do well in places where they can run at large, and the hens take more pains to rear their chicks, being so to speak[5] set free from slavery. And other birds there are that will not breed in captivity. The analogy of these cases to that of human slaves can hardly have escaped the notice of the writer.

The distinction between the slaves who are chained and those who are not appears the more striking from Columella's references to the lock-up chamber or slave-prison. His predecessors pass lightly over this matter, but he gives it the fullest recognition. The *ergastulum* should be a chamber[6] below ground level, as healthy as you can get, lighted by a number of slits in the wall so high above the floor as to be out of a man's reach. This dungeon is only for the refractory slaves, chained and constantly inspected. For the more submissive ones cabins (*cellae*) are provided in healthy spots near their work but not so scattered as to make observation difficult. There is even a bath

---

[1] XI 1 § 18 *more optimi pastoris...idem quod ille diligens opilio.*

[2] *valetudinarium* XI 1 § 18, XII 1 § 6, 3 §§ 7, 8.

[3] IV 3 § 1 *quosdam emacitas in armentis, quosdam exercet in comparandis mancipiis; de tuendis nulla cura tangit.* Cf I 4 § 7.

[4] XII 3 especially §§ 1, 8, cf *praef* § 9. He refers to Xenophon.

[5] VIII 11 § 2 *tamquam servitio liberatae,* also 12 and 15 § 7 *parere cunctantur in servitute.*

[6] 1 6 § 3 *vinctis quam saluberrimum subterraneum ergastulum, plurimis idque angustis illustratum fenestris atque a terra sic editis ne manu contingi possint.* Cf XI 1 §§ 22.

house[1], which the staff are allowed to use on holidays only: much bathing is weakening. Whether on an average farm the chained or unchained slaves are assumed to be the majority is not quite clear; probably the unchained, to judge by the general tone of the precepts. But that a lock-up is part of the normal establishment is clear enough. And it is to be noted that in one passage[2] *ergastula* are mentioned in ill-omened juxtaposition with citizens enslaved by their creditors. Whether it is implied that unhappy debtors were still liable to be locked up as slaves in creditors' dungeons as of old, is not easy to say. Columella is capable of rhetorical flourishes now and then. It is safer to suppose that he is referring to two forms of slave-labour; first, the working off arrears of debt[3] by labour of a servile kind; second, the wholesale slave-gang system suggested by the significant word *ergastula*. Or are we to read into it a reference to the kidnapping[4] of wayfarers which Augustus and Tiberius had striven to put down? Before we leave the subject of the slave-staff it is well to note that no prospect of freedom is held out, at least to the males. Fertility, as we have seen, might lead to manumission of females. But we are not told what use they were likely to make of their freedom, when they had got it. My belief is that they stayed on the estate as tolerated humble dependants; for they would have no other home. Some were natives of the place, and the imported ones would have lost all touch with their native lands. Perhaps the care of poultry[5] is a specimen of the various minor functions in which they could make themselves useful. At all events they were free from fetters and the lash. And the men too may have been occasionally manumitted on the same sort of terms. Silence does not prove a negative. For instance, we hear of *peculium*, the slave's quasi-property, only incidentally[6] as being derived from *pecus*. Yet we are not entitled to say that slaves were not free to make savings under the system of Columella.

Though the *vilicus* appears in this treatise as the normal head of the management, there are signs that this was not the last word in estate-organization. That he is sometimes[7] referred to as being the landlord's agent (*actor*), but usually not, rather suggests that he could be, and often was, confined to a more restricted sphere of duty, namely

---

[1] I 6 § 19 *rusticis balneis.*

[2] I 3 § 12 [our land-grabbers scorn moderation and buy up *fines gentium* so vast that they cannot even ride round them] *sed proculcandos pecudibus et vastandos feris derelinquunt, aut occupatos nexu civium et ergastulis tenent.* Schneider explains *nexu* etc as = *civibus ob aes alienum nexis.* Surely at this date it cannot be used in the strictly technical sense. See p 269.

[3] Like the *obaerarii* or *obaerati* of Varro I 17 § 2. See on that passage p 180.

[4] *suppressio.* See Index.

[5] VIII 2 § 7 *anus sedula* may serve as *custos vagantium.*   [6] VI *praef* § 4.

[7] I 8 § 5, 7 § 7, but in XII 3 § 6 for instance *actores* are not = *vilici.* Schneider.

the purely agricultural superintendence of the farm in hand. This would make him a mere farm-bailiff, directing operations on the land, but with little or no responsibility for such matters as finance. And in a few passages we have mention of a *procurator*. This term must be taken in its ordinary sense[1] as signifying the landlord's 'attorney' or full legal representative. He is to keep an eye on the management, for instance[2] the threshing-floor, if the master is not at hand. The position of his quarters indicates his importance: as the steward's lodging is to be where he can watch goings-out and comings-in, so that of the *procurator* is to be where[3] he can have a near view of the steward as well as doings in general. Judging from the common practice of the day, it is probable that he would be a freedman. Now, why does Columella, after referring to him thus early in the treatise, proceed to ignore him afterwards? The only reasonable explanation that occurs to me is that the appointment of such an official would only be necessary in exceptional cases: in short, that in speaking of a *procurator* he implies an unexpressed reservation 'supposing such a person to be employed.' Circumstances that might lead to such an appointment are not far to seek. The landlord might be abroad for a long time on public duty or private business. There might be large transactions pending (purchases, sales, litigation, etc) in connexion with the estate or neighbourhood; in the case of a very large estate this was not unlikely. The estate might be one of several owned by the same lord, and the *procurator* intermittently resident on one or other as from time to time required. Or lastly the services of an agent with full legal powers may have been desirable in dealing with free tenantry. If a landlord had a number of tenant farmers on his estates, it is most unlikely that his *vilici*, slaves as they were, would be able to keep a firm hand[4] on them : and the fact of his letting his farms surely suggests that he would not desire to have much rent-collecting or exaction of services to do himself.

One point in which Columella's system seems to record a change from earlier usage may be found in the comparative disuse of letting out special jobs to contractors. In one passage[5], when discussing the trenching-work required in *pastinatio*, and devices for preventing the disputes arising from bad execution of the same, he refers to *conductor* as well as *dominus*. The interests of the two are liable to clash, and he tries to shew a means of ensuring a fair settlement between the

---

[1] See Cic *de oratore* I § 249, *pro Tullio* § 17. [2] I 6 § 23.

[3] I 6 § 7 *procuratori supra ianuam ob easdem causas : et is tamen vilicum observet ex vicino*. Cf Plin *epist* III 19 § 2.

[4] In Columella's time. At a later date this could hardly be said, as the position of *coloni* became worse.

[5] III 13 §§ 12, 13. Cf Dig XLIII 24 § 15[1].

parties without going to law. I understand the *conductor* to be a man who has contracted for the job at an agreed price, and *exactor operis* just below to be the landlord, whose business it is to get full value for his money. Thus *conductor* here will be the same as the *redemptor* so often employed in the scheme of Cato. I cannot find further traces of him in Columella. Nor is the sale of a hanging[1] crop or a season's lambs to a speculator referred to. But we have other authority for believing that contracts of this kind were not obsolete, and it is probable that the same is true of contracts for special operations. That such arrangements were nevertheless much rarer than in Cato's time seems to be a fair inference. The manifest reluctance[2] to hire external labour also points to the desire of getting, so far as possible, all farming operations performed by the actual farm-staff. If I have rightly judged the position of tenant farmers, it is evident that their stipulated services would be an important help in enabling the landlord to dispense with employment of contractors' gangs on the farm. This was in itself desirable: that the presence of outsiders was unsettling to your own slaves had long been remarked, and in the more elaborate organization of Columella's day disturbing influences would be more apprehensively regarded than ever.

It is hardly necessary to follow out all the details of this complicated system and enumerate the various special functions assigned to the members of the staff. To get good foremen even at high prices was one of the leading principles: an instance[3] is seen in the case of vineyards, where we hear of a thoroughly competent *vinitor*, whose price is reckoned at about £80 of our money, the estimated value of about 4½ acres of land. The main point is that it is a system of slave labour on a large scale, and that Columella, well aware that such labour is in general wasteful, endeavours to make it remunerative by strict order and discipline. He knows very well that current lamentations over the supposed exhaustion[4] of the earth's fertility are mere evasions of the true causes of rural decay, neglect and ignorance. He knows that intensive cultivation[5] pays well, and cites striking instances. But the public for whom he writes is evidently not the men on small holdings, largely market-gardeners[6], who were able to make a living with or without slave-help, at all events when within reach of urban markets.

---

[1] A good instance in Pliny *NH* XIV 49, 50.

[2] III 21 § 10 (of hurry resulting from want of forethought) *cogitque plures operas quantocumque pretio conducere.*

[3] III 3 § 8.

[4] I *praef* §§ 1, 2, II 1. Cf III 3 § 4 with Varro I 44 § 1.

[5] I 3 § 9 *nec dubium quin minus reddat laxus ager non recte cultus quam angustus eximie,* IV 3 § 6.

[6] For milk-delivery see Calpurnius *ecl* IV 25-6 *et lac venale per urbem non tacitus porta.* For cheese Verg *G* III 402.

He addresses men of wealth, most of whom were proud of their position as landlords, but presumably not unwilling to make their estates more remunerative, provided the effort did not give them too much trouble. This condition was the real difficulty; and it is hard to believe that Columella, when insisting on the frequent presence of the master's eye, was sanguine enough to expect a general response. His attitude towards pastoral industry seems decidedly less enthusiastic than that of his predecessors. Stock[1] must be kept on the farm, partly to eat off your own fodder-crops, but chiefly for the sake of supplying manure for the arable land. In quoting Cato's famous saying on the profitableness of grazing, he agrees that nothing pays so quickly as good grazing, and that moderately good grazing pays well enough. But if, as some versions have it, he really said that even bad grazing was the next best thing for a farmer, Columella respectfully dissents. The breeding and fattening of all manner of animals for luxurious tables[2] remains much the same as in the treatise of Varro. A curious caution is given[3] in discussing the fattening of thrushes. They are to be fed with 'dried figs beaten up with fine meal, as much as they can eat or more. Some people chew the figs before giving them to the birds. But it is hardly worth while to do this if you have a large number to feed, for it costs money to hire[4] persons to do the chewing, and the sweet taste makes them swallow a good deal themselves.' Now, why hire labour for such a purpose? Is it because slaves would swallow so much of the sweet stuff that your thrushes would never fatten?

It is well known that importation of corn from abroad led to great changes in Italian agriculture in the second century BC. The first was the formation of great estates worked by slave-gangs, which seems to have begun as an attempt to compete with foreign large-scale farming in the general production of food-stuffs. If so, it was gradually discovered that it did not pay to grow cereal crops for the market, unscrupulous in slave-driving though the master might be. Therefore attention was turned to the development on a larger scale of the existing culture of the vine and olive and the keeping of great flocks and herds. Food for these last had to be found on the farm in the winter, and more and more it became usual only to grow cereals as fodder for the stock, of course including the slaves. No doubt there was a demand for the better sorts, such as wheat, in all the country towns, but the farms in their immediate neighbourhood would supply the need. That Columella assumes produce of this kind to be normally consumed on the place, is indicated by his recommending[5] barley as good food for all live-stock, and for slaves when mixed with wheat. Also by his

[1] VI *praef* §§ 3–5.   [2] Also bee-keeping.   [3] VIII 10 §§ 3, 4.
[4] *quia nec parvo conducuntur qui mandant...etc.*   [5] II 9 §§ 14, 16.

treating the delicate[1] white wheat, much fancied in Rome, as a degenerate variety, not worth the growing by a practical farmer. His instructions for storage shew the same point of view. The structure and principles of granaries[2] are discussed at length, and the possibility of long storage[3] is contemplated. The difficulties of transport by land had certainly been an important influence in the changes of Roman husbandry, telling against movements of bulky produce. Hence the value attached[4] to situations near the seaboard or a navigable stream (the latter not a condition often to be realized in Italy) by Columella and his predecessors. Military roads served the traveller as well as the armies, but took no regard[5] of agricultural needs. Moreover they had special[6] drawbacks. Wayfarers had a knack of pilfering from farms on the route, and someone or other was always turning up to seek lodging and entertainment. Thus it was wise not to plant your villa close to one of these trunk roads, or your pocket was likely to suffer. But to have a decent approach[7] by a country road was a great convenience, facilitating the landlord's periodical visits and the carriage of goods to and from the estate.

Certain words call for brief notice. Thus *opera*, the average day's work of an average worker, is Columella's regular labour-unit in terms of which he expresses the labour-cost[8] of an undertaking. In no other writer is this more marked. Occasionally *operae* occurs in the well-known concrete sense[9] of the 'hands' themselves. The *magistri* mentioned are not always the foremen spoken of above, but sometimes[10] directors or teachers in a general sense or even as a sort of synonym for *professores*. To recur once again to *colonus*, the word, as in other writers, often means simply 'cultivator,' not 'tenant-farmer.' The latter special sense occurs in a passage[11] which would be useful evidence for the history of farm-tenancies, if it were not doubtful whether the text is sound.

There remains a question, much more than a merely literary problem, as to the true relation of Columella to Vergil. That he constantly quotes the poet, and cites him as an authority on agriculture, is a striking fact. One instance will shew the deep veneration with which he regards the great master. In speaking[12] of the attention to local qualities of climate and soil needed in choosing an estate, he

---

[1] *siligo*, II 6 § 2, 9 § 13.   [2] I 6 §§ 9–17.
[3] II 20 § 6 *frumenta, si in annos reconduntur,...sin protinus usui destinantur...*etc.
[4] I 2 § 3.   [5] As Plutarch *C Gracc* 7 says εὐθεῖαι γὰρ ἤγοντο διὰ τῶν χωρίων ἀτρεμεῖς.
[6] I 5 §§ 6, 7.   [7] I 3 §§ 3, 4.   [8] II 13 § 7 *consummatio operarum*.
[9] II 21 § 10.   [10] I *praef* § 12, XI I § 12.
[11] I *praef* § 17 (of the non-urban population in old times) *qui rura colerent administrarentve opera colonorum*. The last three words are not in some MSS.
[12] I 4 § 4, Verg *G* I 51–3.

quotes lines from the first *Georgic,* the matter of which is quite traditional, common property. But he speaks of Vergil (to name the
poet[1] was unnecessary) as a most realistic[2] bard, to be trusted as an
oracle. Nay, so irresistible is to him the influence of Vergil, that he
must needs cast his own tenth book into hexameter verse: the subject
of that book is gardens, a topic on which Vergil had confessedly[3] not
fully said his say. And yet in the treatment of the land-question there
is a fundamental difference between the two writers. Columella's
system is based on slave labour organized to ensure the completest
efficiency : Vergil practically ignores slavery altogether. Columella
advises you to let land to tenant farmers whenever you cannot effectively superintend the working of slave-organizations under stewards :
Vergil ignores this solution also, and seems vaguely to contemplate a
return to the system of small farms owned and worked by free yeomen
in an idealized past. Columella is concerned to see that capital invested
in land is so employed as to bring in a good economic return : Vergil
dreams of the revival of a failing race, and possible economic success
and rustic wellbeing are to him not so much ends as means. The
contrast is striking enough. In the chapter on Vergil I have already
pointed out that the poet had at once captured the adoration of the
Roman world. It was not only in quotations or allusions, or in the
incense of praise, that his supremacy was held in evidence so long as
Latin literature remained alive. His influence affected prose style also,
and subtle reminiscences of Vergilian flavour may be traced in Tacitus.
But all this is very different from the practice of citing him as an authority on a special subject, as Columella did and the elder Pliny did
after him.

I would venture to connect this practice with the Roman habit of
viewing their own literature as inspired by Greek models and so tending to move on parallel lines. Cicero was not content to be a Roman
Demosthenes ; he must needs try to be a Roman Plato too, if not also
a Roman Aristotle. Now citation of the Homeric poems as a recognized authority on all manner of subjects, not to mention casual illustrations, runs through Greek literature. Plato and Aristotle are good
instances. It is surely not surprising that we find Roman writers
patriotically willing to cite their own great poet, more especially as
the *Georgics* lay ready to hand. In the next generation after Columella, Quintilian framed his criticism[4] of the two literatures (as food for
oratorical students) on frankly parallel lines. Vergil is the pair to
Homer : second to the prince of singers, but a good second : and he is
quoted and cited throughout the treatise as Homer is in Aristotle's

---

[1] So the Greeks often refer to Homer as The Poet.   [2] *verissimo vati velut oraculo.*
[3] Verg *G* IV 116 foll.   [4] Quintil X 1 §§ 46–131, especially §§ 85–6.

Rhetoric. True, the cases are not really parallel. Whatever preexistent material may have served to build up the Homeric poems, they are at least not didactic poems, made up of precepts largely derived from technical writers, and refined into poetic form with mature and laborious skill. To quote the *Georgics*, not only for personal observation of facts but for guiding precepts, is often to quote a secondary authority in a noble dress, and serves but for adornment. But in such a consideration there would be nothing to discourage Roman literary men. To challenge Vergil's authority on a rustic subject remained the prerogative of Seneca.

Additional note to page 263

Varro *de lingua Latina* VII § 105 says *liber qui suas operas in servitutem pro pecunia quadam debebat dum solveret nexus vocatur, ut ab aere obaeratus.* This antiquarian note is of interest as illustrating the meaning of *operae*, and the former position of the debtor as a temporary slave.

AGE OF THE FLAVIAN AND ANTONINE EMPERORS

XXXIV. GENERAL INTRODUCTION.

It is not easy to find a satisfactory line of division between the period of the Flavian emperors and that of the adoptive series that came after them. The Plebeian Flavians had no family claim, through birth or adoption, to a preeminent position in the Roman world, and the rise of Vespasian to power was indeed a revolution. Henceforth, though outward forms and machinery remained, the real control of the empire rested with those supported directly or indirectly by the great armies. But the sound administrative policy set going by the common sense of Vespasian long maintained the imperial fabric in strength, and it is commonly held that from 69 to 180 AD was the Empire's golden age. Nevertheless its vitality was already ebbing, and the calamities that beset it in the days of Marcus Aurelius found it unable to renew its vigour after holding in check its barbarian invaders. The Flavian-Antonine period must be treated as one, and from the point of view of the present inquiry certain significant facts must always be borne in mind. The Italian element in the armies was becoming less and less. Military policy consisted chiefly in defence of the frontiers, for the annexations of Trajan were not lasting, and they exhausted strength needed for defence. It was an ominous sign that the Roman power of assimilation was failing. Mixed armies of imperfectly Romanized soldiery, whether as conquerors or as settlers, could not spread Roman civilization in the same thorough way as it had become at length established in Spain or southern Gaul. To spread it extensively and not intensively meant a weakening of Roman grasp; and at some points[1] it seems as if the influx of barbarism was felt to be a menace in time of peace, not effectively counteracted by the peaceful penetration of Rome.

Now, if the protection of Italy by chiefly alien swords was to relieve the imperial centre from the heavy blood-tax borne by it in the old days of Roman expansion, surely it remained an Italian function or duty to provide carriers[2] of Roman civilization, that is, if border lands

---

[1] See Tacitus *Germ* 41 on the exceptionally favourable treatment of the Hermunduri, with Schweitzer-Sidler's notes.

[2] Seneca *ad Helviam* 7 § 7 refers to the colonies sent out to the provinces in earlier times, and is rhetorically exaggerated.

were to be solidly Romanized as a moral bulwark against barbarism.
But this duty could only be performed by a healthy and vigorous Italy,
and Italy[1] was not healthy and vigorous. Internal security left the
people free to go on in the same ways as they had now been following
for generations, and those ways, as we have seen, did not tend to the
revival of a free rural population. Country towns were not as yet in
manifest decay, but there were now no imperial politics, and municipal
politics, ever petty and self-regarding, offered no stimulus to arouse a
larger and common interest. Municipalities looked for benefactors, and
were still able to find them. In this period we meet with institutions
of a charitable kind, some even promoted by the imperial government,
for the benefit of orphans and children of the poor. This was a credit
to the humanity of the age, but surely a palliative of social ailments,
not a proof of sound condition. In Rome there was life, but it was
cosmopolitan life. Rome was the capital of the Roman world, not of
Italy. In the eyes of jealous patriots it seemed that what Rome herself
needed was a thorough Romanizing. It was not from the great wicked
city, thronged with adventurers[2] of every sort, largely Oriental Greeks,
and hordes of freedmen, that the better Roman influences could spread
abroad. Nor were the old Provinces, such as Spain and southern Gaul,
where Roman civilization had long been supreme, in a position to
assimilate[3] and Romanize the ruder border-lands by the Rhine and
Danube. They had no energies to spare: moreover, they too depended on the central government, and the seat of that government
was Rome.

Italy alone could have vitalized the empire by moral influence, creating in the vast fabric a spiritual unity, and making a great machine
into something more or less like a nation,—that is, if she had been
qualified for acting such a part. But Italy had never been a nation
herself. The result of the great Italian war of 90 and 89 BC had been
to merge Italy in Rome, not Rome in Italy. Italians, now Romans,
henceforth shared the exploitation of the subject countries and the
hatred of oppressed peoples. But under the constitution of the Republic
politics became more of a farce the more the franchise was extended, and
the most obvious effect of Italian enfranchisement was to increase the
number of those who directly or indirectly made a living out of provincial
wrongs. The Provinces swarmed with bloodsuckers of every kind. The
establishment of the Empire at length did something to relieve the
sufferings of the Provinces. But it was found necessary to recognize
Italy as a privileged imperial land. In modern times such privilege

[1] Cf Nissen *Italische Landeskunde* vol II pp 128-30.
[2] A notable utterance on this topic is Seneca *ad Helviam* 6 §§ 2, 3. See Mayor's notes on
Juvenal III 58 foll.
[3] See Tacitus *Germ* 29 for interesting matter bearing on these points.

would take the form of political rights and responsibilities. But political life was dead, and privilege could only mean local liberties, exemption from burdens, and the like. And in the long run the maintenance or abolition of privilege would have to depend on the success or failure of the system. Now the emperors of the first two centuries of the Empire did their best to maintain the privileged position of Italy. But even in the time of Augustus it was already becoming clear that Romanized Italy depended on Rome and that Rome, so far as the Senate and Magistrates were concerned, could not provide for the efficient administration of Italy or even of Rome itself. Then began the long gradual process by which Italy, like the rest of the empire, passed more and more under the control of the imperial machine. In the period we are now considering this was steadily going on, for brief reactions, such as that under Nerva, did not really check it, and Italy was well on the way to become no more than a Province.

The feature of this period most important in connexion with the present inquiry is the evidence[1] that emperors were as a rule painfully conscious of Italian decay. Alive to the dangers involved in its continuance, they accepted the responsibility of doing what they could to arrest it. Their efforts took various forms, chiefly (a) the direct encouragement of farming (b) relief of poverty (c) measures for providing more rural population or preventing emigration of that still existing. It is evident that the aim was to place and keep more free rustics on the land. In the numerous allotments of land to discharged soldiers a number of odd pieces[2] (*subsiciva*), not included in the lots assigned, were left over, and had been occupied by squatters. Vespasian, rigidly economical in the face of threatened state-bankruptcy, had the titles inquired into, and resumed and sold those pieces where no valid grant could be shewn. Either this was not fully carried out, or some squatters must have been allowed to hold on as 'possessors,' probably paying a quit-rent to the treasury. For Domitian[3] found some such people still in occupation and converted their tenure into proprietorship, on the ground that long possession had established a prescriptive right. Nerva tried to go further[4] by buying land and planting agricultural colonies: but little or nothing was really effected in his brief reign. In relief of poverty it was a notable extension to look beyond the city of Rome,

---

[1] The numerous references need not be given here. They can be found in H. Schiller's *Geschichte der Römischen Kaiserzeit*.

[2] Schiller I 515, 534. See Hyginus gromat I p 133, Frontinus *ibid* pp 53-4, and the rescript of Domitian in Girard, *textes* part I ch 4 § 5. Suetonius *Dom* 9.

[3] Domitian also made ordinances forbidding new vineyards in Italy and enjoining the destruction of those in the Provinces. But these were not carried out. Schiller I 533. Suet *Dom* 7, 14, Stat *silv* IV 3 11-12.

[4] Schiller I 540.

where corn-doles had long existed, and continued to exist. The plan adopted was for the state to advance money at low rates of interest to landowners in municipal areas, and to let the interest received form a permanent endowment for the benefit of poor parents and orphans. We must remember that to have children born did not imply a legal obligation to rear them, and that the prospect of help from such funds was a distinct encouragement to do so. Whether any great results were achieved by this form of charity must remain doubtful: flattering assurances[1] to Trajan on the point can no more be accepted without reserve than those addressed to Augustus on the success of his reforms, or to Domitian on his promotion of morality. But it seems certain that private charity was stimulated by imperial action, and that the total sums applied in this manner were very large. Begun by Nerva, carried out[2] by Trajan, extended by Hadrian and Antoninus Pius, the control of these endowments was more centralized by Marcus. In his time great dearth in Italy had made distress more acute, and the hour was at hand when the inner disorders of the empire would cause all such permanent foundations to fail and disappear. They may well have relieved many individual cases of indigence, but we can hardly suppose their general effect on the Italian population to have been a healthy one. They must have tended to deaden enterprise and relax self-help, for they were too much after the pauperizing model long established in Rome. The provision of cheap loan-capital for landowners may or may not have been a boon in the long run.

The increase of rustic population through excess of births over deaths could not be realized in a day, even if the measures taken to promote it were successful. So we find Trajan[3] not only founding colonies in Italy but forbidding colonists to be drawn from Italy for settlement in the Provinces; a restriction said to have been[4] disregarded by Marcus. But one important sequel of the frontier wars of Marcus, in which German mercenaries were employed, was the transplanting[5] of large numbers of German captives into Italy. Such removals had occurred before, but seldom and on a small scale. This wholesale transplantation under Marcus made a precedent for many similar movements later on. It may be taken for granted that the emperor did not turn out Italians in order to find room for the new settlers. It is also probable that these were bound to military service. The great military colonies of later date, formed of whole tribes or nations settled near the frontiers, certainly held their lands on military tenure. Such was the system of frontier defence gradually forced upon Rome through

---

[1] Plin *paneg* 26–8. [2] Schiller 1 566, 623, 630, 656.
[3] Schiller 1 566. [4] Capitolinus *M Aurel* 11 § 7. The text is in some doubt.
[5] Schiller 1 651.

the failure of native imperial forces sufficient for the purpose: and this failure was first conspicuous in Italy. Among the various measures taken by emperors to interest more persons in promoting Italian agriculture we may notice Trajan's[1] ordinance, that Provincials who aspired to become Roman Senators must shew themselves true children of Rome by investing one third of their property in Italian land. The order seems to have been operative, but the reduction[2] of the fixed minimum proportion from $\frac{1}{3}$ to $\frac{1}{4}$ by Marcus looks as if the first rule had been found too onerous. There is no reason to think that the state of rural Italy was materially bettered by these well-meant efforts. And the introduction of barbarian settlers, who had to be kept bound to the soil in order to be readily available when needed for military service, tended to give the rustic population a more and more stationary character. It was in fact becoming more usual to let farms to free *coloni*; but the *coloni*, though personally free, were losing freedom of movement.

NOTE ON EMIGRATION FROM ITALY.

In the *Journal of Roman Studies* (vol VIII) I have discussed the question whether the emigration from Italy to the Provinces was to a serious extent agricultural in character, and in particular whether we can believe it to have carried abroad real working rustics in large numbers. Are we to see in it an important effective cause of the falling-off of the free rustic population of Italy? That the volume of emigration was large may be freely granted; also that settlements of discharged soldiers took place from time to time. Nor does it seem doubtful that many of the emigrants became possessors of farm-lands[3] in the Provinces. But that such persons were working rustics, depending on their own labour, is by no means clear. And, if they were not, the fact of their holding land abroad does not bear directly on the decay of the working farmer class in Italy. That commerce and finance and exploitation in general were the main occupations of Italian[4] emigrants, I do not think can be seriously doubted. And that many of them combined landholding with their other enterprises is probable enough.

Professor Reid kindly reminds me that soldiers from Italy, whose term of service expired while they were still in a Province, were apt to settle down there in considerable numbers. The case of Carteia in Spain is well known, and that of Avido, also in Spain, was probably of the same nature. These were not regular Colonies. So too in Africa Marius seems to have left behind him communities of soldiers not regularly organized[5] as *coloniae*. When the

---

[1] Schiller I 566. Plin *epist* VI 19 depicts the situation fully. The aim was to make them feel Italy their *patria*. See the jealousy of rich Provincials shewn by senators, Tac *Ann* XI 23.

[2] Schiller I 656.

[3] The remarkable community of Lamasba is referred to below in a note after chapter XXXVII.

[4] The *locus classicus* on emigrant Romans is Cic *pro Fonteio* §§ 11–13, which belongs to 69 BC. Cf Sallust *Iug* 21, 26, 47.

[5] That is, allottees of land distributed *viritim*.

town of Uchi Maius received the title of *colonia* from the emperor Severus, it called itself[1] *colonia Mariana*, like the one founded by Marius in Corsica. And the same title appears in the case[2] of Thibari. With these African settlements we may connect the law carried by Saturninus in 100 BC to provide the veterans of Marius with allotments of land in Africa, on the scale of 100 *iugera* for each man. If this record[3] is to be trusted (and the doubtful points cannot be discussed here), the natural inference is that farms of considerable size are meant, for the working of which no small amount of labour would be required. Nor is this surprising, for the soldiers of Marius were at the time masters of the situation, and not likely to be content with small grants. Whether the allotments proposed were in Africa or in Cisalpine Gaul[4] is not quite certain. Marius seems to have left Africa in the winter of 105–4 BC. Since then he had been engaged in the war with the northern barbarians, and the lands recovered from the invaders were in question. Still, the proposal may have referred to Africa, for it is certain that the connexion of Marius with that Province was remembered[5] long after. The important point is that the persons to be gratified were not civilian peasants but discharged veterans of the New Model army, professionalized by Marius himself. Neither the retired professional mercenaries of Greco-Macedonian armies, nor the military colonists of Sulla, give us reason to believe that such men would regard hard and monotonous labour with their own hands as a suitable reward for the toils and perils of their years of military service. Surely they looked forward to a life of comparative ease, with slaves to labour under their orders. If they kept their hold on their farms, they would become persons of some importance in their own provincial neighbourhood. Such were the *milites* or *veterani* whom we find often mentioned under the later Empire: and these too were evidently not labourers but landlords and directors.

Therefore I hold that the class of men, many of them Italians by descent, whom we find holding land in various Provinces and living on the profits of the same, were mostly if not all either soldier-settlers or persons to whom landholding was one of several enterprises of exploitation. That the mere Italian peasant emigrated in such numbers as seriously to promote the falling-off of the free rustic population of Italy, is a thesis that I cannot consider as proved or probable.

XXXV. MUSONIUS.

In earlier chapters I have found it necessary to examine the views of philosophers on the subject of agriculture and agricultural labour, holding it important to note the attitude of great thinkers towards these matters. And indeed a good deal is to be gleaned from Plato and Aristotle. Free speculations on the nature of the State included not only strictly political inquiries, but social and economic also. But in the Macedonian period, when Greek states no longer enjoyed unrestricted freedom of movement and policy, a change came over philosophy. The tendency of the schools that now shewed most vital energy, such as the Epicurean and Stoic, was to concern themselves

[1] Inscription, Dessau 1334, CIL VIII 15454.
[2] Dessau 6790.   [3] [Victor] *de viris illustribus* 73 § 1, cf § 5.
[4] Cf Appian *civ* I 29 § 2.
[5] *Bellum Afr* 32, 35, 56, Dion Cass XLIII 4 § 2.

with the Individual rather than the State. The nature of Man, and his possibilities of happiness, became more and more engrossing topics. As the political conditions under which men had to live were now manifestly imposed by circumstances over which the ordinary citizen had no control, the happiness of the Individual could no longer be dependent on success in political ambitions and the free play of civic life. It had to be sought in himself, independent of circumstances. The result was that bold questioning and the search for truth ceased to be the prime function of philosophic schools, and the formation of character took the first place. Hence the elaboration of systems meant to regulate a man's life by implanting in him a fixed conception of the world in which he had to live, and his relation to the great universe of which he and his immediate surroundings formed a part. And this implied a movement which may be roughly described as from questioning to dogma. The teacher became more of a preacher, his disciples more of a congregation of the faithful; and more and more the efficiency of his ministrations came to depend on his own personal influence, which we often call magnetism.

When Greek literature and thought became firmly established in Rome during the second century BC, it was just this dogmatic treatment of moral questions that gave philosophy a hold on a people far more interested in conduct than in speculation. The Roman attempts, often clumsy enough, to translate principle into practice were, and continued to be, various in spirit and success. Stoicism in particular blended most readily with the harder and more virile types of Roman character, and found a peculiarly sympathetic reception among eminent lawyers. The reigns of the first emperors were not favourable to moral philosophy; but the accession of Nero set literature, and with it moralizing, in motion once more. A kind of eclectic Stoicism came into fashion, a Roman product, of which Seneca was the chief representative. A touch of timeserving was needed to adapt Greek theories for practical use in the world of imperial Rome. Seneca was both a courtier and a wealthy landowner, and was one of the victims of Nero's tyranny. We have seen that while preaching Stoic doctrine, for instance on the relations of master and slave, he shews little interest in agriculture for its own sake or in the conditions of agricultural labour. It is interesting to contrast with his attitude that of another Stoic, a man of more uncompromising and consistent type, whose life was partly contemporaneous with that of Seneca, and who wrote only a few years later under the Flavian emperors.

Musonius[1] **Rufus**, already a teacher of repute in Nero's time,

---

[1] For details of his life see Mayor on Pliny *epp* III 11. Cf Ritter and Preller *hist Philos,* Champagny *Les Césars* IV I § I.

seems to have kept himself clear of conspiracies and intrigues, recognizing the necessity of the monarchy and devoting himself to his profession of moral guide to young men. But any great reputation was dangerous in Nero's later years, and a pretext was found for banishing the philosopher in 65. Under Galba he returned to Rome, still convinced of the efficacy of moral suasion, witnessed the bloody successions of emperors in 69, and risked his life in an ill-timed effort to stay the advance of Vespasian's soldiery by discoursing on the blessings of peace. Vespasian seems to have allowed him to remain in Rome, and he is said to have been tutor to Titus. Yet he had not shrunk from bringing to justice an informer guilty of the judicial murder of a brother Stoic, and he was generally regarded as the noblest of Roman teachers, both in principles and in practice. He has been spoken of as a forerunner of Epictetus and Marcus Aurelius. Evidently no timeserver, he seems to have made allowance for human needs and human weakness in the application of strict moral rules. It is a great pity that we have no complete authentic works of his surviving: but some of the reports by a pupil or pupils have come down to us. One of these extracts[1] is so complete in itself, and so striking in its view of agriculture and agricultural labour, that I have translated it here. We are to bear in mind that the opinions expressed in it belong to a time when a small number of great landlords owned a large part (and that the most attractive) of Italy, and vast estates in the provinces as well. It is the luxurious and slave-ridden world of Petronius and Seneca that we must keep before us in considering the advice of Musonius; advice which we cannot simply ignore, however much we may see in this good man a voice crying in the wilderness.

'There is also another resource[2], nowise inferior to the above, one that might reasonably be deemed superior to it, at least for a man of strong body: I mean that derived from the land, whether the farmer owns it or not. For we see that there are many who, though cultivating land owned by the state[3] or by other persons, are yet able to support not only themselves but wives and children; while there are some who by the devoted industry of their own hands[4] attain to great abundance in this way of life. For the earth responds most fairly and justly to the care bestowed upon her, returning manifold what she receives and providing a plenty of all things necessary to life for him that will labour; and she does it consistently with a man's self-respect and dignity. For nobody, other than an effeminate weakling, would describe any of the operations of husbandry as disgraceful or incom-

---

[1] Preserved by Stobaeus *flor* LVI 18. It is in Greek, the classic language of Philosophy, as the *Meditations* of Marcus Aurelius, etc.

[2] πόρος, a means of livelihood.   [3] ἢ δημοσίαν ἢ ἰδιωτικήν.

[4] αὐτουργικοὶ καὶ φιλόπονοι ὄντες.

patible with manly excellence. Are not planting ploughing vine-dressing honourable works? And sowing reaping threshing, are not these all liberal pursuits, suited to good men? Nay, the shepherd's life, if it did not degrade Hesiod or hinder him from winning divine favour and poetic renown, neither will it hinder others. For my part, I hold this to be the best of all the tasks comprised in husbandry, inasmuch as it affords the soul more leisure for pondering and investigating what concerns mental culture. For all tasks that bend the body and keep it fully on the strain do at the same time force the soul to give them its whole attention, or nearly so, sharing as it does the strain of the body: but all those that permit the body to escape excessive strain do not prevent the soul from reasoning out important questions and from improving its own wisdom by such reasonings, a result which is the special aim of every philosopher. This is why I set such special value on the art of shepherds. If however a man does[1] combine tillage with philosophy, I hold no other life comparable with this, and no other means of livelihood preferable to it. Surely it is more according to nature to get your sustenance from Earth, our nurse and mother, than from some other source. Surely it is more manly[2] to live on a farm than to sit idle in a city. Surely out-of-door pursuits are healthier than sheltered retirement. Which, pray, is the freeman's choice, to meet his needs by receiving from others, or by contrivance of his own? Why, it is thought far more dignified to be able to satisfy your own requirements unaided than with aid of others. So true is it that to live by husbandry, of course with due respect[3] to what is good and honourable, is beautiful and conducive to happiness and divine favour. Hence it was that the god (Delphic Apollo) proclaimed[4] that Myson of Chenae was a wise man and greeted Aglaus of Psophis as a happy one; for these both led rustic lives, working with their own hands and not spending their time in cities. Surely then it is a worthy ambition to follow these men's example and devote ourselves to husbandry in earnest.

'Some may think it a monstrous notion that a man of educative power, qualified to lead youths on to philosophy, should till the soil and do bodily labour like a rustic. And, if it had been the fact that tilling the soil hinders the pursuit of philosophy or the lending help to others in that pursuit, the notion would have been monstrous indeed. But, as things are, if young men could see their teacher at work in the country, demonstrating in practice the principle to which reason guides us, namely that bodily toil and suffering are preferable to dependence on others for our food, I think it would be more helpful to them than

---

[1] εἴ γε μὴν ἅμα φιλοσοφεῖ τις καὶ γεωργεῖ.

[2] τοῦ καθῆσθαι ἐν πόλει τὸ ζῆν ἐν χωρίῳ.   [3] σύν γε τῷ καλοκαγαθίας μὴ ὀλιγωρεῖν.

[4] These are stock instances of happiness in rustic life. For references see notes in Frazer's *Pausanias* VIII 24 § 13, X 24 § 1.

# of rustic labour 279

attendance at his lectures in town. What is to hinder the pupil, while he works at his teacher's side, from catching his utterances on self-control or justice or fortitude? For the right pursuit of philosophy is not promoted by much talking, and young men are under no necessity to learn off the mass of speculation on these topics, an accomplishment of which the Professors[1] are so vain. For such discourses are indeed sufficient to use up a man's lifetime: but it is possible to pick up the most indispensable and useful points even when one is engaged in the work of husbandry, especially as the work will not be unceasing but admits periods of rest. Now I am well aware that few will be willing to receive instruction by this method: but it is better that the majority of youths who profess the pursuit of philosophy should never attend a philosopher at all, I mean those unsound effeminate creatures whose presence at the classes is a stain upon the name of philosophy. For of those that have a genuine love of philosophy not one would be unwilling to spend his time with a good man on a farm, aye though that farm were one most difficult[2] to work; seeing that he would reap great advantages from this employment. He would have the company of his teacher night and day; he would be removed from the evils of city life, which are a stumbling-block to the pursuit of philosophy; his conduct, good or bad, could not escape notice (and nothing benefits a pupil more than this); moreover, to be under the eye of a good man when eating and drinking and sleeping is a great benefit.'

At this point the writer digresses for a moment to quote some lines of Theognis and to interpret them in a sense favourable to his own views. He then continues 'And let no one say that husbandry is a hindrance to learning or teaching. Surely it is not so, if we reflect that under these conditions the pupil enjoys most fully the company of his teacher while the teacher has the fullest control of his pupil. Such then being the state of the case, it is clear that of the philosopher's resources none is more useful or more becoming than that drawn from husbandry.'

In this extract three points simply stand for principles dear to all sincere Stoics; (1) the duty and benefit of living 'according to Nature,' (2) the duty and benefit of self-sufficiency and not depending on the support of others, (3) the duty and satisfaction of continued self-improvement. Consistent practice on these lines would go far to produce the Stoic ideal, the Wise Man, happy and perfect in his assurance and dignity. But the attempt to combine all these in a ' back to the land ' scheme of moral betterment has surely in it a marked personal note. It is the dream of a singular man in the surroundings of a rotten civilization; a civilization more rotten, and a dream more utopian, than

[1] σοφιστάς. [2] χαλεπώτατον.

the dreamer could possibly know. Aspirations towards a healthy out-
door life had been felt by many before Musonius. Admiration of rustic
pursuits was no new thing, but it was generally freedom from worries,
with the occasional diversions of the chase, that were attractive to the
town-bred man. Ploughing and digging, and the responsible charge of
flocks and herds, had long been almost entirely left to slaves, and
Musonius is driven to confess that few youths of the class from which
he drew pupils would be willing to undertake such occupations. It was
useless to urge that bodily labour is not degrading: that it is exhausting, and engrosses the whole attention, he could not deny. He falls
back on pastoral duties as light and allowing leisure for serious dis-
course. The suggestion seems unreal, though sincere, when we remember that Italian shepherds had to fight wolves and brigands.
Moreover, the preference of grazing to tillage was in no small degree
due to the fewer persons employed in it, and the stockmen were a
notoriously rough class. Even the idealized shepherds of the bucolic
poets exhibit a coarseness not congenial to conversation savouring of
virtue. But to a Stoic preacher who could try to pacify a licentious
soldiery the notion of using pastoral pursuits as a means to moral
excellence may well have seemed a reasonable proposal.

It is at least clear that the futility of philosophy as administered
by lecturers in Rome had made a strong impression on Musonius. The
fashionable company to whom the discourses were addressed, whether
they for the moment shed some of their self-satisfaction or not, were
seldom or never induced to remodel their worthless lives. So Musonius
urges them to break away from solemn trifling and take to rustic
labour. He probably chose this remedy as one specially Roman, following the tradition of the heroes of ancient Rome. But no artificial
revival of this kind was possible, whatever his generous optimism
might say. His contemporary the elder Pliny, who was content to
glorify the vanished past and deplore the present, had a truer appreciation of the facts. Farm-work as a means of bringing personal influence to bear, treating body and mind together, a sort of 'Wisdom
while you dig,' was in such a society a merely fantastic proposal. The
importance of farming and food-production was a commonplace, but
the vocation of Musonius was moralizing and character-production.
There is no reason to think that he had any practical knowledge of
agriculture. His austere life proves nothing of the kind. The only
remark that shews acquaintance with conditions of landholding is his
reference to the farmers who make a living on hired land. And this is
in too general terms to have any historical value.

XXXVI. PLINY THE ELDER.

Among the writers of this period who refer to agricultural matters the most important is the **elder Pliny,** who contrived in a life of public service[1] in various departments to amass a prodigious quantity of miscellaneous learning and to write many erudite works. His *naturalis historia,* an extraordinary compilation of encyclopaedic scope, contains numerous references to agriculture, particularly in the eighteenth book. He collected and repeated the gleanings from his omnivorous reading, and the result is more remarkable for variety and bulk than for choice and digestion. As a recorder he is helpful, preserving as he does a vast number of details, some not otherwise preserved, others of use in checking or supplementing other versions. Far removed as the book is from being a smooth and readable literary work, the moralizing rhetoric of the age shews its influence not only in the constant effort to wring a lesson of some kind out of the topic of the moment, but in the longer sermonizing passages that lead up to some subject on which the writer feels deeply. One of these[2] occurs in introducing agriculture, and in pursuing the subject he loses no opportunity of contrasting a degenerate present with a better past. We need not take his lamentations at their full face-value, but that they were in the main justified is not open to doubt. It has been so often necessary to cite him in earlier chapters, that we shall not have to dwell upon him at great length here.

The functions of compiler and antiquarian are apt to coincide very closely, and it is in his picture of the earlier conditions of Roman and Italian farming that Pliny's evidence is most interesting. The old traditions[3] of the simple and manly yeomen, each tilling his own little plot of ground, content with his seven *iugera* of land or even with two in the earliest times, Cincinnatus and the rest of the farmer-heroes, to whom their native soil, proud of her noble sons, responded[4] with a bounteous fertility that she denies to the heartless labour of slave-gangs on modern *latifundia,*—these are the topics on which he enlarges with a rhetorical or even poetic warmth. The ruin of Italy, nay of Provinces too, through the land-grabbing and formation of vast estates, is denounced[5] in a classic passage. He sees no end to the process. Six landlords held between them half the Province of Africa in the time of Nero. Wanting money, the emperor put them to death for the sake of

---

[1] He was in command of the fleet at Misenum in 79 AD when the great eruption of Vesuvius took place. He persisted in approaching it, and met his death. The family belonged to the colony of Novum Comum in Transpadane Gaul, now part of Italy.

[2] *NH* XVIII 1–5.   [3] *NH* XVIII 7, 18, 20.   [4] *NH* XVIII 19, 21, 36.

[5] *NH* XVIII 35.

their property. He does not add, but doubtless reflected, that such measures only added to the resources controlled by a tyrant ruler, not a desirable object. We may add further that such iniquities inevitably disposed virtuous emperors to leave the land-monopolizers a free hand, perhaps unwillingly; but these gentry were not breaking the law by buying land, and an emperor conscious of the burden of administration, and desiring to carry on his work undisturbed by internal disloyalty, had strong reasons for not provoking wealthy capitalists. To conciliate them, and if possible to engage their cooperation in schemes designed for the public good according to the ideas of the time, was to proceed on the line of least resistance.

Among the traditional precepts handed on by Pliny from Cato and others are many with which we are already familiar. Such is the rule of Regulus[1], that in buying a farm regard must be had to the healthiness of the situation as well as to the richness of the soil. Another is the need of keeping a due proportion[2] between farm-house and farm. Great men of the late Republic, Lucullus and Scaevola, erred on this point in opposite directions: Marius on the other hand laid out a *villa* so skilfully that Sulla said 'here was a man at last with eyes in his head.' The value of the master's eye is another old friend. We have also seen above that Mago's[3] advice, when you buy a farm, to sell your town house, was not a policy to be followed by Romans of quality, who felt it a duty not to cut themselves off from touch with public affairs. Another tradition is that of the sentiment of the olden time, holding it criminal[4] to slay man's fellow-worker, the ox. In referring to the technical skill required in a steward, a favourite topic of Cato, Pliny gives his own view[5] briefly, 'the master ought to set the greatest store by his steward, but the fellow should not be aware of it.' The calculation of labour-cost[6] in terms of *operae*, as with others, so with him, is a regular way of reckoning. And we meet once more the saying that, while good cultivation is necessary, too high farming does not pay. He illustrates this by an instance[7] of comparatively modern date. A man of very humble origin, who rose through military merit to the consulship, was rewarded by Augustus with a large sum of money: this he spent on buying land[8] in Picenum and fancy-farming. In this course he ran through his property, and his heir did not think it worth his while to claim the succession. The general tendency of all these precepts and anecdotes is to commend moderation and to rebuke the

---

[1] *NH* XVIII 27–8.   [2] *NH* XVIII 32.   [3] *NH* XVIII 35.

[4] *NH* VIII 180. In Aelian *var hist* this is recorded (v 14) as an old rule in Attica.

[5] *NH* XVIII 36.

[6] *NH* XIX 60 *octo iugerum operis palari iustum est* is a good instance. This verb *palare* =to dig should be added to dictionaries.

[7] *NH* XVIII 37–8.   [8] *agros...coemendo colendoque in gloriam.*

foolish ambition of land-proud capitalists of his own day. His praise of the ancient ways and regret for their disappearance do not suggest any hope of their revival. To Pliny as to others it was only too clear that legends of conquering consuls setting their own hands to the plough had no practical bearing on the conditions of the present age.

Thoughtful men[1] could not ignore the fact that the decline in production of cereal crops left Italy exposed to risk of famine. At any moment storms might wreck the corn-fleets from Egypt or Africa, and the strategic value of Egypt[2] as a vital food-centre had been shewn quite recently in strengthening the cause of Vespasian. No wonder Pliny is uneasy, and looks back regretfully[3] to the time when Italy was not fed by the Provinces, when thrifty citizens grew their own staple foodstuffs, and corn was plentiful and cheap. He quotes some prices from the time of the great Punic wars and earlier, which shew the remarkable cheapness of wine oil dried figs and flesh, as well as of various grains. This result was not due to great estates owned by individual landlords[4] who elbowed out their neighbours, but to the willing work of noble citizens tilling their little holdings. To look for similar returns from the task-work of chained and branded slaves is a sheer libel on Mother Earth. That he treats at great length of agricultural details, not only of grain-crops in their various kinds, but fruits, vegetables, indeed everything he can think of, and all the processes of cultivation, is due to his encyclopaedic bent, and need not detain us here. When he tells us[5] that vine-growing was a comparatively late development among the Romans, who long were content with grain-growing, it is a passing sigh over a vanished age of simple life. The meaning of words changes and records the change of things. When the Twelve Tables[6] spoke of *hortus*, it was not a garden in the modern sense, a place of pleasure and luxury, that was meant, but a poor man's small holding. By that venerable code it was made a criminal offence[7] to cut or graze off under cover of night the crops raised on a man's plough-land. A man whose farm was badly cultivated was disgraced by the censors. For, as Cato[8] said, there is no life like the farmer's for breeding sturdy men to make efficient soldiers and loyal citizens. The gist of these utterances, picked out of the mass, is that Pliny would like to see Italy able to provide for her own feeding and her own defence, but knows very well that no such ideal is within the range of hope.

His interest in agriculture such as he saw it around him is shewn in recording recent or contemporary doings, such as that of the man

---

[1] So Tiberius in Tac *ann* III 54.   [2] Tac *hist* III 8 *Aegyptus, claustra annonae.*
[3] *NH* XVIII 15 foll.
[4] *ibid* 17 *nec e latifundiis singulorum contingebat arcentium vicinos.*
[5] *NH* XVIII 24.   [6] *NH* XIX 50–1.   [7] *NH* XVIII 12.   [8] *NH* XVIII 11, 26.

mentioned above who squandered a fortune on ill-judged farming. A more successful venture[1] was that of Remmius Palaemon, apparently in the time of Claudius. He was a freedman, not a farmer, but a schoolmaster (*grammaticus*) of repute, a vainglorious fellow. He bought some land, not of the best quality and let down by bad farming. To farm this he engaged another freedman, one Acilius Sthenelus, who had the vineyards thoroughly overhauled (*pastinatis de integro*). Before eight years were out, he was able to sell a hanging crop for half as much again as it had cost him to buy the land, and within ten years he sold the land itself to Seneca (not a man for fancy prices) for four times as much as he had given for it. Truly a fine speculation. Sthenelus had carried out another of the same kind[2] on his own account. We must note that both were in the vine-culture, not in corn-growing, and the appearance of freedmen, probably oriental Greeks, as leaders of agricultural enterprise in Italy. There is nothing to shew that these undertakings were on a large scale: the land in Sthenelus' own case is stated as not more than 60 *iugera*. But no doubt he was, like many of his tribe, a keen man of business[3] and not too proud or preoccupied to give close attention to the matter in hand. Such a man would get the utmost out of his slaves and check waste: he would keep a tight grip on a slave steward if (which we are not told) he found it necessary to employ one at all. For Pliny, as for most Romans, a profitable speculation had great charms. He cannot resist repeating the old Greek story[4] of the sage who demonstrated his practical wisdom by making a 'corner' in olive-presses, foreseeing a 'bumper' crop. Only he turns it round, making it a 'corner' in oil, in view of a poor crop and high prices, and tells it not of Thales but of Democritus.

There were of course many principles of agriculture that no economic or social changes could affect. The 'oracle' of Cato, as to the importance[5] of thorough and repeated ploughing followed by liberal manuring, was true under all conditions. But just for a moment the veil is lifted to remind us that in the upland districts there was still an Italy agriculturally, as socially, very different from the lowland arable of which we generally think when speaking of Italian farming. 'Ploughing on hillsides[6] is cross-wise, and so toilsome to man that he even has to do ox-team's work: at least the mountain peoples[7] use the mattock for tillage instead of the plough, and do without the ox.' It is to be regretted that we have so little evidence as to the condition of

---

[1] *NH* XIV 49, 50.   [2] *NH* XIV 48.
[3] Such as the *agricola strenuus* depicted in the letter of Marcus to Fronto (p 29 Naber), who has *omnia ad usum magis quam ad voluptatem*.
[4] *NH* XVIII 273-4. Aristotle *Politics* I 11.   [5] *NH* XVIII 174.
[6] *NH* XVIII 178 ...*transverso monte*.
[7] *certe sine hoc animali montanae gentes sarculis arant.*

the dalesmen, other than the passages of such writers as Horace and Juvenal, who refer to them as rustic folk a sojourn among whom is a refreshing experience after the noise and bustle of Rome. For it seems certain that in these upland retreats there survived whatever was left of genuine Italian life, and we should like to be able to form some notion of its quantity; that is, whether the population of freemen on small holdings, living mostly on the produce of their own land, was numerically an important element in the total population of Italy. That great stretches of hill-forest were in regular use simply as summer pastures, and that the bulk of the arable lands were held in great estates, and slaves employed in both departments, we hear in wearisome iteration. But to get a true picture of the country as a whole is, in the absence of statistics, not possible.

I have not been able to discover in Pliny any definite repugnance to slavery as a system. It is true that he is alive to the evils of the domestic slavery prevalent in his day. The brigades of slaves (*mancipiorum legiones*)[1] filling the mansions of the rich, pilfering at every turn, so that nothing is safe unless put under lock and seal, are a nuisance and a demoralizing influence. They are an alien throng (*turba externa*) in a Roman household; a sad contrast[2] to the olden time, when each family had its one slave, attached to his master's clan, when the whole household lived in common, and nothing had to be locked up. But this is only one of Pliny's moralizing outbreaks, and it is the abuse and overgrowth of slavery, not slavery in itself, that he is denouncing. In speaking of agriculture he says 'to have farms cultivated by slave-gangs[3] is a most evil thing, as indeed are all acts performed by those who have no hope.' Here the comparative inefficiency of workers who see no prospect of bettering their condition is plainly recognized; but it is the economic defect, not the outrage on a common humanity, that inspires the consciously futile protest. And at the very end of his great book, when he breaks out into a farewell panegyric[4] on Italy, and enumerates the various elements of her preeminence among the countries of the world, he includes the supply of slave-labour[5] in the list. Spain perhaps comes next, but here too the organized employment[6] of slaves is one of the facts that are adduced to justify her praise. Now I do not imagine that Pliny was a hard unkindly man. But he evidently accepted slavery as an established institution, one of the

---

[1] *NH* XXXIII 26–7.
[2] *aliter apud antiquos singuli Marcipores Luciporesve dominorum gentiles omnem victum in promiscuo habebant.*
[3] *NH* XVIII 36 *coli rura ab ergastulis pessimum est, et quicquid agitur a desperantibus.*
[4] *NH* XXXVII 201–3.
[5] *principatum naturae optinet…viris feminis ducibus militibus servitiis…etc.*
[6] *servorum exercitio.*

economic bases of society. He saw its inferiority to free labour, but a passing protest seemed to him enough. Had he been asked, Why don't you recommend free labour directly? I think he would have answered, Where are you going to find it in any quantity? And it is obvious that, slave labour once assumed, the great thing was to have enough of it. Nor again have I found him using *colonus* in the sense of tenant farmer. In that of 'cultivator' it occurs several times, as in the quotation[1] from Cato, that to call a man *bonum colonum* was of old the height of praise. Figuratively it appears in comparisons, as when the guilt of the slayer of an ox is emphasized[2] by the addition 'as if he had made away with his *colonus*.' So of the fertilizing Nile he says 'discharging the duty[3] of a *colonus*.' In the passage where he warns his readers against too high farming[4] he remarks 'There are some crops that it does not pay to gather, unless the owner is employing his own children or a *colonus* of his own or hands that have on other grounds to be fed—I mean, if you balance the cost against the gain.' Here it is just possible that he means 'a tenant of his own,' that is a tenant long attached to the estate, like the *coloni indigenae* of Columella: but I think it is quite neutral, and probably he has in mind either a relative or a slave. The 'persons for whose keep he is responsible' sums up to the effect that if you have mouths to fill you may as well use their labour, for it will add nothing to your labour-bill. So far as I have seen, the difference between ownership and tenancy is not a point of interest to Pliny.

In continuation of what has been said above as to the relations of Vergil and Columella, it is necessary to discuss briefly the attitude of Pliny towards these two writers. The indices to the *Natural History* at once disclose the fact that citations of Vergil[5] are about six times as numerous as those of Columella. Indeed he seldom refers to the latter; very often to Varro, even more often to Cato. The frequent references to Vergil may reasonably be explained as arising from a wish to claim whenever possible the moral support of the now recognized chief figure of Roman literature. This was all the more easy, inasmuch as Vergil's precepts in the *Georgics*[6] are mostly old or borrowed doctrine cast into a perfect form. Columella had used them in a like spirit, but in dealing with the labour-question he faced facts, not only instructing his readers in the technical processes of agriculture, but setting forth the forms of

---

[1] *NH* xviii 11.   [2] *NH* viii 180 *tamquam colono suo interempto.*

[3] *NH* xviii 167 *coloni vice fungens.*

[4] *NH* xviii 38 *praeterquam subole suo colono aut pascendis alioqui colente domino aliquas messis colligere non expedit, si computetur impendium operae.*

[5] In *NH* xviii 120 he cites Vergil as giving a piece of advice based on the usage of the Po country. Pliny as a Transpadane may have been prejudiced in Vergil's favour and possibly jealous of the Spanish Columella.

[6] In *NH* xviii 170 he cites Verg *G* i 53, calling it *oraculum illud,* but with a textual slip.

labour-organization by which those processes were to be carried on. Now Pliny records an immense mass of technical detail, but of labour-organization he says hardly anything; for his laments over a vanished past are only of use in relieving his own feelings. And yet the labour-question, and the tenancy-question connected therewith, were the central issues of the agricultural problem. It was not the knowledge of technical details that was conspicuously lacking, but the will and means to apply knowledge already copious. Not what to do, but how to get it done, was the question which Columella tried to answer and Pliny, like Vergil, did not really face. It is curious to turn out the eight distinct references to Columella in Pliny. In none of these passages is there a single word of approval, and the general tone of them is indifferent and grudging. Sometimes the words seem to suggest that his authority is not of much weight, or pointedly remark that it stands quite alone. In one place[1] he is flatly accused of ignorance. When we consider that Pliny speaks of Varro with high respect, and positively worships Cato and Vergil, it is clear that there must have been some special reason for this unfriendly and half-contemptuous attitude. The work of Columella did not deserve such treatment. It evidently held its ground in spite of sneers, for Palladius in the fourth century cites it repeatedly as one of the leading authorities. It is not difficult to conjecture possible causes for the attitude of Pliny: but none of those that occur to me is sufficient, even if true, to justify it. I must leave it as one of the weak points in the *Natural History*.

XXXVII. TACITUS.

P Cornelius Tacitus, one of the great figures of Roman literature, passed through the time of the Flavian emperors, but his activity as a writer belonged chiefly to the reign of Trajan. Like most historians, he gave his attention to public and imperial affairs, and we get from him very little as to the conditions of labour. Of emperors and their doings evil or good, of the upper classes and their reactionary sympathies, their intrigues and perils, we hear enough: but of the poor wage-earners[2] and slaves hardly anything, for to one who still regretted the Republic while accepting the Empire, an aristocrat at heart, the lower orders were of no more importance than they had been to Cicero. Indeed they were now less worthy of notice, as free political life had ceased and the city rabble, no longer needed for voting and rioting, had

---

[1] *NH* XVIII 70.

[2] The passing mention in *Annals* XVI 13 of the great mortality among the *servitia* and *ingenua plebes* in the plague of 65 AD is a good specimen. The two classes are often thus spoken of together. Cf Sueton *Claud* 22, *Nero* 22.

merely to be fed and amused. A populace of some sort was a necessary element in the imperial capital: that it was in fact a mongrel mob could not be helped, and year by year it became through manumissions of slaves a mass of more and more cosmopolitan pauperism. The Provinces and the frontier armies were matters of deep interest, but the wars of the succession after Nero only served to exhibit with irresistible stress the comparative unimportance of Italy. Tacitus, a Roman of good family, born in Italy if not in Rome, dignified and critical by temperament, was not the man to follow the fashion of idle and showy rhetoric. He does not waste time and effort in vainly deploring the loss of a state of things that could not be restored. That the present condition of Italy grieved him, we may feel sure. But he viewed all things in a spirit of lofty resignation. That he was led to contrast the real or assumed virtues of German barbarians with the flagrant vices of Roman life was about the limit of his condescension to be a preacher: and it is not necessary to assume that the pointing of a moral was the sole motive of his tract on the land and tribes of Germany.

I have already referred to the uneasiness of Tiberius as to the food-supply[1] of Rome, dependent on importations of corn which were liable to be interrupted by foul weather and losses at sea. The risk was real enough, and the great artificial harbours constructed at the Tiber mouth by Claudius and Trajan were chiefly meant to provide accommodation for corn-fleets close at hand, with large granaries to store cargoes[2] in reserve. The slave rising of 24 AD in south-eastern Italy, and its suppression, have also been mentioned[3] above. These passages, and a passing reference to the unproductiveness[4] of the soil (of Italy) are significant of the inefficiency of Italian agriculture in the time of Tiberius. But in reporting these matters Tacitus writes as historian, not as a contemporary witness, and enough has been said of them above. A curious passage, not yet referred to, is that describing the campaign[5] against money-lenders in 33 AD. A law passed by Julius Caesar in BC 49 with the object of relieving the financial crisis without resorting to a general cancelling of debts, long obsolete, was raked up again, and there was widespread alarm, for most senators had money out on loan. It seems that some trials and condemnations actually took place, and that estates of the guilty were actually seized and sold for cash under the provisions of a disused law. Further trouble at once followed, for

---

[1] *Annals* III 54.

[2] This policy bore fruit in the possibility of forming reserves in the next period. See Spart *Severus* 8 § 5, 23 § 2.

[3] *Annals* IV 27.   [4] *Annals* IV 6 *infecunditati terrarum*.

[5] *Annals* VI 16, 17. Caesar's law is described as *de modo credendi possidendique intra Italiam*. Nipperdey holds that it cannot be the law of BC 49, but must be an unknown law, not of temporary effect. See his note.

there was a general calling in of mortgages, while cash was scarce, the proceeds of the late sales having passed into one or other of the state treasuries. Eighteen months grace had been granted to enable offending capitalists to arrange their affairs in conformity with the law. Evidently these gentry were in no hurry to reinvest their money as it came in, but waited for a fall in the price of land, certain to occur as a consequence of dearer money. In order to guard against such a result, the Senate had ordered that each (that is, each paid-off creditor,) should invest ⅔ of his loanable capital in Italian real estate, and that each debtor[1] should repay ⅔ of his debt at once. But the creditors were demanding payment in full, and it did not look well for the debtors to weaken their own credit (by practically confessing insolvency). So there was great excitement, followed by uproar in the praetor's court: and the measures intended to relieve the crisis—the arrangements for sale and purchase—had just the opposite effect. For the capitalists had locked up all their money with a view to the (eventual) purchase of land. The quantity of land thrown on the market sent prices down, and the more encumbered a man was the more difficult he found it to dispose of his land (that is, at a price that would clear him of debt). Numbers of people were ruined, and the situation was only saved by Tiberius, who advanced a great sum of money to be used in loans for three years free of interest, secured in each case on real estate[2] of twice the value. Thus confidence was restored and private credit gradually revived. But, Tacitus adds, the purchase of land on the lines of the Senate's order was never carried through: in such matters it is the way of the world to begin with zeal and end with indifference.

If I have rightly given the sense of this passage, it furnishes some points of interest. It sets before us a state of things in which a number of landowners have raised money by mortgaging their real estate, disregarding the provisions (whatever they were) of a law practically disused. This reminds us that one very general use of Italian land was as a security on which money could at need be raised. It was the only real security always available, and this inclined people to keep their hold on it, though as a direct income-producer it seldom gave good returns. No doubt they had to pay on their borrowings a higher rate[3] of interest than they got on their capital invested in land. To be forced suddenly to sell their lands in a glutted market was manifest ruin; for the whole strength of their position lay in the justified assumption that

---

[1] Nipperdey's restoration of this sentence with the help of Suet *Tib* 48 seems to me quite certain.
[2] *si debitor populo in duplum praediis cavisset.* The precedent of Augustus is mentioned in Sueton *Aug* 41.
[3] See Cicero *in Catil* II § 18.

the capital value of their land in the market exceeded the amount of their mortgage debts. Otherwise, who would have lent them the money on that security? We can hardly avoid the suspicion that the frequent use of land as a pledge may have had something to do with that unsatisfactory condition of agriculture on which the evidence of Latin writers has driven us to dwell. The mortgagor, once he had got the money advanced, had less interest in the landed security: the mortgagee, so long as he got his good return on the money lent, was unconcerned to see that his debtor's income was maintained; and that, in taking a mortgage, he had insisted on a large margin of security for his capital, is not to be doubted. For what purpose these loans were generally contracted, we are not told. Those who borrowed money to waste it in extravagance would surely have found it more business-like to sell their land outright. The number of those who preferred to keep it, though encumbered on onerous terms, simply from social pride, cannot have been really large; but they would hardly make wise landlords. Probably some men raised money to employ it in speculations[1] that seemed to offer rich returns. So long as the empire stood strong, mercantile speculation was far-reaching and vigorous. But those engaged in this line of business would seldom be able to find large sums in ready cash at short notice. Hence to them, as to spendthrifts, the sudden calling in of mortgages was a grave inconvenience.

The picture of the wily capitalists, hoarding their money till the 'slump' in land-values had fully developed, is one of all 'civilized' peoples and ages. What is notable on this particular occasion is the sequel according to Tacitus. Once their design of profiting by their neighbours' necessities was checked by the intervention of Tiberius, the investment in real estate was no longer attractive. The Senate's order was not enforced and the money-lenders could, and did, reserve their ready cash for use in some more remunerative form of investment. The slackness of the Senate may have been partly due to careless neglect, as the words seem to suggest. But it may be suspected that some members of that body had private reasons for wishing the Order of the House not to be seriously enforced. Tacitus remarks that, on the matter being laid before the Fathers, they were thrown into a flutter, since there was hardly one among them[2] that had not broken the law. This surely refers to the time-honoured trick of Roman senators, who, forbidden to engage in commerce (and money-lending was closely connected with commerce), evaded the restriction in various ways, such as holding shares in companies or lending through their freedmen as agents. So now, seeking

---

[1] See the case of Sittius in Cic *pro Sulla* §§ 56–9. Such financial opportunities were evidently few in the later Empire.

[2] *trepidique patres (neque enim quisquam tali culpa vacuus)*...etc.

a high rate of interest on their capital, they did not wish to lock up any more of it in land. Most of them would already own enough real estate for social purposes. From this episode we have some right to infer that in the period of the early Empire it had already become clear that very extensive landowning in Italy was an unwise policy for men who wanted a large income. Yet the preferential position of Italy had not ceased to be a fact; and even in the time of Trajan we have seen an imperial ordinance bidding new senators from the Provinces to invest ⅓ of their fortunes in Italian land. This might raise prices for the moment, but it had nothing directly to do with promoting agriculture. Practical farming seems to have been passing more and more into the hands of humbler persons, often freedmen, who treated it as a serious business.

That the attention of Tacitus had been directed to the methods of capitalists in Italy, and therewith to money-lending, land-holding, and slavery, may be gathered from the remarks on these subjects in his *Germany*. He writes, as Herodotus and others had done before him, taking particular notice of customs differing from those prevalent in his own surroundings. Thus he notes[1] the absence of money-lending at interest. He describes the system of communal ownership of land by village-units, and its periodic redistribution among the members of the community. The wide stretches of open plains[2] enable the Germans to put fresh fields under tillage year by year, leaving the rest in fallow (no doubt as rough pasture). Intensive culture is unknown. To wring the utmost out of the soil by the sweat of their brow is not their aim: they have no orchards or gardens or fenced paddocks, but are content to raise a crop of corn. All this is in marked contrast with Italian conditions. Even to get rid of fallows was an ambition of agriculturists in Italy, and a rotation-system[3] had been devised to this end. And, whatever may have been the case in prehistoric times, full property in land had long been established by the Roman Law, and there was in the Italian land-system no trace of redistribution for short terms of use. In treating of slavery, the first point made is its connexion with the inveterate German habit of gambling. Losers will end by staking their own freedom on a last throw; if this also fails, they will submit to be fettered and sold. To the Roman this seems a false notion of honour. He adds that to take advantage of this sort of slave-winning is not approved by German sentiment: hence the winner combines[5] scruples with profit by selling a slave of this class into foreign lands.

[1] *Germ* 26.
[2] See Schweitzer-Sidler's notes, and cf the remarks of Caesar *BG* IV 1, VI 22
[3] See Pliny *NH* XVIII 259 and Conington's notes on Verg *G* I 71–83. Varro I 44 § 3.
[4] *Germ* 24.
[5] *servos condicionis huius per commercia tradunt, ut se quoque pudore victoriae exsolvant.*

Other slaves are not employed in Roman fashion as an organized staff of domestics. Each has a lodging and home of his own: his lord requires of him a fixed rent[1] of so much corn or live-stock or clothing, as of a tenant: and he renders no service beyond this. Housework is done by a man's own wife and family. Slaves are seldom flogged or chained or put to task-work. The German may kill his slave, but it will not be as a penalty for disobedience, but in a fit of rage. Freedmen are of little more account than slaves, and are only of influence at the courts of the kings who rule some of the tribes. There they rise above the freeborn and noble: but in general the inferiority of freedmen serves to mark the superiority of the freeborn.

Tacitus had held an important official post in Belgic Gaul or one of the so-called 'Germanies' along the Rhine, and had been at pains to learn all he could of the independent barbarians to the East. The Rhine frontier was one of the Roman borders that needed most careful watching, and Roman readers took an uneasy interest in the doings of the warrior tribes whose numbers, in contrast to their own falling birthrate, were ever renewed and increased by alarming fertility. He was not alone in perceiving the contrasts between Italian and German institutions and habits, or in reading morals therefrom, expressed or implied. Germans had been employed as mercenary soldiers by Julius Caesar, and were destined to become one of the chief elements of the Roman armies. But in Italy they were perhaps more directly known as slaves. We have just seen that Tacitus speaks of a regular selling of slaves over the German border, and another passage[2] incidentally illustrates this fact in a curious manner. In the course of his conquest of Britain, Agricola established military posts on the NW coast over against Ireland. It seems to have been in one of these that a cohort of Usipi were stationed. They had been raised in the Roman Germanies, and apparently sent over in a hurry. Not liking the service, they killed their officer and the old soldiers set to train them, seized three vessels, and put to sea. After various adventures and sufferings in a voyage round the north of Britain, they fell into the hands of some tribes of northern Germany, who took them for pirates—those that were left of them. Of the fate reserved for some of these Tacitus remarks 'Some were sold as slaves[3] and, passing from purchaser to purchaser, eventually reached the Roman bank (of the Rhine), where their extraordinary story aroused much interest.' Such were the strange possibilities in the northern seas and lands where the Roman and the German met.

---

[1] *Germ* 25 *frumenti modum dominus aut pecoris aut vestis ut colono iniungit, et servus hactenus paret.* The *colonus* here is clearly a tenant, his German analogue a serf.

[2] *Agricola* 28.

[3] *per commercia venumdatos et in nostram usque ripam mutatione ementium adductos.*

NOTE ON AN AFRICAN INSCRIPTION.

It may be convenient to notice here an inscription[1] relative to irrigation in Africa. In all parts of the empire subject to drought the supply of water to farmers was a matter of importance, as it is in most Mediterranean countries to-day. Good soils, that would otherwise have lain waste, were thus turned to account. In the African Provinces much was done to meet this need, as the remains of works for storage of water clearly testify. The period 69–180 AD seems to have been marked by a considerable extension of cultivation in these parts, and particularly in southern Numidia, which at that time was included in the Province Africa. In this district, between Sitifis (Setif) and Trajan's great city Thamugadi (Timgad), lay the commune of Lamasba[2], the members of which appear to have been mainly engaged in agriculture. There has been preserved a large portion of a great inscription dealing with the water-rights of their several farms. There is nothing to suggest that the holders of these plots were tenants under great landlords. They seem to be owners, not in the full sense of Roman civil law, but on the regular provincial[3] footing, subject to tribute. To determine the shares of the several plots in the common water-supply was probably the most urgent problem of local politics in this community.

The date of the inscription has been placed in the reign of Elagabalus; but it is obviously based on earlier conditions and not improbably a revision of an earlier scheme. It deals with the several plots one by one, fixing the number of hours[4] during which the water is to be turned on to each, and making allowance for variation of the supply according to the season of the year. A remarkable feature of this elaborate scheme is the division of the plots into those below the water level into which the water finds its way by natural flow (*declives*), and those above water level (*acclives*). To the latter it is clear that the water must have been raised by mechanical means, and the scale of hours fixed evidently makes allowance for the slower delivery accomplished thereby. For the 'descendent' water was to be left flowing for fewer hours than the 'ascendent.' As a specimen of the care taken in such a community to prevent water-grabbing by unscrupulous members this record is a document of high interest. That many others of similar purport existed, and have only been lost to us by the chances of time, is perhaps no rash guess.

The water-leet is called *aqua Claudiana*. The regulations are issued by the local senate and people (*decreto ordinis et colonorum*), for the place had a local[5] government. Names of 43 possessors remain on the surviving portion of the stone. In form they are generally Roman[6]. It is noted that only three of them have a *praenomen*. Of the quality of the men it is not easy to infer anything. Some may perhaps have been Italians. Whether they, or some of them, were working farmers must remain doubtful. At all events they do not seem to belong to the class of *coloni* of whom we shall have to speak below, but to be strictly cultivating possessors. What labour they employed it is hardly possible to guess.

---

[1] CIL VIII 18587, Ephem epigr VII 788, where it is annotated by Mommsen and others.
[2] Mentioned in two routes of the *Itinerarium Antoninum*.
[3] Cf Gaius II 7, 21, and below, note on p 351.   [4] Cf Digest VIII 6 § 7, XLIII 20 §§ 2, 5.
[5] See Marquardt *Stvw* I, index under *Lamasba*.
[6] Were they perhaps *veterani*? That there were a number of these settled in Africa is attested by Cod Th XI 1 § 28 (400), cf XII 1 § 45 (358).

XXXVIII. FRONTINUS.

Sextus Julius Frontinus, a good specimen of the competent departmental officers in the imperial service, was not only a distinguished military commander but an engineer and a writer of some merit. His little treatise[1] on the aqueducts of Rome has for us points of interest. From it we can form some notion of the importance of the great waterworks, not only to the city but to the country for some miles in certain directions. For water-stealing by the illicit tapping of the main channels was practised outside as well as within the walls. Landowners[2] did it to irrigate their gardens, and the underlings of the staff (*aquarii*) connived at the fraud: to prevent this abuse was one of the troubles of the *curator*. But in certain places water was delivered by branch supplies from certain aqueducts. This of course had to be duly licensed, and license was only granted when the flow of water in the particular aqueduct was normally sufficient to allow the local privilege without reducing the regular discharge in Rome. The municipality of Tibur[3] seems to have had an old right to a branch of the *Anio vetus*. The *aqua Crabra* had been a spring serving Tusculum[4], but in recent times the Roman *aquarii* had led off some of its water into the *Tepula*, and made illicit profit out of the supply thus increased in volume. Frontinus himself with the emperor's approval redressed the grievance, and the full supply of the *Crabra* again served the Tusculan landlords. The jealous attention given to the water-works is illustrated by the decrees[5] of the Senate in the time of the Republic and of emperors since, by which grants of water-rights can only be made to individuals named in the grant, and do not pass to heirs or assigns: the water must only be drawn from the reservoir named, and used on the estate for which the license is specifically granted.

The office of *curator aquarum* was manifestly no sinecure. It was not merely that constant precautions had to be taken against the stealing of the water. An immense staff[6] had to be kept to their duties, and the cleansing and repair of the channels needed prompt and continuous attention. And it seems that some of the landowners through whose estates the aqueducts passed gave much trouble[7] to the administration. Either they erected buildings in the strips of land reserved as legal margin on each side of a channel, or they planted trees there,

---

[1] Written 97 AD, under Nerva.

[2] *de aquis* 75. Formerly this offence was punished by confiscating the land so watered, *ibid* 97.

[3] *de aquis* 6.   [4] *de aquis* 9.

[5] *de aquis* 107–10. But according to Digest XLIII 20 § 1^{39-43} (Ulpian) the grant was sometimes not *personis* but *praediis*, and so perpetual.

[6] *de aquis* 105, 116–8.   [7] *de aquis* 120, 124–8.

thus damaging the fabric; or they drove local roads over it; or again they blocked the access to working parties engaged in the duties of upkeep. Frontinus quotes decrees of the Senate dealing with these abuses and providing penalties for persons guilty of such selfish and reckless conduct. But to legislate was one thing, to enforce the law was another. Yet the unaccommodating[1] landlords had no excuse for their behaviour. It was not a question of 'nationalizing' the side strips, though that would have been amply justified in the interests of the state. But the fact is that the old practice of Republican days was extremely tender of private rights. If a landlord made objection to selling a part of his estate, they took over the whole block and paid him for it. Then they marked off the portions required for the service, and resold the remainder. Thus the state was left unchallenged owner of the part retained for public use. But the absence of any legal or moral claim has not availed to stop encroachments: the draining away of the water still goes on, with or without leave, and even the channels and pipes themselves are pierced. No wonder that more severe and detailed legislation was found necessary in the time of Augustus. The writer ends by recognizing the unfairness of suddenly enforcing a law the long disuse of which has led many to presume upon continued impunity for breaking it. He therefore has been reviving it gradually, and hopes that offenders will not force him to execute it with rigour.

What stands out clearly in this picture of the water-service is the utter lack of public spirit imputed to the landowners near Rome by a careful and responsible public servant of good repute. There is none of the sermonizing of Seneca or the sneers and lamentations of Pliny. Frontinus takes things as they are, finds them bad, and means to do his best to improve them, while avoiding the temptations of the new broom. That a great quantity of water was being, and had long been, diverted from the public aqueducts to serve suburban villas and gardens, is certain. What we do not learn is whether much or any of this was used for the market-gardens of the humble folk who grew[2] garden-stuff for the Roman market. It is the old story,—little or nothing about the poor, save when in the form of a city rabble they achieve distinction as a public burden and nuisance. It does however seem fairly certain that licenses to abstract water were only granted as a matter of special favour. Therefore, so far as licensed abstraction went, it is most probable that influential owners of *suburbana* were the only beneficiaries. Theft of water with connivance[3] of the staff was

---

[1] *impotentia possessorum.*

[2] *holitores* as in Horace *epist* I 18 36. Later called *hortulani* as in Apuleius *metam* IX 31-2, 39-42. Girard, *textes* part III ch 4 § I e, gives an interesting case of a *colonus hortorum olitoriorum* between Rome and Ostia, belonging to a *collegium*. The man is probably a freedman.

[3] *de aquis* 112-5.

only possible for those who could afford to bribe. There remains the alternative of taking it by eluding or defying the vigilance of the staff. Is it probable that the poor market-gardener ventured to do this? Not often, I fancy: we can only guess, and I doubt whether much of the intercepted water came his way. There was it is true one aqueduct[1] .the water of which was of poor quality. It was a work of Augustus, intended to supply the great pond (*naumachia*) in which sham sea-fights were held to amuse the public. When not so employed, this water was made available for irrigation of gardens. This was on the western or Vatican side of the Tiber. Many rich men had pleasure-gardens in that part, and we cannot be sure that even this water was in practice serving any economic purpose.

XXXIX. INSCRIPTIONS RELATIVE TO *ALIMENTA*.

It is impossible to leave unnoticed the inscriptions[2] of this period relative to *alimenta*, and Mommsen's interpretation[3] of the two chief ones, though their connexion with my present subject is not very close. In the bronze tablets recording respectively the declarations of estate-values in the communes of Ligures Baebiani (101 AD) and Veleia (103 AD), made with the view of ascertaining the securities upon which the capital endowment was to be advanced, we have interesting details of this ingenious scheme for perpetuating charity. But neither these, nor some minor inscribed records of bequests, nor again the experience of Pliny the younger in a benefaction[4] of the same kind, give us direct evidence on labour-questions. It is in connexion with tenure of land and management of estates that these documents mainly concern us. The fact that there was felt to be a call for charities to encourage the rearing of children was assuredly not a sign of social or economic wellbeing; but this I have remarked above.

The following points stand out clearly in the interpretation of Mommsen. The growth of large estates as against small is shewn in both the tablets as having gone far by the time of Trajan: but not so far as modern writers have imagined. In the case of the Ligures Baebiani there is record of a considerable number of properties of moderate value, indeed they are in a majority. At Veleia, though small estates have not disappeared, there are more large ones, and the process of absorption has evidently been more active. This was not strange, for the former case belongs to the Hirpinian hill country of southern Italy, the latter to the slopes of the Apennine near Placentia,

---

[1] *de aquis* 11, cf also 92.   [2] Wilmanns *exempla* 2844–8.
[3] *Hermes* XIX pp 393–416.   [4] Plin *epist* VII 18.

including some of the rich plain of the Po. The latter would naturally attract capital more than the former. I have more than once remarked that in the upland districts agricultural conditions were far less revolutionized than in the lowlands. This seems to be an instance in point: but the evidence is not complete. There is nothing to shew that the estates named in these tablets were the sole landed properties of their several owners. Nor is it probable. To own estates in different parts of the country was a well understood policy of landlords. How we are to draw conclusions as to the prevalence of great estates from a few isolated local instances, without a statement of the entire landed properties of the persons named, I cannot see. That writers of the Empire, when they speak of *latifundia*, are seldom thinking of the crude and brutal plantation-system of an earlier time, is very true. Those vast arable farms with their huge slave-gangs were now out of fashion, and Mommsen points out that our records are practically silent as to large-scale arable farming. We are not to suppose that it was extinct, but it was probably rare.

The most valuable part of this paper is its recognition of the vital change in Italian agriculture, the transfer of farming from a basis of ownership to one of tenancy. The yeoman or owner-cultivator of olden time had been driven out or made a rare figure in the most eligible parts of Italy. The great plantations, which had largely superseded the small-scale farms, had in their turn proved economic failures. Both these systems, in most respects strongly contrasted, had one point in common: the land was cultivated by or for the owner, and for his own account. But the failure of the large-scale plantation-system did not so react as to bring back small ownership. Large ownership still remained, supported as it was by the social importance attached to land-owning, and occasionally by governmental action directed to encourage investment in Italian land. Large owners long struggled to keep their estates in hand under stewards farming for their masters' account. But this plan was doomed to failure, because the care and attention necessary to make it pay were in most cases greater than landlords were willing to bestow. By Columella's time this fact was already becoming evident. He could only advise the landlords to be other than he found them, and meanwhile point to an alternative, namely application of the tenancy-system. It was this latter plan that more and more found favour. The landlord could live in town and draw his rents, himself free to pursue his own occupations. The tenant-farmer was only bound by the terms of his lease; and, being resident, was able to exact the full labour of his staff and prevent waste and robbery. The custom was for the landlord to provide[1] the equipment

---

[1] Mommsen *op cit* p 410. See index under *instrumentum*.

(*instrumentum*) of the farm, or at least most of it, including slaves. Thus he was in a sense partner of his tenant, finding most of the working capital. Whether he had a claim to a money rent only, or to a share of crops also, depended on the terms of letting. It seems that rents were often in arrear, and that attempts to recover sums due by selling up tenants' goods did not always cover the debts.

The typical tenant-farmer was certainly a 'small man.' To let the whole of a large estate to a 'big man' with plenty of capital was not the practice in Italy. Why? I think the main reason was that a big capitalist who wanted to get the highest return on his money could at this time do better for himself in other ventures: if set upon a land-enterprise, he could find far more attractive openings in some of the Provinces. Anyhow, as Mommsen says, 'Grosspacht' never became acclimatized in Italy, though we find it on Imperial domains, for instance in Africa. In connexion with this matter I am led to remark that small tenancy 'Kleinpacht' seems to have existed in two forms, perhaps indistinguishable in law, but different in their practical effect. When a landlord, letting parcels of a big estate to tenants, kept in hand the chief *villa* and its appurtenances as a sort of Manor Farm, and tenants fell into arrear with their rent, he had a ready means of indemnifying himself without 'selling up' his old tenants and having possibly much difficulty in finding better new ones. He could commute arrears of rent into obligations of service[1] on the Manor Farm. Most tenants would probably be only too glad to get rid of the immediate burden of debt. It would seem a better course than to borrow for that purpose money on which interest would have to be paid, even supposing that anyone would be willing to lend to a poor tenant confessedly in difficulties. And such an arrangement would furnish the landlord with a fixed amount of labour (and labour was becoming scarcer) on very favourable terms—he or his agent would see to that. But it was not really necessary to reserve a 'Manor Farm' at all, and a man owning land in several districts would hardly do so in every estate, if in any. Such a landlord could not readily solve the arrears-problem by commutation. He was almost compelled[2] to 'sell up' a hopeless defaulter: and, since most of the stock had probably been supplied by himself, there would not be much for him to sell. That such cases did occur, we know for certain; the old tenant went, being free to move, and to find a good new one was no easy matter, particularly as the land was sure to have been left in a bad state. Arrears of farm-rents had a regular phrase (*reliqua colonorum*) assigned to them,

---

[1] Whether we have in Columella a direct reference to this method is a question I have discussed in the chapter on that author. However answered, it does not affect the present passage. See the chapter on the African inscriptions.

[2] See the case cited in the chapter on Pliny the younger.

and there is good reason to believe that they were a common source of trouble. It has been well said[1] that landlords in Italy were often as badly off as their tenants. The truth is that the whole agricultural interest was going downhill.

If the tenant-farmer was, as we see, becoming more and more the central figure of Italian agriculture, we must next inquire how he stood in relation to labour. It is *a priori* probable that a man will be more ready to work with his own hands on a farm of his own than on one hired: no man is more alive to the difference of *meum* and *alienum* than the tiller of the soil. It is therefore not wonderful that we find tenant-farmers employing slave labour. From the custom of having slaves as well as other stock supplied by the landlord we may fairly infer that tenants were, at least generally, not to be had on other terms. Mommsen remarks[2] that actual handwork on the land was more and more directed rather than performed by the small tenants. Thus it came to be more and more done by unfree persons. This recognizes, no doubt rightly, that the system of great estates let in portions to tenants was not favourable to a revival of free rustic labour, but told effectively against it. He also points out[3] that under Roman Law it was possible for a landlord and his slave to stand in the mutual relation of lessor and lessee. Such a slave lessee is distinct from the free tenant *colonus*. It appears that there were two forms of this relation. The slave might be farming on his own[4] account, paying a rent and taking the farm-profits as his *peculium*. In this case he is in the eye of the law *quasi colonus*. Or he might be farming on his master's account; then he is *vilicus*. In both cases he is assumed to have under him slave-labourers supplied[5] by the landlord, and it seems that the name *vilicus* was sometimes loosely applied even in the former case. In the latter case he cannot have been very different from the steward of a large estate worked for owner's account. I can only conclude that he was put in charge of a smaller farm-unit and left more to his own devices. Probably this arrangement would be resorted to only when an ordinary free tenant was not to be had; and satisfactory ones were evidently not common in the time of the younger Pliny.

So far as I can see, in this period landlords were gradually ceasing to keep a direct control over the management of their own estates, but the changes in progress did not tend to a rehabilitation of free labour.

---

[1] By H Blümner in Müller's *Handbuch* ed 3, IV ii 2 p 544.

[2] Mommsen *op cit* p 416. See the chapter on evidence from the Digest.

[3] Mommsen *op cit* p 412.

[4] Digest XXXIII 7 § 20[1] *non fide dominica sed mercede. ibid* § 12[3] *qui quasi colonus in agro erat.*

[5] Dig XXXIII 7 § 20[3] *praedia ut instructa sunt cum dotibus et reliquis colonorum et vilicorum et mancipiis et pecore omni legavit et peculiis et cum actore.* Cf also XL 7 § 40[5].

One detail needs a brief special consideration. The landlord's agent (*actor*) is often mentioned, and it is clear that the *actor* was generally a slave. But there is reference to the possible case[1] of an *actor* living (like his master) in town, not on the farms, and having a wife[2] and daughter. This suggests a freedman, not a slave, and such cases may have been fairly numerous. Another point for notice is the question of *vincti, alligati, compediti*, in this period. Mommsen[3] treats the chaining of field-slaves as being quite exceptional, in fact a punishment, in Italy under the Empire. Surely it was always in some sense a punishment. From what Columella[4] says of the normal employment of chained labourers in vineyard-work I can not admit that the evidence justifies Mommsen's assertion. That there was a growing reluctance to use such barbarous methods, and that local usage varied in various parts of the country, is certain.

XL. DION CHRYSOSTOM.

We have seen that there is no lack of evidence as to the lamentable condition of Italian agriculture in a large part of the country. But things were no better in certain Provinces, more particularly in Greece. Plutarch deplores[5] the decay and depopulation of his native land, but the most vivid and significant picture preserved to us is one conveyed in a public address[6] by the famous lecturer **Dion of Prusa**, better known as Dion[7] Chrysostom. It describes conditions in the once prosperous island of Euboea. The speaker professes to have been cast ashore there in a storm, and to have been entertained with extraordinary kindness by some honest rustics who were living an industrious and harmless life in the upland parts, the rocky shore of which was notorious as a scene of shipwrecks. There were two connected households, squatters in the lonely waste, producing by their own exertions everything they needed, and of course patterns of every amiable virtue. The lecturer recounts the story of these interesting people as told him by his host. How much of it is due to his own imagination, or put together out of various stories, we cannot judge: but it is manifest that what concerns us is to feel satisfied that the experiences described were possible, and not grotesquely improbable, in their setting of place and time. I venture to accept the story as a sketch of what might very well have happened, whether it actually did so or not.

[1] Dig XXXIII 7 § 20⁴.
[2] But that *uxor* was sometimes loosely used of a slave's *contubernalis* is true. Wallon II 207, cf Paulus *Sent* III 6 §§ 38, 40, Dig XXXIII 7 § 12⁷, ³³.
[3] Mommsen *op cit* p 409.   [4] Columella I 9 § 4.
[5] Plut *de defectu oraculorum* 8.   [6] oratio VII, *Euboicus seu venator*.
[7] A contemporary of the younger Pliny, flourished about 100 AD.

We live mostly by the chase, said the hunter, with very little tillage. This croft (χωρίον) does not belong to us either by inheritance or purchase. Our fathers, though freemen, were poor like ourselves, just hired herdsmen, in charge of the herds of a rich man who owned wide farm-lands and all these mountains. When he died, his estate was confiscated: It is said that the emperor[1] made away with him to get his property. Well, they drove off his live-stock for slaughter, and our few oxen with them, and never paid our wages. So we did the best we could, taking advantage of the resources of the neighbourhood in summer and winter. Since childhood I have only once visited the city[2]. A man turned up one day demanding money. We had none, and I told him so on my oath. He bade me come with him to the city. There I was arraigned before the mob as a squatter on the public land, without a grant from the people, and without any payment. It was hinted that we were wreckers, and had put together a fine property through that wicked trade. We were said to have valuable farms and abundance of flocks and herds, beasts of burden, slaves. But a wiser speaker took a different line. He urged that those who turned the public land to good account were public benefactors and deserved encouragement. He pointed out that two thirds of their territory was lying waste through neglect and lack of population. He was himself a large landowner: whoever was willing to cultivate his land was welcome to do so free of charge,—indeed he would reward him for his pains—the improvement would be worth it. He proposed a plan for inducing citizens to reclaim the derelict lands, rent-free for ten years, and after that rented at a moderate share of the crops. To aliens less favourable terms might be offered, but with a prospect of citizenship in case of reclamation on a large scale. By such a policy the evils of idleness and poverty would be got rid of. These considerations he enforced by pointing to the pitiful state of the city itself. Outside the gates you find, not a suburb but a hideous desert. Within the walls we grow crops and graze beasts on the sites of the gymnasium and the market-place. Statues of gods and heroes are smothered in the growing corn. Yet we are forsooth to expel these hard-working folks and to leave men nothing to do but to rob or steal.

The rustic, being called upon to state his own case, described the poverty of the squatter families, the innocence of their lives, their services to shipwrecked seafarers, and so forth. On the last topic he received a dramatic confirmation from a man in the crowd, who had himself been one of a party of castaways hospitably relieved three years before by these very people. So all ended well. The stress laid on the

[1] I think Nero is meant here.
[2] Mahaffy, *Silver Age* p 329, thinks Carystos is meant, though it might be Chalcis.

simple rusticity of the rustic, and the mutual distrust and mean jealousy
of the townsfolk, shew in numerous touches that we have in this narrative a highly coloured scene. But the picture of the decayed city, with
its ancient walls a world too wide for its shrunk population, is com-
panion to that of the deserted countryside. Both panels of this mournful
diptych could have been paralleled in the case of many a city and territory in Italy and Greece. The moral reflexions, in which the lecturer
proceeds to apply the lessons of the narrative, are significant. He enlarges on the superiority of the poor to the rich in many virtues, un-
selfishness in particular. Poverty in itself is not naturally an evil. If
men will only work with their own hands, they may supply their own
needs, and live a life worthy of freemen. The word αὐτουργεῖν occurs
more than once in this spirited appeal, shewing clearly that Dion had
detected the plague-spot in the civilization of his day. But he honestly
admits the grave difficulties that beset artisans in the various trades
practised in towns. They lack necessary[1] capital: everything has to
be paid for, food clothing lodging fuel and what not, for they get
nothing free but water, and own nothing but their bodies. Yet we cannot advise them to engage in foul degrading vocations. We desire them
to live honourably, not to sink below the standards of the greedy
usurer or the owners of lodging-houses or ships or gangs of slaves.
What then are we to do with the decent poor? Shall we have to propose turning them out of the cities and settling them on allotments in
the country? Tradition tells us rural settlement prevailed throughout
Attica of yore: and the system worked well, producing citizens of a
better and more discreet type than the town-bred mechanics who
thronged the Assemblies and law-courts of Athens.

It may be said that Dion is a mere itinerant philosopher, who
travels about seeing the world and proposing impracticable remedies
for contemporary evils in popular sermons to idle audiences. But he
knew his trade, and his trade was to make his hearers 'feel better' for
attending his discourses. When he portrays the follies or vices of the
age, he is dealing with matters of common knowledge, and not likely
to misrepresent facts seriously. When he suggests remedies, it matters
little that there is no possibility of applying them. Present company
are always excepted, and the townsfolk who listened to the preacher
would neither resent his strictures on city life nor have the slightest
intention of setting their own hands to the spade or plough. That
there was a kind of moral reaction[2] in this period, and that lecturers

---

[1] ἀφορμῆς. This passage seems openly to recognize the ruinous competition of slave labour
under capitalists, which the single artisan was unable to face. The admission is so far as I
know very rare in ancient writers. That Dion's mind was greatly exercised on the subject of
slavery in general, is shewn by Orations X, XIV, XV, and many scattered references elsewhere.

[2] See the chapter on Musonius.

and essayists contributed something to the revival of healthier public sentiment, I do not dispute; though I think too much success is some-times[1] ascribed to their good intentions. At any rate they cannot be credited with improving the conditions of rustic life. To the farmer the voice of the great world outside was represented by the collectors of rents and taxes, the exactors of services, not by the sympathetic homilies of popular teachers.

XLI. NEW TESTAMENT WRITERS.

The authors of the books of the New Testament, whom it is convenient to view together as a group of witnesses bearing on the condition of a part of the Roman East under the early Empire, supply some interesting matter. We read of an agriculture that includes corn-growing, the culture of vines, and pastoral industry: the olive, and above all the fig-tree, appear as normal objects of the countryside. Plough spade and sickle, storehouse threshing-floor and winepress, are the familiar appliances of rustic life, as they had been from time immemorial. Farmers need not only hard work, but watchfulness and forethought, for the business of their lives. Live stock have to be protected from beasts of prey, and need endless care. And the rustic's outlook is ever clouded by the fear of drought and murrain. All this is an ordinary picture, common to many lands: only the anxiety about water-supply is perhaps specially Oriental. The ox and the ass are the chief beasts of draught and burden. In short, country life goes on as of old, and much as it still does after many changes of rulers.

From the way in which farmers are generally spoken of I infer that they are normally peasant[2] landowners. That is to say, not tenants of an individual landlord, but holding their farms with power of sale and right of succession, liable to tribute. The Roman state is strictly speaking the owner, having succeeded to the royal ownership assumed by the Seleucid kings. But that there was also letting[3] of estates to tenant-farmers is clear, for we read of collection of rents. At the same time we find it suggested, apparently as a moral rather than legal obligation, that the toiling farmer has the first claim[4] on the produce, and the ox is not to be muzzled. Such passages, and others insisting on honesty and the duty of labour, keep us firmly reminded of the moral aims pervading the works of these writers. In other words, they are more concerned to define what ought to be than to record what is. Many of the significant references to rustic matters occur in parables.

---

[1] As in Archbishop Trench's charming *Lectures on Plutarch* pp 10, 77 foll.
[2] Matt 21 §§ 28–30. I cannot feel sure of this general inference.
[3] Matt 21 §§ 33–41, Mar 12 §§ 1–9, Luk 20 §§ 9–16.
[4] 1 Cor 9 §§ 7—10, 1 Tim 5 § 18, 11 Tim 2 § 6.

But we must not forget that a parable would have little force if its details were not realistic.

Of the figures appearing on the agricultural scene we may distinguish the wealthy landlord[1], whether farming for his own account or letting his land to tenants: the steward[2] farming for his lord's account: the tenant-farmer: probably the free peasant on a small holding of his own. Labour is represented by the farmer working with his own hands, and by persons employed simply as labourers. These last are either freemen or slaves. Slavery is assumed as a normal condition, but a reader can hardly help being struck by the notable passages in which the wage-earner appears as a means of illustrating an important point. Does the occurrence of such passages suggest that in these Oriental surroundings wage-service was as common a system as bond-service, perhaps even more so? I hesitate to draw this conclusion, for the following reason. Accepting the fact of slavery (as the writers do), there was not much to be said beyond enjoining humanity on masters and conscientious and respectful service on slaves. But the relation between hirer and hired, presumably a bargain, opened up far-reaching issues of equity, transcending questions of formal law. Hence we hear much about it. That the workman is worthy of his meat ($\dot{\epsilon}\rho\gamma\dot{\alpha}\tau\eta\varsigma\ldots\tau\rho o\phi\hat{\eta}\varsigma$) is a proposition of which we have an earlier[3] version, referring to slaves. The cowardice of the hireling shepherd points a notable moral. The rich who defraud the reaper of his hire[4] meet with scathing denunciation. For to him that worketh the reward is not reckoned[5] of grace but of debt.

This last proposition seems to furnish a key to the remarkable parable[6] of the Labourers in the Vineyard, which has been subjected to many diverse interpretations. If we accept the view that the wages represent the Kingdom of God, and that this reward is granted not of debt but of grace, it is clear that great stress is laid on the autocratic position of the householder ($o\dot{\iota}\kappa o\delta\epsilon\sigma\pi\dot{o}\tau\eta\varsigma$). His treatment of the hired labourers is an assertion of entire indifference to what we call 'economic' considerations. How it is to be interpreted as equitable, theologians must decide, or be content to leave modern handworkers to draw their own conclusions. My interest in the matter may be shewn in the question whether this householder is to be regarded as a typical figure, or not. I trust I am guilty of no irreverence in saying that to me he seems a purely hypothetical character. That is to say that I take the gist of the parable to be this: if an employer chose to deal with his

---

[1] Luk 12 §§ 16–9, etc.   [2] $o\dot{\iota}\kappa o\nu\dot{o}\mu o\varsigma$, Luk 12 §§ 42–8, 16 §§ 1–12, 1 Cor 4 § 2.
[3] [Aristotle] *Econ* I 5 § 3 $\delta o\dot{\upsilon}\lambda\omega\ \delta\dot{\epsilon}\ \mu\iota\sigma\theta\dot{o}\varsigma\ \tau\rho o\phi\dot{\eta}$.   [4] James 5 § 4.
[5] Rom 4 § 4.
[6] Matt 20 §§ 1–16. Abp Trench, *Notes on the Parables*, has cleared away a mass of perverse interpretations.

hirelings on such arbitrary principles, he would be acting within his rights. I do not infer that such conduct was likely in ordinary life, or even that a concrete case of its occurrence had ever been known. I cannot believe that in a country where debts[1] and usury are referred to as matters of course, and where masters entrusted money[2] to their slaves for purposes of trade, where sales of land[3] were an ordinary business transaction, a sane individualistic capitalist would act as the man in this parable. Those who think differently must clear up their own difficulties. I would add that this parable, the details of which seem to me non-realistic, only occurs in one of the Gospels. Is it possible that it is based on some current Oriental story?

XLII. MARTIAL AND JUVENAL.

Among the witnesses, other than technical writers, from whom we get evidence as to the conditions of agriculture under the Empire, are two poets, Martial and Juvenal. The latter, a native of Aquinum in the old Volscian part of Latium, never shook off the influence of his connexion with rural Italy. The former, a native of Bilbilis in Spain, was one of the gifted provincials who came to Rome as the literary centre of the world. He spent more than thirty years there, and made an unrivalled name as a writer of epigrams, but his heart was in Spain. The attitude of these two men towards the facts of their time is very different, and the difference affects the value of their evidence. In the satires of Juvenal indignant rhetoric takes up a high moral position, and declaims fiercely against abominations. Now this attitude is beset with temptations to overstate an evil rather than weaken effect. Moreover, in imperial Rome it was necessary to be very careful: not only were personal references dangerous, but it was above all things necessary to avoid provoking the Emperor. Yet even Emperors could (and did) view attacks upon their predecessors with indifference or approval: while vicious contemporaries were not likely to put on the cap if their deceased counterparts were assailed. So the satirist, confining his strictures mainly to the past, is not often a contemporary witness of the first order. It is fortunate that his references to rustic conditions are not much affected by this limitation: but they mostly refer to the past. **Martial** on the contrary is a mere man of his time. His business is not to censure, still less to reform, but to find themes for light verse such as will hit the taste of average Roman readers. He soon discovered that scandal was the one staple topic of interest, and exploited it as a source of 'copy' down to the foulest dregs. Most of the charac-

---

[1] Matt 6 § 12, Luk 7 § 41, 16 § 5.   [2] Matt 25 §§ 14–30, Luk 19 §§ 12–26.
[3] Acts 1 § 18, 4 §§ 34–7.

ters exposed appear under fictitious Greek names, but doubtless Roman gossips applied the filthy imputations to each other. We need not suppose that Martial's ruling passion was for bawdy epigram. But he knew what would hit the taste of an idle and libidinous world. For himself, nothing is clearer than that he found life in the great city a sore trial, not solely from the oppressive climate at certain seasons of the year. He was too clever a man not to suffer weariness in such surroundings. He had to practice the servility habitually displayed by poor men towards the rich and influential, but he did not like it. It seems to have been through patronage that he got together sufficient wealth to enable him eventually to retire to his native country. The din and dirt and chronic unrest of Rome were to him, as to Juvenal, an abomination: and from these ever-present evils there was, for dwellers in mean houses or crowded blocks of sordid flats, no escape. Both writers agree that the Rome of those days was only fit for the wealthy to live in. Secure in his grand mansion on one of the healthiest sites, with plenty of elbow-room, guarded against unwelcome intrusions by a host of slaves and escorted by them in public, the millionaire could take his life easily: he could even sleep. Martial had his way to make as a man of letters, and needed to keep brain and nerves in working order. For this, occasional retirement from the urban pandemonium was necessary. So he managed to acquire a little suburban[1] property, where he could spend days in peace and quiet. Many of his friends did the same. To keep such a place, however small, in good order, and to grow some country produce, however little, it was necessary to have a resident[2] *vilicus*. He had also a *vilica*, and there would probably be a slave or two under them. The poet was now better off, and doing as others did. These *suburbana*, retreats for the weary, were evidently numerous. Their agricultural significance was small. Martial often pokes fun at the owners who withdraw to the country for a holiday, taking with them[3] their supplies of eatables bought in the markets of Rome. Clearly the city markets were well supplied: and this indicates the existence of another class of suburban properties, market-gardens on a business footing, of which we hear little directly. An industry of this kind springs up round every great centre of population: how far it can extend depends on the available means of delivering the produce in fair marketable condition. Round Rome it had no doubt existed for centuries, and was probably one of the most economically sound agricultural undertakings in central Italy. That it was conducted on a small scale and was prosperous may be the reason why it attracted little notice in literature.

---

[1] Often referred to. See Friedländer's index under *Nomentanus*, and cf VIII 61, IX 18, 97.
[2] I 55, X 48.   [3] III 47 etc. Cf VII 31, XII 72.

Though Martial cannot be regarded as an authority on Italian agriculture, it so happens that passages of his works are important and instructive, particularly in connexion with matters of land-management and farm-labour. He gives point to his epigrams by short and vivid touches, above all by telling contrasts. Now this style of writing loses most of its force if the details lack reality. He was therefore little tempted to go beyond the truth in matters of ordinary non-bestial life, such as agricultural conditions; we may accept him as a good witness. To begin with an all-important topic, let us see what we get from him on the management of land, either for the landlord's account under a slave *vilicus*, or by letting it to a free *colonus*. In explaining the gloomy bearing of Selius, he remarks[1] that it is not due to recent losses: his wife and his goods and his slaves are all safe, and he is not suffering from any failures of a tenant or a steward. Here *colonus* as opposed to *vilicus* must mean a free tenant, who might be behindhand with his rent or with service due under his lease. The opposition occurs elsewhere, as when he refers[2] to the produce sent in to a rich man in Rome from his country estates by his steward or tenant. So too on the birthday of an eminent advocate all his clients and dependants send gifts; among them[3] the hunter sends a hare, the fisherman some fish, and the *colonus* a kid. The *venator* and *piscator* are very likely his slaves. In protesting[4] against the plague of kissing as it strikes a man on return to Rome, he says, 'all the neighbours kiss you, and the *colonus* too with his hairy unsavoury mouth.' It seems to imply that the rustic tenant would come to Town to pay his respects to his landlord. Barring the kiss, the duty of welcoming the squire makes one think of times not long gone by in England. In one passage[5] there is a touch suggestive of almost medieval relations. How Linus has managed to get through a large inherited fortune, is a mystery in need of an explanation. He has not been a victim of the temptations of the great wicked city. No, he has always lived in a country town, where economy was not only possible but easy. Everything he needed was to be had cheap or gratis, and there was nothing to lead him into extravagant ways. Now among the instances of cheapness is the means of satisfying his sexual passions when they become unruly. At such moments either the *vilica* or the *duri nupta coloni* served his turn. The steward's consort would be his slave, and there is no more to be said: but the tenant-farmer's wife, presumably a free woman, is on a different footing. There is no suggestion of hoodwinking the husband, for the situation is treated as

---

[1] II 11 *nihil colonus vilicusque decoxit.* This may imply that the *vilicus* was a *servus quasi colonus* liable to a rent and in arrears. See notes pp 299, 311. But I do not venture to draw this inference.

[2] VII 31.   [3] X 87. Cf Juv IV 25–6, Digest XXXII § 99, XXXIII 7 § 12[13, 13], etc.
[4] XII 59.   [5] IV 66.

a matter of course. It would rather seem that the landlord is represented as relying on the complaisance of a dependent boor. If I interpret the passage rightly, we have in it a vivid side-light on the position of some at least of the *coloni* of the first century AD. That *vilici* and *coloni* alike were usually clumsy rustics of small manual skill, is suggested by two passages[1] in which they are credited with bungling workmanship in wood or stone. Perhaps we may detect reference to a *colonus* in an epigram on a man who spends his money lavishly on his own debaucheries but is meanly niggardly to necessitous friends. It says 'you sell ancestral lands to pay for a passing gratification of your lust, while your friend, left in the lurch, is tilling land[2] that is not his own.' That is, you might have made him a present of a little farm, as many another has done; but you have left him to sink into a mere *colonus*. Enough has now been said to shew that these tenant-farmers were a humble and dependent class of men, and that the picture drawn from passages of Martial corresponds to that drawn above in Weber's interpretation of Columella.

It is not necessary to set out with the same fulness all the evidence of Martial on agricultural matters regarded from various points of view. The frequent reference to the land is a striking fact: like his fellow-countryman Columella, he was clearly interested in the land-system of Italy. He shews wide knowledge of the special products of different districts; a knowledge probably picked up at first in the markets of Rome, and afterwards increased by experience. No writer draws the line more distinctly between productive and unproductive estates. That we hear very much more of the latter is no wonder: so long as the supremacy of Rome was unshaken, and money poured into Italy, a great part of the country was held by wealthy owners to whom profit was a less urgent motive than pleasure or pride. To what lengths ostentation could go is seen[3] in the perverse fancy of a millionaire to have a real *rus in urbe* with grounds about his town house so spacious that they included a real vineyard: here in sheltered seclusion he could have a vintage in Rome. This is in truth the same vulgar ambition as that (much commoner) of the man who prides himself on treating guests at his country mansion to every luxury procurable in Rome. It is merely inverted.

At this point it is natural to ask whence came the vast sums lavished on these and other forms of luxury. Italy was not a great manufacturing country. The regular dues from the Provinces flowed into the treasuries, not openly into private pockets. Yet a good deal of these monies no doubt did in the end become the reward of individuals, as salaries or amounts payable to contractors, etc. These however would

---

[1] VI 73, X 92.   [2] IX 2 *haud sua desertus rura sodalis arat.*   [3] XII 57.

not by themselves suffice to account for the immense squandering that evidently took place. A source of incomes, probably much more productive than we might at first sight imagine, existed in the huge estates owned by wealthy Romans in the lands beyond the seas. Martial refers[1] to such properties at Patrae in Achaia, in Egypt, etc. The returns from these estates, however badly managed, were in the total probably very large. And they were no new thing. In Varro and in Cicero's letters we find them treated as a matter of course: the case of Atticus and his lands in Epirus is well known. Pliny[2] tells us of the case of Pompey, and also of the six land-monopolizers whom Nero found in possession of 50 % of the Province of Africa. The practice of usury in the subject countries was no longer so widespread or so remunerative as it had been in the last period of the Republic, but it had not ceased, and the same is true of the farming of revenues. Commerce was active: but we are rather concerned with the means of paying for imported goods than with the fact of importation. The anxiety as to the supply of corn from abroad shews itself in the gossip[3] of quidnuncs as to the fleet of freight-ships coming from Alexandria. Puteoli and Ostia were doubtless very busy; all we need note is that someone must have made money[4] in the business of transport and delivery. These considerations may serve to explain the presence of so much 'money in the country' as we say, and the resulting extravagance. But all this social and economic fabric rested on the security guaranteed by the imperial forces on land and sea.

One of Martial's epigrams[5] is of special interest as describing a manifestly exceptional estate. It was at or near Baiae, the famous seaside pleasure-resort, which had been the scene of costly fancies and luxurious living for more than a hundred years. The point of the poem lies in the striking contrast of this place compared with the unproductive *suburbanum*[6] of another owner, which is kept going by supplies from the Roman market. For the place is a genuine unsophisticated country farm, producing corn and wine and good store of firewood, and breeding cattle swine sheep and various kinds of poultry and pigeons. When rustic neighbours come to pay their respects, they bring presents, such as honey in the comb, cheese, dormice, a kid, a capon. The daughters[7] of honest tenants bring baskets of eggs. The *villa* is a centre of hospitality; even the slaves are well fed. The presence of a slave-household brought from Town is particularly dwelt on: what with fishing and trapping and with 'light work' in the garden, these spoilt

---

[1] v 35, x 14, etc.   [2] Plin *NH* xviii § 35.   [3] ix 35.
[4] See Juv xiv 267–302 on the risks faced by speculators in sea-borne commerce.
[5] iii 58.   [6] iii 47.
[7] *dona matrum* 'presents from their mothers.' Eggs, I think. Cf vii 31 and Juv xi 70–1 The conjecture *ova matrum* (Paley) is good.

menials, even my lord's pet eunuch, are happy enough. There are also
young home-bred slaves (*vernae*) probably the offspring of the farm-
slaves. The topsyturvydom of this epigram is so striking that one may
suspect Martial of laughing in his sleeve at the eccentric friend whose
farm he is praising. In any case this cannot be taken seriously as a
realistic picture of a country seat practically agricultural. The owner
evidently drew his income from other sources. And the sort of man
who treated himself to an eunuch can hardly have been much of a
farmer, even near Baiae. The mention of *probi coloni* illustrates what
has been said above as to tenants, and that a farm could be described
in such words as *rure vero barbaroque* is a candid admission that in too
many instances a place of the kind could only by courtesy be styled a
farm, since the intrusion of 'civilization' (that is, of refined and luxurious
urban elements) destroyed its practical rustic character. That the estate
in question produced enough to feed the owner and his guests, his domestics brought from Rome, and the resident rustic staff as well, is
credible. But there is nothing to shew that it produced any surplus for
the markets: it may have done something in this direction, but that it
really paid its way, yielding a moderate return on the capital sunk in
land slaves and other farm-stock, is utterly incredible.

Whether in town or country, the life sketched by Martial is that
of a society resting on a basis of slavery. At the same time the supply
of new slaves[1] was not so plentiful as it had been in days before the
Roman Peace under Augustus. Serviceable rustic slaves were valuable
nowadays. Addressing Faustinus, the wealthy owner of the above
Baian *villa* and several others, the poet says 'you can send this book[2]
to Marcellinus, who is now at the end of his campaign in the North
and has leisure to read: but let your messenger be a dainty Greek
page. Marcellinus will requite you by sending you a slave. captive
from the Danube country, who has the making of a shepherd in him,
to tend the flocks on your estate by Tibur.' Each friend is to send the
other what the other lacks and he is in a position to supply. This is a
single instance; but the suggested *do ut des* is significant. As wars
became rarer, and prisoners fewer, the disposal of captives would be a
perquisite of more and more value. That the normal treatment of
slaves was becoming more and more humane, is certain. But whether
humanitarian sentiment in Stoic forms, as preached by Seneca and
others, had much to do with this result, is more doubtful. The wisdom
of not provoking discontent among the slaves, particularly in the
country, was well understood. The decline of the free rustic popula-

---

[1] The story of the Usipian deserters who found their way back into Roman hands by
way of the slave-market is a curious episode of 83 AD. Tac *Agr* 28. See the chapter on
Tacitus.   [2] VII 80.

tion had made the absence of a regular police force a danger not to be ignored. Improved conditions were probably in most cases due to self-interest and caution much more than to humane sentiment. In Martial's day we may gather from numerous indications that in general the lot of slaves was not a hard one if we except the legal right of self-disposal. Urban domestics were often sadly spoilt, and were apt to give themselves great airs outside the house or to callers at the door. But I believe that in respect of comfort and happiness the position of a steward with a slave-staff in charge of a country place owned by a rich man was in most cases far pleasanter. Subject to the preparation for the master's occasional visits and entertainment of his guests, these men were left very much to their own devices. The site of the *villa* had been chosen for its advantages. So long as enough work was done to satisfy the owner, they, his caretakers, enjoyed gratis for the whole year[1] the privileges and pleasures which he paid for dearly and seldom used.

It seems certain that it was on such estates that most of the slave-breeding took place. It was becoming a more regular practice, as we see from Columella. And it had advantages from several points of view. The slave allowed to mate with a female partner and produce children was more effectively tied to the place than the unmated labourer on a plantation was by his chain. So long as the little *vernae* were not brutally treated (and it seems to have been a tradition to treat them well), the parents were much less likely to join in any rebellious schemes. And, after all, the young of slaves were worth money, if sold; while, if kept by the old master, they would work in what was the only home they had known: they would be easier to train and manage than some raw barbarian from Germany or Britain or the Sudan. But it must not be forgotten that the recognition of slave-breeding foreboded the eventual decline of slavery—personal slavery—as an institution, at least for purposes of rustic life. I know of no direct evidence[2] as to the class or classes from which the unfree *coloni* of the later Empire were drawn. But it seems to me extremely probable that many of the *coloni* of the period with which we are just now concerned were homebred slaves manumitted and kept on the

---

[1] x 30, of a charming seaside *villa* at Formiae. *o ianitores vilicique felices, dominis parantur ista, serviunt vobis.* In Dig XXXIII 7 § 15[2] we hear of *mulier villae custos perpetua.*

[2] The note of Mommsen, *Hermes* XIX 412, deals with the case of *servi quasi coloni* farming parcels of land, recognized in the writings of jurists. It seems that they farmed either at their own risk or for owner's account [*fide dominica*]. In the former case they could have a tenant's agreement like the free *coloni*. In the latter they were only *vilici* and therefore part of the *instrumentum*. Here I think we may see beginnings of the unfree colonate. But Mommsen does not touch the point of manumission. It seems to me that an agreement with a slave must at first have been revocable at the pleasure of the *dominus*, and its growth into a binding lease was probably connected in many instances with manumission.

estate as tenants. This conjecture finds a reason for manumission, as the freedman would be capable of a legal relation, which the slave was not. The freedman's son would be *ingenuus*, and would represent, in his economic bondage under cover of legal freedom, a natural stage in the transition from the personal slave to the predial serf.

That there were *vernae* on the small suburban properties, the rest-retreats of Martial and many others, is not to be doubted. But they can hardly have been very numerous. These little places were often but poorly kept up. The owners were seldom wealthy men, able to maintain many slaves. Economy and quiet were desired by men who could not afford ostentation. The normal use of the epithet *sordidus*[1] (not peculiar to Martial) in speaking of such places, and indeed of small farmsteads in general, is characteristic of them and of the undress life led there. The house was sometimes in bad condition. To patch up a leaky roof[2] a present of a load of tiles was welcome. A man buys a place the house (*casa*) on which is horribly dark and old: the poet remarks that it is close to the pleasure-garden (*hortos*) of a rich man. This explains the purchase: the buyer will put up with bad lodging for the prospect of good dinners at his neighbour's table. The difficulty of finding a purchaser for an estate of bad sanitary record, and the damage done to riparian farms by the Tiber floods, are instances[3] of the ordinary troubles of the little landowners near Rome. A peculiar nuisance, common in Italy, was the presence in some corner of a field of the tomb[4] of some former owner or his family. A slice of the land, so many feet in length and breadth, was often reserved[5] as not to pass with the inheritance. What the heir never owned, that he could not sell. So, when the property changed hands, the new owner had no right to remove what to him might be nothing but a hindrance to convenient tillage. Altars[6] taken over from a predecessor may also have been troublesome at times, but their removal was probably less difficult.

The picture of agricultural conditions to be drawn from Juvenal agrees with that drawn from Martial. But, as said above, the point of view is different in the satirist, whose business it is to denounce evils, and who is liable to fall into rhetorical exaggeration. And to a native of central Italy the tradition of a healthier state of things in earlier ages was naturally a more important part of his background than it could be to a man from Spain. Hence we find vivid scenes[7] drawn from

---

[1] I 55 *hoc petit, esse sui nec magni ruris arator, sordidaque in parvis otia rebus amat.* And often.

[2] VII 36, XI 34.   [3] I 85, X 85. Cf Pliny *epist* VIII 17.

[4] X 61, XI 48. The title *de sepulchro violato*, Dig XLVII 12, will illustrate this.

[5] The form HNS (*heredem non sequitur*) is common in sepulchral inscriptions.

[6] X 92.   [7] Juv XIV 161-71.

legend, shewing good old Romans, men of distinction, working on the land themselves and rearing well-fed families (slaves included) on the produce of meagre little plots of two *iugera*. An ex-consul[1] breaks off his labours on a hillside, shoulders his mattock, and joins a rustic feast at the house of a relative. The hill-folk of the Abruzzi are patterns of thrifty contentment, ready to earn their bread[2] with the plough. But the civic duties are not forgotten. The citizen has a double function. He serves the state in arms and receives a patch of land[3] as his reward for wounds suffered. He has to attend the Assembly before his wounds[4] are fully healed. In short, he is a peasant soldier who does a public duty in both peace and war. The vital need of the present day[5] is that parents should rear sons of this type. Here we have the moral which these scenes, and the frequent references to ancient heroes, are meant to impress on contemporaries. A striking instance[6] from historical times is that of Marius, who is represented as having risen from the position of a wage-earning farm-labourer to be the saviour of Rome from the barbarians of the North. But the men of the olden time led simple lives, free from the extravagance and luxury of these days and therefore from the temptations and ailments that now abound. The only wholesome surroundings[7] now are to be found in out-of-the way country corners or the homes of such frugal citizens as Juvenal himself. But these are mere islets in a sea of wantonness bred in security: luxury is deadlier[8] than the sword, and the conquered world is being avenged in the ruin of its conqueror. Perhaps no symptom on which he enlarges is more significant and sinister from his own point of view than that betrayed in a passing reference by the verbal contrast[9] between *paganus* and *miles*. The peasant is no longer soldier: and in this fact the weightiest movements of some 250 years of Roman history are virtually implied.

So much for an appeal to the Roman past. But Juvenal, like Vergil before him, was not content with this. He looks back to the primitive age[10] of man's appearance on earth and idealizes the state of things in this picture also. Mankind, rude healthy and chaste, had not yet reached the notion of private property: therefore theft was unknown. The moral is not pressed in the passage where this description occurs; but it is worth noting because the greed of men in imperial Rome, and particularly in the form of land-grabbing and

---

[1] XI 86–9.   [2] XIV 179–81.   [3] XIV 159–63.   [4] II 73–4.   [5] XIV 70–2.
[6] VIII 245 foll. For the error in this tradition see Madvig, *kleine philologische Schriften* No 10.
[7] III 223–9.   [8] VI 287–95, cf XI 77–131.
[9] XVI 32–4. See Hardy on Plin *epist* x 86 B, Shuckburgh on Sueton *Aug* 27, Tac *hist* III 24 *vos, nisi vincitis, pagani*. This use is common in the Digest.
[10] VI 1–18, XV 147–58.

villa-building, is a favourite topic in the satires. All this side of contemporary life, viewed as the fruit of artificial appetites and unnecessary passions, is evidence of a degeneracy that has been going on ever
since the beginnings of society. And the worst of it is that those who
thrive on present conditions are the corrupt the servile and the mean,
from whom no improvement can be hoped for. Juvenal's picture of
present facts as he sees them is quite enough to justify his pessimism.
As a means of arresting degeneration he is only able to suggest a
change[1] of mind, in fact to urge people to be other than they are.
But he cannot shew where the initiative is to be found. Certainly not
in the mongrel free populace of Rome, a rabble of parasites and
beggars. Nor in the ranks of the wealthy freedmen into whose hands
the chief opportunities of enrichment have passed, thanks to the imperial jealousy of genuine Romans and preference of supple aliens.
These freedmen are the typical capitalists: they buy up everything,
land included; and Romans who despise these upstarts have nevertheless to fawn on them. Nor again are leaders to be found in the surviving remnant of old families. It is a sad pity, but pride of birth,
while indisposing them to useful industry, does not prevent them from
debauchery or from degrading themselves in public. Financial ruin
and charges of high treason are destroying them: even were this not
so, who would look to such persons for a wholesome example? Neither
religion with its formalities and excitements, nor philosophy with its
professors belying their moral preaching, could furnish the means of
effecting the change of heart needed for vital reform.

No, it was not from the imperial capital, the reeking hotbed of
wickedness, that any good could come. And when Juvenal turns to
the country it is remarkable how little comfort he seems to find in the
rural conditions of Italy. Like other writers, he refers to the immense
estates[2] that extended over a great part of the country, both arable
and grazing lands (*saltus*), the latter in particular being of monstrous
size. We cannot get from him any hint that the land-monopoly, the
canker of the later Republic, had been effectually checked. Nor indeed
had it. One of the ways in which rich patrons[3] rewarded clients for
services, honourable or (as he suggests) often dishonourable, was to
give the dependant a small landed estate. The practice was not new.
Maecenas had given Horace his Sabine farm. But the man who gave
away acres must have had plenty of acres to give. True, some of the
great landlords had earned[4] their estates by success in an honourable
profession: but the satirist is naturally more impressed by the cases of
those, generally freedmen, whose possessions are the fruit of corrupt

---

[1] X 356-66.   [2] VII 188-9, IX 54-5, etc.   [3] IX 59-62.
[4] VII 188-9, case of Quintilian.

compliance or ignoble trades. These upstarts, like the Trimalchio of Petronius, live to display their wealth, and the acquisition of lands[1] and erection of costly villas are a means to this end. The fashion set by them is followed by others, and over-buying and over-building are the cause of bankruptcies. Two passages[2] indicate the continued existence of an atrocious evil notorious in the earlier period of the *latifundia*, the practice of compelling small holders to part with their land by various outrages. The live stock belonging to a rich neighbour are driven on to the poor man's farm until the damage thus caused to his crops forces him to sell—of course at the aggressor's price. A simpler form, ejectment without pretence of purchase, is mentioned as an instance of the difficulties in the way of getting legal redress, at least for civilians. There would be little point in mentioning such wrongs as conceivable possibilities: surely they must have occurred now and then in real life. The truth, I take it, was that the great landlord owning a host of slaves had always at disposal a force well able to carry out his territorial ambitions; and possession of power was a temptation to use it. The employment of slaves in rural border-raids was no new thing, and the slave, having himself nothing to lose, probably found zest in a change of occupation.

In Juvenal agriculture appears as carried on by slave labour, and the employment of supplementary wage-earners is ignored; not unnaturally, for it was not necessary to refer to it. The satirist himself[3] has rustic slaves, and is proud that they are rustic, when they on a special occasion come in to wait at his table in Rome. Slaves are of course included[4] in the stock of an estate, great or small, given or sold. All this is commonplace: what is more to the satirist's purpose is the mention[5] of a member of an illustrious old family who has come down in the world so low as to tend another man's flocks for hire. And this is brought in as a contrast to the purse-proud insolence of a wealthy freedman. But more remarkable is the absence of any reference to tenant *coloni*. Even the word *colonus* does not occur in any shade of meaning. This too may fairly be accounted for by the fact that little could have been got out of references to the system for the purposes of his argument. It was, as he knew, small peasant landowners, not tenants, that had been the backbone of old Rome; and it was this class, viewed with the sympathetic eye of one sighing for perished glories, that he would have liked to restore. It is a satirist's bent to wish for the unattainable and protest against the inevitable. For himself, he can sing the praises of rustic simplicity and cheapness and

---

[1] XIV 86–95, 140 foll, 274–5. Cf X 225–6 etc.
[2] XIV 140–55, XVI 36–9. Cf Seneca *epist* 90 § 39.
[3] XI 151 foll.   [4] VI 149–52, IX 59–62.   [5] I 107–8.

denounce the luxury and extravagance of Roman society, though he dare not assail living individuals. And in exposing the rottenness of the civilization around him he attacks the very vices that had grown to such portentous heights through the development of slavery. Idleness bore its fruit, not only in the debauchery and gambling that fostered unholy greed and crimes committed to procure the money that was ever vanishing, but in the degradation of honest labour. Pampered menials were arrogant, poor citizens servile. And vast tracts of Italian land bore witness to the mournful fact that the land system, so far from affording a sound basis for social and economic betterment, was itself one of the worst elements of the situation.

At this stage it is well to recall the relation between agriculture and military service, the farmer-soldier ideal. The long-since existing tendency for the soldier to become a professional, while the free farmer class was decaying, had never obliterated the impression of this ideal on Roman minds. The belief that gymnastic exercises on Greek models were no effective substitute for regular manual labour in the open air as guarantees of military 'fitness' is still strong in Juvenal. It shews itself in his pictures of life in Rome, where such exercises were practised for the purpose of 'keeping fit' and 'getting an appetite,' much as they are now. Followed by baths and massage and luxurious appliances of every kind, this treatment enabled the jaded city-dweller to minimize the enervating effects of idleness relieved by excitements and debauchery. He significantly lays stress on the fact that these habits were as common among women as among men. The usual allowance must be made for a satirist's exaggeration; but the general truth of the picture is not to be doubted. The city life was no preparation for the camp with its rough appliances and ever-present need for the readiness to endure cheerfully the hardships of the field. The toughness of the farm-labourer was proverbial: the Latin word *durus* is his conventional epithet. In other words, he was a model of healthy hardness and vigour. Now to Juvenal, as to others, the best object of desire[1] was *mens sana in corpore sano*, and he well knew that to secure the second gave the best hope of securing the first. We might then expect him to recommend field work as the surest way to get and keep vigorous health. Yet I cannot find any indication of this precept save the advice to a friend to get out of Rome and settle on a garden-plot in the country. He says 'there live devoted[2] to your clod-pick; be the *vilicus* of a well-tended garden.' I presume he means 'be your own steward, and lend a hand in tillage as a steward would do.' But an average *vilicus* would be more concerned to get work out of his underlings than to exert himself, and Juvenal is not very explicit in

---

[1] x 356.   [2] III 223-9, *bidentis amans.*

his advice, the main point being to get his friend out of Rome. I have
reserved for comparison with this passage one from Martial[1]. In a
couplet on a pair of *halteres* (something rather like dumb-bells) he says
'Why waste the strength of arms by use of silly dumb-bells? If a man
wants exercise, he had better go and dig in a vineyard.' This is much
plainer, but one may doubt whether it is seriously meant to be an
ordinary rule of life. Probably it is no more than a sneer at gymnastic
exercises. For Martial well knew that muscle developed by the practice
of athletics[2] is very different from the bodily firmness and capacity for
continuous effort under varying conditions that is produced by a life
of hard manual labour. And the impression left on a reader's mind
by epigrammatist and satirist alike is that in Rome and in the most
favoured and accessible parts of Italy the blessing of 'corporal soundness' was tending to become a monopoly of slaves. For when Juvenal
declares[3] that nowadays the rough *fossor*, though shackled with a
heavy chain, turns up his nose at the garden-stuff that fed a Manius
Curius in the olden days, hankering after the savoury fleshpots of the
cook-shop, we need not take him too seriously.

XLIII. PLINY THE YOUNGER.

The **younger Pliny**, one of the generation who remembered Vespasian, lived through the dark later years of Domitian, and rejoiced
in the better times of Nerva and Trajan, is one of our most important
witnesses. Not being a technical writer on agriculture, it was not his
business to dwell on what ought to be done rather than what was being
done. Being himself a great landowner as well as a man of wide interests and high reputation, he knew the problems of contemporary
land-management from experience, and speaks with intelligence and
authority. He was not a man of robust constitution, and like many
others he found much refreshment in rural sojournings. He is remarkable for keen appreciation of beautiful scenery. Adopted by his
uncle, the author of the *Natural History*, well-educated and in touch
with the literary circles and the best social life of Rome, his letters
illustrate the intellectual and moral influences that prevailed in cultivated households of honest gentlemen. In particular he is to us perhaps
the very best example of the humanizing tendency of the current
philosophies of the day in relation to the subject of slavery. He is

[1] Mart XIV 49 *exercet melius vinea fossa viros.*
[2] See his use of *ingenuus* = not fit for hard work, III 46, X 47, following Ovid, and cf the
lines to a slave IX 92.
[3] Juv XI 77–81.

deeply interested in promoting manumissions[1] whenever he gets a chance. His tender concern for the welfare of his slaves constantly meets us, and he is only consoled for the death of one by reflecting that the man was manumitted in time[2] and so died free. In fact he does not regard slavery as a normally life-long condition ; and he allows his slaves to make informal wills and respects their disposition of their savings among their fellows[3] in the household, which is to slaves a sort of commonwealth. Masters who don't feel the loss of their slaves are really not human. But this all refers to domestics, and does not touch the case of the field-hand toiling on the farm.

A transaction[4] in reference to the sale of some land by the lake of Como, Pliny's own neighbourhood, illustrates the normal changes of ownership that were going on, and his own generous nature. An old lady, an intimate friend of his mother, wanted to have a property in that lovely district. Pliny gave her the offer of any of his land at her own price, reserving only certain parcels for sentimental reasons. Before (as it seems) any bargain was made, a friend died and left $\frac{5}{12}$ of his estate to Pliny, including some land such as the old lady desired. Pliny at once sent his freedman Hermes to offer her the suitable parcels for sale. She promptly clinched the bargain with Hermes at a figure which turned out to be only $\frac{7}{9}$ of the full value. Pliny's attention was called to this, but he stood by the act of his freedman and ratified the sale. The *publicani* who were then farming the 5 °/₀ duty on successions soon appeared, and claimed the 5 °/₀ as reckoned on estimated full value of the property. The old lady settled with them on these terms, and then insisted on paying to Pliny the full value, not the bargained price; which offer he, not to be outdone, gracefully declined. Such was the course of a commonplace transaction, carried out by exceptional people in an unselfish spirit. We are most certainly not to suppose that this sort of thing was common in land-dealings. Another letter[5] shews us how a well-meant benefaction might fail in its aim for want of means in the beneficiary. An old slave-woman, once Pliny's wet-nurse, had evidently been manumitted, and he made her a present of a small farm (*agellum*) to provide her maintenance. At that time its market value was ample to secure this. But things went wrong. For some reason the yearly returns fell, and the market value fell also. Whether the old woman had tried to manage it herself and failed, or whether a bad tenant had let down the cultivation, does not plainly appear. At any rate Pliny was greatly relieved when a friend, presumably one living near the place, under-

---

[1] See *epist* IV 10, VII 16, 32, VIII 16.   [2] Cf Martial I 101, VI 29.
[3] An important limitation, on which see Wallon III 55.
[4] VII 11, 14.   [5] VI 3.

took to direct the cultivation of the farm. He expresses his confidence
that under the new management the holding would recover its value.
For his own credit, not less than for the advantage of his nurse, he
wishes to see it produce its utmost. These little holdings no doubt
needed very skilful management, and I suspect that idle slaves were
in this case the cause of the trouble. Slaves commonly went with land,
and I do not think the generous donor would give his old nurse the
bare land without the needful labour. The old 'Mammy' could not
control them, and Pliny's friend saved the situation.

Trajan's order, requiring Provincial candidates for office to invest
a third[1] of their property in Italian real estate, and the artificial rise
of prices for the time, has been dealt with above. Pliny advised a
friend, if he would be not sorry[2] to part with his Italian estates, to
sell now at the top of the market and buy land in the Provinces,
where prices would be correspondingly lowered. Of the risks attendant
on landowning in Italy he was well aware, and one letter[3] on the pros
and cons of a tempting purchase must be translated in full. He writes
thus to a friend.

'I am doing as usual, asking your advice on a matter of business.
There are now for sale some landed properties that border on farms
of mine and indeed run into them. There are about them many points
that tempt me, but some equally important that repel me. The temptations are these. First, to round off my estate would be in itself an
improvement. Secondly, it would be a pleasure, and a real economy
to boot, to make one trip and one expense serve for a visit to both
properties, to keep both under the same[4] legal agent, indeed almost
under the same stewards, and to use only one of the granges as my
furnished house, just keeping the other in repair. I am taking into
account the cost of furniture, of chief servants, fancy gardeners, artisans,
and even hunting[5] outfit : for it makes a vast difference whether items
like these are concentrated in one spot or are scattered in separate
places. On the other hand I fear it may be rash to expose so large a
property to the same local climatic risks. It seems safer to encounter
the changes of fortune by not holding too much land in one neighbourhood. Moreover, it is a very pleasant thing to have change of
scene and climate, and so too is the mere touring about from one of
your estates to another. Then comes the chief issue on which I am
trying to make up my mind. The farms are productive, the soil rich,
the water-supply good ; they contain pastures, vineyards, and wood-

---

[1] VI 19.   [2] *si paenitet te Italicorum praediorum.*   [3] III 19.

[4] *sub eodem procuratore ac paene isdem actoribus habere.* The *actores* seem to be = *vilici*,
under the newer name. *procurator* a much more important person. See *paneg* 36 for the
two as grades in the imperial private service. Cf chapter on Columella p 264.

[5] *atriensium, topiariorum, fabrorum, atque etiam venatorii instrumenti.*

lands that afford timber, from which there is a small but regular return. A favoured land, you see : but it is suffering from the weakness[1] of those who farm it. For the late landlord several times distrained[2] on the tenants' goods, lessening their arrears[3] of rent for the moment, but draining their substance for the future : the failure of this sent up the arrears once more. So they will have to be equipped[4] with labour ; which will cost all the more because only trusty slaves will do. As for chained slaves, I never keep them on my estates, and in those parts nobody does. I have now only to tell you the probable price. It is three million sesterces, though at one time it was five million : but, what with the present scarcity[5] of tenants and the prevailing agricultural depression, the returns from the farms have fallen, and so has the market value. You will want to know whether I can raise easily even the three millions. It is true that nearly all I have is invested[6] in land ; still I have some money out at interest, and I shall have no trouble in borrowing. I shall get it from my mother-in-law, who lets me use her cash as if it were my own. So pray don't let this consideration influence you, provided the others do not gainsay my project ; I beg you to weigh them most carefully. For of experience and foresight you have plenty and to spare as a guide in general business, particularly in the placing of investments.'

The glimpses of agricultural conditions that we get from Pliny's letters do not as a rule give us a cheerful picture. Most of his land seems to have been under vines, and the vintage[7] was often poor, sometimes a failure. Drought and hailstorms played havoc[8] with the crops. When there was a bountiful vintage, of course the wine made a poor price. Hence the returns from the farms are small, and unsafe[9] at that. So he replies to similar complaints of friends. When he is at any of his country places he generally has to face a chorus of grumbling[10] tenants. He was sometimes utterly puzzled what to do. If inclined to make abatements[11] of rent, he is uneasily aware that this remedy may only put off the evil day. If tenants do not recover their solvency

---

[1] *sed haec felicitas terrae inbecillis cultoribus fatigatur.* No doubt lack of sufficient capital is meant.

[2] See Digest xx 2 §§ 4, 7, for *pignora* on farms.   [3] *reliqua colonorum.*

[4] *sunt ergo instruendi eo pluris quod frugi mancipiis : nam nec ipse usquam vinctos habeo nec ibi quisquam.* I take *instruendi* as referring to *agri* just above. The slaves are a normal part of *instrumentum fundi.*

[5] *hac paenuria colonorum.* Not the tenants' poverty. Cf VII 30 § 3.

[6] *sum quidem prope totus in praediis.*

[7] Daubeny, *Lectures* p 147, regards this great variation as normal in modern experience, and vineyards as the least lucrative kind of husbandry.

[8] VIII 15, IX 28, IV 6, X 8 § 5.   [9] II 4 § 3.

[10] *querellae rusticorum,* V 14 § 8, VII 30 § 3, IX 36 § 6.

[11] *remissiones,* IX 37 § 2, X 8 § 5.

(and he knows that they seldom do), he will have to change his policy[1], for they are ruining the land by bad husbandry. For himself, he is no farmer. When on a country estate, watching the progress of the vintage, he potters about[2] in a rather purposeless manner, glad to retire to his study where he can listen to his reader or dictate to his secretary : if he can produce[3] a few lines, that is his crop. It would seem that not all his farms were let to tenants. In one letter he speaks of his town-slaves[4] being employed as overseers or gangers of the rustic hands, and remarks that one of his occupations is to pay surprise visits to these fellows. We can guess what a drag upon Italian agriculture the slavery-system really was : here is a man full of considerate humanity, devoted to the wellbeing of his slaves, who cannot trust one of them to see that others do their work.

But that letting to tenants was his usual plan is evident from the number of his references to the trouble they gave him. It was not always clear whether to get rid of them or to keep them (and if the latter, on what terms,) offered the less disastrous solution of an awkward problem. In one letter[5] he gives the following excuse for his inability to be present in Rome on the occasion of a friend's succeeding to the consulship. 'You won't take it ill of me, particularly as I am compelled[6] to see to the letting of some farms, a business that means making an arrangement for several years, and will drive me to adopt a fresh policy. For in the five years[7] just past the arrears have grown, in spite of large abatements granted. Hence most (of the tenants) take no further trouble to reduce their liabilities, having lost hope of ever meeting them in full : they grab and use up everything that grows, reckoning that henceforth it is not they[8] who would profit by economy. So as the evils increase I must find remedies to meet them. And the only possible plan is to let these farms[9] not at a cash rent but on shares, and then to employ some of my staff as task-masters to watch the crops. Besides, there is no fairer source of income than the returns rendered by soil climate and season. True, this plan requires mighty honesty, keen eyes, and a host of hands. Still I must make the trial ; I must act as in a chronic malady, and use every possible treatment to promote a change.'

[1] As de Coulanges remarks pp 17-8, Pliny does not propose to get rid of them, but to keep them as partiary tenants. They would be in his debt. He uses the expression *aeris alieni* IX 37 § 2. He would have to find *instrumentum* for them.

[2] IX 20 § 2.   [3] IX 16.   [4] IX 20 § 2 *obrepere urbanis qui nunc rusticis praesunt.*

[5] IX 37.   [6] *necessitas locandorum praediorum plures annos ordinatura.*

[7] *priore lustro.* The *lustrum* or *quinquennium* was the common term of leases, and recognized in law books. Cf Digest XII 1 § 4[1], XIX 2 § 24, etc.

[8] *ut qui iam putent se non sibi parcere.*

[9] *si non nummo sed partibus locem, ac deinde ex meis aliquos operis exactores custodes fructibus ponam.* His new tenants would be *coloni partiarii.*

No doubt there were many landlords more effectively qualified to wring an income out of rustic estates than this delicate and gentle literary man. Indeed he knew this himself and made no secret of it. Writing to a friend[1] he says 'When others go to visit their estates, it is to come back the richer ; when I do so, it is to come back the poorer for the trip.' He then tells the story of a recent experience. He had disposed of the year's vintage on some estate (evidently the hanging crop) by auction to some speculative buyers, who were tempted by the apparent prospects of a rise in price to follow. Things did not turn out as expected, and Pliny felt bound to make some abatement in the covenanted price. Whether this was simply owing to his own scrupulous love of fair dealing, or whether some stipulation in the contract of sale had automatically become operative, does not seem quite clear : I should give him the benefit of the doubt. How to make the abatement equitably, so as to treat each case with perfect fairness, was a difficult problem. For, as he shews at length, the circumstances of different cases differed widely, and a mere 'flat rate' remission of so much per cent all round would not have worked out so as to give equal relief to all. After careful calculation he devised a scheme that satisfied his conscientious wish to act fairly by each and all. Of course this left him a large sum out of pocket, but he thought that the general approval of the neighbourhood and the gratitude of the relieved speculators were well worth the money. For to have a good name among the local dealers was good business for the future. Many an honest gentleman since Pliny's time has similarly consoled himself for his losses of honour, and some of them have not missed their well-earned recompense.

Among his many country properties, a certain Tuscan *villa* was one of his favourite resorts. In a long description of it and its various attractions he mentions[2] incidentally that the Tiber, which ran right through the estate, was available for barges in winter and spring, and thus enabled them to send their farm-produce by water-carriage to Rome. This confirms the evidence of other writers, as does also the letter describing the wide-spread devastation[3] caused by a Tiber flood. More notable as throwing light on conditions of life in rural Italy is a letter[4] in reply to a correspondent who had written to inform him of the disappearance of a Roman of position and property when on a journey, apparently in the Tiber country. The man was known to have reached Ocriculum, but after that all trace of him was lost. Pliny had small hopes from the inquiry that it was proposed to conduct. He cites a similar case from his own acquaintance years before. A fellow-burgess of Comum had got military promotion as centurion through

[1] VIII 2.   [2] V 6 § 12.   [3] VIII 17.   [4] VI 25.

the influence of Pliny, who made him a present of money when he set
out, apparently for Rome, to take up his office. Nothing more was
ever heard of him. But Pliny adds that in this case, as in the one just
reported, the slaves escorting their master also disappeared. Therefore
he leaves it an open question, whether[1] the slaves murdered their
master and escaped undetected, or whether the whole party on either
occasion were murdered by a robber band. The lack of a regular con-
stabulary in Italy had been, and still was, a grave defect in Roman
administration. To account for this neglect we must remember that
rich men always relied on their slave-escort for protection. If the poor
man travelled, he was not worth[2] robbing ; his danger was the chance
of being kidnapped and sold for a slave, and we have seen that some
of the early emperors tried to put down this abuse. The danger to a
traveller from his own slaves was perhaps greater on a journey than
at home ; but it was of the same kind, inseparable from slavery, and
was most cruelly dealt with by the law. Meanwhile brigandage seems
never to have been thoroughly extinguished in Italy or the Provinces[3].

In spite of these drawbacks to life and movement in a great slave-
holding community, there is nothing that strikes a reader more in
Pliny's letters than the easy acceptance of present conditions. Under
Trajan the empire seemed so secure and strong, that unpleasant occurrences could be regarded as only of local importance. That the
free population of Italy could no longer defend in arms what their
forefathers had won, was manifest. But custom was making it seem
natural to rely on armies raised in the Provinces; all the more so perhaps as emperors were being supplied by Spain. That slavery itself
was one of the cankers that were eating out the vitality of the Roman
empire, does not seem to have occurred to Pliny or other writers of
the day. Philosophers had got so far as to protest against its worst
abuses and vindicate the claims of a common humanity. Christian
apostles, in the circles reached by them, preached also obedience[4] and
an honesty above eye-service as the virtues of a slave. But in both of
these contrasted doctrines the teachers were mainly if not exclusively
thinking of domestics, not of farm-hands. There was however one
imperial department in which the distinction between slave and free
still rigidly followed old traditional rules; and it was one much more
likely to have to deal with cases of rustic slaves than of domestics.
This was the army. The immemorial rule, that no slave could be a
soldier, had never been broken save under the pressure of a few great

[1] *interceptusne sit a suis an cum suis dubium.*   [2] Cf Juvenal x 19-22.
[3] Fronto, when appointed to govern Asia, one of the most peaceful Provinces, at once
looked out for a military officer to deal with *latrones.* Fronto p 169 Naber.
[4] Paul *Ephes* 6 §§ 5 foll, *Coloss* 3 §§ 22 foll, 1 Pet 2 §§ 18 foll.

temporary emergencies, or by the evasions incident to occasions of
civil warfare. It still remained in force. When Pliny was governor of
the Province of Bithynia and Pontus he had to deal with a question
arising out of this rule. Recruiting was in progress, and two slaves
were discovered among the men enlisted. They had already taken the
military oath, but were not yet embodied in any corps. Pliny reported
the case[1] to Trajan, and asked for instructions. The emperor sent a
careful answer. 'If they were called up (*lecti*), then the recruiting
officer did wrong: if they were furnished as substitutes[2] (*vicarii dati*),
the fault is with those who sent them : but if they presented themselves as volunteers, well knowing[3] their disqualification, they must be
punished. That they are not as yet embodied, matters little. For they
were bound to have given a true account of their extraction on the
day when they came up for inspection.' What came of it we do not
know. But it is no rash guess that the prospect of escaping into
the ranks of the army would be attractive[4] to a sturdy rustic slave,
and that a recruiting officer might ask few questions when he saw a
chance of getting exceptionally fine recruits. Probably the two detected suffered the capital penalty. Such was still the rigid attitude of
the great soldier-emperor, determined not to confess the overstraining
of the empire's man-power. But the time was not far distant when
Marcus, beset by the great pestilence and at his wits' end for an army
of defence, would enrol slaves[5] and ruffians of any kind to fight for
Rome.

It is not necessary to cite the numerous references in the letters to
slaves and slavery that are not connected with agriculture. Nor need
I pursue in detail the circumstances of one of his generous public
benefactions, the alimentary endowment[6] for freeborn children, probably at Comum. It has been mentioned in another chapter, and its
chief point of interest is in the elaborate machinery employed to secure
the perpetuity of the charity. To leave money to the municipality was
to risk its being squandered. To leave them land meant that the
estate would not be carefully managed. What he did was to convey[7]
the property in some land to a representative of the burgesses, and to
take it back subject to a rent-charge considerably less than the yearly
value of the land. Thus the endowment was safe, for the margin al-

---

[1] x 29, 30, with Hardy's notes.
[2] The first reference to a practice that was common later.
[3] *cum haberent condicionis suae conscientiam.*
[4] On the other hand we hear of free citizens trying to shirk army service earlier than this.
Cf Sueton *Aug* 24, *Tib* 8.
[5] Capitolinus *Marcus* 21 §§ 6, 7.   [6] VII 18.
[7] *actori publico mancipavi.* See chapter on the *alimenta* of Trajan's time. References to
municipal benefactions are very numerous in the Digest.

lowed would ensure that the land would not be allowed to drop out of cultivation. An interesting glimpse of municipal patriotism, active and passive. The only other detail I have to note is that he regularly uses the term *colonus* as 'tenant-farmer.' I have not found a single instance of the older sense 'tiller of the soil.' We cannot argue from Pliny to his contemporaries without some reserve, for he was undoubtedly an exceptional man. But, so far as his evidence goes, it bears out the view that great landlords were giving up the system of slave steward-ships for free tenancies. Owners there still were who kept their estates in hand, farming themselves or by deputy for their own ac-count. But that some of these were men of a humbler class, freedmen to wit, we have seen reason to believe from references in the elder Pliny. Perhaps they were many, and some may even have worked with their own hands. Be this as it may, slave labour[1] was still the staple appliance of agriculture, and whenever there were slaves for sale there were always buyers.

XLIV. SUETONIUS AND OTHERS.

Suetonius, whose Lives of the first twelve emperors contain much interesting and important matter, stands in relation to the present inquiry on the same footing as most of the regular historians. He flourished in the times of Trajan and Hadrian, and therefore what remains of his writings is not contemporary evidence. But he was a student and a careful compiler from numerous works now lost. The number of passages in which he refers to matters directly or indirectly bearing on rustic life and labour is not large, and most of them have been cited in other chapters, where they find a place in connexion with the context. He can be dealt with very briefly here.

The close connexion between wars and the supply of slaves is marked in the doings of Julius[2] Caesar. Gaulish and British captives were (as Caesar himself records) no small part of the booty won in his northern campaigns. He rewarded his men after a victory with a prisoner apiece: these would soon be sold to the dealers who followed the army, and most of them would find their way to the Roman slave-market. To gratify friendly princes or provincial communities, he sent them large bodies of slaves as presents. So his victims served instead of cash to win adherents for their new master. And these natives of the North would certainly be used for heavy rough work, mostly as farm-hands. When Augustus, loth to enlarge the empire,

---

[1] As we have seen above, the tenant *coloni* employed slave labour. Whether they worked with their own hands, or confined themselves to direction, probably varied in various cases.

[2] Sueton *Julius* 26, 28.

felt constrained to teach restless tribes a lesson, he imposed a reserve-
condition[1] on the sale of prisoners taken: they were not to be employed in districts near their old homes, and not to be manumitted
before thirty years. Most of these would probably also be brought to
Italy for the same kind of service. Yet, as we have seen, there was
kidnapping[2] of freemen in Italy; probably a sign that slaves were
already become dear. That their numbers had been reduced in the
civil wars, not only by death but by manumission, is fairly certain. In
the war with Sextus Pompeius it was found necessary[3] to manumit
20,000 slaves to serve as oarsmen in the fleet. Suetonius also records
that Augustus when emperor had trouble with the unwillingness of
Romans to be called up for military duty. He had to deal sharply[4]
with an *eques* who cut off the thumbs of his two sons to incapacitate
them. The abuse of the public corn-doles was a grave evil. Men got
rid of the burden of maintaining old slaves by manumitting them and
so making them, as freedmen-citizens, entitled to a share of the doles.
This was shifting the burden of feeding useless mouths on to the
state. Augustus saw that the vast importation of corn for this bounty
tended to discourage[5] Italian agriculture, and thought of abolishing
the whole system of *frumentationes*. But he had to give up the project,
being convinced that the system would be restored. He really desired
to revive agriculture, and it was surely with this aim that he advanced
capital sums[6] to landlords free of interest on good security for the
principal. The growth of humane sentiment toward slaves is marked
by the ordinance of Claudius[7] against some very cruel practices of
slaveowners. And we are reminded that penal servitude was now a
regular institution in the Roman empire by Nero's order[8] for bringing
prisoners from all parts to carry out some colossal works in Italy, and
for fixing condemnation to hard labour as the normal penalty of crime.

In the Lives of the three Flavian emperors there are one or two
passages of interest. At this distance of time it is not easy to appreciate the effect on the sentiments of Roman society of the extinction
of the Julio-Claudian house, and the accession of a thoroughly plebeian
one, resting on the support of the army and readily accepted by the
Provinces. Suetonius, like Tacitus, was near enough to the revolutionary year 69 AD to understand the momentous nature of the crises
that brought Vespasian to the head of affairs. He takes pains to
describe[9] the descent of the new emperor from a Sabine family of no

---

[1] *Aug* 21 *sub lege...ne in vicina regione servirent neve intra tricesimum annum libera-
rentur.* See Shuckburgh's note.

[2] *Aug* 32, *Tiber* 8.   [3] *Aug* 16.   [4] *Aug* 24.

[5] *Aug* 42 *quod earum* [*frumentationum*] *fiducia cultura agrorum cessaret.*

[6] *Aug* 41 *usum eius* (*pecuniae*) *gratuitum iis qui cavere in duplum possent.*

[7] *Claud* 25.   [8] *Nero* 31.   [9] *Vesp* 1.

remarkable distinction. For two generations they had combined with
fair success the common Roman professions of military service and
finance. They were respectable people of good local standing. But
there was another story relative to a generation further back. It was
said that Vespasian's greatgrandfather (this takes us back to Republican days) had been a contractor[1] for rustic labour. He was a
headman or 'boss' of working-parties such as are wont to pass year
after year from Umbria into the Sabine country to serve as farm-
labourers. Of this story Suetonius could not discover any confirmation. But that there had been, and perhaps still was, some such supply
of migratory labour available, is a piece of evidence not to be ignored.
Vespasian himself was a soldier who steadily rose in the usual official
career till he reached the coveted post of governor of Africa. After a
term of honest but undistinguished rule, he came back no richer than
he went, indeed he was very nearly bankrupt. He was driven to mortgage all his landed estate, and to become for a time a slave-dealer[2],
in order to live in the style that his official rank required. The implied disgrace of resorting to a gainful but socially despised trade is at
least evidence of the continual demand for human chattels. Of two
acts of Domitian[3], his futile ordinance to check vine-growing, and his
grant of the remaining odd remnants of Italian land to present occupants, enough has been said above.

It is not necessary to collect the numerous passages in writers of
this period that illustrate the growing change of view as to slavery in
general. The point made by moralists, that moral bondage is more
degrading than physical (for the latter need not be really degrading),
came with not less force from Epictetus the slave than from Seneca
the noble Roman. It is however worth while just to note the frequent
references to cases of philosophers and other distinguished literary
men who had either actually been slaves or had at some time in their
lives been forced to earn their daily bread by bodily labour. Such
cases are, Cleanthes[4] drawing water for wages, Plautus[5] hired by the
baker to grind at his mill, and Protagoras[6] earning his living as a
common porter. In one passage several slaves[7] are enumerated who
became philosophers. Now, what is the significance of these and other
references of the same import? I suggest that they have just the same

---

[1] *mancipem operarum quae ex Umbria in Sabinos ad culturam agrorum quotannis com-
meare soleant.*

[2] *Vesp* 4 *ad mangonicos quaestus.* Hence his nickname *mulio,* for which as a sign of
indigence cf Gellius XV 4.

[3] *Domit* 7, 9. See p 272.

[4] Fronto p 144 Naber, cf Seneca *epist* 44 § 3.

[5] Sueton *fragm* p 24 Reifferscheid, Gellius III 3.

[6] Gellius V 3.   [7] Gellius II 18.

bearing as the general principles of common humanity argumenta-
tively pressed by the Stoic and other schools of thought. The sermonizing of Seneca is a good specimen. But discussion of principles
in the abstract was never the strong point of Roman society, and citation of concrete instances would serve to give reality to views that
were only too often regarded as the visionary speculations of chattering Greeks. That Roman authors, down to the last age of Roman
literature, expressed the longing for a more wholesome state of agriculture by everlasting references to Cincinnatus and the rest of the
traditional rustic heroes, is another recognition of this method. The
notion that courage and contempt of death could be fostered by the
spectacle of gladiators rested on much the same basis. True, there is
nothing in the above considerations that directly bears upon rustic
labour as such: but hints that 'a man's a man for a' that' are not to
be ignored when they make their appearance in the midst of a slave-
holding society.

XLV. APULEIUS.

The Province of Africa was in this period a flourishing part of the
empire, giving signs of its coming importance in the next generation,
when it produced several emperors. It was in fact a sort of successor
of Spain, and like Spain it enjoyed the advantage of not fronting on
the usual seats of war to the North and East. One of the most remarkable literary figures of the age was the African[1] L Apuleius of
Madaura, who travelled widely as student and lecturer, and was well
acquainted with Greece and Italy. A philosopher of the mystical-
Platonist type, he was in touch with practical life through his study of
the Law, and was for some time a pleader in Rome. His native Province[2] was notoriously addicted to litigation, and a modern scholar[3]
has shewn that the works of Apuleius abound in legal phraseology
and are coloured with juristic notions. Now, it was not possible to
go far in considering property and rights without coming upon
questions relative to land: moreover, he himself owned land in Africa.
Accordingly we find in him some references to land, and even to
rustic labour and conditions of rural life. And, though his *Metamorphoses* is a fantastic romance, there is no reason to doubt that incidents
and scenes (other than supernatural) are true to facts observed by the
writer, and therefore admissible as evidence of a general kind. An

---

[1] Madaura was in the Numidian part of the Province, near the Gaetulian border. See
the *Apologia* 24. Oea, referred to below, was in the eastern strip, on the coast.

[2] Juvenal VII 148–9 *nutricula causidicorum Africa*.

[3] F Norden *Apuleius von Madaura und das Römische Privatrecht* (Teubner 1912).

instance may be found in the case of the ass, that is the hero of the story transformed into that shape by magic. He is to be sold, and the waggish auctioneer[1] says to a possible bidder 'I am well aware that it is a criminal offence to sell you a Roman citizen for a slave: but why not buy a good and trusty slave that will serve you as a helper both at home and abroad?' Here we have a recognition of the fact of kidnapping, which is referred to elsewhere in the book; that in cases of Roman victims the law took a very serious view of the offence; while the point of the pleasantry lies in the circumstance that neither auctioneer nor company present are aware that the ass is a transformed man, liable to regain his human shape by magical disenchantment.

The scene of the *Metamorphoses* is laid in Greece, and the anecdotes included in it do not give us a favourable picture of that part of the Roman empire. There was surely nothing to tempt the writer to misrepresent the condition of the country by packing his descriptions with unreal details: he would thus have weakened the effect of his romance. Wealth in the hands of a few, surrounded by a pauper majority; shrunken towns, each with its more or less degraded rabble; general insecurity for life liberty and property; a cruel and arbitrary use of power; a spiritless acquiescence in this pitiful state of things, relieved by the excitements of superstition and obscenity: such was Roman Greece as Apuleius saw it. No doubt there was Roman Law to enforce honesty and order. But the administration of justice seldom, if ever, reaches the standard of legislation; and as yet the tendency of the Roman government was to interfere as little as possible with local authorities. Greece in particular had always been treated with special indulgence, in recognition of her glorious past. Whether the effects of this favour were conducive to the wellbeing of the country, may fairly be doubted. The insane vanity of Nero, masquerading as Liberator of Greece, had surely done more harm than good. Hadrian's benefactions to Athens, dictated by sentimental antiquarianism, could not improve the general condition of the country, however satisfactory they might be to what was now an University town living on students and tourists.

One of the first things that strikes a reader of this book is the matter-of-fact way in which brigandage[2] is taken for granted. These robbers work in organized bands under chosen captains, have regular strongholds as bases of operations, draw recruits from the poverty-stricken peasantry or slaves, and do not hesitate to attack and plunder great mansions, relying on the cowardice or indifference (or perhaps

---

[1] *Metamorphoses* VIII 24. See Norden's remarks pp 83–4.
[2] See for instance *Metam* IV 9, VI 31, VII 4, 9.

treachery) of the rich owner's slaves. Murder is to them a mere trifle, and their ingenuity in torturing is fiendish. No doubt their activities are somewhat exaggerated as a convenient part of the machinery of the story, but the lament of Plutarch and the Euboic idyll of Dion forbid us to regard these brigand-scenes as pure fiction. They are another side of the same picture of distressful Greece. Nor is the impression produced thereby at all weakened by a specimen of military[1] insolence. Greece was not a Province in which a large army was kept, but all Governors had some armed force to support their authority. The story introduces the ass with his present owner, a gardener, on his back. They are met by a swaggering bully of a soldier, who inquires where they are going. He asks this in Latin. The gardener makes no reply, not knowing Latin. The angry soldier knocks him off the ass, and repeats his question in Greek. On being told that they are on their way to the nearest town, he seizes the ass on the pretext of being wanted for fatigue duty in the service of the Governor, and will listen to no entreaties. Just as he is preparing to break the gardener's skull, the gardener trips him up and pounds him to some purpose. He shams dead, while the gardener hurries off and takes refuge with a friend in the town. The soldier follows, and stirs up his mates, who induce the local magistrates to take up the matter and give them satisfaction. The gardener's retreat is betrayed by a neighbour, and clever concealment nullified by an indiscretion of the ass. The wretched gardener is found and haled off to prison awaiting execution, while the soldier takes possession of the ass. This story again is surely not grotesque and incredible fiction. More likely it is made up from details heard by the African during his sojourn in Greece. If scenes of this kind were possible, the outlook of humble rustics[2] can hardly have been a cheerful one.

That perils of robbers and military insolence were not the only troubles of the countryside, is shewn by the following anecdote[3] describing the brutal encroachments of a big landlord on poorer neighbours. A landowner, apparently a man of moderate means, had three sons, well-educated and well-behaved youths, who were close friends of a poor man with a little cottage of his own. Bordering on this man's little holding was the large and fertile landed estate belonging to a rich and powerful neighbour in the prime of life. This rich man, turning the fame of his ancestors to bad account, strong in the support

---

[1] *Metam* IX 39-42.

[2] It seems certain that the convenience of humble rustics was little regarded by the upper classes. Even Marcus Aurelius (in Fronto p 35 Naber) confesses to the reckless scattering of a flock of sheep and to having been taken for a mounted brigand.

[3] *Metam* IX 35-8. This is a case of *periculum mortis ab hominis potentis crudelitate aut odio*, referred to Digest XXXIX 6 § 3 [Paulus] as a risk like that of war or brigandage.

of party cliques, in fact an autocrat[1] within the jurisdiction of the town, was given to making raids on the poverty of his humble neighbour. He slaughtered his flocks, drove off his oxen, and trampled down his crops before they were ripe, till he had robbed him of all the fruit of his thrift. His next desire was to expel him altogether from his patch of soil: so he got up a baseless dispute over boundaries, and claimed the whole of the land as his own. The poor man, though diffident by nature, was bent upon keeping his hereditary ground if only for his own burial. The claim upset him greatly, and he entreated a number of his friends to attend at the settlement[2] of boundaries. Among those present were the three brothers mentioned above, who came to do their little best in the cause of their injured friend. But the rich man, unabashed by the presence of a number of citizens, treated all efforts at conciliation with open contempt, and swore that he would order his slaves to pick the poor man up by the ears and chuck him ever so far from his cottage in less than no time. The bystanders were greatly incensed at this brutal utterance. One of the three brothers dared to say ' It's no good your bullying and threatening like this just because you are a man of influence; don't forget that even poor[3] men have found in the laws guarding freemen's rights a protector against the outrages of the rich.' Upon this the enraged tyrant let loose his ferocious dogs[4] and set them on the company. A horrible scene followed. One of the three youths was torn to pieces, and the others also perished ; one of them slain by the rich man himself, the other, after avenging his brother, by his own hand.

The mere aggression of the rich landlord on the poor is interesting as adding another instance of the encroachments to the occurrence of which many other writers testify. The most remarkable feature of the story is the insolent disregard of the Law shewn by the rich man from first to last. That the governor of the Province could prevent or punish such outrages, if his attention were called to them, is not to be doubted. But he could not be everywhere at once, and it is not likely that many of the poorer class would be forward to report such doings and appear as accusers of influential persons. The rich probably sympathized with their own class, and a poor man shrank from a criminal prosecution that would in any event expose him to their vengeance afterwards. True, the poor were the majority. But it was a very old principle of Roman policy to entrust the effective control of municipalities to the burgesses of property, men who had something to lose and who, being a minority, would earn their local

---

[1] *cuncta facile faciens in civitate.*   [2] Norden pp 161–3.

[3] *cum alioquin pauperes etiam liberali legum praesidio de insolentia locupletium consueverint vindicari.*

[4] Fierce dogs seem to have been a marked feature of country life. See VIII 17, IX 2.

supremacy by a self-interested obedience to the central government. Thus local magnates (their evil day was not yet come) were left very much to their own devices, and most provincial governors cared too much for their own ease and comfort to display an inquisitive zeal. Moreover, so far as the rich thought it judicious to keep the poorer contented, it would be the town rabble that profited chiefly if not exclusively by their liberalities: the more isolated rustic was more liable to suffer from their land-proud greediness. We must picture them as overbearing and arbitrary slaveholders, practically uncontrolled; and the worst specimens among them as an ever-present terror to a cowed and indigent peasantry. We are not to suppose that things were as bad as this in all parts of Greece, but that there was little or nothing to prevent their becoming so, even in happier districts.

From time immemorial the Greek tendency had been to congregate in towns, and after the early fall of the landowning aristocracies this tendency was strengthened by democratic movements. The country as a whole was never able to feed its population. But the population was now greatly reduced. Given due security, perhaps the rustics might now have been able to feed the towns. And that they were to some extent doing so may be inferred from the fact that the chief peasant figure in the rural life of the *Metamorphoses* is the market-gardener[1]. If he is but left in peace, he seems to be doing fairly well. It is natural at this point to inquire whether a *hortulanus* might not also be a *colonus*, the former name connoting his occupation and the latter his legal position in relation to the land. Both terms often occur, but they seem to be quite distinct: I can find nothing to justify the application of both to the same person. And yet I cannot feel certain that Apuleius always means a tenant-farmer[2] under a landlord whenever he uses the word *colonus*. Probably he does, as Norden seems to think. In any case the gardener is evidently in a smaller way of business than the average *colonus*, and it may be that his little scrap of land is his own. He certainly works[3] with his own hands, and I find nothing to suggest that he is an employer of slaves, or that he himself is not free. That the tenant-farmers were often *coloni partiarii*, bound to deliver to their landlord a fixed share of their produce in kind, is highly probable. But this does not exclude the payment of money rents as well. Local usage probably varied in different districts. It is true that Apuleius several times[4] uses *partiarius* metaphorically,

---

[1] *hortulanus*, see IV 3, IX 31–2, 39–42.

[2] See V 17, VII 15, VIII 17, 29, 31. Cf Norden pp 88–9.

[3] IX 32. Cf the case of small farmers in Africa, *Apol* 17, 23.

[4] See IV 30, VIII 26. Cf Norden p 89, and pp 84–5 on metaphorical use of the legal term *postliminium*, which occurs also in Rutilius *de reditu* I 214.

but this only shews his addiction to legal language, and is no proof of the prevalence of the share-system in Greece. The *coloni*, nominally free, were as yet only bound to the soil by the practical difficulty of clearing themselves from the obligations that encumbered them and checked freedom of movement. But they were now near to the time when they were made fixtures by law.

Another work of Apuleius furnishes matter of interest, the so-called *Apologia*, a speech in his own defence when tried on a charge of magical arts about the year 158 AD. That the accused was in no little danger from this criminal prosecution has been shewn[1] by Norden. What concerns us is the reference to rustic affairs that the speaker is led to make in the course of his argument, when demolishing some of the allegations of his enemies. The trial was in Africa at the regular provincial assize, and the conditions referred to are African. Apuleius, as a man of note in his native Province, takes high ground to manifest his confidence in the strength of his case. The prosecution want to draw him into an unseemly squabble over side-issues. As the chief alleged instance of his magic was connected with his marriage to a rich lady, a widow of mature age, whom he was said to have bewitched, being at the time a young man in need, it had evidently been thought necessary to discuss his financial position as throwing light upon his motives. If at the same time he could be represented as having acted in defiance of well-known laws, so much the better. If we may trust the bold refutation of Apuleius, they entangled themselves in a contradiction and betrayed their own blind malice. His reply[2] is as follows. 'Whether you keep slaves to cultivate your farm, or whether you have an arrangement with your neighbours for exchange[3] of labour, I do not know and do not want to know. But you (profess to) know that at Oea, on the same day, I manumitted three slaves: this was one of the things you laid to my charge, and your counsel brought it up against me, though a moment before he had said that when I came to Oea I had with me but a single slave. Now, will you have the goodness to explain how, having but one, I could manumit three,—unless this too is an effect of magic. Was there ever such monstrous lying, whether from blindness or force of habit? He says, Apuleius brought one slave with him to Oea. Then, after babbling a few words, he adds that Apuleius manumitted three in one day at Oea. If he had said that I brought with me three, and granted freedom to them all, even that would not have deserved[4] belief. But, suppose

---

[1] Norden pp 26–7.   [2] *Apologia* 17.
[3] *an ipse mutuarias operas cum vicinis tuis cambies.*
[4] Because of the strict rules of the laws passed to check manumission. Gaius I §§ 42–7. Norden p 86.

I had done so, what then? would not three freedmen be as sure a mark of wealth as three slaves of indigence?'

After this outburst the speaker is at pains to point out that to do with few slaves is a philosopher's part, commended by examples not of philosophers only but of men famed in Roman history. The well-worn topic of the schools, that to need little is true riches, is set forth at large, with instances in illustration. He then asserts[1] that he inherited a considerable property from his father, which has been much reduced by the cost of his journeys and expenses as a student and gifts to deserving friends. After this he turns upon his adversary. 'But you and the men of your uneducated rustic class are worth just what your property is worth and no more, like trees that bear no fruit and are worth only the value of the timber in their stems. Henceforth you had better not taunt any man with his poverty. Your father left you nothing but a tiny farm at Zarat, and it is but the other day that you were taking the opportunity of a shower of rain to give it a good ploughing with the help of a single ass, and made it a three-days[2] job. What has kept you on your legs is the quite recent windfalls of inheritances from kinsmen who died one after another.' These personalities, in the true vein of ancient advocacy, do not tell us much, but it is interesting to note that the skilled pleader, a distinguished man of the world, quite naturally sneers at his opponent for having been a poor working farmer. Whether this was an especially effective taunt in the Province Africa, the home of great estates, it is hardly possible to guess.

Of small farmers in Africa, working their own land, we have, probably by accident, hardly any other record. But the reference above, to neighbours taking turns to help one another on their farms, comes in so much as a matter of course that we may perhaps conclude that there were such small free farmers, at least in some parts of the Province. For slaves we need no special evidence. But the lady whom Apuleius had married seems to have been a large slaveowner as well as a large landowner. He declares that he with difficulty persuaded her to quiet the claims of her sons by making over to them a great part of her estate in land and other goods; and one item consists[3] of 400 slaves. We have also a reference to *ergastula* in a passage where he is protesting that to charge him with practising magic arts with the privity of fifteen slaves is on the face of it ridiculous[4]. 'Why, 15

---

[1] *Apol* 23.   [2] *triduo exarabas*, to mark the smallness of the *agellus*.
[3] *Apol* 93.
[4] *Apol* 47 XV *liberi homines populus est, totidem servi familia, totidem vincti ergastulum.* See Norden p 87. *ergastulum* = the inmates of a lock-up, regarded as a body. See quotations from Columella p 263 and Pliny p 285, Mayor on Juvenal XIV 24, and cf Lucan II 95. So *operae* is used = 'hands.'

free men make a community, 15 slaves make a household, and 15 chained ones a lock-up.' I take these *vincti* to be troublesome slaves, not debtors. Again, in refuting the suggestion that he had bewitched the lady, he states as proof of her sanity that at the very time when she is said to have been out of her mind she most intelligently audited and passed the accounts of her stewards[1] and other head-servants on her estates. And in general it has been well said[2] that Apuleius, with all his wide interest in all manner of things, did not feel driven to inquire into the right or wrong of slavery in itself. He took it as he found it in the Roman world of his day. That he had eyes to see some of its most obvious horrors, may be inferred from the description[3] of the condition of slaves in a flour-mill, put into the mouth of the man-ass. But with the humanitarian movements of these times he shews no sympathy; and he can depict abominable scenes of cruelty and bestiality without any warmth of serious indignation.

[1] *viliconum, Apol* 87. Cf *Metam* VIII 22.
[2] Norden p 81.　　　　　　　　　　[3] *Metam* IX 12.

COMMODUS TO DIOCLETIAN

XLVI. GENERAL INTRODUCTION.

The death of Marcus Aurelius in 180 AD brings us to the beginning of a long period of troubles, in which the growing weakness of the empire was exposed, the principate-system of Augustus finally failed under the predominance of military power, and the imperial government was left to be reorganized by Diocletian on a more Oriental model. There is no doubt that during some hundred years the internal wellbeing of the Roman empire was being lowered, and that the parts most open to barbarian invasion suffered terribly. But the pressure of taxation to supply military needs bore heavily on all parts and impaired the vitality of the whole. Reactions there were now and then, when a strong man, or even a well-meaning one, became emperor and had a few years in which to combat present evils and for the moment check them. But the average duration of reigns was very brief; emperors were generally murdered or slain in battle; from 249 to 283 the chief function of an emperor was to lead his army against barbarian invaders. It is a remarkable fact that the first half of this unhappy century was the classical period of Roman jurisprudence. The important post of Praetorian Prefect, which began with a dignified military command and was more and more becoming the chief ministry of the Empire, was again and again held by eminent jurists. But in the long run the civil power could not stand against the jealousy of the military, and the murder of Ulpian in 228 practically ends the series of great lawyer-ministers, leaving the sword in undisputed control. The authorities for this century of troubles are meagre and unsatisfactory. With the help of contemporary inscriptions, modern writers are able to compose some sort of a history of the times, so far as public events and governmental activities are concerned. But the literature of private life, the source of our best evidence on agricultural labour, is for the time at an end, and the facts of farm life were not of the kind thought worthy of record in inscriptions.

There is therefore nothing to be done but to glean the few scraps of information that in any way bear upon the condition of tillers of the soil in this period. They are as a rule of little value, and they come from writers of little authority. But it is something if they are of a piece with the general record of these unhappy times. Even the imperial biographies of Marius Maximus survive only in the meagre abstracts of later writers, and modern historians are quite unable to reconstruct any clear picture of the inner life of the period 180–284 AD owing to the lack of materials.

The most significant piece of information relates to Pertinax. We are told[1] that one of the useful reforms contemplated by him was the reclamation of waste lands throughout the empire. He ordained that any one might occupy derelict lands, even on the imperial estates: on careful cultivation thereof, the farmer was to become owner[2]. For a space of ten years he was to be exempt from all taxation, and his ownership was to be guaranteed against future disturbance. This passage is good evidence of the decay of agriculture, agreeing with what we have learnt from other sources. But we cannot gather from it that the well-meant design had any practical effect. Pertinax was only emperor for the inside of three months, and could not realize his virtuous aspirations. About 80 years later we find Aurelian[3] planning the development of waste lands in Etruria, and Probus[4] giving allotments in the wilds of Isauria to his veterans as settlers with obligation of military service. There can be little doubt that the depopulation and decline of cultivation, made sadly manifest in the calamitous times of Marcus Aurelius, had never ceased to undermine the vital forces of the empire. How to fill up deserted lands, and make them productive of food and revenue, was the problem that every serious ruler had to face. And there was in fact only one resource available to meet the need. The native population of the empire, stationary at best, had been further reduced by pestilence and famine, and was not able to fill up the spaces laid waste by frontier wars. Hence the policy of bringing in masses of barbarians, adopted by Marcus, had to be repeated again and again.

We must not confuse these settlements with the immigrations of conquering tribes that occurred later. Rome was still superior to her adversaries in military organization and skill, and under fairly equal conditions able to defeat them in pitched battles. Thus Claudius II gained great victories over the Goths, and the biographer[5] tells us of the sequel. 'The Roman provinces were filled with barbarian slaves and Scythian tillers of the soil. The Goth was turned into a settler on the barbarian frontier. There was not a single district but had some Gothic slave whose bondage attested the triumph.' Here we seem to have the echo of a somewhat boastful contemporary version. The mention of both slaves and frontier colonists is to be noted. We have no statistics to guide us in an attempt to estimate the relative numbers of the two classes. But the settlement of defeated barbarians on the

---

[1] Herodian II 4 § 6.   [2] δεσπότης.
[3] Vopisc *Aurel* 48 § 2.   [4] Vopisc *Probus* 16 § 6.
[5] Trebell *Claud* 9 §§ 4, 5. *Scythicis* is an emendation. *senibus* MSS.

frontier as Roman subjects is clearly regarded as a worthy achievement. So indeed it might have been, had it been possible to civilize
them as Romans, only profiting by the introduction of new blood. But
this process was no longer possible: its opposite, the barbarizing of
Roman lands, steadily went on. Claudius only reigned about two
years. The great soldier who followed him in 270–5, Aurelian, had a
plan for employing prisoners of war[1] on the cultivation of waste lands
in Italy itself, but we have no reason to think that much came of it.
And the true state of things was confessed in his abandonment of
Trajan's great Province of Dacia. Aurelian withdrew[2] the army and the
provincials, whom he settled south of the Danube in Moesia ; putting
the best face he could on this retirement by giving Moesia the name
of Dacia.

These phenomena attest an obvious truth, sometimes ignored, that
territorial expansion needs something more than military conquest to
give it lasting effect. In order to hold conquered lands the conquerors
must either occupy them or thoroughly assimilate the native population. Emperors in this period became aware that they could do neither.
Alexander Severus (222–35) gained a great victory[3] over the Persians
and took a number of prisoners. It was a tradition of Persian kings
not to let their subjects pass into foreign slavery, and Alexander allowed them to redeem these captives by a money payment. This he
used partly in compensating the masters of those who had already
passed into private ownership, and the rest he paid into the treasury.
This conciliatory policy may have been wise. In any case the treasury
was in this age chronically in need of ready money. But dealing with
the great oriental monarchy was a simpler undertaking than that of
dealing with the rude peoples of the North, who pressed on in tribal
units, offering no central power with which to negotiate. Probus (276–82)
seems to have been sorely troubled by their variety and independence
of action. We hear that when operating in Thrace he settled 100,000
Bastarnae[4] on Roman soil, and that all these kept faith with him. But
he went on to transplant large bodies of Gepidae Gruthungi and Vandals. These all broke their faith. While Probus was busy putting
down pretenders in other parts of the empire, they went on raiding
expeditions at large by land and sea, defying and damaging the power
of Rome. True, the emperor broke them by force of arms, and drove
the remnant back to their wilds: but we can see what the biographer
ignores, that such raids did mischief which the empire was in no condition to repair. What were the terms made with these barbarians, to

---

[1] *familias captivas.*   [2] Vopisc *Aurel* 39 § 7.

[3] Lamprid *Alex* 55 §§ 2, 3, cf Trebell *Gallien* 9 § 5.

[4] Vopisc *Probus* 18 §§ 1, 2. See Zosimus 1 71 and No v of the *Panegyrici* cap 18 for
other versions, in which the raiders are called Franks.

which the Bastarnae faithfully adhered, we are not told. Probably the grant of lands carried with it the duty of furnishing recruits to Roman armies and accepting the command of Roman officers.

In connexion with agricultural conditions we must not omit to notice the change that was passing over Roman armies. The straits to which Marcus had been reduced by the years of plague and losses in the field had compelled him to raise fresh troops by any means, enrolling slaves, hiring barbarian mercenaries, and so forth. With this miscellaneous force he just managed to hold his ground in the North. But the army never recovered its old tone. The period 180–284 shews it going from bad to worse. It is full of sectional jealousy and losing all sense of common imperial duty; only effective when some one strong man destroys his rivals and is for the moment supreme. The rise and fall of pretenders[1] is a main topic of the imperial history. As from the foundation of the Empire, the numbers of the army were inadequate for defence against simultaneous attacks on several frontiers. The lack of cooperation among their enemies, and the mobility of Roman frontier armies, had sufficed to keep invaders at bay. But as pressure became more continuous it was more difficult to meet the needs of the moment by moving armies to and fro. More and more they took on the character of garrisons, their chief camps grew into towns, local recruits filled up their ranks, and they were less and less available for service as field-armies. But it was obviously necessary that the country round about their quarters should be under cultivation, in order to supply them with at least part of their food. It may safely be assumed that this department was carefully attended to in the formation of all these military stations. And it seems that under the new conditions one of the evils that had hitherto embarrassed the empire was gradually brought to an end. For the fact remains that, after all the wholesale waste of lives in the bloody wars of the third century, it was still possible to raise great and efficient armies. Reorganized by Diocletian and Constantine, the empire proved able to defend itself for many years yet, even in the West. The new system may have been oppressive to the civil population, but it certainly revived military strength. This could not have been achieved without an improvement in the supply of man-power. It has been maintained[2] that this improvement was due to the permanent settlements of barbarians, mostly of German race, within the territories of the empire during the third century. Whether planted on the vacant lands as alien settlers (*inquilini*)[3] on easy terms, but bound to provide recruits for the army, or

[1] Even the extreme license of the soldiery, in deposing and murdering their own nominee, occurs repeatedly, and was no doubt one of the chief evils that prompted the reforms of Diocletian.

[2] O Seeck, *Untergang der antiken Welt* book II ch 6.   [3] See index under the word.

enlisted from the first and settled in permanent stations, they were year by year raising large families and turning deserted borderlands into nurseries of imperial soldiers. This picture may be somewhat overdrawn, but it has the merit of accounting for the phenomena. Without some explanation of the kind it is very hard to understand how the empire came to survive at all. With it, the sequel appears natural and intelligible. These barbarians were so far Romanized as to be proud of becoming Romans: the empire was barbarized so far as to lend itself to institutions of a more and more un-Roman character, and to lose the remaining traditions of literature and art: and when ruder barbarians in the fifth century assailed the empire in the West they found the control of government already in the hands of kinsmen of their own.

If we are to take the very meagre gleanings from the general records of this period and combine them with the information gathered from the African inscriptions referred to below, we can provisionally form some sort of notion of the various classes of labour employed on the land. First, there were *coloni*, freemen[1] in the eye of the law, however much local conditions, or the terms of their tenancies and the tendency for tenancies to become hereditary, may have limited the practical use of their legal freedom. Secondly, there were, at least in some parts, protected occupants encouraged to turn to account parcels of land that had for some reason or other lain idle. Thirdly, there were also rustic slaves who did most of the work on large farms. The stipulated services of tenants[2] at certain seasons to some extent supplemented their labour, at least in some parts: and the falling supply of slaves tended to make such auxiliary services more important. For the value of agricultural land depends mainly on the available supply of labour. Fourthly, chiefly if not entirely in the northern Provinces, a number of barbarians had been planted upon Roman soil. Some entered peacefully and settled down as willing subjects of the empire on vacant lands assigned to them. Some had surrendered after defeat in battle, and came in as prisoners. But, instead of making them rustic slaves on the old model, Marcus had found a new and better use for them. A new status, that of *inquilini*[3] or 'alien denizens' was created, inferior to that of free *coloni* but above that of slaves. They seem to have been generally left to cultivate plots of land, paying a share of the produce, and to have been attached to the soil, grouped under Roman landlords or chief-tenants. They had their wives and families,

---

[1] See chapter on evidence of the Digest.

[2] See chapter on the African inscriptions.

. [3] This matter is ably treated at length by Seeck *op cit* vol I pp 578–83. That they were distinct from *coloni* and *servi* is clear from the later constitutions in Cod Theod V 17, 18. (9, 10), XII 19, and Cod Just XI 48 § 13.

and their sons recruited Roman armies. Lastly, we have no right to assume that small cultivating owners[1] were wholly extinct, though there can hardly have been many of them.

We have an account[2] of the rising in Africa (238 AD) which, so far as it goes, gives us a little light on the agricultural situation there in the middle of this period. The barbarian emperor Maximin was represented in the Province by a *procurator fisci* whose oppressions provoked a conspiracy against him. Some young men of good and wealthy families drew together a number of persons who had suffered wrong. They ordered their slaves[3] from the farms to assemble with clubs and axes. In obedience[4] to their masters' orders they gathered in the town before daybreak, and formed a great mob. For Africa is naturally a populous[5] country; so the tillers of the soil were numerous. After dawn the young leaders told the mass of the slaves to follow them as being a section of the general throng: they were to conceal their weapons for the present, but valiantly to resist any attack on their masters. The latter then met the procurator and assassinated him. Hereupon his guards drew their swords meaning to avenge the murder, but the countrymen in support of their masters[6] fell upon them with their rustic weapons and easily routed them. After this the young leaders, having gone too far to draw back, openly rebelled against Maximin and proclaimed the proconsul Gordian Roman emperor. In this passage we have before us young men of landlord families, apparently holding large estates and working them with slave labour. They are evidently on good terms with their slaves. Of tenant farmers there is no mention: but there is a general reference to support given by other persons, already wronged or afraid of suffering wrong. The Latin biographer[7], who drew from Herodian, speaks of the murder as the work of 'the rustic common folk[8] and certain soldiers.' Now Frontinus[9], writing in the latter part of the first century AD, tells us that in Africa on their great estates individuals had 'a considerable population[10] of common folk.' The language can hardly refer to slaves: and a reference to levying recruits[11] for the army plainly forbids such an interpretation. But it does not imply that there were no slaves employed on those great estates; the writer is not thinking of the free-or-slave labour question. In regard to the writers who record this

---

[1] We shall find some reference to them later in the Codes.
[2] Herodian VII 4 §§ 3–6.   [3] τοὺς ἐκ τῶν ἀγρῶν οἰκέτας.
[4] πεισθέντες κελεύουσι τοῖς δεσπόταις.
[5] φύσει γὰρ πολυάνθρωπος οὖσα ἡ Λιβύη πολλοὺς εἶχε τοὺς τὴν γῆν γεωργοῦντας.
[6] ὑπερμαχόμενοι τῶν δεσποτῶν.   [7] Capitolinus *Maximin* 13 § 4, 14 § 1.
[8] *per rusticanam plebem deinde et quosdam milites interemptus est.*
[9] Frontin gromat p 53.   [10] *non exiguum populum plebeium.*
[11] *legere tironem ex vico.*

particular episode, are we to suppose that by 'slaves' Herodian loosely means *coloni*? Surely not. Then does Capitolinus by 'rustic common folk' mean slaves? I cannot believe it. More probably the writer, contemporary with Diocletian and Constantine, uses a loose expression without any precise meaning. If we are to attempt any inference from the language of Herodian, we must accept him as a witness that in Africa, or at least in parts of Africa, agriculture was still being carried on by slave labour. This does not exclude the existence of a small-tenancy system side by side with it. And the state of things disclosed[1] in the African inscriptions referred to above is consistent with both systems: for that the manor-farm on a great estate employed a slave staff for its regular operations, and drew from tenants' services only the help needed at certain seasons, seems the only possible conclusion from the evidence. Therefore, while agreeing with Heisterbergk[2] that the narrative of Herodian shews the populousness of Africa, we need not go so far as to ignore the fact of a considerable farm-slave element in the Province.

Meanwhile there are signs that rural Italy was suffering from the disorders and insecurity that had so often hindered the prosperity of agriculture. Even under the strong reign of Severus, with a larger standing army in Italy than ever before, a daring brigand[3] remained at large for two years and was only captured by treachery. Though we do not hear of his attacking farmers directly, such a disturbance must have been bad for all country folk. That he black-mailed them is probable: that they were plundered and maltreated by the licentious soldiery employed against him, is as nearly certain as can be from what we know of the soldiery of this time.

XLVII. THE AFRICAN INSCRIPTIONS.

Certain inscriptions[4] from the Roman Province of Africa, dating from the second and third centuries AD or at least referring to matters of that period, throw some light upon the management of great imperial domains in that part of the world. To discuss these in full one by one would be beyond the scope of this work, and would require several chapters of intolerable length. I shall content myself with giving a short account of each case, confined to those details

---

[1] This evidence has come to hand since Heisterbergk wrote (1876) *Die Entstehung des Colonats*.

[2] *op cit* pp 116–8.

[3] Dion Cass epit LXXVI 10. For this story Dion is a contemporary witness.

[4] The special treatises on these documents are fully mentioned in Girard's *Textes de droit Romain*, ed 4, 1913. An essay on the *Colons du saltus Burunitanus* in Esmein's *Mélanges* (1886) is still of great value.

which have direct bearing on my subject and which can be gathered with reasonable certainty from the often mutilated texts. French and German savants have contributed freely to the deciphering and inter-pretation, with happy results: but some of the proposed 'restorations' are much too bold to serve as a basis for further argument. After the details, I purpose to consider the points common to these in-teresting cases, and their place in the history of agriculture and agricultural labour under the earlier Roman Empire, say from Trajan to Severus.

(1) The inscription of Henschir Mettich[1] belongs to the year 116–7 AD, at the end of Trajan's reign. It deals with a domain called *fundus villae magnae Variani*, and does not refer to it by the term *saltus* at all. There is no reference to arrears of rent, the *reliqua colonorum* of which we often hear in the jurists and other writers. In-deed there is no mention of money-rents, unless we reckon as such the little dues (4 *as* per head) payable for grazing stock on the common pasture. The *coloni* are *partiarii*, paying certain shares (generally $\frac{1}{3}$) of their yearly produce as rent. These are paid, not to an imperial official but to the lords or head-tenants of the estate (*dominis aut con-ductoribus eius fundi*) or to their stewards (*vilicis*). It seems certain therefore that it was the chief tenants who were responsible to the imperial treasury for the amounts annually due, and that upon them rested the troublesome duty of collection. That this charge was a new one, laid upon them by Trajan, is perhaps possible, but hardly probable. For this statute regulating the domain (a *lex data*) is expressly declared to be modelled on a *lex Manciana*[2], which can hardly be other than a set of regulations issued by a former owner of the estate, and adopted with modifications by the imperial agents (*procuratores*) specially appointed to organize it as an imperial domain. In Roman practice it was usual to follow convenient precedents. How long the estate had become Crown-property, and by what process, inheritance purchase confiscation etc, we do not know. Nor is it certain whether the new statute was prepared as a matter of course on the cessation of private ownership, or whether it was issued in response to an appeal to the emperor complaining of oppressive exactions on the part of the head-tenants. But of the latter situation there is no sign, and I am inclined to accept the former alternative. In that case it appears necessary to suppose that the system of letting a great estate to one or a few great lessees, who might and did sublet parcels to small

[1] Text in Girard's *Textes de droit Romain* part III chapter 6.
[2] We seem to have the names of two former owners, Varianus and Mancia. For the retention of names of former owners see Dittenberger in *Orientis Graeci inscriptiones selectae* No 669 note 18. Rostowzew *Gesch des Röm colonates* ch 4 rejects this view and makes the *lex Manciana* an imperial law.

tenant farmers, was not unknown in the practice of great private landlords. This may well have been the case in Africa, still populous and
prosperous, though such a system never took root in depopulated and
failing Italy. It required willingness on the part of men of substance
to risk their capital in a speculation that could only succeed if good
sub-tenants were to be found. This condition could not be fulfilled in
Italy, but in Africa things were very different.

It is however easier to note this difference by unmistakeable signs
than to ascertain it in detail. One point is clear. The *coloni* on this
domain were bound to render fixed services to the head-tenants at
certain seasons of the year. These services consisted of two days'
work (*operas binas*) at the times of ploughing hoeing and harvest, six
in all. The falling-off in the supply of slaves, despite occasional
captures of prisoners in war, was a consequence of the *pax Romana*,
and how to provide sufficient labour was a standing problem of agriculture. The guarantee of extra labour at seasons of pressure was
doubtless a main consideration with speculators in inducing them to
venture their substance by becoming lessees of large tracts of land.
Of hired labour available for the purpose the statute gives no hint,
nor is it likely that such labourers were to be found in Africa. Thus
the *colonus*, and perhaps his whole household, were bound to certain
compulsory services, and thereby made part of an organization strictly
regulated and liable to further regulation. Further regulation was not
likely to give the peasant farmer more freedom of movement, since the
leading motive of the system was to secure continuous cultivation, and
this could best be secured by long tenancies, tending to become hereditary.
Therefore this statute offers various inducements to keep the peasant
contentedly engaged in bettering his own position by developing the
estate. The head-tenants are strictly forbidden to oppress him by
exacting larger shares of produce or more *operae* than are allowed by
the regulations. He is encouraged to cultivate parcels of waste land, not
included in his farm, by various privileges: in particular, a term of rent-
free years is guaranteed to him in case he plants the land with fruit
trees. This term, varying from five to ten years according to species
of trees, is meant to give him time to get a taste of profit before he becomes liable to rent: its effect in making him loth to move is obvious.

The statute tells us nothing on another important point. From the
jurists and other sources[1] we know that in Italy it was normally the
custom for the stock of a farm let to a *colonus* to be found for the
most part by the landlord. It was held[2] that in taking over this *instrumentum* at a valuation the tenant virtually purchased it, of course not

---

[1] Pliny *epist* III 19 § 7. Digest XIX 2 § 19[2], XXXII § 91[1], XXXIII 7 *passim*.
[2] Dig XIX 2 § 3, and Monro's note.

paying for it in ready money, but standing bound to account for the amount on quitting the tenancy. Thus a small man was left free to employ his own little capital in the actual working of the farm. He could add to the stock, and his additions gave to the landlord a further security for his rent, over and above that given by the sureties usually required. What stock was found by landlords, and what by tenant, was a matter for agreement generally following local convention. But on this African domain we are not told how the question of *instrumentum* was settled. Probably there was a traditional rule so well established that no reference to the point in the statute seemed necessary. The sole landlord was now the emperor. Without some direct evidence to that effect, I can hardly suppose that the provision of farm stock was entrusted to his *procuratores*. On the other hand, if the chief tenants, the *conductores*, were expected to undertake this business, as if they had been landlords, this too seems to call for direct evidence. Possibly the need of finding stock for an African peasant farmer was not so pressing as in Italy: still some equipment was surely required. How it was provided, seems to me a question for answering which we have not as yet sufficient materials. But it may be that on these domains the practical necessity for dealing with it seldom occurred. If, when the formal term of a tenancy expired, the same tenant stayed on either by tacit renewal (*reconductio*) or by grant of a new lease, the stock originally supplied would surely remain for use on the farm, upkeep and renewals of particular articles being of course allowed for. If a farmer's son succeeded him as tenant, the situation would be the same, or very nearly so. Therefore the manifest desire of emperors to keep tenants in permanence probably operated to minimize questions of *instrumentum* to the point of practical insignificance.

That the *coloni* on this estate were themselves hand-workers can hardly be doubted. The *operae* required of them suggest this on any natural interpretation. But there is nothing to shew that they did not employ[1] slave labour—if and when they could get it. We are not to assume that they were all on one dead level of poverty. That the head-tenants kept slaves to work those parts of the domain that they farmed for their own account, is indicated by the mention of their *vilici*, and made certain by the small amount of supplementary labour guaranteed them in the form of tenants' *operae*. Only one direct mention of slaves (*servis dominicis*) occurs in the inscription, and the text is in that place badly mutilated. Partly for the same defect, it seems necessary to avoid discussing certain other details, such as the position of the *stipendiarii* of whom we hear in a broken passage. Nor

---

[1] So Cuq, Seeck, Schulten, rightly I think. But in practice I believe the chance seldom occurred.

do I venture to draw confident inferences from the references to *inquilini* or *coloni inquilini,* or to discover an important distinction between the tenants who actually resided on the estate and those who did not. It may be right to infer a class of small proprietors dwelling around on the skirts of the great domain and hiring parcels of land within it. It may be right to regard the *inquilini* as *coloni* transplanted from abroad and made residents on the estate. But until such conclusions are more surely established it is safer to refrain from building upon them. The general effect of this document is to give us outlines of a system of imperial 'peculiars,' that is of domains on which order and security, necessary for the successful working and continuous cultivation, were not left to the operation of the ordinary law, but guaranteed in each case by what we may call an imperial by-law.

(2) The inscription of Souk el Khmis[1] deals with circumstances between 180 and 183 AD. The rescript of Commodus, and the appeal to which it was the answer, are recorded in it. The imperial estate to which it refers is called *saltus Burunitanus.* A single *conductor* appears to have been the lessee of the whole estate, and it was against his unlawful exactions that the *coloni* appealed. Through the connivance of the responsible *procurator* (corruptly obtained, the *coloni* hint,) this tyrant had compelled them to pay larger shares of produce than were rightly due, and also to render services of men and beasts beyond the amount fixed by statute. This abuse had existed on the estate for some time, but the proceedings of the present *conductor* had made it past all bearing. Evidently there had been some resistance, but official favour had enabled him to employ military force in suppressing it. Violence had been freely used: some persons had been arrested and imprisoned or otherwise maltreated; others had been severely beaten, among them even Roman citizens. Hence the appeal. It is to be noted that the appellants in no way dispute their liability to pay shares of produce (*partes agrarias*) or to render labour-services at the usual seasons of pressure (*operarum praebitionem iugorumve*). They refer to a clause in a *lex Hadriana,* regulating these dues. It is against the exaction of more than this statute allows that they venture to protest. They judiciously point out to the emperor that such doings are injurious to the financial interest[2] of his treasury (*in perniciem rationum tuarum*), that is, they will end by ruining the estate as a source of steady revenue. The officials of the central department in Rome were evidently of the same opinion, for the rescript of Com-

[1] Text in Girard, part I chapter 4 § 10.
[2] This significant hint seems to have been almost normal in such petitions. A good instance is the petition of Scaptoparene (see index, *Inscriptions*).

modus[1] plainly ordered his *procuratores* to follow closely the rules and policy applicable to the domains, permitting no exactions in transgression of the standing regulations (*contra perpetuam formam*). In short, he reaffirmed the statute of Hadrian.

In this document also we hear nothing of tenants' arrears or of money-rents. Naturally enough, for the *coloni* are *partiarii* whose rent is a share of produce. In connexion with such tenants the difficulty[2] of *reliqua* does not easily arise. They are labouring peasants, who describe themselves as *homines rustici tenues manuum nostrarum operis victum tolerantes*. Of course they are posing as injured innocents. Perhaps they were: at any rate the great officials in Rome would look kindly on humble peasants who only asked protection in order to go on unmolested, producing the food which it was their duty to produce, —food, by the by, of the need of which the Roman mob was a standing reminder. Of *vilici* or ordinary slaves this document says nothing, for it had no need to do so; but the right to *operae* at certain seasons implies slave labour on the head-tenant's own farm, probably attached to the chief *villa* or *palatium*. In a notable phrase at the end of their appeal the *coloni* speak of themselves[3] as 'your peasants, home-bred slaves and foster-children of your domains' (*rustici tui vernulae et alumni saltuum tuorum*). Surely this implies, not only that they are *coloni Caesaris*, standing in a direct relation to the emperor whose protection[4] they implore against the *conductores agrorum fiscalium*; but also that their connexion with the estate is an old-established one, passing from fathers to sons, a hereditary tie which they have at present no wish to see broken.

In this case the circumstances that led to the setting-up of the inscription are clear enough. Evidently the appeal represented a great effort, both in the way of organizing concerted action on the part of the peasant farmers, and in overcoming the hindrances to its presentation which would be created by the interested ingenuity of those whose acts were thereby called in question. The imperial officials in the Provinces were often secretly in league with those in authority at Rome, and to have procured an imperial rescript in favour of the appellants was a great triumph, perhaps a rare one. The *forma perpetua* containing the regulations governing the estate was, we learn,

---

[1] It is perhaps worth noting that under Commodus the transport of corn from Africa was specially provided for by the creation of a *classis Africana* for that purpose. See Lamprid *Commodus* 17 §§ 7, 8.

[2] De Coulanges pp 10 foll deals with this point at length, but I think he pushes his conclusions too far.

[3] Cf the Aragueni (see index, *Inscriptions*) παροίκων καὶ γεωργῶν τῶν ὑμετέρων.

[4] Dig I 19 § 3[1] is of a later date, but refers to a protective rescript of Antoninus Pius. Cf XLIX 14 § 47[1], L 6 § 6[11]. See Schulten in *Hermes* XLI pp 11-16.

already posted up on a bronze tablet. It had been disregarded: and
now it was an obvious precaution to record that the emperor had
ordered those regulations to be observed in future. How long the
effect of this rescript lasted we are left to guess. Officials changed,
and reaffirmation of principles could not guarantee permanent reform
of practice. Still, the policy of the central bureau, when not warped
by corrupt influence, was consistent and clear. To keep these imperial
' peculiars' on such a footing as to insure steady returns was an un-
doubted need: and, after the extreme strain on the resources of the
empire imposed by the calamitous times of Marcus, it was in the reign
of Commodus a greater need than ever.

(3) The Gazr Mezuâr inscription[1], very fragmentary and in some
points variously interpreted, belongs to the same period (181 AD). A
few details seem sufficiently certain to be of use here. The estate in
question is imperial property, apparently one of the domanial units
revealed to us by these African documents. It seems to record another
case of appeal against unlawful exaction of *operae*, probably by a
conductor or *conductores*. It also was successful. But it is notable that
the lawful amount of *operae* to be rendered by *coloni* on this estate
was just double of that fixed in the other cases—four at each of the
seasons of pressure, twelve in all. We can only infer that the task-
scale varied on various estates for reasons unknown to us. One fragment, if a probable restoration[2] is to be accepted, conveys the impression of a despairing threat on the part of the appellants. It suggests
that on failure of redress they may be driven to return to their homes
where they can make their abode in freedom. On the face of it, this
is an assertion of freedom of movement, a valuable piece of evidence,
if it can be trusted. We may safely go so far as to note that it is at
least not inconsistent with other indications pointing to the same
conclusion. We may even remark that the suggestion of going home
in search of freedom agrees better with the notion that these *coloni*
were African natives than with the supposition of their Italian origin.
The Roman citizens on the Burunitan estate will not support the
latter view, for they are mentioned as exceptional. Seeck (rightly, I
think,) urges that Italy was in sore need of men and had none to spare
for populous Africa. I would add that the emigration of Italians to
the Provinces as working farmers seems to require more proof than
has yet been produced. As officials, as traders, as financiers and petty
usurers, as exploiters of other men's labour, they abounded in the
subject countries; but, so far as I can learn, not as labourers. Many
of them no doubt held landed estates, for instance in the southern
parts of Spain and Gaul. But when we meet with loose general ex-

[1] CIL VIII 14428.   [2] [*domum rev*]*ertamur ubi libere morari possimus.*

pressions[1] such as 'The Roman is dwelling in every land that he has conquered,' we must not let them tempt us into overestimating the number of Italian settlers taking an active part in the operations of provincial agriculture.

(4) The inscription of Ain Ouassel[2] belongs to the end of the reign of Severus. The text is much broken, but information of no small importance can be gathered from what remains. Severus was himself a native of Africa, and may have taken a personal interest in the subject of this ordinance. In point of form the document chiefly consists of a quoted communication (*sermo*) from the emperor's *procuratores*[3], one of whom, a freedman, saw to its publication in an inscription on an *ara legis divi Hadriani*. A copy of the *lex Hadriana*, or at least the relevant clauses thereof, was included. The matter on which the emperor's decision is announced was the question of the right to occupy and cultivate rough lands (*rudes agri*)[4], which are defined as lands either simply waste or such as the *conductores* have neglected to cultivate for at least ten years preceding. These lands are included in no less than five different *saltus* mentioned by proper names, and the scope of the ordinance is wider than in the cases referred to above. It appears that, while it may have contained some modifications or extensions of the provisions of the *lex Hadriana*, its main bearing was to reaffirm and apply the privileges granted by that statute. It is not rash to infer that we have here evidence of a set of regulations for all or many of the African domains, forming a part of Hadrian's great work of reorganization.

If the remaining words of this inscription are rightly interpreted, as I think they are, it seems that the policy of encouraging the cultivation of waste and derelict lands was at this time being revived by the government. We have seen it at work in Trajan's time, promoted by guarantee of privileges and temporary exemption from burdens. But the persons then encouraged to undertake the work of reclamation were to all appearance only the *coloni* at the time resident on the estate. In the case of these five *saltus*, the offer seems to be made more widely, at least so far as the remaining text may justify such conclusions. It reads like an attempt to attract enterprising squatters of any kind from any quarter. They are offered not merely undisturbed occupation and a heritable tenure of some sort, but actual *possessio*.

---

[1] Seneca *ad Helviam* 7 § 7 *ubicumque vicit Romanus habitat.*

[2] Text in Girard, part III chapter 6.

[3] From comparing the remains of the next inscription (5) it appears that the emperor is Hadrian.

[4] Cf *agrum rudem provincialem* in Hyginus, Gromat I 203. In the later empire we find legislation to promote such cultivation. See cod Th V 11 § 8 (365 AD), § 12 (388–392), 14 § 30 (386).

Now this right, which fills a whole important chapter in Roman law, was one protected by special legal remedies, and even on an imperial domain can hardly have been a matter of indifference. It was quite distinct from mere *possessio naturalis*[1], which was all that the ordinary *colonus* enjoyed on his own behalf. This new-type squatter is allowed the same privilege of so many years of grace, free of rent, at the outset of his enterprise, that we have noted above. The details are somewhat different. For olives the free term is ten years : for fruit trees (*poma*, here mentioned without reference to vines) it is seven years. It is expressly provided that the *divisio*, which implies the partiary system of tenancy, shall apply only to such *poma* as are actually brought[2] to market. This suggests that in the past attempts to levy the quota as a proportional share of the gross crop, without regard to the needs of the grower's own household, had been found to discourage reclamation. It has been pointed out that the effect of the new policy would be to create a sort of perpetual leasehold, similar to that known by the Greek term *emphyteusis*, which is found fully established in the later empire. But the land was not all under fruit-crops. The disposal of corn crops is regulated in a singular clause thus. 'Any shares of dry[3] crops that shall be due are, during the first five years of occupation, to be delivered to the head-tenant within whose holding[4] the land occupied is situate. After the lapse of that time they are to go to the account (of the Treasury[5]).' Why is the *conductor* to receive these *partes aridae?* It is reasonably suggested that the intention was to obviate initial obstruction on the part of the big lessee, and thus to give the reclamation-project a fair start.

For we have no right to assume that the parcels of land thrown open to occupation had hitherto been included[6] in no tenancy. The whole import of the document shews that they often belonged to this or that area held by one or other of the big lessees. That there was at least one *conductor* to each of the five *saltus* seems certain. That there was only one to each, is perhaps probable, but hardly to be gathered from the text. Now, so long as the *conductor* regularly paid his fixed rent (*canon*) and accounted for the taxes (*tributa*) due from the estate, why should the imperial authority step in to take pieces of land (and that the poorest land) out of his direct control? The

---

[1] Dig xli 3 § 33[1]. Of course the *dominus* could possess *per colonum*. See Buckland, *Elementary Principles* § 38 p 77.

[2] *quae venibunt a possessoribus.*   [3] For *aridi fructus* cf Digest xlix 14 § 50.

[4] *in cuius conductione agrum occupaverit.*

[5] *rationi (bus fisci)* gives the sense. But *rationi* simply may be correct, cf Digest ii 14 § 42, etc.

[6] Girard cites Rostowzew's opinion that the right to occupy abandoned land as well as old wastes was an extension of the *lex Manciana* by the *lex Hadriana*.

answer to this is that the Roman law[1] recognized the right of a private landlord to require of his tenants that they should not 'let down' the land leased to them: and proof of neglected cultivation might operate to bar a tenant's claim for abatement of rent. What was the right of an ordinary landlord was not likely to be waived by an emperor: though his domains might be administered in fact by a special set of fiscal regulations, he claimed a right analogous to that recognized by the ordinary law, and none could challenge its exercise. A big lessee might often find that parts of his holding could not be cultivated at a profit under existing conditions. Slave labour was careless and inefficient; it was in these times also costly, so costly that it only paid to employ it on generous soils. The task-work of *coloni* did not amount to much, and it was no doubt rendered grudgingly. He was tempted to economize in slaves[2] and to employ his reduced staff on the best land only. We need not suppose that he got an abatement of his fixed rent from the fiscal authorities: he was most unlikely to attract their attention by making such a claim. He had made his bargain with eyes presumably open. That he had agreed to the *canon* assures us that it must have been low enough to leave him a comfortable margin for profit. We may be fairly sure that he sat quiet and did what seemed to pay him best.

In the remaining text of this statute there is no reference to *operae* due from the new squatters, and nothing is said of *coloni*. This does not seem to be due to injury of the stone. The persons for whose benefit the statute is enacted are apparently a new or newly recognized element[3] in the population of these domains, not *coloni*. But the rights offered to them are expressly referred to as rights granted by the statute of Hadrian. If so, then the *lex Hadriana* contemplated the establishment of a new peasant class, not *coloni*, and the present statute was merely a revival of Hadrian's scheme. The men are eventually to pay shares of crops, and Schulten's[4] view, that they are on the way to become *coloni*, is possible, if not probable. When he remarks that they might find the position of *coloni* a doubtful boon, we need not challenge his opinion.

(5) The inscription of Ain el Djemala[5], a later discovery (1906) is of special importance as belonging to the same neighbourhood as the

---

[1] See Dig XIX 2 §§ 15³, 24², 25³, 51ᵖʳ, 54¹.

[2] Later legislation to prevent this neglect of poorer land. Cod Th v 14 § 34 (394 AD), x 3 § 4 (383), XI 1 § 4 (337), etc.

[3] Prof Buckland writes to me that he believes these squatters were to be owners, not *coloni*, owners in the only sense possible in non-Italic soil, paying *tributum*. The words *frui possidere* used to describe their right are the technical words for provincial ownership. Cf Gaius II 7.

[4] In *Hermes* XXIX pp 215, 224.   [5] Girard, part III chapter 6.

preceding one. It is a document of Hadrian's time. It refers to the same group of estates as the above, and deals with the same matter, the right to cultivate waste or derelict parcels of land. Indeed the connexion of the two inscriptions is so close that the parts preserved of each can be safely used to fill gaps in the text of the other. In a few points this inscription, the earlier in date, supplies further detail. The most notable is that another estate, a *saltus* or *fundus Neronianus*, is mentioned in it, and not in the later one. Thus it would seem that it referred to six estates, a curious coincidence, when we recall the six great African landlords made away with by Nero. Another little addition is that waste lands are defined as marshy or wooded. Also that the land is spoken of as fit for growing olives vines and corn-crops, which supplements a mutilated portion of the Ain Ouassel stone. But in one point the difference between the two is on the face of it difficult to reconcile. In addressing the imperial *procuratores* the applicants base their request on the *lex Manciana*, the benefit of which they seek to enjoy[1] as used on the neighbouring *saltus Neronianus*. Here the broken text is thought to have contained a reference to the enhanced prosperity of that estate owing to the concession. In any case we may fairly conclude that the *lex Manciana* was well known in the district, and its regulations regarded by the farmers as favourable to their interests. But the reply to their petition does not refer to it as the immediate basis of the decision given. The communication (*sermo*) of Hadrian's procurators is cited as the ground of the leave granted for cultivation of waste lands. Yet the broken sentence at the end of the inscription seems at least to shew that the rules of the *lex Manciana* were still recognized as a standard, confirmed and perhaps incorporated, or referred to by name, in the *lex Hadriana* itself. It is ingeniously suggested that the farmers rest their case on the *Manciana* because the *Hadriana* was as yet unknown to them; while the reply refers to Hadrian's statute as authority. Whether the *saltus* or *fundus Neronianus*, on which the Mancian regulations were in force, is another estate-unit similar to the five named both here and in the later inscription, is a point on which I have some doubts, too little connected with my subject for discussion here. The general scope of the concession granted by Hadrian is the same as the later one of Severus.

If Hadrian issued a statute or statutes regulating the terms of occupancy on the African domains, and some attempts to evade it were met by its reaffirmation under Commodus, it is quite natural that neglect or evasion of it in some other respects should be met by reaffirmation under Severus. This consideration will account for the identity of the concessions granted in these two inscriptions. And it

---

[1] *lege Manciana condicione saltus Neroniani vicini nobis.*

agrees perfectly with the evidence of later legislation in the Theodosian code. The normal course of events is, legislation to protect the poorer classes of cultivators, then evasion of the law by the selfish rich, then reenactment of evaded laws, generally with increased penalties. That under the administrative system of the domains much the same phenomena should occur, is only what we might expect.

XLVIII. DISCUSSION OF THE ABOVE INSCRIPTIONS.

In reviewing the state of things revealed to us by these inscriptions we must carefully bear in mind that they relate solely to the Province Africa. Conditions there were in many ways exceptional. When Rome took over this territory after the destruction of Carthage in 146 BC, it was probably a country divided for the most part into great estates worked on the Carthaginian system by slave labour. Gradually the land came more and more into the hands of Roman capitalists, to whose opulence Horace refers. Pliny tells us that in Nero's time six[1] great landlords possessed half the entire area of the Province, when that emperor found a pretext for putting them to death and confiscating their estates. Henceforth the ruling emperor was the predominating landlord[2] in a Province of immense importance, in particular as a chief granary of Rome. We are not to suppose that any change in the system of large units was ever contemplated. Punic traditions, probably based on experience, favoured the system; though the Punic language, still spoken, seems to have been chiefly confined to the seaboard districts. What the change of lordship effected was not only to the financial advantage of the imperial treasury: it also put an end to the creation of what were a sort of little principalities that might some day cause serious trouble. At this point we are tempted to wonder whether the great landlords, before the sweeping measure of Nero, had taken any steps towards introducing a new organization in the management of their estates. Trajan's statute refers to a *lex Manciana* and adopts a number of its regulations. These regulations clearly contemplate a system of head-tenants and sub-tenants, of whom the latter seem to be actual working farmers living of the labour of their own hands, as those who some 65 years later described themselves in appealing to Commodus. The former have stewards in charge of the cultivation of the 'manor farms' attached to the principal farmsteads, and evidently employ gangs of slaves: but at special seasons have a

[1] It is tempting to identify these with the six mentioned in Nos (2) and (4) above.
[2] For the vast extent of imperial estates, particularly in Africa, see Hirschfeld, *der Grundbesitz der Römischen Kaiser*, in his *Kleine Schriften*.

right to a limited amount[1] of task-labour from the free sub-tenants of
the small farms. That these labour-conditions were devised to meet a
difficulty in procuring enough slaves to carry on the cultivation of the
whole big estate, is an inference hardly to be resisted. That we find it
on more than one estate indicates that for the time it was serving its
purpose. But, in admitting that it probably began under the rule of
great private landlords, we must not lose sight of the fact that it was
liable to grievous abuse, and that even the regulations of Hadrian did
not remove the necessity of pitiful appeals for redress.

An important characteristic of these estates was that they were
outside the municipal[2] system. Each of the so-called *civitates* had its
own charter or statute (*lex*) conforming more or less closely to a
common[3] model, under which the municipal authorities could regulate
the management of lands within its territory. But these great estates
were independent[4] of such local jurisdictions. And this independence
would seem to date from the times of private ownership, before the
conversion of many of them into imperial domains. Mommsen thought
that this separate treatment of them as 'peculiars' began in Italy
under the Republic, and was due to the influence of the land-owning
aristocracy, who were bent upon admitting no such concurrent authority on their *latifundia*. This may have been so, and the extension
of large-scale possessions to the Provinces may have carried the system
abroad. At all events there it was, and it suited the convenience of a
grasping emperor: he had only to get rid of the present possessor and
carry on the administration of the domain as before: his agents stepped
into the place of those employed by the late landlord, and only slight
modification of the current regulations would be required. He issued
a statute for management of 'crown-property' as he would for a municipality. It was in effect a local law, and it does not appear that the
common law administered by the ordinary courts could override it.
The imperial *procurator* was practically the magistrate charged with
its administration in addition to his financial duties, for government
and extraction of revenue were really two sides of the same function.
Obviously the interests of the emperor, of his agent, of the head-tenants,
and of the peasant cultivators, were not the same. But the peasant,
who wanted to pay as little as possible, and the emperor who wanted

[1] De Coulanges seems hardly to recognize how small was the amount of *operae*, a few
days in the year. But in his tenth chapter he shews how vastly the system was extended (so
many days a week) in the early Middle Age.

[2] Mommsen in *Hermes* XV pp 391-6.

[3] Such as the *lex coloniae Genetivae Iuliae* of 44 BC, and the *leges* of Salpensa and Malaca
of 81-4 AD. Girard, and Bruns' *Fontes*.

[4] Esmein p 309 well refers to the passages in Lachmann's *Feldmesser*, Frontinus p 53 and
Siculus Flaccus p 164. Cf Hirschfeld l.c. p 558.

to receive steady returns—as large as possible, but above all things steady—had a common interest in preventing unlawful exactions, by which a stable income was imperilled and the prosperity of the cultivator impaired. On the other hand the *procurator* and the *conductor* could only make illicit profits through combining to rob the emperor by squeezing his *coloni.* How to accomplish this was no doubt a matter of delicate calculation. How much oppression would the *coloni* stand without resorting to the troublesome and risky process of an appeal? We only hear of one or two appeals made with success. Of those that were made and rejected or foiled by various arts, and of those abandoned in despair at an early stage, we get no record. Yet that such cases did occur, perhaps not seldom, we may be reasonably sure.

It is well to remember that Columella, in whose treatise letting of farms to tenants first appears, not as an occasional expedient but as part of a reasoned scheme of estate-management, makes provision for a *procurator*[1] as well as a *vilicus.* One duty of the former is to keep an eye on the latter. In the management of great estates an atmosphere of mistrust is perhaps to some extent unavoidable. In an agricultural system based on slave labour, this mistrust begins at the very bottom of the structure and reaches to the very top, as is shewn by all experience ancient and modern. Industry in slaves, diligence and honesty in agents and stewards, are not to be relied on when these subordinates have no share in the profit derived from the practice of such virtues. And mistrust of slaves and freedmen did not imply a simple trust in free tenants. Columella only advises[2] letting to tenants in circumstances that make it impracticable to cultivate profitably by a slave-staff under a steward. The plan is a sort of last resort, and it can only work well if the tenants stay on continuously. Therefore care should be taken to make the position of the *coloni* permanently attractive. This advice is primarily designed for Italy, but its principles are of general application, and no doubt justified by experience. Their extension to *latifundia* abroad, coupled with a falling-off in the supply of slaves, led to similar results: great estates might still be in part worked by slave labour under stewards, but letting parcels to small tenants became a more and more vital feature of the system. But to deal directly from a distance with a number of such peasant farmers would be a troublesome business. We need not wonder that it became customary to let large blocks of land, even whole *latifundia*, to big lessees, speculative men who undertook the subletting and rent-collecting of part of their holdings, while they could work the central manor-farm by slave labour on their own account, and generally exploit the situation for their own profit. Thus, as once the *latifundium* had absorbed little properties,

---

[1] Colum I 6 §§ 7, 8.   [2] Colum I 7.

so now its subdivision was generating little tenancies, with chief-tenants as a sort of middlemen between the *dominus* and the *coloni*. To protect the *colonus*, the powers of the *conductor*[1] had to be strictly limited: to ease the labour-problem and retain the *conductor*, a certain amount of task-work had to be required of the *colonus*. And this last condition was ominous of the coming serfdom.

If the economic situation and the convenience of non-resident landlords operated to produce a widespread system of letting to small tenants, it was naturally an object to levy the rents in such a form as would best secure a safe and regular return. To exact a fixed money-rent would mean that the peasant must spend time in marketing his produce in order to procure the necessary cash, and thereby lessen the time spent in actual farm-labour. In bad years he would look for an abatement of his rent, nor would it be easy to satisfy him: here was material for disputes and discontent. Such difficulties were known in Italy and elsewhere, and jurists recognized[2] an advantage of the 'partiary' system in this connexion. An abatement of rent due in a particular year need not imply that the landlord lost the amount of abatement for good and all. If the next year produced a 'bumper' crop, the landlord was entitled to claim restitution of last year's abatement in addition to the yearly rent. This too, it seems, in the case of a tenant sitting at a fixed money-rent. But the *partiarius colonus* is on another footing: he shares gain and loss with the *dominus*, with whom he is a quasi-partner[3]. It was surely considerations of this kind that led to the adoption of the share-rent system on these great African estates. By fixing the proportion on a moderate scale, the peasant was fairly certain to be able to pay his rent, and he would not be harassed with money transactions dependent on the fluctuations in the price of corn. Under such conditions he was more likely to be contented and to stay on where he was, and that this should be so was precisely what the landlord desired. On the other hand the big *conductor* might pay rent either in coin or kind. He was a speculator, doubtless well able to take care of his own interests: probably the normal case was that he agreed to a fixed cash payment, and only took the lease on terms that left him a good prospect of making it a remunerative venture. But on this point there is need of further evidence.

When the emperor took over an estate of this kind, such an exist-

---

[1] *conductor* and *coloni* are both bound by the statute for the *fundus* or *saltus*. In theory both are tenants of the emperor, in practice the *conductor* has the upper hand, as Cuq points out.

[2] Compare Dig XIX 2 § 15[4] with § 25[6].

[3] *quasi societatis iure*. Of course not a real *socius*. See Index, *colonia partiaria*, and Vinogradoff, *Growth of the Manor* note 91 on p 109.

ing organization would be admirably fitted to continue under the fiscal administration. Apparently this is just what happened. One small but important improvement would be automatically produced by the change. The *coloni* would now become *coloni Caesaris*[1], and whatever protection against exactions of *conductores* they may have enjoyed under the sway of their former lords was henceforth not less likely to be granted and much more certain of effect. To the fiscal officials any course of action tending to encourage permanent tenancies and steady returns would on the face of it be welcome: for it was likely to save them trouble, if not to bring them credit. The only influence liable to incline them in another direction was corruption in some form or other, leading them to connive at misdeeds of the local agents secretly in league with the head-lessees on the spot. That cases of such connivance occurred in the period from Trajan to Severus is not to be doubted. During the following period of confusion they probably became frequent. But it was not until Diocletian introduced a more elaborate imperial system, and increased imperial burdens to defray its greater cost, that the evil reached its height. Then the corruption of officials tainted all departments, and was the canker ever gnawing at the vital forces of the empire. But that this deadly corruption was a sudden growth out of an existing purity is not to be imagined. All this is merely an illustration of that oldest of political truisms, that to keep practice conformable to principle is supremely difficult. The only power that seems to be of any effect in checking the decay of departmental virtue is the power of public opinion. Now a real public opinion cannot be said to have existed in the Roman Empire; and, had it existed, there was no organ through which it could be expressed. And the Head of the State, let him be ever so devoted to the common weal, was too overburdened with manifold responsibilities to be able to give personal attention to each complaint and prescribe an equitable remedy.

How far we are entitled to trace a movement of policy by the contents of these African inscriptions is doubtful. They are too few, and too much alike. Perhaps we may venture to detect a real step onward in the latest of them.. The renewal of the encouragement of squatter-settlers[2] on derelict lands does surely point to a growing consciousness that the food-question was becoming a more and more serious one. Perhaps it may be taken to suggest that the system of leasing the African domains to big *conductores* had lately been found failing in

---

[1] See Dig I 19 § 3[1], an opinion of Callistratus, a jurist of the time of Severus. That in some sense or other the *coloni* were tenants of the emperor seems certain. See CIL VIII 8425 (Pertinax), 8426 (Caracalla), also 8702, 8777. And Esmein pp 313-5.

[2] This becomes an important subject of legislation in the Theodosian code. See Cod Th V 11 § 8, 14 § 30.

efficiency. But it is rash to infer much from a single case: and the African Severus may have followed an exceptional policy in his native province. It is when we look back from the times of the later Empire, with its frantic legislation to bind *coloni* to the soil, and to enforce the cultivation of every patch of arable ground, that we are tempted to detect in every record symptoms of the coming constraint. As yet the central government had not laid its cramping and sterilizing hand on every part of its vast dominions. Moreover the demands on African productivity had not yet reached their extreme limit. There was as yet no Constantinople, and Egypt still shared with Africa the function of supplying food to Rome. Thus it is probably reasonable to believe that the condition of the working tenant-farmers was in this age a tolerable[1] one. If those on the great domains were bit by bit bound to their holdings, it was probably with their own consent, so far at least that, seeing no better alternative, they became stationary and more or less dependent peasants. In other parts of Africa, for instance near Carthage, we hear of wealthy landowners employing bodies of slaves. Some of these men may well have been Italians: at least they took a leading part later in the rising against Maximin and the elevation of Gordian.

In connexion with the evidence of this group of inscriptions it may be not out of place to say a few words on the view set forth by Heisterbergk, that the origin of the later serf-colonate was Provincial, not Italian. He argues[2] that what ruined small-scale farming in Italy was above all things the exemption of Italian land from taxation. Landlords were not constrained by the yearly exaction of dues to make the best economic use of their estates. Vain land-pride and carelessness were not checked: mismanagement and waste had free course, and small cultivation declined. The fall in free rustic population was both effect and cause. In the younger Pliny's time good tenants were already hard to find, but great landlords owned parks and mansions everywhere. In the Provinces nearly all the land was subject to imperial taxation in kind or in money, and owners could not afford to let it lie idle. The practical control of vast estates was not possible from a distance. The direction of agriculture, especially of extensive farming (corn etc) from a fixed centre was little less difficult. There was therefore strong inducement to delegate the business of cultivation to tenants, and to let the difference in amount between their rents and the yearly imperial dues represent the landlord's profit. Thus the spread of *latifundia* swallowed up small holdings in the

---

[1] See de Coulanges pp 140–4, where this view is more strongly expressed.
[2] *Die Entstehung des Colonats* pp 70 foll, citing especially Frontinus Gromat I p 35 and Columella III 3 § 11.

Provinces as in Italy; but it converted small owners into small tenants, and did not merge the holdings into large slave-gang plantations or throw them into pasture. The plan of leasing a large estate as a whole to a big head-tenant, or establishing him in the central 'manor farm,' was quite consistent with the general design, and this theory accounts for the presence of a population of free *coloni*, whom later legislation might and did bind fast to the soil.

This argument has both ingenuity and force, but we can only assent to it with considerable reservations. Letting to free *coloni* was a practice long used in Italy, and in the first century AD was evidently becoming more common. It was but natural that it should appear in the Provinces. Still, taken by itself, there is no obvious reason why it should develope into serfdom. With the admitted scarcity and rising value of labour, why was it that the freeman did not improve his position in relation to his lord, indeed to capitalists in general? I think the presence of the big lessee, the *conductor*, an employer of slave labour, had not a little to do with it. Labour as such was despised. The requirement of task-work to supplement that of slaves on the 'manor farm' was not likely to make labour more esteemed. Yet to get his little holding the *colonus* had to put up with this condition. It may be significant that we hear nothing of *coloni* working for wages in spare time. Was it likely that they would do so? Then, when the *conductor* came to be employed as collector of rents and other dues on the estate, his opportunities of illicit exaction gave him more and more power over them; and, combined with their reluctance to migrate and sacrifice the fruits of past labour, reduced them[1] more and more to a state of *de facto* dependence. At the worst they would be semi-servile in fact, though free in law; at the best they would have this outlook, without any apparent alternative to escape their fate. This, I imagine, was the unhappy situation that was afterwards recognized by law.

I must not omit to point out that I have said practically nothing on the subject[2] of municipal lands and their administration by the authorities of the several *res publicae* or *civitates*. Of the importance of this matter I am well aware, more particularly in connexion with the development of *emphyteusis* under the perpetual leases granted by the municipalities. In a general history of the imperial economics this topic would surely claim a significant place. But it seems to have little or no bearing on the labour conditions with which I am primarily concerned, while it would add greatly to the bulk of a treatise already too long. So too the incidence of taxation, and the effects of degrada-

---

[1] This is very nearly the view of Wallon III 264 'le Colonat à l'origine ne fut pas un droit mais un fait.' Ib 266.

[2] I have made some reference to it below in the chapter on the *Digest*.

tion[1] of the currency, influences that both played a sinister part in imperial economics, belong properly to a larger theme. Even the writers on land-surveying etc, the *agrimensores* or *gromatici*, only touch my subject here and there when it is necessary to speak of tenures, which cannot be ignored in relation to labour-questions. All these matters are thoroughly and suggestively treated in Seeck's great history of the Decline and Fall of the ancient world. Another topic left out of discussion is the practical difference, if any, between the terms[2] *fundus* and *saltus* in the imperial domains. I can find no satisfactory materials for defining it, and it does not appear to bear any relation to the labour-question. The meaning of the term *inquilinus* is a more important matter. If we are to accept Seeck's ingenious conclusions[3], it follows that this term, regularly used by the jurists of a house-tenant (urban) as opposed to *colonus* a tenant of land (rustic), in the course of the second century began to put on a new meaning. Marcus settled large numbers of barbarians on Roman soil. These 'indwellers' were labelled as *inquilini*, a word implying that they were imported aliens, distinct from the proper residents. An analogous distinction existed in municipalities between unprivileged 'indwellers' (*incolae*) and real *municipes*. Now a jurist's opinion[4] in the first half of the third century speaks of *inquilini* as attached (*adhaerent*) to landed estates, and only capable of being bequeathed to a legatee by inclusion in the landed estate: and it refers to a rescript of Marcus and Commodus dealing with a point of detail connected with this rule of law. Thus the inquilinate seems to have been a new condition implying attachment to the soil, long before the colonate acquired a similar character. For the very few passages, in which the fixed and dependent nature of the colonate is apparently recognized before the time of Constantine, are with some reason suspected of having been tampered with by the compilers of the Digest, or are susceptible of a different interpretation. It is clear that this intricate question cannot be fully discussed here. If these rustic *inquilini* were in their origin barbarian settlers, perhaps two conclusions regarding them may be reasonable. First, they seem to be distinct from slaves, the personal property of individual owners. For the evidence, so far as it goes, makes them attached[5]

---

[1] This is fully treated by Seeck, bk III c 5.

[2] In the Ain el Djemala inscription we have them used indifferently. It is not clear that the usage in various provinces was identical. See Vinogradoff *Growth of the Manor* pp 69, 70.

[3] Given in a long note, vol I pp 5, 8-83.

[4] Marcian in Dig xxx § 112[pr]. Cf L 15 § 4[8] (Title *de censibus*) *si quis inquilinum vel colonum non fuerit professus* etc, where the mention of *colonum* is suspected of interpolation by Seeck.

[5] Dig xxx § 112[pr] *si quis inquilinos sine praediis quibus adhaerent legaverit, inutile est legatum* (Marcian). Esmein p 313 takes them to be really slaves, but I cannot follow him.

to the land, and only transferable therewith. Secondly, they are surely labourers, tilling with their own hands the holdings assigned to them. If this view of them be sound, we may see in them the beginnings of a serf class. But it does not follow that the later colonate was a direct growth from this beginning. We have noted above several other causes contributing to that growth; in particular the state of *de facto* fixity combined with increasing dependence, in which the free *colonus* was gradually losing his freedom. Whether the later colonate will ever receive satisfactory explanation in the form of a simple and convincing theory, I cannot tell: at present it seems best to admit candidly that, among the various influences tending to produce the known result, I do not see my way[1] to distinguish one as supremely important, and to ignore the effect of others. The opinion[2] of de Coulanges, that the origin of the later colonate is mainly to be sought in the gradual effect of custom (local custom), eventually recognized (not created) by law, is perhaps the soundest attempt at a brief expression of the truth.

XLIX. THE JURISTS OF THE DIGEST.

For the position of the *colonus* in Roman Law during the period known as that of the 'classic' Jurists we naturally find our chief source of evidence in the Digest. And it is not surprising that here and there we find passages bearing on labour-questions more or less directly. But in using this evidence it is most necessary to keep in mind the nature and scope of this great compilation. First, it is not a collection of laws. Actual laws were placed in the Codex, based on previous Codes such as the Theodosian (439 AD), after a careful process of sifting and editing, with additions to complete the work. This great task was performed by Justinian's commissioners in 14 months or less. The Justinian Code was confirmed and published in 529 AD, and finally in a revised form rather more than five years later. Secondly, the Digest is a collection of opinions of lawyers whose competence and authority had been officially recognized, and whose *responsa* carried weight in the Roman courts. From early times interpretation had been found indispensable in the administration of the law; and in the course of centuries, both by opinions on cases and by formal treatises, there had grown up such a mass of written jurisprudence as no man could master. These writings were specially copious in the 'classic' period (say from Hadrian to Alexander 117–235). Actual laws are sometimes cited in the form of imperial decisions, finally settling some

---

[1] This conclusion, I am pleased to find, had been forestalled by Esmein p 307.
[2] *Le Colonat Romain* pp 125, 132.

disputed point. But the normal product of discussion is the opinion of this or that eminent jurist as to what is sound law in a particular question. The different opinions of different authorities are often quoted side by side. If this were all, we might congratulate ourselves on having simply a collection of authentic extracts from named authors, conveying their views in their own words. And no doubt many of the extracts are of this character.

But the position is not in fact so simple as this. Tribonian and his fellow-commissioners were set to work at the end of the year 530. Their task was completed and the *Digesta* published with imperial confirmation at the end of 533. Now the juristic literature in existence, of which the Digest was to be an epitome superseding its own sources, was of such prodigious bulk that three years cannot have been sufficient for the work. To read, abstract, classify, and so far as possible to harmonize, this mass of complicated material, was a duty surely needing a much longer time for its satisfactory performance. Moreover, as this official Corpus of jurisprudence was designed for reference and citation as an authority in the courts, it had to be[1] brought up to date. That this necessity greatly increased the commissioners' burden is obvious: nor less so, that it was a duty peculiarly difficult to discharge in haste, and liable, if hurried, to result in obscurities inconsistencies and oversights. That much of the Digest has suffered from overhaste in its production is now generally admitted. Its evidence is therefore to be used with caution. But on the subject of *coloni* the main points of interest are attested by witnesses of high authority, such as Ulpian, in cited passages not reasonably suspected of interpolation. And it is not necessary to follow up a host of details. We have only to reconstruct from the law-sources the characteristic features of agriculture and rustic tenancy as it existed before the time of Diocletian ; and these features are on the whole significant and clear. Fortunately we are not entirely dependent on collection and comparison of scattered references from all parts of the great compilation. One title (XIX 2 *locati conducti*)[2] furnishes us with a quantity of relevant matter classified under one head by the editors themselves.

First and foremost it stands out quite clear that the *colonus* is a free man, who enters into a legal contract as lessee with lessor, and that landlord and tenant are equally bound by the terms of the lease. If any clause requires interpretation owing to special circumstances having arisen, the jurist endeavours to lay down the principles by which the court should be guided to an equitable decision. For in-

---

[1] In fact, as we say, *edited*.
[2] Of this Title there is a useful little edition by the late C H Monro.

stance, any fact by which the productiveness of a farm and therewith the solvency of the tenant are impaired may lead to a dispute. Care is therefore taken to relieve the tenant of responsibility for damage inflicted by irresistible force (natural or human)[1] or due to the land-lord's fault. But defects of climate and soil[2] give no claim to relief, since he is presumed to have taken the farm with his eyes open: nor does the failure of worn-out fruit trees, which tenants were regularly bound by their covenant to replace. The chief rights of the landlord[3] are the proper cultivation of the farm and regular payment of the rent. In these the law duly protects him. The tenant is bound not to let down the land by neglect, or to defraud[4] the landlord by misappro-priating what does not belong to him: rent is secured normally by sureties (*fideiussores*)[5] found by the tenant at the time of leasing, or sometimes by the fact that all property of his on the farm is expressly pledged[6] to the lessor on this account. Thus it is the aim of the law to guard the presumably poorer and humbler party against hard treat-ment, while it protects the man of property against fraud. In other words, it aims at strict enforcement of the terms[7] of lease, while in-clined to construe genuinely doubtful points or mistakes in favour[8] of the party bound. That landlord and tenant, even in cases of fixed money rent, have a certain community[9] of interest, seems recognized in the fact that some legal remedies against third persons (for ma-licious damage etc) could in some cases be employed[10] by either land-lord or tenant. In short, the latter is a thoroughly free and responsible person.

That a tenant should be protected against disturbance[11] was a matter of course. During the term of his lease he has a right to make his lawful profit on the farm : the landlord is not only bound to allow him full enjoyment (*frui licere*), but to prevent molestation by a third party over whom he has control. Indeed the tenant farmer has in some relations a more positive protection than the landlord himself. Thus a person who has right of *usus* over an estate may in certain circum-stances refuse[12] to admit the *dominus*; but not the *colonus* or his staff of slaves employed in the farm-work. Change of ownership can perhaps

---

[1] XIX 2 § 15[2], 25[6], also § 15[1, 8]. [2] XIX 2 § 15[2, 5].
[3] XIX 2 §§ 15[3], 24[2], 25[3], 51[pr], 54[1]. [4] XVII 2 § 46, XLIV 7 § 34[2], XLVII 2 § 68[5].
[5] XIX 2 § 54[pr], XX 6 § 14, etc. [6] XX 1 § 21[pr], XLIII 32, 33, XLVII 2 § 62[3].
[7] XIX 2 §§ 9[2, 3], 23, 51[pr], XLV 1 § 89. [8] XIX 2 § 52, cf XLIX 14 § 50.
[9] XIX 2 § 25[6] (Gaius?).
[10] IX 2 § 27[14], XLVII 2 § 83[1], § 10 § 5[4]. Compare also XIX 2 § 60[5], XLVII 2 § 52[8]. I cannot deal with the difficult legal questions involved here. See Buckland's *Elementary principles* § 135.
[11] XIX 2 §§ 15[8], 24[4], 25[1], XXXIII 4 § 1[15].
[12] VII 8 §§ 10[4], 11. Having nothing to do with the *fructus*, the usuary cannot interfere with the *colonus*.

never be a matter of indifference to the sitting tenant of a farm. But it is the lawyer's aim to see that the passing of the property shall not impair the tenant's rights under his current lease. A lease sometimes contained clauses fixing the terms (such as a money forfeit)[1] on which the contract might be broken; in fact a cross-guarantee between the parties, securing the tenant against damage by premature ejectment and the landlord against damage by the tenant's premature quitting. The jurists often appeal to local custom as a means of equitable decision on disputed points. But one customary principle seems to be recognized[2] as of general validity, the rule of *reconductio.* If, on expiration of a lease, the tenant holds on and the landlord allows him to remain, it is regarded as a renewal of the contract by bare agreement (*nudo consensu*). No set form of lease is necessary; but this tacit contract holds good only from year to year. Another fact significant as to the position of the *colonus* is that he is assumed to have the right to sublet[3] the farm: questions that would in that case arise are dealt with as matters of course. I suppose that a lease might be so drawn as to bar any such right, but that in practice it was always or generally admitted. Again, it is a sign of his genuinely independent position in the eye of the law that his own oath, if required of him, may be accepted[4] as a counter-active plea (*exceptio iurisiurandi*) in his own defence, when sued by his landlord for damage done on the farm.

On the economic side we have first to remark that the *colonus* is represented as normally a man of small means. It is true that in the Digest *conductor* and *colonus* are not clearly[5] distinguished, as we find them in the African inscriptions and in the later law. For the former is simply the counterpart of *locator*, properly connoting the relation between the contracting parties: *colonus* expresses the fact that the cultivation (*colere*) of land belonging to another devolves upon him by virtue of the contract. Every *colonus* is a *conductor*, but not every *conductor* a *colonus.* Now custom, recognized by the lawyers, provided a means of supplying the small man's need of capital. To set him up in a farm, the landlord equipped him with a certain stock (*instrumentum*). This he took over at a valuation, not paying ready money for it, but accepting liability[6] to account for the value at the end of his tenancy. The stock or plant included[7] implements and animals (oxen, slaves,

---

[1] XIX 2 § 54[1].

[2] XIX 2 §§ 13[11], 14. The normal term of a lease was 5 years (*lustrum, quinquennium*).

[3] XIX 2 § 24[1], XLI 2 § 30[6], XLIII 16 § 20. So in law of 224 AD, cod Iust IV 65 § 6.

[4] XII 2 § 28[6].

[5] XIX 2 § 25[3], XL 7 § 40[5]. Compare the language of XXXIV 3 § 16 with § 18.

[6] XIX 2 §§ 3, 54[2].

[7] XIX 2 § 19[2], XXXII §§ 91[1], 93[2], 101[1], XXXIII 7 *passim*, esp § 4. For the *vilicus*, XXXIII 7 §§ 18[4], 20[1]. A woman caretaker, *ibid* § 15[2].

etc), and a miscellaneous array of things, of course varying with the nature of the farm and local custom. To this nucleus he had inevitably to add belongings[1] of his own, which were likely to increase with time if the farm prospered in his hands. His rent[2] might be either a fixed yearly payment in cash or produce, or a proportionate share of produce varying from year to year. The money-rent[3] seems to have been the usual plan, and it was in connexion therewith that claims for abatement generally arose. The impression left by the frequent references to *reliqua* in the Digest, and the experiences of the younger Pliny, is that tenant-farmers in Italy were habitually behind with their rents and claiming[4] *remissio*. This is probably true of the period (say) 100–250 AD, with which we are here concerned. It was probably a time of great difficulty for both landlords and tenants, at least outside the range of suburban market-gardening. Signs are not lacking that want of sufficient capital[5] cramped the vigour of agriculture directly and indirectly. Improvements might so raise the standard of cultivation on an estate as to leave an awkward problem for the owner. Its upkeep on its present level might need a large capital ; tenants of means were not easy to find, and subdivision into smaller holdings would not in all circumstances provide a satisfactory solution. Moreover, if the man of means was not unlikely to act independently, in defiance of the landlord, the small man was more likely to take opportunities of misappropriating things to which he was not entitled.

All these difficulties, and others, suggest no great prosperity in Italian agriculture of the period. That on certain soils farming did not pay, was as well known[6] to the jurists as to other writers. And one great cause of agricultural decline appears in their incidental remarks as clearly as in literature. It was the devotion of much of the best land in the best situations to the unproductive parks and pleasure-grounds of the rich. This can hardly be laid to the account of the still favoured financial position of Italy as compared with the Provinces, for we find the same state of things existing late in the fourth century, when Italy had long been provincialized and taxed accordingly. It was fashion, and fashion of long standing, that caused this evil. And this cause was itself an effect of the conditions of investment. The syndicates for exploiting provincial dues had gone with the Republic.

---

[1] XXXIII 7 § 24.   [2] XIX 2 §§ 19[3], 25[6].

[3] XXXIII 7 §§ 18[4], 20[1], XLVII 2 § 26[1]. I note that de Coulanges p 14 holds that the contract rested solely on the basis of a fixed money rent, citing (p 12) Gaius III 142, Dig XIX 2 § 2[pr] (Gaius). But I am not satisfied that cases of rent in kind were not subject to legal remedy. See Monro on Dig XIX 2 § 19[3], and Pliny *epist* IX 37 § 3. And Vinogradoff, *Growth of the Manor* note 91 on p 109.

[4] See XIX 2 § 15.   [5] XIII 7 § 25, XXXI § 86[1].

[6] VII 1 § 41, XXVII 9 § 13[pr].

State contracts and industrial enterprises were not enough to employ all the available capital. The ownership of land, now that politics were not a school of ambition, was more than ever the chief source of social importance. A man who could afford to own vast unremunerative estates was a great personage. We may add that such estates, being unremunerative, were less likely to attract the fatal attention of bad emperors, while good rulers deliberately encouraged rich men to invest fortunes in them as being an evidence of loyalty to the government. The uneconomic rural conditions thus created are plainly referred to in the staid remarks of the jurists. We read of estates owned for pleasure (*voluptaria praedia*)[1]: of cases where it may be doubted[2] whether the *fundus* does not rather belong to the *villa* than the *villa* to the *fundus*: and the use of the work *praetorium*[3] (= great mansion, palace, 'Court') for the lord's headquarters on his demesne becomes almost official in the mouth of lawyers. Meanwhile great estates abroad could be, and were, profitable to their owners, who drew rent from tenants and were normally non-resident. Yet *praetoria* were sometimes found even in the Provinces.

In connexion with this topic it is natural to consider the questions of upkeep and improvements. The former is simple. As the tenant has the disposal of the crops raised and gathered (*fructus*), he is bound[4] to till the soil, to keep up the stock of plants, and to see that the drainage of the farm is in working order. Further detail is unnecessary, as his liability must be gauged by the state of the farm when he took it over. Improvements look to the future. From the lawyers we get only the legal point of view, which is of some interest as proving that the subject was of sufficient importance not to be overlooked. Now it seems certain that a *conductor* or *colonus* had a right of action to recover[5] from the *dominus* not only compensation for unexhausted improvements, but his whole outlay on them, if shewn to have been beneficial. Or his claim might rest on the fact that the project had been approved[6] by the landlord. But it might happen that a work beneficial to the particular estate was detrimental to a neighbouring one. In such a case, against whom—landlord or tenant—had the owner of that estate a legal remedy? It was held that, if the tenant had carried out the work in question[7] without his landlord's knowledge, he alone was liable. If, as some held, the landlord was bound to provide a particular remedy, he could recover the amount paid under this head from his tenant. To insure the owner

---

[1] VII 1 § 13[4].   [2] VII 4 §§ 8, 10.

[3] XXXII § 91[1], L 16 § 198. Cf Juvenal 1 75, Suet *Aug* 72, Gaius 37, Palladius 1 8, 11, 24, 33.

[4] VII 1 § 13, XII 2 § 28[6], XIX 2 §§ 25[5], 29, XLVII 2 §§ 26[1], 62[8], 7 § 9.

[5] XIX 2 §§ 55[1], 61[pr].   [6] XLIII 24 § 13[6].   [7] XXXIX 3 §§ 42[2,3], 5.

against loss from the acts of his lessee was evidently an object of the first importance, and this is in harmony with the Roman lawyers' intense respect for rights of property. The general impression left on the reader of their utterances on this subject is that a landlord, after providing a considerable *instrumentum*, had done all that could reasonably be expected from him. Improvements, the desirability of which was usually discovered through the tenant's experience, were normally regarded as the tenant's business : it was only necessary to prevent the landlord from arbitrarily confiscating what the tenant had done to improve his property. Obviously such 'improvements' were likely to occasion disputes as to the value of the work done : but it was the custom of the countryside to refer technical questions of this kind to the arbitration of an impartial umpire (*vir bonus*), no doubt a neighbour familiar with local circumstances. On the whole, it does not appear that the law treated the *colonus* badly under this head, and the difficulty of securing good tenants may be supposed to have guaranteed him against unfair administration.

A great many more details illustrating the position of *coloni* as they appear in the Digest could be added here, but I think the above will be found ample for my purpose. The next topic to be dealt with is that of labour, so far as the references of the lawyers give us any information. First it is to be noted that the two systems[1] of estate-management, that of cultivation for landlord's account by his *actor* or *vilicus*, and that of letting to tenant farmers, were existing side by side. The latter plan was to all appearance more commonly followed than it would seem to have been in the time of Columella, but the former was still working. A confident opinion as to the comparative frequency[2] of the two systems is hardly to be formed on Digest evidence : for in rustic matters the interest of lawyers was almost solely concerned with the relations of landlord and tenant. What an owner did with his own property on his own account was almost entirely his own business. There are signs that a certain change in the traditional nomenclature represents a real change of function in the case of landlords' managers. The term *actor* is superseding[3] *vilicus*, but the *vilicus* still remains. He would seem to be now more of a mere farm-bailiff, charged with the cultivation of some part or parts of an estate that are not let to tenants. It may even be that he is left with a free hand and only required to pay a fixed[4] yearly return. If so, this arrangement is not easily to be distinguished from the case of a slave *colonus*

---

[1] Alternative, XX I § 32.

[2] A curious case is the putting in an *imaginarius colonus* [of course at a high nominal rent] in order to raise the selling price of a farm. XIX I § 49 (jurist of 4th cent), earlier in Fr Vat § 13.

[3] See XXXII § 41⁵, XXXIV 4 § 31ᵖʳ.   [4] XXXIII 7 §§ 18⁴, 20¹, XL 7 § 40⁵.

or *quasi colonus*[1] occupying a farm. The financial and general supervision of the estate is in the hands of the *actor*[2], who collects all dues, including rents of *coloni*, and is held to full account[3] for all these receipts as well as for the contents of the store-rooms. He is a slave, but a valuable and trusted man: it is significant that the manumission[4] of *actores* is not seldom mentioned. Evidently the qualities looked for in such an agent were observed to develope most readily under a prospect of freedom. But, so long as he remained *actor* of an estate, he could be regarded as part of it: in a bequest the testator could include him as a part[5], and often did so: and indeed his peculiar knowledge of local detail must often have been an important element in its value. To employ such a person in the management of an estate, with powerful inducements to good conduct, may have solved many a difficult problem. We may perhaps guess that it made the employment of a qualified legal agent (*procurator*) less often necessary, at least if the *actor* contrived to avoid friction with his master's free tenants.

Whether an estate was farmed for the owner by his manager, or let to tenants, or partly on one system partly on the other, it is clear that slave-labour is assumed as the normal basis of working. For the *colonus* takes over slaves supplied by the *dominus* as an item of the *instrumentum*. And there was nothing to prevent him from adding slaves of his own, if he could afford it and thought it worth his while to employ a larger staff. Whether such additions were often or ever made, we must not expect the lawyers to tell us; but we do now and then hear[6] of a slave who is the tenant's own. Such a slave might as part of the tenant's goods be pledged to the landlord as security for his rent, but he would not be a part of the estate of which the landlord could dispose by sale or bequest. In such a case the slaves might be regarded[7] as accessories of the *fundus*, if it were so agreed. This raised questions as to the degree of connexion that should be treated as qualifying a slave to be considered an appurtenance of a farm. The answer was in effect that he must be a member of the regular staff. Mere temporary employment on the place did not so attach him, mere temporary absence on duty elsewhere did not detach him. A further question was whether all slaves in any sort of employment on the place were included, or only such as were actually engaged in farm work proper, cultivation of the soil, not those employed in various

[1] xv 3 § 16, XXXIII 7 § 12³, 8 § 23³.   [2] *servus actor*, his *rationes*, XL 7 § 40ᵖʳ, ⁴, ⁵.
[3] His *reliqua*, XXXII §§ 91ᵖʳ, 97.   [4] XXXIV 1 § 18³, 3 § 12, XL 7 § 40 *passim*.
[5] XXXII §§ 41², 91ᵖʳ, XXXIII 7 §§ 12³⁸, 20³, ⁴, 22¹. These refer to *legata*, in which particular intention could be expressed, cf XXXII § 91¹.
[6] IX 2 § 27⁹, ¹¹, XIX 2 § 30⁴.
[7] XXI 1 § 32, XXVIII 5 § 35³, XXXII §§ 60³, 68³, XXXIII 7 § 20.

subsidiary[1] industries. These questions the jurists discussed fully, but we cannot follow them here, as their legal importance is chiefly in connexion with property and can hardly have affected seriously the position of tenants. But it is interesting to observe that the lawyers were feeling the necessity of attempting some practical classification. The distinction[2] between *urbana* and *rustica mancipia* was old enough as a loose conversational or literary one. But, when rights of inheritance or legacy of such valuable property were involved, it became important to define (if possible) the essential characteristics of a 'rustic' slave.

That the condition of the rustic slave was improving, and generally far better than it had been on the *latifundia* of Republican days, seems indicated by the jurists' speaking of a slave as *colonus* or *quasi colonus* without any suggestion of strangeness in the relation. We may assume that only slaves of exceptional capacity and merit would be placed in a position of economic (if not legal) equality with free tenants. Still the growth of such a custom can hardly have been without some effect on the condition of rustic slaves in general. It was not new in the second century: it is referred to by a jurist[3] of the Augustan age. The increasing difficulty of getting either good tenants or good slaves no doubt induced landlords to entrust farms to men who could and would work them profitably, whether freemen or slaves. And a slave had in agriculture, as in trades and finance, a point in his favour: his person and his goods[4] remained in his master's power. If by skilled and honest management he relieved his master of trouble and worry, and contributed by regular payment of rent to assure his income, it was reasonable to look for gratitude expressed, on the usual Roman lines, in his master's will. Manumission, perhaps accompanied by bequest[5] of the very farm that he had worked so well, was a probable reward. May we not guess that some of the best farming carried on in Italy under the earlier Empire was achieved by trusted slaves, in whom servile apathy was overcome by hope? Such a farmer-slave would surely have under him[6] slave labourers, the property of his master; and he would have the strongest possible motives for tact and skill in their management, while his own capacity had been developed by practical experience. I can point to no arrangement in Roman agriculture so calculated to make it efficient on a basis of slavery as this.

[1] See above on Martial pp 307–10.
[2] XXXII § 99, XXXIII 7 *passim*, esp § 25[1]. Buckland, *Slavery* p 6.
[3] Alfenus Varus in Dig XV 3 § 16.
[4] Hence the frequent references to *peculia*. See XXXIII 8 *de peculio legato*, where from §§ 6[pr], 8[pr], it appears that his *peculium* might include land and houses. Cf de Coulanges pp 55–6, 66–7, 135–6.
[5] XXXII § 97 etc.　　　　　　　[6] XXXIII 7 § 12[3] etc.

H. A.

24

The services (*operae*) of a slave, due to his owner or to some one in place of his owner, were a property capable of valuation, and therefore could be let and hired at a price. That is, the person to whom they were due could commute[1] them for a *merces*. This might, as in the corresponding Greek case of ἀποφορά, be a paying business, if a slave had been bought cheap and trained so as to earn good wages. It was common enough in various trades: what concerns us is that the plan was evidently in use in the rustic world also. Now this is notable. We naturally ask, if the man's services were worth so much to the hirer, why should they not have been worth as much (or even a little more) to his own master? Why should it pay to let him rather than to use him yourself? Of course the owner might have more slaves than he needed at the moment: or the hirer might be led by temporary need of labour to offer a fancy price for the accommodation: or two masters on neighbouring farms might engage in a reciprocity of cross-hirings to suit their mutual convenience at certain seasons. Further possibilities might be suggested, but are such occasional explanations sufficient to account for the prevalence of this hiring-system? I think not. Surely the principal influence, steadily operating in this direction, was one that implied an admission of the economic failure of slavery. If A's slave worked for B so well that it paid A to let him do so and to receive a rent for his services, it follows that the slave had some inducement to exert his powers more fully as B's hireling than in the course of ordinary duty under his own master. Either the nature and conditions of the work under B were pleasanter, or he received something for himself over and above the stipulated sum claimed by his master. In other words, as a mere slave he did not do his best: as a hired man he felt some of the stimulus that a free man gets from the prospect of his wage. So Slavery, already philanthropically questioned, was in this confession economically condemned.

These points considered, we are not surprised to find mention of slaves letting out their own[2] *operae*. This must imply the consent of their masters, and it is perhaps not rash to see in such a situation a sign of weakening in the effective authority of masters. A master whose interest is bound up with the fullest development of his slave's powers (as rentable property exposed to competition) will hardly act the martinet without forecasting the possible damage to his own pocket. A slave who knows that his master draws an income from his efficiency is in a strong position for gradually extorting privileges till he attains no small degree of independence. We may perhaps find traces of such an advance in the arrangement by which a slave hires

[1] VII 7 § 3 *in hominis usu fructu operae sunt et ob operas mercedes* (Gaius), XII 6 § 55.
[2] VII 1 §§ 25, 26, XIX 2 § 60[7] (Labeo, time of Augustus, cited by Javolenus).

his own *operae*[1] from his master. He will thus make a profit out of hiring himself: in fact he is openly declaring that he will not work at full power for his master, but only compound with him for output on the scale of an ordinary slave. This arrangement was common in arts and handicrafts, and not specially characteristic of Rome. In rustic life, the slave put into a farm as tenant[2] at a fixed rent, and taking profit and loss, may furnish an instance. Whether such cases were frequent we do not know. The general impression left by the Digest passages on hiring and letting of slaves is that, when we read of *mercennarii,* it is generally if not always hireling[3] slaves, not free wage-earners, that are meant. In a passage[4] where *servus* occurs as well as *mercennarius,* it is reference to the owner as well as to the hirer that necessitates the addition. If I have interpreted these points aright, the picture suggested is a state of things in which the rustic slave was steadily improving his position, supplying hired labour, at times entrusted with the charge of a farm, and with a fair prospect of becoming by manumission under his owner's will a free *colonus,* or even his own landlord. How far this picture is really characteristic of rustic Italy, or of the Provinces (such as Gaul or Spain), is what one would like to know, but I can find no evidence.

In the foregoing paragraphs I have refrained from inquiring whether the *colonus* as he appears in the Digest was a farmer who worked with his own hands, or merely an employer and director of labour. The reason is that I have found in the texts no evidence whatever on the point. It was not the jurist's business. We are left to guess at the truth as best we may, and we can only start from consideration of the farmer's own interest, and assume that the average farmer knew his own interest and was guided thereby. Now, being bound to pay rent in some form or other and to make good any deficiencies in the *instrumentum* at the end of his tenancy, he had every inducement to get all he could out of the land while he held it. How best to do this, was his problem. And the answer no doubt varied according to the size of the farm, the kind of crops that could profitably be raised there, and the number and quality of the staff. In some rough operations, his constant presence on one spot and sharing the actual work might get the most out of his men. Where nicety of skill was the main thing, he might better spend his time in direction and minute watching of the hands. On a fairly large farm he would have enough to do as director. We may reasonably guess that he only toiled with his own hands if he thought it would pay him to do so.

---

[1] XL 7 § 14^{pr} *mercedem referre pro operis suis* (Alfenus), cf XLV 3 § 18^{3}.

[2] XXXIII 7 §§ 18^{4}, 20^{1}. *mercede* or *pensionis certa quantitate* as opposed to *fide dominica.*

[3] VIII 6 § 20, XLIII 16 § 1^{20}, 24 § 3^{pr}.   [4] XLIII 24 § 5^{11}.

This *a priori* guesswork is not satisfactory. But I see nothing else to be said; for the African inscriptions do not help us. The circumstances of those great domains were exceptional.

So far we have been viewing agriculture as proceeding in times and under conditions assumed to be more or less normal, without taking account of the various disturbing elements in rustic life, by which both landlords and tenants were liable to suffer vexation and loss. Yet these were not a few. Even a lawyer could not ignore wild beasts. Wolves carried off some of A's pigs. Dogs kept by B, *colonus* of a neighbouring *villa*, for protection of his own flocks, rescued the pigs. A legal question[1] at once arises: are the rescued pigs regarded as wild game, and therefore belonging to the owner of the dogs? No, says the jurist. They were still within reach; A had not given them up for lost; if B tries to retain them, the law provides remedies to make him give them up. I presume that B would have a claim to some reward for his services. But the lawyer is silent, confining his opinion to the one question of property. References to depredations of robbers or brigands (*latrones, grassatores,*) occur often, and quite as a matter of course. The police of rural Italy, not to mention the Provinces, was an old scandal. Stock-thieves, who lifted a farmer's cattle sheep or goats, and sometimes his crops, were important enough to have a descriptive name (*abigei*)[2] and a title of the Digest to themselves. That bad neighbours made themselves unpleasant in many ways, and that their presence gave a bad name to properties near them, was an experience of all lands and all ages: but the jurists treat it gravely[3] as a lawyer's matter. Concealment of such a detrimental fact[4] by the seller of an estate made the sale voidable. The rich (old offenders in this kind) were by a rescript of Hadrian[5] awarded differential punishment for removing landmarks: in their case the purpose of encroachment was not a matter open to doubt.

In one connexion the use of force as an embarrassing feature of rustic life was a subject of peculiar interest to the jurists, and had long been so. This was in relation to questions of possession. In Roman law *possessio* held a very important place. All that need be said of it here is that the fact of possession, or lack of it, seriously affected the position of litigants in disputes as to property. Great ingenuity was exercised in definition and in laying down rules for ascertaining the fact. Now among the means employed in gaining or recovering possession none was more striking or more effective than the use of force. Special legal remedies had been provided to deal with such violence;

[1] XLI 1 § 44.   [2] XLVII 14, cf XLVIII 19 § 16[7], XLIX 16 § 5[2].
[3] In XIX 2 § 25[4] (Gaius?) the tenant is held to blame for wilful damage done by a neighbour with whom he has a quarrel.
[4] XVIII 1 § 35[8].   [5] XLVII 21 § 2.

interdicta issued by the praetor, to forbid it, or to reinstate a claimant dislodged by his rival, or simply to state the exact issue raised in a particular case. On conformity or disobedience to the praetor's order the case was formally tried in court: the question of law mainly turned on questions of fact. What concerns us is that force was solemnly classified under two heads, *vis* and *vis armata*. Each of these had its own proper interdict at least as early as the time of Cicero, and they occupy a whole title[1] in the Digest. Clearly the use of force was no negligible matter. That it was a danger or at least a nuisance to owners or claimants of property, is not less clear. But how did it touch the *colonus?* He was, as such, neither owner nor claimant of the property of his farm. He had in his own capacity[2] no possession either. But, as tenant of a particular owner, his presence operated[3] to secure the possession of his landlord. Hence to oust him by force broke the landlord's possession; whether rightly or wrongly, the law had to decide. Now it is obvious that, in cases where serious affrays resulted from intrusion, a tenant might suffer grave damage to his goods and person. The intruders (often a gang of slaves) would seldom be so punctiliously gentle as to do no harm at all. Therefore, having regard to the amount of interest in this subject shewn by the lawyers, we cannot omit the use of force in matters of possession from the list of rustic embarrassments.

Another cause of annoyance was connected with servitudes, such as rights of way and water, which were frequent subjects of dispute in country districts. Whether regarded as rights or as burdens, the principles governing them were a topic that engaged the minute and laborious attention[4] of the lawyers. Now it is evident that a right of way or water through an estate, though a material advantage to a neighbouring estate served by the convenience, might be a material disadvantage to the one over which the right extended. Also that the annoyance might be indefinitely increased or lessened by the cantankerous or considerate user of the right by the person or persons enjoying it. When we consider that servitudes were already an important department of jurisprudence in Republican days, and see how great a space they occupy in the Digest, we can hardly resist the conclusion that country proprietors found in them a fertile subject of quarrels. But surely the quarrels of landlords over a matter of this kind could not be carried on without occasional and perhaps frequent disturbances and injury to the tenants on the land. Even if the law provided means

---

[1] XLIII 16, *de vi et de vi armata.*
[2] XLI 3 § 33[1] etc. [3] XLI 2 §§ 3[8, 12], 25[1], etc.
[4] VIII 3 *de servitutibus praediorum rusticorum.* Specimens of inscribed notices of servitudes, Girard *textes* part III ch 3 § 1.

of getting compensation for any damage done to a tenant's crops or other goods in the course of attempts to enforce or defeat a claimed servitude, was the average *colonus* a man readily to seek compensation in the law-courts? I think not. But, if not, he would depend solely on the goodwill of his own landlord, supposing the latter to have got the upper hand in the main dispute. On the whole, I strongly suspect that in practice these quarrels over rustic servitudes were a greater nuisance to farmers than might be supposed. So far as I know, we have no statement of the farmer's point of view. Another intermittent but damaging occurrence was the occasional passage of soldiery, whose discipline was often lax. We might easily forget the depredations and general misconduct of these unruly ruffians, and imagine that such annoyances only became noticeable in a later period. But the jurists do not allow us to forget[1] the military requisitions for supply of troops on the march, the payment for which is not clearly provided, and would at best be a cause of trouble; or the pilferings of the men, compensation for which was probably not to be had. It would be farmers in northern Italy and the frontier-provinces that were the chief sufferers.

Damage by natural disturbances or by fires may happen in any age or country. That Italy in particular was exposed to the effect of floods and earthquakes, we know. Accordingly the lawyers are seriously concerned with the legal and equitable questions arising out of such events. It was not merely the claim of tenants[2] to abatement of rent that called for a statement of principles. Beside the sudden effects of earthquakes torrents or fires, there were the slower processes of streams changing their courses[3] and gradual land-slides on the slopes of hills. These movements generally affected the proprietary relations of neighbouring landlords, taking away land from one, sometimes giving to another. Here was a fine opening for ingenious jurists, of which they took full advantage. The growth of estates by alluvion, and loss by erosion, was a favourite topic, the operation of which, and the questions thereby raised, are so earnestly treated as to shew their great importance in country life. Of fire-damage, due to malice or neglect, no more need be said; nor of many other minor matters.

But, when all the above drawbacks have been allowed for, it is still probably true that scarcity of labour was a far greater difficulty for farmers. We hear very little directly of this trouble, as it raised no point

---

[1] VII 1 § 27[3], XIX 2 § 15[2] (Ulpian). The abuse of the quartering of troops was no new evil in the Provinces. We hear of it from Cicero. In the third century AD we have the notable petitions from Scaptoparene in Thrace (238) text in Mommsen *ges Schr* II 174–6, and from the Aragueni in Asia Minor (244–7), text in Dittenberger *Or Graec inscr* No 519. For Italy in 5th century see on Symmachus.

[2] XIX 2 §§ 9[3], 15.   [3] XLI 1 § 7[1–6], etc.

of law. Very significant[1] however are the attempts of the Senate and certain emperors to put down an inveterate scandal which is surely good indirect evidence of the scarcity. It consisted in the harbouring[2] of runaway slaves on the estates of other landlords. A runaway from one estate was of course not protected and fed on another estate from motives of philanthropy. The slave would be well aware that severe punishment awaited him if recovered by his owner, and therefore be willing to work for a new master who might, if displeased, surrender him any day. The landlords guilty of this treason to the interests of their class were probably the same as those who harboured[3] brigands, another practice injurious to peaceful agriculture both in Italy and abroad. Another inconvenience, affecting all trades and all parts of the empire in various degrees, was the local difference in the money-value[4] of commodities in different markets. This was sometimes great: and that it was troublesome to farmers may be inferred from the particular mention of wine oil and corn as cases in point. No doubt dealers had the advantage over producers, as they generally have, through possessing a more than local knowledge of necessary facts. These middlemen however could not be dispensed with, as experience shewed, and one of the later jurists[5] openly recognized. Facilities for borrowing, and rates of interest, varied greatly in various centres. But all these market questions do not seem to have been so acute as to be a public danger until the ruinous debasement of the currency in the time of Gallienus. A few references may be found to peculiar usages of country life in particular Provinces. Thus we read that in Arabia[6] farms were sometimes 'boycotted,' any person cultivating such a farm being threatened with assassination. In Egypt[7] special care had to be taken to protect the dykes regulating the distribution of Nile water. Both these offences were summarily dealt with by the provincial governor, and the penalty was death. Here we have one more proof of the anxiety of the imperial government to insure the greatest possible production of food. The empire was always hungry,—and so were the barbarians. And the northern frontier provinces could not feed both themselves and the armies.

While speaking of landlords and tenants we must not forget that all over the empire considerable areas of land were owned by municipalities, and dealt with at the discretion of the local authorities. Variety of systems was no doubt dictated by variety of local circumstances:

---

[1] XI 4 § 1[1], cf Paulus *sent* I 6 *a* § 5.

[2] Dealt with later in the Codes as a frequent evil. For early medieval laws on the point see de Coulanges p 152.

[3] XLVII 9 §§ 3[3], 16, Paulus *sent* V 3 § 4.   [4] XIII 4 § 3.

[5] Callistratus in L 11 § 2, quoting Plato *rep* 371 *a–c*.

[6] XLVII 11 § 9.   [7] XLVII 11 § 10, cf cod Th IX 32 § 1, cod Just IX 38.

but one characteristic was so general as to deserve special attention on the part of jurists. This was the system of perpetual leaseholds[1] at a fixed (and undoubtedly beneficial) rent, heritable and transferable to assigns. So long as the tenant regularly paid the *vectigal*, his occupation was not to be disturbed. It was evidently the desire of the municipal authorities to have a certain income to reckon with: for the sake of certainty they would put up with something less than a rackrent. There were also other lands owned by these *civitates* that were let on the system[2] in use by private landlords; the normal term probably being five years. Of these no more need be said here. Beneficial leases under a municipality were liable to corrupt management. It had been found necessary[3] to disqualify members of the local Senate (*decuriones*) from holding such leases, that they might not share out the common lands among themselves on beneficial terms. But this prohibition was not enough. The town worthies put in men of straw[4] as nominal tenants, through whom they enjoyed the benefits of the leases. So this evasion also had to be met by revoking the ill-gotten privilege. But disturbance of tenancies was not to be lightly allowed, so it appears that a reference to the emperor[5] was necessary before such revocation could take place. This system of perpetual leases is of interest, not as indicating different methods of cultivation from those practised on private estates, but as betraying a tendency to fixity[6] already existing, destined to spread and to take other forms, and to become the fatal characteristic of the later Empire. Another striking piece of evidence in the same direction occurs in connexion with the lessees (*publicani*) of various state dues (*vectigalia publica*) farmed out in the usual way. In the first half of the third century the jurist Paulus attests[7] the fact that, in case it was found that the right of collecting such dues, hitherto very profitable to the lessees, could only be let at a lower lump sum than hitherto, the old lessees were held bound to continue their contract at the old price. But Callistratus, contemporary or nearly so, tells us that this was not so, and quotes[8] a rescript of Hadrian (117–138 AD) condemning the practice as tyrannical and likely to deter men from entering into so treacherous a bargain. It appears that other[9]

---

[1] *agri vectigales* or (as the title calls them by a later name) *emphyteuticarii.* VI 3 §§ 1, 2, XIX 1 § 13[6], XLIII 9 § 1, L 16 § 219. Large blocks were also hired by middlemen (*mancipes*) and sublet in parcels to *coloni,* XIX 2 § 53.

[2] VI 3 §§ 1, 3.   [3] L 8 § 2[1].

[4] *subiectis aliorum nominibus.*   [5] XXXIX 4 § 11[1], *auctoritate principali.*

[6] Gaius III 145 concludes that the contract in these leases is one of letting and hiring, not of purchase and sale. That is, it includes everything save the bare *dominium,* notably *possessio,* and, as Prof Buckland points out to me, covenants usual in such cases could be enforced by the *actio ex locato.*

[7] XXXIX 4 § 11[5].   [8] XLIX 14 § 3[6].

[9] *principalibus rescriptis.* From the text I infer that these are later than Hadrian.

emperors had forbidden it, but there is no proof that they succeeded in stopping it. At all events the resort to coercion in a matter of contract like this reveals the presence of a belief in compulsory fixity, ominous of the coming imperial paralysis, though of course not so understood at the time. It did not directly affect agriculture as yet; but its application to agriculture was destined to be a symptom and a cause of the empire's decline and fall.

Another group of tenancies, the number and importance of which was quietly increasing, was that known as *praedia Caesaris*[1], *fundi fiscales*, and so forth. We need not discuss the departmental differences and various names of these estates. The tenants, whether small men or *conductores* on a large scale who sublet in parcels[2] to *coloni*, held either directly or indirectly from the emperor. We have seen specimens in Africa, the Province in which the crown-properties were exceptionally large. What chiefly concerns us here is the imperial land-policy. It seems clear that its first aim was to keep these estates permanently occupied by good solvent tenants. The surest means to this end was to give these estates a good name, to create a general impression that on imperial farms a man had a better chance of thriving than on those of average private landlords. Now the 'state,' that is the emperor or his departmental chiefs, could favour crown-tenants in various ways without making a material sacrifice of a financial kind. In particular, the treatment of crown-estates as what we call 'peculiars,' in which local disputes were settled, not by resort to the courts of ordinary law, but administratively[3] by the emperor's *procuratores*, was probably a great relief; above all to the humbler *coloni*, whom we may surely assume to have been a class averse to litigation. No doubt a *procurator* might be corrupted and unjust. But he was probably far more effectually watched than ordinary magistrates; and, if the worst came to the worst, there was as we have seen the hope of a successful appeal to the emperor. Another favour consisted in the exemption of Caesar's tenants from various burdensome official duties in municipalities, the so-called *munera*, which often entailed great expense. This is mentioned by a jurist[4] near the end of the second century: they are only to perform such duties so far as not to cause loss to the treasury. Another[5], somewhat later, says that their exemption is granted in order that they may be more suitable tenants of treasury-farms. This exemption is one more evidence of the well-known fact that in this age municipal offices were beginning to be evaded[6] as ruinous, and no longer sought

---

[1] XXX § 39[10], XIX 2 § 49.   [2] XLIX 14 § 47[1] (Paulus).

[3] XLIII 8 § 2[4] (Ulpian), a very important passage.

[4] Papirius Justus in L 1 § 38[1], *muneribus fungi sine damno fisci oportere.*

[5] Callistratus in L 6 § 6[11], *ut idoniores praediis fiscalibus habeantur.*

[6] References are endless. Most significant is L 4 § 4 (Ulpian) *honores qui indicuntur.*

as an honour. We must note that, if this *immunitas* relieved the crown-tenants, it left all the more burdens to be borne by those who enjoyed no such relief. And this cannot have been good for agriculture in general.

It is not to be supposed that the *fiscus*[1] was a slack and easy landlord. Goods of debtors were promptly seized to cover liabilities: attempts to evade payment of *tributa* by a private agreement[2] between mortgagor and mortgagee were quashed: a rescript[3] of Marcus and Verus insisted on the treasury share ($\frac{1}{2}$) of treasure trove: and so on. But there are signs of a reasonable and considerate policy, in not pressing demands so as to inflict hardship. Trajan[4] had set a good example, and good emperors followed it. We may fairly guess that this moderation in financial dealings was not wholly laid aside in the management of imperial estates. Nor is it to be imagined that the advantages of imperial tenants were exactly the same in all parts of the empire. In Provinces through which armies had to move it is probable that *coloni Caesaris* would suffer less[5] than ordinary farmers from military annoyances. But on the routes to and from a seat of war it is obvious that the imperial post-service would be subjected to exceptional strain. Now this service was at the best of times[6] a cause of vexations and losses to the farmers along the line of traffic. The staff made good all deficiencies in their requirements by taking beasts fodder vehicles etc wherever they could find them: what they restored was much the worse for wear, and compensation, if ever got, was tardy and inadequate. The repair of roads was another pretext for exaction. It is hardly to be doubted that in these respects imperial tenants suffered less than others. Some emperors[7] took steps to ease the burden, which had been found too oppressive to the roadside estates. But this seems to have been no more than relief from official requisitions: irregular 'commandeering' was the worst evil, and we have no reason to think that it was effectually suppressed. It appears in the next period as a rampant abuse, vainly forbidden by the laws of the Theodosian code.

L. THE LATER COLONATE, ITS PLACE IN ROMAN HISTORY.

In the endeavour to extract from scattered and fragmentary evidence some notion of agricultural conditions in the Roman empire before and after Diocletian we are left with two imperfect pictures, so strongly contrasted as to suggest a suspicion of their truth. We can hardly

[1] Title XLIX 14 *de iure fisci*.   [2] II 14 § 42 (Papinian).
[3] XLIX 14 § 3[10].   [4] XLVIII 22 § 1, cf XLIX 14 §§ 47, 50, (Paulus).
[5] That they did sometimes suffer may be inferred from the case of the Aragueni (p 374) who describe themselves as πάροικοι and γεωργοί (=*inquilini* and *coloni*) of the emperor.
[6] L 5 §§ 10, 11, etc.
[7] See Spartian *Hadrian* 7 § 5, Capitolinus *Anton* 12 § 3, Spartian *Severus* 14 § 2.

believe that the system known as the later Colonate appeared in full force as a sudden phenomenon. Nor indeed are we compelled to fly so directly in the face of historical experience. That we have no narrative of the steps that led to this momentous change, is surely due to the inability of contemporaries to discern the future effect of tendencies operating silently[1] and piecemeal. What seems at the moment insignificant, even if observed, is seldom recorded, and very seldom intentionally. Hence after generations, seeking to trace effects to causes, are puzzled by defects of record. Their only resource is to supplement, so far as possible, defective record by general consideration of the history of the time in question and cautious inference therefrom : in fact to get at the true meaning of fragmentary admissions in relation to their historical setting. The chief topic to be dealt with here from this point of view is the character of the Roman Empire in several aspects. For among all the anxieties of the government during these troubled centuries the one that never ceased was the fear of failure in supplies of food.

The character of the Roman Empire had been largely determined by the fact that it arose from the overthrow of a government that had long been practically aristocratic. The popular movements that contributed to this result only revealed the impossibility of establishing anything like a democracy, and the unreality of any power save the power of the sword. The great dissembler Augustus concealed a virtual autocracy by conciliatory handling of the remains of the nobility. But the Senate, to which he left or gave many powers, was never capable of bearing a vital part in the administration, and its influence continued to dwindle under his successors. The master of the army was the master of the empire, and influence was more and more vested in those who were able to guide his policy. That these might be, and sometimes were, not born Romans at all, but imperial freedmen generally of Greek or mixed-Greek origin, was a very significant fact. In particular, it marked and encouraged the growth of departmental bureaus, permanent and efficient beyond the standard of previous Roman experience. But the price of this efficiency was centralization, a condition that carried with it inevitable dangers, owing to the vast extent of the empire. In modern times the fashionable remedy suggested for over-centralization is devolution of powers to local governments controlling areas of considerable size. Or, in cases of aggregation, the existing powers left to states merged in a confederation are considerable. In any case, the subordinate units are free to act within their several

---

[1] De Coulanges makes it his main thesis that the later colonate was a creation of custom, at length recognized by law. My conclusions here were reached before reading his fine treatise.

limited spheres, and the central government respects their 'autonomy,' only interfering in emergencies to enforce the fulfilment of definite common obligations.

But, if it had been desired to gain any such relief by a system of devolution within the Roman empire, this would have meant the recognition of 'autonomy' in the Provinces. And this was inconceivable. The extension of Roman dominion had been achieved by dividing Rome's adversaries. Once conquered, it was the interest or policy of the central power to keep them in hand by preventing the growth of self-conscious cohesion in the several units. Each Province was, as the word implied, a department of the Roman system, ruled by a succession of Roman governors. It looked to Rome for orders, for redress of grievances, for protection at need. If the advance of Rome destroyed no true nations, her government at least made the development of truly national characteristics impossible, while she herself formed no Roman nation. Thus, for better or worse, the empire was non-national. But, as we have already seen, the decline of Italy made it more and more clear that the strength of the empire lay in the Provinces. Now, having no share in initiative and no responsibility, the Provinces steadily lost vitality under Roman civilization, and became more and more helplessly dependent on the central power. As the strain on the empire became greater, the possibility of relief by devolution grew less : but more centralization was no cure for what was already a disease.

That local government of a kind existed in the empire is true enough ; also that it was one of the most striking and important features of the system. But it was municipal, and tended rather to subdivide than to unite. It was the outcome of a civilization profoundly urban in its origins and ideas. The notion that a city was a state was by no means confined to the independent cities of early Greece. Whether it voluntarily merged itself in a League or lived on as a subordinate unit in the system of a dominant power, the city and its territory were politically one. Within their several boundaries the townsmen and rustic citizens of each city were subject to the authorities of that community. Beyond their own boundary they were aliens under the authorities of another city. It is no wonder that jealousies between neighbour cities were often extreme, and that Roman intervention was often needed to keep the peace between rivals. But the system suited Roman policy. In the East and wherever cities existed they were taken over as administrative units and as convenient centres of taxation : in the West it was found useful and practicable to introduce urban centres into tribes and cantons, and even in certain districts to attach[1] local populations to existing cities as dependent hamlets. And,

---

[1] *attributi* or *contributi*. See Mommsen, *Staatsrecht* III, *die attribuirten Orte.*

so long as the imperial government was able to guard the frontiers and avert the shock of disturbances of the Roman peace, the empire held its own in apparent prosperity. To some historians the period of the 'Antonines' (say about 100–170 AD) has seemed a sort of Golden Age. But signs are not lacking that the municipal system had seen its best days. The severe strain on imperial resources in the time of Marcus left behind it general exhaustion. The decay of local patriotism marked the pressure of poverty and loss of vitality in the cities. More and more their importance became that of mere taxation-centres, in which the evasion of duty was the chief preoccupation: they could not re-invigorate the empire, nor the empire them.

Another characteristic of the empire, not less significant than those mentioned above, was this: taken as a whole, it was non-industrial. Manufactures existed here and there, and products of various kinds were exchanged between various parts of the empire. So far as the ordinary population was concerned, the Roman world might well have supplied its own needs. But this was not enough. The armies, though perilously small for the work they had to do, were a heavy burden. The imperial civil service as it became more elaborate did not become less costly. The waste of resources on unremunerative buildings and shows in cities, above all in Rome, and the ceaseless expense of feeding a worthless rabble, were a serious drain: ordained by established custom, maintained by vanity, to economize on these follies would seem a con-fession of weakness. Nor should the extravagance of the rich, and of many emperors, be forgotten: this created a demand for luxuries chiefly imported from the East; precious stones, delicate fabrics, spices, per-fumes, rare woods, ivory, and so forth. Rome had no goods to export in payment for such things, and the scarcity of return-cargoes must have added heavily to the cost of carriage. There was on this account a steady drain of specie to the East, and this had to be met by a corresponding drain of specie to Rome. In one form or another this meant money drawn from the Provinces, for which the Provinces re-ceived hardly the bare pretence of an equivalent, or a better security for peace.

Thus the empire, created by conquest and absorption, administered by bureaucratic centralization, rested on force; a force partly real and still present, partly traditional, derived from a victorious past. The belief in Rome as the eternal city went for much, and we hear of no misgivings as to the soundness of a civilization which expressed itself in a constant excess of consumption over production. Naturally enough, under such conditions, the imperial system became more and more what it really was from the first, a vast machine. It was not a league of cooperating units, each containing a vital principle of growth, and furnishing the power of recovery from disaster. Its apathetic parts looked passively to the centre for guidance or relief, depending on the perfection of a government whose imperfection was assured by attempting a task beyond the reach of human faculty and virtue. The exposure of the empire's weakness came about through collision with the forces of northern barbarism. What a machine could do, that it did, and its final failure was due to maladies that made vain all efforts to renew its internal strength.

The wars with the northern barbarians brought out with singular clearness two important facts, already known but not sufficiently taken into account. First, that the enemy were increasing in numbers while the people of the empire were in most parts stationary or even declining. Bloody victories, when gained, did practically nothing to redress the balance. Secondly, that at the back of this embarrassing situation lay a food-question of extreme seriousness and complexity. More and more food was needed for the armies, and the rustics of the empire, even when fitted for military service, could not be spared from the farms without danger to the food-supply. The demands of the commissariat were probably far greater than we might on the face of it suppose; for an advance into the enemy's territory did not ease matters. Little or nothing was found to eat: indeed it was the pressure of a growing population on the means of subsistence that drove the hungry German tribes to face the Roman sword in quest of abundant food and the wine and oil of the South and West. The attempt of Marcus and others after him, to solve the problems of the moment by enlisting barbarians in Roman armies, was no permanent solution. The aliens too had to be fed, and their pay in money could not be deferred. Meanwhile the taxation of the empire inevitably grew, and the productive industries had to stagger along under heavier burdens. The progressive increase of these is sufficiently illustrated in the history of *indictiones*. At first an *indictio* was no more than an occasional[1] impost of so much corn levied by imperial proclamation on landed properties in order to meet exceptional scarcity in Rome. But it was in addition to the regular *tributum*, and was of course most likely to occur in years when scarcity prevailed. No wonder it was already felt onerous[2] in the time of Trajan. Pressure on imperial resources caused it not only to become more frequent, and eventually normal: it was extended[3] to include other products, and became a regular burden of

---

[1] Cf Dig XXXIII 2 § 28 *indictiones temporariae* [Paulus], XIX 1 § 13⁶ [Ulpian].
[2] Pliny *paneg* 29 (of imperial subjects) *nec novis indictionibus pressi ad vetera tributa deficiunt.*
[3] Hence cod Theod has a title *de superindictionibus.*

almost universal application, and ended by furnishing a new chronological unit, the Indiction-period of 15 years.

That agriculture, already none too prosperous, suffered heavily
under this capricious impost in the second century, seems to me a fact
beyond all doubt. And, not being then a general imperial tax, it fell
upon those provinces that were still flourishing producers of corn.
Debasement of currency already lowered the value of money-taxes,
and tempted emperors to extend the system of dues in kind. Under
Diocletian and Galerius things came to a head. Vast increase of taxation was called for under the new system, and it was mainly taxation
in kind. Already the failure of agriculture was notorious, and attempts
had been made to enforce cultivation of derelict lands. The new taxation only aggravated present evils, and in despair of milder measures
Constantine attached the *coloni* to the soil. Important as the legal
foundation of the later serf-colonate, this law is historically still more
important as a recognition of past failure which nothing had availed
to check. He saw no way of preventing a general stampede from the
farms save to forbid it as illegal, and to employ the whole machinery
of the empire in enforcing the new law. This policy was only a part
of the general tendency to fix everything in a rigid framework, to make
all occupations hereditary, that became normal in the later Empire.
The Codes are a standing record of the principle that the remedy for
failure of legislation was more legislation of the same kind. Hard-
pressed emperors needed all the resources they could muster, particularly food. They had no breathing-space to try whether more freedom
might not promote enterprise and increase production, even had such
a policy come within their view. Hence the cramping crystallizing
process went on with the certainty of fate. The government, unable
to develope existing industry, simply squeezed it to exhaustion.

How came it that the government was able to do this? How came
it that agricultural tenants could be converted into stationary serfs
without causing a general upheaval[1] and immediate dissolution of the
empire? Mainly, I think, because the act of Constantine was no more
than a recognition *de iure* of a condition already created *de facto* by
a long course of servilizing influences. Also because it was the apparent
interest, not only of the imperial treasury but of the great proprietors
generally, to tie down to the soil[2] the cultivators of their estates. Labour
was now more valuable than land. In corn-growing Africa the importance attached to the task-work of sub-tenants was a confession of

---

[1] The rising of the Bagaudae in Gaul, at least partly due to agricultural distress, had been
put down by Maximian in 285–6. See Schiller III pp 124–6.

[2] It is true that the *colonus* was guaranteed against disturbance, but I think de Coulanges
pp 114–7, 123 makes too much of this.

this. And, law or no law, things had to move in one or other direction. Either the landlord and head-lessee had to win further control of the tenants, or the tenants must become less dependent. Only the former alternative was possible in the circumstances ; and the full meaning of the change that turned *de facto* dependence into legal constraint may be stated as a recognition of the *colonus* as labourer rather than tenant. Whether the settlement of barbarians as domiciled aliens in some Provinces under strict conditions of farm-labour had anything to do with the creation of this new semi-servile status, seems hardly to be decided on defective evidence. At all events it cannot have hindered it. And we must make full allowance for the effect of various conditions in various Provinces. If we rightly suppose that the position of *coloni* had been growing weaker for some time before the act of Constantine, this does not imply that the process was due to the same causes operating alike in all parts of the empire in the same degree. The evidence of the Theodosian Code shews many local differences of phe-nomena in the fourth and fifth centuries ; and it is not credible that there was a greater uniformity in the conditions of the preceding age. Laws might aim at uniformity, but they could not alter facts.

My conclusion therefore is that the general character of the imperial system was the main cause of the later serf-colonate. However much the degradation of free farm-tenants, or the admission of slaves to tenancies, or the settlement of barbarians under conditions of service, may have contributed to the result, it was the mechanical nature of the system as a whole that gave effect to them all. After Trajan the rulers of the empire became more and more conscious that the problem before them was one of conservation, and that extension was at an end. Hadrian saw this, and strove to perfect the internal organization. By the time of Aurelian it was found necessary to surrender territory as a further measure of security. We can hardly doubt that under such conditions the machine of internal administration operated more me-chanically than ever. Then, when the reforms of Diocletian made fresh taxation necessary to defray their cost, an agricultural crisis was pro-duced by the turning of the imperial screw. The hierarchy of officials justified their existence by squeezing an assured revenue out of a population unable to resist but able to remove. There was no other source of revenue to take the place of the land : moreover, it was agricultural produce in kind that was required. Therefore the central bureaucracy, unchecked by any public opinion, did after its wont. In that selfish and servile world each one took care of his own skin. Compulsion was the rule : the *coloni* must be made to produce food : therefore they must be bound fast to the soil, or the empire would starve—and the officials with it.

ADDITIONAL NOTES TO CHAPTER L.

I cannot lose this opportunity of referring to a very interesting little book by M. Augé-Laribé, *L'évolution de la France agricole* [Paris 1912]. Much of it bears directly on the labour-question, and sets forth the difficulties hindering its solution. It is peculiarly valuable to a student of the question in the ancient world, because it lays great stress on the effect of causes arising from modern conditions. Causes operating in both ancient and modern times are thereby made more readily and clearly perceptible. Such modern influences in particular as the vast development of transport, the concentration of machine-industries in towns, and the constant attraction of better and more continuous wage-earning, by which the rustic is drawn to urban centres, are highly significant. The difference from ancient conditions is so great in degree that it practically almost amounts to a difference in kind. So too in the material resources of agriculture: the development of farm-machinery has superseded much hand-labour, while Science has increased the possible returns from a given portion of soil.

Most significant of all from my point of view is the author's insistence on the *irregularity* of wage-earning in rustic life as an active cause of the flitting of wage-earners to the towns. This brings it home to a student that a system of rustic slavery implies a set of conditions incompatible with such an economic migration; and also that the employment of slaves by urban craftsmen would not leave many eligible openings for immigrant rustics. It is fully consistent with my view that the wage-earning rustic was a rare figure in the Greco-Roman world.

It is perhaps in the remedies proposed by the author for present evils (and for the resulting depopulation of the countryside) that the contrast of ancient and modern is most clearly marked. Bureaucratic the French administrative system may be: but it is not the expression of a despotism that enslaves its citizens in the frantic effort to maintain itself against pressure from without. For individuals and organizations are free to think speak and act, and so to promote what seems likely to do good. Initiative and invention are not deadened by the fear that betterment will only serve as a pretext for increase of burdens. Stationary by instinct the French peasant proprietor may be: but he is free to move if he will, and no one dare propose to tie him to the soil by law.

Nor can I omit a reference to a paper of the late Prof Pelham on *The Imperial domains and the Colonate* (1890, in volume of Essays, Oxford 1911). The simplicity of the solution there offered is most attractive, and the general value of the treatise great. But I do not think it a final solution of the problem. Not only are there variations of detail in the domains known to us from the African inscriptions (some of them found since 1890). That some of the regulations may have been taken over from those of former private owners is a point not considered. And there is no mention of the notable requisition of the services of *coloni* as mere retainers, to which Caesar refers without comment (above pp 183, 254). Therefore, while I welcome the proposition that the system of the Imperial domains had much to do with the creation of the later Colonate, I still think that earlier and more deep-seated causes cannot safely be ignored. Perhaps this is partly because I am looking at the matter from a labour point of view.

FROM DIOCLETIAN

LI. GENERAL INTRODUCTION.

If we desire to treat History as the study of causation in the affairs of mankind—and this is its most fruitful task—we shall find no more striking illustration of its difficulties than the agricultural system of the later Roman Empire. In the new model of Diocletian and Constantine we see the imperial administration reorganized in new forms[1] deliberately adopted : policy expresses itself, after a century of disturbance, in a clear breach with the past. But, when Constantine in 332 legislates[2] to prevent *coloni* from migrating, he refers to a class of men who are not their own masters but subject to control (*iuris alieni*), though he distinguishes them from slaves. Evidently he is not creating a new class : his intention is to prevent an existing class from evading its present responsibilities. They are by the fact of their birth attached as cultivators to their native soil. With this tie of *origo*[3] goes liability to a certain proportion of imperial tax (*capitatio*). This is mentioned as a matter of course. Now we know that such serf-*coloni* formed at least a large part of the rustic population under the later Empire. We cannot but see that the loss of the power of free migration is the vital difference that marks off these tied farmers from the tenant farmers of an earlier period, the class whom Columella advised landlords to retain if possible. For these men cannot move on if they would. How came they to be in this strange condition, in fact neither slave nor free, so that Constantine had merely to crystallize relations already existing[4] and the institution of serf-tenancy became a regular part of the system? If we are to form any notion of the conditions of farm labour in this period, we must form some notion of the causes that produced the later or dependent colonate. And this is no simple matter : on few subjects has the divergence of opinions been more marked than on this. I have stated my own conclusions above, and further considerations are adduced in this chapter.

Our chief source of evidence is the collection of legal acts of the Christian emperors issued by authority in the year 438, and known as the *codex Theodosianus*. It covers a period of more than a hundred

---

[1] There were in the latter half of the third century some signs of the coming reconstruction. But they came to no effect.

[2] Cod Th v 17 (9) § 1 *apud quemcumque colonus iuris alieni fuerit inventus, is non solum eundem origini suae restituat verum super eodem capitationem temporis agnoscat...* etc. Runaway *coloni* are to be chained like slaves. *iuris alieni* = the control of someone other than the person harbouring him. The *colonus* is legally dependent, though nominally free.

[3] See Weber, *Agrargeschichte* pp 256 foll.   [4] See Seeck II 320 foll, 330 foll.

years, and innumerable references to the land-questions attest the continual anxiety of the imperial government to secure adequate cultivation of every possible acre of land. Contemporary history may suggest motives for this nervousness. The increased expenses of the court and the administrative system made it necessary to raise more taxes than ever for the civil services. The armies, now mainly composed of Germans and other barbarians, were necessary for imperial defence, but very costly to equip pay and feed. Whether they were mercenaries drawing wages, or aliens settled as Roman subjects within the empire on lands held by tenure of military service, they were either a burden on the treasury or a doubtful element of the population that must at all costs be kept in good humour. On a few occasions Roman victories furnished numbers of barbarian prisoners to the slave-market. These would be dispersed over various districts, generally at some distance from the troubled frontiers, and the rustic slaves of whom we hear were doubtless in great part procured in this way. But that the rustic population consisted largely of actual slaves we have no reason to believe. Of estates worked on a vast scale by slave labour we hear nothing. Naturally; for the social and economic conditions favourable to that system had long passed away. Slaves were no longer plentiful, markets were no longer free. Under the Empire, the pride of great landlords needed a strong mixture of caution; under a greedy or spendthrift emperor the display of material wealth was apt to be dangerous. In the century of confusion before Diocletian agriculture had been much interrupted in many parts of the empire, and much land had gone out of cultivation. So serious was the situation in the later part of that period, that Aurelian[1] imposed upon municipal senates the burden of providing for the cultivation of derelict farms.

When a taxpayer is required to pay a fixed amount in a stable currency, he knows his liability. So long as he can meet it, any surplus income remains in his hands, and he has a fair chance of improving his economic position by thrift. If what the state really wants is (say) corn, it can use its tax-revenue to purchase corn in the open market. But this assumes that the producer is free to stand out for the best price he can get, and that he will be paid in money on the purchasing power of which he can rely for his own needs. This last condition had ceased to exist[2] in the Roman empire. Not to mention earlier tamperings with the currency, since the middle of the third century its state had been deplorable. Things had now gone so far that the value of the fixed money taxes seriously reduced the income derived

---

[1] Cod Just XI 59 § 1, in which Constantine, finding the *civitatum ordines* unequal to this burden, extends the liability to other landlords also.

[2] See Seeck II 214 foll, 223, 249, IV 88.

from them : the government was literally paid in its own coin. The policy of Diocletian was to extend an old practice of exacting payment in kind, and this became the principal method[1] of imperial taxation. We must bear in mind that the supply of corn for the city of Rome, the *annona urbis*, went on as before, though the practical importance of Rome was steadily sinking. Diocletian made it no longer the residence of emperors, and Constantine founded another capital in the East : but Rome was still fed by corn-tributes from the Provinces, chiefly from Africa and Egypt. When the New Rome on the Bosporus was fully equipped as an imperial capital, Egypt was made liable for the corn-supply of the Constantinopolitan populace. Old Rome had then to rely almost entirely on Africa, with occasional help from other sources. Italy itself[2] was now reduced to the common level, cut up into provinces, and liable for furnishing supplies of food. But it was divided into two separate regions: the northern, officially named *Italia*, or *annonariae regiones*, in which a good deal of corn was grown, had to deliver its *annona* at Mediolanum (Milan) the new imperial head-quarters: the southern, *suburbicariae* (or *urbicariae*) *regiones*, in which little corn was grown, sent supplies of pigs cattle wine firewood lime etc to Rome. The northern *annona*, like that from other provinces, helped to maintain military forces and the host of officials employed by the government. For it soon became the practice to pay salaries in kind. In the pitiful state of the currency this rude method offered the best guarantee for receipt of a definite value.

Unhappily this exaction and distribution in kind was at best a wasteful process. At worst it was simply ruinous. The empire was subject to constant menace of attack, and was in dire need of the largest possible income raised on the most economical system. If the ultimate basis of imperial strength was to be found in the food-producers, it was all-important to give the farming classes a feeling of security sufficient to encourage industry and enterprise, and at all costs to avoid reducing them to despair. Nor was the new census as designed by Diocletian on the face of it an unjust and evil institution. Taking account of arable lands and of the persons employed in cultivating them, it aimed at creating a fixed number[3] of agricultural units each of which should be liable to furnish the same amount of yearly dues in kind. But it is obvious that to carry out this doctrinaire scheme with uniform neatness and precision was not possible. To deal fairly with agriculture a minute attention to local differences and special peculiarities was necessary, and this attention could not be given on

---

[1] Seeck II 249, 284. See Cod Th XI 2 §§ 1–5 (dates 365–389), not in Cod Just.

[2] Heisterbergk p 59 with references. Seeck, *Schatzungsordnung* pp 302–5.

[3] The details of this system are fully discussed in Seeck's great article, *die Schatzungsordnung Diocletians*, in the Ztschr für social und Wirthschaftsgeschichte 1896.

so vast a scale. Perhaps careful observation and correction of errors might have produced a reasonable degree of perfection in a long period of unbroken peace : but no such period was at hand. The same strain that drove the imperial government to the new taxation also prevented any effective control of its working.

It is perhaps inevitable that the exaction of dues in kind should lead to abuses. At all events, abuses in this department were no new thing: the sufferings of such Provinces as Sicily and Asia were notorious in the time of the Republic. A stricter control had made the state of things much better in the first two centuries of the Empire. The exploitation of the Provincials was generally checked, and the imperial government was not as yet driven by desperate financial straits to turn extortioner itself. Caracalla's law of 212, extending the Roman franchise[1] to all free inhabitants, was a symptom of conscious need, for it brought all estates under the Roman succession-tax. At the same time it did away with the old distinction between the ruling Roman people and the subject nationalities: henceforth, wherever there was oppression within the Roman world, it necessarily fell upon Roman[2] citizens. Time had been when the Roman citizen, free to move into any part of the Roman dominions and to acquire property there[3] under protection of Roman law, made full use of the opportunities afforded him, to the disadvantage of the subject natives. Now all alike were the helpless subjects of a government that they could neither reform nor supersede ; a government whose one leading idea was to bring all institutions into fixed grooves in which they should move mechanically year after year, unsusceptible of growth or decay. True, the plan was absurd, and some few observers may have detected its absurdity. But the power of challenging centralized officialism and evoking expression of public opinion, never more than rudimentary in the Roman state, was now simply extinct. Things had come to such a pass that, speaking generally, a citizen's choice lay between two alternatives. Either he must bear an active part in the system that was squeezing out the vital economic forces of the empire, making whenever possible a profit for himself out of a salary or illicit gains ; or he must submit passively to all such extortions as the system, worked by men whose duty and interest alike tended to make them merciless, was certain to inflict. The oppressors, though numerous, could only be few in proportion to

---

[1] Digest I 5 § 17, Dion Cass LXXVII 9 § 5. Schiller *Geschichte* I pp 750–1 thinks that military motives had much to do with it, as adding to the citizen troops. What is supposed to be a copy of the edict itself has been found in a papyrus, see Girard, *textes* part I ch 4 § 12. The text is in the Giessen papyri No 40. It seems certain that the lowest class of *peregrini* (the *dediticii*) were not included in the grant.

[2] See Seeck II 323. Cf Lactant *mort pers* 23 § 5, Victor *Caes* 39 § 31.

[3] Through the *ius commercii*.

the whole free population. Therefore the vast majority stood officially condemned to lives of penury and wretchedness. The system became more hard-set and the outlook more hopeless with the lapse of time.

The dues exacted from the various parts of the empire varied in quality[1] according to local conditions, and to some extent in methods of collection. In the frontier Provinces the quantity was sometimes reduced[2] by remissions, when a district ravaged by invaders was relieved for a few years that it might recover its normal productiveness. The details of these variations are beyond the scope of the present inquiry. The general principle underlying the whole system was the fixing of taxation-units equal in liability, and the organizing of collection in municipal groups. Each municipal town or *civitas* was the administrative centre of a district, and stood charged in the imperial ledgers as liable for the returns from a certain number of units, this number being that recorded as existing at the last quinquennial census. For the collection the chief municipal authorities were responsible; and they had to hand over the amount due to the imperial authorities, whether they had received it in full or not. Already burdened with strictly municipal liabilities, the members of municipal senates (*curiales*) were crushed by this additional and incalculable pressure. Unable to resist, they generally took the course of so using their functions and powers as to protect their own interests as far as possible. One obvious precaution was to see that the number of taxable units[3] in their district was not fixed too high by the census officials. This precaution was certainly not overlooked, and success in keeping down the number may well have been the chief reason why the system was able to go on so long. The *curiales* were mostly considerable landlords, residing in their town and letting their land to tenants. But there were other landlords, smaller men, some also resident in the towns, others in the country. We still hear of men farming land[4] of their own, and it seems that some of these held and farmed other land also, as *coloni* of larger landlords. When any question arose as to the number of units for the tax on which this or that farm was liable, it is clear that the interests of different classes might easily clash. And the *curiales* undoubtedly took care[5] that their own and those of their friends did not suffer.

These remarks imply that the system practically worked in favour

[1] Seeck, *Schatzungsordnung*, cited above.

[2] A long title in cod Th is devoted to remissions, XI 28, consisting of temporary laws. And these deal chiefly with Italian and African Provinces, notably §§ 7, 12, with Campania. They date from 395 to 436.

[3] In the panegyric (No VIII cap II) on Constantine we have mention of a reduction of 7000 *capita* for relief of a district in Gaul.

[4] Cod Th XI 1 § 14. Cf. Seeck, *Schatzungsordnung* pp 315-6.

[5] Compare the conduct of the magistrates of Antioch in the evidence of Libanius cited below.

of the richer classes[1] as against the poorer. And so it certainly did, not only in the time of revision at the census each fifth year, but on other occasions. If an invasion or some other great disaster led the emperor to grant temporary relief, this would normally take the form of reducing the number of taxable units in the district for a certain period. But the local authorities were left to apportion this reduction[2] among the several estates, and the poor farmers had no representative to see that they got their fair share of relief. Moreover, outside taxation, the farmers were often subjected to heavy burdens and damage by the irregular requisitions of imperial officials. For instance, the staff of the imperial post-service (*cursus publicus*)[3] were a terror. They pressed the goods of farmers into the service of their department on various pretexts, and exacted labour on upkeep of roads and stations. For their tyranny there was no effective compensation or redress. Like other officials, they could be bought off by bribes: but this meant that the various exactions[4] were shifted from the shoulders of the rich to those of the poor. Another iniquity, the revival of a very old[5] abuse, was connected with the question of transport, an important consideration in the case of dues in kind, often bulky. For instance, in the case of corn, the place at which it had to be delivered might easily count for more in estimating the actual pressure of the burden than the amount of grain levied. In making the arrangements for delivery there were openings for favouritism and bribery. Circumstances varied greatly in various parts of the empire. In some Provinces delivery was made at a military depot within easy reach. Transport by sea from Egypt or Africa was carried on by gilds[6] of shippers, who became more and more organized and regulated by law. But in many parts good roads were few, and laid out for strategic reasons; the country roads inconvenient and rough: and for transport in bulk the post-service provided no machinery available for the use of private persons.

It is not necessary here to follow out in detail all the particular discomforts and grievances of the farming classes under the system devised by Diocletian and developed by his successors. Enough has been said to shew that they were great, and to remove all ground for wondering that the area of arable land actually under tillage, and with it population, continued to decline. Constantine's law confirming the bondage of *coloni* to the soil by forbidding movement was the confession

---

[1] See for instance cod Th XIII 10 § 1.   [2] See below, in section on Salvian.
[3] See Ammianus XIX 11 § 3, Victor *Caesares* 13 §§ 5, 6. A long title cod Th VIII 5 is devoted to the *cursus*, containing 66 laws from 315 to 407, and other references abound.
[4] Cf cod Th XI 16 § 3 (324), § 4 (328).
[5] Cf Cic II *in Verr* III § 190, Tac *Agr* 19. Cf cod Th XI 1 § 22 (386), with Godefroi's notes, also §§ 11 (365) and 21 (385), XIV 4 § 4 (367).
[6] See the title *de naviculariis*, cod Th XIII 5, including 38 laws.

of a widespread evil, but no remedy. Repeated legislation to the same
purpose only recorded and continued the failure. When all the resources
of evasion were exhausted, the pauperized serf fled to a town and
depended for a living on the pitiful doles of private or ecclesiastical
charity, or turned brigand and took precarious toll of those who still
had something to lose. In either case he was an additional burden on
a society that already had more than it could bear. In 382 we find an
attempt[1] made to put down 'sturdy beggars.' The law rewarded anyone who procured the conviction of such persons by handing over the
offenders to him. An ex-slave became the approver's own slave, and
one who had nothing of his own beyond his freeborn quality was granted
to him as his *colonus* for life. But this law seems to have been ineffectual
like others. Desertion of farms might to some extent be checked, but
mendicity and brigandage remained.

There was however another movement, later in time and less in
volume, but not less serious as affecting the practical working of the
imperial machine. With the increase of poverty life in municipal towns
became less attractive. Local eminence was no longer an object of
ambition ; for to local burdens, once cheerfully borne, was now added
a load of imperial responsibilities which lay heavy on all men of property,
and which they could neither shake off nor control. In hope of evading
them, well-to-do citizens took refuge[2] in the country, either on estates
of their own or under the protection of great landlords already settled
there. But to allow this would mean the depletion of the local senates
(*curiae*) on whose services as revenue-collectors the financial system of
the empire depended. To prevent men qualified for the position of
curiales from escaping that duty was the aim of legislation[3] which by
repeated enactments confessed its own failure. That there were country
magnates, men of influence (*potentes*), whose protection might seem
able to screen municipal defaulters, is a point to be noted. They were
the great *possessores*[4] (a term no longer applied to small men), who
held large estates organized on a sort of manorial model, and sometimes ruled them like little principalities, territorial lordships[5] standing
in direct relations with the central authorities and not hampered by
inclusion in the general municipal scheme. Such 'peculiars' had existed
under the earlier Empire, and evidently continued to exist: the Crown-

---

[1] Cod Th XIV 18 *de mendicantibus non invalidis*.

[2] If I rightly interpret Dig L 5 § 1² (Ulpian) cases had occurred earlier of men liable to
office even pretending to be mere *coloni* in order to evade liability (*ad colonos praediorum se
transtulerunt*. See Dirksen under *transferre*).

[3] Very significant is the law cod Th XVI 5 § 48 (410) by which even heretics are held to
curial duty.

[4] See Seeck, *Schatzungsordnung* pp 315-6, De Coulanges p 119.

[5] See Weber, *Agrargeschichte* pp 266-7.

lands of the emperors, especially in Africa, were the most signal cases. But the great private Possessor could not secure to his domain the various exemptions[1] that emperors conferred on theirs. He had to collect and pay over[2] the dues from his estate, as a municipal magistrate did from the district round his town-centre. But he had a more immediate and personal interest in the wellbeing of all his tenants and dependants, whose presence and prosperity gave to his land by far the greater part[3] of its value.

That territorial magnates should be free to build up a perhaps dangerous power in various corners of the empire by gathering dependants round them, could hardly be viewed with approval by the jealousy of emperors. Not only was the system of letting land in parcels to tenants spreading, but the power of the landlords over them was increasing, long before Constantine took the final step of treating them as attached permanently to the soil. Whether they were the landlord's free tenants who had gradually lost through economic weakness the effective use of freedom ; or small freeholders who had found it worth their while to part with their holdings to a big man and become his tenants for the sake of enjoying his protection ; or former slaves to whom small farms had been entrusted on various conditions; they were in a sort of economic bondage. Doubtless most of them lived from hand to mouth, but we have no reason to believe that poverty, so long as they had plenty to live on, was the motive[4] that made them wish to give up their holdings and try their luck elsewhere. It was the cruel pressure of Diocletian's new taxation, and the army of officials employed to enforce it, that drove them to despair. A contemporary witness[5] tells us, referring to this very matter, ' the excess of receivers over givers was becoming so marked that farms were being abandoned, and tillages falling to woodland, the resources of the tenants being exhausted by the hugeness[6] of the imposts.' And this evidence does not stand alone. So Constantine sought a remedy in prevention of movement, binding down the tenants to the soil. Henceforth the land to which a *colonus*[7] was attached by birth, and the *colonus* himself, were to be legally and economically inseparable. Attempts at evading the new rule were persistently met by later[8] legislation. The motive of such attempts may be found by remembering that depopulation was

---

[1] Cf cod Th XI 16 *passim*.

[2] A rule of 366, or later according to Mommsen, cod Th XI 1 § 14, cod Just XI 48 § 4.

[3] Cf cod Th XIII 10 § 3, retained in cod Just XI 48 § 2, plainly recognizing this.

[4] See the advantages of the colonate summed up in de Coulanges p 144, and cf *ibid* p 139.

[5] Lactantius *de mort pers* 7 § 3.   [6] *enormitate indictionum.*

[7] Cf Augustin *de civ Dei* X 1 *coloni, qui condicionem debent genitali solo, propter agri culturam sub dominio possessorum.*

[8] Cf cod Th V 17 (9) §§ 1, 2 (332), etc.

steadily lowering the value of land and raising that of labour. If an individual landlord could add to the value of his own estate by getting more *coloni* settled on it, withdrawn from other estates, he might profit by the transaction: but the government, whose policy was to keep the greatest possible area under cultivation, could not allow one part to be denuded of labourers to suit the interest of the owner of another part.

When the law stepped in to deprive the tenant, already far gone in dependence on his landlord, of such freedom of movement as he still retained, it is remarkable that rustic slaves were not at the same time legally attached to the soil. That inconvenience was caused by masters selling them when and where they chose, is shewn by Constantine's law[1] of 327, allowing such sales to take place only within the limits of the Province where they had been employed. No doubt their removal upset the arrangements for that part of a taxable unit in which the number of adult heads[2] was taken into account, and so had to be checked. But it seems not to have been till the time of Valentinian[3], somewhere between 367 and 375, that the sale of a farm-slave off the land was directly prohibited, like that of a *colonus*. In referring to this matter, the significance of the difference of dates is thus brought out[4] by Seeck: 'That this measure was carried through much sooner in the case of the small farmers than in that of the farm-slaves, is very characteristic of the spirit of that age. Where court favour is the deciding factor that governs the entire policy, the government is even more reluctant to limit the proprietary rights of the great landlord[5] than the liberties of the small man.' This is very true, but we must not forget that in both cases the binding of the labourer to the soil did in fact restrict the landlord's freedom of disposal. He as well as his dependants came under a system not designed to promote his private convenience or interest, but to guarantee a maximum of total cultivation in the interest of the empire as a whole. So we find that he was not allowed[6] to raise at will the rents of his tenants: they could sue their landlord (a right which in practice was probably not worth much), and even when this right was restricted[7] in 396 they still retained it in respect of unfair increases of rent and criminal cases. So too, if he acquired extra slaves, either by receiving them as volunteers from derelict farms or in virtue of an imperial grant, it was strictly ordained[8]

---

[1] Cod Th XI 3 § 2.   [2] The *capitatio*.   [3] Cod Just XI 48 § 7.

[4] *Schatzungsordnung* pp 313–4.

[5] Rostowzew *Geschichte des Röm Colonates* pp 381–97 traces the abandonment of the policy of favouring *coloni*, and adoption of reliance on great possessors, as a result of the pressing difficulties of the collection of revenue.

[6] Cod Just XI 50 § 1 (Constantine).   [7] Cod Just XI 50 § 2.

[8] Cod Th XI 1 § 12 (365).

that such acquisition carried with it the tax-liability for the whole of the derelict land. The landlord was therefore kept firmly in the grip of the central power, and not left free to build up a little principality by consolidating at will all the labour-resources that he could annex as dependants. Moreover he was watched by a host of imperial agents and spies whose interests could only be reconciled with his own by the costly method of recurrent bribery.

When we return to the main question of the actual farm-labour, and ask who toiled with their own hands to raise crops, we find ourselves in a curious position. The evidence, whether legal or literary, leaves us in no doubt that the tenant farmer of this period was normally himself a labourer. And yet it is not easy to cite passages in which this is directly affirmed. The pompous and affected language of the imperial laws is throughout a bad medium for conveying simple facts ; nor was the question, who did the work, of any interest to the central authority, concerned solely with the regular exaction of the apportioned dues. The real proof that *coloni*, whether still holding some land of their own or merely tenants, and *inquilini*, whether solely barbarian dependants or not, were actual handworkers, is to be found in legitimate inference from certain facts. First, the increase in the value of labour compared with the decline in that of land. The binding of tenant to soil was a confession of this. Secondly, the general poverty of the farmers[1] and their helplessness against oppression and wrong. Of this the description of Salvian gives a striking, if rhetorical, picture, and it is implied in many laws designed[2] for their protection. That persons in so weak an economic position could have carried on their business as mere directors of slave-labour is surely inconceivable : and we are to remember that not only they themselves but their families also were bound to the soil. It was their presence, that is to say their labour, that gave value to the land, and so paid the taxes. Hence it was that in forming taxable units (*capita*) it was generally the practice to include in the reckoning[3] not only the productive area (*iugatio*) but also the ‘heads’ that stocked it (*capitatio*). In other words, productiveness must in the interest of the state be actual, not merely potential.

The importance of keeping the real locally-bound *coloni* strictly to their business of food-production was fully recognized in the regulations for recruiting the armies. Landlords, required to furnish[4] recruits, were

---

[1] Wallon, *Esclavage* III 266, 282.

[2] For instance cod Th XI 11 (date somewhere 368–373), IV 13 §§ 2, 3 (321). Also XI 7–10, 16 § 10, etc.

[3] Seeck, *Schatzungsordnung* pp 285–308, with an account of local variations. For instance, in Africa and Egypt there was no *capitatio*.

[4] See cod Th VII 13 § 7, 8 (375, 380). Even the imperial estates made liable, ibid § 12 (397). Dill p 196. In 379 Theodosius had to raise recruits from γεωργοί, Libanius XXIV 16.

free to name some of their *coloni* for that purpose. But there was no fear that they would be eager to do this, for the work of their tenants was what gave value to their properties. And the imperial officers charged with recruiting duty were ordered[1] (and this in 400, when the need of soldiers was extreme) not to accept fugitive tenants belonging to an estate (*indigenis*): these no doubt if found were to be returned to their lords. The military levy was to fall upon sons of veterans, for in this class as in others no effort was spared to make the ways of life hereditary; or on wastrels (*vagos*)[2], of whom the laws often make mention; or generally on persons manifestly by the circumstances of their birth (*origo*) liable to army service. Here we have the service still in principle confined to freemen. But it is not to be doubted that many a slave (and these would be nearly all rustic slaves) passed muster with officers hasting to make up their tale of men, and so entered the army. At a much later date (529) we find Justinian[3] contemplating cases of slaves recruited with the consent of their owners, in short furnished as recruits. He enacts that such men are to be declared *ingenui*[4], that is freeborn not freedmen, the master losing all rights over them : but, if they are efficient soldiers, they are to remain in the service. And the power of commuting[5] the obligation of furnishing a recruit for a payment of money, which was to some extent allowed, introduced a method of recruiting[6] by purchase. A recruit being demanded, it did not follow that the emperor got either the particular man (inspected of course and passed as fit) or a fixed cash-commutation. The recruiting officer conveniently happened to have a man or two at disposal, picked up in the course of his tour. The landlord, anxious to keep his own staff intact, came to terms with the officer for one of these as substitute. These officers knew when they could drive hard bargains, and did not lose their chances. In a law of 375, this system is directly referred to, and an attempt is made to regulate it[7] on an equitable footing. To abolish it was clearly impossible. Eventually the state undertook to work it officially, and bought its own 'bodies' (*corpora*, like σώματα, of slaves) with the composition-money or *aurum temonarium*. That some of these 'bodies' were escaped slaves is highly

---

[1] Cod Th VII 18 § 10, cf VIII 2 § 3 (380). See Seeck II 490–1.
[2] Cod Th VIII 2 § 3. By long use the word had become quite official. Cf *inopes ac vagi* in Tac *ann* IV 4, etc.   [3] Cod Just XII 33 § 6.
[4] De Coulanges pp 168–9 points out that in the early Middle Age we find *ingenui* = *coloni*.
[5] *temonaria functio*. See Dirksen under *temo*. Cod Th XI 16 §§ 14, 15, 18, cf VII 13 § 7, VI 26 § 14.   [6] Wallon III 149, 476.
[7] Cod Th VII 13 § 7, where occur the words *cum corpora postulantur* opposed to *aurum*. For the money-commutation (*adaeratio*) often accepted from the landlords see Mommsen *Ges Schr* VI p 254 *Das Röm Militärwesen seit Diocletian*. Also Rostowzew in the *Journal of Roman Studies* vol VIII on *Synteleia tironon*, and Wagner on Ammianus XIX 11 § 7.

probable. Some may have been stray barbarians, not included in the various barbarian corps which more and more came to form the backbone of the Roman army. But the majority would probably be indigent wretches to whom any change seemed better than the miserable lives open to them in the meanest functions of the decaying civilization of the towns. In any case such recruits[1] would be but a poor substitute for the pick of the rustic population.

The same anxiety to spare the rustics unnecessary exactions, that they might not sink under their present burdens, appears in other regulations. The subordinates employed in the public services such as the Post, or as attendants on functionaries, were tempted to ease their own duties by demanding contributions from the helpless country-folk. This we find forbidden[2] in 321 as interfering with the farmers' right to procure and carry home things required for agriculture. So too a whole Title[3] in the *Codex* is devoted to the prevention of *super-exactiones*, a form of extortion often practised by officials, chiefly by the use of false weights and measures or by foul play with the official receipts. The laws forbidding practices of this kind seem to belong to the latter part of the fourth century and the earlier part of the fifth. But the evil was clearly of old standing, and the laws almost certainly vain. That illicit exactions were a particular affliction of the poorer rustics, who could not bribe the officials, is confessed[4] by a law of 362, which ordains that the burdens of supplying beasts fodder etc for service of the Post, upkeep of the roads and so forth, are to be laid on all *possessores* alike. Further enactments follow in 401 and 408. But these rules for equitable distribution of burdens, even if carried out, only spread them over all landowners and *coloni*. All the upper ranks[5] of the imperial service carried exemption from *sordida munera* in some form or other, and personal grants of exemption were often granted as a favour. It is true that such exemption only extended to the life of the grantee, that exemptions were revocable, and that in course of time extreme necessities led to revocations. But all this did not operate to relieve the unhappy rustic on whom the whole imperial fabric rested. The rich might have to lose their privileges, but it was too late for the poor to gain a benefit. That the underlings of provincial governors were a terror to farmers, levying on them illicit services and generally blackmailing them for their own profit, is clear from the law[6] (some-

---

[1] Cf Vegetius *rei milit* I 7, of the disasters caused by slovenly recruiting, *dum indicti possessoribus tirones per gratiam aut dissimulationem probantium tales sociantur armis quales domini habere fastidiunt.*

[2] Cod Th IV 13 §§ 2, 3, kept with variants in cod Just IV 61 § 5.

[3] Cod Th XI 8.   [4] Cod Th XI 16 § 10, 17 §§ 2–4.

[5] For the special position of imperial senators see Dill pp 126, 166, 196, 218 foll.

[6] Cod Th XI 11, kept with some omissions in cod Just XI 55 § 2.

where 368–373) announcing severe punishment for the offence and declaring that it had become a regular practice. The law of 328, enacting[1] that no farmer (*agricola*) was to be impressed for special service in the seasons of seed-time or harvest, is on rather a different footing. It expressly justifies the prohibition on the ground of agricultural necessity: in short, it is not to protect the farmer, but to leave him no excuse for not producing food.

A great critic[2] has commented severely on the intellectual stagnation that fell upon the Roman empire and was one of the most effective causes of its decline. That literature fed upon the past and dwindled into general imbecility is commonly recognized: but the lack of material inventions and the paucity of improvements is perhaps not less significant than the decay of literature and art. The department of agriculture was no exception to this sterile traditionality. Since the days of Varro there had been no considerable change. So far as labour is concerned, the system of Columella can hardly be called an advance ; for it employs directly none but slave labour, a resource already beginning to fail, and causing landlords to seek help from the development of tenancies. In modern times the dearness of labour has stimulated human ingenuity to produce machines by which the efficiency of human labour is increased and therefore fewer hands required for a given output. But in the world under the Roman supremacy centuries went by with hardly any modification of the mechanical equipment. A small exception may perhaps be found in a sort of rudimentary reaping-machine. It was briefly referred to by the elder Pliny[3] in the first century of our era, and described by Palladius in the fourth. The device was in use on the large estates in the lowlands of Gaul, and was perhaps a Gaulish invention. It is said to have been a labour-saving[4] appliance. From the description it seems to have been clumsy ; and, since it cut off the ears and left the straw standing, it was only suited to farms on which no special use was made of the straw. Its structure (for it was driven by an ox from behind) must have made it unworkable on sloping ground. That we hear nothing of its general adoption may be due to these or other defects. But I believe there is no record of attempts to improve the original design. The lack of interest in improvement of tools has been noted as a phenomenon accompanying the dependence on slave labour. And when under the Roman empire we see the free tenant passing into the condition of a serf-tenant, we are witnessing a process that steadily tended to reduce him to the moral labour-level of the apathetic and hopeless slave. To make the

[1] Cod Th XI 16 § 4, cod Just XI 48 § 1.
[2] Seeck I, chapter on *die Ausrottung der Besten*.
[3] Pliny *NH* XVIII 296. Palladius VII 2.   [4] *hoc compendio.* Pall.

agriculture of a district more prosperous was to attract the attention of greedy officials. To resist their illicit extortions was to attract the attention of the central government, whose growing needs were ever tempting it to squeeze more and more out of its subjects. Why then should the rustic, tied to the soil, trouble himself to seek more economical methods, the profits of which, if ever realized, he was not himself likely to enjoy?

LII. LIBANIUS.

In order to get so far as possible a living picture of the conditions of rustic life and labour we must glean the scattered notices preserved to us in the writers of the period of decline. Due allowance must be made for the general artificiality and rhetorical bent of authors trained in the still fashionable schools of composition and style. For even private letters were commonly written as models destined eventually to be read and admired by the public, while in controversial works and public addresses the tendency to attitudinize was dominant. The circulation of literary trivialities and exchange of cheap compliments, especially prevalent in Gaul, was kept up to the last by self-satisfied cliques when the barbarians were already established in the heart of the empire. Nevertheless valuable side-lights on questions of fact are thrown from several points of view. This evidence agrees with that drawn from the imperial laws, and is in so far better for our purpose that it deals almost exclusively with the present. When it looks to the future, it is in the form of petition or advice; while the normal substance of the laws is to confess the existence of monstrous abuses by threatening offenders with penalties ever more and more severe, and enjoining reforms that no penalties could enforce. A writer very characteristic of his age (about 315–400) is the 'sophist' Libanius, who passed most of his later years at Antioch, the luxurious chief city of the East. For matters under his immediate observation he is a good authority, and may help us to form a notion of the extent to which imperial ordinances were practically operative in the eastern parts of the empire.

Two of the 'orations,' or written addresses, of Libanius are particularly interesting as appeals to the emperor Theodosius for redress of malpractices affecting the rustic population and impairing the financial resources of the empire. The earlier[1] (about 385) exposes gross misdeeds of the city magistrates of Antioch What with the falling of old houses and clearing of sites for new buildings there were great quantities of mixed rubbish to be removed and deposited else-

[1] *Orat* 50. I take the date given by Förster.

where. Apparently there was now no sufficient staff of public slaves at disposal; at all events the city authorities resorted to illegal means for procuring the removal. When the country folk came into town to dispose of their produce, the magistrates requisitioned their carts asses mules (and themselves as drivers) for this work. Thus the time of the poor rustics was wasted, their carts and sacks damaged, and they and their beasts sent back to their homes in a state of utter exhaustion. No law empowered the city magnates to act thus. From small beginnings a sort of usage had been created, which nothing short of imperial ordinance could now break and abolish. That the magistrates were conscious of doing wrong was shewn by what they avoided doing. They did not impress slaves or carts from houses in the city. They did not exact like services from the military or powerful landlords. Nor did they lay the burden on the estates[1] of the municipality, the rents from which were part of the revenues of Antioch. Favour is only justified by equity; and there is, says Libanius, no equity in sparing the luxurious rich by ruining the poor. So he entreats his most gracious[2] Majesty to protect the farms as much as the cities, or rather more. For the country is in fact the foundation on which cities rest. Without it they could never have existed: and now it is on the rise and fall of rural wellbeing that urban prosperity depends. This appeal speaks for itself. But it is significant that the skilled pleader thinks it wise to end on a note of imperial interest. 'Moreover, Sire, it is from the country that your tribute is drawn. It is to the cities that you address your orders[3] for taxation, but the cities have to raise it from the country. Therefore, to protect the farmers is to preserve your interests, and to maltreat the farmers is to betray them.'

In the oration numbered 47 the abuse dealt with is of a very different kind. The date is 391 or 392, and the subject is the 'protections' (*patrocinia*)[4] of villages. The pressure of imperial taxation and the abuses accompanying its collection had driven the villagers to seek help in resisting the visits of the tax-gatherers. This help was generally found in placing the village under the protection of some powerful person, commonly a retired soldier, who acted as a rallying-centre and leader, probably in most cases backed by some retainers of his own class. Of course these men did not undertake opposition to the public authorities for nothing. But it seems that their exactions were, at least in the earlier stages, found to be less burdensome than those of the official collectors. The situation thus created was as follows. The local

---

[1] For such properties see cod Th x 3.   [2] φιλανθρωπότατε βασιλεῦ.

[3] § 36 γράμμασι, which I take to be = *indictiones*.

[4] In cod Th the title xi 24 is *de patrociniis vicorum*, and the laws range from 360 to 415. Cod Just xi 54 shews that the evil was still in existence in 468.

senators (*curiales*) whose turn it was to collect the dues from the district under their municipality (a duty that they were not allowed to shirk) went out to the villages for the purpose. They were beaten off[1] by use of force, often wounded as well as foiled. They were still bound to pay over the tax, which they had not received, to the imperial treasury. In these latter days default of payment rendered them liable to cruel scourging. So the unhappy *curiales* had to sell their own property to make up the amount due. The loss of their means strikes them out of the *curia* for lack of the legal qualification. And this was not only a loss to their particular city: it damaged imperial interests, bound up as the whole system was with maintaining unimpaired the supply of qualified *curiales*. The evil of these 'protections' was, according to Libanius, great and widespread. The protectors had become a great curse to the villagers themselves by their tyranny and exactions. Their lawless sway had turned[2] farmers into brigands, and taught them to use iron not for tools of tillage but for weapons of bloodshed. And the trouble was not confined to villages where the land belonged to a number of small owners: it extended also to those[3] under one big proprietor. The argument that the villagers have a right to seek help in resistance to extortion, is only sound if the means employed are fair. To justify this limitation two significant analogies[4] are applied. Cities near the imperial frontier must not call in the foreign enemy to aid them in settling their differences with each other: they must seek help within the empire. A slave must not invoke the aid of casual bystanders against ill-usage: he stands in no relation to outsiders, and must look to his master for redress. The full bearing of these considerations is seen when we remember that the farmers are serf-tenants. They are owned[5] by masters, as the municipal city exists only in and for the empire, and the slave has no legal personality apart from his lord.

It is a fact, says[6] Libanius, that through such evasion of their liabilities on the part of the rustics many houses have been ruined. He is surely referring to the *curiales* and other landlords resident in the city, the numbers of which class it was the imperial policy to maintain at full strength. In moral indignation[7] he urges the iniquity of beggaring poor souls who have nothing to live on but the income from their lands. ' Say I have an estate, inherited or bought, farmed by sensible tenants who humbly faced the ups and downs of Fortune under my considerate care. Must you then stir them up by agitation, arousing unlooked-for conflicts, and reducing men of good family to indigence ? ' This appeal

---

[1] *Orat* 47 §§ 8–10. Zulueta (see below) points out that the protection given by the patrons was exerted quite as much by improper influence on judges as by use of force.

[2] § 6 τοῦτο καὶ λῃστὰς γεωργοὺς ἐποίησε.   [3] § 11 ἀλλὰ καὶ οἷς εἷς ὁ δεσπότης.

[4] §§ 19–21.   [5] § 24 ὧν εἰσιν (οἱ γεωργοί).

[6] §§ 17, 18.   [7] § 34.

H. A.   26

would not sound overdrawn in the society of that age, though it might fall somewhat coldly upon modern ears. But the most notable point in this oration is the nature of the remedy[1] for which the writer pleads, and which none but the emperor can supply. It is simply to enforce the existing law. Some years before, probably in 368, the emperor Valens had strictly forbidden[2] the 'protections' that were the cause of this trouble. So now the appeal to Theodosius is 'give the law sinews, make it a law indeed[3] and not a bare exhortation.' For, if it is not to be observed, it had better be repealed. That a leading writer of the day could so state the case to the ruler of the Roman world is a fact to be borne in mind by readers of the imperial laws.

LIII. SYMMACHUS

In passing on to **Q. Aurelius Symmachus**[4] (about 345–405) we find ourselves in very different surroundings. The scene is in Italy, and the author a man of the highest station in what was still regarded as the true centre of the Roman world. He was *praefectus urbi* in 384–5, consul in 391, and the leading figure in Roman society and literary circles. From the bulky collection of his letters, and the forty reports (*relationes*) addressed to the emperor by him as city prefect, we get much interesting evidence as to the condition of rural Italy and the anxieties of the corn-supply of Rome. With his championship of the old religion, by which he is best known, we have here nothing to do; and his literary affectations, characteristic of most writers of the later Empire, do not discredit him as a witness. A remarkable feature of his letters is their general triviality and absence of direct reference to the momentous events that were happening in many parts of the empire. His attention is almost wholly absorbed by matters with which he was immediately connected, his public duties, his private affairs, the interests of his relatives and friends, or the exchange of compliments. His time is mostly passed either in Rome or at one or other of his numerous country seats: for he was one of the great land-lords of his day, and the condition of Italian agriculture was of great importance to him. As a representative of the landed interest and as

---

[1] §§ 36-8 δὸς δὴ νεῦρα τῷ νόμῳ καὶ ποίησον αὐτὸν ὡς ἀληθῶς νόμον ἀντὶ ψιλῆς προση-γορίας... etc.   [2] Cod Th XI 24 § 2 (Valens).

[3] Note that the law Cod Th XII 1 § 128, sternly forbidding *militares viri* to interfere with *curiales* or to use any violence to leading men in the municipalities, is dated 392 July 31. Also that it is retained in Cod Just X 32 § 42. Zulueta *de patrociniis vicorum* pp 38–40 concludes that it is uncertain to what emperor Libanius is appealing, and places the date in 386–9 AD. He finds the reference in Cod Th V 17 § 2 (Theodosius), not in XI 24 § 2.

[4] The leading authority on Symmachus is O Seeck. In particular the dating of many of the letters in his great edition (MGH, Berlin 1883) is often helpful.

a self-conscious letter-writer he resembles the younger Pliny, but is weaker and set in a less happy age.

A topic constantly recurring[1] in his correspondence is the apprehension of famine in Rome and the disturbances certain to arise therefrom. The distribution of imperial powers among several seats of government (of which Rome was not one) since the changes of Diocletian had left to the ancient capital only a sort of traditional primacy. The central bureaus were elsewhere, and Rome was only the effective capital of the southern division of Italy. Yet the moral force of her great past was still a living influence that expressed itself in various ways, notably in the growth of the Papacy out of the Roman bishopric. For centuries it had been the licensed lodging of a pauperized mob, fed by doles to keep them quiet, enjoying luxurious baths at nominal cost, and entertained with exciting or bloody shows in the circus or amphitheatre. This rabble had either to be kept alive and amused or got rid of; but the latter alternative would surely have reduced Rome to the condition of a dead city. It was morally impossible for a Roman emperor to initiate so ominous a policy. So the wasteful abomination dragged on, and every hitch in the corn-supply alarmed not only the *praefectus annonae* but the *praefectus urbi* with the prospect of bread riots. And the assignment of the Egyptian corn to supply Constantinople made Rome more than ever dependent on the fortunes of the African[2] harvest. When this failed, it was only by great departmental energy that temporary shortage was made good by importations[3] from Macedonia Sardinia or Spain or even by some surplus from Egypt. Even lower Italy, where little corn was grown, was at a pinch made to yield some. But bad seasons were not the only cause of short supplies. The acts of enemies might starve out Rome, as the rebellion of Gildo in Africa (397–8) nearly did. Moreover the slackness and greed of officials[4] sometimes ruined the efficiency of the department, and 'profiteering' was practised by unscrupulous[5] capitalists. Nor even with good harvests abroad were the prefects always at ease, since the corn-fleets might be delayed or scattered by foul weather, and meanwhile the consumption did not cease. And it sometimes happened that the cargoes were damaged and the public health suffered[6] from unwholesome food. Among these various cares the *praefectura annonae* was no bed of roses. No wonder the worthy Symmachus tells us of private cnarity[7] to relieve the necessities of the poor, and even gives a hint of voluntary

[1] See *epist* II 6, 7, 52, IV 5 (4), 18, 21, IX 14, 114 (124), X 2, 21, *relat* 3 §§ 15–18, 9 § 7, 18, 35, 37.
[2] *epist* III 55, 82, IV 54, 74, VII 38, 68, *relat* 18.
[3] *epist* II 6, III 55, 82, IX 42, VII 68, *relat* 9, 18, 37.
[4] *epist* VII 66, IX 10, *relat* 18.   [5] *epist* II 55, IV 68.
[6] *epist* VI 15 (14).   [7] *epist* VI 15 (14), VII 18, 68. Seeck, V 284, 555.

rationing at the tables of the rich. But in appealing to the gods for succour he rather suggests that human benevolence would be unequal to the strain.

That agriculture was not on a sound footing in most of Italy is evident from several passages in the letters. In one of the earliest (before 376) he tells his father that, though he finds Campania charming, he should like to join him at Praeneste. 'But' he adds 'I am in trouble about my property. I must go and inspect it wherever it lies, not in hope of making it remunerative, but in order to realize the promise of the land by further outlay. For things are nowadays come to such a pass[1] that an owner has to feed the farm that once fed him.' Some of the references to the management of estates are rather obscure. In speaking of one near Tibur he mentions[2] stewards (*vilicorum*) and complains of their neglect. 'The land is badly farmed, and great part of the returns (*fructuum*) is in arrear (*debetur*): the *coloni* have no means left[3] to enable them to clear their accounts or to carry on cultivation.' The exact status of these stewards and tenants and their relations to each other are far from clear, and the case may have been a peculiar one. Again, writing to bespeak the good offices of an influential man on behalf of an applicant, he says 'I do this for him rather as a duty[4] than as an act of free grace, for he is a farm-tenant of mine.' The tenant's name is Theodulus, which invites a conjecture that this was a case of an oriental Greek slave placed as tenant on a farm, either for his master's account, or for his own at a rent, and afterwards manumitted. A reference to *servi*, dependants (*obnoxii*)[5] who are owing him rents which his agents on the distant estate in question do not take the trouble to collect, may point to the same sort of arrangement. In another passage he mentions[6] a man who was for a long time *colonus* under a certain landlord, but here too the lack of detail forbids inference as to the exact nature of the relation. That slave labour was still employed on some Italian farms appears from a request[7] for help in recovering some runaways. They may have been house slaves, but if a neighbouring landlord gave them shelter no doubt he made them pay for it in work. The control of slaves in the country was never easy, and the quasi-military discipline described by Columella was a confession of this. And it was only on a large scale that a staff of overseers sufficient to work it could be provided. The time for it was indeed

---

[1] *epist* I 5 *ut rus quod solebat alere nunc alatur.* Cf cod Th XI 1 § 4.

[2] *epist* VI 82 (81).

[3] *nihilque iam colonis superest facultatum quod aut rationi opituletur aut cultui.*

[4] *epist* VII 56 *cum sit colonus agrorum meorum atque illi debita magis quam precaria cura praestetur.*

[5] *epist* IX 6. Cf IX 11.   [6] *epist* IX 47 (50).

[7] *epist* IX 140 (X 18).

gone by. Slaves employed in hunting[1] are mentioned by Symmachus
as by Pliny. No doubt they took to this occupation with zest. The
degeneracy of hunting by deputy is contemptuously noted as a sign
of the times by the soldier critic[2] Ammianus. But it was no new thing.

That the general state of the countryside was hardly favourable to
the quiet development of agriculture may be gathered from many
notices. For instance, when he would have been glad to be out of
Rome for the good of his health, he complains[3] that the prevalence
of brigandage in the country near forces him to stay in the city. A
friend urges him to come back to Rome for fear of a violent raid on an
estate apparently suburban: he can only reply[4] that a breach of
possession during his absence will not hold good in law. Whether the
militaris impressio[5] on his farm at Ostia, to which he casually refers,
was the raid of foreign foes suddenly landing on that coast, or the lawless outrage of imperial troops, is not certain: I rather suspect the
latter. For, fifteen years later (398), after the overthrow of Gildo, he
writes[6] that the soldiers are all back from Africa, and the Appian way is
clear: here the meaning seems plain. And his endeavour[7] to prevent the
commandeering of an old friend's house at Ariminum for military
quarters is significant of the high-handed treatment of civilians by
army men in those days, of which we have other evidence. Nevertheless men were still willing to buy estates. Symmachus himself was
still adding to his vast possessions. We see him in treaty[8] for a place
in Samnium, where there was apparently some queer practice on the
part of the seller: in another case he is annoyed[9] that his partner in a
joint purchase has contrived to secure the whole bargain as sole
transferee, and rather sulkily offers to waive his legal claims on being
reimbursed what he has already paid to the transferor. It seems strange
that a man who, beside his numerous properties in Italy, owned estates[10]
in Mauretania (where he complains that the governors allow his interests
to suffer) and in Sicily (where the lessee is called *conductor*, probably a
tenant in chief subletting to *coloni*), should have had an appetite for
more investments of doubtful economic value. But other investments
were evidently very hard to find in an age when industry and commerce
were fettered by the compulsory gild-system. And a man of influence
like Symmachus was better able than one of the common herd to
protect his own interests by the favour of powerful officials.

[1] *epist* VIII 2. Plin *epist* I 6, V 6 § 46.
[2] Amm Marc XXVIII 4 § 18 *alienis laboribus venaturi.*   [3] *epist* II 22.   [4] *epist* V 18.
[5] *epist* II 52. Cf the cases contemplated in Dig XIX 2 §§ 13[7], 15[2].   [6] *epist* VII 38.
[7] *epist* IX 45 (48).   [8] *epist* VI 11.   [9] *epist* IX 27 (30).
[10] *epist* VII 66, IX 49 (52). In the law of 414 Cod Th XVI 5 § 54 we have these *conductores privatorum* opposed to *conductores domus nostrae* in Africa. See above, chapter on
the African inscriptions.

We get glimpses of the condition of agriculture in Italy under the strain of events. It must be borne in mind that Italy was no longer exempt from the land-burdens of the imperial system. For many years, certainly from 383 to 398, Rome was hardly ever free from the fear of famine. It was necessary to scrape together all the spare food that could be found in the country in order to eke out the often interrupted importations from abroad. The decline of food-production in rich Campania is indicated by many scattered references. The district was probably too much given over to vines, and a great part of it occupied by unproductive villas. In 396 Symmachus is relieved to know that the corn-supply of Rome is assured, at least for twenty days. He goes on to mention[1] that corn has been transferred from Apulia to Campania. Whether this was for Campanian consumption, or eventually to be forwarded to Rome, is not stated. I am inclined to the former alternative by the consideration of the quarrel between Tarracina and Puteoli referred to below. That corn should have been brought from Apulia[2] is a striking fact. A great part of that province was taken up by pastures and olive-yards. It can only have had corn to spare by reason of sparse population and good crops. If we had the whole story of this affair, the explanation might prove to be simpler than it can be now. In 397 he writes[3] to a friend that the Apulians are having a bad time. They are erroneously supposed to be in for a good harvest, and so are being required to supply corn. This will be stripping the province without materially helping the state. For winter is coming on, and there is not time left to bring such a great crop of ripeness. Symmachus had friends dependent on property in Apulia. Writing some four years later[4] he refers to this estate as rated for taxation on a higher scale than its income would warrant: he asks the local governor to see that it shall not be crushed by 'public burdens.'

For to Symmachus, as to all or most men in this passive and cruelly selfish age, the first thought was to protect their own interests and those of their friends by engaging the favour of the powerful. Many of the passages cited above illustrate this, and many more could be given. The candour of some of his applications is remarkable. On behalf of one dependant in trouble he says[5] to the person addressed 'but he will get more help from the partiality of your judgment, for he really has some right on his side.' To another he writes[6] that of course right is always to be considered, but in dealing with *nobiles probabilesque personas* a judge should feel free to qualify strict rules,

---

[1] *epist* VI 12.

[2] In *quality* the Apulian wheat was thought excellent. Varro *RR* 1 2 § 6.

[3] *epist* IX 29.   [4] *epist* VII 126 *res...non tam reditu ampla quam censu.*

[5] *epist* IX 11 *sed maior opitulatio ex tui arbitrii favore proveniet, cum causae eius etiam iustitia non desit.*   [6] *epist* IX 37 (40).

letting the fairness of his decision appear[1] in the distinction made. This proposition introduces a request on behalf of his sister. Some farms of hers are overburdened with the dues exacted by the state, and are now empty for lack of tenants. Only the governor's sanction can give them the relief needed to restore them to solvency; and Symmachus trusts that his friend will do the right thing by the lady. In another case[2] he asks favour for a dependant, significantly adding a request that his friend will see to it that the case does not come before another judge. Now, what chance of asserting their own rights had humble folk in general, and poor working farmers in particular, when governors and judges of all sorts were solicited like this by men whose goodwill was worth securing,—men for the most part unscrupulous greedy and prone to bear grudges, not such as the virtuous and kindly Symmachus? Perhaps nothing shews the selfishness of the rich more than their attempts to shirk the duty of furnishing recruits for the army. Yet we find in one letter[3] a request to a provincial governor to check the activities of the recruiting agents. That the writer accuses these latter of overstepping their legal powers can only be viewed with some suspicion, considering his readiness to use private influence. Early in 398, when a force was being raised to operate against Gildo, it was thought necessary to enlist slaves from the city households. The protests[4] of their owners, in which Symmachus shared, were loud: the compensation allowance was too low, and so forth. Yet, if any one was interested in suppressing the rebel, it was surely these wealthy men.

That the obligation of providing for the sustenance of the idle populace of Rome was not only a worry to officials but a heavy burden on farmers in the Provinces whence the supplies were drawn, needs no detailed proof. But they were used to the burden, and bore it quietly in average years. A very bad season might produce dearth even in Africa, and call for exceptional measures[5] of relief on the part of emperors. So Trajan had relieved Egypt. It was however an extreme step to ease the pressure in Rome by expelling[6] all temporary residents, as was actually done during the famine of 383. These would be nearly all from the Provinces, and Symmachus uneasily refers[7] to the resentment that the expulsion was certain to provoke. But in this age a rebellion of provincials to gain redress of their own particular grievances was not a conceivable policy. When discontent expressed itself in something more than a local riot, it needed a head in the form of a pretender making a bid for imperial power. But we are not to suppose

---

[1] *ut perspiciatur in discretione iudicium.*   [2] *epist* IX 47 (50).
[3] *epist* IX 10.   [4] *epist* VI 59 (58), 65 (64).   [5] *epist* IV 74.   [6] *epist* II 7.
[7] *quanto nobis odio provinciarum constat illa securitas.*

that Rome, and later Constantinople, stood quite alone in receipt of
food-favours. The case of two Italian municipalities, reported on[1] by
Symmachus in 384–5, proves the contrary, and we have no ground for
assuming that they were the only instances. The important port-town
of Puteoli was granted 150000 *modii* of corn yearly towards the feeding
of the city by Constantine. Constans cut down the allowance to 75000.
Constantius raised it again to 100000. Under Julian a complication
arose. The governor of Campania found Tarracina in sore straits
(evidently for food) because of the failure[2] of the supplies due from the
towns long assigned for that purpose. Now Tarracina had a special
claim to support, since it provided Rome with firewood for heating the
baths and lime for the repair of the walls. It seems that the governor
felt bound to keep this town alive, but had no new resources on which
he could draw. So he took 5700 *modii* from the allowance of Puteoli
and gave them to Tarracina. Final settlement was referred to Julian,
but not reached before his death in the Persian war (363). The next
stage was that a deputation from Capua[3] addressed the emperor Gratian,
confining themselves to complaint of their own losses. By this one-
sided representation they procured an imperial order, that the amount
of corn allowance which Cerealis[4] had claimed for the people of Rome
should be given back to all the cities deprived of it by his act. But
under this order the total recovered for sustenance of the provincials
only reached 38000 *modii* of corn that had been added to the stores of
the eternal city. So Puteoli refused to hand over even the 5700 to
Tarracina. And the provincial governor did not go carefully into the
terms of the order, but ruled in favour of Puteoli. An appeal followed,
and it came out that the grant of 5700 to Tarracina was not an ordinary
bounty but an earmarked[5] sum granted in consideration of services to
Rome. The governor did not feel able either to confirm it or to take
it away. Therefore the matter was referred to the emperors for a final
settlement. This strange story gives us a momentary glimpse of things
that make no figure in general histories. The abject dependence of the
municipalities on imperial favour stands out clearly: not less so the
precarious nature of such favours, a feature of the time amply illustrated
by the later imperial laws, numbers of which were simply issued to
withdraw privileges previously granted, under the stress of needs that

---

[1] *relatio* 40.

[2] *quod nihil subsidii decreta dudum oppida conferebant.* This seems to imply a previous
grant to Tarracina, levied on other towns. Cf *relat* 37 *decretae provinciae*, referring to supply
of Rome.

[3] *Capuana legatio.* Meaning *Campanian*, I take it.

[4] Neratius Cerealis, praef annonae 328, praef urbi 352–3, consul 358. Godefroi's Pro-
sopographia, Wilmanns inscr 1085, and cod Th XIV 24. The order is given thus, *cum
frumenti numerum, quem Cerealis ex multis urbibus Romano populo vindicarat, restitui
omnibus.*   [5] *secretum.*

made it impossible to maintain them. Again, we see that in addition
to the normal jealousy of neighbours the competition for imperial favour
was an influence tending to hinder rather than promote cohesion :
tending in fact to weaken the fabric now menaced by the tribal barbarians. Above all, this affair strongly suggests the partiality of the
central government to town populations. The farmers of the municipal
territories were certainly liable to the land-burdens, and were the ultimate basis of imperial finance : but of them there is not a word. Lastly,
we may suppose that inter-municipal disputes such as this were not
of very frequent occurrence : but we have no reason to believe that
this Campanian case was unique.

LIV. AMMIANUS.

In **Ammianus Marcellinus** (about 330 to 400) we have an oriental
Greek from Antioch who passed a great part of his life in the military
service of the empire. He had travelled much, campaigned in Gaul
and the East, and was an observant man of wide interests, and in his
history impartial to the best of his power. Whether in deliberate
criticisms, or in casual references, he is an exceptionally qualified and
honest witness as to the state of things in the empire. On one important
point his evidence is of special value. All through the surviving portion
of his work (353–378) he leaves us in no doubt that the internal evils
of the empire were weakening it more than the pressure of barbarians
from without. He does not argue this in a section devoted to the topic,
but he takes occasion to notice the abuses that impaired the prosperity
of the Provinces or led directly to grave disasters. The corruption
jealousy greed cruelty and general misrule of officials high and low
was no secret to him. That the ultimate sufferers from their misdeeds
were the poor, and more particularly the poor farmers, may be gathered
from many passages. That the centre of this all-pervading disease lay
in the imperial court, a focus of intrigue and jobbery that the very
best of emperors could never effectively check, he was surely aware.
At least it is only on this assumption that we get the full flavour of
his references to court-intrigues and his criticisms of emperors, his
balanced discussions of their good and bad qualities and the effects of
their policy and practice. In truth the whole system was breaking
down. It lasted longer in the East than in the West, because the
eastern peoples were more thoroughly tamed. They had been used
to despotic government long before the coming of Rome. And the
assaults of external enemies were more formidable and persistent in
the North and West than in the South and East. Yet, so long as the
empire held together, imperial despotism was inevitable. Neither
Ammianus nor any other writer of that age did or could offer a possible

alternative. Christianity might capture the empire and spread among the barbarians, but it had no constructive solution for the problems of imperial government.

A remarkably plain-spoken passage[1] occurs in reference to the events of 356, where he describes the administration of Julian in Gaul. By his victories over the Germans he relieved the impoverished Gauls, but this was by no means his only benefit. For instance, where he found at his first coming a tax-unit[2] of 25 gold pieces demanded as the *tributum*, at his departure (360) he left things so much improved that seven of these sufficed to meet all dues. Great was the joy in Gaul. As a particular example of his thoughtful care, Ammianus cites his policy in the matter of arrears of tribute. There were occasions, especially in provinces liable to invasion, when it was certain that such arrears could not be recovered in the ordinary course. It was not to the interest of the central government to ruin or turn adrift farmers whose places it would not be easy to fill. This consideration was no doubt used to procure from emperors orders of remission, *indulgentiae*[3] as they were called. Julian to the last would not give relief by thus waiving the imperial rights. 'For he was aware[4] that the effect of that step would be to put money into the pockets of the rich; the universal practice, as everyone knows, being for the poor to be made to pay up the due amount in full directly the order of collection is issued, and allowed no time of grace.' It seems then that it was not the amount of the imperial taxation, but the iniquities perpetrated in connexion with its collection, that were the real burden crushing the vitality of the Provinces. So thought Julian, rightly: and in the next year we find him firmly upholding his principles in the face of exceptional difficulties. The emperor Constantius had felt compelled to make Julian Caesar, and to place him at the head of the Western section of the empire. But his jealousy and fear of the Caesar's winning glory in Gaul led him to surround Julian with officers devoted to himself and secretly encouraged to hamper their titular chief in every possible way. The court of Constantius was a hotbed of intrigue and calumny. Private reports of the doings of Julian were being regularly received. Any reforms that he was able to make in Gaul had to be effected in the teeth of imperial malignity.

---

[1] XVI 5 §§ 14, 15.

[2] Seeck, *Schatzungsordnung* p 306, keeps the MS reading *capitulis* here. See his remarks, and for the word *capitulum* cf cod Th XI 16 § 15 (382) *capituli atque temonis necessitas*, ibid § 14 *capitulariae sive...temonariae functionis*.

[3] The title cod Th XI 28 is *de indulgentiis debitorum*.

[4] *norat enim hoc facto se aliquid locupletibus additurum, cum constet ubique pauperes inter ipsa indictorum exordia solvere universa sine laxamento conpelli.* We shall return to this point in connexion with Salvian.

A flagrant instance[1] is seen in the efforts made to thwart his reforming energy during the winter of 357–8. After defeating and humbling aggressive German tribes, he set himself to relieve the distress of the landowners, who had suffered great losses. There was at the time a great need of money. The praetorian prefect of the Gauls, Florentius, proposed to raise the sums required[2] by an additional levy, and procured from Constantius an order to that effect. Julian would rather die than allow this. He knew what would happen in carrying it out, and that such 'precautions' (*provisiones*)[3] or rather destructions (*eversiones*) had often brought provinces into the extremities of want. The Prefect, to whose department the matter in strictness belonged, protested loudly, relying on the powers given him by Constantius. But Julian stood firm, and tried to soothe him by calmly proving that there was no necessity for the proposed measure. Careful calculations shewed that the normal impost (*capitatio*) would produce enough to furnish the needful supplies, and something to spare. He would have nothing to do with the order[4] for an extra levy. The Prefect duly reported this to Constantius, who reprimanded the Caesar for his obstinacy. Julian replied that the provincials had been exposed to ravages from various quarters, and that if they were still able to render the usual dues[5] the government had reason to be thankful. To wring more out of men in distress by punishments was impossible. And he did manage to prevent extraordinary exactions in Gaul. In the winter of 358–9 he continued the same policy. He saw to the equitable assessment[6] of the tribute, and kept at bay the horde of rascally officials who made fortunes[7] out of injuring the people. The corruption of the law-courts he checked by hearing the important cases himself. No wonder that in an age of Christian emperors the virtuous pagan earned a reputation as a restorer of Roman greatness far beyond the boundaries of Gaul. Whether the fact that adherents of polytheism were now chiefly to be found among rustics (*pagani*) had anything to do with Julian's clear appreciation of the sufferings of countryfolk, is a question on which I cannot venture to offer an opinion.

That all or most of the corn levied by imperial taxation was in the frontier Provinces required for the military commissariat is well known, and the granaries for storing it were a leading feature of permanent camps and garrison towns. The feeding of armies in the field, always

---

[1] XVII 3.

[2] *quicquid in capitatione deesset ex conquisitis se supplere. conquisita* are the sums produced by a *superindictio* raising the amount to be levied. Cf cod Th XI 1 § 36, and title XI 6 *de superindicto.*

[3] Cf XXX 5 § 6 *provisorum*, cod Th XII 1 § 169 *tuae provisionis...incrementis.*

[4] *indictionale augmentum.*   [5] *sollemnia...nedum incrementa.*

[6] XVIII 1.   [7] *quorum patrimonia publicae clades augebant.*

wasteful, no doubt consumed a great deal. In the case of Gaul (for to
live on the country was starvation to a force invading wild Germany)
the quantity to be brought up to the front seems to have been normally
more than Gaul could spare. It was usual to rely on the harvests[1] of
Britain. Transport was the main difficulty. Saxon pirates infested the
narrow seas, and the navigation of the Rhine was blocked by Franks.
Julian's energy cleared away these obstacles, and saw to the erection
or repair of granaries in the Rhineland towns to receive the British
corn. These measures enabled him to do without making extra demands
on the farmers of Gaul, a step sometimes unavoidable when there was
war on the frontiers. Of course such commandeering was very unpopular, and wise generals avoided it whenever possible. Ammianus
draws particular attention[2] to this matter when narrating the campaign
of Theodosius in Mauretania (373). He forbade the levy of supplies
from the provincials, announcing that he would make the stores of the
enemy[3] provide the commissariat, and the landowners were delighted.

Among the interesting references that occur in the course of the
work are some that throw further light on the conditions of life in the
parts of the empire subject to invasion. It is not necessary to cite the
frequent mention of various kinds of fortified posts from great strongholds to mere blockhouses. These remind us that the strength of the
imperial armies could never be so maintained as to guard the frontier
at all times on all points. Barbarian raiders slipped through[4] the inevitable gaps, and wide stretches of country were laid waste long before
sufficient forces could be gathered to expel them. We do not need
the descriptions of their cruel ravages to convince us that agriculture
near the Danube or Rhine borders was a perilous calling. If the farmer
were not carried away into bondage or slain, he was left robbed of his
all, and in imminent danger of starving: for the barbarians ate up
everything, and hunger was a principal motive in leading them to come
and warning them to return home. Naturally it was the custom in
these borderlands to provide fortified refuges here and there in which
local farmers could find temporary shelter with their belongings, and
homesteads of any importance were more or less equipped for defence.
This was the state of things even in Mauretania. We read of a farm[5]
(*fundus*) which the brother of Firmus the rebel leader (373) 'built up
after the fashion of a city'; also of one girt with a strong[6] wall, a very

---

[1] XVIII 2 § 2 and references in Wagner's edition. Schiller, *Kaiserzeit* II p 313.

[2] XXIX 5 §§ 10–13.   [3] *messes et condita hostium virtutis nostrorum horrea esse.*

[4] As when in Pannonia (373) they crossed the Danube and *occupatam circa messem
agrestem adortae sunt plebem*, XXIX 6 § 6.

[5] XXIX 5 § 13 *in modum urbis exstruxit.*

[6] XXIX 5 § 25 *muro circumdatum valido.* In XXX 10 § 4 we find *Murocincta* as the
name of a *villa* and *Triturrita* in Rutilius *de reditu* I 527, 615. Cf cases in Caesar's time,
Bell Afr 9, 40, 65.

secure refuge for the Moors, to destroy which Theodosius had to employ battering-rams. These are not the only instances. And forts (*castella*) and walled towns are often referred to. Along the northern borders the necessity for such precautions was much greater. Still it seems that few if any in the latter part of the fourth century foresaw that frontier defences would at no distant date give way before the barbarian flood. A high imperial official, with whose corrupt connivance[1] gross wrongs had been perpetrated (370) in Africa, on being superseded in office withdrew to his native Rhineland, and 'devoted himself[2] to rural affairs.' The retired ease for which he apparently hoped was soon ended, though not by barbarian raiders. The malignity of a praetorian prefect tracked him to his retreat and by persecution drove him to suicide.

This last episode may remind us that the weakening of the empire was not wholly due to failure of an economic kind or to decay of military skill. The farmers might raise crops enough, the armies might prove their superiority in the field, but nevertheless the great organism was in decline. A general mistrust, fatal to loyal cooperation for the common good, was the moral canker by which the exertions of farmer and soldier were hampered and rendered vain. Officials seeking to ruin each other, emperors turning to murders and confiscations as a source of revenue, all classes bound fast in rigid corporations or gilds under laws which it was their study to evade; the failure of individual enterprise, lacking the joy of individual freedom, and the stimulus of expected reward; in short, everyone ready to sacrifice his neighbour to save his own skin: how was a society characterized by such phenomena to maintain a moral advantage over the rude barbarians? That it was now protected by alien swords, that aliens were even commanding[3] the Roman armies, was not the main cause of its overthrow. As a rule these barbarians kept their bargain, and shed their blood freely for the empire that enlisted them in masses. But we must distinguish between two or three different classes of these alien defenders. The mere mercenaries need not detain us. More significant were the contingents taken over in large bodies by agreement with the tribes. A good instance[4] is that of the year 376, when a vast host of Goths sought leave to pass the Danube with the hope of settling on vacant lands south of the river. We are told that the Roman commanders on that front got over their first alarm and took the line that really the emperor was in luck. Here was a huge supply of recruits[5] brought to him from the ends of the earth, an unlooked-for reinforcement ready to be blended with his own troops, and to make up an unconquerable army. Instead of spending

---

[1] xxviii 6 § 8.   [2] xxx 2 § 10 *negotiis se ruralibus dedit.*

[3] There was much jealousy on this score, and a powerful reaction, as after the death of Valentinian in 375, but even then the foreign element prevailed. Schiller II 389.

[4] xxxi 4 §§ 4, 5.   [5] *ex ultimis terris tot tirocinia.* Cf xix 11 § 7.

the yearly payments of the provinces[1] on filling up the ranks, the treasury would gain a great sum of gold. It would seem that they reported to the emperor in favour of the request, for Valens granted the petition of a Gothic embassy. Arrangements were made for transporting them over the river, and it was understood that they had leave to settle in the parts of Thrace. But now troubles began. Greedy Roman officials fleeced and maltreated the hungry horde, who were at length driven into rebellion. With the sequel, the great battle (378) near Adrianople, and the death of Valens, we are not here concerned. But the account[2] of their ravages in Thrace gives us a picture of the countryside in a harassed province and of the slave labour employed. The rebels, unable to take fortified places by regular siege, overran the country in raiding bands. Captives guided them to places stocked with food. But they were especially encouraged and strengthened by the great number of people of their own race who came pouring in to join them. Ammianus describes[3] these deserters as men who had long before been sold (into slavery of course) by traders, and with them very many whom at the time of their passing the river, when they were perishing of hunger, they had bartered for thin wine or worthless scraps of bread.

This scene may serve to remind us that slavery and the sale of slaves to Roman dealers were recognized features of German tribal life as described by Tacitus. It also gives us a glimpse of the way in which opportunities of imperial advantage could be wasted or turned into calamities by the unpatriotic and selfish greed of Roman officials. In this case potential recruits were turned into actual enemies; and the barbarian slaves, who should have been tilling Thracian fields in the interest of Rome, were left to guide and recruit the hostile army of their kinsmen. It must not be supposed that all schemes for raising barbarian troops in large bodies were thus by gross mismanagement brought to a disastrous end. The value of sound flesh and blood in the ranks was well understood, and a successful campaign against German tribes could be made profitable from this point of view. Thus in 377, when Gratian had a whole tribe at his mercy, he required of them a contingent[4] of sturdy recruits to be incorporated in Roman army-units, on delivery of whom he set free the rest to return to their native homes. That such recruits became under Roman discipline so far Romanized as to provide efficient armies is clear from the victories that still delayed

[1] *et pro militari supplemento, quod provinciatim annuum pendebatur, thesauris accederet auri cumulus magnus.* I hope I am right in referring this to the *temonaria functio* or obligation of paying the *temo* = the price of a recruit. Cod Th XI 16 §§ 14, 15.

[2] XXXI 6 § 5.

[3] *dudum a mercatoribus venundati, adiectis plurimis quos primo transgressu necati inedia vino exili vel panis frustris mutavere vilissimis.*

[4] XXXI 10 § 17, *iuventute valida nostris tirociniis permiscenda.*

the fall of the empire. But 'Roman' was becoming more than ever a mere name-label: there had never been a Roman nation. Of the third class of alien soldiery little need be said. Military colonists of barbarian origin had for a long time past been brought into the empire, some as frontier guards holding land on condition of army service, others more in the interior, even[1] in Italy; and these latter undoubtedly furnished many recruits, on whatever terms. The general result may be summed up in saying that, when the barbarian invaders at last came to stay, they found their kindred already there at home.

LV. CLAUDIAN.

In **Claudian**, who wrote about 400, we have another oriental Greek, who wrote chiefly in Latin with far more mastery of that language than Ammianus. Stilicho his patron, the great barbarian head of the Roman army, was at the height of his power, and Claudian's most congenial occupation was to sing his praises and denounce his opponents. He was also poet laureate of the feeble emperor Honorius. Writing mainly on contemporary themes, he is, if allowance be made for his bias, a witness worth citing; but the passages relevant to the present subject are naturally few. In common with other writers of the later ages of Rome he is constantly looking back to a great and glorious past, contrasting painfully with that present which he nevertheless is striving to glorify. Thus he not only refers with enthusiasm[2] to the old heroes of Roman history and legend, the common material of Roman literature, but even dreams[3] of a golden age to be, when the earth of her own accord shall render all good things in abundance to a people living happily in communistic brotherhood. This fancy however is no more than a piece of unreal rhetoric, an echo of Vergil. It is inspired by the victories of Stilicho, and the world-dominion under which this beatific vision is to be realized is—the rule of Honorius.

In January 395 the great Theodosius died, and the empire was divided between his two sons. In November, Rufinus, who dominated Arcadius at Constantinople, was murdered. His place was soon taken by the eunuch Eutropius. On these two personages Claudian poured out a flood of invective, speaking for Stilicho and the West. The greed of Rufinus is depicted[4] as ruinous to the landed interests. 'The fertility of his land was the ruin of the landlord: a good crop[5] made the farmers tremble. He drives men from their homes, and thrusts them out of

---

[1] XXVIII 5 § 15 of Theodosius defeating Alamanni, *pluribus caesis, quoscumque cepit ad Italiam iussu principis misit, ubi fertilibus pagis acceptis iam tributarii circumcolunt Padum.* 370 AD. Cf XXXI 9 § 4, 377 AD, and XX 4 § 1, 360 AD.

[2] For instance, *in Rufinum* I 200–5, *de bello Gildon* 105–12, *de IV cos Honor* 412–8.

[3] *in Rufin* I 380–2.   [4] *in Rufin* I 189–92.   [5] *metuenda colonis fertilitas.*

their ancestral borders, either robbing the living or seizing the estates of the dead.' The jealousy of the West expresses itself in a passage[1] referring to the famine created in Rome by the rebellion of Gildo in Africa. Honorius (that is Stilicho) is effusively praised for its relief by importations from other Provinces, chiefly from Gaul. That, owing to the claim of the New Rome to the corn of Egypt, the Old Rome should be so dependent on Africa, is a situation indignantly resented[2] in eloquent lines. A symptom ominous of imperial failure was the attempt to wrest eastern Illyricum from the rule of Arcadius (407–8) an enterprise[3] secretly concerted between Stilicho and Alaric. Fugitives from Epirus sought refuge in Italy. Stilicho treated them as prisoners of war from an enemy's country, and handed them over to Italian landlords as slaves or *coloni*. When Alaric and his Goths moved towards Italy, some of these refugees, aided by a law issued for their protection, found their way home again. Claudian unblushingly declares[4] that none but Stilicho will be able to heal the empire's wound: 'at length the *colonus* will return to his own borders and the court will once more be enriched by the tributes of Illyricum.'

A Roman view of the intruding barbarians and their capacity of peaceful settlement is in one place[5] put into the mouth of Bellona the war-goddess. She addresses a Gothic chief in bitter sarcasm. 'Go and be a thorough ploughman, cleaving the soil: teach your comrades to lay aside the sword and toil at the hoe. Your Gruthungians[6] will make fine cultivators, and tend vineyards in accordance with the seasons.' She taunts him with degenerating from the good old habits of his race, war and plunder, and scornfully describes him as one captured[7] by the glamour of fair dealing, who had rather live as a serf on what is granted him than as a lord on what he takes by force. In short, he is a coward. Now no doubt there were Goths and others, Huns in particular, of this war-loving work-hating type approved by the war-goddess. But abundant evidence shews that many, perhaps most, of the barbarians were quite ready to settle down in peace and produce their own food. When Claudian himself speaks[8] of the 'Teuton's ploughshare' as one of the agencies producing corn that relieved famine in Rome, he is most likely referring to the many Germans already settled in Gaul as well as to inhabitants of the 'Germanies,' the two provinces along the Rhine.

A curious passage[9] in the poem on the Gothic war and Stilicho's

[1] *in Eutrop* I 401–9.   [2] *de bello Gildon* 49–74.

[3] See Bury, *Later Roman empire* I 108-9, Seeck, *Untergang* V 379–80, Dill, *Roman Society* p 233, Wallon, *Esclavage* III 276–7. The affair is referred to in cod Th X 10 § 25 (Dec 408).

[4] *de cos Stilichonis* II 204–7.   [5] *in Eutrop* II 194–210.

[6] *bene rura Gruthungus excolet et certo disponet sidere vites.*

[7] *quem detinet aequi gloria concessoque cupit vixisse colonus quam dominus rapto.*

[8] *in Eutrop* I 406 *Teutonicus vomer.*   [9] *de bell Goth* 450–68.

defeat of Alaric at Pollentia (402) is of interest in connexion with the Roman army and the recruiting system. Of the confidence revived in Rome by the appearance of Stilicho and his troops a vivid picture is drawn, and he continues 'henceforth[1] no more pitiful conscription, no more of reapers laying down the sickle and wielding the inglorious javelin...nor the mean clamorous jangling of amateur leaders: no, this is the presence of a genuine manhood, a genuine commander, a scene of war in real life.' If this means anything, it implies that hasty levies[2] of raw countrymen were notoriously unfit to face hordes of barbarian tribesmen in the field. True, no doubt; professional training had been the basis of efficiency in Roman armies ever since the days of Marius. But the words surely suggest further that conscription within the empire was in Claudian's time not found a success, that is in producing a supply of fit recruits to keep the legions up to strength. This also was doubtless true, as much other evidence attests, and was the main reason why the 'Roman' soldiery of the period were mostly barbarians. But here, as usual, the witness of the court-poet is in the form of admission rather than statement. His business was to be more Roman than Rome. It remains only to mention two similes, one of which perhaps refers to free labour. An old crone[3] has 'poor girls' under her engaged in weaving. They beg for a little holiday, but she keeps them at work 'to earn their joint livelihood.' This may be a scene from life, but is more likely an echo from earlier poetry. When he illustrates[4] the effect of Stilicho's coming on the peoples rising against Rome by comparing them to slaves, deceived by false report of their lord's death, and caught revelling by him when he unexpectedly returns, it is a scene that might be enacted in any age. The little poem on the old man of Verona is famous as a picture of humble contentment in rustic life. But the main point of it as evidence is that the case is exceptional.

LVI. VEGETIUS.

Vegetius, a contemporary of Ammianus and Claudian, is credited with two surviving works, one on the military system, the other on veterinary practice. Both are largely compilations, and belong to the class of technical writings which formed a great part of the literature of this age. In discussing army matters the author looks back with regret to the sounder conditions of the past. Speaking[5] of the quality of recruits, he says 'It can surely never have been matter of doubt that

[1] *non iam dilectus miseri nec falce per agros deposita iaculum vibrans ignobile messor... sed vera iuventus, verus ductor adest et vivida Martis imago.*
[2] Cf Vegetius *rei milit* I 7, of disasters in recent times, *dum longa pax militem incuriosius legit.*
[3] *in Eutrop* II 370–5.   [4] *de bell Goth* 366–72.   [5] *epitoma rei militaris* I 3.

the common countryfolk are more fit (than townsfolk) to bear arms,
reared as they are in toil under the open sky, able to stand the heat of
the sun and caring not for the shade, with no experience of baths or
knowledge of luxuries, straightforward and frugal, with limbs hardened
to endure any kind of toil; for the wearing of armour, digging of
trenches, and carrying their kit, are continuations of rustic habit.' It
is true that sometimes town-bred recruits have to be levied, but they
need long and careful training to fit them for active service. True, the
Romans of old went out to war from the city. But luxury was unknown
in those days: the farmer of today was the warrior of tomorrow, by
change of weapons. Cincinnatus went straight from the plough to
be dictator. A little after, speaking[1] of the standard of height, he
tells us that it has always been usual to have a standard tested by
actual measurement, below which no recruit was passed for service in
certain crack units. But there were then[2] larger numbers to draw from,
and more men followed the combatant service, for the civil service[3] had
not as yet carried off the pick of those in military age. Therefore, if
circumstances require it, strength rather than height should be the
first consideration. I am loth to infer much[4] from this passage, the
period referred to in 'then' being undefined. What it does shew is that
in the writer's own time a considerable number of men of military age
(Romans being meant) were attracted by the civil career of the new
imperial service, which in all its grades was technically styled[5] a *militia*.
Nor does it appear certain that in preferring the rustic recruit to the
urban Vegetius implies the existence of a plentiful supply of the former
among the subjects of the empire. His words rather suggest to me the
opposite conclusion, which is in agreement with the evidence from other
sources.

Turning to the veterinary work (*ars mulomedicinae*) we come upon
a chapter devoted[6] to the management of horses. It is well to keep a
free space near the stable for the beasts to get exercise by rolling, for
they need exercise. 'And for this end it is very helpful to have them
mounted[7] often and ridden gently. Unskilful riders spoil both their

[1] *rei milit* I 5, *senos pedes vel certe quinos et denas uncias* [has not *ad* fallen out before
senos?]. In a law of 367, cod Th VII 13 § 3 *in quinque pedibus et septem unciis*.

[2] *tunc*. When? From I 28 it might be inferred that he looks back to the first Punic war.
But I do not think so.

[3] *necdum enim civilis pars florentiorem abduxerat iuventutem*. So I 7 *civilia sectantur
officia*.

[4] The assertion that *Martius calor* has not subsided (I 28), accepted by Seeck I 413,
seems to me rhetorical bravado. Much more likely is the view (*ib* 414) that the improved
standard of recruits in the fifth century was due to prevalence of barbarians.

[5] Seeck II 88 foll. Hence army service was called *militia armata*.

[6] *mulomed* I 56 §§ 11–13.

[7] *si saepius et cum moderatione animalia sedeantur*. For *sederi* cf § 35 *sub honesto sessore*,
Spart Hadr 22 § 6, cod Th IX 30 § 3.

paces and their temper. Most mischievous is the recklessness[1] of slaves. When the master is not there, they urge his horses to gallop, using spur as well as whip, in matches of speed with their mates or in fiercely-contested races against outsiders: it never occurs to them to halt or check their mounts. For they give no thought[2] to what is their master's loss, being well content that it falls on him. A careful owner will most strictly forbid such doings, and will only allow his cattle to be handled by suitable grooms who are gentle and understand their management.' We must bear in mind that the horse was not used in agriculture or as an ordinary beast of burden. Horse-breeding was kept up to supply chargers for war, racers for the circus, mounts for men of the wealthier classes in hunting or occasionally for exercise, for solemn processions and such like. When Vegetius treats of a stable or stud of horses, he has in mind the establishment of a gentleman of means, and it is worth noting that such an establishment could be contemplated by a writer of about 400 AD. This harmonizes with the picture of Italian conditions that we get from the letters of Symmachus and other sources. A few rich were very rich, the many poor usually very poor. The carelessness, wastefulness, thievishness, of slaves is a very old story, and in the middle of the fourth century had been bitterly referred to[3] by the emperor Julian. That Vegetius does not advise the owner of these slave grooms to make a *vilicus* responsible for seeing that his orders are obeyed, is probably due to the rigidly technical character of the treatise: he is not writing on the management of estates.

[1] *servorum impatientia.*
[2] *neque enim de damno domini cogitant, quod eidem contingere gratulantur.*
[3] Julian *orat* VII p 232 a–b.

CHRISTIAN WRITERS

LVII. LACTANTIUS.

When we turn to the Christian writers, whom it is convenient to take by themselves, we pass into a different atmosphere. Of rhetoric there is plenty, for most of them had been subjected to the same literary influences as their Pagan contemporaries. But there is a marked difference of spirit, more especially in one respect very important from the point of view of the present inquiry. Christianity might counsel submission to the powers that be: it might recognize slavery as an institution: it might enjoin on the slave to render something beyond eyeservice to his legal master. But it could never shake off the fundamental doctrine of the equal position of all men before their Almighty Ruler, and the prospect of coming life in another world, in which the standards and privileges dominating the present one would go for nothing. Therefore a Christian writer differed from the Pagan in his attitude towards the poor and oppressed. He could sympathize with them, not as a kindly though condescending patron, but as one conscious of no abiding superiority in himself. The warmth with which the Christian witnesses speak is genuine enough. The picture may be somewhat overdrawn or too highly coloured, and we must allow for some exaggeration, but in general it is surely true to fact.

First comes **Lactantius**, who has already[1] been once quoted. Writing under Constantine, he speaks of the Diocletian or Galerian persecution as a contemporary. The passage[2] to be cited here describes the appalling cruelty of the fiscal exactions ordered by Galerius to meet the pressing need of the government for more money. It was after the abdication of Diocletian and Maximian in 305. The troubles that ensued had no doubt helped to render financial necessities extreme. The remark, that he now practised against all men the lessons of cruelty learnt in tormenting the Christians, must refer to Galerius. The account of the census[3], presumably that of 307, is as follows. 'What brought disaster on the people and mourning on all alike, was the sudden letting loose of the census on the provinces and cities. Census-officers, sparing nothing, spread all over the land, and the scenes were such as when

---

[1] Above, p 393.   [2] *de mortibus persecutorum* 22-3.
[3] For the *census* under the new system, first in 297 and then every fifth year, see Seeck II pp 263 foll. It was only concerned with the land and taxation units liable to the levy of *annona*. De Coulanges pp 75-85 urges that the system already described by Ulpian in Dig L 15 §§ 3, 4, is much the same, and points out that monastic records shew it still surviving in the early Middle Age. But practice, rather than principle, is here in question.

an enemy invades a country and enslaves the inhabitants. There was measuring of fields clod by clod, counting of vines and fruit trees, cataloguing of every sort of animals, recording of the human[1] heads. In the municipalities (*civitatibus*) the common folk of town and country put on the same[2] footing, everywhere the marketplace crammed with the households assembled, every householder with his children and slaves. The sounds of scourging and torturing filled the air. Sons were being strung up to betray parents; all the most trusty slaves tortured to give evidence against their masters, and wives against husbands. If all these means had failed, men were tortured for evidence against themselves, and when they broke down under the stress of pain they were credited with admissions[3] never made by them. No plea of age or infirmity availed them: informations were laid against the invalids and cripples: the ages of individuals were recorded by guess, years added to those of the young and subtracted from those of the old. All the world was filled with mourning and grief.' In short, Romans and Roman subjects were dealt with as men of old dealt with conquered foes. 'The next step was the paying[4] of moneys for heads, a ransom for a life. But the whole business was not entrusted to the same body of officials (*censitoribus*); one batch was followed by others, who were expected to make further discoveries: a continual doubling of demands went on, not that they discovered more, but that they made additions arbitrarily, for fear they might seem to have been sent to no purpose. All the while the numbers of live stock were falling, and mankind dying; yet none the less tribute was being paid on behalf of the dead, for one had to pay for leave to live or even to die. The only survivors were the beggars from whom nothing could be wrung, immune for the time from wrongs of any sort by their pitiful destitution.' He goes on to declare that, in order to prevent evasion of the census on pretence of indigence, a number of these poor wretches were taken out to sea and drowned.

In this picture[5] we may reasonably detect high colouring and perhaps downright exaggeration. Probably the grouping together of horrors reported piecemeal from various quarters has given to the description as a whole a somewhat deceptive universality. That the imperial system, though gradually losing ground, held its own against

[1] *hominum capita.* In most provinces the taxable unit was fixed by taking account of the number of able-bodied on each estate as well as of the acreage. Seeck II 266 foll, also *Schatzung* pp 285-7.

[2] The urban taxation was conducted in each town by the local *decemprimi*, aldermen, and was quite distinct.

[3] *adscribebantur quae non habebantur* may mean 'were put on the record as owning what they did not own.'

[4] *pecuniae pro capitibus pendebantur.* The *capita* here seem to have a double sense.

[5] De Coulanges pp 75-6 treats it severely on the score of Christian prejudice.

unorganized barbarism for several more centuries, seems proof positive
that no utter destruction of the economic fabric took place in the census
to which Lactantius refers. But that the pressure exerted by the central
power, and the responsive severity of officials, were extreme, and that
the opportunities for extortion were seized and cruelly used, may fairly
be taken for fact on his authority. This was not the beginning of
sufferings to the unhappy tillers of the soil, nor was it the end. One
census might be more ruinous to their wellbeing than another: it was
always exhausting, and kept the farmers in terror. But they had not
as yet reached the stage of thinking it better to bear the yoke of barbarian chieftains than to remain under the corrupt and senseless
maladministration of imperial Rome.

LVIII. SULPICIUS SEVERUS.

The life and doings of the famous saint of Gaul, Martin of Tours,
a Pannonian by birth, were chronicled by **Sulpicius Severus**, writing
soon after 400, in an enthusiastic biography still in existence. In another
work occurs a passage[1] narrating one of his hero's many miracles; and
the story is too artlessly illustrative of the behaviour of the military
and the state of things on the public roads, not to be mentioned here.
Martin was travelling on his ecclesiastical duties, riding on an ass with
friends in company. The rest being for a moment detained, Martin
went on alone for a space. Just then a government car (*fiscalis raeda*)
occupied by a party of soldiers was coming along the road. The mules
drawing it shied at the unfamiliar figure of the saint in his rough and
dark dress. They got entangled in their harness, and the difficulty of
disentangling them infuriated the soldiers, who were in a hurry. Down
they jumped and fell upon Martin with whips and staves. He said not
a word, but took their blows with marvellous patience, and his apparent
indifference only enraged them the more. His companions picked him
up all battered and bloody, and were hastening to quit the scene of
the assault, when the soldiers, on trying to make a fresh start, were
the victims of a miracle. No amount of beating would induce the mules
to stir. Supernatural influence was suspected and made certain by
discovery of the saint's identity. Abject repentance was followed by
gracious forgiveness, and mules and soldiers resumed their journey.
Now the point of interest to us is the matter-of-fact way in which this
encounter is narrated. That a party of the military should bully peaceful civilians on the high road is too commonplace an event to evoke
any special comment or censure. But it is clearly an edifying fact that
violence offered to a holy man did not escape divine punishment. There

[1] Sulp Sev *dial* II 3.

is no suggestion that similar brutality to an ordinary rustic would have met with any punishment human or divine. Laws framed for the protection of provincials[1] against illegal exactions and to prevent encroachments of the military[2] remained on the statute-book, but in remote country parts they were dead letters. It is interesting to recall that Martin had in his youth served for some years as a soldier. As the son of a veteran, his enrolment[3] came in the ordinary course. But, though he is said to have been efficient, he did not like the profession and got his discharge with relief. His life covered about the last three quarters of the fourth century.

LIX. SALVIAN.

The calamities that befel the Roman world in the fourth century led to much recrimination between Pagan and Christian, each blaming the other for misfortunes generally regarded as the signal expression of divine wrath. Symmachus had been answered by Ambrose, and Christian interpretation of the course of human history produced its classic in Augustine's great work *de civitate Dei* early in the fifth century. About the same time Orosius wrote his earnest but grotesque *historiae adversus paganos*, an arbitrary and superficial distortion of history, interesting as a specimen of partisan composition. But it is not till the middle of the century that we come upon a Christian author who gives us a graphic picture of the sufferings of the people in a Province of the empire, and a working theory of their causes, strictly from a pious Christian's point of view. This is **Salvian**, an elder of the Church at Massalia. His evidence is cited by all historians, and must be repeated here. The main thesis is that all the woes and calamities of the age are judgments of God provoked by the gross immorality[4] of the Roman world. So far from imputing all vices and crimes to the Heathen and the Pagan, he regards them as shared by all men : but he draws a sharp line between those who sin in ignorance, knowing no better, and those who profess the principles of a pure Christianity and yet sin against the light that is in them. For the barbarians are either Heathen or Heretics (he is thinking of the Arians), while in the empire the Orthodox church prevails. And yet the barbarians prosper, while the empire decays. Why? simply because even in their religious darkness the barbarians are morally superior to the Romans. For our present purpose it is the economic and social phenomena as depicted by Salvian that are of interest, and I proceed to give an abstract of the

---

[1] For instance cod Th VII 1 § 12, VIII 5, XI 10, 11.   [2] Cod Th VII 20 § 7.

[3] Sulp Sev *vita S Martini* 2 § 5, and cf cod Th VII 22, also 1 § 8. See the note of Seeck II 490.

[4] This view has been challenged by Dill, pp 118-9. But cf Sidonius *epist* v 19, IX 6.

passage[1] in which he expounds his indictment of Roman administration and the corrupt influences by which it is perverted from the promotion of prosperity and happiness to a cause of misery and ruin.

The all-pervading canker is the oppression of the poor by the rich. The heavy burdens of taxation are thrown upon the poor. When any relief is granted, it is intercepted by the rich. Franks Huns Vandals and Goths will have none of these iniquities, and Romans living among those barbarians also escape them. Hence the stream of migration sets from us to them, not from them to us. Indeed our poor folk would migrate in a body, but for the difficulty of transferring their few goods their poor hovels and their families. This drives them to take another course. They put themselves under the guardianship and protection of more powerful persons, surrendering[2] to the rich like prisoners of war, and so to speak passing under their full authority and control. But this protection is made a pretext for spoliation. For the first condition of protection is the assignation[3] of practically their whole substance to their protectors: the children's inheritance is sacrificed to pay for the protection of their parents. The bargain is cruel and onesided, a monstrous and intolerable wrong. For most of these poor wretches, stripped of their little belongings and expelled from their little farms, though they have lost their property, have still to bear the tribute on the properties lost : the possession is withdrawn, but the assessment[3] remains : the ownership is gone, but the burden of taxation is crushing them still. The effects of this evil are incalculable. The intruders (*pervasores*) are settled down (*incubant*) on their properties, while they, poor souls, are paying the tributes on the intruders' behalf. And this condition passes on to their children. So they who have been despoiled by the intrusion[5] of individuals are being done to death by the pressure of the state (*publica adflictione*), and their livelihood is taken from them by squeezing as their property was by robbery. Some, wiser or taught by necessity, losing their homes and little farms through intrusions or driven by the tax-gatherers to abandon them through inability to keep them, find their way to the estates of the powerful, and become[6] serf-tenants (*coloni*) of the rich. Like fugitives from the enemy or the law, not able to retain their social birthright, they bow themselves[7] to the mean lot of mere sojourners : cast out of property and position, they

---

[1] The earlier part of book v of the *de gubernatione Dei*, especially §§ 34–50. The rising of the Bagaudae (286) in Gaul is dealt with §§ 24 foll. See Schiller II pp 124–6.

[2] *dediticios se divitum faciunt et quasi in ius eorum dicionemque trascendunt.*

[3] *addicunt*, a technical law term.   [4] *possessio...capitatio.*

[5] *pervasio* = attack, encroachment. Cf cod Th II 4 §§ 5, 6.

[6] *fundos maiorum expetunt et coloni divitum fiunt.*

[7] *iugo se inquilinae abiectionis addicunt.* See cod Th V 18 (10) *de inquilinis et colonis*, cod Just XI 48 § 13.

have nothing left to call their own, and are no longer their own masters. Nay, it is even worse. For though they are admitted (to the rich men's estates) as strangers (*advenae*), residence operates to make them[1] natives of the place. They are transformed as by a Circe's cup. The lord of the place, who admitted them as outside[2] aliens, begins to treat them as his own (*proprios*): and so men of unquestioned free birth are being turned into slaves. When we are putting our brethren into bondage, is it strange[3] that the barbarians are making bondsmen of us?

This is something beyond[4] mere partisan polemic. It finds the source of misery and weakness in moral decay. Highly coloured, the picture is surely none the less true. The degradation of the rustic population presents itself in two stages. First, the farmer, still owning his little farm (*agellus, rescula*), finds that, what with legal burdens and illegal extortions, his position is intolerable. So he seeks the protection[5] of a powerful neighbour, who exploits his necessities. Apparently he acquires control of the poor man's land, but contrives to do it in such a form as to leave him still liable to payment of the imperial dues. That this iniquity was forbidden[6] by law mattered not: corrupt officials shut their eyes to the doings of the rich. From the *curiales* of the several communities no help was to be looked for. Salvian declares[7] that they were tyrants to a man. And we must not forget that they themselves were forced into office and held responsible for paying in full the dues they were required to collect. The great machine ground all, and its cruel effects were passed on from stronger to weaker, till the peasant was reached and crushed by burdens that he could not transmit to others. The second stage is the inevitable sequel. The poor man's lot is more intolerable than before. His lesson is learnt, and he takes the final step into the status of a rich man's *colonus*. Henceforth his lord is liable[8] for his dues, but he is himself the lord's

---

[1] *fiunt praeiudicio habitationis indigenae*. That is, by prescription they acquire a new *origo*. See cod Th v 17 (9) §§ 1, 2, 18 (10), cod Just XI 64 § 2, 48 § 16.

[2] *extraneos et alienos*; that is, belonging to someone else.

[3] *et miramur si nos barbari capiunt, cum fratres nostros faciamus esse captivos?*

[4] I think de Coulanges is too severe on the rhetoric of Salvian (pp 141-3). After all, the Codes do not give one a favourable picture of the later colonate, and the Empire did fall in the West.

[5] This arrangement was especially frequent in the East. See on Libanius pp 400-1, and cod Th XI 24 *de patrociniis vicorum*, cf cod Just XI 54. But so far as individuals were concerned it was widespread.

[6] Seeck cites cod Th III 1 § 2 [337], XI 1 § 26 [399], 3 §§ 1-5 [319-391], and for the legal tricks used to defeat the rule XI 3 § 3.

[7] *de gub Dei* v § 18 *quae enim sunt non modo urbes sed etiam municipia atque vici ubi non quot curiales fuerint tot tyranni sunt?*

[8] From *adscribere*, to record the liability of the lord, his *coloni* came to be called *adscripticii*. Weber *Agrargeschichte* p 258.

serf, bound to the soil on which his lord places him, nominally free, but unable to stir from the spot[1] to which his labour gives a value. If he runs away, the hue and cry follows him, and he is brought ignominiously back to the servile punishment that awaits him—unless he can make his way to some barbarian tribe. Whether he would find himself so much better off in those surroundings as Salvian seems to imply, must be left doubtful. Any family that he might leave behind would remain in serfage under conditions hardly improved by his desertion.

LX. APOLLINARIS SIDONIUS.

The last of our array of witnesses is **Apollinaris Sidonius**[2] (about 430–480), a writer whose life is singularly illustrative of the confused period in which the Roman empire was tottering and the series of luckless emperors was ended in the West. Britain had been finally lost in the time of Honorius. The Armorican provinces had rebelled, and even now the hold of Rome on them was slight and precarious. The rest of Gaul and much of Spain and Africa had been subject to barbarian inroads, and numbers of the invaders were settled in the country: for instance, the Western Goths were fully established in Aquitania. But the Roman civilization was by no means wiped out. Roman landlords still owned large estates: Romans of culture still peddled with a degenerate rhetoric and exchanged their compositions for mutual admiration. Panegyrics on shadowy emperors were still produced in verse and prose, and the modern reader may often be amazed to note the way in which the troubles of the time could be complacently ignored. Above all, there was the Church, closely connected with Rome, claiming to be Catholic and Orthodox, a stable organization, able to make itself respected by the barbarians. That the latter were Arian heretics was indeed a cause of friction, though the Arians were destined to go under. The conversion of the Franks under the Catholic form did not give Roman Christianity the upper hand till 496. But the power of bishops, ever growing[3] since the days of Constantine, was throughout a powerful influence holding the various communities together, maintaining law and order, and doing much for the protection of their own people. A native of Lugudunum, the chief city of Gaul, Sidonius came of a noble and wealthy family, and his social position evidently helped him in his remarkable career. In 468 he was city prefect at Rome, barely eight years before Odovacar re-

---

[1] Cod Th XI 1 § 26 [399] refers especially to Gaul. He is *servus terrae* in fact, as Weber *Agrargeschichte* p 258 remarks.

[2] In Esmein's *Mélanges* [1886] there is an excellent essay on some of the letters of Sidonius discussed here, forestalling a number of my conclusions.

[3] See Seeck II 175 foll.

moved the last of the titular Western emperors. We find him anxiously concerned[1] with the old food-question, like his predecessor Symmachus, and not less endeavouring to cooperate harmoniously with the *praefectus annonae*. For a hungry rabble, no doubt fewer in number, still hung about the Eternal city, though its services in the way of applause were no longer in appreciable demand.

From about 471 Sidonius was bishop[2] of Arverni (Clermont in Auvergne), and performed his difficult duties with efficiency and dignity, a sincerely pious man with a good deal of the *grand seigneur* about him. Moving about on duty or seeking restful change, he was often visiting country houses, his own or those of friends, receiving or returning hospitality. His references to these visits lead to descriptions[3] of many pleasant places, and pictures of life in the society of cultivated gentlemen to which he belonged. There is hardly any mention of the suffering farmers of whom Salvian speaks so eloquently. Yet I hesitate to charge Salvian with gross exaggeration and imaginative untruth. Not only do the two men look from different points of view. Sidonius is writing some twenty years later than Salvian, and much had happened in the meantime. The defeat of Attila in 451 by the armies of the Romans and Western Goths had not only saved Gaul from the Huns, but had greatly improved the relations between Goth and Roman. And it is to be noted that, in a passage[4] mentioning the victory of the allies and the reception of Thorismund the Gothic king as a guest at Lugudunum, Sidonius praises his correspondent[5] for his share in lightening the burdens of the landowners. Now Salvian knows nothing of the battle of 451, and indeed does not regard the Huns as being necessarily enemies of Rome. It seems certain that for the rustics things were changed for the better. Not that the farmer was his own master, but that the great Roman taxing-machine was no longer in effective action. A great part of Gaul had passed under Teutonic lords. If the subjects were exposed to their caprice, it was of a more personal character, varying with individuals and likely to be modified by their personal qualities. This was a very different thing from the pressure of the Roman official hierarchy, the lower grades of which were themselves squeezed to satisfy the demands of the higher, and not in a position to spare their victims, however merciful their own inclinations might be.

But though the establishment of barbarian kingdoms, once the raiding invasions were over, had its good side from the working farmer's point of view, much of the old imperial system still lingered on. The

---

[1] Sidon *epist* I 10.
[2] See Dill, *Roman Society in the last century of the Western Empire*, p 179.
[3] See *epist* II 2, 9, 14, IV 24, VIII 4.   [4] *epist* VII 12 § 3.
[5] *quia sic habenas Galliarum moderarere ut possessor exhaustus tributario iugo relevaretur.*

power of the Catholic Church stood in the way of complete revolution, and the Church was already[1] a landowner. Roman traditions died hard, and among them it is interesting to note the exertion of private interest on behalf of individuals and causes in which an honourable patron felt some concern. Thus we find Sidonius writing[2] on behalf of a friend who wants to buy back an ancestral estate with which recent troubles have compelled him to part. Great stress is laid on the point that the man is not grasping at pecuniary profit but actuated by sentimental considerations : in short, the transaction proposed is not a commercial one. The person addressed is entreated to use his influence[3] in the applicant's favour ; and we can only infer that he is asked to put pressure on the present owner to part with the property, probably to take for it less than the market price. Another letter[4] is to a bishop, into whose district (*territorium*) the bearer, a deacon, fled for refuge to escape a Gothic raid. There he scratched a bit of church-land and sowed a little corn. He wants to get in his crop without deductions. The bishop is asked to treat him with the consideration usually shewn to the faithful[5] ; that is, not to require of him the season's rent[6]. If this favour is granted him, the squatter reckons that he will do as well as if he were farming in his own district, and will be duly grateful. Very likely a fair request, but Sidonius does not leave it to the mere sense of fairness in a brother bishop. To another bishop he writes a long letter[7] of thanks for his thoughtful munificence. After the devastation of a Gothic raid, further damage had been suffered by fires among the crops. The ensuing distress affected many parts of Gaul, and to relieve it this worthy sent far and wide bountiful gifts of corn. The happy results of his action have earned the gratitude of numerous cities, and Sidonius is the mouthpiece of his own Arverni. The affair illustrates the beneficence of good ecclesiastics in troubled times. For Gaul was not enjoying tranquil repose. The barbarians were restless, and the relations[8] between their kings and the failing empire were not always friendly. Religious differences too played a part in preventing the coalescence of Gallo-Roman and Teuton. The good bishop just referred to is praised by Sidonius as a successful converter of heretics.

The fine country houses with their vineyards and oliveyards and general atmosphere of comfort and plenty shew plainly that the invasions and raids had not desolated all the countryside. The first need of the invaders was food. Wanton destruction was not in their own interest, and the requisitioning of food-stuffs was probably their chief offence, naturally resented by those who had sown and reaped for their

[1] Instances in *epist* III 1, VI 10.　　[2] *epist* III 5.　　[3] *suffragio vestro.*　　[4] *epist* VI 10.
[5] *domesticis fidei*, already, it seems, a stereotyped phrase. See Ducange.
[6] *debitum glaebae canonem.*　　[7] *epist* VI 12.　　[8] See Dill, book IV ch 3.

own consumption. If we admit this supposition, it follows that their operations, like those of other successful invaders, would be directed mainly to the lowland districts, where most of the food-stuffs were produced. Now the country houses of Sidonius and his friends were, at least most of them, situated in hilly country, often at a considerable distance from the main[1] roads, among pleasant surroundings which these kindly and cultivated gentlemen were well qualified to enjoy. It is evident that some, perhaps many, of these snug retreats were not seriously[2] molested, at all events in southern and south-eastern Gaul. Roughly speaking, the old and most thoroughly Romanized provinces, the chief cities of which were Lugudunum and Narbo, were still seats (indeed the chief seats) of Roman civilization. It was there that the culture of the age survived in literary effort sedulously feeding on the products and traditions of the past. Sidonius thinks it a pity[3] that men of education and refinement should be disposed to bury their talents and capacity for public service in rural retreats, whether suburban or remote. The truth probably was that town life had ceased to be attractive to men unconcerned in trade and not warmly interested in religious partisanship. The lord of a country manor, surrounded by his dependants, could fill his store-rooms and granaries[4] with the produce of their labour. He still had slaves[5] to wait on him, sometimes even to work on the land. With reasonable kindliness and care on his part, he could be assured of comfort and respect, the head of a happy rustic community. The mansions of these gentry, sometimes architecturally[6] fine buildings, were planted in spots chosen for local advantages, and the library was almost as normal a part of the establishment as the larder. Some of the owners of these places gave quite as much of their time and attention to literary trifling as to the management of their estates. The writing of letters, self-conscious and meant for publication, after the example of Pliny the younger, was a practice of Sidonius. The best specimen of this kind is perhaps the long epistle[7] in which he describes minutely a place among the foot-hills of the Alps. Every attraction of nature seconded by art is particularized, down to the drowsy tinkling of the bells on the mountain flocks accompanied by the shepherd's pipe. No doubt the effective agriculture[8] of Gaul had little in common with these Arcadian scenes. The toiling *coloni*, serfs of a barbarian chief or a Roman noble, were all the while producing

[1] *aggeres publici*, cf *epist* II 9 § 2, IV 24 § 2. It is an official expression, used by jurists.
[2] No doubt some were castles, more or less defensible. The *burgus* of Leontius by the Garonne was such, cf *carm* XXII 121–5.
[3] *epist* I 6, VII 15, VIII 8.   [4] *epist* II 14.
[5] *epist* IV 9 § 1, VII 14 § 11. *liberti* mentioned VII 16. See Dill p 178.
[6] *epist* VIII 4 § 1.   [7] *epist* II 2. Cf Dill pp 168–72.
[8] In *epist* III 9 is a curious case of a farmer who owned slaves and in his slack simplicity let them be enticed away to Britain.

the food needed to support the population; and it is a convincing proof of the superficiality of Sidonius as an observer of his age that he practically ignores them.

To attempt a full description of society in Roman Gaul of the fifth century is quite beyond my scope. It has already been admirably done by Sir Samuel Dill. But there are a few points remaining to be discussed as relevant to my subject. That the decline of the middle class, and the passing of large areas of land into few hands, was a process forwarded by inability to pay debts incurred, is extremely probable. It had been going on for many centuries. But I do not see that the evidence of Sidonius suggests that this evil was in his time especially prevalent. The case cited[1] is peculiar. The borrower is expressly stated not to have mortgaged any of his land. The loan was only secured by a written bond which fixed the interest[2] at 12 °/₀ per annum. This had been ten years in arrear, and the total debt was now doubled. The debtor fell ill, and pressure was put on him by officials employed to collect debts. I infer that the lack of real security prompted this dunning of a sick man, for fear the personal security might lapse by his death. Sidonius, a friend of the creditor, undertook to plead with him for at least some stay of action. This man had lately been ordained, and Sidonius (not yet himself in orders, I think,) was evidently surprised to note the simple religious life led by him in his country villa. And he needed little entreaty, but acted up to what he considered his duty to a brother Christian. He not only granted further time for payment, but remitted the whole of the accrued interest, claiming only the principal sum lent. Such conduct may have been, and probably was, exceptional; but I cannot argue from it that heartless usurers were eating up the small landowners of Gaul.

So too the case of the young man[3] of good position who cast off a slave mistress and wedded a young lady of good family, reputation, and property, may have been exceptional. Sidonius takes it all very coolly, and mildly improves the occasion. A far more interesting affair is one in a lower station of life, of which I must say a few words. In a brief letter[4] to his friend Pudens he says 'The son of your nurse has raped my nurse's daughter: it is a shocking business, and would have made bad blood between you and me, only that I saw at once you did not know what to do in the matter. You begin by clearing yourself of connivance, and then condescend to ask me to condone a fault committed in hot passion. This I grant, but only on these terms, that you release[5] the ravisher from the status of a Sojourner, to which he belongs

---

[1] Dill p 220, citing *epist* IV 24. See Esmein pp 377–83 for the legal points of the case.
[2] *centesima*, that is 1 °/₀ *per mensem*, I suppose.
[3] *epist* IX 6. See Dill pp 174–5.   [4] *epist* V 19.
[5] *sub condicione concedo, si stupratorem pro domino iam patronus originali solvas inquilinatu.*

by birth; thus becoming his patron instead of his lord. The woman is free already. And to give her the position of a wedded wife, and not the plaything of caprice, there is but one way. Our scamp for whom you intercede must become your Client[1] and cease to be a Tributary, thus acquiring the quality of an ordinary Commoner rather than that of a Serf.' Sidonius is as usual ready to make the best[2] of a bad job. From his proposal I draw the following conclusions. First, as to the nurses. The *nutrix*, like the Greek τροφός, held a position of trust and respect in the household, consecrated by immemorial tradition. No slave had a higher claim to manumission, if she desired it. It would seem that Sidonius' 'mammy' was ending her days as a freedwoman, and hence her daughter was free. It looks as if the nurse of Pudens were still a slave, and her son an *inquilinus* on the estate of Pudens. He may very well have been tenant of a small holding, practically a serf-tenant. Pudens is still his *dominus*. His quality of *inquilinus* attaches to him in virtue of his *origo*; that is, he is registered in the census-books[3] as a human unit belonging to a particular estate and taken into account in estimating taxation-units. Therefore he is *tributarius*[4]. Sidonius proposes to divest him of the character of serf and make him an ordinary Roman citizen. The difference this would make is probably a purely legal one. Being at present a Serf, probably in strict law a slave also, his connexion with the girl is a *contubernium*. His manumission[5] (for such it really is) will enable him to convert it into a *matrimonium*, carrying the usual legal responsibilities. The practical change in his economic position will probably be nil. He will still remain a dependent *colonus*, but he may perhaps enjoy the privilege of paying his own share[6] of taxes. That Sidonius speaks of his present condition first as Inquilinate and then as Colonate, is one of many proofs that the two terms now connoted virtually[7] the same thing. Such had already been stated as a fact in a law of Honorius, which was retained by Tribonian in the code of Justinian. Whether the *inquilini* were barbarian bondsmen (*hörige*), tenants bound to the soil like *coloni*

---

[1] *mox cliens factus e tributario plebeiam potius incipiat habere personam quam colonariam.*

[2] He calls his solution *compositio seu satisfactio*. Esmein pp 364 foll shews that *compositio* was now a regular expression for the practice of avoiding the strict Roman Law, under barbarian and ecclesiastical influences.

[3] See Index, *inquilini*, and de Coulanges pp 65, 74, 85.

[4] See de Coulanges pp 100–1.

[5] See this question fully discussed by Esmein pp 370–5. Also the doubts of de Coulanges pp 101, 104.

[6] For this point see Seeck, *Schatzungsordnung* pp 314–5.

[7] Cod Th v 18[10] *si quis colonus originalis vel inquilinus...*etc. And below, *originarius* [419]. Cod Just XI 48 § 13 *inquilinos colonosve, quorum quantum ad originem pertinet vindicandam indiscreta eademque paene videtur esse condicio, licet sit discrimen in nomine,...*etc, and § 14 *causam originis et proprietatis.* The limiting word *paene* may refer to difference in mode of payment of taxes. These laws, retained in cod Just, date from 400.

but the personal property of their landlords, as Seeck holds; or usually descendants of *coloni*, as Weber thought; is more than I can venture to decide. I do not think that either hypothesis[1] exhausts all the possibilities, and the point is not material to the present inquiry. In any case it can hardly be doubted that both classes consisted of men who worked with their own hands, only aided in some cases by slave labour which was far from easy to procure.

LXI. CONCLUDING CHAPTER.

After so long a discussion of the surviving evidence, it is time to sum up the results and see to what conclusions the inquiry leads us in respect of the farm life and labour of the Greco-Roman world. And first as to the figures of the picture, the characters with whose position and fortunes we are concerned. We find three classes, owner farmer labourer, clearly marked though not so as to be mutually exclusive. We can only begin with ownership in some form, however rudimentary; for the claim to resist encroachment on a more or less ill-defined area is a phenomenon of even the rude life of hunter-tribes. How private property grew out of common ownership is a question beyond the range of the present inquiry. It is enough that the owner, whether a clan or a family or an individual, has a recognized right to use the thing owned (here land) and to debar others from doing so. But it is clear that he may also be the actual manager of its use: he may even supply in person all the labour needed for turning it to account: in short, he may be his own farmer and his own labourer. And legend asserts or implies that such was the primitive condition of man when he passed from nomadic to settled existence. Differentiation of function is therefore a product of time and circumstance, a development varying in date and degree among various races and in various portions of the world. Once the stage of civilization is reached at which the regular cultivation of the same piece of land year by year is the normal means of sustaining human life, we meet the simplest economic figure, the peasant who supplies his own needs by his own methods, tilling the soil which in some sense he claims as his own. Whether it is his own permanently as an individual, or temporarily as a member of a village community, is a difference immaterial from the present point of view. Nor does it matter that his method of dealing with the land may be regulated by principles conventional in the society to which he belongs.

Delegation of management is a momentous step, destined to bring important unforeseen consequences. Many reasons may have rendered it necessary or at least convenient. It appears in two forms, the actual and relative dates of which are hardly to be determined with certainty.

[1] Seeck just cited. Weber, *Agrargeschichte* p 257.

Delegation of function 433

Either the owner keeps the profit of the undertaking and bears the loss, or some division of profit and loss between the owner and the manager is the condition of the arrangement between the two parties. Ownership is not abdicated: nor is it easy to see how, without a clear recognition of ownership, any system of delegation could arise. But on the first plan the owner owns not only the land but the service of his delegate. Whether the man be a client bound to his patron by social custom, or an agent earning a wage, or a slave the property of his master, he is merely a servant in charge. He can be superseded at any moment at the landowner's will. The free tenant on the other hand is a creature of contract, and his existence presupposes a community in which the sanctity of deliberate bargains is considerably developed. Whether the tenant's obligation consists in the payment of a fixed rent in money or kind, or in a share of produce varying with the season's crop, does not matter. He is bound by special law, however rudimentary; and it is the interest of the community to see that such law is kept in force: for no one would enter into such bargains if their fulfilment were not reasonably assured. Whether a certain reluctance to enter into such a relation may perhaps account for the rare and doubtful appearance of tenancy in early Roman tradition, or whether it is to be set down simply to defects of record, I do not venture to decide. The landlord's obligation is to allow his tenant the enjoyment and free use of a definite piece of land on certain terms for a stipulated period. Further stipulations, giving him the right to insist on proper cultivation and the return of the land in good condition at the end of the tenancy, were doubtless soon added at the dictation of experience. That tenant farmers with their families usually supplied labour as well as management, is surely not to be doubted. That, in the times when we begin to hear of this class as non-exceptional, they also employed slave labour, is attested: that we do not hear of them as engaging free wage-earners, may or may not be an accidental omission.

Labour, simply as labour, without regard to the possible profit or loss attending its results, was no more an object of desire, engaged in for its own sake, in ancient times than it is now. Domestication of animals, a step implying much attentive care and trouble, was a great advance in the direction of securing a margin of profit on which mankind could rely for sustenance and comfort. The best instance is perhaps that of the ox, whose services, early exploited to the full, were cheaply obtained at the cost of his rearing and keep. Hence he was kept. But in ages of conflict, when might was right, the difference[1]

[1] E Meyer *Kl Schr* p 185 takes the words of Aristotle *Pol* 1 2 § 5 ὁ γὰρ βοῦς ἀντ' οἰκέτου τοῖς πένησίν ἐστιν as proving that even in Ar's time the small farmer had to do without a slave. I think they prove that if he could not afford a slave he must do with an ox only. For the additional protection of the ox see Index. Cf Maine, *Early Law and Custom* pp 249-51.

H. A.

28

between an ox-servant and a man-servant had in practice no existence, and the days of theory were as yet in the far future. A human enemy, captured and spared, could be put to use in the same way as a domesticated ox. His labour, minus the cost of his keep, left a margin of profit to his owner. At the moment of capture, his life was all he had: therefore his conqueror had deprived him of nothing, and the bargain was in his favour, though economically in his owner's interest. No wonder then that our earliest records attest the presence of the slave. Even nomad tribes were attended by slaves[1] in their migrations, nor indeed has this custom been wholly unknown in modern times. On the other hand it is remarkable how very little we hear of wage-earning labour in ancient agriculture. Nothing seems to imply that it was ever a normal resource of cultivation. When employed, it is almost always for special work at seasons of pressure, and it seems to have remained on this footing, with a general tendency to decline. In other words, the margin of profit on the results of wage-earning labour seemed to employers less than that on the results of slave labour, so far as ordinary routine was concerned. And we are not in a position to shew that in their given circumstances their judgment was wrong. But we need to form some notion of the position of the wage-earning labourer in a civilization still primitive.

The main point ever to be borne in mind is that the family household was a close union of persons bound together by ties of blood and religion under a recognized Head. A common interest in the family property carried with it the duty of common labour. The domestic stamp was on everything done and designed. Even the slave had a humble place in the family life, and family religion did not wholly ignore him. He was there, and was meant to stay there. Farm-work was the chief item in the duties of the household, and he bore, and was meant to bear, his full share of it. But the hired labourer stood in no such relation to the household union, however friendly his connexion with his employer might be. He did his work, took his wage, and went: no tie was severed by his going, and any other person of like capacity could fill his place if and when the need for help-service arose. In short, his labour was non-domestic, irregular, occasional: and therefore less likely to receive notice in such records as have come down to us. But if we conclude (as I am inclined to do) that wage-labour was not much employed on the land in early times, we must admit that this is rather an inference than an attested tradition.

The distinction between domestic regular service and non-domestic help-service is essential, and on a small holding from which a family

---

[1] E Meyer *Kl Schriften* p 179 will only use the word *slaves* of a part of these, but the distinction does not matter here.

raised its own sustenance the line of division was easy to draw. Later
economic changes tended to obscure it, and we find Roman jurists[1] of
the Empire striving to discover a full and satisfactory answer to a much
later question, namely the distinction between a domestic and a rustic
slave. But by that time 'domestic' appears as 'urban,' for the effect of
centuries has been to draw a really important line of division, not
between slave and free but between two classes of slaves. There is
however in the conditions of early slavery, when 'domestic' and 'rustic'
were merely two aspects of the same thing, another point not to be
overlooked, since it probably had no little influence on the development
of human bondage. It is this. The human slave differs from the
domesticated ox through possession of what we call reason. If he
wished to escape, he was capable of forming deep-laid plans for that
purpose. Now the captives in border wars would be members of neighbouring tribes. If enslaved, the fact of being still within easy reach of
their kindred was a standing temptation to run away, sure as they
would be of a welcome in their former homes. No kindness, no watchfulness, on the master's part would suffice to deaden or defeat such an
influence. To solve the problem thus created, a way was found by
disposing of captives to aliens more remote and getting slaves brought
from places still further away. This presupposes some commercial intercourse. In the early Greek tradition we meet with this slave-trade
at work as a branch of maritime traffic chiefly in the hands of Phoenician
seamen. In Italy we find a trace of it in the custom[2] of selling 'beyond
Tiber,' that is into alien Etruria. At what stage of civilization exactly
this practice became established it is rash to guess: we cannot get
behind it. The monstrous slave-markets of the historical periods shew
that it developed into a normal institution of the ancient world. But
it is not unreasonable to suppose that an alien from afar was less easily
absorbed into his master's family circle than a man of a neighbouring
community though of another tribe. Are we to see in this the germ
of a change by which the house-slave became less 'domestic' and tended
to become a human chattel?

The exploitation of some men's labour for the maintenance of
others could and did take another form in ages of continual conflict.
Successful invaders did not always drive out or destroy the earlier inhabitants of a conquered land. By retaining them as subjects to till

[1] See Dig XXXII § 99 (Paulus), and XXXIII 7 *passim*, especially § 25[1].

[2] That religious scruple was opposed to keeping members of the same race-unit in slavery
is most probable. This *trans Tiberim* rule is known from Gellius XX 1 § 47, referring to
debt-slaves. Greeks however, even when abhorring the enslavement of Greek by Greek in
principle, did not discontinue the practice. E Meyer *Kl Schr* p 202 compares the medieval
scruple in reference to brother Christians. See also his remarks p 177. For Hebrew law and
custom see *Encyclopaedia Biblica* (1903) vol IV and Hastings' *Dictionary of the Bible* (1902)
vol IV, articles *Slavery*.

the soil, and making the support of their rulers the first charge upon
their produce, the conquerors provided for their own comfort and
became a leisured noble class. In the Greek world we find such aristocracies of a permanently military character, as in Laconia and Thessaly.
Colonial expansion reproduced the same or very similar phenomena
abroad, as in the cases of Heraclea Pontica and Syracuse. The serfdom
of such subject populations was a very different thing[1] from slavery.
It had nothing domestic about it. There is no reason to suppose that
the serf was under any constraint beyond the regular performance of
certain fixed duties, conditions imposed by the state on its subjects,
not the personal orders of an individual owner. In some cases at least
the serf seems to have enjoyed a measure of protection[2] under public
law. Whether the original Roman *plebs* stood on much the same footing
as the Greek serfs is perhaps doubtful, but their condition presents
certain analogies. The main truth is that the desire of conquerors to
profit by the labour of the conquered was and is an appetite almost
universal: moral revulsion against crude forms of this exploitation is
of modern, chiefly English, origin; even now it is in no small degree
a lesson from the economic experience of ages. But it is well to remember that we use 'serfdom' also as the name for the condition of
rural peasantry in the later Roman Empire, and that this again is a
different relation. For it is not a case of conquered people serving
their conquerors. Rather is it an affliction of those who by blood or
franchise represent the conquering people. Step by step they sink under
the loss of effective freedom, though nominally free, bound down by
economic and social forces; influences that operate with the slow certainty of fate until their triumph is finally registered by imperial law.

That the institution of Property is a matter of slow growth, is now
generally admitted by sincere inquirers. It had reached a considerable
stage of development when a clan or household (still more when an
individual) was recognized as having an exclusive right to dispose of
this or that material object presumably useful to others also. For
instance, in the right of an owner to do as he would with an ox or a slave.
Individual property in land was certainly a later development, the ap-
propriation being effected by a combination of personal acquisitiveness
with economic convenience. From my present point of view the chief
interest of the property-question is in its connexion with debt-slavery.
That farmers, exposed to the vicissitudes of seasons, are peculiarly
liable to incur debts, is well known from experience ancient and modern.
But ancient Law, if rudimentary, was also rigid; and tradition depicts
for us the small peasant as a victim of the wealthy whose larger capital

[1] Different also from the position of a food-producer class in a great territorial state, being based on local conditions.
[2] Illustrated with great clearness in the provisions of the Gortyn laws.

enabled them to outlast the pressure of bad times. How far the details of this picture are to be taken literally as evidence of solid fact has not unreasonably been doubted. But that a farmer in straits could pledge not only his land but his person as security for a debt seems hardly open to question. For we find the practice still existing in historical periods, and political pressure exerted to procure mitigation of the ancient severity. Now, if a man gave himself in bondage to a creditor until such time as his debt should be discharged, he became that creditor's slave for a period that might only end with his own life. Here we have another way in which the man of property could get the disposal of regular labour without buying a slave in the market or turning to work himself. A later form of the practice, in which a debtor worked off his liability[1] by service at an estimated rate, a method of liquidation by the accumulation of unpaid wages, seems to have been a compromise avoiding actual slavery. Evidently subsequent to the abolition of debt-slavery, it died out in Italy, perhaps partly owing to the troublesome friction that would surely arise in enforcing the obligation.

It is natural to ask, if we find small trace of eagerness to labour in person on the land, and ample tradition of readiness to devolve that labour on slaves and subjects, how comes it that we find agriculture in honour, traditionally regarded as the manual labour beyond all others not unworthy of a freeman? To reply that human life is supported by the produce of the land is no sufficient answer. To recognize the fact of necessity does not account for the sentiment of dignity. Now, in the formation of such unions as may fairly be called States, the commonest if not universal phenomenon is the connexion of full citizenship with ownership of land. Political movement towards democracy is most significantly expressed in the struggles of landless members of inferior right to gain political equality. Whether the claim is for allotments of land, carrying a share of voting-power, or for divorcing the voting-power from landholding, does not matter much here. At any rate it was the rule that no alien could own land within the territory of the state, and state and territory were coextensive. Only special treaties between states, or a solemn act of the sovran power in a state, could create exceptions to the rule. From this situation I would start in attempting to find some answer to the above question. In a village community I think it is generally agreed that all true members had a share of the produce, the great majority as cultivators, holding lots of land, not as tenants at will or by contract, but in their own right, though the parcels might be allotted differently from time to time. If a few craftsmen were left to specialize in necessary trades for the service of

---

[1] Varro *RR* I 17 § 2 on *obaerarii* or *obaerati*.

all, and drew their share in the form of sustenance provided by the cultivating members, the arrangement presented no insuperable difficulty on a small scale. But the tillers of the soil were the persons on whose exertions the life of the community primarily and obviously depended. The formation of a larger unit, a State, probably by some successful warrior chief, made a great change in the situation. A city stronghold established a centre of state life and government, and villages exchanged the privileges and perils of isolation for the position of local hamlets attached to the common centre of the state, and in this new connexion developing what we may fairly call political consciousness. Under the new dispensation, what with growth of markets, the invention of coined money, and greater general security, the movement towards individual property proceeded fast. Noble families engrossed much of the best land: and tradition[1] credibly informs us that in one mode or other they imposed the labour of cultivation on the poorer citizens, of course on very onerous terms.

At this point in the inquiry some help may be got from taking the military view. War, at least defensive war, was a possibility ever present. Kings, and the aristocracies that followed them, had as their prime function to secure the safety of the state. A sort of regular force was provided by the obligation of army service that rested upon all full citizens. The warrior nobles and their kinsmen formed a nucleus. But the free peasant farmers were indispensable in the ranks, and, as their farms usually lay near the frontier, they furnished a hardy and willing militia for border warfare. The craftsmen, smith potter cobbler etc, were now more concentrated in the city, and were always regarded as ill-fitted for service in the field. Naturally the classes that bore a direct part in defence of the state stood higher in general esteem. But to say this is not to say that bodily labour on the land was, as labour, honoured for its own sake. The honour belonged to those who, owning land, either worked it with their own hands or employed the labour of others. I can find no trace of traditional respect for the labourer as labourer until a much later age, when a dearth of free rustic labourers had begun to be felt. Then it appeared in the form of yearning[2] for a vanished past, side by side with humanitarian views in relation to

[1] The relative importance of land and the means of cultivation [especially oxen] in early times, the power thus gained by chiefs granting cattle to tenants, and the connexion of these phenomena with legends of debt-slavery, are instructively discussed in Maine's *Early history of Institutions*, lecture VI.

[2] Mr G G Coulton kindly reminds me of an analogy observable in the history of Art. It is progressive on simple lines up to a certain point. Then it begins to ramify, and differences of taste become more acute. Hence an anarchy of taste, driving men to yearn (like Ruskin, Morris, etc.) for the old simplicity. So the peasant up to a point is useful and noble. But fresh currents of civilization alter his position. Then men yearn for the old simplicity, only defective through being essentially simple.

slavery. Meanwhile a stage had been traversed in which slavery was recognized as necessary in spite of its admitted evils, and therefore requiring justification; a movement most clearly illustrated by the special pleading of Aristotle. That great writer was fully alive to the manifold merits of the farmer class as citizens and producers, but his trust in the power of self-interest proves him a confirmed individualist. How to combine self-interest with patriotic devotion to the common welfare is the vital problem, even now only solved ideally on paper. That coldly-reasoned conclusions of thinkers were really the foundation of the esteem in which we find the working farmer held, I cannot believe. Much more likely is it that it sprang mainly from immemorial tradition of a time when ownership and cultivation went together, and that theory merely absorbed and revived what was still an indistinct impression in the minds of men.

The Greeks had a significant word, αὐτουργός, the usage of which may serve to illustrate my meaning. That it connotes the fact of a man's bearing a personal part in this or that work is clear on the face of it. That no other person also bears a part, is sometimes implied by the context, but it is not necessarily contained in the word itself. To put it differently, he does his own work, not necessarily all his own work. I note two points in connexion with it that seem to me important. First, it is so often used as descriptive of rustic labour that it seems to have carried with it associations of farm-life: most of the other uses are almost metaphorical, some distinctly so. Secondly, I have never found it applied to the case of a slave. Why? I think, because it conveyed the further notion of working not only yourself but for yourself. If in some passages it is not quite certain that an owner (rather than a tenant) is referred to, surely this extension of meaning is not such as to cause surprise. It is not enough to suggest serious doubt that the common and full sense of the word was that a man did work with his own hands on his own account on his own land. This was the character to which immemorial tradition pointed; and, whenever tenancy under landlords began, the word fitted the working tenant-farmer well enough. The Romans had the tradition in the most definite form, though Latin furnished no equivalent word. Their literature, moralizing by examples and unapt for theory, used it as material for centuries. But neither in the Greek world nor in Italy can I detect any reason for believing that the peasant farmer, idealized by later ages, is rightly to be conceived as a person unwilling to employ slave labour—if and when he could get it. The tradition, in which rustic slaves appear from very early times, seems to me far more credible than late legends of a primitive golden age in which there were no slaves at all. That a man, to be enslaved, must first have been free, is a piece of speculation with which I am not here concerned.

Tradition then, looking back to times when landowner and citizen were normally but different sides of the same character, both terms alike implying the duty of fighting for the state, idealized and glorified this character with great but pardonable exaggeration of virtues probably not merely fictitious. The peasant citizen and producer was its hero. As the devolution of bodily labour upon slaves or hirelings became more common with the increase of commerce and urban life, and the solid worth of a patriot peasantry became more evident in the hour of its decay, men turned with regret to the past. And the contrast of the real present with an idealized past naturally found a significant difference in the greater or less willingness of men to work with their own hands, particularly on the land. But it was the labour of free citizens, each bearing an active part in the common responsibilities of the state and enjoying its common protection, that was glorified, not labour as in itself meritorious or healthy. The wholesomeness of rustic toil was not ignored, but to urge it as a motive for bodily exertion was a notion developed by town-bred thinkers. That it coloured later tradition is not wonderful: its recognition is most clearly expressed in the admission of superior 'corporal soundness' in the sparely-fed and hard-worked slave or wage-earner. But labour as labour was never, so far as I can learn, dignified and respected in Greco-Roman civilization. Poverty, not choice, might compel a man to do all his own work; but, if he could and did employ hired or slave labour also, then he was an αὐτουργὸς none the less. This I hold to be an underlying fact that Roman tradition in particular is calculated to obscure. It was voluntary labour, performed in a citizen's own interest and therefore a service to the state, that received sentimental esteem.

The power of military influences in ancient states is often cited as a sufficient explanation of the social fact that non-military bodily labour was generally regarded with more or less contempt. The army being the state in arms, the inferiority of those who did not form part of it though able-bodied was manifest to all. This is true as far as it goes, but there was something more behind. Why does not the same phenomenon appear in modern states with conscript armies, such as France or Italy or above all Switzerland? I think the true answer is only to be found by noting a difference between ancient and modern views as to the nature and limits of voluntary action. It is only of states in which membership is fairly to be called citizenship that I am speaking; and as usual it is Greek conditions and Greek words that supply distinct evidence. Not that the Roman conditions were materially different, but they were perhaps less clearly conceived, and

the record is less authentic and clear. Now, beyond the loyal obedience
due from citizen to state, any sort of constraint determining the action
of one free man by the will of others was feared and resented to a
degree of which we cannot easily form an adequate notion. In the
gradual emancipation of the commons from the dominion of privileged
nobles, the long struggle gave a passionate intensity to the natural
appetite for freedom. And the essence of freedom was the power of
self-disposal. This power was liable to be lost permanently by sale
into slavery, but also from time to time by the effect of temporary
engagements. The most obvious instance of the latter condition was
the bondage created by unpaid debt. Hence the persistent and eventually successful fight to make it illegal to take a borrower's person as
security for his debt. But, suppose the debt cancelled by the seizure
of his goods, the man was left a pauper. His only resource was to
work for wages, and this placed him for the time of his engagement at
the full disposal[1] of his employer. If he was not a master's slave for
good and all, he would be passing from master to master, ever freshly
reminded of the fact that his daily necessities subjected him to the
will of others, nullifying his freeman's power of self-disposal. If he
worked side by side with slaves, there was a further grievance. For
the slave, in whom his owner had sunk capital, had to be kept fed and
housed to retard his depreciation: the free labourer depended[2] on his
wage, liable to fail. The situation, thus crudely stated, was intolerable.
In practice it was met, first by devotion to handicrafts as a means of
livelihood in which the winning of custom by skill relieved the worker
from direct dependence on a single master; but also by allotments of
land in annexed territory, and sometimes (as at Athens) by multipli-
cation of paid state-employments.

Of ordinary artisans, as distinct from artists, it may be said that
their position varied according as their special trades were more or less
esteemed by contemporary sentiment. The successful could and did
employ[3] helpers, usually slaves. In urban populations they were an
important element, particularly in those where military considerations
were not predominant. The accumulation of capital, and the introduction of industries on a larger scale in factory-workshops with staffs of
slaves, may have affected some trades to their disadvantage, but on
the whole the small-scale craftsmen seem generally[4] to have held their

[1] Mr Zimmern, *The Greek Commonwealth* pp 265 foll, has some interesting remarks on
craftsmen as wage-earners, and points out their preference for serving the state rather than
private employers. The latter plan would have put them almost in the position of slaves.

[2] When food was provided, we must reckon it as part of his wage.

[3] A vast number of Greek records of manumission refer to such cases.

[4] See Francotte, *L'Industrie dans la Grèce ancienne* book II chap 5, *La concurrence
servile*. I cannot follow E Meyer *Kl Schr* pp 198–201. And the oft-cited passage of Timaeus

ground. Unskilled labour on the other hand was generally despised. It was as a matter of course chiefly performed by slaves. If a citizen was compelled by want to hire out his bodily strength, this was not voluntary: complete submission to another's will, even for a short time, made the relation on his part virtually servile. Accordingly philosophers, when they came to discuss such topics, came to the conclusion that the need of such unskilled labour proved slavery to be 'according to nature,' a necessary appliance of human society. When the Stoic defined a slave as a lifelong hireling, he gave sharp expression to what had long been felt as a true analogy. For, if the slave was a lifelong hireling, the hireling must be a temporary slave. Romans could borrow the thought, but with them practice had preceded theory.

In making comparisons between wage-earning ancient and modern we come upon a difficulty which it is hardly possible to set aside or overcome. A slave could be hired from his owner, just as a freeman could be hired from himself. The difference between the two cases would be clearly marked[1] in the modern world, and language would leave no room for misunderstanding. But many passages in ancient writers leave it quite uncertain whether the hirelings referred to are free or slave. The point is an important one, particularly to inquirers who attempt to estimate the relative economic efficiency of free and slave labour. For the immediate interest of the freeman is to get a maximum of wage for a minimum of work: the ultimate interest of the hired slave was often to improve his own prospect of manumission. The custom was to allow the slave to retain a small portion of his wage. Now this stimulus to exertion was manifestly to the interest of the employer, who may even have made it a part of his bargain with the owner. The slave, alive to the chance of laying up a little store for the eventual purchase of his freedom, was induced to work well in order to be kept employed on these terms. The owner drew a steady income from his capital sunk in slaves, and the system was thus convenient to all parties. We may add that, by causing a slave to take thought for his own future, this plan encouraged him to take reasonable care of his own health, and so far retarded his progressive deterioration as an investment; while his owner stood to recover the slave's hoarded wage-portion in the form of redemption-money on manumission of his worn-out slave. There is reason to think that slave labour under these conditions was often more efficient than free. Unhappily we have no direct discussion of the question from ancient observers, who did not

(Athen VI 264 d), where free Phocians object to slaves taking their employment, refers solely to domestic and personal attendance.

[1] Of this there is abundant American evidence from writers on Slavery. The hired slave sometimes got a higher wage than the hired freeman.

take this point of view, though well aware of the influence of prospective manumission in producing contentment.

But how far was this comparatively genial arrangement applicable to the ruder forms of unskilled labour? Take for instance mining. Freemen would have none of it, and the inhuman practices of exploiters were notorious. Yet hired slaves were freely employed. Owners knew that their slaves were likely to waste rapidly under the methods in use, and at Athens a common stipulation was that on the expiry of a contract the gang hired should be returned in equal number, the employer making good the losses certain to occur in their ranks. Here we have the mere human chattel, hopeless and helpless, never likely to receive anything but his keep, as an engine receives its fuel and oil, but differing in this, that he was liable to cruel punishment. Such labourers could not work for a freedom that they had no prospect of living to enjoy. And how about the case of agriculture? That freemen did work for wages on farms we know, but we hear very little of them, and that little almost entirely as helpers at certain seasons. So far as I have been able to learn, free wage-labour did not really compete with slave labour in agriculture: moreover the hired man might be a hired slave, while migratory harvesters, probably freemen, appear at least in some cases as gangs hired for the job under a ganger of their own, responsible to the employer for their conduct and efficiency. Most significant is the almost complete absence of evidence that rustic slaves had any prospect of manumission. In former chapters I have commented on this fact and noted the few faint indications of such an arrangement. At all events the crude plantation-system, while it lasted, was a work-to-death system, though worn-out survivors may have had a better lot than miners, if allowed to exist as old retainers on the estate. But cultivation by slave labour for the purpose of raising an income for the landlord was, even in its later improved organization, a system implying brutal callousness, if not downright cruelty. Slave stewards and overseers, at the mercy of the master themselves, were naturally less concerned to spare the common hands than to escape the master's wrath. When writers on agriculture urge that on all grounds it is wise to keep punishments down to a minimum, the point of their advice is surely a censure of contemporary practice.

Now in modern times, humanitarian considerations being assumed, the prevailing point of view has been more and more a strictly economic and industrial one. It has been assumed that the freedom of an individual consists first and foremost in the freedom to dispose of his own labour on the best available terms. And this freedom rests on freedom to move from place to place in search of the best labour-market from time to time. But the movement and the bargaining have been regarded as strictly voluntary, as in a certain sense they are. The power to migrate or emigrate with the view of 'bettering himself' is conferred on the wage-earner by modern facilities for travel, and new countries readily absorb additional labour. But experience has shewn that free bargaining for wages is not seldom illusory, since the man of capital can bide his time, while the poor man cannot. Still, when every allowance has been made on this score, it is true that the modern labourer, through freedom of movement, has far more power of self-disposal than the wage-earner of the Greco-Roman world. That his position is strengthened and assured by the possession of political power, is not without ancient analogies: but a difference in degree if not in kind is created by the wide extension of the franchise in modern states, and its complete separation in principle from the ownership of land. That is, the basis of citizenship is domicile: for citizen parentage is not required, but easily supplemented[1] by legal nationalization. Moreover, religion is no longer a necessary family inheritance, but the choice of individuals who can generally gratify their preferential sentiments in surroundings other than their birthplace. Compare this position with the narrow franchises of antiquity and their ineffectiveness on any large scale, their normally hereditary character, the local and domestic limitation of religious ties, the restricted facilities for travel, not to mention its ever-present perils. Remember that to reside in another state as an alien did not, in default of special treaty or act of legislative grace, give the resident any claim to civic rights in his place of residence, while misfortune might at any time reduce him to slavery in a foreign land. Surely under such conditions the limits of purely voluntary action were narrow indeed. The lure of the wage and the fear of unemployment are often a severe form of pressure, but they are, as fetters on freedom, a mere nothing in comparison with this.

Considerations such as those set forth in the preceding paragraphs shew that in treating of ancient agriculture and farm-labour we are apparently faced by a curious paradox. Cultivation of land (including the keeping of live stock) is an honourable pursuit. That good health, sustenance, even comfort and profit, are its natural attendants, is not doubted. But the position of the labouring hands is painful and mean, so much so that a common punishment for urban house-slaves was to send them to work on a farm. The rustic slave's lot differed for the better from that of the mine-slave in the healthier nature of the occupation, but in little else. And this degradation inevitably reacted on the estimate of rustic wage-earners, whenever employed. There may have been less repugnance to work side by side with slaves than has

[1] See Whitaker's Almanack, and the exposure of an impudent agency for the purpose in the *Times* 15 Sept 1914.

been felt in modern times, when a marked colour-line implied the disgrace of a 'white' man doing 'niggers' work.' But it is not to be doubted that in agriculture as in other occupations the presence of slavery did degrade labour, at all events so soon as agriculture put on anything of an industrial character. The really 'respectable' person was the man who directed the operations, the γεωργός, *agricola,* or *colonus* (in the original sense): he was the man who worked the land and made it yield crops, whether he took part in the actual digging and ploughing or not. The larger the scale, the more he confined himself to direction, necessarily ; but he was the producer, a pillar of public economy, none the less. He had provided the labour, bought or hired ; in effect, the labour was his own. With the toiling yeoman farmer of tradition he had this in common, that both worked for themselves, not for another. And this position, attractive in all societies, was marked out with peculiar distinctness through the institution of slavery underlying the social fabric. Exploitation of man by man, the first beginnings of which elude our search and are only ascertained by inference, suggests some sort of superiority in the upper party. At all events the master, the man who has the upper hand, gets the credit of achievement, and in agriculture as elsewhere the subordinate operative is inevitably forgotten. It is from this point of view that we must regard the fine Roman legends of sturdy farmer-citizens, the fathers of the Republic. They are idylls conveying truth, dressed up by the imagination of a later age: and have their place in the region where history and poetry meet and blend. We must not gather from them that slavery was exceptional or a fact of no importance. Tradition habitually ignores what is normal and therefore assumed. The fairer inference is that, as I have already remarked, slavery was in those early days still a family institution, not an industrial system.

Some help towards the understanding of the different position of manual labour in ancient times as compared with modern may be got by considering Abolitionism. That a slave is a man, and as such not to be wholly ignored in respect of the claims of common humanity ; that slave-labour is listless and ineffective, giving poor returns in proportion to the strength employed ; these conclusions, moral and economic, were reached by the thinkers of the ancient world while their civilization was in full bloom. Why then do we find no movement corresponding to the Abolitionism of modern times ? Two things were obviously necessary for such a movement ; the motive to inspire it, and the force to give effect to it. Let men once be convinced that slavery is both wrong and unprofitable, and let them have the power to insist on putting an end to it, Abolitionism in some form or other is the necessary result.

Now in speaking of ancient conditions we must never lose sight of the fact that in its origin slavery was a favour. By the undissembled rule of force the conquered only retained his life through the mercy of the conqueror. By a contract tacit or expressed he was pledged for life to the service and profit of his master. And the master could, if his interest pointed that way, make over his rights to a third party. Hence the growth of a slave-market, and the relation of master and slave no longer was normally that of individual conqueror and conquered. But the original notion was by no means extinct, and it continued to colour the current view of slavery as 'natural,' a thing of course, an unquestioned social fact. Nor was there anything in the condition of the slave to arouse a feeling of horror, so long as patriarchal rule prevailed. If the Head of the family possessed absolute power over the slave, his power over members of the family in general was in kind the same. The bondman, a humble dependant rather than a mere chattel, was in a sense also a member of the family and under the protection of the household gods. What was there for an observer, let him be ever so kind-hearted, to object to? Accordingly, as the state developed, it too kept slaves of its own, employing them in mean functions for which it was needful to have a staff always at hand. In short, the institution was taken for granted, and growing intercourse with foreigners only served to reveal its universal prevalence.

How came it then that in course of time humanitarian scruples arose, and questioners were found to argue that the system was 'unnatural' and wrong? The answer must be sought in the application of an originally domestic institution to industrial ends. Once the stage was reached at which the products of labour were habitually put on the market, and the producer got his living by their regular sale, it was soon discovered that to produce and deal on a larger scale was more economical, and therefore more profitable, than on a smaller one. In the handicrafts this was so obvious that slave assistants were commonly kept by tradesmen: it was important to be sure of having the necessary help when wanted. The same was the case in the professions based on special training: the surgeon, the architect, the surveyor, the banker, employed slave subordinates, and had often been slaves themselves. In all these departments, not to mention domestic service, the position of the slave was affected by two important considerations. First, he was one of a few, and under immediate observation, so that escape from servitude was practically impossible. Secondly, there was a reasonable chance of earning manumission by long faithful service. But there were occupations in which it was far more difficult to reconcile the interests of the slave with those of the master. Such were the exploitation of mines and quarries, in which labour was simply applied

in the form of brute force under direction. The direction, usually entrusted to slave or freedman overseers, was generally unsympathetic,
sometimes cruel ; for the overseer's first thought was to please his
master, even if he could only do so by working the slaves to death.
The extension of agriculture as a means of profit rather than subsistence
created conditions of the same kind in this occupation. It was here
that the monstrous abuses incidental to slavery were most strikingly
displayed. For, while quarries and mines were only worked in a few
localities, the plan of working great landed estates by the labour of
slave-gangs was applicable to vast areas of the best soil. And in Africa
Sicily and Italy we find it so applied for the profit of the nobles and
capitalists of a conquering race.

The evils of this system may be set down to the account of obsequious
stewards heartlessly wringing profit for their masters out of human
flesh and blood. But we must not ignore two considerations which
suggest that the root of the evil lay not in the caprice or greed of individuals but in the attempt to carry on rural industry by slave labour
at all. In the country, opportunities of escape were many ; the slave-
prison and the fetters could hardly be dispensed with if you meant
to keep your farm-hands at disposal. And manumission, as a means
of encouraging good service, was evidently not of much avail in country
places. For after long years of exhausting labour the worn-out slave
would be unable to earn a living by hard bodily work ; and he knew
no other. He had been bought as a flesh-and-blood machine ; as such,
to manumit him while still efficient would be a sacrifice of sunk capital
for which nobody was prepared. It seems that the ordinary practice
was to keep him at work till he could work no longer, and then to let
him linger on the estate as an invalid retainer, feeding on what he
could get and decaying in peace. But the industrializing of agriculture,
heartlessly selfish in its aims, tempted landlords to shirk the unprofitable
maintenance of spent labourers. When a slave was no longer worth
his keep, it might pay to sell him at once for what he would fetch.
There was thus a mouth less to be fed, and the problem of how to turn
the remnant of his strength to account was shifted on to his new owner.
This plan, approved by the elder Cato as a detail of farm-economy,
marks the change of relations between master and slave in rustic life.
The old domestic relation has disappeared in the brutal exploitation
of a human animal for immediate profit. The crudely industrial system
reproduced on great estates the horrid phenomena of the quarry and
the mine.

That humane and thoughtful men should be disgusted with such
doings was inevitable, and disgust was soon reinforced by reasonable
alarm. For tillage was not the sole occupation of rustic enterprise. It

was found that in many districts grazing paid better than tillage, and the two could be worked together remuneratively on a large scale. The charge of flocks and herds, shifting their pasture according to seasons, led to employment of able-bodied slaves in a duty responsible and at the same time removed from immediate control for months together. These slave herdsmen, hardy and used to a free life in wild uplands, had to face wolves and robbers, and therefore to bear arms. We need not dwell on the danger from such a class menacing the peace of a country unprotected by rural police. It was real enough. Being slaves, they had nothing but their lives to lose, and their lives it was their owners' interest to protect. Meanwhile the unescorted traveller was at their mercy, and any peasants within reach would pay black-mail to escape their raids. Yet nothing was done to get rid of the nuisance and peril of this state of things. Servile risings were clumsily put down with appalling bloodshed, and left to recur. Meanwhile the free population of the countryside diminished, and prosperity could not be restored by new slave-gangs. Such was notoriously the condition of a great part of rural Italy under the later Republic, and contemporary evidence clearly shews that the improvement effected under the Empire was slight.

Now, when experience had proved the blighting influence of slavery, why was there no movement to do away with the system altogether? Truth is, there was at present no basis to start from. The moral en-thusiasm, often sincere, that has inspired such movements in modern times, had no effective existence. Moral considerations were almost entirely confined to a section of rich or cultivated society. It was not expected that the common herd should rise above the meanest motives of crude self-interest. The artisan, who either employed, or hoped soon to employ, a slave or two, was not likely to condemn slavery: the parasitic loafer was not likely to welcome a mass of new competitors for the doles and bribes that he undeservedly enjoyed. During the last century of the Roman Republic no opposition to slavery as an institu-tion could have arisen from the urban populace. And the wealthier classes were interested in slavery. Religion did not touch the question. A few scrupulous and thoughtful men might have supported an anti-slavery movement, had there been one; but we have not the smallest reason to think that any individual ever dreamt of starting humanitarian propaganda on his own account and at his own risk. There was no place in the ancient world for the reformer of this type. Even those leaders whose policy offered advantages to the free masses, such as the Gracchi or some Spartan kings, did not so fare in their enterprises as to encourage imitation. As for appealing to the slaves themselves, it was only desperate adventurers who did so, and that only to use their force in promoting criminal designs. Such cases only served to justify the cruel execution of cruel laws for protecting masters and the state in general from the imminent slave-peril. If we turn from the city, in which what passed for politics ran its troubled and futile course, to the countryside, we are at once in a scene from which all political life had departed. The farmer-citizens grew fewer and fewer, and the great majority of them were virtually disfranchised by distance. Nor were they likely to favour any movement that seemed to be for the benefit of slaves.

The establishment of the Empire did not, indeed could not, produce any material change in the way of arousing effective sentiment hostile to slavery. But it did much to promote internal order and far-reaching peace. Under the new model of government the corrupt circles of nobles and greedy capitalists were no longer in absolute control of the civilized world, and it might seem that there was now some chance of dealing with the canker of slavery. But no such movement was the result. Old notions remained in full vigour. Augustus had his hands too full, and the need of conciliating private interests was too pressing, for him to disturb them, even had he been minded to do so. And who else could take the initiative? But the fate of two moral influences is worth noting. Stoicism, the creed of not a few ardent spirits, might profess to rise superior to worldly distinctions and advantages and assert the potential dignity of man even in the humblest condition of life. But it was always a creed of the few: its aloofness, tending to a certain arrogance, made it unfitted[1] to lead a great reform: it neither would nor could furnish the machinery of zealous propaganda. In the earlier Empire we find it politically allied with malcontent cliques in which smouldering resentment at the restraints on 'freedom' expressed itself by idealizing the Republic and hoping for a reaction. Thus it lost itself in impracticable dreams, and the hand of emperors under provocation sometimes fell heavily on its most virtuous men. The spread of Christianity came later, and was not diverted from its aims by a social affinity with the upper classes. Slaves bore no small part in its expansion to the West, and it was free to operate steadily as a humanitarian influence. But its claim to universality naturally exposed it to grave suspicion in a world that knew religion only as an affair of each several community, with a sort of overlordship vested in the conquering gods of Rome. Though it was a Church and not a philosophic system, though meant for all mankind and not for a

---

[1] Compare Wendell Phillips 'Before this there had been among us scattered and single abolitionists, earnest and able men; sometimes, like Wythe of Virginia, in high places. The Quakers and Covenanters had never intermitted their testimony against slavery. But Garrison was the first man to begin a *movement* designed to annihilate slavery.' Speech at G's funeral 1879.

cultivated few, it could only win its way by accepting civilization[1] in the main as it stood. Therefore it was compelled to accept slavery as an institution, and to content itself with inculcating humanity on masters and conscientious devotion to duty on slaves. If Abolitionism was to spring from this seed, a long time had to be spent in waiting for the harvest.

Yet the establishment of the Empire did lead to effects that in their turn served as contributory causes undermining the old slave-system, particularly[2] in agriculture. In a more peaceful age fewer slaves were brought to market, and this meant higher prices and put a premium on the economical employment of bought labour. To meet the situation, agricultural policy was developed on two lines, each of which was the improvement or extension of an existing practice. One was the more scientific organization of the labour-staff, so as to get better results from an equal amount of labour. The other was a more frequent resort to the plan of letting farms to tenants, whenever that arrangement seemed favourable to the landlord's interest. Of these developments we have direct information from Columella, who still prefers the former plan wherever feasible. But it was with the system of tenancies on various conditions that the future really lay. I have endeavoured above to sketch the process[3] by which tenants were gradually reduced to a condition of dependency on their landlords, and the difficulty of finding and keeping good tenants that was the other side of the movement. A very significant detail is the fact that slaves were put into farms[4] as tenants: that this was no unusual practice is clear from the way in which the classical jurists refer to it as a matter of course. And so things slowly moved on, with ups and downs, the tenants slave or free becoming more and more bondsmen of the land, liable to task-services and not free to move at will. Thus by usage, and eventually by law, a system of serfdom was established, while personal slavery declined.

Looked at from an Abolitionist point of view, we are here dealing with a sheer evasion of the slavery-question. But this was inevitable. The imperial government, which alone had the power necessary for attempting solutions of grave problems, was doomed to become more

[1] Prof Bury, *Idea of Progress* p 275, points out that Guizot noted that Christianity did not in its early stages aim at any improvement of social conditions.

[2] The conclusions reached in this paragraph are in agreement with E Meyer *Kl Schr* pp 151-2, 155, 205, 209. But he seems to put the decline of the slave-gang system rather earlier than I venture to do.

[3] We must bear in mind that a tenant was naturally unwilling to work for a margin of profit not to be retained by himself. Hence the tendency to find means of constraining him to do so.

[4] *coloni* or *quasi coloni*, cf Dig XV 3 § 16, XXXIII 8 § 23³, or XXXIII 7 §§ 12³, 18⁴, 20¹, and numerous other references.

and more mechanical. Under great strains in the third century it lost its vital forces to such a degree that it was powerless for internal betterment. The later despotic Empire, seeing the failure of past policy, could find no better way than to do as before[1], only more mechanically and more thoroughly. What little of freedom of movement and of self-disposal still remained to the toiling classes accordingly disappeared. Once a certain number had been slaves; now none were practically free. Diminution of personal slavery had not increased personal freedom. The attempt to confine all labour to fixed grooves and rigid rules was a last desperate effort to control and employ the resources of ancient civilization, in the hope of thus finding means sufficient to endure the ever-growing strain upon the empire. This system might serve its purpose for the moment, but it was a vain device, killing enterprise and working out its own ruin through its own stagnation. In agriculture, on which the whole fabric rested, its effects were particularly ruinous: for in no occupation is there greater need of constant forethought and loving care, which the prospect of private advantage alone can guarantee. All these phenomena may assure us that as yet there was no clear understanding of the value of free self-disposal as the economic basis of society. From the moral point of view no genuine progress was to be looked for in a stagnant age. The transition from normal slavery to gild-bondage and normal land-serfdom does not seem to have been affected by the spiritual levelling of Christianity. But that as she gained power, the Church did something to mitigate[2] the hardness of the time, is not to be doubted.

I need not dwell at length on the contrast presented by modern anti-slavery movements. The influence of religion, personal and humanitarian, is alone enough to account for the new spirit aroused and organized by Clarkson and Wilberforce. To put down the slave-trade because it was wrong was a momentous step, and emancipation its inevitable corollary, costly though it might be. That the reform was carried out two generations before the handworking masses of England gained political power is a most notable fact. For it is not possible to connect the achievement with the natural jealousy of free labour objecting to competition of slave labour. In the United States the motives for Abolition were necessarily more mixed, but sincere fanatics,

---

[1] The compulsory tenure of municipal offices is commonly cited as illustrating the pressure even on men of means. It began in the second century. See Dig L 1 § 38[6], 2 § 1 [Ulpian], 4 § 14[6] [Callistratus citing Hadrian], and many other passages. Notable is L 4 § 4[1] *honores qui indicuntur* [Ulpian].

[2] This topic is the subject of Churchill Babington's Hulsean dissertation, Cambridge 1846. I learn that a pamphlet by Brecht, *Sklaverei und Christentum*, takes a less favourable view, but have not seen it. The survival of the colonate and its heavy burdens in the early Middle Age are treated by de Coulanges, particularly in connexion with the estates of the Church.

religious and violent, were the leaders of the crusade. But the repugnance of free labour to the recognition of slavery in any part of the Republic (and it was this sentiment that furnished the necessary voting-power) was not so purely philanthropic. Students of American history are well aware of the moral change brought about by a single mechanical invention in the southern states. The economic advantages of the cotton-gin made slavery so profitable that existing tendencies towards emancipation died out in the South. A new life was given to a confessed evil, and the developed plantation-system, industrialized for the profit of a few, went down the road of fate to end in tragedy. The result of the great civil war at all events settled one question. Henceforth labour was to stand on a footing of self-disposal and wage-earning, with freedom to improve its conditions on those lines. The solution, obtained at an awful cost, was final for the time: what will be its ultimate outcome is at present (1919) a matter of some doubt, for reasons not to be discussed here.

The fact that Abolitionism is a phenomenon of the modern[1] world, and not of the ancient, will not seem insignificant to those who have read widely in the ancient writers and remarked how very little we hear of free wage-earning labour. If we deduct the references to independent artisans practising trades on a small scale (and their cases are not relevant here), what we hear of mere wage-earners is very little indeed. And of this little again only a part concerns agriculture. I take it that we may fairly draw one conclusion from this: the wishes of the free wage-earning class, whatever their numbers may have been, were practically of no account in the ancient world. From first to last the primitive law of superior force, the 'good old rule' of which slavery was a product, was tacitly accepted. Civilization might undergo changes of character, periods of peace might alternate with periods of war: still bondage and labour were closely connected in men's minds, and honest labour as such commanded no respect. How could it? Of a golden age, in which all men were free and slavery unknown, we have nothing that can be called evidence. The curtain rises on a world in which one man is at the full disposal of another. What is at first a small domestic matter contains the germ of later developments; and in the case of agriculture we see clearly how demands of an industrial nature transformed single bondservice into the wholesale and brutal exploitation of human chattels in slave-gangs. We have no good reason to believe that men ever in the ancient world abstained from

[1] The slow progress of emancipation is referred to by E Meyer *Kl Schr* p 178, of course from a very different point of view. He mentions that slavery was not completely forbidden in Prussia till 1857, and is against its abolition in German colonies. Seeley in his *Life of Stein* points out that the armies of Frederic the Great were mainly recruited from serfs.

employing slave labour out of humanitarian scruples. Scarcity of slaves, or lack of means to buy them, were certainly the main restrictive influences. The institution was always there, ready for extension and adaptation as changing conditions might suggest. If ancient civilization did not rest on a basis of slavery, on what did it rest? Assuredly not on free self-disposal. The man free to dispose of himself claimed the right to dispose of others, up to the limits of his own power and will. In this there is nothing wonderful. We need not flatter ourselves that the rule of force is now extinct. True, personal bondage to individuals is forbidden by law, but effective freedom of self-disposal, perhaps an impossible dream, is not yet realized: only its absence is dissembled under modern forms.

When I say that ancient civilization rested on a basis of slavery, the condition present to my mind is this. A social and political structure requires for its stability a reasonably sound economic foundation. This foundation is found in the assured and regular use of natural resources. And this use implies the constant presence of an obedient labour-force that can be set to work and kept working as and when needed. This force is now more and more supplied by machinery, the drudge that cannot strike. Antiquity made the slave its quasi-mechanical drudge: the more or less of slavery at a given moment simply depended on circumstances.

In returning to my original questions, whether the growth of Greco-Roman civilization was in fact achieved through the system of slavery, and whether it could conceivably have been accomplished without slavery, I have I think given my answer to the first, that is, so far as agriculture is concerned. And agriculture was the vital industry, on which the whole fabric principally rested. As to the second question, I can give no satisfactory answer. For my part, I agree with those who hold that, in the conditions of antiquity as depicted in our traditions and inferred by modern inquirers, slavery in some form and degree was an indispensable condition of progress. States, organizations of a lasting kind, had to be established by force. Captive labour, added to the resources of conquerors, seems to be a powerful means of increasing their economic strength and abridging the wasteful periods of conflict. But, once the stage had been reached at which a state was sufficiently stable and strong to provide for order within and to repel invaders, a slave-system became a canker, economic, social, ultimately political. I believe that the maladies from which the old Greco-Roman civilization suffered, and which in the end brought about its decay and fall, were indirectly or directly due to this taint more than to any other cause. I know of no case ancient or modern in which a people have attained to a sound and lasting prosperity by exploiting the servitude of other men. Serfdom or slavery, it matters not. So far as human experience has gone, it appears that all such conditions are eventually ruinous[1] to the rulers.

For it is not merely the degradation of manual labour that results from slavery. The deadening of inventive genius and economic improvements is fatally promoted through the tendency to remedy all shortcomings by simply using up more flesh and blood. Man abdicates a most important function of his reason, and accepts a mere superiority of animal over animal. This is surely not following the true law of his development. It is from this point of view that the great scientific inventions of modern times present an encouraging spectacle, as the earlier abuses of their exploitation are gradually overcome, and the operative citizen vindicates his claims as a human being. That ancient slavery did in some ways act for good by guaranteeing leisure to classes some of whom employed it well, may be freely admitted. But I do not think we can sincerely extend the admission to include the case of Politics, whatever Greek philosophers may have thought. Nor can we without reservations apply it in the field of Art. On the other hand Literature surely owed much to the artificial leisure created by slavery. Even in its most natural utterances Greco-Roman literature is the voice of classes privileged because free, not restrained by the cramping influences of workaday life and needs. Its partisan spirit is the spirit of the upper strata of society, ignoring the feelings, and often the existence, of the unfree toilers below. In the main aristocratic, it tells us next to nothing of the real sentiments of even the free masses, particularly on the labour-questions that have now for some time increasingly occupied the public mind. That we are, for good or for evil, viewing all matters of human interest on a different plane from that of the 'classic' writers, is a consideration that students of the Past are in duty bound never to forget.

But, when we are told[2] that ancient civilization in its early stages (as seen in the Homeric poems etc) may fairly be labelled as Medieval, while it may be called Modern when in its full bloom, we shall do well to pause before accepting a dogma that may imply more than we are prepared to grant. That mankind had to make a fresh start in the Middle Ages, ancient civilization having run its course and failed, is a proposition dangerously true. If it implies that the 'free' labour of modern times is not a direct development from ancient slavery, so far good. If we are to hold that ancient slave labour and modern free labour, when and so far as each is a factor of economic importance, are practically identical phenomena of capitalism eager to make a profit

[1] The Turk and his Rayahs furnishes a very striking illustration.
[2] E Meyer, *Kl Schr* p 188.

out of cheap labour, we may ask—is the parallelism so exact as it is thus represented to be? When we are told that the capitalist would nowadays prefer to employ slave labour if it were to be had, and that the legal form in which labour is supplied is a secondary consideration from the economic point of view, we begin to hesitate: is this really true? Was not the ineffectiveness of slave labour detected in ancient times? Was it not proved to demonstration in America, as attested by the evidence of both Northern and Southern witnesses? To reply that what capital wants is not mere slave labour but efficient slave labour, would be no answer. Capital is not, and never was, blind to the inefficiency of slave labour as compared with free labour. In the pursuit of profit it needs a supply of labour at its immediate and certain disposal; therefore it takes what it can get. In the ancient world the unquestioned institution of slavery offered a source of supply, not ideal, but such as could be relied on. Therefore capital employed slavery to extend its operations, simply turning existing conditions to account. And the admission, that the most flourishing period of Greco-Roman civilization was also the period in which slavery reached its greatest development, is surely a virtual denial that the basis of that civilization was free labour. That is, free wage-earning labour. For the independent farmer or artisan had nothing to do with the matter: he worked for himself, not for another, and was on a different plane from either wage-earner or slave. If he did not employ either wage-earner or slave, it was because he found such help too costly or a doubtful boon.

The case of agriculture at once reveals what was found to be the strong point of slave labour, the feasibility of employing it in large masses. Much of the work consisted in the mere mechanical use of brute force, and one overseer could direct many hands. In operations dependent on the seasons, the labour must be at hand to utilize opportunities. The choice lay between slaves not working with a will and free wage-earners not likely to be on the spot when wanted. Why were slaves preferred? Because their presence in sufficient number could be relied on in the existing conditions of the world. The history of industrial agriculture was a long tale of effort so to organize slave labour as to get out of it the greatest possible margin of profit. Not that slavery was thought preferable in itself; but a means of wholesale cultivation had to be found, and the then available resources of civilization offered no other. When the supply of slaves began to fail, landlords sought a remedy in letting some or all of their land to tenant farmers (extending an old practice), not in attempting to farm on their own account with hired labour. Hired labour remained as before, an occasional appliance to meet temporary needs.

The use of the terms Medieval and Modern as labels[1] for ancient civilization in two clearly marked stages has, I repeat, just enough truth in it to be dangerous. As a rhetorical flourish it may pass. But it conveys by suggestion much that cannot be accepted. No doubt it is not meant to imply that what we call the Middle Ages is to be ignored. But it inevitably tends to stifle a belief in historical continuity, a faith in which is the soul of historical inquiry as generally understood in the present day. That modern labour-conditions shew a powerful reaction against medieval, is obvious : that medieval conditions have not influenced the modes of this reaction, is to me incredible. I do not believe that the modern free wage-earning system could have grown out of the ancient slave-labour system, had there been no such intervening period as the 'Middle Ages.' That the aims of the capitalist ancient and modern are the same, is a mere truism: but is not the same true of the medieval capitalist also ?

That the wage-earning handworker often finds his freedom of self-disposal limited in practice, though his position is very far removed from slavery, I have pointed out above. Also, that modern facilities for movement have helped materially to assert and enlarge his freedom. From this point of view the discovery of the New World was the turning-point of European history. But in course of time capitalistic phenomena appeared there also, and on a larger scale. And now, almost the whole world over, the handworker is striving, not only for higher wages but for more complete self-disposal. This necessitates some control of the industries in which he works. Individual effort being vain, he forms unions to guard his interests. The unions, acting by strike-pressure, come into conflict with governments representing the state. The next step is to employ political pressure by gaining and using votes under representative systems, so as to remodel legislation and administration in a sense favourable to the handworker. This movement, now well under way in the most civilized countries, is not perhaps socialistic in principle, and we do not yet know how far it is likely to take that turn. In order to fight exploitation, the handworker has to surrender a good deal of his individual freedom: whether he will be content to surrender a good deal more, the coming age will see. This much at least is clear,—the handworking wage-earners are no longer, as in the ancient world, a class of no account. That they have wrung so many great concessions from unwilling capitalists seems to me a proof that their freedom, even under medieval[2] restrictions, had

[1] Since writing this section I have found in Prof Bury's *Idea of Progress* pp 269–70 a passage which seems to justify the objection here raised, though it occurs in a different connexion.

[2] It is perhaps hardly necessary to refer to the great economic disturbance caused by the Black Death in fourteenth century England.

always in it something real, some quality that sharply distinguished it from ancient slavery. In ancient slavery I can see no germ out of which betterment of labour-conditions could conceivably arise. It simply had to die, and modern attempts to revive it have had to die also.

In the foregoing pages I have recognized two lines of distinction. One is that commonly admitted, the line that parts freeman from slave. The other is that between free wage-earner and slave. In looking back from modern circumstances to ancient, the latter is much the more important. For, now that slavery in the proper sense has been abolished by modern civilized peoples, the conditions of wage-earning stand out as presenting the most momentous issues of the present age. To the statesmen the questions raised are full of anxiety as to the probable influence of present policies on future wellbeing. A student of Greco-Roman civilization must ask himself whether modern labour-questions and their attempted solutions may not indirectly furnish help in appraising and judging the conditions of the past. Now it so happens that in the case of agriculture recent events in Russia possess very marked significance, and it is therefore hardly possible to leave them unnoticed here.

It seems to be established[1] beyond reasonable doubt that the genuine and effective doctrine of Leninite Bolshevism, in its definition of the 'working class,' excludes the peasantry. They are not 'proletarian.' That is, the great majority of peasants have something. This each wants to keep, and if possible to augment. In short, they are Individualists. Now Bolshevism builds on dogmas of Marxian Socialism, however much it may warp their application, however widely it may depart from Marxian theory in its choice of methods. Therefore it sees in the peasants only a class of petty bourgeoisie with the anti-socialistic instincts of that hated class, and will spare no effort to exclude them from political power. It disfranchises employers, even though the work they do is productive and useful to society. We need go no further: these principles of the Bolshevik creed, be it prophetic vision or be it crazy fanaticism blind to the facts of human nature and devoid of all practical sense of proportion, are enough for my present purpose. It results from them that all wage-earning is wrong: no man has the right to employ another man for his own purposes: that the relation benefits both employer and employed, even if true, is a

---

[1] John Spargo, *Bolshevism, the enemy of political and industrial Democracy*. London, J Murray 1919. I think I may accept the author's evidence on the points here referred to, confirmed as it is by other observers. See his remarks pp 69, 156, 275, 278, in particular. That the same sharp distinction between peasant and wage-earner is drawn by the Socialists in other countries also, and is to them a stumblingblock, is clearly to be seen in King and Okey's *Italy today*. See appendix.

consideration[1] wholly irrelevant. For it is promised that the new civilization, recast on the Bolshevik model, will leave no room for wage-service of one man to another.

I am not to criticize this scheme of social and economic life, but to look at it coolly as an illustrative fact. It is surely a significant thing that, while slavery and serfdom are now reckoned as virtually obsolete phenomena of the past, the old distinction, between the man who works himself for himself and the man who works for another, is still before us as the vital line of division in labour-questions. Bloodshed and torture as means of enforcing the dogma may be confined to Russia, but the distinction is at the bottom of industrial unrest all over the world. Most significant of all is the admission that peasant landholders are not a 'proletariate.' Of course they are not. But to philosophers and statesmen of antiquity they appeared as an all-important class, not only as producers of food but as a solid element of population, promoting the stability of state governments. This stability was favourable to continuity of policy and enabled all interests to thrive in peace. Have the development of machinery and transport in recent times so far altered the conditions of agriculture that this is no longer the case? In other words, is the agricultural labourer, the present wage-earner, to supersede the peasant landholder as the dominant figure of rustic life? Is the large-scale farmer to survive only as the impotent figure-head of rural enterprises? Is a political proletariate competent to regulate the conduct of an industry directly dependent on soil climate and seasons? Wherever man is in immediate contact with forces of nature, in farm-life as in seafaring, the bodily energies of many can only be effective through subordination to the mind of one. How far, under the modern factory system, where the mill goes on as usual in all weathers, direction by wage-earners may be a practicable proposition, I cannot tell. That such a plan would be a failure on a farm, I have no doubt whatever.

My general conclusion then is that the old distinction observable under Greco-Roman civilization was in itself a sound one. Yet it led to no lasting and satisfactory solution of agricultural labour-problems. Many causes no doubt contributed to this failure; but the lack of a satisfactory labour-system was probably the greatest. Neither slavery nor serfdom was capable of meeting the need, and the wage-earning system never grew so as efficiently to supersede them. Now, after centuries of the wage-system, we are uneasily asking ourselves whether modern civilization is gravely endangered through the failure of this

[1] A remarkable article in the *Times* of 10 May 1920 describes the influences tending in the opposite direction in the United States, particularly the workman's prospect of proprietorship.

system also. It seems that in agriculture at least there are two possible alternatives, either a final settlement of the wage-question on a footing satisfactory to the labourer, or a return to αὐτουργία. Probably neither of these will be found to exclude the other or to be equally applicable to the circumstances of all countries. That communal ownership and shifting tenure can be revived seems impossible under modern conditions, whatever some Socialists may fancy. On the other hand voluntary cooperation in marketing seems to have a great future before it. Of a movement in that direction I have found no traces among the ancients : but modern developments in the way of transport may remove many difficulties. At any rate it is in such efforts of adaptation and compromise that expert agriculturists seem to be looking for help. As to labour, slavery and serfdom being excluded from modern civilized states, the coming problem is how to secure the performance of agricultural work. The choice lies between attractive wage-conditions, appealing to individual interest, and the Socialist scheme of tasks carried out under official direction, assumed to be in the best interests of a whole community. Both plans offer a substitute for the crude compulsory methods vainly employed in the ancient world. Which plan is the more suited to the demands of human nature, whether self-disposal or communism is to be the dominant aim and note of society, coming generations must decide.

APPENDIX.

SOME BYZANTINE AUTHORITIES.

To follow up the history of agricultural labour under the so-called Byzantine empire, after the Roman empire had fallen in the West, is beyond my scope. Yet there are certain matters on which light is thrown by surviving documents that it is hardly possible wholly to ignore. That the position of the agricultural classes did not follow the same lines of development in East and West, is in itself a fact worth noting, though not surprising. It may be said to run parallel with the general fate of the two sections of the once Roman world. In the West[1] the growth of what we call Feudalism and the rise of new nation-states are the phenomena that in the course of centuries gradually produced our modern Europe. In the East the Empire long preserved its organization, declining in efficiency and power, but rallying again and again, serving as a bulwark of Christian Europe, and not extinguished finally till 1453. It might perhaps have been guessed that the conditions of rustic life would undergo some change, for the system of the later Roman colonate was already shewing signs of coming failure in the time of Arcadius and Honorius. The need of some system more favourable to individual energy and enterprise, more to be trusted for production of food, was surely not to be ignored. Food must have been a need of extreme urgency, with armies constantly engaged in northern or eastern wars, and the mouths of Constantinople ever hungry at home. After the Saracen conquest of Egypt in the seventh century, the food-resources on which the government could rely must have been seriously reduced, and the need greater than ever. Thus we are not to wonder if we find indications of great interest taken in agriculture, and direct evidence of reversion to a better land-system than that of the later Roman colonate.

A. GEOPONICA.

The curious collection known as **Geoponica**[2] comes down to us in a text attributed to the tenth century, which is supposed to be a badly-edited version of an earlier work probably of the sixth or early seventh century. It is in a scrap-book form, consisting of precepts on a vast number of topics, the matter under each heading being professedly drawn from the doctrine of some author or authors whose names are prefixed. Some of these are Byzantine writers, others of much earlier date, including Democritus and Hippocrates, and the Roman Varro. Modern critics consider these citations of names untrustworthy, the collector or editor having dealt very carelessly with the work of his predecessors. I can

---

[1] For the survival of the colonate in the West see de Coulanges pp 145–86.
[2] See Krumbacher's history of Byzantine Literature in Iwan Müller's Handbuch, and Oder's article in Pauly-Wissowa.

only say that an examination of the chapters that are of special interest to me fully bears out this censure. I would add that a reference to the index shews that Cato Columella Pliny (elder) and Palladius are never cited, and express my suspicion that the omission of names is not always a proof that those authors were disregarded as sources. The general character of the work is unscientific and feeble, abounding in quackery and superstition. Technical and dogmatic, it has nevertheless an air of unreality, perhaps due in part to the later editor, but probably in part to the original compiler, whose name is given as Cassianus Bassus, a lawyer (σχολαστικός), apparently a Byzantine.

It has been remarked that the cultivation of corn fills but a small space in the Geoponica, being evidently quite a subordinate department of farm-life as there contemplated. Is this an indication that Constantinople was still drawing plenty of corn from Egypt, and may we infer that this feature is due to the original compiler, writing before the loss of that granary-province? I do not venture to answer the question.

The passages interesting from my point of view occur in the second book, where some reference, scanty and obscure though it be, is made to labour and labourers. A chapter (2) on the classes of labourers suited for various kinds of work is a good specimen of this unsatisfactory treatise. It is labelled Βάρωνος, but we may well hesitate to ascribe the substance to Varro. The rules given are for the most part quite commonplace, and I cannot trace them in Varro's res rustica. On the other hand some of them correspond to precepts of Columella. Whether this is their real source, or whether they are traditional rules handed down carelessly by previous compilers, perhaps on even earlier authority, I see no sure means of determining. The doctrine that boys (παῖδες) should be employed in field-labour (ἐργασία), to watch and learn from their experienced elders, and the remark that their suppleness fits them better for stooping jobs (weeding etc), is new to me. Varro[1] at least puts the minimum age for field-hands at 22. Perhaps this doctrine comes from some later authority, of a time when the old supply of adult field-hands was evidently failing.

Another chapter, labelled as drawn from Florentinus (? first half of third century), deals with the qualifications and duties of the ἐπίτροπος or οἰκονόμος, the Roman vilicus. This chapter (44) is also quite commonplace, and can be copiously illustrated out of many authors, from Xenophon and Cato to Columella and Pliny. The exact meaning of one passage (§ 3) is not clear to me, but its general drift is in agreement with the rest. The notable point about the chapter is that it discusses the steward and his staff as forming the ordinary establishment of a farm. Are we to infer that this system was normal at the time when the compiler put together the precepts under this head? Or is this a case of unintelligent compilation, a mere passing-on of doctrines practically obsolete by a town-bred writer in his study? I cannot tell. The consideration of further details may give some help towards a judgment.

The next chapter (45), with the same label, treats of the steward's diary and the organization of the hands (ἐργάται). The main doctrine is that every day must have its task, and every plan be punctually carried out, since one delay

[1] Varro RR I 17 §§ 3, 4.

upsets the whole course (τὴν τῆς ἐργασίας τάξιν) and is bad for both crops and land. This again is stale enough, and may be illustrated from Cato and Columella. The rules for organizing the hands in groups of suitable size, so as to get a maximum of efficiency with a minimum of overseers, agree closely with what we find in Columella. Thus there is a strong probability that the labour intended is that of slaves.

In chapter 46, with same label, the subject is one of scale (περὶ μέτρου ἐργασίας), the expression of several operations in terms of labour-units (ἐργασίαι, operae). This also is an old story, capable of much illustration from earlier writers. The work contemplated is that of a vineyard. The way in which the hands (ἐργάται) are referred to is more suited to a slave-staff than to wage-earners.

So too in chapter 47, with same label. It is περὶ τῆς τῶν γεωργῶν ὑγιείας, enjoining general care of the men's health and prescribing remedies for various ailments. It seems taken for granted that the hands will submit to the treatment imposed. Remembering the traditional interest of the master in his slaves' health, we can hardly doubt that slaves are meant here.

Chapter 48, labelled as drawn from Didymus (? fourth or fifth century), is a warning against ill-considered transplantation from better spots to less wholesome ones. The reverse order is the right one. This rule applies not only to plants (φυτά) but to farm-workers (γεωργόι) also. The principle can be traced back to earlier writers. It seems assumed that the men, like the plants, can be removed at the master's will. Probably slaves are meant, and we may recall the objections of Varro and Columella to risking slave-property in malarious spots.

Chapter 49, labelled Βάρωνος, asserts the necessity of keeping such artisans as smiths carpenters and potters on the farm or near at hand. The tools have to be kept in good order, and visits to the town waste time. That this precept comes from Varro I 16 §§ 3, 4, seems more than doubtful: reference will shew that the passages differ considerably.

I would add that the argument prefixed to book III, a farmer's calendar, at least in Beckh's text, gives a list of the months from January to December, attaching to each Roman name the corresponding Egyptian one. The editor apparently accepts this double list as genuine. If it be so, has the fact any bearing on the relations between Constantinople and Egypt referred to above?

B. THE FARMER'S LAW.

The so-called 'Farmer's Law,' νόμος γεωργικός, is now assigned by the critics to the time of the Iconoclast emperors, say about 740 AD. It is an official document of limited scope, not a general regulative code governing agricultural conditions in all parts of the eastern empire. Its text origin arrangement and the bearing of its evidence have been much discussed, and it will suffice here to refer to the articles of Mr Ashburner[1] on the subject. What

[1] In the *Journal of Hellenic Studies* 1910 and 1912. There the views of Zachariä are discussed.

concerns me is the position of farmers under the Byzantine empire in the eighth century as compared with that of the fourth or fifth century *coloni*, and the different lines of development followed by country life in East and West. Therefore it is only necessary to consider some of the main features of the picture revealed to us by various details of the Farmer's Law.

The first point that strikes a reader is that the serf[1] *colonus* has apparently disappeared. Land is held by free owners, who either themselves provide for its cultivation or let it to tenants who take over that duty. The normal organization is in districts (χωρία) each of which contains a number of landowners, who either farm their own land or, if short of means (ἄποροι), let it to other better-equipped farmers of the same district. Thus the transactions are locally limited, and the chief object of the law is to prevent misdeeds that might prejudically affect the prosperity of the local farmers. These are in a sense partners or commoners (κοινωνοί), the 'commonalty' (κοινότης) of the district, which is a taxation-unit with its members jointly liable. The district seems to be regarded as originally common and then divided into members' lots, with a part reserved perhaps as common pasture. Redivision is contemplated, and the lots seem to belong rather to the family than to the individual. To judge from the tone of the rules, it seems certain that the farmers and their families are a class working with their own hands. But there are also wage-earning labourers, and slaves owned or hired for farm work. Tenancy on shares, like the partiary system in Roman Law, appears as an established practice, and in one passage (clause 16) Mr Ashburner detects a farmer employed at a salary, in short a *mercennarius*.

Thus we find existing what are a kind of village communities, the land-owning farmers in which are free to let land to each other and also to exchange farms if they see fit to do so. How far they are free to flit from one commune to another remains doubtful. And there is no indication that they are at liberty to dispose of their own land-rights to outsiders. There appears however side by side with these communal units another system of tenancies in which individual farmers hire land from great landlords. Naturally the position of such tenants is different from that of tenants under communal owners: the matter is treated at some length by Mr Ashburner. What proportion the corn crop generally bore to other produce in the agriculture of the Byzantine empire contemplated by these regulations, the document does not enable us to judge. Vineyards and figyards were clearly an important department, and also gardens for vegetables and fruit. Live stock, and damage done to them and by them, are the subject of many clauses, nor is woodland forgotten. But the olive does not appear. So far as one may guess, the farming was probably of a mixed character. The penalties assigned for offences are often barbarous, including not only death by hanging or burning but blinding and other mutilations of oriental use. At the same time the ecclesiastical spirit of the Eastern empire finds expression in the bestowal of a curse on one guilty of cheating, referring I suppose primarily to undiscovered fraud.

[1] The truth seems to be that serfage had never become so widespread in the East as in the West, as Mr Bouchier, *Syria as a Roman Province* p 181, points out.

The state of things inferred from the provisions of the 'Farmer's Law' is so remarkable in itself, and so different from the course of rustic development in the West, that we are driven to seek an explanation of some kind. Many influences may have contributed to produce so striking a differentiation. But one can hardly help suspecting that there was some one great influence at work in the eastern empire, to which the surprising change noted above was mainly due. In his *History of the later Roman Empire*[1] Professor Bury has offered a conjectural solution of the problem. It is to be sought in the changes brought about in the national character and the external history of the Empire. Since the middle of the sixth century north-west Asia Minor and the Balkan country had been filled with Slavonic settlers, and other parts with other new colonists. Now the new settlers, particularly the Slavs, were not used to the colonate system or the rigid bond of hereditary occupations, and emperors busied in imperial defence on the North and East knew better than to force upon them an unwelcome system. Invasions had reduced the populations of frontier provinces and shattered the old state of serfdom. Resettlement on a large scale had to be carried out within the empire, and under new conditions to suit the changed character of the population. Among the new elements that produced this change the most important was the coming of the Slavs.

For the Slavs had themselves no institution corresponding to the German *laeti*. Slaves indeed they had, but not free cultivators attached to the soil. Therefore they could not, like the Germans in the West, adapt themselves to the Roman colonate; accordingly their intrusion led to its abolition. In support of this view the well-known Slavonic peasant communities are cited as evidence. Nor can it be denied that this consideration has some weight. But, while we may provisionally accept the conclusion that Slavonic influences had something, perhaps much, to do with the new turn given to the conditions of rustic life in the East, we must not press it so far as to infer that the colonate-system was extinct there. In no case could the 'Farmer's Law' fairly be used to prove the negative: and moreover it is apparently the case according to Mr Ashburner that the document is not a complete agricultural code for all agricultural classes within the empire. If it is 'concerned exclusively with a village community, composed of farmers who cultivate their own lands,' it cannot prove the non-existence of other rustic conditions different in kind. Colonate seems to have disappeared, while slavery has not. But that is the utmost we can say. The slave at least is still there. As to the important question, whether the farmers contemplated in the Law enjoy a real freedom of movement, as has been thought, it is best to refer a reader to the cautious reserve of Mr Ashburner.

The one general inference that I venture to draw from these two authorities is that, however much or little the conditions of agriculture may have changed in the surviving Eastern part of the Roman empire, the employment of slave labour still remained.

[1] Vol II pp 418–421.

C. EXTRACTS FROM MODERN BOOKS.

(1) Hume, Essay XI, *Of the populousness of antient nations.*

We must now consider what disadvantages the antients lay under with regard to populousness, and what checks they received from their political maxims and institutions. There are commonly compensations in every human condition; and tho' these compensations be not always perfectly equal, yet they serve, at least, to restrain the prevailing principle. To compare them and estimate their influence, is indeed very difficult, even where they take place in the same age, and in neighbouring countries: But where several ages have intervened, and only scattered lights are afforded us by antient authors; what can we do but amuse ourselves by talking, *pro* and *con*, on an interesting subject, and thereby correcting all hasty and violent determinations?

MODERN ITALIAN CONDITIONS.

(2) Bolton King and Thomas Okey, *Italy today.*

In *Italy today*, Messrs **Bolton King and Thomas Okey** furnish a most interesting collection of facts relative to Italian rural conditions. The extent to which the phenomena of antiquity reappear in the details of this careful treatise is most striking. Italy being the central land of my inquiry, and convinced as I am that the great variety of local conditions is even now not sufficiently recognized in Roman Histories, this excellent book is of peculiar value. In the course of (say) fifteen centuries Italy and her people have passed through strange vicissitudes, not merely political: a great change has taken place in the range of agricultural products: yet old phenomena of rural life meet the inquirer at every turn. Surely this cannot be dismissed lightly as a casual coincidence. I cannot find room to set out the resemblances in detail, so I append a short table of reference to passages in the book that have impressed me most. Supplementary to this, as a vivid illustration of conditions in a mountain district, the first three chapters of *In the Abruzzi*, by **Anne Macdonell**, are decidedly helpful. For instance, it appears that the old migratory pasturage still existed in full force down to quite recent times, but the late conversion of much Apulian lowland from pasture to tillage has seriously affected the position of the highland shepherds by reducing the area available for winter grazing. The chapter on brigandage has also some instructive passages.

REFERENCES TO *Italy today.*

Peasant contrasted with wage-earner, pp 64–6, 72, 74, 126, 166–8, 171–2, 175–6, 200, 312, and Index under *mezzaiuoli* and *peasants*. Agricultural classes, pp 164–6. Partiaries, pp 168, 173. Emphyteusis, p 173. Improvements, p 173. Farming through steward, pp 174–5. Tenancies, pp 168–74, and Index under *peasants*. Rents in kind, p 171. Debt of various classes, pp 182–4, 366, 376. Taxes, p 140. Gangs of labourers, pp 166, 376. Wages, pp 126, 128, 168, 174, 366, 369–71. Food in wage, p 370. Emigration, pp 371, 396. Self-help in rural districts, pp 184–6, 376. Charities, pp 220 foll, 379 foll. Socialists and Peasantry, pp 64–6, 170, 172, cf 71–2.

(3) **R E Prothero,** *The pleasant land of France*. London 1908.

Chapters (essays) II and III, *French farming* and *Tenant-right and agrarian outrage in France*, contain much of interest.

pp 91–2 Social advantages of the system of peasant proprietors. A training[1] to the rural population. Element of stability. The answer to agitators 'Cela est bien, mais il faut cultiver notre jardin.' Difficulties which beset its artificial creation. *Métayage* (under present conditions) has proved the best shelter for tenant-farmers against the agricultural storm. Need of implicit confidence between landlord and working partner.

pp 98–9 Tenant-right in Santerre (Picardy). Tenant considers himself a co-proprietor of the land. Former payment of rent in kind taken to be a sign of joint ownership. Now in money, but calculated upon market price of corn. Landlord's loss of control. High money value of *droit de marché*.

p 104 Traces of Roman occupation. Roman soldier followed by farmer. 'Under the empire the *colonus* was not a slave, but the owner of slaves: he held his land in perpetuity; he could not leave it. He paid a fixed rent in kind, which could not be raised. Tenant-right therefore is explained as the recognition by the Frankish conquerors of this hereditary claim to the perpetual occupation of the soil.' [One of the various explanations offered.]

p 119 Severe legislation failed to get rid of tenant-right, but since 1791 it has been recognized, and so its importance decreased. Under the *ancien régime* leases were short—9 years—and precarious. They were governed by the Roman law maxim *emptori fundi necesse non est stare colonum*. That is, if property changed hands during the continuance of the lease, the new owner might evict the tenant. The *Code Civil* confirms law of 1791—dispossession only if provision has been made (in lease) for it.

In general, land-tenures vary very greatly in the various provinces.

(4) **G G Coulton,** *Social life in Britain from the Conquest to the Reformation*. Cambridge 1918.

In Section VI *Manor and Cottage* are a number of extracts throwing light on the rustic conditions of their times.

1. *A model Manor* pp 301–6, describing the organization of an estate, with the duties of the several officials and departmental servants. Watchful diligence and economy, strict accountability and honesty are insisted on, that the rights of the Lord may not be impaired.

2. *The Manorial court*, pp 306–8.

3. *The peasant's fare*, p 308.

4. *Incidents of the countryside*, p 309.

7. *Decay of yeomanry*, pp 310–12. (Latimer.)

8. *Decay of husbandry*, pp 312–14. (Sir T More.)

All these passages are of great interest as shewing how a number of pheno-

---

[1] Sir W. Herringham, *A Physician in France*, pp 167–8 on Peasantry as a strength to the State.

mena observable in the case of ancient estates are repeated under medieval conditions. The typical Manor with its elaborate hierarchy and rules, the struggles of the small yeoman, the encroachments of big landlords, the special difficulties of small-scale tillage caused by growth of large-scale pasturage, the increase of wastrels and sturdy beggars, are all notable points, worthy the attention of a student of ancient farm life and labour.

The Big Man and the Small Farmer.

(5) **Clifton Johnson**, *From the St Lawrence to Virginia*. New York 1913, p 21. Chapter on the Adirondack winter.

(Conversation in an up-country store.)

'I worked for Rockefeller most of that season. You know he has a big estate down below here a ways. There used to be farmhouses—yes and villages on it, but he bought the owners all out, or froze 'em out. One feller was determined not to sell, and as a sample of how things was made uncomfortable for him I heard tell that two men came to his house once and made him a present of some venison. They had hardly gone when the game warden dropped in and arrested him for havin' venison in his house. All such tricks was worked on him, and he spent every cent he was worth fighting lawsuits. People wa'n't allowed to fish on the property, and the women wa'n't allowed to pick berries on it. A good deal of hard feeling was stirred up, and Rockefeller would scoot from the train to his house, and pull the curtains down, 'fraid they'd shoot him. Oh! he was awful scairt.'

Eastern Europe.

(6) **Marion L Newbigin DSc**, *Geographical aspects of Balkan problems*. London 1915.

Turks—'not all their virtues, not all their military strength, have saved them from the slow sapping of vitality due to their divorce alike from the actual tilling of the land and from trade and commerce....He has been within the (Balkan) peninsula a parasite, chiefly upon the ploughing peasant, and the effect has been to implant in the mind of that peasant a passion for agriculture, for the undisturbed possession of a patch of freehold, which is probably as strong here as it has ever been in the world.' p 137.

Thessaly—'the landowners are almost always absentees, appearing only at the time of harvest' (originally Turks, now mostly Greeks) 'who have taken little personal interest in the land' (no great improvement in condition of cultivator). (So in Bosnia—better in Serbia and Bulgaria) 'lands mostly worked by the peasants on the half-shares system.' p 175.

Albania—(poverty extreme—temporary emigration of the males, frequent in poor regions) 'young Alb[s] often leave their country during the winter, going to work in Greece or elsewhere as field labourers, and returning to their mountains in the spring.' pp 183–4.

Generally—small holdings mostly in the Balkan states.

D. LIST OF SOME BOOKS USED.

This list does not pretend to be complete. Many other works are referred to here and there in the notes on the text. But I feel bound to mention the names of some, particularly those dealing with conditions that did or still do exist in the modern world. Miscellaneous reading of this kind has been to me a great help in the endeavour to understand the full bearing of ancient evidence, and (I hope) to judge it fairly. It is on the presentation and criticism of that evidence that I depend: for the great handbooks of Antiquities do not help me much. The practice of making a statement and giving in support of it a reference or references is on the face of it sound. But, when the witnesses cited are authors writing under widely various conditions of time and place and personal circumstances, it is necessary whenever possible to appraise each one separately. And when the aim is, not to write a technical treatise on 'scientific' lines, but to describe what is a highly important background of a great civilization, a separate treatment of witnesses needs no apology. I cannot cite in detail the references to conditions in a number of countries, for instance India and China, but I have given them by page or chapter so as to be consulted with ease.

(1) AGRICULTURE AND RUSTIC LIFE AND LABOUR.

M Weber, *Die Römische Agrargeschichte*, Stuttgart 1891.
C Daubeny, *Lectures on Roman husbandry*, Oxford 1857.
Ll Storr-Best, *Varro on farming*, translated with Introduction commentary and excursus, London 1912.
E de Laveleye, *Primitive Property*, English translation 1878.
H Blümner, article 'Landwirtschaft' in I Müller's *Handbuch* VI ii 2, ed 3 pp 533 foll.
A E Zimmern, *The Greek Commonwealth*, Oxford 1911.
Büchsenschütz, *Besitz und Erwerb*, Halle 1869.
Columella of Husbandry, translation (anonymous), London 1745.

(2) ECONOMIC AND SOCIAL MATTERS.

Adam Smith, *Wealth of Nations, passim.*
H Nissen, *Italische Landeskunde*, Berlin 1883–1902.
K W Nitzsch, *Geschichte der Römischen Republik*, vol II, Leipzig 1885.
L Bloch, *Soziale Kämpfe im alten Rom*, ed III Berlin 1913.
David Hume, *Essays*, ed 1760 (Essay XI of the populousness of antient nations).
J Beloch, *Die Bevölkerung der Griechisch-Römischen Welt*, Leipzig 1886.
H Francotte, *L'Industrie dans la Grèce ancienne*, Bruxelles 1900–1.
O Seeck, *Geschichte des Untergangs der antiken Welt*, Berlin 1897–1913.
O Seeck, 'Die Schatzungsordnung Diocletians,' in *Zeitschrift für Social- und Wirthschaftsgeschichte*, Weimar 1896.
H Schiller, *Geschichte der Römischen Kaiserzeit*, Gotha 1883–7.
S Dill, *Roman society in the last century of the Western Empire*, London 1898.
G Gilbert, *Handbuch der Griechischen Staatsalterthümer*, vol II, Leipzig 1885.

(3) LAW AND THE LATER COLONATE.

Several of the books named under other heads deal with legal points, for instance Beauchet, Lipsius, Meier and Schömann, Calderini, M Clerc.

The Digest and Codex Justinianus have been used in the text of Mommsen and P Krüger.

The Codex Theodosianus in text of Mommsen and P M Meyer, Berlin 1905 and in Ritter's edition of Godefroi, Leipzig 1736–45.

P Girard, *Textes de droit Romain*, ed 4 Paris 1913.

F Zulueta, 'De Patrociniis vicorum,' in Vinogradoff's *Oxford Studies*, Oxford 1909.

M Rostowzew, *Studien zur Geschichte des Römischen Colonates*, Leipzig and Berlin 1910.

B Heisterbergk, *Die Entstehung des Colonats*, Leipzig 1876.

A Esmein, *Mélanges d'histoire du Droit*, Paris 1886.

Fustel de Coulanges, 'Le Colonat Romain,' in his *Recherches sur quelques problèmes d'histoire*, Paris 1885.

H F Pelham, *Essays* (No XIII), Oxford 1911.

I am sorry that inability to procure copies has prevented me from consulting the following works:

Beaudouin, *Les grands domaines dans l'empire Romain*, Paris 1899.

Bolkestein, *de colonatu Romano eiusque origine*, Amsterdam 1906.

(4) MANUMISSION AND KINDRED TOPICS.

A Calderini, *La manomissione e la condizione dei liberti in Grecia*, Milan 1908.

M Clerc, *Les métèques Athéniens*, Paris 1893.

L Beauchet, *Droit privé de la République Athénienne*, Paris 1897.

J H Lipsius, *Das Attische Recht etc*, Leipzig 1905.

Meier und Schömann, *Der Attische Process*, Berlin 1883–7.

Mommsen, *Römisches Staatsrecht*.

G Haenel, *Corpus legum*, Leipzig 1857.

C G Bruns, *Fontes Iuris Romani antiqui*.

Dareste, Haussoullier, Th Reinach, *Recueil des inscriptions juridiques Grecques*, Paris 1904. (Laws of Gortyn.)

Wescher et Foucart, *Inscriptions de Delphes*, Paris 1863.

Wilamowitz-Möllendorf, 'Demotika der Metöken,' in *Hermes* 1887.

(5) SLAVERY AND SLAVE TRADE.

H Wallon, *Histoire de l'esclavage dans l'antiquité*, ed 2 Paris 1879.

J K Ingram, *A history of slavery and serfdom*, London 1895.

E H Minns, *Scythians and Greeks*, Cambridge 1913 (pages 438, 440, 461, 465, 471, 567).

V A Smith, *The early history of India*, Oxford 1914 (pages 100–1, 177–8, 441).

M S Evans, *Black and White in the Southern States*, London 1915.

„ *Black and White in South-east Africa*, ed 2 London 1916.

470

J E Cairnes, *The Slave Power*, ed 2 London and Cambridge 1863.

W W Buckland, *The Roman Law of Slavery*, Cambridge 1908.

W E Hardenburg, *The Putumayo, the Devil's Paradise*, with extracts from Sir R Casement's report, London and Leipzig 1912.

H W Nevinson, *A modern Slavery*, London and New York 1906.

Sidney Low, *Egypt in transition* (see under *Medieval and Modern conditions*).

Mrs M A Handley, *Roughing it in Southern India*, London 1911 (pages 193–4).

(6) MEDIEVAL AND MODERN CONDITIONS.

Books illustrating matters of rustic life, peasant proprietorship, agricultural wage-labour, etc.

Bolton King and Thomas Okey, *Italy today*, new ed London 1909.

R E Prothero, *The pleasant land of France*, London 1908 (Essays II and III).

Anne Macdonell, *In the Abruzzi*, London 1908 (chapters 1–3).

G Renwick, *Finland today*, London 1911 (pages 59, 60).

Sir J D Rees, *The real India*, London 1908.

Marion L Newbigin, *Geographical aspects of Balkan problems*, London 1915.

Ralph Butler, *The new eastern Europe*, London 1919 (chapter VII).

John Spargo, *Bolshevism, the enemy of political and industrial democracy*, London 1919 (pages 69, 156, 275, 278).

W H Dawson, *The evolution of modern Germany*, London 1908 (chapters XIII, XIV).

P Vinogradoff, *The growth of the Manor*, ed 2 London 1911.

G G Coulton, *Social life in Britain from the Conquest to the Reformation*, Cambridge 1918 (Section VI).

Mary Bateson, *Medieval England 1066–1350*, London 1903.

Sidney Low, *Egypt in transition*, London 1914 (pages 60–2, 240–1).

Sidney Low, *A vision of India*, ed 2 London 1907 (chapter XXIII).

Sir A Fraser, *Among Indian Rajahs and Ryots*, ed 3 London 1912 (pages 185, 191–210).

J Macgowan, *Men and Manners in modern China*, London 1912 (pages 17 foll, 189–96, 275–7).

M Augé-Laribé, *L'évolution de la France agricole*, Paris 1912.

(7) SPECIAL AMERICAN SECTION.

H Baerlein, *Mexico, the land of unrest*, London 1914 (chapters VIII, XI).

F L Olmsted, *A journey in the seaboard slave States* (1853–4), ed 2 New York 1904 (pages 240, 282, vol II pages 155, 198, 237).

H R Helper, *The impending crisis of the South* (*economic*), New York 1857.

B B Munford, *Virginia's attitude towards Slavery and Secession*, ed 2 London 1910 (pages 133–4 etc).

W Archer, *Through Afro-America, an English reading of the Race-problem*, London 1910.

A H Stone, *Studies in the American Race-problem*, London 1908 printed in New York.

F F Browne, *The everyday life of Abraham Lincoln*, London 1914 (pages 348–9).

G P Fisher, *The colonial era in America*, London 1892 (pages 254, 259).

J Rodway, *Guiana*, London 1912 (of Indians, pages 224–5).

J Creelman, *Diaz, Master of Mexico*, New York 1911 (pages 401–5).

E R Turner, *The Negro in Pennsylvania* 1639–1861, Washington 1911.

Social and economic forces in American history, New York and London 1913 (by several authors).

J F Rhodes, *History of the United States from* 1850, London 1893–1906.

C R Enock, *The Republics of Central and South America*, London and New York 1913.

INDICES

Where the reference is less direct, the figure is given in brackets

I GENERAL

474

II LIST OF WORDS AND PHRASES

A. GREEK

480

οἰκέται 30, 39, 64, 110, 341
οἰκεύς, οἰκῆες 17, 21, 30
οἰκογενεῖς 129
οἰκοδεσπότης 304
οἰκονόμος 461
ὀπώρα 108, 111
ὄρη 111
ὅροι 107

παραμονά 123
πάροικοι 347, 378
πενέστης 37, 116
περίοικοι 94
πρόκλησις 110

σκαφεύς 35, [116]

στάσις 66
στρατιώτας 116
συνοικία 108
σώματα 122, 396

τεμένη 111
τεχνῖται 68, 98
τροφή 75, 95, 304

φελλεύς 47, 83
φιάλη 237
φύσις 34-5

χορηγία 86, [93]
χρηματιστική 98
χωρία 463

B. LATIN

abigei 372
actor 258, 263, 299, 300, 319, 324, 367-8
adaeratio 396
addicere 424
adscribere, adscripticii 425
adsidui 10, 152, 253
advenae 425
aedificare 214
agellus 215-6, 219, 243, 318, 334, 425
aggeres publici 429
agrestes 199, 200, 230
agricola 227, 230, 284, 398, 445
agri fiscales 347
agri rudes 349
agri vectigales 376
alimenta 296 foll., 324
alligati [see compediti]
annonariae regiones 388
annona urbis 388, [402-3], 427
aquarii 294
arare, arator 195, 197-8, 214, 219, 227, 248, 308, 312
aridi fructus, partes aridae 350
artes 188, 193
artifex 245
asinarius 172, 227
atriensis 246, 250, 319
attributi 380
auctoritas principalis 376

bubulcus 172
burgus 429

calcarius 172
canon 350-1, [356], 428
capita 395, 421
capitatio 386, 395, 411, [421], 424, [431]
capitulum 410
capulator 172
casa 312
castella 413
censitores 421
civilis pars 418
classes, decuriae 261
colere 184, 230, 253, 267, 364

coloni Caesaris 208-9, [293?], 347, 355, 357, 377-8
coloni indigenae 252, [347], 396
colonia partiaria 211, 321, 332, 343, 347, [350], 356, [463]
colonia, place to which colonus belongs 258
colonia [settlement], official sense, 133, [141], 152
colonus as serf-labourer 383-4, 392, 394, 401, 416, 424-5, 429, 431
colonus as sub-tenant 195, 209, 343-52, 355-6, 359, 376-7
colonus becoming bound to the soil [161], 201, 210-2, 257, 274, 333, 344-52, 356, 358-9, 383-4, 386-99, [404], 415-6, 450
colonus, cultivator 133, 167, 183, 195, 215, 230, [233], 249, 267, 286, [293], [364], 445
colonus, free but dependent 161, 183, [195], 209, 254, [264], 307-8, 312, 340, 358-9, 404
colonus imaginarius 367
colonus may sublet farm 364
colonus, mean economic and social position of 195, 235-6, 243, 246-7, 255, 307-8, 364
colonus, member of a colonia 293
colonus originalis 431
colonus, tenant farmer [free in law and fact] 139, 157-8, 183-4, 194-5, 202, [208], 210, 215-6, 221, 224, 233-5, 243, 246, 252-5, [267], 286, [292], 295, 315, 325, 332, 362-3, 364, 366-7, 371-3
colonus, veteran allottee 155-6, [215], 223, 249, [293?]
colonus, yeoman farmer 230
compediti alligati vincti 166, 172, [218], 220, 227, 248, [252], 260-3, 300, 320, 334-5
compositio 431
conductor 264-5, 343, 345-51, 355-7, 359, 364, 366, 377, 405
conductum 247
conquisita 411
contubernalis, contubernium 258, 300
corpora 396

III LIST OF PASSAGES CITED

Demosthenes (*contd.*)

Digest

Digest (*contd.*)

Diodorus

Dion Cassius

Dion Chrysostom

Dionysius

Euripides

IV MODERN AUTHORITIES

V COUNTRIES, PLACES AND PEOPLES

492

41653